Composers on Music

AN ANTHOLOGY
OF COMPOSERS' WRITINGS
from PALESTRINA *to* COPLAND

EDITED BY SAM MORGENSTERN

GREENWOOD PRESS, PUBLISHERS
NEW YORK

Ref.

ML
90
M4
1969

TO *Adrienne Foulke*

CONTENTS

Chapter II

Chapter VI

Chapter VII

Chapter VIII

Chapter IX

INTRODUCTION

Much of what has been written about music is the work of theorists, performers, critics, musicologists, or aestheticians concerned with all the arts. This book, however, originated from the idea that the composers, the men nearest their craft, have had things of perhaps paramount interest to say about practically all facets of their art. If music, most abstract of all the arts, can indeed be concretized into words— and how often have the pros and cons of this been argued!—then the craftsmen themselves may be best equipped to speak, even if one must thereby forgo some degree of objectivity.

While this volume is limited to composers' writings on their own and others' music, the temptation to wander farther afield has been very real. It would have been interesting, for example, to include an important early theorist, such as Guido d'Arezzo, from the eleventh century, or later, Jean Paul, who influenced Schumann so strongly. But as non-composers, they have not come within the scope of this book.

On the other hand, one soon discovers that some of the most prolific composers have written next to nothing about their art. The reader will find Bach and Handel conspicuously absent. What little of their writing is extant consists chiefly of ornate dedications and routine business letters, though some pithy sayings of Bach have survived in anecdotes.[1] This is not to say that their musical output consumed every moment of their working time, but rather that they were either not interested or not adept in verbalizing about their art. Wagner, on the other hand, has left volumes of literary work (to say nothing of the libretti for his operas which he wrote himself) that nearly equal his music in quantity; Liszt, though occupied with a prodigious amount of composition, wrote essays and books on almost every conceivable musical subject; Schumann and Berlioz found time to be professional music critics as well as highly productive composers. Indeed, the nineteenth century seems to have been particularly rich in composers of a literary bent.

The complete literary works of some composers—Weber, Schumann, Wagner and Liszt, for instance—have been collected in numbers

---

[1] See Hans T. David and Arthur Mendel, *The Bach Reader*, New York, W. W. Norton, 1945, pp. 32 ff.

of volumes that are easily accessible in most large libraries. The inclusion here of others has meant long research among widely scattered sources: letters, prefaces, magazine articles, lectures, biographies and autobiographies.

Instruction books and treatises on methods have yielded valuable material. Couperin's *L'Art de toucher le clavecin* and Carl Philipp Emanuel Bach's more detailed and searching *Versuch über die wahre Art das Clavier zu spielen* carry as much contemporary interest, what with the revival of harpsichord playing, as they did in the eighteenth century. The twentieth century composer-teacher is less occupied with method and more concerned with the aesthetics of music. Hindemith's *Unterweisung im Tonsatz* is a thorough study of modern counterpoint and harmony, but the lectures he gave at Harvard, called *A Musician's World*, deal with pure aesthetics and style. Similarly, Copland's collection of Harvard lectures, *Music and Imagination*, Stravinsky's *Poetics of Music*, and Vaughan Williams' *National Music*, drawn from a course he gave at Bryn Mawr College, avoid the technical aspects of music for the most part.

Much of the material presented here is translated into English for the first time. When existing translations have been used, an occasional word has been altered for the sake of greater precision or clarity; in a few instances, a complete retranslation was required to make the material more comprehensible to the modern reader. For example, Caccini's foreword to his *Le Nuove Musiche* was published in later editions of Playford's *Introduction to the Skill of Music*, but the style, expression and even the musical terms of the early English version rendered it obsolete. Had the old English style preserved the flavor of Caccini's old Italian, one might have been tempted to retain it, but it did no more than add confusion to an already complicated original.

Also, upon close comparison with the originals, some of the Monteverdi translations were found wanting; they have been changed into what, hopefully, more nearly coincides with what Monteverdi meant to say. An effort to adhere to the literary style of certain other composers—the occasionally staccato manner of Ravel, Satie's quaint turn of phrase, for instance—finally inclined the editor to agree with La Rochefoucauld when he maintained that "Les traductions sont comme les femmes: lorsqu'elles sont belles, elles ne sont pas fidèles, et lorsq'elles sont fidèles, elles ne sont pas belles."

In certain long essays, considerations of space have made cuts necessary. Falla's study of *cante jondo* is vitally interesting, but too long to include *in toto* in a book which seeks to cover nearly ninety composers and give adequate hearing to all. Every page of Chavez' book on music and electricity, one of the few thorough discussions of a comparatively new phenomenon, has something of interest, but only brief sections, giving the reader a survey of the subject, have been culled; if these excerpts lead him to a complete reading of the book, so much the better. The same holds for Hindemith, Honegger, Krenek, Sessions and others. By the same token, the not infrequently purple prose or the philosophical digressions not pertinent to the subject in hand were pruned from Liszt's writings; the tirades and polemics which interlard Wagner's most acute observations on music and drama have—perhaps only to good effect—been largely eliminated.

Short cuts have been indicated by the usual three dots, longer omissions by a centered dash, editorial interpolations are enclosed within brackets; and the number at the end of an excerpt guides the reader to the List of Sources at the end of the book.

Headings are supplied by the editor in most cases, but it was not thought necessary to indicate the few instances where these are taken from the composer's own title. The data as to source, time and place, are given under the headings as fully as they could be ascertained; almost all footnotes are supplied by the editor, but where they are by either the composer or the editor of the source they are so marked.

The composers are chronologically arranged, and for the sake of convenience the selections are grouped into chapters of approximately equal length. Attempts at arranging the material according to contents, schools, countries, epochs, have proved futile in view of the widely varying availability and the diversity of the material. Within each composer's section, however, the order is roughly as follows: general topics, comments on specific composers (in historical sequence), and writings about his own music.

The composer's writing style, as will be seen, often not only reflects his personality, but can also reveal a striking affinity with his musical style and capture the flavor of his period in history. Mozart's full-blooded, racy letters, interspersed with earthy expletives, echo the lustiness of the Salzburg of his day. The rational clarity of eighteenth century music in France finds its counterpart both in the subject matter and the lucid exposition of the writings of Rameau, Grétry, Couperin and Rousseau. And the return to, or rather the inheritance of, this reasonableness and clarity is manifest in the writings of Satie, Debussy and Ravel. Soul-searching, to which Beethoven was so given, bursts into full flower with the late nineteenth century romantics. *Sturm und Drang,* utter darkness and overpowering lights are as much a part of Mahler's letters as they are of his symphonies. In our time, Albert Roussel may speculate on the relation of inspiration to composition, but the dominant contemporary trend is the matter-of-fact approach, the divorce of mystery from composing, an attitude that permeates the writings of such men as Aaron Copland, Virgil Thomson, and Hindemith.

Rarely has the professional composer been able to earn a living solely through composition. Often he has turned to journalism to supplement his income, proving himself a gifted writer as well as composer. With his crisp, sometimes cynical epigrams, Debussy could admirably sum up a large musical idea or even the entire works of a given composer. More impassioned and opinionated, sometimes even losing a sense of (musical) proportion, Hugo Wolf wrote his reviews with vigor and verve. In the United States today, Virgil Thomson, in his brilliant reviews and magazine articles, has not only written with spice and an uncanny feeling for the word, but has documented for us the whole contemporary musical scene. An avowed Francophile, he follows in the Gallic tradition of clarity, succinctness, and a freedom of illusion to which he adds an American forthrightness.

In trying to cover as many aspects of music as possible, it transpired that, though certain periods stressed certain forms of music, opera—or the combination of music and drama in one guise or another—runs like a continuous thread through almost the entire history of our Western music. As Gounod once remarked, "The Composer, to achieve a successful career, must create it through composing operas." He was referring to France, but the observation is surely as valid for Italy also. Already in the early eighteenth century, when opera had hardly had a chance to develop, Marcello was satirizing its corruption and decay in Venice; Gluck was writing manifestoes on its reform; the famous "Guerre des Bouffons" was raging between the adherents of Piccini and Gluck, and Rousseau was in the midst of it. Later in the same century, Mozart's letters, particularly the one to his father describing work in progress on *The Abduction from the Seraglio*, are most illuminating from a technical angle. Little over a half century later, Wagner was fulminating over the decadence of opera and propounding his formulas for reform by the volume.

The correspondence covering twenty-five years of collaboration between Strauss and Hofmannsthal is a textbook on opera construction. These letters, incidentally, reflect the various metamorphoses of Strauss: his change from a highly romantic, to an intensely realistic, to practically a neo-classic composer; his inflation of the orchestra beyond Wagnerian proportions, and the later reduction of his instrumentation to little more than chamber music ensemble size; his early disregard for the capacity of the human voice which he swamped under a mammoth instrumentation, and then his adoption of unaccompanied dialogue as practiced by Mozart and French *opéra comique.*

Verdi's and Puccini's letters are a mine of information on the problems of opera composing; on the relation of librettist to composer; on the attitude of these Italians to the tide of Wagnerian music drama which flooded Italy as it did France, where Debussy and some of his colleagues tried to stem it; and on opera business, in general.

The mating of music and the word occupies an important place in the writings of some composers. In *A Plaine and Easie Introduction to Practicalle Musicke* Morley condemned some of his predecessors for misplaced stresses and accents, and he codified a set of rules for correct prosody. Telemann, Gluck, Grétry, Weber and Moussorgsky had much to say on the subject, Weber and Grétry expanding on correct declamation.

An interest in folk music and its relation to serious composition arose in the nineteenth century. The Russian "Five," following in the wake of Glinka's pioneering, championed the cause of folklore and folk song as subject matter for developing a national Russian music. In the twentieth century, Bartók and Kodály approached folk music from a scientific point of view, went out into the Hungarian countryside to collect authentic folk melodies and carefully recorded their findings. Bartók's comments on the unauthenticity of the gypsy tunes used by Liszt in his Rhapsodies and by Brahms in his arrangements are especially enlightening. Vaughan Williams, both in his compositions and his published lectures, has sponsored the renaissance of English folk song. Jazz as a serious musical form was taken up by Gershwin, and its special affinity for the French is commented on in several instances by Milhaud.

In all periods, suggestions and even rules for performance are given by many composers. Byrd and Caccini were naturally preoccupied with singing, the latter emphasizing voice production and the monodic style. The operatic composers, Weber and Rossini, discussed the requirements of the opera singer. Concomitant with the interest in vocal matters is the attention given to keyboard playing. Not only did C. P. E. Bach and Couperin write treatises on the subject, but Frescobaldi had a word to say on organ playing and harpsichord performance. The popularity of the concert pianist in the nineteenth century brought about a wealth of literature on keyboard technique. Schumann devoted a number of articles to Liszt's incomparable pianism, while Glinka found him less satisfactory than John Field, the quiet performer, precursor of the Chopin style of playing. With the rise of the virtuoso conductor in the latter part of the nineteenth century appeared, first, Wagner's ideas on what makes a good conductor, then the precepts of Mahler and Strauss.

Added to these varied elements is the leaven of controversy. Rameau developed a theory of harmony which was summarily repudiated by Rousseau. Weber was outraged when a work of his was compared to Beethoven's; he felt that the direction Beethoven was taking in his later years would doom him to oblivion. The Wagnerites reviled the Brahmsians, and both were rejected by the French. Today Schoenberg has his ardent disciples and partisans, but is sharply opposed by Hindemith. And so on. Yet these clashes strike the spark that vitalizes music.

Finally, a word on the problem of choice which the compiler of such a book as this must face: despite the fact that nothing can be found in the writing of certain composers who should be represented because of their place in music history, the quotable material from only a few composers could fill more than one volume. Balance and variety can be the sole criteria of selection. Where the same subject has been treated by a group of composers, particularly of the same period, the quotation which has seemed to cover the topic most thoroughly, concisely or effectively has been chosen. Obviously, the ingredients of music—melody, harmony and rhythm—and the forms enumerated above, have been discussed again and again through the centuries. It is the difference in point of view and in stress that lends interest to the same basic material, sheds new light on it, and gives this book, it is hoped, its reason for being.

An anthology like this could not have been created without the help and encouragement of many kind friends. I want to thank Philip Miller, of the Music Reference Division of the New York Public Library, and his staff for invaluable aid generously given. Gladys Chamberlain and Mary Lee Daniels, formerly of the Music Library Branch at 58th Street, gave me unreservedly of their time and effort and turned over to me all the resources of their collection. Herbert Weinstock read and advised me on large portions of the manuscript. Frances Keene and

Ludovico Calderrara were helpful in the Caccini translations. Harry Cumpson and Jean Karsavina translated Balakirev's letters from the Russian. Adrienne Foulke read the manuscript as it was being written and again on its completion.

Acknowledgment is made elsewhere to the many publishers, composers, and other holders of copyrighted material who consented to the use of selections for this book. If through oversight any permissions were not obtained, I hope those concerned will accept our apologies. In a few cases, after all reasonable efforts, it was found impossible to trace the present holders of the rights to material.

My gratitude goes to all who have contributed to the production of what I hope will be both a useful and an interesting source of information.

S.M.

New York, July, 1956

I

PALESTRINA
BYRD
CACCINI
MORLEY
MONTEVERDI
FRESCOBALDI
SCHÜTZ
PURCELL
COUPERIN
TELEMANN
RAMEAU
MARCELLO

GIOVANNI PIERLUIGI DA PALESTRINA
1525(?)-1594

In his *Mémoires* Berlioz observes that the religious music of Palestrina does not differ from his secular compositions, and to underline the point, cites musical examples.[1] Busoni makes the same statement in his sketch for a preface to *Dr. Faustus*. We also know that Palestrina wrote Masses on secular songs, and for *L'Homme Armé* actually retained the original title.

Some years after the appearance of his religious motets, Palestrina published a volume of madrigals to secular texts of indifferent character. Yet the greater part of his career was spent in the service of the church, and he was, understandably, most prolific in his output of religious music. His *Missa Papae Marcelli* was considered by church authorities to be one of the greatest examples of pure church music.

Great religious composer that he was, Palestrina did not lack a keen business sense either in his professional or personal life. After a series of family misfortunes—the death of his first wife, two sons and brothers—he decided to become a priest. Although he actually received the tonsure, he soon thereafter abandoned that life to marry a wealthy woman into whose fur business he entered.

He exhibits the same lively practicality in the following dedications of his motets to high-ranking churchmen, and they may perhaps be considered more politic than sincere.

SECULAR AND SACRED TEXTS

Dedication to Cardinal Carpi of *First Book of Motets*, 1563

Our wisest mortals have decided that music should give zest to divine worship, so that those whom pious devotion to religious practice has led to the temple might remain there to delight in voices blending in harmony.

If men take great pains to compose beautiful music for profane songs, they should devote at least as much thought to sacred song, nay, even more than to mere worldly matters.

[1] See p. 119.

Therefore, though well aware of my feeble powers, I have held
nothing more desirable than that whatever is sung throughout the year,
according to the season, should be agreeable to the ear by virtue of its
vocal beauty, insofar as it lay in my power to make it so.   [1]

Dedication to Pope Gregory XIII of *Fourth Book*
of Motets (containing settings of the
Song of Songs), 1584

There exists a vast mass of love songs of the poets, written in a
fashion entirely foreign to the profession and name of Christian. They
are the songs of men ruled by passion, and a great number of musicians,
corrupters of youth, make them the concern of their art and their industry; in proportion as they flourish through praise of their skill, so
do they offend good and serious-minded men by the depraved taste of
their work. I blush and grieve to think that once I was of their number. But, while I cannot change the past, nor undo what is done, I
have mended my ways. Therefore I have labored on songs which have
been written in praise of Our Lord, Jesus Christ, and His Most Holy
Virgin Mother, Mary; and I have now produced a work which treats
of the divine love of Christ and His Spouse the Soul, the Canticle of
Solomon.   [2]

MUSIC AND BUSINESS

Dedication to Pope Sixtus V of *Lamentations*, 1588

Worldly cares of any kind, Most Holy Father, are adverse to the
Muses, and particularly those which arise from a lack of private means.
For, when the latter afford a sufficiency (and to ask more is the mark
of a greedy and intemperate man), the mind can more easily detach
itself from other cares; if not, the fault lies within. Those who have
known the necessity of laboring to provide this sufficiency, according
to their station and way of life, know full well how it distracts the
mind from learning, and from a study of the liberal arts.

Certainly I have known this experience all my life, and more
especially at present. Yet I thank the Divine Goodness, first, that the
course is now almost finished, and the goal in sight; secondly, that in
the midst of the greatest difficulties, I have never interrupted my study
of music. Dedicated to the profession since boyhood, and engrossed
in it to the best of my abilities and energies, indeed what other interest could I have had? Would that my progress had equalled my
labor and my diligence!

I have composed and published much; a great deal more is lying by me, which I am hindered from publishing because of the straitened means of which I have spoken. It would require no small expenditure, especially were the larger notes and letters used, as church publications properly demand.

Meanwhile, I have only been able to publish, in this small format, those *Lamentations* of the Prophet Jeremiah which are usually sung in choral form in the churches during Holy Week.

This work I offer to Your Holiness with that humility due the exalted Pastor of the Universal Catholic Church, outstanding in holiness and admirable in authority.   [3]

WILLIAM BYRD

1543–1623

In his *Plaine and Easie Introduction to Practicalle Musicke*, Thomas Morley speaks of Byrd as "never without reverence to be named of the musicians." His contemporaries considered Byrd a tremendously important composer, and the record of his death refers to him as a "Father of Musicke."

A student of Thomas Tallis, he shared with his master the honorary post of organist in the Chapel Royal, and in common with Tallis, he received a patent from Queen Elizabeth granting them sole rights to print and sell music and music paper for twenty-one years. These privileges accorded Byrd, a practicing Catholic in a militantly Protestant England, also attest to his reputation as a musician.

Though he wrote extensively for the virginals and string instruments—abundant examples of the former are included in the *Fitzwilliam Virginal Book*, and *My Ladye Nevells Booke* consists entirely of his virginal works—his interest in vocal literature and its performance, so eloquently expressed in the following quotations, is manifest in his vast output of choral music, madrigals and songs. He wrote three Masses for the Catholic Church, a Protestant service, over two hundred motets and gradualia, psalms, anthems and the *Turbae* for a Passion according to Saint John.

He had a very keen feeling for song, his vocal lines fitting beautifully to the text, its innate rhythm and design superseding the regular meter of the music.

Byrd has often been compared to Palestrina. Both men, living to a ripe old age, wrote prolifically for the church. However, Palestrina is smooth and polished, while Byrd is vigorous and varied, as well as harmonically more daring and original.

SINGING

From: *Psalmes, Sonets & Songs*, 1588

Reasons briefly set downe by th'auctor, to perswade every one to learne to sing.

First it is a Knowledge easely taught, and quickly learned where there is a good Master, and an apt Scoller.

2. The exercise of singing is delightfull to Nature & good to preserve the health of Man.

3. It doth strengthen all the parts of the brest, & doth open the pipes.

4. It is a singular good remedie for a stutting & stammering in the speech.

5. It is the best meanes to procure a perfect pronunciation & to make a good Orator.

6. It is the onely way to know where Nature hath bestowed the benefit of a good voyce: which guift is so rare, as there is not one among a thousand, that hath it: and in many, that excellent guift is lost, because they want Art to expresse Nature.

7. There is not any Musicke of Instruments whatsoever, comparable to that which is made of the voyces of Men, where the voyces are good, and the same well sorted and ordered.

8. The better the voyce is, the meeter it is to honour and serve God therewith: and the voyce of man is chiefly to be imployed to that ende.

omnis spiritus laudet Dominum.

Since singing is so good a thing
I wish all men would learne to sing. [1]

PERFORMING AND LISTENING

Preface to *Psalmes, Songs, and Sonnets,* 1611

To all true lovers of Musicke, W. Byrd wisheth all true happinesse both temporall and eternall.

Being excited by your kinde acceptance of my former travailes in Musicke, I am thereby much incouraged to commend to you these my last labours, for myne *ultimum vale.* Wherein I hope you shall finde Musicke to content every humour: either melancholy, merry, or mixt of both.

Onely this I desire; that you will be but as carefull to heare them well expressed as I have been both in the Composing and correcting of them. Otherwise the best Song that ever was made will seeme harsh and unpleasant, for that the well expressing of them, either by Voyces, or Instruments, is the life of our labours, which is seldome or never well performed at the first singing or playing. Besides a song that is well and artificially made cannot be well perceived nor understood at the first hearing, but the oftner you shall heare it, the better

cause of liking you will discover: and commonly that Song is best
esteemed with which our eares are most acquainted. As I have done
my best endeavour to give you content, so I beseech you satisfie my
desire in hearing them well expressed, and then I doubt not, for Art
and Ayre both of skilfull and ignorant they will deserve liking. *Vale.*

Thine, W. Byrd   [2]

GIULIO CACCINI

1550–1610

In the latter half of the sixteenth century, Europe began to see a violent reaction to over-elaborate counterpoint, and a tendency toward both a simple musical style and the natural expression of words and emotions. Reform expressed itself not only in the church, through the Council of Trent, but also in secular music. The artists of the Renaissance were striving to revive antiquity, and no mention was to be found in Greek literature of counterpoint, a product of the Middle Ages.

Caccini gave impetus to this change by exploiting the solo voice in the monodic style, the *stile rappresentativo*, in his most important work, the collection of arias and madrigals appropriately known as *Le Nuove Musiche*. In his preface to this work he expressed the principles of the new style and advanced the practice of monodic singing. He is supposed to have had a beautiful voice which, naturally enough, he was reluctant to subordinate. Counterpoint militated against the soloist while, conversely, an outstanding solo part would have marred the counterpoint in a vocal ensemble. In his music Caccini allowed the instrument to accompany the voices only with chords. His songs for solo voice and basso continuo were a novelty in the Florence and Rome of his time.

Also active in the invention of opera, Caccini set Rinuccini's *Euridice* (1600) to music; this was the first opera to be printed, although not the first to be composed. He wrote scenes to words by Count Bardi, at whose palace in Florence there gathered the most famous poets and musicians of the day, united in the attempt to restore Greek drama with appropriate music. Out of their endeavors, opera was born.

THE BEGINNINGS OF THE MONODIC STYLE

From: Preface to Le Nuove Musiche, 1614

To the readers: If heretofore I did not publish the results of my musical studies in the noble style of singing, learned from my mas-

9

ter, the famous Scipione della Palla, nor the madrigals and arias composed by me at different times, it was because I did not see fit to do
so, as it seemed to me that these pieces had been honored sufficiently,
and because I see them performed continuously—more often than
they deserve—by the most famous singers in Italy, as well as by other
noble persons, amateurs of this profession. But now I see many of
them corrupted and ruined; also, those long vocal roulades (single
and double) which I invented to avoid the customary old style of
passages, more suited to wind and string instruments than to the
voice, I also see are misused, redoubled and intermingled one with
another, and I find an indifferent use of the rise and fall of the
voice, of the exclamations, trills and *gruppi*, and other similar ornaments of the good style of singing. For these reasons I have been
forced, as well as urged by my friends, to have my music published.
My purpose in this introduction to my first publication is to set before
my readers the causes which led me to the adoption of this style of
singing for the solo voice, and since no music has been written in
recent times that is endowed with that complete grace I feel resounding
in my soul, I have wished also to leave some trace of it in these compositions, that others may achieve perfection, as a small spark sometimes generates a great flame.

I can truly say that I learned more than I learned in thirty years'
study of counterpoint from the wise discussions I heard when there
flourished in Florence the brilliant *Camerata* of the illustrious Giovanni Bardi, Count of Vernio, which I frequented, and where there
gathered not only a great part of the nobility, but also the best
musicians and men of genius, poets and philosophers of the city. These
learned gentlemen always encouraged me, and with clear reasoning
persuaded me not to adhere to that type of music which, not permitting the words to be clearly understood, distorts the idea and the
line [prosody], now lengthening, now shortening the syllables in order
to make them fit the counterpoint, that destroyer of poetry. They
urged me to adhere instead to that style so highly lauded by Plato and
other philosophers who maintained that music is nothing if not words
and rhythm first, and sound last, and not the contrary. For, if one is
to penetrate other people's minds and produce those wonderful effects admired by the writers, it cannot be achieved by counterpoint
in modern music, especially not when one voice sings above a string
accompaniment, and not a word is understood because of the multitude
of passages on both long and short syllables, the only purpose being
that the singers be lauded by the populace and declared great.

Having seen, as I say, that such music and such musicians gave no pleasure other than that which harmony could give the ear, since without the words being understood, it could not move the intellect, the thought came to me to introduce a kind of music through which one could express oneself in harmony, using . . . a certain noble carelessness in the song, passing sometimes through dissonances, yet keeping the notes of the bass steady, except when I wanted to observe the common usage; and, as they do not well serve any other purpose, the inner voices might be played on an instrument to express some feeling. This is why I then created these songs for a solo voice, as it seemed to me it had more power to please and move the listener than many voices singing together; thus I composed the madrigals "Perfidissimo volto," "Vedrò'l mio Sol," "Dovrò dunque morire," and similar pieces, and especially the aria on the eclogue of Sannazaro, "Itene a l'ombra degli ameni faggi," in that same style I used later for the fables which were sung in concerts in Florence.

These madrigals and arias were received in the *Camerata* with enthusiastic applause, and I was exhorted to continue along the same lines; therefore I decided to move to Rome and present them there. I performed these madrigals and arias for many gentlemen who had gathered at the home of Signor Nero Neri, and especially for Signor Lione Strozzi, and all of them can testify as to how greatly they urged me to continue on the project I had undertaken, even going so far as to tell me how, until then, they had never heard the harmony of a solo voice over a single stringed instrument that could move the soul with such power as did these madrigals.

Returning to Florence, I observed that at that time musicians were setting certain songs to vulgar words which, to my mind, were neither appropriate nor well regarded by people of taste. It then occurred to me to compose a few songs in the style of an aria to be played with several stringed instruments in order to lift the spirits of the listener. I expressed this thought to many gentlemen of the city, whereupon they courteously obliged me with poems of diverse lengths. I must mention especially Signor Gabriello Chiabrera who gave me quite a few verses of great variety, on which from time to time I composed several arias. These arias have not been unwelcome throughout all Italy, and now everyone is using that style when composing for a solo voice. This is true particularly here in Florence where I have been living for thirty-seven years under the patronage of these worthy princes, and where anyone who has so wished, has been able to see and hear at his pleasure all that I have accomplished in these studies.

In the madrigals as well as in the arias I have always sought to have the music follow the meaning of the words, searching out those more or less expressive chords, according to the sentiments they should convey, and trying particularly to give them grace by concealing as much as I could the craft of counterpoint; and I placed the consonant harmonies on the long syllables, avoiding the short ones, and observed the same rule in making the passages of division, although, in order to embellish, I have sometimes put in a few chromatics up to the value of a quarter note or at most a half note, chiefly over short syllables. These are permissible, since they pass quickly and are not division passages, but give a certain additional grace, and this I also did because every rule can suffer a few exceptions. But, as I said before, I think that these long roulades have been wrongly used; the passages were not written because they were necessary to the proper style of singing, but rather, I think, to titillate the ears of those who understand little of what it means to sing with expression; if they did know, they would surely abhor such passages . . . Accordingly, I introduced these roulades only in music which is less emotional, on long syllables and not on short ones, and in final cadences; my only other observation concerning the vowels being that in such long roulades, the vowel *u* is sung to better effect by the soprano voice than by the tenor, and the vowel *i* is better for the tenor than the vowel *u*. With all the other vowels I follow common usage, although the open ones are more sonorous than the closed, and are also more adaptable and more easily used . . . I have used [counterpoint] only to harmonize two parts, to avoid certain notable errors and soften certain dissonances, to accentuate expression rather than to use craft. One can see that an aria or a madrigal, composed in such a style, will produce a better effect and will please the taste of him who hears it more if it follows the meaning of the words than if it contains all the arts of counterpoint. And there is no better way to be convinced of this than to try it.   [1]

THOMAS MORLEY

1557–1603

A pupil of William Byrd, Morley dedicated his remarkable theoretical work, *A Plaine and Easie Introduction to Practicalle Musicke*, to his master. This treatise deals exhaustively with standardized sixteenth century musical theory, and contains an authoritative study of modal music. Written in Socratic vein, its questions and answers lend it charm and informality, and exhibit the author's keen wit.

Although he is known primarily for his gay lively madrigals, brimful of Elizabethan vigor and lustiness, Morley composed a fair amount of serious church music; his setting of the English Burial Service was in constant use until superseded by Purcell's. He also published the "first book of consort lessons," which can be called the first true chamber music.

Possibly he was acquainted with Shakespeare. For a time they lived near one another, and the document is still extant in which they were assessed a certain tax, and against which they both successfully protested. Morley composed one or two songs for Shakespeare's plays. Curiously enough, the text of "It was a lover and his lass" from *As You Like It* is to be found in Morley's *First Book of Ayres*, published twenty-three years before the first folio edition of the play.

From: *A Plaine and Easie Introduction to*
Practicalle Musicke, 1597

THE FANTASIE

The most principal and chiefest kind of music which is made without a ditty is the fantasie, that is, when a musician taketh a point [theme] at his pleasure, and wresteth and turneth it as he list, making either much or little of it according as shall seeme best in his own conceit. In this may more art be shown than in any other music, because the composer is tide to nothing but that he may add, deminish and alter at his pleasure. And this kind will beare any allowances whatsoever tolerable in other musicke, except changing the ayre & leaving the key, which in fantasie may never be suffered.   [1]

FUGAL COMPOSITION

If a man would study, he might upon it [a point] find varietie enough to fill up many sheets of paper: yea, though it were given to all the musicians of the world, they might compose upon it, and not one of their compositions be like unto that of another. And you shall find no point so well handled by any man, either Composer or Organist, but with studie either he himselfe or some other might make it much better. [2]

SIGHT SINGING

But supper being ended, and Musicke bookes, according to the custome being brought to the table: the mistresse of the house presented me with a part, earnestly requesting me to sing. But when after manie excuses, I protested unfainedly that I could not: everie one began to wonder. Yea, some whispered to others, demanding how I was brought up: so that upon shame of mine ignorance, I go nowe to seeke out mine olde frinde, master *Gnorimus*, to make my selfe his scholler. [3]

Singing extempore upon a plainsong is in deede a peece of cunning, and very necessarie to be perfectly practiced by him who meaneth to be a composer. [4]

TESSITURA AND TRANSPOSITION

Likewise take a voice being never so good, and cause it sing above the naturall reach, it will make an unpleasing and sweete [?] noise, displeasing both the singer because of the straining, and the hearer because of the wildenes of the sound: even so, if songes of the high key be sung in a low pitch, & they of the low key sung in the high pitch, though it will not be so offensive as the other, yet will it not breed so much contentment in the hearer as otherwise it would do. [5]

WORDS AND MUSIC

It followeth to shew you how to dispose your musicke according to the nature of the words which you are therein to expresse, as whatsoever matter it be which you have in hand, such a kind of musicke must you frame to it. You must therefore if you have a grave matter, applie a grave kind of musicke to it, if a merrie subject you must make your musicke also merrie. For it will be a great absurditie to use a sad harmonie to a merrie matter, or a merrie harmonie to a sad lamentable or tragical dittie. You must then when you would expresse any word signifying hardnesse, crueltie, bitternesse, and other such like, make the harmonie like unto it, that is, somwhat harsh and hard but yet so it offend not. Likewise, when any of your words shal expresse complaint, dolor, repentance, sighs, teares and such like, let your harmonie be sad and doleful. . . .

Also if the subject be light, you must cause your musicke go in motions, which carrie with them a celeritie or quicknesse of time, as minimes, crotchets and quavers: if it be lamentable, the note must go in slow and heavie motions, as semibreves, breves and such like, and of all this you shall finde examples everie where in the works of the good musicians. Moreover you must have a care that when your matter signifieth ascending, high heaven, and such like, you make your musicke ascend: and by the contrarie when your dittie speaketh of descending lowenes, depth, hell, and others such, you must make your musicke descend, for as it will be thought a great absurditie to talke of heaven and point downwarde to the earth: so will it be counted great incongruitie if a musician upon the wordes *hee ascended into heaven* should cause his musicke descend, or by the contrarie upon the descension should cause his musicke to ascend. We must also have a care to applie the notes to the wordes, as in singing there be no barbarisme committed: that is, that we cause no sillable which is by nature short be expressed by manie notes or one long note, nor no long sillable be expressed with a shorte note, but in this fault do the practitioners erre more grosselie, then in any other, for you shal find few songes wherein the penult sillables of these words, *Dominus, Angelus, filius, miraculum, gloria,* and such like are not expressed with a long note, yea many times with a whole dossen of notes, and though one should speak of fortie he should not say much amiss, which is a grosse barbarisme, & yet might be easelie amended. We must also take heed of seperating any part of a word from another by a rest, as som dunces have not slackt to do, yea one whose name is Johannes Dunstable (an ancient English author) hath not only devided the sentence, but in the very middle of a word hath made two long rests.   [6]

MOTET AND MADRIGAL

I say that all musicke for voices (for onlie of that kinde have we hetherto spoken) is made either for a dittie or without a dittie, if it bee with a dittie, it is either grave or light, the grave ditties they have still kept in one kind, so that whatsoever musicke be made upon it, is comprehended under the name of a Motet: a Motet is properlie a song made for the church, either upon some hymne or Antheme, or such like, and that name I take to have beene given to that kinde of musicke in opposition to the other which they called *Canto firmo*, and we do commonlie call plainsong, for as nothing is more opposit to standing and firmnes then motion, so did they give the Motet that name of moving,[1] because it is in a manner quight contrarie to the other, which after some sort, and in respect of the other standeth still. This kind of al others which are made on a ditty, requireth most art, and moveth and causeth most strange effects in the hearer, being aptlie framed for the dittie and well expressed by the singer, for it will draw the auditor (and speciallie the skilfull auditor) into a devout and reverent kind of consideration of him for whose praise it was made. But I see not what passions or motions it can stirre up, being sung as most men doe commonlie sing it: that is, leaving out the dittie and singing onely the bare note, as it were a musicke made onelie for instruments, which will in deed shew the nature of the musicke, but never carrie the spirit and (as it were) that livelie soule which the dittie giveth, but of this enough. And to returne to the expressing of the ditty, the matter is now come to that state that though a song be never so wel made & never so aptlie applied to the words, yet shall you hardlie find singers to expresse it as it ought to be, for most of our church men (so they can crie louder in ý quier than their fellowes) care for no more, whereas by the contrarie, they ought to studie howe to vowell and sing cleane, expressing their wordes with devotion and passion, whereby to draw the hearer as it were in chaines of gold by the eares to the consideration of holie things. But this for the most part, you shall find amongest them, that let them continue never so long in the church, yea though it were twentie yeares, they will never studie to sing better then they did the first day of their preferment to that place, so that it should seeme that having obtained the living which they sought for, they have little or no care at all either of their owne credit, or well discharging of that dutie whereby they have their maintenance. But to returne to our Motets, if you compose in this kind, you must cause your harmonie to carrie a majestie taking discordes and bindings so often as you canne, but let it be in long notes, for the nature of it will not beare short notes and quicke motions, which denotate a kind of wantonnes.

This musicke (a lamentable case) being the chiefest both for art and utilitie, is notwithstanding little esteemed, and in small request with the greatest number of those who most highly seeme to favor art, which is the cause that the composers of musick who otherwise would

---

[1] Motet is derived from French *mot*, not from 'motion.'

follow the depth of their skill, in this kinde are compelled for lack of *maecenates* to put on another humor, and follow that kind whereunto they have neither beene brought up, nor yet (except so much as they can learne by seeing other mens works in an unknown tounge) doe perfectlie understand ý nature of it, such be the newfangled opinions of our countrey men, who will highlie esteeme whatsoever commeth from beyond the seas, and speciallie from Italie, be it never so simple, contemning that which is done at home though it be never so excellent. Nor yet is that fault of esteeming so highlie the light musicke particular to us in England, but generall through the world, which is the cause that the musitions in all countries and chiefly in Italy, have imploied most of their studies in it: whereupon a learned man of our time writing upon *Cicero* his dreame of *Scipio* saith, that the musicians of this age instead of drawing the minds of men to the consideration of heaven and heavenlie thinges, doe by the contrarie set wide open the gates of hell, causing such as delight in the exercise of their art tumble headlong into perdition.

This much for Motets, under which I comprehend all grave and sober musicke; the light musicke hath beene of late more deepely dived into, so that there is no vanitie which in it hath not beene followed to the full, but the best kind of it is termed *Madrigal,* a word for the etymologie of which I can give no reason, yet use sheweth that it is a kinde of musicke made upon songs and sonnets, such as *Petrarcha* and many Poets of our time have excelled in. This kinde of musicke weare not so much disalowable if the Poets who compose the ditties would abstaine from some obscenities, which all honest eares abhor, and sometime from blasphemies to such as this, *ch'altro di te iddio non voglio* [other than you I'll have no god] which no man (at least who hath any hope of salvation) can sing without trembling. As for the musick it is next unto the Motet, the most artificiall and to men of understanding most delightfull. If therefore you will compose in this kind you must possesse your selfe with an amorous humor (for in no composition shal you prove admirable except you put on, and possesse your selfe wholy with that vaine wherein you compose) so that you must in your musicke be wavering like the wind, sometime wanton, sometime drooping, sometime grave and staide, otherwhile effeminat, you may maintaine points and revert them, use triplaes [triple time] and shew the verie uttermost of your varietie, and the more varietie you shew the better shal you please. In this kind our age excelleth, so that if you would imitate any, I would appoint you these for guides: Alfonso Ferrabosco for deepe skill, Luca Marenzio for good ayre and fine invention, Horatio Vecchi, Stephano Venturi, Ruggiero Giovanelli, and

John Croce,[1] with divers others who are verie good, but not so generalie good as these.

[7]

[1] Alfonso Ferrabosco (1543–1588), born and died in Bologna, lived in England, with interruptions, from ca. 1562–1578; Luca Marenzio's (1553–1599) madrigals were introduced to England in 1588; Orazio Vecchi (1550–1605), composer of the madrigal opera *Il Amfiparnasso* (c. 1594); Steffano Venturi, Venetian madrigalist of the sixteenth century; Ruggiero Giovanelli (c. 1560–1625), successor of Palestrina at St. Peter's in Rome; Giovanni della Croce (1558–1609), master of the chapel at St. Mark's, Venice.

CLAUDIO MONTEVERDI

1567–1643

Although today the dramatic impact of Monteverdi's operas is less intense than it must have been when they were new, the music still retains an unimpaired freshness and beauty. Those still occasionally revived—*Orfeo* (1607) and the *Incoronazione di Poppea* (1642)—are a cross between oratorio and opera and hence perhaps more effective in concert form than when staged. Yet Monteverdi was aware of the necessary ingredients of a good libretto: witness his witty letter to Alessandro Striggio, dissecting a libretto, *The Marriage of Thetis and Peleus*, which did not meet with his approval.

Monteverdi's vocal line is always emotionally expressive and his orchestra colorful. The use of pizzicato and tremolo in the opera orchestra is reputedly his invention. Also, he was the first to use a fairly complete orchestra in opera. His efforts to fuse drama and music into a complete whole were repeated in the eighteenth century by Gluck, and again in the nineteenth, by Wagner.

The prefaces to his books of madrigals declare his musical credo. Here he lashes back at Artusi, the academic critic of his free modulations, of his conscious breaking of the age-old rules. He advises the composer to write what he feels, not what the laws prescribe. His *Second Practice*, a proposed complete answer to Artusi, never appeared for lack of time. Monteverdi was more amply defended by his brother, Giulio Cesare, in the "Dichiarazione" (Declaration) included in the *Scherzi Musicali*, published in Venice, in 1607.

One of the best known and best loved of Italian madrigals is his *Lasciate mi morire*, written both as a lament for his opera *Arianna* and as a five-part madrigal. Here, as in most of his vocal works, the significance of the words dictates the melodic line. High and low notes are employed for words representing height and depth, nature is musically imitated, the sigh and the sob are put to music. Textual meaning is paramount. As Monteverdi says: "Let the word be master of the melody, not its slave."

A DEFENSE OF MODERN MUSIC

Preface to *Fifth Book of Madrigals*, 1605

To the reader: Do not be surprised if I allow these madrigals to go to press without first answering the remarks made by Artusi about certain small details in them. Being in the service of His Serene Highness of Mantua, I do not have the necessary time at my disposal. Nevertheless, I have written my answer, to let it be known that I do not write things by accident. As soon as it is copied, it will appear under the title of *Second Practice* or *On the Perfection of Modern Music*, and will astonish some people for whom there can exist no other "practice" than that taught by Zarlino. But they may rest assured that, as far as consonances and dissonances are concerned, there is another point of view to be considered besides the already existing one, and that this other point of view is justified by the satisfaction it gives both to the ear and to the intelligence. I wanted to tell you this, so that the title *Second Practice* should not be used by others and, also, so that creative spirits may in the meantime search out new things relative to harmony, and be assured that the modern composer builds his works on the basis of truth.   [1]

REQUIREMENTS OF AN OPERA LIBRETTO

From: Letter to Alessandro Striggio the Younger[1]
Venice, December 9, 1616

At the outset I would say that, in general, music should be mistress of the air and not only of water, which in my language means that the themes outlined in this fable are all crude and earth-bound, seriously lacking in beautiful harmonies, since the harmonies will be confined to the coarsest blasts of the winds of the earth, painful to hear and painful to play on the stage. Here I leave the verdict to your exquisite and very intelligent taste; for, as a result of this fault, three guitars would be needed instead of one; in place of one harp, three, and so on. Instead of a delicate voice, a forced one would be required. Besides, in my opinion, the imitation of speech would have to be supported by wind instruments rather than by delicate stringed instruments, since, I believe, the harmonies of Tritons and other marine gods should be given to trombones and trumpets, not to guitars or to the harpsichord and the harp. In actuality, being maritime, the action takes place outside the city, and Plato teaches us that *cithara debet esse in civitate et*

---

[1] The librettist of *Orfeo*.

thibia in agris (the guitar belongs in the city and the flute in the fields). So, either delicate instruments will be inappropriate, or the appropriate instruments will not be delicate.

In addition, I have noticed that there are twenty performers, Cupids, Zephyrs and Sirens. Thus, many sopranos would be needed. It must not be forgotten that the Winds, that is to say, the Zephyrs and the Boreae, must sing, too. How, my dear sir, can I imitate the speech of the Winds, if they do not talk? And how can I induce emotion in them? Arianna moved us because she was a woman, Orfeo because he was a man, not a Wind. Harmonies imitate these personages themselves, but one cannot, by means of melodic line, realize the windstorm, the bleating of lambs, the neighing of horses, and so on. To repeat, harmonies do not imitate the speech of the Winds because it does not exist.

Further, the ballets scattered through this fable have not one rhythm to which one can dance. The entire fable, because of my ignorance which is not negligible, does not move me at all, and it is with difficulty that I even understand it. I do not feel that it brings me naturally to an ending which moves me. *Arianna* moved me to a real lament; *Orfeo* stirred me to a true prayer, but I do not know what the aim of this fable is. What, then, does Your Illustrious Highness wish music to do for it? [2]

THE IMITATION OF NATURE

From: Letter to an unknown addressee,
Venice, October 22, 1633

The title of the book will be as follows: *Melody or Second Musical Practice*. By "Second" I mean, "from the modern aspect." "First" denotes "from the aspect of antiquity." I divide the book into three parts which correspond to the three divisions of melody. In the first, I speak of line, in the second, of harmony, and in the third, of rhythm. I am of the opinion that it will not be unwelcome to the public for, during the course of my practical work, I discovered, when I was about to write "Ariadne's Lament," that I was unable to find any book which could instruct me in the method of the imitation of nature, or which could even have made clear to me that I should be an imitator of nature. The sole exception was Plato, one of whose ideas was, however, so obscure that, with my weak sight and at such great distance, I could hardly apprehend the little he could teach me. I must say that it has cost me great effort to complete the laborious work necessary to achieve what little I have accomplished in the imitation of nature. And for this reason, I hope I shall not cause displeasure. If I should succeed in bringing this work to a conclusion, as I so dearly wish, I should count myself happy to be praised less for modern compositions than for those in the traditional style. And for this presumption I beg forgiveness anew. [3]

THE INVENTION OF THE AGITATO STYLE

From: Preface to *Eighth Book of Madrigals:*
Madrigali guerrieri ed amorosi, 1638

I consider the principal passions or emotions of the soul to be three, namely, anger, serenity, and humility. The best philosophers affirm this; the very nature of our voice, with its high, low and middle ranges, shows it; and the art of music clearly manifests it in these three terms: agitated, soft and moderate. I have not been able to find an example of the agitated style in the works of past composers, but I have discovered many of the soft and moderate types. However, Plato describes the first in the third book of his *Rhetoric* in these words: "Take that harmony which would fittingly imitate the brave man going to war." [*Republic,* 399 A] Knowing that contrasts are what move our souls, and that such is the aim of all good music—as Boethius asserts: "Music is a part of us, and either ennobles or degrades our behavior" —I set myself with no little study and zeal to rediscover this style.

Considering that all the best philosophers maintain that the pyrrhic or fast tempo was used for agitated, warlike dances, and contrariwise, the slow, spondaic tempo for their opposites, I thought about the semibreve [whole note] and proposed that each semibreve correspond to a spondee. Reducing this to sixteen semichromes [sixteenth notes], struck one after another and joined to words expressing anger and scorn, I could hear in this short example a resemblance to the emotion I was seeking, although the words did not follow the rapid beat of the instrument.

To arrive at a better proof, I resorted to the divine Tasso, as the poet who expresses most appropriately and naturally in words the emotions he wishes to depict, and I chose his description of the combat between Tancred and Clorinda as the theme for my music expressing the contrary passions aroused by war, prayer and death.

In the year 1624 I had this work performed before the most eminent citizens of Venice, at the house of the Most Illustrious and Excellent Signor Girolamo Mocenigo, noble knight and servant of the Most

Serene Republic and my special patron and protector. It was received with much applause and was highly praised.

Having met with success in my method of depicting anger, I proceeded with even greater zeal in my investigations and wrote divers compositions, both ecclesiastical and chamber works. These found such favor with other composers that they not only *spoke* their praise but, to my great joy and honor, *wrote* it by imitating my work. Consequently, it has seemed wise to let it be known that the investigation and the first efforts in this style—so necessary to the art of music, and without which it can rightly be said that music has been imperfect up to now, having had but two styles, soft and moderate—originated with me. [4]

GIROLAMO FRESCOBALDI
1583-1643

Frescobaldi is the greatest name of Italian keyboard music. Just as Caccini created a new style of singing, as Monteverdi first composed truly dramatic music, so Frescobaldi introduced the idiomatic keyboard style both for the organ and the harpsichord. His free counterpoint, his dramatic manner of playing his music, mark him as the foremost protagonist of the new ideas. And he was the first to put his ideas about keyboard playing on paper.

He was the most accomplished organist of his era. When he played services at St. Peter's in Rome, he is said to have attracted audiences of as many as thirty thousand people.

It is felt that the great classical period of organ playing began with Frescobaldi. Hence, his remarks on seventeenth century playing style quoted here have contemporary validity, as have those of the later Couperin [1] and Carl Philipp Emanuel Bach.[2]

HARPSICHORD PLAYING

Preface to *Toccatas and Partitas, Book I*, 1615

I well know how performers like to indulge in impressive ornaments and many passages. Therefore I take the liberty of adding the following observations to these, my modest products, which I herewith publish. However, I wish to add that I fully recognize the merits of others and maintain the greatest respect for their abilities. May the benevolent, studious reader receive kindly observations that are made with the best intentions.

1. These pieces should not be played to a strict beat any more than modern madrigals which, though difficult, are made easier by taking the beat now slower, now faster, and by even pausing altogether in accordance with the expression and meaning of the text.

2. I not only saw to it that the toccatas should be rich in passages and ornaments, but that their various sections should be playable sepa-

[1] See page 35. [2] See page 56.

rately. Thus the performer need not play the whole toccata through, but may finish at his discretion.

3. The beginning of the toccatas should be played slowly and arpeggiando. However, thereafter the notes of the chords must be struck together and also in the case of appoggiaturas and dissonances. Should this result in an impression of emptiness, the chords may be struck again at the discretion of the performer.

4. In trills and passages, whether they proceed scale- or leapwise, the last note should be held, no matter if this note be an eighth or sixteenth or different from the following note. This will prevent confusing one passage with the next.

5. The tempo of cadences, even where they are written in smaller note values, should be retarded. The approach to the end of a passage or cadence should likewise be taken more adagio.

6. A passage should end and be separated from the next at the point where a consonance occurs, written in quarter notes for both hands.

Where a trill occurs in one hand—right or left—at the same time as a passage in the other, the two should not be played note against note. The trill should be played fast and the passage slowly and *espressivo* in order to avoid confusion.

7. Passages in eighth and sixteenth notes occurring concomitantly in both hands should not be played too fast. The second of every two sixteenth notes should be dotted slightly (not the first).

8. Before a passage in sixteenth notes written for both hands, one should pause slightly on the preceding note even though it is black [short]. One should then courageously plunge into the passage, thus displaying the virtuosity of the hands to greater advantage.

9. It would be wise to choose a broad tempo for partitas that contain passages and expressive sections. This should also be observed in the toccatas. But partitas which contain no passages should be taken rather fast. It must be left to the discretion and good taste of the player to hit on exactly the right tempo to bring out the spirit and perfection of this style of playing.

The passacaglia movements may be played separately. The tempo of one movement should be adapted to that of the other. The same obtains for the ciaconnas.[1]   [1]

---

[1] The last paragraph is an addition to the edition of 1637.

ORGAN PLAYING

Preface to *Fiori musicali*, 1635

To the Reader: Having always desired to help students in the profession with whatever talent God has granted me, I have demonstrated this desire through my books which contain all manner of capriccios and inventions, printed partly in tablature and partly in score. It has been my constant wish that all those who read and study my works should derive satisfaction and profit from them. Concerning this new book I wish only to say that my main purpose was to compose pieces in such a style as would assist organists in their verses [interludes] in masses and vespers. Their knowledge of these will prove useful; they may employ them at will, and in the *canzoni* and *ricercari* may finish at any cadence, should the pieces seem too long.

I believe it will greatly benefit the player to play from the score, not only in order to familiarize himself thoroughly with this style of composition, but also because in this way the true artist will be differentiated from the ignoramus.

I need add no more except to say that experience is the best teacher. He who wishes to advance in his art should endeavor to apply what I say here. The truth of what I say he will see from the benefit he derives from it.

1. Trills or expressive passages occurring in the toccatas should be played quietly (adagio); eighth notes appearing in the parts should be taken somewhat faster, the beat being slowed down where trills reappear. In a word, the player should use his own judgment and taste.

2. The beginning of a toccata is to be played slowly even when it consists of eighth notes, and then faster in relation to its passages.

3. The Kyries may be played rapidly or slowly according to the feeling of the performer.

4. It should also be mentioned that some of the verses [interludes], though intended for the Kyrie, may also be used in other contexts at the discretion of the performer.

5. The *cantus firmus* is to be played legato but should this prove impracticable for the hands, the performer may break the line. However, I have tried to make it as easy for the player as I could.   [2]

HEINRICH SCHÜTZ

1585–1672

Born exactly one century before Bach, Schütz was one of his most important forerunners. His work falls between the unaccompanied choral music of Palestrina, Vittoria, and Byrd, and the unaccompanied choral music of Bach.

In 1609 he went to Italy and for four years studied with Giovanni Gabrieli. Twenty years later, during the Thirty Years' War, he made a second journey to Venice where he became acquainted with the new developments of Monteverdi. While there, he wrote the choral works in the Italian style which he mentions in the preface to his *Symphoniae sacrae*, thus introducing the Italian baroque style of writing to his native Germany. He also set to music Rinuccini's libretto for *Dafne*—previously set by Peri and Caccini—which had been translated into German, thereby actually giving Germany its first opera. The score is no longer extant.

Primarily a religious composer, Schütz set the *Psalms of David*, the Passions—precursors of the Bach Passions—and other liturgical texts.

TEMPO IN THE NEW STYLE

From: Preface to *The Psalms of David* (for 8
and more parts), 1619

Since I have set these *Psalms* in the *stilo recitativo* which until now has been almost unknown in Germany, and since the Psalms, having many words, call for a continuous declamation without long repetition, I would ask those who are unfamiliar with this style to be sure not to hurry the beat. It would be best to adhere to a moderate tempo, so that the words may be clearly understood. Otherwise, there will ensue a most unpleasant harmony, all too like a *battaglia di mosche* [a battle of flies] and wholly at variance with the composer's intention.

[1]

COMPOSING NEW MUSIC FOR THE CHURCH

From: Preface to *The Psalms of David* (for 4 parts), 1628

Although these new melodies for the late Dr. Cornelius Becker's *Book of Psalms* possess little art or value, they were not created without difficulties.

First, since I had to follow the manner of the old church tunes and yet comply with the requirements of the music of today, I did not always use double-whole and whole notes, but mostly half-, quarter-, and eighth-notes. Thus, the singing will not only be more lively, but the words less protracted, better understood, and the psalm sooner finished. These faster notes, if sung according to the present fashion in their proper beat, will not detract from the gravity of the song; even the old church tunes, though notated in long notes, are now being sung with a faster beat in Christian assemblies.

Secondly, instead of rests, I have used a comma after each verse because, in this kind of composition, the rests are not strictly observed, and such arias and melodies can be sung with more grace when they follow the meaning of the words. However, if someone should find these melodies too secular, or if a composer or organist wishes to use them for a chorale, he may set the descant (the chief part) to longer notes and interpose rests. This, I hope, will prove satisfactory.

Finally, dear reader, if my labor pleases you, may you use it to praise God the All-Highest; but if one or the other tune displease you, then use, instead, the old, familiar melodies which you will find listed in the index to this book, or else try to help others compose better melodies and publish them to the greater Glory of God. *Vale.*   [2]

THE MODERN ITALIAN STYLE IN GERMANY

Preface to *Symphoniae Sacrae, Book II*, 1647

I need not detain you with the tale of how, in the year 1629, during my second sojourn in Italy where I lived for some time, I indited—with the little talent God gave me—after the musical manner then in vogue there, a little Latin work for one, two and three vocal parts, accompanied by two violins or similar instruments, and within a short time had it published in Venice under the title *Symphoniae Sacrae*.

Inasmuch as parts of the work which were imported into Germany found such favor among our musicians, and were performed in the most excellent places to German texts instead of Latin, I was spurred on to compose such a work in our German mother tongue. After prolonged beginnings, I finally finished it, with God's help, along with much other work.

However, until now I have been prevented from sending it to press because of the miserable conditions prevailing in our dear fatherland which adversely affect all the arts, music included; and even more importantly, because the modern Italian style of composition and performance (with which, as the sagacious Signor Claudio Monteverdi remarks in the preface to his *Eighth Book of Madrigals*,[1] music is said finally to have reached its perfection) has remained largely unknown in this country.

Experience has proved that the modern Italian manner of composition and its proper tempo, with its many black notes, does not in most cases lend itself to use by Germans who have not been trained for it. Believing one had composed really good works in this style, one has often found them so violated and corrupted in performance that they offered a sensitive ear nothing but boredom and distaste, and called down unjustified opprobrium on the composer and on the German nation, the inference being that we are entirely unskilled in the noble art of music—and certain foreigners have more than once leveled such accusations at us.

As only a few manuscript copies of my little work were extant (it was dedicated to the then Highborn Prince and Lord, Christian V of Denmark and Norway, Prince of the Goths and Wends, as may be seen from the affixed letter of dedication), and as I learned that many sections, carelessly and improperly copied, had got into the hands of eminent musicians, I was forced to revise it carefully and have it published for those who may find pleasure in it.

I hope that intelligent musicians who have been trained in good schools will appreciate the labor I have spent on it, and not be entirely displeased by the newly introduced style, [for] to please them alone, next to God, these present few copies are being brought to light.

As for others, above all those of us Germans who do not know how properly to perform this modern music, with its black notes and steady, prolonged bowing on the violin, and who, albeit untrained, still wish to play this way I herewith kindly request them not to be ashamed to seek instruction from experts in this style and not to shirk home practice before they undertake a public performance of any of these pieces. Otherwise they and the author—though he be innocent— may receive unexpected ridicule rather than praise.

While in the Concerto "Es steh Gott auf" I have to a degree followed Signor Claudio Monteverdi's madrigal "Armato il cuor"[2] as

[1] See p. 22.   [2] *Scherzi Musicali* (Venice, 1632), No. 8.

well as one of his *ciaconne* (with two tenor parts),[1] I leave it to those familiar with the aforementioned compositions to judge to what extent I have done this. However, let no one suspect the rest of my work unduly, for I am not prone to deck my cap with strange feathers.

Finally, should God grant me longer life, I hereby promise—with His gracious aid—to publish soon more of my humble works, among them such as may be most effectively used by those who are not and do not intend to become professional musicians. *Vale.*   [3]

COUNTERPOINT *VERSUS* THOROUGHBASS

Preface to *Geistliche Chormusik* (for 5–7 parts, with optional BC), 1648

Kind Reader: It is obvious that since the *stilo concertato* over a basso continuo came from Italy to the notice of us Germans, it has been greatly favored by us and has found more followers than any previous style; various and sundry musical works, published in Germany and found in bookstalls, amply testify to this. Far be it from me to disapprove of this. Indeed, I recognize among us many who are interested and well-skilled in music, whose fame I do not begrudge, but willingly grant. Nevertheless, no musician, trained in a good school in the most difficult study of counterpoint, can start on any other kind of composition and handle it correctly, unless he has first trained himself sufficiently in the style without basso continuo and has also mastered all the prerequisites for regular composition, such as: disposition of the modes; simple, mixed and inverted fugues; double counterpoint; different styles for different kinds of music; part writing; connection of themes, and so on, of which the learned theoreticians write profusely and in which students of counterpoint are being orally trained in technical schools. No composition of even an experienced composer lacking such a background (even though it may appear as heavenly harmony to ears not properly trained in music) can stand up or be judged better than an empty shell.

All this has led me once more to write a little work without basso continuo, thereby perhaps to refresh some composers, especially German beginners, and encourage them to crack this hard nut (in which the true kernel and proper foundation of good counterpoint is to be found) and first to pass this test, before they attempt the *stilo concertato.* In Italy, which is the true university of music (where in my youth I laid the foundation for this profession), it was customary for

[1] Ibid., No. 9

beginners first to work out and perform certain sacred or secular pieces without basso continuo, and I assume that this excellent procedure is still observed there. Therefore I hope that these remarks intended to stimulate music and further our nation's glory will be well received by everyone and not taken as intending any belittlement.

I must also mention that this style in church music without basso continuo (which I have therefore called *Geistliche Chormusik*) is not uniform throughout: some of these compositions are meant for solo voices; some for a full chorus with vocal and instrumental parts; and some are written so that the parts should not be duplicated or triplicated, but split into separate vocal and instrumental parts, and thus may be effectively performed on the organ or even in several choruses (if it be a composition of eight, twelve or more parts). Specimens of these types may be found in my present work, composed for a few parts only (to some parts in the final numbers I have not added the text for this reason), and the intelligent musician can recognize this in the earlier pieces and will know how to proceed properly with the later ones.

Here and now I want to say and publicly to request that no one take the above remarks to mean that I want to nominate or recommend this or any other of my published musical works—the little value of which I admit—as a text or a safe model. I would rather direct everyone toward the Italian style which has been canonized, as it were, by the most eminent composers, and toward other old and new classical writers, whose excellent and incomparable works will (for all those who copy and study them diligently) shine as a bright light . . . and lead them on the right path to the study of counterpoint. Furthermore, I hope, and have some reason to believe, that a musician [1] who is well known to me and who is an expert both in theory and practice, will shortly publish some treatises on these subjects which will be useful and profitable, especially to us Germans. I shall not fail to promote this endeavor zealously, so that it may benefit musical study in general.

Finally, should one or another organist glance at my little work composed without basso continuo, and perhaps want to reduce it in tablature or score, I hope he will not have to repent of the time and labor thus spent, but that his efforts will aid in spreading this sort of music more widely.

God be with us all. [4]

[1] Most likely a reference to Marco Scacchi (c. 1595–c. 1686), capellmeister in Warsaw.

HENRY PURCELL

1658-1695

The rosy future for his country's music which Purcell foretold in his dedication to *Dioclesian* did not materialize. He himself brought the golden age of English choral and instrumental polyphony to its zenith. After him English music deteriorated, its practitioners imitating continental styles virtually until its resurrection in the twentieth century.

Purcell's theatrical gifts are manifest in his incidental music to *The Faerie Queen, King Arthur, The Tempest,* and other plays. Yet it is his *Dido and Aeneas* which is most widely and appreciatively known. Not the first attempt at English opera, *Dido and Aeneas* has remained almost the only one to achieve lasting fame and it has retained its freshness through the centuries.

THE MODERN ITALIAN STYLE IN ENGLAND

Preface to *Sonatas of III Parts,* 1683 [This preface was probably written for Purcell by John Playford]

Ingenuous Reader: Instead of an elaborate harangue on the beauty and the charms of Musick (which after all the learned Enconions that words can contrive commends it self best by the performance of a skilful hand, and an angelical voice:) I shall say but a very few things by way of Preface, concerning the following Book, and its Author: for its Author, he has faithfully endeavour'd a just imitation of the most fam'd Italian Masters; [1] principally, to bring the seriousness and gravity of that sort of Musick into vogue, and reputation among our Countrymen, whose humor, 'tis time now, should begin to loath the levity, and balladry of our neighbours: The attempt he confesses to be bold, and

[1] It is difficult to ascertain which Italian works Purcell refers to as models here; so few had reached England prior to the *Sonatas'* appearance in 1683. He may have had in mind Giovanni Battista Vitali, whose sonatas greatly resemble his own; or Lelio Colista, the only Italian composer he mentions in his additions to Playford.

daring, there being Pens and Artists of more eminent abilities, much better qualify'd for the imployment than his, or himself, which he well hopes these his weak endeavours, will in due time provoke, and enflame to a more accurate undertaking. He is not asham'd to own his unskilfulness in the Italian language; but that's the unhappiness of his Education, which cannot justly be accounted his fault, however he thinks he may warrantably affirm, that he is not mistaken in the power of the Italian Notes, or elegancy of their Compositions, which he would recommend to the English Artists. There has been neit' ·r care, nor industry wanting, as well in contriving, as revising the whole Work; which had been abroad in this world much sooner, but that he has now thought fit to cause the whole Thorough Bass to be Engraven, which was a thing quite besides his first Resolutions. It remains only that the English Practitioner be enform'd, that he will find a few terms of Art perhaps unusual to him, the chief of which are the following: *Adagio* and *Grave*, which import nothing but a very slow movement: *Presto Largo, Poco Largo*, or *Largo* by it self, a middle movement: *Allegro*, and *Vivace*, a very brisk, swift, or fast movement: *Piano*, soft. The Author has no more to add, but his hearty wishes, that his Book may fall into no other hands but theirs who carry Musical Souls about them; for he is willing to flatter himself into a belief, that with such his labours will seem neither unpleasant, nor unprofitable. *Vale.* [1]

ENGLISH MUSIC IN ITS NONAGE

From: Dedication to the Duke of Somerset of *The Prophetess, or the History of Dioclesian,* 1690 [This Dedication was written for Purcell by Dryden]

Musick and Poetry have ever been acknowledg'd Sisters, which walking hand in hand, support each other; As Poetry is the harmony of Words, so Musick is that of Notes; and as Poetry is a Rise above Prose and Oratory, so is Musick the exaltation of Poetry. Both of them may excel apart, but sure they are most excellent when they are joyn'd, because nothing is then wanting to either of their Perfections: for thus they appear like Wit and Beauty in the same Person. Poetry and Painting have arrived to their perfection in our own Country: Musick is yet but in its Nonage, a forward Child, which gives hope of what it may be hereafter in *England,* when the Masters of it shall find more Encouragement. 'Tis now learning *Italian,* which is its best Master, and studying a little of the *French* Air to give it somewhat more of Gayety and Fashion. Thus being farther from the Sun, we are of later Growth than our Neighbour Countries, and must be content to shake off our Barbarity by degrees. The present Age seems already dispos'd to be refin'd, and to distinguish betwixt wild Fancy, and a just, numerous Composition.   [2]

COMPOSING UPON A GROUND

From: Purcell's additions to Playford's Introduction to the Skill of Musick

One thing that was forgot to be spoken of in its proper Place, I think necessary to say a little of now, which is Composing upon a Ground,[1] a very easy thing to do, and requires but little Judgment; as 'tis generally used in *Chacones*, and often the *Ground* is four notes gradually descending, but to maintain *Fuges* upon it would be difficult, being confin'd like a *Canon* to a *Plain Song*. There are also pretty *Dividing Grounds* (of whom the *Italians* were the first *Inventors* to *Single Songs*, or *Songs* of Two Parts, which to do neatly, requires considerable Pains, and the best way to be acquainted with 'em, is to Score much, and chuse the best Authors.   [3]

[1] These remarks on *ground bass*—a constantly recurring bass phrase over which are set a varying harmony and melody—are quoted from the 1700 edition of Playford's *Introduction*. Purcell was a master of *ground bass*, as illustrated in his fourfold use of it in *Dido and Aeneas*, notably in Dido's lament, and in his *Chaconne* for strings.

FRANÇOIS COUPERIN

1668–1733

Added to its quaintness, charm, and humanity, Couperin's *L'art de Toucher le Clavecin* contains cogent remarks on touch, fingering, and the execution of ornaments, the last such an important facet of French keyboard music of the period. The series of eight harpsichord *Préludes* at the end of the treatise are not only felicitous works, but excellent examples of his principles of instruction. In his *Suites*, Bach shows the influence of Couperin both in form and content.

The most renowned member of a highly musical family, François Couperin is known as Couperin le Grand to distinguish him from an uncle of the same name. An organist as well as harpsichordist, he played the organ in the Church of St. Gervais from his eighteenth year until his death. His compositions, reflections of his twofold ability, include elegant, courtly harpsichord music as well as religious vocal music, *Élévations*, *Leçons de Ténèbres*, and motets.

Besides the instructive monograph on harpsichord playing, part of which is quoted here, Couperin wrote another didactic work on the art of harmonization, *Règle pour l'Accompagnement*.

From: *The Art of Playing the Harpsichord*, 1717

THE BEGINNER AT THE HARPSICHORD

The proper age to start children is from six to seven years, not that this excludes older people, but naturally, in order to mold and develop the hands for playing the harpsichord, the sooner one begins, the better, and since grace is necessary for it, one should begin with the position of the body.

To be seated at the proper height, the underside of the elbows, the wrists and the fingers should be kept on one level. One should choose a chair accordingly.

An appropriately high support should be placed under the feet of young people and adjusted as they grow, so that their feet do not dangle in the air, and they can keep the body correctly balanced.

An adult should sit about nine inches from the keyboard, measuring from the waist, and young people proportionately less. The middle of the body and the middle of the keyboard should correspond.

When seated at the harpsichord, the body should be turned slightly to the right. The knees should not be pressed together too much, the feet should be kept parallel, and above all, the right foot should be kept well forward.

As for facial grimaces, one can correct them by placing a mirror on the reading desk of the spinet or harpsichord.

If the player keeps his wrist too high, the only remedy I have found is to have someone hold a flexible stick so that it passes above the faulty wrist and at the same time below the other wrist. If the trouble is the reverse, the opposite should be done. One must absolutely not allow the stick to cramp the player. Little by little the fault will correct itself. I have found this invention very useful.

It is better and more sensible not to beat time with the head, the body or the feet. One should have an easy manner at the harpsichord and avoid either staring fixedly at any object, or looking too vague; in short, one should look at the audience, if there is any, as if one were occupied with nothing else. This advice is only for those who play without the help of their scores.

Very young people should at first use a spinet or only one keyboard of the harpsichord, the one or the other being very lightly quilled. This is of paramount importance, for good execution depends much more on flexibility and great freedom of the fingers than on strength. If a child is allowed to begin playing on two keyboards, it will of necessity strain its small hands in order to make the keys sound; badly placed hands and a hard touch will be the result.

Softness of touch depends on keeping the fingers as close as possible to the keys. It stands to reason (experience aside) that a hand which drops from a height will give a much dryer stroke, and that therefore the quill will produce a much harder sound from the string, than if the hand is kept close to the keys.

During the first lessons it is recommended that the child practice only with the instructor present. Children are too easily distracted to discipline themselves to hold their hands in the prescribed position. At the beginning of children's study I actually keep the key of the instrument on which I am instructing them as a precautionary measure, so that in my absence they can not spoil in a moment what I have so carefully set in three quarters of a hour.

Apart from the usual ornaments such as shakes, mordents, and *ports-de-voix* [appogiaturas from below combined with mordents], I have always had my students do little finger exercises, either passages of varied arpeggios, beginning with the simplest and in the easiest keys, and by degrees leading them to the greatest dexterity and the most difficult keys. These little exercises, which cannot be repeated too often, are so many parts ready to fall in place and form a whole, and can be used on many occasions.

People who begin late or who have been badly taught must take care, since their muscles may have become stiff or acquired bad habits, to relax them, or have someone else relax them, before they sit down to the harpsichord; that is, they should stretch or have their fingers stretched in all directions. This also helps alert the mind, and one is more free.   [1]

LEARNING THE NOTES

One should begin to teach children notation only after they have a number of pieces in their fingers. It is nearly impossible that, while they are looking at their notes, their fingers should not get out of position, fumble, or that the ornaments themselves should not be changed. Besides, memory is developed in learning things by heart.

[2]

A MUSICIAN'S HANDS

Men who wish to arrive at a certain degree of perfection should never do any work which is harmful to their hands. Women's hands, because they do no such work, are generally better. I have already said that muscular flexibility contributes much more to good playing than strength. My proof is evidenced by the difference between women's hands and men's hands. A man's left hand, which he uses less in his work, is commonly the more supple at the harpsichord. [3]

MEASURE AND RHYTHM

I find that we confuse measure with what is known as cadence or rhythm. Measure defines the quantity and equality of the time, and cadence is properly the spirit or the soul which must be combined with it. Italian *sonades* [popular at the time] are hardly susceptible to cadence. But all our airs for violin, our pieces for harpsichord, for viols, etc., describe and seem to want to express this spirit. Since we have never devised symbols to communicate our particular ideas, we try to remedy this by indications such as *Tendrement, Vivement*, etc., which suggest more or less what we would like to have heard. I wish someone would take the trouble to translate our indications for the benefit of foreigners, and thus allow them to judge the excellence of our instrumental music.

As for the delicate pieces which are played on the harpsichord, it is wise not to play them quite as slowly as they are played on other instruments, because of the short duration of harpsichord tones, and because expression and taste are retained whether the tempo is fast or slow. [4]

GEORG PHILIPP TELEMANN

1681–1767

Georg Philipp Telemann was one of the most cosmopolitan embodiments of the musical life of his time. Unlike Bach, who was known primarily in Germany, and Handel, whose musical activities were centered in England, Telemann, a personal friend of both, was the all-European figure of the eighteenth century. He founded or revived the Collegia Musica in Leipzig, Frankfurt and Hamburg, thereby inaugurating concert life as we know it. He was, with equal distinction, director of church and court music.

To call him prolific as a composer would be an understatement. No one has so far compiled a list of his complete works which probably run into many thousands: about sixty operas, fifty passions, a thousand French Overtures and cantatas and myriad chamber and orchestral pieces. Not all of this survives, nor does everything extant represent him at his best, but the abundance of his invention, his thorough (though self-taught) workmanship, and his alertness in matters of style and taste made him one of the best-loved composers of his time throughout Europe from France to Russia.

Telemann was equally skilled in the French and Italian manner, and spanned the styles of his era from late Baroque practices to the galant and the sentimental; in his last works (for example, the monodrama *Ino*, 1765), he touched on the classical.

MUSIC AND WORDS

From: Preface to T. E. Schubart's *Fortsetzung des harmonischen Gottesdienstes*, 1731

Just as not everyone is born a poet, so every poet cannot write texts adaptable to music, and especially sacred music. It would be desirable for experts to explore this question. But meanwhile, the esteemed author of the present Cantatas has given the world a model which contains every beauty requisite to such compositions. The ideas and phrases from Scripture, the simple vitality of the arias, the constant variety of emotion, the recitatives neither too long drawn-out nor too abrupt, the avoidance of too many dangling phrases, especially at full and half cadences in arias, and other such features testify to the truth of what I say. It has been my good fortune to set my music to such excellent texts, and I am resolved to make the best use of them. I pray God may grant me the strength to do so for His greater glory and for the service of mankind.   [1]

From: *Autobiography* in Mattheson's *Ehrenpforte,* 1740

POLISH MUSIC

In Pless, a dominion of the Court of Promnitz in upper Silesia, where the Court used to repair for six months, as well as in Cracow, I became familiar with Polish and Hanakian music in their true, barbaric beauty. In the public taverns the band would consist of a fiddle strapped to the body, a Polish bagpipe, a bass trombone and a regal. The fiddle was tuned a third higher than usual, and could thus outscream any six ordinary violins. At places of better repute the regal was omitted, but the number of fiddles and bagpipes was augmented. Indeed, once I found thirty-six bagpipes and eight fiddles together. One can hardly believe with what inspiration bagpipers and fiddlers improvise while the dancers rest. An observant person could pick up enough ideas from them in a week to last a lifetime. In short, this music contains much valuable material, if it is properly treated.

In time I wrote various grand concertos and trios in this manner which I clothed in Italian dress, with divers adagios and allegros.   [2]

DUTIES OF A MUSICIAN

Until now I could have been compared to the cook who has many pots on the stove but serves from only one at a time. But now I was to serve everything at once—to show my knowledge of various instruments and my ability with voice and pen. The original intention at Eisenach was to install only an instrumental ensemble, the members of which were chosen by Herr Pantaleon Hebenstreit whom I can never praise enough, and to whom I was assigned as concert master. I had to play the violin and other instruments both at table and in the chamber, while Hebenstreit bore the title of director. He also fiddled in the chamber and was heard on his admirable cembalon. But after His Grace, the Duke, had found pleasure in some church cantatas which I had sung alone, a chapel was started, and I was ordered to contract for the necessary singers who had also to double as violinists. Upon their arrival I was appointed conductor, at the same time continuing my former duties. I must say that this chapel, largely arranged in the French manner, surpassed even the Paris opera orchestra which I had recently heard and which has a great reputation.

At this point I must call attention to Herr Hebenstreit's violinistic skill which certainly placed him among masters of the first rank. Whenever we were to perform a concerto together, I used to lock myself up a few days before. Fiddle in hand, shirtsleeve rolled up on my left arm to which I applied nerve-strengthening salves, I acted as my own teacher so that I might in some measure equal his power. And lo, it did help me to improve considerably. Since I composed everything for all the performances (save a few contributions by him), one can easily imagine how much I must have written.   [3]

PROGRESS IN MUSIC

From: Correspondence with Carl Heinrich Graun
about Rameau, 1751–52

If there is nothing new to be found in melody then we must seek novelty in harmony.   [4]

JEAN PHILIPPE RAMEAU
1683–1764

Celebrated as a composer, Rameau was equally famous as a theorist; his *Traité de l'Harmonie* is considered an important contribution to musical science. Among his other significant theoretical works are *Le Nouveau Système de Musique* and the *Dissertation sur les différents Méthodes d'Accompagnement pour le Clavecin ou pour l'Orgue*. He discovered chord inversion and established a principle of root progression that was not dependent on the real bass of the music. He founded his system of harmony on the tones of the common chord (thirds).

Rameau was a product of the Age of Reason, yet he consistently extolled feeling and instinct. He worshipped nature, and what he considered the artificialities of Italian music did not appeal to him. In the then raging battle over French versus Italian music—*La Guerre des Bouffons*, it was called—he championed the French and thereby incurred the wrath of Rousseau and the Encyclopedists.

As a composer he was a genuine innovator, applying new harmonies and rhythms, striking modulations and new orchestral effects in his operas and instrumental pieces. He discovered the independent powers of functional harmony which heretofore had always been more or less accidental, and not only explored it theoretically in his books but demonstrated it in his music. By making melody derive from harmony, he paved the way for the practice of Classical and Romantic music.

From: *Le Nouveau Système de musique théorique*, 1726

ON COMPOSITION

While composing music is not the time to recall the rules which might hold our genius in bondage. We must have recourse to the rules only when our genius and our ear seem to deny what we are seeking. [1]

We may note that the semi-skilled generally use a chord because it is familiar to them or pleases them, but the expert uses it only to the extent that he feels its power. [2]

We all have our habitual "modulations" into which we lapse when we lack the knowledge which might divert us from them to good purpose. We are accustomed to go through a mode in a certain fashion, to pass to the other, etc. However, all expressions are not alike, the connection between one phrase and another is not always the same, their qualities do not always have the same power, etc.　　　　[3]

TASTE

It is often by seeing and hearing musical works (operas and other good musical compositions), rather than by rules, that taste is formed.

[4]

From: *Observations sur notre instinct pour la musique et sur son principe,* 1734

HARMONY

To enjoy the effects of music fully, we must completely lose ourselves in it; to judge it, we must relate it to the source through which we are affected by it. This source is nature. Nature endows us with the feeling that moves us in all our musical experiences; we might call her gift *instinct.* Let us allow instinct to inform our judgments, let us see what mysteries it unfolds to us before we pronounce our verdicts, and if there are still men sufficiently self-assured to dare make judgments on their own authority, there is reason to hope that none will be found weak enough to listen to them.

A mind preoccupied, while listening to music, is never free enough to judge it. For instance, if we think to attribute the essential beauty of this art to changes from high to low, from fast to slow, soft to loud— means which do give variety to sounds—we will judge everything according to this prejudice, without considering how weak these means are, or what scant merit there is in making use of them; we will fail to perceive that they are foreign to harmony, which is the sole basis of music and the true source of its glorious effects.

A truly sensitive spirit must judge quite differently! If the spirit is not moved by the power of the expression, by the vivid colors of which the harmonist alone is capable, then it is not absolutely satisfied. The spirit may, of course, lend itself to whatever may entertain it, but it must evaluate things in proportion to the impact the given experience exerts.

Harmony alone can stir the emotions. It is the one source from which melody directly emanates, and draws its power. Contrasts between high and low, etc., make only superficial modifications in a melody; they add almost nothing . . .

If the imitation of noise and motion is not used as frequently in our music as in Italian music, it is because with us the main object is feeling. Feeling has no pre-determined rhythms, and consequently cannot be everywhere reduced to a regular measure without losing that verity which is its charm. The musical expression of the physical lies in beat and rhythm; that which touches the emotions comes, on the contrary, from harmony and its inflections, a fact which we must carefully weigh before deciding what should carry the balance.

The comic genre almost never aims to express emotion and consequently is the one genre that lends itself to those cadenced rhythms by which we do honor to Italian music. We do not always notice, however, how our own musicians have made felicitous use of them. Our enjoyment of the few attempts which the delicacy of French taste has permitted our composers to risk, has proved how easily we can excel in this genre.   [5]

INSTINCT

In music the ear obeys only nature. It takes account of neither measure nor range. Instinct alone leads it.   [6]

Whether a novice or the most experienced person in music, the moment one sings an improvisation, one ordinarily places the first tone in the middle register of the voice and then continues up, even though the voice range above or below this first tone is about equal; this is completely consistent with the resonance of any sounding body from which all emanating overtones are above its fundamental tone which one thinks one is hearing alone.

On the other hand, inexperienced as one may be, one hardly ever fails, when improvising on an instrument, immediately to play, ever ascending, the perfect chord made up of the overtones [harmonics] of the sounding body, the major form of which is always preferred to the minor, unless the latter is suggested by some reminiscence.   [7]

Often we think we hear in music only what exists in the words, or in the interpretation we wish to give them. We try to subject music to forced inflections, but that is not the way to be able to judge it. On the contrary, we must not think but let ourselves be carried away by the feeling which the music inspires; without our thinking at all, this feeling will become the basis of our judgment. As for reason, everybody possesses it nowadays; we have just discovered it in the bosom of nature itself. We have even proved that instinct constantly recalls it to us, both in our actions and in our speech. When reason and instinct are reconciled, there will be no higher appeal. [8]

RHYTHM

From: *Code de musique pratique*, 1760

Of all the elements united in the performance of music, rhythm is the one most natural to us, as it is equally natural to all animals. If this is so, why then do we accuse so many people of lacking an ear for rhythm?

If rhythm consists only in the regularity of movement, let us examine both the movements of animals and our own, such as walking or moving some part of the body. Where reflection or will do not affect them, the movements will always be regular. But if we wish to make someone follow a prescribed rhythm, in which case his mind is preoccupied with a rhythm unfamiliar to him, where thinking, in other words, destroys the natural functioning, should we be surprised that he seems insensitive to it?

Wait until that person completely gets the knack of subjecting the movement to the beat, and we will no longer find him rebellious. Or, let us allow him to prescribe for himself a repeated movement of the hand without thinking about it; let us make him perform something which is familiar to him based on this movement, be it music or dance step, each note or step corresponding to each movement, and soon we will see that we were mistaken about him. Let us lead him in this fashion by degrees. Above all, let us not hurry him. Let us better judge the effects of nature. Let us not attribute to him the stumbling-blocks which we ourselves put in his way, and soon we will find the ear which we have denied him. [9]

BENEDETTO MARCELLO

1686–1739

Intellectuals and cultivated people of the seventeenth and eighteenth centuries carried on endless discussions about opera, one of the most popular musical forms of the times. Its decay from models of antiquity was constantly criticized, the relative importance of music and poetry in the form heatedly debated.

Marcello, lawyer, poet, violinist, singer, and composer, was at once an intellectual and a professional musician. His main work was the *Estro poetico-armonico*, a series of paraphrases on the first fifty Psalms. He also composed concertos, sonatas, madrigals and cantatas.

Il Teatro alla Moda, a volume of twenty-four chapters, from which the following excerpts are taken, is a biting, witty satire on the theater of the day, particularly the Venetian opera.

Its complete title reads: "Theater à la mode, or a sure and easy method for effectively composing and performing Italian operas in the modern manner, in which is given useful and necessary advice to poets, composers, musicians of either sex, impresarios, instrumentalists, engineers, painters, decorators, comedians, tailors, pages, extras, prompters, copyists, the protectors and mothers of female virtuosos, and other persons belonging to the theater."

From: *Il teatro alla moda,* 1720

INSTRUCTIONS FOR LIBRETTISTS

A writer of operatic librettos, if he wishes to be modern, must not have read the Greek and Latin classic authors, nor should he do so in the future. After all, the old Greeks and Romans never read modern writers.

Nor should he have the slightest knowledge of Italian meter and verse. At most he might possibly admit he "had somewhere heard" that verses must consist of seven or eleven syllables. This amply suffices, and he can then suit his fancy by making verses of three, five, nine, thirteen, or even fifteen syllables.

He should, on the other hand, boast that he has had thorough school-

46

ing in mathematics, painting, chemistry, medicine, law, etc., and should then confess that his genius so strongly compelled him to it, that he just *had* to become a poet. Yet he need not have the slightest acquaintance with the various rules concerning correct accentuation or the making of good rhymes. He need not have any command of poetical language. Mythology and history can be closed books to him. To make up for this, as frequently as possible he will employ in his works technical terms from the above-named sciences, or from others, though they may have no relation whatsoever to the world of Poetry. He should call Dante, Petrarch, and Ariosto obscure, clumsy, and dull poets whose works, accordingly, he should never, or only very seldom, use as examples. Instead, the modern librettist should acquire a large collection of contemporary writings; from these he should borrow sentiments, thoughts, and entire verses. This sort of theft he should refer to as "laudable imitation."

Before the librettist begins writing, he should ask the impresario for a detailed list of the number and kind of stage sets and decorations he wishes to see employed. The librettist will then incorporate all these into his drama. He should always be on the alert for elaborate scenes such as sacrifices, sumptuous banquets, supernatural apparitions, or other spectacles. In connection with these, the librettist will consult with the theater engineer to discover how many dialogues, monologues, and arias will be needed to pad each scene of this type, so that all technical problems of staging can be worked out without haste. The disintegration of the drama as an entity and the intense boredom of the audience are without importance compared to these considerations.

He should write the entire opera without preconceived plan, but rather proceed verse by verse. For, if the audience never understands the plot, it can be counted on to be attentive to the very end. One thing any able modern librettist must strive for: he must frequently have all characters of the piece on the stage at the same time, even though no one knows why. One by one, they may then leave the stage, singing the usual canzonetta.

The librettist should not worry about the ability of the performers, but much more about whether the impresario has at his disposal a good bear or lion, an able nightingale, genuine-looking bolts of lightning, earthquakes, storms, etc.

For the finale of his opera he should write a magnificent scene with more elaborate effects, so that the audience will not walk out before the work is half over. He should conclude with the customary chorus in praise of the sun, moon, or impresario. [1]

INSTRUCTIONS FOR COMPOSERS

The modern composer should know no rules of composition aside from some vague generalities. He need not understand numerical proportions in relation to music, the advantages of contrary motion, or the disadvantages of tritones or hexachords with the b-natural. He need not know how many modes there are, or how to distinguish them, or how they are divided, or what their characteristics are. Instead, in this connection he might declare that there are only two modes, namely major and minor; the former with the major third and the latter with the minor third. He need not digress to point out what the ancients understood by a major and minor tone.

He will see no difference between diatonic, chromatic, and enharmonic [1] genera, but he must contrive to jumble all three within a single canzonetta. With such a modernistic confusion he can distinguish himself over the composers of antiquity.

Before he actually starts to write the music, the composer should call upon all female singers in the company and offer to include anything they might care to have, such as arias without a bass in the accompaniment, *furlanette*, rigadoons, etc., with the violins, the bear, and the extras accompanying in unison.

He must not permit himself to read the entire libretto, which might confuse him. Instead, he should compose it verse by verse and immediately insist that all arias be rewritten [by the librettist]. This is the only way he will be able to utilize every melody that has popped into his head during the summer. If the words to these arias again fail to fit the notes properly—this commonly happens—he will continue to harass the librettist until the latter satisfies him completely.

All arias should have an instrumental accompaniment and care should be taken to have every part move in exactly the same note values, whether eighths, sixteenths, or thirty-seconds. Noise is what counts in modern music, not harmonious sound which would consist mainly of diverse note values, and the interchange of tied and accented notes. To avoid this true kind of harmony, the modern composer should employ nothing more daring than a four-three suspension, and that only in the cadence. If this seems to him a bit old-fashioned, he can make up for it by finishing the piece with all instruments playing in unison.

[1] *Enharmonic*, since Nicola Vicentino (1511–72), had meant the use of smaller intervals than halftones.

He must not forget that happy and sad arias should alternate throughout the opera, from beginning to end, regardless of any meaning of text, music, or stage action.

If nouns such as "father," "empire," "love," "arena," "kingdom," "beauty," "courage," "heart," appear in the aria, the modern composer should write long coloraturas over them. This applies also to "no," "without," "already," and other adverbs. This serves to introduce a little change from the old custom of using coloratura passages only over words expressing motion or emotion, for instance, "torment," "sorrow," "song," "fly," "fall."

He should lend his services to the impresario for very little, mindful that thousands of *scudi* must be paid to famous singers. He should be satisfied with less pay than the least of them, though he should not tolerate the injustice of receiving less than the theater bear or the extras.   [2]

II

ROUSSEAU
C. P. E. BACH
GLUCK
HAYDN
GRÉTRY
MOZART
BEETHOVEN
SPOHR
WEBER
ROSSINI
SCHUBERT
DONIZETTI

JEAN JACQUES ROUSSEAU

1712–1778

Philosopher, educator, historian, novelist, botanist, Rousseau was also a musician and composer. His *Écrites sur la Musique*, a volume devoted to musical essays and polemics, included his famous "Lettre sur la Musique Française" in which he emphatically defended Italian music as opposed to French in the "Guerre des Bouffons." His *Confessions* contain many musical references, and *Emile*, his novel on the education of youth, devotes a chapter to music. Rousseau also wrote musical articles for Diderot's *Encyclopédie* and a *Dictionnaire de Musique*. He devised a new system of musical notation which, because of a number of discrepancies, never became acceptable to musicians.

In the articles quoted below he contests several theories propounded by Rameau, namely, that musical effects and melody stem from natural harmonics alone, and that its own bass is inherent in every melody. His opinions on the relation between sound and color (occasioned by Louis-Bertrand Castel's alleged invention of a color harpsichord and color music in 1725) were passionately opposed by Grétry.[1]

Owing to lack of training he was a dilettante composer, yet his opera *Le Devin du village* (1752) was extremely successful and praised by many, among them Gluck. His literary works brought him fame, but he earned his living primarily as a music copyist.

From: *Essai sur l'origine des langues,* 1753

MELODY AND HARMONY

Everybody in the world takes pleasure in listening to beautiful sounds, but if this experience is not enlivened by melodic inflections which are familiar, it will not be a pleasure nor will it change into sensuous enjoyment. To our way of thinking, the most beautiful melodies will always indifferently affect the ear which is not accustomed to them. Here is a language that requires the dictionary.

Harmony, properly so called, is in an even less favorable position

[1] See p. 74.

53

than melody. Having but conventional beauties, it in no way flatters
inexperienced ears. A long habit of listening is necessary to sense and
savor it. Untutored ears hear only noise in our consonances. When
the natural proportions are altered, it is not surprising that the natural
pleasure no longer exists . . .

M. Rameau claims that upper voices of a certain simplicity naturally
suggest their basses, and that a person having a good though unpracticed ear will sing this bass spontaneously. This is the prejudice of a
musician, and is belied by all experience. Not only will he who has
never heard either bass or harmony fail to find this harmony or this
bass by himself, but they will displease him if he does hear them; he
will much prefer a simple unison.

Harmony itself is inadequate even for expressions which seem to
depend solely on it. Thunder, the murmur of waters, wind and storms
are badly conveyed by simple chords. No matter what one does, the
sound itself says nothing to the mind; things themselves must speak
to be understood. In every imitation, a kind of extra commentary must
be added to the voice of nature. The musician who tries to convey
noises by sound deceives himself. He knows neither the weakness nor
the strength of his art, and he judges without taste or insight. Teach
him that he must interpret noise through natural song, that if he
wishes to make frogs croak, he must make them sing. For it is not
enough that he imitate; he must move and please, without which his
dull imitation is nothing and, provoking interest in no one, his efforts
will make no impression.   [1]

SOUNDS AND COLORS

There are no absurdities to which, in the arts, material observations
have not given rise. In the analysis of sound, the same relations have
been found as in that of light. Immediately they have been seized
upon without regard for experience or reason. The sense of the system
has been completely confused, and for want of knowing how to paint
with the ears, people have presumed to sing with their eyes. I have
seen the famous harpsichord on which music may supposedly be made
with colors. Not to recognize that the effect of colors is in their
permanence while that of sounds is in their succession, is to be unaware
of the workings of nature.

All the wealth of coloring displays itself at once over the face of
the earth. All can be seen at a first glance, yet the more one looks,
the more one is enchanted; one has only endlessly to contemplate and
to admire.

It is not the same with sound. Nature does not always analyze or separate overtones. On the contrary, she hides them under the semblance of a unison, or, if at times she separates them in the modulated song of man or the warbling of birds, the tones pour forth successively, one after the other. She inspires songs and not chords; she dictates melody and not harmony. Colors are the attire of inanimate things; all matter is colored. But sounds announce movement; the voice proclaims a sentient being. Only animated bodies sing. It is not the automatic flute player who plays the flute, it is the manipulator who measures the breath and makes the fingers move.

Each sense, then, has its proper field. The field of sound is time, that of sight is space. To multiply sounds heard at one time, or to develop colors one after the other, is to change their economy, to substitute the eye for the ear, and the ear for the eye.   [2]

THE FUNCTION OF MUSIC

One of the greatest advantages of the musician is that of being able to paint the things one cannot hear, while it is impossible for the painter to represent what one cannot see; and the greatest marvel of an art, which is only produced by movement, is to be able to create the image of repose. Sleep, the calm of the night, solitude and silence itself enter into the pictures of music. We know that noise can produce the effect of silence, and silence the effect of noise, as when one falls asleep at a dull, monotonous reading, and awakens the moment it stops. But music acts more intimately upon us, by arousing through one sense feelings similar to those which can be aroused through another. And since the relation cannot be perceptible unless the impression be strong, painting, deprived of this strength, cannot give to music the reflections which the latter can draw from painting. Though all nature be asleep, he who contemplates it is not sleeping, and the art of the musician consists in substituting for the unconscious image of an object that of the movements which its presence arouses in the heart of the beholder. Not only can it agitate the sea, animate the flames of a fire, make the brooks flow, the rains fall, and swell the torrents; it can paint the horror of a desert, darken the walls of a subterranean prison, calm the tempest, render the air tranquil and serene and, through the orchestra, diffuse a new freshness through the woods. It does not represent these things directly, but it excites in one's soul the same feelings one experiences on seeing them.   [3]

CARL PHILIPP EMANUEL BACH

1714–1788

Though the contemporary pianoforte allows techniques different from those of the keyboard instruments of Emanuel Bach's time, the precepts he laid down in his *Versuch über die wahre Art das Clavier zu spielen* (1753–62), are still valid. His advice to solo performers and accompanists is as applicable to today's executants as to Bach's own students. One of the greatest keyboard players of his age, he "raised the art of performance through teaching and practice to its perfection," to quote the poet Klopstock.

Because it was nearly impossible to sustain long notes on the keyboard instruments of the period, the organ excepted, both the soloist and accompanist often turned composer or improviser, adding embellishments to fill in the pauses occasioned by long notes in a melodic line. Singers and other instrumentalists took up the practice. In Bach's chapter on embellishments, he tried to correct the ensuing bad taste and lack of uniformity and clarity. He cited the French school, Rameau in particular, as masters of correct and precise ornamentation. It is interesting to compare this chapter with Saint-Saëns' study, quoted elsewhere in this book,[1] where the French composer bewails how vague the old embellishment signs are to the contemporary musician.

As a composer, C. P. E. Bach brought order to sonata form. He definitely established the three-movement plan, and the three-part first movement (exposition, development and recapitulation), which Haydn, Mozart and Beethoven perfected.[2] Though generally known as the exponent of the pre-classical school of writing, he made use, particularly in his sacred works, of the most intricate forms of counterpoint. An innovator, he was yet the pupil of his father Johann Sebastian Bach, whom he defended passionately in the last years of his life, *vide* his letter comparing his father and Handel.

[1] See p. 229.   [2] See pp. 70, 90.

From: *Essay on the True Art of Playing
Keyboard Instruments*, 1753–62

EMBELLISHMENTS

No one disputes the need for embellishments. This is evident from the great numbers of them to be found everywhere. They are, in fact, indispensable. Consider their many uses: they connect and enliven tones and impart stress and accent; they make music pleasing and command our close attention. Expression is heightened by them; let a piece be sad, joyful or otherwise, and they will lend fitting assistance. Embellishments provide opportunities for fine performance as well as much of its subject matter. They improve mediocre compositions. Without them the best melody is empty and ineffective, the clearest content clouded.

In view of their many commendable services, it is unfortunate that there are also poor embellishments and that good ones are sometimes used too frequently and ineptly.

Because of this, it has always been better for composers to specify the proper embellishments unmistakably, instead of leaving their selection to the whims of tasteless performers.

In justice to the French, it must be said that they notate their ornaments with painstaking accuracy. So do the masters of the keyboard in Germany, without embellishing to excess. Who knows but that our moderation with respect to both the number and kind of ornaments is the influence which has led the French to abandon their earlier practice of decorating almost every note, to the detriment of clarity and noble simplicity?   [1]

PERFORMANCE

Keyboard players whose chief asset is mere technique are clearly at a disadvantage. A performer may have the most agile fingers, be competent at single and double trills, master the art of fingering, read skillfully at sight regardless of key, and transpose extemporaneously without the slightest difficulty; he may play tenths, even twelfths, or runs, cross hands in every conceivable manner, and excel in other related matters; yet he may be something less than a clear, pleasing, or stirring keyboard player. More often than not, one meets technicians, nimble players by profession, who possess all these qualifications and indeed astound us with their prowess without ever touching our sensibilities. They overwhelm our hearing without satisfying it and stun the mind without moving it. In writing this, I do not wish to discredit the praiseworthy skill of reading at sight. A commendable ability, I urge its practice on everyone. A mere technician, however, can lay no claim to the rewards of those who gently move the ear rather than the eye, the heart rather than the ear, and lead it where they will. Of course it is only rarely possible to reveal the true content and feeling of a piece on its first reading. Even the most practiced orchestras often require more than one rehearsal cf certain pieces which, to judge from the notes alone, are very easy. Most technicians do nothing more than play notes. And how the continuity and flow of the melody suffer, even when the harmony remains unmolested! It is to the advantage of the keyboard that dexterity be developed beyond the limits of other instruments. But finger velocity must never be misused. It should be reserved for those passages that call for it, without advancing the tempo of the piece as a whole.

In what does good performance consist? The ability, through singing or playing, to make the ear conscious of the true content and feeling of a composition. Any passage can be so radically changed by modifying its performance that it will scarcely be recognizable.

The subject matter of performance is the loudness or softness of tones, the touch, the snap, legato and staccato execution, the vibrato, arpeggiation, the holding of tones, the retard and acceleration. Lack of these elements or inept use of them makes for poor performance.

Good performance, then, occurs when one hears all notes and their embellishments played in correct time with fitting volume produced by a touch which is related to the true content of a piece. Herein lies the rounded, pure, flowing manner of playing which makes for clarity and expressiveness . . . In rapid passages, every tone must be played with a fitting pressure or the effect will be turgid and chaotic. . . .[1] A well-rounded manner of performance can be most readily discerned from the playing of rapid pieces which contain alternating light and heavy runs of equal speed. Keyboard players are often found whose ready fingers serve them well in loud runs, but desert them, through lack of control, in the soft ones, thereby making for indistinctness. The performers grow nervous, speed onward, and lose control . . .

In general, the briskness of allegros is expressed by detached notes, and the tenderness of adagios by broad, slurred notes. The performer must keep in mind that these characteristic features of allegros and adagios are to be given consideration even when a composition is not

---

[1] The rest of the paragraph is from the edition of 1787.

so marked, as well as when the performer has not yet gained an adequate understanding of the emotional content of a work. I use the expression, "in general," advisedly, for I am well aware that all kinds of execution may appear in any tempo.

There are many who play stickily, as if they had glue between their fingers. Their touch is lethargic; they hold their notes too long. Others, in an attempt to correct this, release the keys too soon, as if they burned them. Both are wrong. Midway between these extremes is best. Here again I speak in general, for every kind of touch has its use.

In order to arrive at an understanding of the true content and feeling of a piece and, in the absence of indications, to decide on the correct manner of performance, be it slurred, detached or what not, and further, to learn the precautions that must be heeded in introducing ornaments, it is advisable that every opportunity be seized to listen to soloists and ensembles. This is all the more true as these details of beauty often depend on extraneous factors. The volume and time-value of ornaments must be determined by the feeling to be achieved. In order to avoid vagueness, rests as well as notes must be given their exact value at fermate and cadences. Yet purposeful violations of the beat are often exceptionally beautiful. However, a distinction in their use must be observed: in solo performance and in ensembles made up of only a few understanding players, manipulations are permissible which affect the tempo itself; here, the group will be less apt to go astray than to become attentive to and adopt the change; but in large ensembles made up of motley players, the manipulations must be addressed to the bar alone without touching on the broader pace.[1] When a composer ends a movement in a different key, he usually wants the following movement to begin forthwith. Other reasons as well may require an uninterrupted attack. It is customary to indicate such a procedure by placing only one instead of the usual two bar lines at the end of the movement.

The pace of a composition, which is usually indicated by several generally accepted Italian expressions, is based on its general content as well as on the fastest notes and passages it contains. Due consideration of these factors will prevent an allegro from being rushed and an adagio from being dragged . . .

To learn the essentials of good performance, it is advisable to listen to accomplished musicians. Above all, lose no opportunity to hear artistic singing. In so doing, the keyboard player will learn to

[1] The rest of the paragraph is from the edition of 1787.

think in terms of song. Indeed, it is a good practice to sing instrumental melodies in order to reach an understanding of their correct performance. This way of learning is of far greater value than reading voluminous tomes or listening to learned discourses. In the latter one finds such terms as Nature, Taste, Song, and Melody, although their authors are often incapable of putting together as many as two natural, tasteful, singing, melodic tones, for these authors dispense their alms and endowments with completely infelicitous arbitrariness.

A musician cannot move others unless he too is moved. He must feel all the emotions that he hopes to arouse in his audience, for the revealing of his own humor will stimulate a like mood in the listener. In languishing, sad passages, the performer must languish and grow sad. Thus will the expression of the piece be more clearly perceived by the audience.[1] Here, however, the error of a sluggish, dragging performance, caused by an excess of emotion and melancholy, must be avoided. Similarly, in lively, joyous passages, the executant must again put himself into the appropriate mood. Constantly varying the passions, he will barely quiet one before he rouses another. Above all, he must discharge this office in a piece which is highly expressive by nature, whether it be by him or by someone else. In the latter case, he must make certain that he assumes the emotion which the composer intended in writing it. It is principally in improvisations or fantasias that the keyboard player can best master the feelings of his audience.

Those who maintain that all this can be accomplished without gesture will retract their words when, owing to their own insensibility, they find themselves obliged to sit like statues before their instruments. Ugly grimaces are, of course, inappropriate and harmful; but suitable expressions help the listener to understand our meaning. Those opposed to this stand are often incapable of doing justice, despite their technique, to their own otherwise worthy compositions. Unable to bring out the content of their works, they remain ignorant of it. But let someone else play these, a person of delicate, sensitive insight, who knows the meaning of good performance, and the composer will learn, to his astonishment, that there is more in his music than he had ever known or believed. Good performance can, in fact, improve and gain praise for even an average composition.

It can be seen from the many emotions which music portrays, that the accomplished musician must have special endowments and be capable of employing them wisely. He must carefully appraise his audience, its attitude toward the expressive content of his program, the

---

[1] This sentence is a footnote added to the edition of 1787.

recital hall itself, and other additional factors. Nature has wisely provided music with every kind of appeal so that all might share in its enjoyment. It thus becomes the duty of the performer to satisfy, to the best of his ability, every last kind of listener.   [2]

ACCOMPANIMENT

The fewer the parts in a piece, the finer must be its accompaniment. Hence, a solo or an aria provides the best opportunity to judge an accompanist. He must take great pains to catch, in his accompaniment, all the nuances of the principal part. Indeed, it is difficult to say whether accompanist or soloist deserves greater credit. The latter may have taken a long time to prepare his piece which, after the present fashion, he himself must compose. Nevertheless, he cannot count on the applause of his audience, for it is only through a good accompaniment that his performance will be brought to life.

On the other hand, the accompanist is usually given much less time; he is allowed only a cursory examination of the piece, but must support and enhance extemporaneously all the beauty on which so much time and care have been expended by the principal performer. Nevertheless, the soloist takes all bravos to himself and gives no credit to his accompanist. But he is right, for he knows that ignorant custom directs these bravos to him alone . . .

It is sometimes necessary and not out of order for the accompanist to discuss a piece with the performer of the principal part before its performance, and to let him decide on the liberties that are to be taken in the accompaniment. Some soloists want the accompanist to be greatly restricted, others not. Since opinion varies so greatly and it is up to the principal part to decide, the safest procedure is to seek a preliminary understanding.

An accompanist must be careful to observe whether the high and low registers of the singer or instrumentalist whom he accompanies are equally loud, and whether his tones are just as clear from a distance as they are from near-by. If they are not, he must modify his playing in order not to cover the weak tones with a loud accompaniment . . .

A forte in a tutti passage is to be differentiated from a forte that accompanies a soloist. The latter must be accurately proportioned to the strength of the principal part, but the former can, of course, be played much louder.   [3]

From: *Autobiography*, 1773

COMMISSIONED MUSIC

Having been obliged to compose most of my works for particular individuals and for the public, I have been placed under more restraint in these works than in the few pieces I have written for my own pleasure. Indeed, sometimes I have been compelled to follow very ludicrous instructions; still, it is possible that these far from agreeable suggestions may have inspired my creative imagination with a variety of ideas which probably would never otherwise have occurred to me.

[4]

CRITICISM

How seldom do we meet with a proper amount of sympathy, knowledge, honesty and courage in a critic—four qualities they ought, in any event, to possess to some extent. It is sad indeed for the world of music that criticism, in many respects so useful, should often be the occupation of persons in no way endowed with these qualities.   [5]

COMPARISON BETWEEN J. S. BACH AND HANDEL

Letter to J. J. Eschenburg, Hamburg, January 21, 1786

I am very much obliged to you, dear Professor, for your *Handel*. With Mr. Burney, I am dissatisfied on several scores. The same thing happens to Handel that happens to others when you want to idolize them: it works usually to their detriment.

Comparisons are difficult and not even necessary. Here, during Handel's time, Keiser surpassed him by far in vocal composition, and Handel would never have become a Hasse, Graun, etc. in this [kind of composition], even had he lived at the same time as these artists. Nor was it necessary that he should; he was great enough, especially in his oratorios.

But to write about organ playing that *he had surpassed my father:* this should not have been said by a man who lives in England where the organ is of slight value, *N.B.*, without pedals, and by one who has, as a consequence, no insight into what constitutes the excellence of organ playing; who perhaps never saw or heard any works for the organ; who, finally, certainly does not know my father's works for the keyboard and more especially for the organ, and in these the obbligato use of the pedal to which now the chief melody, now the alto or the tenor voice is given, [as] always in fugues where *no voice is ever abandoned* and the most difficult passages occur while the feet are occupied with the greatest fire and brilliance, *enfin*, innumerable things about which Burney knows nothing.

Hasse, Faustina, Quantz and others who knew Handel well and heard him play, said in 1728 or 1729,[1] when my father made a public appearance in Dresden: Bach has brought organ playing to its greatest perfection. (*Vide* Quantz's *Method*.)

Seriously, the differences could hardly be greater. Did Handel ever write trios for two manuals and pedals? Did he write fugues for five or six voices for keyboard alone? Certainly not. Consequently, no comparison can be made in this respect, the disparity being too great. People need only look at the clavier and organ compositions of both men!

Excuse my chatter and scribble! The drollest thing of all is the King's gracious precautionary measure, thanks to which everything that Handel wrote in his youth is being preserved. I do not wish to compare myself to Handel, but recently I burned a ream or more of my old compositions and am glad that they no longer exist.

Pray continue to love, all the foregoing notwithstanding,

Your most devoted
Bach

[6]

[1] This performance took place on September 14, 1731.

CHRISTOPH WILLIBALD GLUCK

1714–1787

The present controversy over opera librettos in English or in their original language lends contemporary interest to Gluck's letters to the editor of the *Mercure de France* and to the Duke of Braganza. Through extensive travel, Gluck came under the influence of Italian, French and German opera, as well as of English oratorio as composed by Handel, and so was well equipped to evaluate the importance of the word in dramatic musical composition.

His own first works were patterned after the current Italian opera, with its ornamental arias, its absence of dramatic content and paucity of sense. However, at the suggestion of the librettist Calzabigi, who offered him the libretto of *Orpheus*, he readily turned against the conventions of Italian opera. Gluck actually tried to implement, in his own century, the aims of the early seventeenth century opera as expressed in the program of Count Bardi and the Florentine *Camerata*, and as practiced by Monteverdi. His orchestra, dramatic action and words were to be given the importance until then usurped by the singer alone. *Orpheus and Eurydice* (1762, revised 1774) was one of the first results of this change in his thinking.

The preface to his *Alceste* (1767) is the manifesto of Gluck's new direction in musical thought. Thereafter, his works express a simplicity and grandeur which expose, by contrast, the artifice of his first Italian models.

ON OPERA REFORM

Dedication of *Alceste* to Duke Leopold of Tuscany, 1769

Your Royal Highness: When I undertook to compose music for *Alceste*, I proposed to abolish entirely all those abuses introduced by the injudicious vanity of singers or by the excessive complaisance of conductors, abuses which have so long disfigured the Italian opera and made it the most ridiculous and tiresome of all entertainments, instead of the most splendid and beautiful. My purpose was to restrict music to its true office, that of ministering to the expression of the poetry and to the situations of the plot, without interrupting the action or smothering it by superfluous ornamentation. I thought the music should accomplish what brilliancy of color and a skilfully adapted contrast of light and shade achieve in a correct and well-designed drawing, by animating the figures without distorting their contours. I wished, therefore, not to arrest an actor in the most exciting moment of his dialogue by making him wait for a wearisome *ritornello* nor, in the midst of half-uttered words, to detain him on a favorite note, whether this aimed to display his fine voice and flexibility in some long passage, or to make him pause till the orchestra gave him time to take breath for a cadenza. I did not feel I should hurry rapidly over the second part of an aria, possibly the most impassioned and important of all, in order to be able to repeat regularly four times over the words of the first part, thus making the aria end where in all probability the sense did not end, and all this for the convenience of the singer, to enable him to vary a passage according to his caprice. In short, I have striven to banish the abuses against which reason and good sense have so long protested in vain.

My idea was that the overture should prepare the spectators for the plot and give some indication of its nature; that the concerted instruments should be regulated according to the interest and passion of the drama; and that in a dialogue there should be no excessive gap between aria and recitative, lest the meaning of a passage be perverted or the force and warmth of the action implausibly interrupted.

Further, I thought that my most strenuous efforts must be directed at the achievement of a noble simplicity, thus avoiding any show of difficulty at the expense of clarity. I did not consider a mere display of novelty valuable unless naturally suggested by the situation and the expression, and on this point no rule in composition exists that I would not gladly sacrifice in favor of the effect produced.

Such are my principles. Fortunately, the libretto was wonderfully suited to my purpose, for the celebrated author [Calzabigi] had conceived a fresh and vigorous dramatic plot and had replaced flowery descriptions, superfluous similes, and cold, sententious morality by the language of the heart, by strong passions, interesting situations, and an ever-varying spectacle.

Success has crowned my convictions, and the unanimous approval of so enlightened a city as Vienna clearly shows that simplicity, truth and nature are the great touchstones of the beautiful in all artistic creation. The most highly respected persons have asked me repeatedly to publish my opera, yet I am fully aware of the risks I incur in combatting widely held prejudices. This is why I must arm myself with the mighty protection of your Royal Highness's name, and therefore I entreat the favor of being permitted to prefix it to my opera, for that august name justly enjoys the respect of all enlightened Europe. . . .

Only a great protector of the fine arts—reigning over a nation which enjoys renown for having rescued the arts from universal oppression and for producing the grandest works in each field in a city which is always the first to cast off the yoke of vulgar prejudice to proceed onward to perfection—can undertake the reforms of that noble drama in which all the fine arts play so large a role. When these reforms are effected, the glory will at least be mine of having set in motion the first stone, and obtained the public testimony of your illustrious patronage.

I have the honor to declare myself, with the utmost devotion, your Royal Highness's

Grateful and obedient servant,

Christoforo Gluck [1]

TRUTH IN MUSIC

From: Dedication of *Paride ed Elena* to Don Giovanni,
Duke of Braganza, October 30, 1770

Almost imperceptible differences distinguish Raphael from the common herd of painters, and the slightest alteration in an outline, that would in no way destroy the likeness in a caricature, can entirely disfigure the portrait of a lovely woman. By changing very little in the expression of my aria *Che farò senza Euridice*, it might be turned into a saltarello for puppets. A note more or less sustained, a neglected *rinforzo* carelessly omitted either in the music or in a vocal passage, an appoggiatura out of place, a shake, a passage, a run can easily ruin a whole scene in such an opera, whereas such things do not harm, or may even improve, the common run of operas.

When truth is sought, it must be varied in accordance with the subject we have to work out, and the greatest beauties of melody and harmony become defects and imperfections when used out of place. [2]

MUSIC AND LIBRETTO

From: Letter to the Editor of the *Mercure de France*,
published February 1, 1773

Whatever talent a composer may possess, he can write only indifferent music if the poet does not arouse in him that enthusiasm without
which productions in every artistic field must be feeble and languid.

Imitation of nature is the acknowledged aim which all ought to
seek. I strive to attain this and my music, always as simple and natural
as I can possibly make it, only tends to enhance the expression and to
add force to the declamation of the poetry. For this reason, I do not
employ those shakes, passages and cadences which Italians use so
lavishly. Their language, which quite suits this style, is by no means
suitable for me; no doubt it has many other merits, but I was born
in Germany and do not consider that any study on my part either
of Italian or French entitles me to appreciate the delicate shades which
cause a preference for one language rather than another, and I think
that a foreigner ought to refrain from judging between them. I feel
I may say, however, that the language which suits me best is the
one which enables the poet to furnish me with the most varied means
of expressing the passions.   [3]

JOSEPH HAYDN

1732-1809

Usually considered a composer of the classical period of music, Haydn is much more than that. He bridged, in his long and industrious life, the final years of the baroque, the entire classical and the beginnings of the romantic periods, and his music bears the imprint of all three. He was not only the father of the modern symphony, but an innovator generally. Speaking to Georg August Griesinger of his thirty years in the employ of the Esterházys, when he had constantly to compose music for the entertainment of his princes, Haydn remarked: "There was no one near me to confuse or torment me, thus I was obliged to be original." His letters stress the importance of originality above all rules, and in his works the student will find all manner of harmonic daring and newness in form.

He came truly into his own in his last works—the symphonies he composed for the impresario Salomon, in London, and the oratorios, the fruits of his sojourn in England, where the oratorio had enjoyed immense popularity from the time of Handel.

His letter to Superintendent Rott, quoted below, is one of the many manifestations of his friendship and respect for Mozart. Theirs was a reciprocal influence: Mozart benefited from Haydn in his string quartets, while Haydn admitted Mozart's superiority in dramatic composition.

Some of the following quotations are taken from Griesinger's *Biographische Notizen über Joseph Haydn* (Leipzig, 1809). Griesinger was attached to the Saxonian Legation in Vienna in 1799; a personal friend of Gottfried Härtel, he served as a kind of agent between Haydn and Breitkopf & Härtel, the great music publishing house. During the last ten years of the composer's life, a close friendship developed between the two men, one fruit of which was the aforementioned biographical sketch. The quotations are reported by Griesinger as verbatim utterances of Haydn.

ON MUSICAL RULES

[Haydn was told that Albrechtsberger wanted all consecutive fifths banished from strict part-writing. He answered:]

What do you mean? Art is free, and must not be confined by technical fetters. The ear—naturally, the cultured ear—must be the judge, and I feel myself as authorized as anybody else to make up rules. Such artificialities have no value; I should rather someone try to write a truly new minuet. [1]

From: Letter to the *Tonkünstlersocietät*, Vienna, 1779

The free arts and the beautiful science of composition will not tolerate technical chains. The mind and soul must be free. [2]

Remark to Dies, 1805

If an idea strikes me as beautiful and satisfactory to the ear and heart, I would far rather overlook a grammatical error than sacrifice what is beautiful to mere pedantic trifling. [3]

ON COMPOSITION

From: Griesinger's *Biographische Notizen*, 1809

I would sit down [at the piano], and begin to improvise, whether my spirits were sad or happy, serious or playful. Once I had captured an idea, I strove with all my might to develop and sustain it in conformity with the rules of art. In this way I tried to help myself, and this is where so many of our newer composers fall short: they string one little piece onto another and break off when they have scarcely started. Nothing remains in one's heart after one has listened to such compositions. [4]

I was never a quick writer and always composed with care and diligence. However, such works are lasting, and the connoisseur knows this immediately from the score. When Cherubini would look over some of my manuscripts, he would always recognize those passages which deserved special marks of distinction. [5]

CARL PHILIPP EMANUEL BACH [1]

From: Griesinger's *Biographische Notizen*, 1809

I could not tear myself away from my clavier until I had played them all through, and whoever knows me thoroughly will find that I owe a great deal to Emanuel Bach, that I understood and eagerly studied him; Emanuel Bach himself at one time complimented me on this score. [6]

MOZART

From: Letter to Franz Rott,[2] Esterház, December 1, 1787

You wish me to write an *opera buffa* for you. Most willingly, if you wish to have a vocal composition for yourself alone. But if it is with a view to producing it on the stage in Prague, I cannot comply with your wish, for all my operas are too closely connected with our personal circle [Prince Esterházy's court in Hungary]. Thus they could never produce the proper effect which I have carefully worked out to accord with the locality. It would be different were I to have the invaluable privilege of composing a new opera for your theatre. But even then I would run grave risks, for scarcely any man could stand beside the great Mozart.

I only wish I could instil in every friend of music, and in great men in particular, the depth of musical sympathy and profound appreciation of Mozart's inimitable music that I myself feel and enjoy. Then nations would vie with each other to possess such a jewel within their frontiers. Prague ought to strive to retain this precious man, but also to remunerate him; for without suitable remuneration, the history of a great genius is sad indeed and gives little encouragement to posterity to exert itself further. It is on this account that so many promising geniuses are lost. It enrages me to think that the unparalleled Mozart is not yet engaged by some imperial or royal court! Forgive my intemperance, but I love the man so dearly! [7]

---

[1] In the late '40s, Haydn became familiar with the *Prussian Sonatas* (1742) by Carl Philipp Emanuel Bach.

[2] Superintendent of Supplies and music patron in Prague.

From: Letter to Johann Michael Puchberg,
London, January, 1792

Because of his [Mozart's] death, I was for some time quite beside myself and could not believe that Providence could have required the presence of this indispensable man in the other world so soon. I only regret that he did not have a chance to convince the still benighted English of the things I preach to them daily.   [8]

BEETHOVEN

From: Letter to the Elector of Cologne,
Vienna, November 23, 1793

I take the liberty of sending to Your Electoral Highness various musical pieces, namely, a quintet, a partita in eight parts, an oboe concerto, variations for the pianoforte, and a fugue, composed by my dear pupil Beethoven, who has been graciously entrusted to me. I flatter myself that these pieces will be kindly received by Your Electoral Highness as worthy proof of his industry outside his regular studies. On the strength of these pieces, connoisseurs and amateurs must own without bias that Beethoven will one day take his place as one of the greatest composers in Europe, and I shall be proud to call myself his master. I only wish that he may still remain with me a while longer.   [9]

HOW "THE SEVEN WORDS OF CHRIST ON THE CROSS" WAS WRITTEN

Preface to the Breitkopf & Härtel edition of 1801 to
which words were added

About fifteen years ago a curate of Cadiz commissioned me to write some pieces of instrumental music on the *Seven Words of Christ on the Cross.*

At that time, it was the custom to perform an oratorio in the Cathedral during Lent and, to give it greater solemnity, it was done with great pomp. The walls, windows and columns were draped in black, and a single lamp, suspended from the center, feebly lighted the sanctuary.

At noon the doors were closed and the orchestra began to play. After the introduction, the Bishop mounted his throne, recited one of the *Seven Words* and made some reflections on it. He then descended, kneeled before the altar, and remained thus for some time. This pause was taken up by the music.

The Bishop then mounted and descended six more times, and each time, after his homily, music was heard.

It was to these ceremonies that the music had to adapt itself.

The problem of composing seven adagios to be performed consecutively, and lasting ten minutes apiece without fatiguing the congregation, was not an easy one to resolve, and I soon recognized the impossibility of confining my music within the circumscribed limits.

My work was written and published without words. Later, I had occasion to add them, which is why the *Oratorio*, as now published by Breitkopf and Härtel, is a complete work and, as to the vocal part, altogether new. The good reception it has had among music lovers gives me the hope that the rest of the public will receive it with the same kindness.   [10]

ANDRÉ ERNEST GRÉTRY

1741–1813

One of the most important opéra comique composers of his time, Grétry devotes a large section of his *Mémoires ou Essais sur la musique* (1789) to a detailed discussion of many of his more than fifty operas. He describes with great charm and vivacity *Les Deux Avares* (1770), *Zémire et Azore* (1771), *L'Amant Jaloux* (1778), *Richard Cœur de Lion* (1784) and other works which, with the exception of occasional excerpts, are almost forgotten today. His general comments on opera, however, might still be of interest to the contemporary theater.

When he turns to consider such subjects as music education and the various facets of composition, his ideas are progressive and at times foreshadow later invention, as, for instance, his essay on color and music quoted here, which gives a foretaste of Wilfrid's Clavilux, Disney's *Fantasia*, the ideas of Scriabin, and even radio.

The autobiographical part of his *Mémoires* gives a vivid picture of eighteenth-century musical life in Rome—as a youngster Grétry won considerable success there—and in Paris. In his other writings—*Réflexions d'un Solitaire* (a supplement to the *Mémoires*) and *De la Verité*—he dilates on republican tenets and the best means of expressing them musically. His life in Paris spanned exciting years in French history—the Revolution and the rise of Napoleon—and many of his musical works celebrated its more important happenings.

The following excerpts are taken from his *Mémoires*.

From: *Mémoires ou Essais sur la musique*, 1789

MUSIC FOR THE THEATER

The theater demands exact musical expression of situation and text because both must be clear: true expression in the music strengthens the situation and allows the words to be heard even over the accompaniment.

Here is what I practice as much as possible in my theatrical compositions: I leave to the singing everything that is only an embellish-

ment or a rounding out of the poetic phrase; melody might weaken
the impact of important words, but it ornaments the rest. If a word
must be clearly understood for the intelligibility of the phrase, let it
be carried by a good note. If you establish a *forte* of one or several
measures in your orchestra, let it be on words already heard, for an
important word, lost against the orchestra, can completely rob a
piece of its meaning.

If the author of a drama, carried away by the exigencies of rhyme,
has given you some lines which are useless or detrimental to the expression, or if you fear that a line in bad taste may repel your audience, render the poet a service by covering the words with a *forte*.

It is difficult, I admit, to follow these precepts by rule of thumb.
Instead, nature must help us to be simple, rich and true in applying
them. But if having evolved a Poetics were enough to make one a
poet, which of us would refuse to be a Boileau? In the theater it is
not enough to write music to words; one must create music with
words.   [1]

ANALOGY BETWEEN COLOR AND SOUND

Father Castel, a Jesuit, invented a harpsichord which displayed colors
instead of producing sounds. Was this harpsichord made up of several
octaves? Was its deepest color black, its highest color white? Did all
the other colors lie between? This I don't know. It would rather
seem that he must have represented the body of sound and its several
parts by prismatic colors or by the rainbow, and that then, by mixing
primary colors, he composed the rest of the octave. Its first octave
being fixed, weren't the higher ones necessarily but a repetition of the
first, shaded more delicately in proportion to their distance from the
first octave? That is how I have pictured Father Castel's harpsichord,
to the existence of which several scholars attest who have not, however, explained its harmonies too fully.   [2]

APPLICATION

We will here show that each scale used in our music has a distinctive character. Thanks to the analogy that exists among all the phenomena of nature, the well-schooled musician may find all colors in
the harmony of sounds. The lowered or flatted tones have the same
effect on the ear as dark, gloomy colors on the eye; the raised or
sharped tones have, on the contrary, an effect similar to that of lively,
bright colors. Between these two extremes we find, in music as well

as in painting, all the colors which are appropriate to the description of varied emotions and characters.

Different emotions color our faces differently. Black and purple indicate fury and rage; purplish red marks anger; pink suits modesty; white denotes candor (here, for the average person, lack of color means the absence of all the vices), while yellow suggests oft-sustained grief . . . I do not doubt that the mingling of these different emotions or characteristics brings out in the face the nuances or interplay of these different colors; nor, in order not to mistake effect for cause, that every differently organized person carries within himself the complexus of his own emotions, and shows us in his face the colors which denote them. See how naturally each person in a play takes on in his costume the colors which suit him! Doesn't this seem to indicate to the musician the tones, the sounds which he should use? All these things are not hard and fast rules, but truth demands of the artist that he observe them, and the man who works by instinct never makes a mistake about them without cause. [3]

RULES

Woe to the artist enslaved by rules who does not dare yield to the flight of his genius. There must be deviations from the rule in order to express almost everything. One must know how to describe the sane man who leaves by the door and the madman who jumps out the window.

If you can achieve what you want only by creating an unusual combination, don't be afraid of enriching theory by one more rule; other artists may later make more effective use of the license you have permitted yourself and will force the most rigidly academic to accept it. Precept has always followed example. However, only the man who is familiar with the rules may sometimes violate them for he alone can know that, in certain cases, the rule is not enough. [4]

MUSIC AND DECLAMATION

Convinced that each speaker had his own tone, his own manner, I schooled myself to reserve to each his character.

I soon perceived that music possessed resources which declamation itself did not. For example, a young girl assures her mother that she has not known love, but while she affects indifference through a simple, monotonous song, the orchestra expresses the torment of her heart in love. Again, suppose a nonentity wishes to express his love or his courage. If he is truly intense about it, he must be permitted the accents of his passion, but meanwhile the orchestra, by its monotony, reveals to us his puny character. In general, the feeling must be in the song; spirit, gestures, and bearing must be reinforced in the accompaniment. [5]

WOLFGANG AMADEUS MOZART

1756–1791

Mozart is revealed as a warm, vigorous human being in his letters, which are spirited and even racy; many of his expressions, typical of the lustiness of his age and environment, are broad almost beyond present-day printability. The letters also reveal his professional attitude toward music which he loved so passionately. He once wrote to his father: "I can more or less adopt or imitate any kind and any style of composition." He did not exaggerate. He was not only a lyric but a truly dramatic composer, a man of the theater, ever conscious of what would please and move his audience. His letters describing the evolution of the *Abduction* may at times seem technical to the lay reader, yet they show his abiding concern for the union of libretto and music. Understandably, Mozart wrote his music to suit the highest capabilities of the best singers at hand, but the dramatic interest of the opera is so strong that, like his other stage works, it has retained unending appeal.

Musically, Mozart was a man of moderation. He created a world of novelty, of color, but he felt that "music . . . must never offend the ear; it must please the hearer; in other words, it must never cease to be music." Although he wrote with amazing swiftness, he could not tolerate shoddiness. Attesting this are his tirade against Clementi's superficial, showy works and his criticism of the Abbé Vogler for his haste and sloppiness in sight reading.

Mozart's respect for Haydn amounted to reverence. The touching dedication of his six quartets to the older master is a tribute to their mutual admiration and deep friendship. Each benefited greatly from the study of the other's works, and they were both frank in admitting the musical debt they owed each other.

PIANOS AND PIANO PLAYING

Letter to his father, Augsburg, October 17/18, 1777

This time I shall begin at once with Stein's pianofortes. Before I had seen any of his make, Späth's claviers had always been my favorites.

But now I much prefer Stein's, for they damp ever so much better than the Regensburg instruments. When I strike hard, I can keep my finger on the note or raise it, but the sound ceases the moment I have produced it. In whatever way I touch the keys, the tone is always even. It never jars, it is never stronger or weaker or entirely absent; in a word, it is always even. It is true that he does not sell a pianoforte of this kind for less than three hundred gulden, but the trouble and the labor which Stein puts into the making of it cannot be paid for. His instruments have special advantage over others in that they are made with escape action. Only one maker in a hundred bothers about this. But without an escapement it is impossible to avoid jangling and vibration after the note is struck. When you touch the keys, the hammers fall back the moment they have struck the strings, whether you hold down the keys or release them. He himself told me that when he has finished making one of these claviers, he sits down to it and tries all kinds of passages, runs and jumps, and he polishes and works away at it until it can do anything. For he labors solely in the interest of music and not for his own profit, otherwise he would soon finish his work. He often says: "If I were not myself such a passionate lover of music and had I not some slight skill on the clavier, I should certainly long ago have lost patience with my work. But I do like an instrument which never lets a player down and which is durable." And his claviers certainly do last. He guarantees that the sounding board will neither break nor split. When he has finished making one for a clavier, he places it in the open air, exposing it to rain, snow, the heat of the sun and all the devils in order that it may crack. Then he inserts wedges and glues them in to make the instrument very strong and firm. He is delighted when it cracks, for he can then be sure that nothing more can happen to it. Indeed, he often cuts into it himself and then glues it together again and strengthens it in this way.   [1]

RUBATO PLAYING

From: Letter to his father, Augsburg, October 23, 1777

In tempo rubato in an Adagio, the left hand should go on playing in strict time!   [2]

SIGHT READING

Letter to his father, Mannheim, January 17, 1778

I should mention that before dinner, he [Abbé Vogler] had scrambled through my concerto [the Piano Concerto in C, K 246] at sight (the one which the daughter of the house plays—written for Countess Lützow). He took the first movement prestissimo—the Andante allegro and the Rondo even more prestissimo. He generally played the bass differently from the way it was written, inventing now and then quite another harmony and melody. Nothing else is possible at that pace, for the eyes cannot see the music nor the hands perform it. Well, what good is that kind of sight reading? The listeners (I mean those who deserve the name) can only say that they have seen music and piano-playing. They hear, think and feel as little during the performance as the player himself. Well, you may easily imagine that it was unendurable. At the same time, I could not bring myself to say to him, *Far too quick!* Besides, it is much easier to play a thing quickly than slowly: in difficult passages you can leave out a few notes without anyone's noticing it. But is that beautiful music? In rapid playing the right and left hands can be changed without anyone's seeing or hearing it; but is that beautiful?

And wherein consists the art of playing *a prima vista?* In this: in playing the piece in the time in which it ought to be played and in playing all the notes, appoggiaturas and so forth, exactly as they are written and with the appropriate expression and taste, so that you might suppose the performer had composed it himself.　　　　[3]

THE DUODRAMA

From: Letter to his father, Mannheim,
November 12, 1778

The Seyler company is here, whom you no doubt already know by reputation; Herr von Dalberg is manager. He refuses to let me go until I have composed a *duodrama* for him; and indeed it did not take me long to make up my mind, for I have always wanted to write a drama of this kind. I cannot remember whether I told you anything about this type of drama the first time I was here. On that occasion I saw a piece of this kind performed twice and was absolutely delighted. Indeed, nothing has ever surprised me so much, for I had always imagined that such a piece would be quite ineffective! You know, of course, that there is no singing in it, only recitation, to which the music is a sort of obbligato accompaniment to a recitative. Now and then the words are spoken while the music goes on, and this produces the finest possible effect. . . . Well, imagine my joy at having to compose just the kind of work I have so much desired.[1] Do you know what I think? I think that most operatic recitatives should be treated

---

[1] Otto Freiherr von Gemmingen's *Semiramis* (K 315e), music lost.

in this way and only sung occasionally, when the words *can be perfectly expressed by the music*. [4]

OPERA

Letter to his father, February 28, 1778

I like an aria to fit a singer as perfectly as a well-tailored suit of clothes. [5]

THE ABDUCTION FROM THE SERAGLIO

Letter to his father, Vienna, September 26, 1781

I thought that it would afford you pleasure if I gave you some idea of my opera [the *Abduction*]. As the original text began with a monologue, I asked Herr Stephanie [1] to make a little arietta out of it and then to put in a duet, instead of making the two chatter together after Osmin's song. As we have given the part of Osmin to Herr Fischer, who certainly has an excellent bass voice (in spite of the fact that the Archbishop told me he sang too low for a bass and that I assured him he would sing higher next time!), we must take advantage of it, particularly as he has the whole Viennese public on his side. But in the original libretto Osmin has only this short song and nothing else except in the trio and the finale; so he has been given an aria in Act I, and he is to have another in Act II. I have explained to Stephanie the words I require for this aria; indeed, I had finished composing most of the music for it before Stephanie knew anything whatever about it. I am enclosing only the beginning and the end which are bound to have a good effect. Osmin's rage is rendered comical by the accompaniment of the Turkish music. In working out the aria I have given full scope now and then to Fischer's beautiful deep notes (in spite of our Salzburg Midas). [2] The passage "Drum beim Barte des Propheten" is indeed in the same tempo, but with quick notes; but as Osmin's rage gradually increases, the allegro assai comes, just when the aria seems to be at an end; this is in a totally different measure and in a different key; the contrast is bound to be very effective. For just as a man in such a towering rage oversteps all the bounds of order, moderation and propriety and completely forgets himself, so must the music, too, forget itself. But passions, whether violent or not, must never be ex-

[1] Gottlieb Stephanie, Jr. (1741–1800) revised the libretto of the *Abduction* from the original of Ch. Fr. Bretzner (1748–1807).

[2] Archbishop Hieronymus Colloredo.

pressed in such a way as to excite disgust, and music, even in the most terrible situations, must never offend the ear; it must please the hearer, or in other words must never cease to be *music*. Therefore, I have gone from F (the key in which the aria is written), not into a remote key, but into a related one, not however, into its nearest relative, D minor, but into the more remote A minor. Let me now turn to Belmonte's aria in A major, "O wie ängstlich, o wie feurig." Would you like to know how I have expressed it, and even indicated his throbbing heart? By the two violins playing in octaves. This is the favorite aria of all those who have heard it, and it is mine also. I wrote expressly to suit Adamberger's voice. You feel the trembling, the faltering; you see how his throbbing breast begins to swell (this I have expressed by a crescendo); you hear the whispering and the sighing, which I have indicated by the first violins with mutes and a flute playing in unison.

The Janissary chorus is, as such, all that can be desired, that is, short, lively and written to please the Viennese. I have sacrificed Constanze's aria a little to the flexible throat of Mlle. Cavalieri, "Trennung war mein banges Los und nun schwimmt mein Aug' in Thränen." I have tried to express her feelings, as far as an Italian bravura aria will allow. I have changed the "Hui" to "schnell," so it now runs thus: "Doch wie schnell schwand meine Freude." I really don't know what our German poets are thinking of. Even if they do not understand the theater, or at all events, operas, they should not make their characters talk as if they were addressing a herd of swine. *Hui*, sow!

Now for the trio at the close of Act I. Pedrillo has passed off his master as an architect, to give him an opportunity to meet his Constanze in the garden. Bassa Selim has taken him into his service. Osmin, the steward, knows nothing of this and, being a rude churl and a sworn foe of all strangers, is impertinent and refuses to let them into the garden. It opens quite abruptly and, because the words lend themselves to it, I have made it a fairly respectable piece of real three-part writing. Then the major key begins at once pianissimo—it must go very quickly—and winds up with a great deal of noise, which is always appropriate at the end of an act. The more noise the better, and the shorter the better, so that the audience has no time to cool down with their applause.

I have sent you only fourteen bars of the overture, which is very short with alternate fortes and pianos, the Turkish music always coming in at the fortes. The overture modulates through different keys, and I doubt whether anyone, even if his previous night had been a sleepless one, could go to sleep over it. Now comes the rub! The first act was finished more than three weeks ago, as was also one aria in

Act II and the drunken duet (*per i signori viennesi*) which consists entirely of *my Turkish tattoo*. But I cannot compose any more, because the whole story is being altered and, to tell the truth, at my own request. At the beginning of Act III there is a charming quintet or rather finale, but I should prefer to have it at the end of Act II. In order to make this practicable, great changes must be made, in fact, an entirely new plot must be introduced—and Stephanie is up to the ears in other work. So we must have a little patience. Everyone abuses Stephanie. It may be that, in my case, he is only very friendly to my face. After all, he is arranging the libretto for me—and what is more, exactly as I want it—so, by Heaven, I do not ask anything more of him. [6]

From: Letter to his father, Vienna, October 13, 1781

Now as to the libretto of the opera [the *Abduction*], you are quite right so far as Stephanie's work is concerned. Still, the poetry is perfectly in keeping with the character of stupid, surly, malicious Osmin. I am well aware that the verse is not of the best, but it fitted in and it agreed so well with the musical ideas which already were buzzing in my head that it could not fail to please me; and I would like to wager that when it is performed, no deficiencies will be found. As for the poetry which was there originally, I really have nothing to say against it. Belmonte's aria "O wie ängstlich" could hardly be better written for music. Except for "Hui" and "Kummer ruht in meinem Schoss" [for sorrow cannot rest], I should say that, in an opera, the poetry must be altogether the obedient daughter of the music. Why do Italian comic operas please everywhere in spite of their miserable libretti—even in Paris, where I myself witnessed their success? Just because there the music reigns supreme and when one listens to it, all else is forgotten. Why, an opera is sure of success when the plot is well worked out, and when the words are written solely for the music, not shoved in here and there to suit some miserable rhyme (which, God knows, never enhances the value of any theatrical performance, be it what it may, but rather detracts from it)—words or even entire verses may ruin the composer's whole idea. Verses are indeed the most indispensable element for music, but rhymes, solely for the sake of rhyming, the most detrimental. Those high and mighty people who set to work in pedantic fashion will always come to grief, both they and their music. The best of all is when a good composer, who understands the stage and is talented enough to make sound suggestions, meets that true phoenix, an able poet; in that case, no fears need be entertained as to the applause even of the ignorant. Poets almost remind me of trumpeters with their professional tricks! If we composers were always to stick so faithfully to our rules (which were very good at a time when no one knew better). we should be concocting music as unpalatable as their libretti.   [7]

THE PIANO CONCERTI, K 413, 414, 415

From: Letter to his father, Vienna, December 28, 1782

These concertos are a happy medium between the too easy and the too difficult; they are brilliant, pleasing to the ear, and natural without being vapid. There are passages here and there from which connoisseurs alone can derive satisfaction; but these passages are written in such a way that the less learned cannot fail to be pleased, even without knowing why.

The golden mean of truth in all things is no longer either known or appreciated. In order to win applause one must write stuff which is so inane that a *fiacre* [cab-driver] could sing it, or so unintelligible that it pleases precisely because no sensible man can understand it. This is not what I have been wanting to discuss with you; I should like to write a book on this, a short introduction to music, illustrated by examples but, I need hardly add, not under my own name.   [8]

CLEMENTI'S PIANO SONATAS

From: Letter to his father, Vienna, June 7, 1783

Well, I have a few words to say to my sister about Clementi's sonatas. Everyone who hears or plays them must feel that, as compositions, they are worthless. They contain no remarkable or striking passages except those in sixths and octaves. And I implore my sister not to practice these passages too much, so that she may not spoil her quiet, even touch and that her hand may not lose its natural lightness, flexibility and smooth rapidity. For after all, what is to be gained by it? Supposing you do manage to play sixths and octaves with the utmost velocity (which no one can accomplish, not even Clementi), you will only produce an atrocious chopping effect and nothing else whatever. Clementi is a charlatan, like all Italians. He writes *Presto* over a sonata or even *Prestissimo* and *Alla breve*, and plays it himself *Allegro* in 4/4 time. I know this is the case, for I have heard him do so. What he really does well are his passages in thirds; but he sweated over them day and night in London. Apart from this, he can do nothing, absolutely nothing, for he has not the slightest expression or taste, still less, feeling.   [9]

PUBLISHING MUSIC

From: Letter to his father, Vienna, February 20, 1784

I must ask you something about which I know nothing whatever. If I have some work printed or engraved at my own expense, how can I protect myself from being cheated by the engraver? For surely he can print off as many copies as he likes and therefore swindle me. The only way to prevent this would be to keep a sharp eye on him. Yet that was impossible in your own case when you had your book[1] printed, for you were at Salzburg and the printer was at Augsburg. Why, I almost feel inclined not to sell any more of my compositions to any engraver, but to have them printed or engraved by subscription at my own expense, as most people do, and in this way make a good profit. I am not doubtful about getting subscribers, for I have already had subscription offers from Paris and Warsaw.   [10]

THE STRING QUARTETS, K 387, 421, 428, 458, 464, 465

Dedication to Joseph Haydn, Vienna, September 1, 1785

To my dear friend Haydn: A father who had decided to send his sons into the great world, thought it his duty to entrust them to the protection and guidance of a man who was very celebrated at the time and who, moreover, happened to be his best friend.

In like manner I send my six sons to you, most celebrated and very dear friend. They are, indeed, the fruit of long and laborious study; but many friends have given me the hope that these children may one day prove a source of consolation to me.

During your last stay in this capital, you yourself, my very dear friend, expressed your approval of these compositions. Your good opinion encourages me to offer them to you and leads me to hope that you will not consider them wholly unworthy of your favor. Please, then, receive them kindly and be to them a father, guide and friend. From this moment I surrender to you all my rights over them. I entreat you, however, be indulgent toward those faults which may have escaped a father's partial eye and, in spite of them, continue your generous friendship towards one who so highly appreciates it. Meanwhile, I remain with all my heart, dearest friend, your most sincere friend,

W. A. Mozart   [11]

[1] *Versuch einer gründlichen Violinschule, 1756.*

LUDWIG VAN BEETHOVEN

1770–1827

The high-flown effusions on Beethoven, for which his biographers and critics are responsible, contrast interestingly with the modest, practical writings of the master himself. Certainly Beethoven lacked neither ideas nor a keen sense of the beautiful in art and at times expressed himself in the most articulate terms on music, yet what he said and his manner of saying it always reflect a direct, workmanlike approach.

The economic problems of the artist naturally concerned him, and his letters and notebooks allude to them constantly. His application for the job of composer to the Vienna opera, quoted below, is only one example of his own search for financial security. Neither he nor Mozart, who tried for similar positions, ever achieved the stability of the "regular job," which generally fell to their inferior contemporaries. Beethoven did not, however, lack publishers. His works were in demand and, as he frankly says, well paid for, so that particularly in later life he was not in want.

The much quoted "Heiligenstädter Testament" and an appreciable portion of his correspondence deal with his bodily afflictions, especially with his deafness from which stemmed, in great part, his neurotic social behavior. Yet these disabilities did not prevent his being very aware of the political or technical trends of his time. For example, he did not underestimate the value of Mälzel's metronome in aiding the correct interpretation of the composer's wishes, although he twitted Mälzel in an amusing round and in a movement of the *Eighth Symphony* (the themes of both are practically identical).

Beethoven was also solidly aware of the importance of his own work. If he was not given to purple prose in discussing it, he knew its quality and place in the history of music, as his remarks about *Fidelio* testify.

MUSIC AND BUSINESS

From: Letter to Franz Anton Hoffmeister, Vienna, *ca.*
January 15, 1801

There should be a single Art Exchange in the world, to which the artist would simply send his works and be given in return as much as he needs. As it is, one has to be half a merchant on top of everything else, and how badly one goes about it! [1]

From: Draft of a contract, *ca.* February, 1809

It must be the aim and aspiration of every true artist to place himself in a position in which, undisturbed by other duties or by economic considerations . . . he can devote himself to the composition of larger works and present these to the public upon their completion. Meanwhile, he must also bear in mind his old age and endeavor to make adequate provision for that period of his life. [2]

COMPOSITION

From: Letter to Friedrich Treitschke, Vienna, April, 1814

The cursed concert which I was partly forced into by my bad [financial] situation has set me back with the opera [*Fidelio*, third version]. The Cantata, too, that I wanted to perform there has robbed me of five or six days. Now everything has to be done at once. I could write something new much faster than add to the old, as I was wont to do. In my instrumental music, too, I always have the whole in my mind; here, however, the whole is to a certain extent divided, and I have to think myself anew into the music. [3]

From: Letter to George Thomson, Vienna, February 19, 1813

I am not in the habit of altering my compositions once they are finished. I have never done this, for I hold firmly that the slightest change alters the character of the composition. [4]

From: Letter to Archduke Rudolph,
Vienna, July 1, 1823

I hope that Your Imperial Highness will continue especially to practice writing down your ideas straight away at the piano; for this purpose, there should be a small table beside the piano. In this way the imagination is strengthened, and one also learns to pin down the remotest ideas at once. It is likewise necessary to write without a piano. Nor should it pain but rather please Your Imperial Highness to find yourself absorbed in this art, at times to elaborate a simple melody, a chorale with simple and again with more varied figurations in counterpoint, and so on, to more difficult exercises. We develop gradually the capacity to represent exactly what we wish to represent, what we feel within us, which is a need characteristic of all superior persons.   [5]

From the Notebooks [1818]

In order to write true church music, look through all the church chorales, those of the monks, and so on, to find the most accurate translations of all the sections, also the perfect prosody of all the Christian and Catholic psalms and canticles generally.   [6]

From a Written Conversation with
Louis Schlösser (1822 or 1823)

I carry my thoughts about with me for a long time, often for a very long time, before writing them down. I can rely on my memory for this and can be sure that, once I have grasped a theme, I shall not forget it even years later. I change many things, discard others, and try again and again until I am satisfied; then, in my head, I begin to elaborate the work in its breadth, its narrowness, its height, its depth and, since I am aware of what I want to do, the underlying idea never deserts me. It rises, it grows, I hear and see the image in front of me from every angle, as if it had been cast [like sculpture], and only the labor of writing it down remains, a labor which need not take long, but varies according to the time at my disposal, since I very often work on several things at the same time. Yet I can always be sure that I shall not confuse one with another. You may ask me where I obtain my ideas. I cannot answer this with any certainty: they come unbidden, spontaneously or unspontaneously. I may grasp them with my hands in the open air, while walking in the woods, in the stillness of night, at early morning. Stimulated by those moods which poets turn into words, I turn my ideas into tones which resound, roar and rage until at last they stand before me in the form of notes.   [7]

From: Archduke Rudolph's Book of Instruction, *ca.* 1816

Many maintain that every movement in a minor key must end of necessity in the same mode. *Nego.* On the contrary, I find that precisely the soft scales of the major at the end have a delightful, uncommonly calming effect. Joy follows on sorrow, and sunshine on rain. With this I feel as though I look toward the mild, silver glance of the shining evening star.   [8]

From a statement to Georg August Griesinger, *ca.* 1824

My *Fidelio* was not understood by the public, but I know that it will yet be valued; nevertheless, although I know what *Fidelio* is worth, I know just as clearly that the symphony is my true element. When sounds stir within me, I always hear the full orchestra; I know what to expect of instrumentalists, who are capable of almost everything, but with vocal compositions I must always keep asking myself: can this be sung? . . .   [9]

Notes on the *Pastoral Symphony,* 1807

It is left to the listener to discover the situation. *Sinfonia caracteristica* or a reminiscence of country life. Every kind of painting loses by being carried too far in instrumental music. *Sinfonia pastorella.* Anyone who has the faintest idea of country life will not need many descriptive titles to be able to imagine for himself what the author intends. Even without a description one will be able to recognize it all, for it is [a record of] sentiments rather than a painting in sounds.   [10]

THE ORGAN

From: a · Written Conversation with Karl Gottlieb
Freudenberg, organist in Breslau, *ca.* 1825

I, too, played the organ frequently in my youth, but ·my nerves could not withstand the power of this gigantic instrument. I should place an organist who is master of his instrument at the very head of all virtuosi.   [11]

TRANSCRIPTIONS

From: Letter to Breitkopf & Härtel,
Vienna, July 13, 1802

With respect to transcriptions and arrangements, I am now sincerely pleased that you refused them. The unnatural fury which possesses us to transplant even things written for the piano to string instruments, instruments so entirely opposed to each other, should certainly come to an end. It is my firm opinion that only Mozart could translate his own works from the piano to other instruments—Haydn likewise—and without wishing to join company with these two great men, I believe that it is also true of my piano sonatas. The fact that whole passages must be omitted or changed is an additional difficulty, and this great stumbling-block can be overcome only by the master himself or at least by one who has no less skill and inventiveness. I have transformed only one of my sonatas [Op. 14, No. 1] into a quartet for string instruments, because I was asked most urgently to do so, and I know for certain that this is a feat others will imitate at their peril.

[12]

PIANOFORTE MUSIC

From: Sketch Book, June 2 [1804]

Finale more and more simple, likewise all my piano music. God knows why my piano music still and always makes the worst impression on me, especially when it is badly played.　　　　　[13]

J. S. BACH

From: Letter to Franz Anton Hoffmeister,
Vienna, ca. January 15, 1801

Your intention to publish the works of Sebastian Bach rejoices my heart which is full of admiration for the great art of this father of harmony, and I hope that your plan will soon be realized. I hope that I myself shall be able to do something for you here, as soon as we hear that golden peace has been declared and as soon as you are ready to collect subscriptions for these works.　　　　　[14]

C. P. E. BACH

From: Letter to Breitkopf & Härtel,
Vienna, July 26, 1809

I have only a few of Emanuel Bach's piano works, and yet some of them must yield to every true artist not only the most lofty pleasure but instruction too. [15]

ON CRITICS

From: Letter to Breitkopf & Härtel,
Vienna, April 22, 1801

Advise your reviewer to show more intelligence and discretion, especially with regard to the products of younger authors, for these reviews could easily discourage men who might otherwise do better work. As for myself, it is true that I am far from having attained such perfection as would exempt me from all criticism, yet at first your reviewer's outcry against me was humiliating. Then, by dint of comparing myself with others, I found it scarcely affected me; I remained quite unmoved and thought, they do not understand it. I was able to remain all the more calm when I observed how, elsewhere, your reviewer extolled men of minor importance who indeed, among the better artists here, are almost lost, decent and hardworking as they may be. [16]

PIANO TEACHING

From: Letter to Karl Czerny [Vienna, 1817]

With regard to his playing: When he [your pupil] is with you, I beg you to wait until he is using the right fingers, keeping the right time and playing the notes more or less correctly, and only then to criticize his rendering. Also, once he has got so far, do not interrupt his playing because of small mistakes but point these out only when he has finished the piece. Although I have given few lessons, I have always followed this method, for it soon forms musicians and this, after all, is one of the foremost aims of art and is less tiring both for master and pupil. [17]

TEMPO MARKINGS AND THE METRONOME

Letter to Ignaz von Mosel [Vienna, 1817]

I am delighted to know that you share my opinion of those headings, inherited from times of musical barbarism, by which we describe the tempo of a movement. What, for example, can be more absurd than 'allegro' which, once and for all, means 'cheerful'? How far removed we often are from this meaning! How often a piece of music expresses the very opposite of its heading! . . . We would do well to dispense with headings. The words which describe the character of the piece are a very different matter. These we could not give up; whereas the tempo is really no more than the body, these refer rather to the spirit of the piece. I have often thought of giving up these absurd terms allegro, andante, adagio, presto. Mälzel's metronome gives us an excellent opportunity to do so. I give you my word, in my future compositions I shall not use them.

It is an altogether different question whether, by doing so, we shall encourage the general use of a metronome, necessary as it is; I hardly think so. But I do not doubt for a moment that we shall be decried as violators of tradition. If this would serve to further our cause, it would still be preferable to being accused of feudalism. I therefore think that it would be best, especially for our countries where music has become a national need and every village schoolmaster must demand the use of a metronome, if Mälzel attempted to dispose of a certain number of metronomes by subscription, at higher prices; and as soon as this number covers his expenses, he will be able to offer the rest of the metronomes required for the national need at so cheap a price that we can surely expect the most general and extensive use of the instrument. It goes without saying that certain persons should take a prominent part in this enterprise, to arouse enthusiasm. As far as I am concerned, you can definitely count on me and with pleasure I await the part you will assign me in the undertaking. [18]

LOUIS SPOHR

1784–1859

Today Spohr is known primarily to violin and clarinet students who play a few of his concertos in conservatory recitals, and to a handful of vocalists who, very occasionally, include one of his songs in their programs. Yet during his lifetime, the chamber works of this prolific composer were constantly performed, and his opera *Jessonda* was repeatedly mounted on practically every German operatic stage.

His *Autobiography* (1860–1) from which the following quotations have been chosen details a vivid picture of the artistic and musical life of his age, and an interesting characterization of Spohr as man and musician. To the twentieth century reader, it may read like an old fashioned novel. The jejune love affairs of the author may appear naïve, his strict morality may paint him as something of a prig, his orthodox adherence to the rules of musical grammar and his holy horror at any infringement of them may class him as a kind of pedant; yet he was a romantic in spirit. He criticized the late Beethoven but that did not prevent him from conducting the *Ninth Symphony* many times; curiously enough, he even produced *Tannhäuser* and *The Flying Dutchman* at Cassel where he was court conductor.

From 1812 to 1815, Spohr lived in Vienna as conductor of the Theatre an der Wien; he and his orchestra participated in the great concert that Beethoven's friends had arranged for his benefit. It took place on December 8, 1813; Beethoven conducted. Spohr's impressions and criticism of Beethoven are quoted below.

THE RUSSIAN IMPERIAL HORN BAND IN ST. PETERSBURG

From: Autobiography

In the first concert, the orchestra consisted of thirty-six violins, twenty bass and double-set wind instruments. In addition to these, the choruses were supported by forty hornists from the Imperial orchestra, each of whom had only one single note to blow. They served in place of an organ and gave the chorus, the notes of which were divided among

them, great firmness and strength. In several soli, their effect was ravishing.

Between the first and second parts of this concert, the Imperial hornists executed an overture by Gluck with a rapidity and exactness which
would have been difficult for stringed instruments; how much the more
so, then, for hornists each of whom blew only one tone! It is hardly
to be believed that they performed the most rapid passages with the
greatest precision, and I could not have conceived it possible had I not
heard it with my own ears. But, as may be imagined, the *Adagio* of the
overture made a greater effect than the *Allegro*, for it is always somewhat unnatural to perform such rapid passages with these living organ
pipes, and one could not help thinking of the thrashings which must
have been inflicted.   [1]

BEETHOVEN IN 1813

Although I had heard much of his conducting, yet it surprised me
greatly. Beethoven was wont to give the signs of expression to his
orchestra by all manner of extraordinary motions of his body. Whenever a *sforzando* occurred, he flung his arms wide, previously crossed
upon his breast. At a *piano*, he bent down, and all the lower in proportion to the softness of tone he wished to achieve. Then when a crescendo
came, he would raise himself again by degrees, and upon the commence-
ment of the forte, would spring bolt upright. To increase the forte yet
more, he would sometimes shout at the orchestra, without being aware
of it.

It was easy to see that the poor deaf maestro could no longer hear
the pianos of his own music. This was particularly remarkable in a passage in the second part of the first "Allegro" of the symphony (No. 7).
At that part there are two holds in quick succession, the second of which
is pianissimo. This Beethoven had probably overlooked, for he again began to give the time before the orchestra had executed this second hold.
Without knowing it, therefore, he was already from ten to twelve bars
in advance of the orchestra when it began the pianissimo. Beethoven,
to signify this in his own way, had crept completely under the desk.
Upon the ensuing crescendo, he again made his appearance, raising
himself continually and then springing up high at the moment when,
according to his calculations, the forte should have begun. As this did
not take place, he looked around him in dismay, stared with astonish-

ment at the orchestra, which was still playing pianissimo, and only re-
covered himself when at length the long-expected forte began, and was
finally audible to himself.

Up to this time [1813], there had been no falling off in Beethoven's
creative powers. But as of this moment, owing to his constantly increasing deafness, he could no longer hear any music, and that must of necessity have had a prejudicial effect upon his creative imagination. His
constant endeavor to be original and to open new paths could no longer,
as formerly, be saved from error by the guidance of the ear. Was it,
then, to be wondered at that his works became more and more eccentric,
disconnected, and incomprehensible? It is true that there are people who
imagine they can understand them, and in their pleasure at that claim,
rank them far above his earlier masterpieces. But I am not of their
number and freely confess that I have never been able to relish the last
works of Beethoven. Yes, I must even reckon the much admired *Ninth
Symphony* among these, the three first movements of which seem to me,
despite some solitary flashes of genius, worse than all the eight previous
symphonies. The fourth movement is, in my opinion, so monstrous and
tasteless and, in its grasp of Schiller's *Ode*, so trivial that I cannot understand how a genius like Beethoven could have written it. I find in it
another proof of what I had already noted in Vienna, that Beethoven
was wanting in aesthetic feeling and in a sense of the beautiful.

As Beethoven had already stopped playing both in public and at
private parties at the time I met him, I had but one opportunity to hear
him when I came informally to the rehearsal of a new Trio (D major, ¾
time) at Beethoven's house. It was by no means enjoyable, for the
pianoforte was woefully out of tune in the first place; this, however,
troubled Beethoven little since he could not hear it. Secondly, of the
former so greatly admired excellence of the virtuoso scarcely anything
was left, in consequence of his total deafness. In the fortes, the poor
deaf man hammered upon the keys in such a way that entire groups
of notes were inaudible, so that one lost all sense of the subject unless
the eye followed the score at the same time. I felt moved with the
deepest sorrow at so harsh a destiny. It is a sad misfortune for anyone
to be deaf. How, then, could a musician endure it without despair?
Beethoven's almost continual melancholy was no longer a riddle to me.

[2]

LONDON, 1820:

THE FIRST USE OF THE BATON

It was still the custom in London at that time, when symphonies and overtures were performed, for the pianist to have the score before him, not exactly to conduct from it but rather to read after and to play in with the orchestra at pleasure,[1] which often produced a very bad effect. The real conductor was the first violin, who gave the tempi and, every now and then when the orchestra began to falter, gave the beat with his bow. Thus a large orchestra, standing so far apart from each other as the members of the Philharmonic, could not possibly be exactly together, and despite the excellence of individual members, the ensemble was much worse than we are accustomed to in Germany. I had therefore resolved that, when my turn came to direct, I would try to remedy this defective system. Fortunately at the morning rehearsal on the day I was to conduct the concert, Mr. Ries took his place at the piano and readily assented to relinquish the score and to remain wholly excluded from all participation in the performance. I then took my stand with the score at a separate music desk in front of the orchestra, drew my directing baton from my coat pocket and gave the signal to begin. Quite alarmed at such a novel procedure, some of the directors wished to protest against it, but when I besought them to grant me at least one trial, they quieted down. The symphonies and overtures that were to be rehearsed were well known to me, and I had already directed their performance in Germany. Therefore, I could not only give the tempi in a very decisive manner, but could indicate all their entries to the wind instruments and horns, which gave them a confidence they had not known hitherto. I also felt free to stop, when the execution did not satisfy me and, in a polite but earnest manner, to remark upon the manner of execution, which remarks Mr. Ries interpreted at my request to the orchestra. Incited thereby to more than usual attention, and given assurance by the conductor's clearly visible manner of marking time, they played with a spirit and correctness such as they had never been heard to achieve until then. The orchestra, surprised and inspired by the result, immediately expressed its collective assent to the new mode of conducting after the first part of the symphony, and thereby overruled all further opposition on the part of the directors. In the vocal pieces also, of which I assumed the conducting at the request of Mr. Ries, leading with the baton was completely successful particularly in the recitative, after I had explained the meaning

[1] A leftover from the epoch of the *continuo*.

of my movements, and the singers repeatedly expressed to me their satisfaction at the precision with which the orchestra now supported them.

The results that evening were more brilliant than I could have hoped. It is true, the audience was at first startled by the novelty and there was considerable whispered comment, but when the music began and the orchestra executed the well known symphony with unusual power and precision, general approbation was shown immediately on the conclusion of the first part by long-sustained applause. The triumph of the baton as a time-giver was decisive, and no conductor was seen seated at the piano any more during the performance of symphonies and overtures.   [3]

CARL MARIA VON WEBER

1786–1826

Weber, the founder of German opera or, more aptly, of German national music, was highly cultured, especially for a musician of his time. He was an avid reader and thoroughly familiar with the works of his contemporaries, Jean Paul and E. T. A. Hoffmann, both of whom he knew well.

A true estimate of Weber is almost impossible without consideration of his writings. In fact, his literary ability contended constantly with his composing and conducting gifts and nearly drew him into the professional writing field. To the musico-literary organization Der Harmonische Verein, we owe the beginning of Weber's writings. This group of artists, founded toward the end of 1810 in Darmstadt, banded together to write on music in general and German music in particular. Various members in different cities acted as agents of the Verein, corresponding with each other, and endeavoring to advertise and popularize one another's musical compositions. Their literary work was more than mutual flattery; it included genuine, wholesome criticism. Actually, these men were the creators of professional musical journalism.

Weber also did battle for German national art in his operas—*Freischütz* particularly. In Dresden, where he was constantly harassed by the popular operatic faction, he created a German style singlehanded which prepared for and had its culmination in the music dramas of Wagner. To the latter, who followed in Weber's footsteps as conductor at the Dresden opera, he was god and mentor.

APPRECIATION

From: Review of E. T. A. Hoffmann's *Undine*

To judge a contemporary work of art correctly demands that calm, unprejudiced mood which, while susceptible to every impression, carefully guards against preconceived opinions or feelings. It requires a mind completely open to the particular work under consideration. Only

97

when his work is viewed in this way is the artist fully equipped to go forth into the world with those feelings and visions which he has created, and which he, the mighty ruler of every passionate emotion, allows us to experience with and through him: pain, pleasure, horror, joy, hope and love. We can very quickly and clearly see whether he has been capable of creating a great structure which will endure, or if, his mind working in momentary, unsteady creative flashes, he has caught our fancy with details only, thereby causing us to forget the work as a whole.

In no type of artistic creation is this more difficult to avoid, and hence more frequently present, than in opera. Obviously, I am referring to the type of opera Germans want: a self-contained work of art in which all elements, contributed by the related arts in collaboration and fused one into the other, disappear and, submerged in various ways, re-emerge to create a new world.

As a rule, single outstanding pieces of the music affect the response to the whole. Seldom do these portions—pleasantly stimulating at first hearing—actually fuse into the overall effect at the close, as they really should, since one should first be won over by a complete work, and then, on closer familiarity, take pleasure in its separate parts.

The nature and inner essence of opera, consisting of wholes within the whole, poses this great problem which only the titans of music have succeeded in overcoming. Every piece of music within it appears, because of its inherent structure, as an independent, organic, self-contained unit. Nevertheless it should merge as a part of the edifice when the latter is viewed in its entirety. Yet it may and should—and this is especially true of the ensemble piece—show various facets conjointly, be a many-visaged Janus head, visible at first glance.

Herein lies the great, profound secret of music which can be felt, yet not expressed. The surging, opposing natures of anger and love, the blissful torment in which salamander and sylph melt in each other's embrace, are herein united. In a word, what love is to mankind, music is to the arts and to mankind as well. For music is truly love itself, the purest, most ethereal language of the emotions, embracing a thousand-fold every color variation in every nuance of emotion, and while it is understood at one and the same time by a thousand different people, it contains but one basic truth. This truth in musical speech, in however unusual a new form it may appear, asserts its rights victoriously in the end. The fate of creative and significant works of art of all epochs demonstrates this frequently and conclusively. For example, nothing more alien than Gluck's creations could have appeared at a time when sensual Italian floods of tone overwhelmed and enervated everybody.

We are now being swallowed up in another, though no less dangerous, fashion of artistic deception. The all-pervasive influences of our time have set up the two extremes, death and sensuality, as rulers. Weighted down by the horrors of war, acquainted with every shade of misery, we seek amusement in only the most vulgar, sensational aspects of artistic life. The theater has become a peepshow in which—anxious to avoid the uneasiness occasioned by true appreciation of a work of art —we sit back comfortably and let a series of scenes be played before us, satisfied to be tickled by trivial jokes and melodies, or hoodwinked by mechanical nonsense which has neither purpose nor sense. Accustomed to shock in our daily life, here again only shock affects us. A gradual emotional development, an ingeniously induced heightening of interest, imply exertion and perhaps boredom, and become, in consequence of our inattention, incomprehensible. [1]

CRITICISM

From: Review of oratorio *Isacco* by Fr. Morlacchi, 1817

Most listeners criticize a work uncharitably or harshly merely because they do not measure it by the standards according to which it was written, or they do not view it from the standpoint from which the composer can see it by virtue of his talent, culture and the conviction and purpose stemming from them.

Ordinarily a German work is as alien and uncomfortable to the Italian mind as an Italian work to the German. Artistic training and familiarity breed in each man a preference and love for the outstanding qualities of his own idiom. However, in any climate, complete truth vanquishes all criticism which must ultimately bow before one single truth.

Criticism is desirable and truly helpful, when, looking kindly through the composer's eyes, it directs him and unravels his secrets, thereby revealing him to himself, since in every human being there exists a pardonable natural bias in favor of his own horizons and capabilities.

It is indeed worthy of praise and recognition when a person, educated according to the artistic tenets and needs of one country, realizes that these do not suffice everywhere. This is already a great step in the right direction, and we must only beware lest we mistake the form for the thing itself. [2]

SPEECH AND SONG

Answer to Müllner's remarks about the melody in
Brünhilde's Song in *Yngurd*, 1817

In my opinion, the first and most sacred duty in singing is the utmost fidelity to diction. None the less, cases occur—in songs less than in extended pieces—where the altogether correct stress of single syllables must perhaps be sacrificed to the complete inner truth of the melody. We cannot fully discuss this here.

As a rule, however, the composer is put in an embarrassing position by the failure of the poet to equalize the speech accent with the prosodic value of the syllables. This dichotomy between verse construction and declamation stands out doubly sharp in the music, where the rhythmic divisions are bound by a much more definite motion in time than even the most conscientious declaimer can express without becoming ridiculously artificial. As compensation, however, music possesses to a far greater degree than speech an aid and a way out, namely the significant emphasis of higher and lower pitch, and often, too, the accent of the beat must be conceded at least a force and effect equal to the pitch of the tone. Further, it is the chief and proper concern of melody to translate and bring out clearly the inner life a word expresses. Here not infrequently, in the anxious search for correctness, the essence of the melody's inner truth is reduced to dryness and sterility. The decision whether the music or the poetry should play the leading role is the rock upon which so many have foundered.   [3]

RHYTHM IN SINGING

From: Article on the metronomic markings to the opera
Euryanthe, 1824

The most difficult problem of all is to unite voice and instruments so that they blend in the rhythmic motion of a piece, and the instruments support and enhance the voice in its emotional expression, for voices and instruments are by their very nature opposed to each other. Because of breathing and articulation, singing calls for a certain fluctuation in the measure which may be compared to the uniform beating of waves against a shore. Instruments (particularly strings) divide the time into sharp segments comparable to the swinging of a pendulum. Truth of expression demands the blending of these contrasting characteristics. The beat should not be a tyrannical restriction or the driving of a mill hammer. On the contrary, it should be to music what the pulse-beat is to the life of man. There is no slow tempo in which passages which demand a faster movement do not occur, and thereby prevent the feeling of dragging. Conversely, there is no presto which does not call for the slower execution of certain passages, so that the expression will not be marred by overzealousness.

In heaven's name, however, let no singer feel himself entitled, because of the above remarks, to that maniacal kind of execution which capriciously distorts every measure, making the listener suffer unbearably, as he might on seeing an acrobat forcibly dislocating all his joints. Pressing forward or holding back in tempo must never give the feeling of jerkiness, jolting or any violence whatsoever. This may occur in a period or a phrase here and there but only in a musical-poetic significance, depending on the vehemence of expression. In a duet, for instance, two contrasting characters may require contrasting characterizations for their emotional expression. The duet between Licinius and the High Priest in *La Vestale* is a good example of the above. The more quietly the High Priest's phrases are sung, the more violently the speeches of Licinius contrast, so much more clearly will the characters stand out and so much greater will be their effect. For all this, we have no means of indication in music. These [interpretative insights] are to be found in the sensitive human breast alone, and if they are lacking there, then neither the metronome, which can only prevent gross blunders, nor our highly inadequate markings will help. (There is so much to be said on the subject of markings that I might be tempted to develop it further were I not warned by frustrating experience.) I consider them superfluous, useless and, I fear, easily misconstrued. Let them remain, but to be used only with caution.   [4]

BEETHOVEN

From: Letter to Hans Georg Nägeli, May 21, 1810
[Repudiating Nägeli's remark that one of
Weber's works reminded him
of Beethoven]

In the first place, I hate everything that bears the stamp of imitation; secondly, my views differ far too much from those of Beethoven ever to come into contact with him. The fiery, almost incredible inventive faculty which inspires him is attended by so many complications in the arrangement of his ideas that it is only his earlier compositions that interest me; the later ones, appear to me a confused chaos, an unintelligible struggle after novelty from which occasionally heavenly flashes of genius dart forth, showing how great he might be if he chose to control his luxuriant fancy.   [5]

ROSSINI

1820

Who would not gladly listen to Rossini's lively flights of fancy, to the piquant titillation of his melodies? But who could be so blind as to attribute to him dramatic truth?   [6]

POET AND COMPOSER

Letter to Friedrich Kind,[1] Dresden, July 28, 1821

The poet and the composer are so blended one into the other that it would be ridiculous to suppose the latter could achieve anything worthwhile without the former.   [7]

[1] Librettist of *Der Freischütz*, who felt his part in the work was not sufficiently recognized.

GIOACCHINO ANTONIO ROSSINI

1792–1868

When one considers that, within the first thirty-seven years of his life, Rossini wrote an almost equal number of operas, one can only conclude that his much-vaunted laziness must have served as a foil for his wit rather than have been an actual defect of character. His letter recounting his utter dilatoriness in composing the overtures to his operas takes on an even more humorous aspect, since today these overtures are more frequently played than the operas they introduced.

With the exception of the *Barber of Seville*—the best example of *opera buffa* extant—most of his other operas have lapsed into oblivion except for sporadic performances. The *Barber's* initial failure due to intrigue and cabal did not disturb Rossini, nor did its success immediately thereafter elate him. He was a worldly man.

Many reasons have been advanced for the cessation of Rossini's musical output from his thirty-seventh year until just before his death when he produced not an opera, but a religious work, the *Stabat Mater*. Perhaps the most reasonable, judging from the fullness of his Paris life, is that he enjoyed living.

THE PRESENT STATE OF MUSIC

Letter to Leopoldo Cicognara, February 12, 1817

Here are my ideas on the present state of music. Ever since the five notes were added to the harpsichord,[1] I have maintained that a dire revolution was brewing in our art which, at that time had reached perfection; for experience has shown that when we wish perforce to achieve the best, we fall into the worst. Haydn had already begun to corrupt purity of taste by introducing strange chords, artificial passages and daring novelties into his compositions, but he still preserved a sublimity and traditional beauty which would seem to excuse his deviations.

[1] Rossini apparently refers to the extension of the keyboard from four and a half to five octaves that took place after 1750.

But after him Cramer and, finally, Beethoven, with their compositions lacking in unity and natural flow and full of arbitrary oddities, corrupted taste in instrumental music completely. And now, for the simple and majestic styles of Sarti, Paisiello and Cimarosa, Mayr has substituted in the theater his own ingenious but vicious harmonies in which the main melody is strangled in deference to the new German school wherein all the young composers have set out to write theater music.

Many of our singers, born outside of Italy, have renounced purity of musical taste which never found roots beyond the confines of Italy, and have adopted the impure style of foreigners to please the capitals of Europe. They have then returned, bringing back and spreading here the germs of bad taste.

Warblings, leaps, trills, jumps, abuses of semitones, clusters of notes, these characterize the singing which now prevails. Therefore meter, the essential part of music, without which melody is incomprehensible and harmony falls into disorder, is ignored and violated by singers. They astound rather than move the public, and whereas in the good old days players sought to make their instruments sing, now our singers endeavor to handle their voices as if they were instruments. The populace, meantime applauding such bad style, makes of music what the Jesuits made of poetry and oratory when they preferred Lucan to Virgil, Seneca to Cicero.

These are my ideas on the current state of music, and I confess to you that I have little hope of seeing this divine art emerge from the corruption in which it is submerged without the total overthrow of existing social institutions and, as you see, the remedy might then be worse than the disease.   [1]

REQUIREMENTS OF AN OPERA SINGER

From: Letter to Ferdinando Guidicini, Bologna,
February 12, 1851

I want to thank you for your kind note in which you ask me a question about music. However, the question is one of expression rather than of substance, and I shall therefore dispose of it briefly. I shall say that, in order to fulfill his part well, the good singer must be only an able *interpreter* of the composer's ideas, seeking to express them with all his skill and investing them with the brilliance inherent in them. In addition, players need only be faithful *executants* of the score as written. But not infrequently it happens that this execution is distorted, often spoiling the ideas of the composer, robbing them of that simplicity of expression which they should have.

The French use the phrase *créer un rôle*. This is French conceit, which is characteristic of those singers who perform a leading rôle in a new opera for the first time and wish to indicate that they are setting an example which is to be followed by other singers who may be called upon to perform the same part. Here again the word *to create* seems hardly appropriate, since *to create* means to *extract from nothing*. The singer, on the other hand, certainly works on something, that is to say, on poetry and on music which are not of his creation.   [2]

RAMEAU

From: Letter to Mme Stephen de la Madeleine, Passy,
September 4, 1862

When you ask me to support the erection of a statue to our immortal Rameau, it is, as we say, "an invitation to a wedding." Believe me, I am an ardent admirer of this illustrious man. He rendered such great services to musical art that one would have to be totally ignorant of them not to grasp eagerly at the only way of honoring him. The dramatic productions, the delightful harpsichord compositions which I have always had performed at my home by their best interpreter, Mme Tardieu, have been and will be the object of my constant admiration and pleasure. *Fiat lux,* I say. Let the statue be raised!

In associating myself with your noble impulse, I send you the expression of my gratitude.   [3]

THE BEST TIME TO COMPOSE AN OVERTURE

Letter to an unknown composer [date unknown]

Wait until the evening before opening night. Nothing primes inspiration more than necessity, whether it be the presence of a copyist waiting for your work or the prodding of an impresario tearing his hair. In my time, all the impresarios in Italy were bald at thirty.

I composed the overture to *Otello* in a little room in the Barbaja palace wherein the baldest and fiercest of directors had forcibly locked me with a lone plate of spaghetti and the threat that I would not be allowed to leave the room alive until I had written the last note.

I wrote the overture to *La Gazza Ladra* the day of its opening in the theater itself, where I was imprisoned by the director and under the surveillance of four stagehands who were instructed to throw my original text through the window, page by page, to the copyists waiting below to transcribe it. In default of pages, they were ordered to throw me out the window bodily.

I did better with *The Barber*. I did not compose an overture, but selected for it one which was meant for a semi-serious opera called *Elisabetta*. The public was completely satisfied.

I composed the overture to *Conte Ory* while fishing, with my feet in the water, and in company of Signor Agnado who talked of Spanish finance. The overture for *William Tell* was composed under more or less similar circumstances. And as for *Mosè*, I did not write one. [4]

MIXED VOICES IN THE CHURCH

Letter to Franz Liszt, Passy, June 23, 1865

I am answering, by return mail, your precious letter of the 17th which proves to me that time and distance have not weakened your affection for the old man of Pesaro. I am writing you in my native language, that being the best suited to bring out and express the feelings of my heart. I began to love and admire you in Vienna in 1822, a recollection so dear to me! The succeeding years have only increased my affection for you. Your determination to enter on an ecclesiastical career has not surprised me. Rather has it inspired me. Oh, my dearest Abbé Liszt, allow me to offer my sincere felicitations on the *holy* road you have taken, which assures you the best possible future. However, I am sure that you will not abandon music in which God has so richly endowed you that the harmony of Heaven will ever be your best escort on this earth.

A propos of music, I do not know if you have heard that I composed a *Messa di Gloria* in four parts which was performed at the palace of my friend, Count Pillet-Will. This Mass was sung by gifted artists of both sexes and accompanied by two pianos and a harmonium. The foremost Parisian composers (among them my poor colleague, Meyerbeer, then still alive) praised it most highly, beyond its deserts. They would like to have me orchestrate it in order to perform it in some Paris cathedral. I am loath to undertake such a work, having put all my scant musical knowledge into this composition and having worked on it with true religious devotion. There exists, I have been told, a *fatal* Bull promulgated by a former Pope which *prohibits* the mingling of the two sexes in the church. Could I ever consent to hearing my poor notes sung out of tune by boy sopranos rather than by women who were educated *ad hoc* for sacred music and who, with their pure, well-pitched voices, would represent (musically speaking) heavenly angels? If it were given me to live in the Vatican as you do, I would throw myself at the feet of my adored Pius IX to plead for the grace of a *new* Bull permitting women to sing in church together with men. Such a step would give new life to sacred music, which is now in total decay. It is my feeling that His Holiness who, I know, loves music and is not ignorant of my name, would acquire new glory in Paradise by issuing such a Bull, and Catholics of every land would bless him for this act of justice (since both sexes mingle in church attendance) and true harmonic sensibility. Our holy religion, though some wretches would like to trample it underfoot, will always remain at its most sublime and music will ever be a great aid to the devout.

As a courageous priest, dear friend, unite with me and let us try to obtain from His Holiness a grace which must lie doubly close to your heart, as a servant of God and as a musician. I realize that I have imposed on you with this lengthy letter. I shall therefore close by blessing you and telling you that no one loves you more than do I.   [5]

FRANZ SCHUBERT
1797-1828

For all his musical fertility—few composers have enjoyed as much—
Schubert had very little to *say* about music. With the exception of a
few poems and a little fantasy called "My Dream," his diaries and letters concern his uneventful, everyday life and the affairs of his close
friends and relatives. The letter to his parents from Steyr, in which he
discusses his songs from *The Lady of the Lake*, was written on one of
his hiking trips, a favorite pastime with him as with many Austrians.

The slighting remark about "one of our greatest German musicians,"
in the panegyric on Salieri, refers to Beethoven. Schubert was merely
expressing the general feeling of the period as well as Salieri's who,
as a disciple of Gluck, felt that Beethoven was a dangerous influence.
Shortly afterwards, however, he reversed himself and became a great
admirer of Beethoven.

SALIERI'S FIFTIETH VIENNA ANNIVERSARY

Entry in his Diary for June 16, 1816

It must be fine and inspiring for a musician to have all his pupils
gathered about him, to see how each strives to give of his best in honor
of the master's jubilee, to hear in all their compositions the simple expressions of Nature, free from all that eccentricity which tends to
govern most composers nowadays, and for which we are indebted—
almost wholly—to one of our greatest German musicians. That eccentricity confuses and confounds, without distinguishing between them,
tragic and comic, sacred and profane, pleasant and unpleasant, heroic
strains and mere noise; it engenders in people not love but madness; it
rouses them to scornful laughter instead of lifting up their thoughts to
God. To have banned these extravagances from the circle of his pupils,
and to have kept them, instead, at the pure source of Nature must be
the greatest satisfaction to a musician who, following in Gluck's steps,
seeks his inspiration in Nature alone, despite the unnatural influences
of the present day.

After fifty years spent in Vienna and nearly as long in the Emperor's service, Herr Salieri celebrated his jubilee, received in recognition from His Majesty a gold medal, and held a big gathering of his pupils of both sexes. [1]

THE LADY OF THE LAKE

From: Letter to his father and stepmother, Steyr, July 25, 1825

In Steyreck we stayed with Countess Weissenwolf, who is a great admirer of my humble self, possesses everything I have written, and sings many of the things very prettily, too. The Walter Scott songs made such a good impression on her that she made it clear she would be by no means displeased, were I to dedicate them to her. But in connection with these, I mean to break with the usual publishing procedure which brings in so little profit. I feel that these songs, bearing as they do the celebrated name of Scott, are likely to arouse more curiosity, and—if I add the English text—should make my name better known in England, too. If only honest dealing were possible with—publishers; but the wise and beneficent regulations of our Government have taken good care that the artist remain the eternal slave of these miserable money-grabbers.

Regarding the letter from Milder, I am very pleased about the good reception accorded *Suleika*, though I wish I could have had a look at the critique myself to see if there were anything to be learned from it. A review, however favorable, can be ridiculous at the same time if the critic lacks average intelligence, as is not seldom the case. [2]

My new songs to Walter Scott's *Lady of the Lake* made a particularly good impression. Everybody was astounded at the piety I expressed in a hymn to the Holy Virgin, and which, it would seem, moves everyone's soul and puts people into a devout frame of mind. I believe this arises from the fact that I never force myself into a devout mood, and never compose such hymns or prayers except when I am unconsciously inspired by Her. Then, however, it is generally real, true devotion. [3]

GAETANO DONIZETTI

1797–1848

In a period of intense rivalry and intrigue among Italian operatic composers, Donizetti's letter of extravagant praise for Bellini's *Norma* and his unenvious recognition of Verdi's talents indicate exceptional high-mindedness. Further evidence of this is to be found in his kind recommendation of Berlioz who had, without apparent justification, impugned the originality of his *Fille du Regiment*.

Donizetti stands midway between Rossini and Verdi in Italian opera history. As prolific as they, and as fluent melodically—he was a master of the bel canto style of composition—he lacked their force and dramatic strength. Of the more than sixty operas he composed, three— *Lucia di Lammermoor*, *Don Pasquale* and *L'Elisir d'Amore*—still remain in the contemporary repertoire, and *La Fille du Regiment* is occasionally performed. The famous sextet from *Lucia* has been played by six of almost everything.

BELLINI'S *NORMA*

Letter to Rubetti, Milan, December 31, 1831

You ask me what artistic events have taken place in Milan lately. The only musical event of extraordinary importance has been the production of *Norma* by the young composer, Vincenzo Bellini. I am happy beyond measure at the splendid reception accorded the above opera at the Scala after its opening on the 26th of this month, a gay and festive reception which was repeated at subsequent performances.

A lucky outcome, all the more significant considering that *Norma* had a somewhat chilly greeting, even, to tell the truth, a hostile one from the numerous public the first evening it was presented. After four evenings, however, an immense crowd besieged boxes, galleries, balconies, orchestra, and filled the vast hall to overflowing, applauding every piece in the opera with tremendous enthusiasm.

Everybody is praising the music of my friend, or rather my brother, Bellini to the skies. Everyone is overwhelmed by his sovereign genius, and is discovering in his work undreamed-of beauties and treasures of sublime harmony. The whole score of *Norma* pleases me immensely, and I have been going to the theater the last four evenings to hear Bellini's opera, remaining through the last scene.

The pieces in *Norma* which struck me most are: the introduction to the first act where the musical ideas are distributed and developed with consummate skill and great knowledge of musical technique. The close of this piece is most original. What truly expert workmanship in the introduction which closes with a strong and vigorous martial chorus, and is most novel in its power and development! The "Casta Diva" is a delicate, enchanting melody. How full of grace and charm is this *cavatina!* The melody lends itself to the most dramatic effects, and the entire instrumental part is worked out with bravura. How utterly beautiful are the recitatives in *Norma!* The duet, "In mia mano alfin tu sei" (Verdi expresses himself similarly) is a marvellous example of dramatic melody. Norma's final scene, "Qual cor tradisti, qual cor perdesti," moved me to tears. Were I to enumerate all the beauties of *Norma* I would never finish this letter. I shall only say that I am completely won over by this moving composition, by the rich elegance of its orchestration, and by the union of the emotional and dramatic with the greatness of inspiration.   [1]

AN ERROR OF BERLIOZ'

Letter to the editor of the *Moniteur Universel*
in Paris, February 16, 1840

An article published in the literary section of your paper today concerning the performance of my *Fille du Regiment* at the Opéra-Comique contains an error as grave as it is odd, one which honor, as well as duty, compels me to correct.

The author of the article does not hesitate to state that my score has already been heard in Italian, at least in great part, and that it is a little opera in imitation of or translated from the *Châlet* by M. Adam.

If M. Berlioz, who rightly places conscientiousness among the first duties of an artist, had taken the trouble to read my score, the poem of which is in fact a translation from the *Châlet*, a score which was engraved and published in Paris by M. Lanner, he would have assured himself that the two operas he cites contain no pieces in common. Allow me to state, in my turn, that the pieces comprising *La Fille du Regiment* were all written expressly for the Opéra-Comique, and that not one of them has figured in any score whatsoever.

I shall be pleased by the correction of this substantial error on which M. Berlioz' entire article is based, and I am confident that, in your complete impartiality, you will not refuse to publish this rectification.   [2]

VERDI

From: Letter to Signora Giuseppina Appiani, Vienna, January 22, 1844

I don't believe it! They tell me (putting it mildly) that you live and breathe only for Verdi, and your letter itself betrays it . . . but I approve your passion. To the degree to which you love artists of great talent I respect you, and I cannot be envious. My heyday is over, and another must take my place. The world wants something new. Others have ceded their places to us and we must cede ours to still others . . . I am more than happy to give mine to people of talent like Verdi. Friends are always worried, but you may rest assured of this young man's success. The Venetians appreciate him as do the Milanese, for the acclaim is the same everywhere. Talent can win esteem all over. In any case, even though his success may not measure up to the complete hopes of his friends, that will not prevent Verdi from occupying shortly one of the most honorable places in the galaxy of composers.   [3]

III

BERLIOZ
GLINKA
MENDELSSOHN
CHOPIN
SCHUMANN

HECTOR BERLIOZ

1803-1869

In the last section of his *Mémoires*, Berlioz has written a few paragraphs of self-evaluation in which he enumerates the prevailing characteristics of his music: "passionate expression, intense ardor, rhythmic animation and unexpected turns." The same, and more, might be said of his literary work. A brilliant writer, master of the colorful phrase, with an overwhelming gift for mordant humor and satire, he was "overpassionate" in his loves and hates. At times he was actually hysterical, romanticizing and exaggerating his feelings. Several stories in the *Mémoires* are colored in the telling, some are fabricated, but all are vivid.

With all this, he was, when necessary, a diplomat of the first order, as witness the tale of his first all-Berlioz concert which he *had* to give in order to attract the attention of his future wife, Harriet Smithson. Also, he had an iron will, and his career was in great measure the result of this. He did not hesitate, for example, to use his position as a celebrated critic to acquaint the world with his own musical and conducting ability. Both were mighty and deserved the publicity.

Berlioz was the father of modern orchestration, and his *Traité d'instrumentation* is still the important authority on the subject. Replete with purple prose, its imagery is often piquant, as, for instance, his aphorism on the effectiveness of combining the orchestra and organ: "The orchestra is Emperor, the organ is Pope. It is wiser not to revive in music the quarrel of the Investitures."

Besides the *Mémoires* and the *Traité*, his writings have been collected in several other volumes, the best known of which are *A travers chants, Les Grotesques de la Musique*, and *Soirées de l'orchestre*. The following quotations are culled from Ernest Newman's edition of the *Mémoires*.

From: *Mémoires*, 1870

THE COMPOSER AND THE PIANO

My father did not wish me to learn the piano, otherwise I should doubtless have swelled the ranks of the innumerable army of famous pianists.

He had no intention of making an artist of me; and I dare say he thought that if I learned the piano I should devote myself too passionately to it, and become more absorbed in music than he wished or intended me to be. I have often felt the want of this accomplishment, as it might have been of the greatest use to me; but when I consider the appalling number of miserable musical platitudes to which the piano has given birth, which would never have seen the light had their authors been limited to pen and paper, I feel grateful to the happy chance which forced me to compose freely and in silence, and has thus delivered me from the tyranny of the fingers, so dangerous to thought, and from the fascination which the ordinary sonorities always exercise on a composer, more or less. Many amateurs have pitied me for this deprivation, but that does not affect me much.   [1]

INSTRUMENTATION AND CONDUCTORS

There is another most important course wanting in all modern conservatories which to my mind is becoming more essential every day, namely, that for instrumentation. That branch of the composer's art has been so greatly developed of late years as to have attracted the attention both of the critics and the public. It has, however, also served only too often to mask the poverty of a composer's ideas, to ape real energy, to counterfeit the power of inspiration, and even in the hands of really able and meritorious writers it has become a pretext for incalculable abuses, monstrous exaggerations, and ridiculous nonsense. It is easy to imagine to what excesses the example of such masters has beguiled their followers. But these very excesses prove the regular and irregular use now made of instrumentation, a blind use in general, and when not led by chance, guided by the most pitiable routine. For it does not follow that, because most composers make more use of instruments than did their predecessors, they are better acquainted with the force, character, and action of each member of the instrumental family, and the various ties of sympathy uniting them. Far from this, many illustrious composers are still quite ignorant of the most elementary part of the science, namely, the *compass* of many of the instruments. One composer, to my certain knowledge, knew nothing of that of the flute. Of that of the brasses in general and trombones in particular they have but a very vague idea; and accordingly you may remark in most modern as in ancient scores, the prudent reserve with which their authors confine themselves to the middle range of those instruments, avoiding with equal care either extremity of the scale. Instrumentation in the present day therefore is like a fashionable foreign language, which many people affect to speak without having learned it, and therefore speak without properly understanding it, and with a great many barbarisms.

Such a class, or course, in conservatories, besides being useful to composition students, would be of great service to those who are called on to become conductors. Indeed, it may readily be imagined that a conductor who is not thoroughly master of all the resources of instrumentation is not very much of a musician, and it is plainly essential that he know at least as much of the *exact compass* and *mechanism* of each instrument as the musicians under his direction, if not more. Otherwise he can only offer them timid suggestions, especially when it is a question of some unusual combination, or bold or difficult passage, about which indolence or incapacity would drive the performer to exclaim: "It cannot be done! There is no such note! It is unplayable!" and other aphorisms in use among ignorant mediocrity in such cases. Then the conductor can answer: "You are mistaken. It is quite feasible. If you set about it in such and such a manner, you will master the difficulty!" or else: "It is certainly difficult, but if it remains an impossibility to you after having worked at it for some days, I can only conclude that you are not master of your instrument, and shall be obliged to have recourse to a more skilful artist!"

In the opposite case—a too frequent one, I must admit—where the composer, for want of proper knowledge, torments the artist, however skilful, by trying to obtain impossibilities, the conductor who is sure of his facts will be able to take the musician's part against the composer, and correct his blunders.

Indeed, while I am on the subject of conductors, I may as well say that it would not be at all a bad plan in a well organized conservatory, as far as possible to teach the art of conducting to composition students especially, so that in an emergency they may conduct the performance of their own works at any rate without making fools of themselves, and distracting the musicians instead of helping them. It is generally supposed that every composer is a born conductor, that is to say, that he knows the art of conducting without having to learn it. Beethoven was an illustrious example of the fallacy of this opinion, and one might name a host of other masters whose compositions are held in general esteem, but who, the moment they take up the baton, neither mark time nor nuance, and would indeed literally bring the musicians to grief if the latter did not quickly perceive the inexperience of their leader and make up their minds to pay no attention to his whirling arms. There are two distinct parts in the work of a conductor: the first and easiest consists simply in conducting the performance of a work already known to the players and which, to use a phrase in vogue at the theaters, has been mounted beforehand. The second consists in directing the study of a work unknown to the performers, clearly setting forth the author's conception and rendering it salient and distinct, obtaining from the band that fidelity, unity, and expression without which there can be no real music and, the technical difficulties once overcome, identifying the players with himself, exciting them by his own zeal, animating them with his own enthusiasm, in short, imparting to them his own inspiration.

But to do this, there is one more art indispensable to the conductor besides the elementary knowledge acquired by study and practice, and those qualities of feeling and instinct which are the gift of nature alone, the absence or presence of which makes the conductor either the composer's best interpreter or his most formidable enemy. This indispensable art is that of *reading the score.*

He who employs a simplified score, or a simple first violin part, as is often done in our day especially in France, cannot detect half the mistakes in the performance and, if he does point out a fault, exposes himself to some such answer as this from the musician addressed: "What do you know about it? You have not got my part,"—one of the least of the inconveniences arising from this deplorable system.

Whence I conclude that if you want to form perfect and genuine conductors, you ought by all means to familiarize them with score-reading, for those who cannot master that difficulty, though they be learned in instrumentation—even composers—and also well up in the mechanisms of rhythmical movement, are really only half masters of their art.   [2]

CHORAL SINGING

Where one ordinary voice is detestable, fifty ordinary voices may be ravishing. A soulless singer paralyzes the most powerful effects of the best composer and renders them ridiculous; on the other hand, the average warmth of feeling which always resides in a really musical multitude brings out the inner flame of the work, and now it lives, whereas a single frigid virtuoso would have killed it.   [3]

PALESTRINA

An able German critic has recently constituted himself the champion of the Sistine Chapel. "Travellers, for the most part," he says, "expect a much more exciting—or I might even say, amusing—kind of music than that which pleases them so much in their own operas; instead of which they hear an ancient plainsong of simple religious character and without any accompaniment. Then these disappointed dilettanti rail against the Sistine Chapel, and declare that the music is utterly uninteresting, and that all the glowing accounts of it are travellers' tales."

We should not go quite so far as these superficial observers. On the contrary, a musician finds the same interest in this music of the past, handed down to us unchanged in style or form, as a painter does in the frescoes of Pompeii. Far from regretting the absence of the trumpets and big drums which have been introduced by the Italian composers of the day to such excess that both dancers and singers think no effect can be produced without them, we must confess that the Sistine Chapel was the only place in Italy where we felt safe from that deplorable innovation, and from the artillery of the manufacturers of *cavatinas*. We grant that the Pope's thirty-two singers, though producing no effect and in fact wholly inaudible in the largest church in the world, suffice for the performance of Palestrina's works in the confined space of the pontifical chapel; we grant that the pure, calm harmony tends to a certain kind of reverie which is not without charm. But the charm is due to the harmonies themselves and is wholly independent of the so-called genius of the composers if, indeed, you can dignify by that name musicians who spent their lives compiling successions of chords like those which constitute a portion of the *Improperia* of Palestrina:

It is quite possible that the musician who wrote these four-part psalms, in which there is neither *melody* nor *rhythm*, and in which the *harmony* is confined to *perfect chords* with a few *suspensions*, may have had some taste and a certain amount of scientific knowledge; but genius—the idea is too absurd!

There are, moreover, people who sincerely believe that Palestrina deliberately wrote in this way in order that his music might be perfectly adapted to his own pious ideal of the words of the text. They would soon see their mistake if they were to hear his madrigals, in which the most frivolous or gallant words are set to exactly the same music as those of the Bible. For example, he has set the words, *Alla riva del Tebro, giovinetto vidd'io vago Pastore* (By the banks of the Tiber, I saw a young shepherd wander), to a solemn chorus, the harmony and general effect of which are identical with those of his so-called religious compositions. The truth is that he could not write any other kind of music; far from pursuing any celestial ideal, his works contain a quantity of formulas adapted from the contrapuntists who preceded him, and of whom he is usually supposed to have been the inspired antagonist. If proof is wanted, look at his *Missa ad fugam.*

How, then, do such works as these, clever though they may be as regards their conquest of contrapuntal difficulties, contribute to the expression of religious feeling? How far are such specimens of the labor of a patient chord-manufacturer indicative of single-minded absorption in the true object of his work? In no way that I can see. The expressive accent of a musical work is not enhanced in any way by its being embodied in a perpetual canon. Beauty and truth of expression gain nothing by the difficulties which the composer may have had to overcome in producing them, any more than his work would have increased in value, had he been suffering physical pain while he was writing it. If Palestrina had lost his hands, and been forced to write with his feet, that fact would in no way have enhanced the value of his works or increased their religious merit.

Nevertheless, the German critic above referred to calls Palestrina's *Improperia* sublime. "The whole ceremony," he says, "the subject in itself, the presence of the Pope and cardinals, the precision and intelligence of the singers, form one of the most imposing and touching sights of Holy Week." True, but that does not convert the music into a work of inspiration and genius.

Some gloomy autumn day, when the dreary north wind is howling, read *Ossian* to the accompaniment of the weird moans of an Aeolian harp hung in the leafless branches of a tree, and you will experience a feeling of intense sadness, an infinite yearning for another state of exist-

ence and intense disgust with the present—in fact, a regular attack of
the "blue devils" and a longing for suicide. This is a much more definite effect than that produced by the music of the Sistine Chapel, and
yet no one ever thought of ranking the makers of Aeolian harps among
the great composers.   [4]

BACH'S *ST. MATTHEW PASSION*

Letter to Desmarest from Berlin, 1843

I was invited by the director to a performance of Sebastian Bach's
Passion. That celebrated work, with which you are no doubt familiar,
is written for two choirs and two orchestras. The singers, at least three
hundred, were arranged upon the steps of a large amphitheater, exactly
like that in the chemistry lecture-room at the Jardin des Plantes; a space
of three or four feet separated the two choirs. The two orchestras,
neither of them large, accompany the voices from the highest steps
behind the chorus, and are consequently somewhat distant from the
conductor, who is placed below, in front, and close beside the piano. I
ought to call it a clavecin, for it has almost the tone of the wretched
instruments of that name used in Bach's time. I do not know if such a
choice is made designedly, but I have remarked in all singing schools,
in the lobbies of theaters, and in fact everywhere, that the piano intended
to accompany the voice is always the most detestable that can be
found. The one which Mendelssohn used at Leipzig in the Gewandhaus
concert-room is the only exception.

You will want to know what the piano-clavecin can be doing *during
the performance* of a work in which the composer has not employed
that instrument at all! Well, it accompanies along with the orchestra, and
probably serves to keep the first rows of the chorus in tune, since they
are supposed not to be able to hear the orchestra properly in the ensemble passages *tutti*, as it is too far back of them. At any rate, this is
the custom. The constant strumming of the chords on this bad piano
produces a wearisome effect by spreading a thick layer of monotony
over the whole, but that is doubtless one reason for not giving it up.
An old custom is so sacred when it is bad!

The singers sit while they are silent, and rise to sing. I think there is
really an advantage in singing standing for the proper emission of the
voice; but it is unfortunate that the singers should weary of this pos-
ture and want to sit down as soon as each has finished, for in a work
like Bach's, where the two choirs not only carry on dialogues but are
also interrupted every instant by solo recitatives, it follows that one side

is always rising and another sitting down, and in the long run this series of ups and downs becomes rather absurd. Besides, it takes away all unexpectedness from certain entries of the choir, because the audience perceives in advance the direction from which the sound will come before it is uttered. I should prefer that the choristers be always seated if they cannot remain standing throughout. But this "impossibility" is among those which vanish instantaneously if the director knows how to say *I will* or *I will not.*

Be this as it may, there was something very imposing in the performance of these vocal masses; the first *tutti* of the two choruses took away my breath, as I did not expect such a powerful burst of harmony. It must, however, be admitted that one wearies of this fine sonority far more quickly than of that of the orchestra, the timbres of voices being less varied than those of instruments. This is easily understood; there are only four kinds of voice, while the number of different instruments is upwards of thirty. . . .

The Germans profess unlimited admiration of Bach's recitatives, but their peculiar virtue perforce escaped me as I did not understand the language and so was unable to appreciate their expression.

Whoever is familiar with our musical customs in Paris must witness, in order to believe, the attention, respect, and even reverence with which German audiences listen to such a composition. Everyone follows the words in the book with his eyes; not a movement among the audience, not a murmur of praise or blame, not a sound of applause; they are at divine service, they are hearing the gospel sung, and they listen in silence, not to the concert but to the service. And really such music ought thus to be listened to. They adore Bach and believe in him, without supposing for a moment that his divinity could ever be called into question. A heretic would horrify them; he is forbidden even to speak of him. God is God and Bach is Bach.   [5]

GLUCK

Of all the ancient composers, Gluck, has, I believe, the least to fear from the incessant revolutions of art. He sacrificed nothing either to the caprices of singers, the exigencies of fashion, or to the inveterate routine with which he had to contend on his arrival in France after his protracted struggles with the Italian theaters. Doubtless his conflicts at Milan, Naples and Parma had increased instead of weakening his strength by revealing its full extent to himself; for, in spite of the fanaticism then prevalent in our French artistic customs, he broke these miserable trammels and trod them underfoot with the greatest ease. True, the clamor of the critics once succeeded in forcing him into a reply but it was the only indiscretion with which he had to reproach himself, and thereafter, as before, he went straight to his goal in silence. We all know what that goal was; we also know that it was never given to any man to succeed more fully. With less conviction or less firmness, it is probable that, despite his natural genius, his degenerate works would not have long survived those of his mediocre rivals now completely forgotten. But truth of expression, purity of style, and grandeur of form belong to all time. Gluck's fine passages will always be fine. Victor Hugo is right: the heart never grows old.   [6]

MOZART OPERAS

I have stated that, when I went up for my first examination at the Conservatory, I was wholly absorbed in the study of dramatic music of the grand school; I should have said of lyrical tragedy, and it was owing to this that my admiration for Mozart was then so lukewarm. Only Gluck and Spontini could excite me. And this was the reason for my tepid regard for the composer of *Don Giovanni*. *Don Giovanni* and *Figaro* were the two Mozart works oftenest played in Paris; but they were always given in Italian, by Italians, at the Italian opera house; that alone was sufficient to prejudice me against them. Their great defect in my eyes was that they seemed to belong to the ultramontane school. Another, more legitimate objection was a passage in the part of Donna Anna which shocked me greatly, where Mozart had inserted a wretched vocalization which is a blot on his brilliant work. It occurs in the allegro of the soprano aria in the second act, *Non mi dir*, a song of intense melancholy in which all the poetry of love is voiced in lamentation and tears, and yet it is made to wind up with such a ridiculous, unseemly phrase that one wonders how the same man could have written both. Donna Anna seems suddenly to have dried her tears and broken out into coarse buffoonery. The words of the passage are *Forse un giorno il cielo ancora sentira-a-a-* (here comes an incredible run, in execrable taste) *pietà di me*. A truly singular form of expression for a noble, outraged woman, to *hope that heaven will one day take pity on her!* . . . I found it difficult to forgive Mozart for this enormity. I now feel I would shed my life's blood if I could thereby erase that shameful page and others of the same kind which disfigure some of his work.

At that time, I received his dramatic doctrines with distrust, therefore, and my enthusiasm fell to just one degree above freezing. Still I felt the warmest admiration for the religious grandeur of the *Magic*

Flute, though I had only heard it in its travestied form as *The Mysteries of Isis.*[1] It was not until afterwards, in fact, that I was able to compare the original score in the Conservatory library with the wretched French *pot-pourri* played at the opera.

As I first heard the works of this great composer under such disadvantageous circumstances, it was only many years later that I was able to appreciate their charm and suave perfection. The wonderful beauty of his quartets and quintets, and of some of his sonatas first converted me to the worship of this angelic genius, whose brightness was slightly dimmed by intercourse with Italians and contrapuntal pedagogues. Even the epithet "shameful" scarcely seems to me strong enough to blast this passage. Mozart has there committed one of the most flagrant crimes recorded in the history of art against passion, feeling, good taste, and good sense.   [7]

CONTRAST BETWEEN *FREISCHÜTZ* AND *OBERON*

If men of genius only knew what love their works inspire! If they only realized with what intense, concentrated devotion a hundred thousand hearts yearn towards them as one, how they would rejoice to receive and surround themselves with such kindred spirits, and how such worship would console them for the bitter envy, petty hatred, and careless indifference which they meet elsewhere!

In spite of his popularity, the stupendous success of the *Freischütz,* and his awareness of his genius, Weber would probably have appreciated such silent, sincere adoration more than anyone. He had written beautiful things which had been coldly received by artists and critics alike. His last opera, *Euryanthe,* had obtained only a moderate success; and he could not but feel anxious as to the fate of *Oberon,* for he must have known it to be a work which could only be truly appreciated by an audience of poets and thinkers. Even Beethoven, the king of kings, had long misunderstood him, so it is easy to realize how, at times, he lost faith in himself, and how it was that the failure of *Oberon* killed him.

The striking contrast between the fate of this glorious work, and that of its eldest brother, the *Freischütz,* is not due to any defects in the favorite of fortune; it is neither vulgar nor petty in form, it owes its brilliancy to no sham effects, to nothing turgid or exaggerated in its expression; in neither the one work nor the other has the composer made the smallest concession to the puerile exigencies of fashion, or to those still more imperious requirements of the singers. He was as

[1] The way it was first mounted in Paris.

simply true, as fearlessly original, as independent of precedent, as regardless of the public, and as determined not to truckle to them, in the *Freischütz* as in *Oberon*. But the former is full of poetry, passion, and contrast. The supernatural element introduces strange and sudden effects. The melody, harmony, and rhythm thunder, burn, and illumine; everything combines to catch and bind the attention. Then too, the characters are taken from daily life, and appeal strongly to popular sympathy; the depiction of recognizable feelings and manners calls for a less exalted style of music which, combined with exquisite workmanship, has a peculiar fascination even for minds which are wont to disdain melodious trifles while, by their very enrichment, they become to the popular mind the perfect ideal of art, and marvels of originality.

In *Oberon*, on the other hand, although human passion again plays a considerable part, the fantastic element is supreme, but it is the fantastic in a calm, fresh, graceful form. Instead of monsters and terrible apparitions we have choruses of spirits of the air, sylphs, fairies, and water-nymphs. And the language of this people—a language entirely their own—which owes its chief charm to its harmonies (its melodies being capriciously vague, with a strange veiled rhythm difficult to follow), is almost unintelligible to the general public. In truth, it is only to be fully appreciated, even among musicians, by those who have studied it deeply and possess, moreover, the gift of vivid imagination.

[8]

THE YOUNG WAGNER

As for the young Kapellmeister, Richard Wagner, who lived for some time in Paris without managing to make himself known except by some articles in the *Gazette Musicale,* his authority was exercised for the first time in assisting me with my rehearsals, which he did with both zeal and good-will. The ceremony of his installation took place the day after my arrival, and when I met him he was in all the intoxication of a very natural delight. After having endured untold privations in France and all the mortifications attendant on obscurity, Wagner, on his return to Saxony, had the boldness to undertake and the good fortune to carry out the composition of both words and music of an opera in five acts, *Rienzi*. It had a brilliant success at Dresden, and was soon followed by the *Flying Dutchman*, an opera in three acts, of which he likewise wrote both words and music. Whatever opinion one may have about the merit of these works, it must be admitted that there are very few men capable of twice accomplishing successfully this double task. It was more than sufficient proof of capacity to attract both attention and interest. The King of Saxony fully understood this, and on the day that he guaranteed Richard Wagner's position by associating him with his principal Kapellmeister, the friends of art might have said to His Majesty what Jean Bart said to Louis XIV when he informed that brave Jack-tar he had made him a Commodore: "Sire, you have done well!"

As *Rienzi* is far longer than most German operas, it is never represented in full. The first two acts are played one evening and the three last on the next. I saw only the second part and, hearing it but once, it was impossible to express a decided opinion about it. I only remember a beautiful prayer sung in the last act by Rienzi and a triumphal march modelled on the magnificent march in *Olympie*, though by no means an imitation of it. I was much struck by the sombre coloring of the *Flying Dutchman*, and by certain stormy effects perfectly appropriate to the subject; but I also remarked an abuse of the tremolo, the more to be regretted in that it had already struck me in *Rienzi*, and because it implied a certain indolence of mind in the author, against which he is not sufficiently on guard. Of all orchestral effects, the sustained tremolo is the most monotonous; it calls for no inventive power on the part of the composer, unless accompanied by some striking idea either above or below it. Be this as it may, however, one must, I repeat, honor the royal consideration that has, so to speak, rescued a young and most gifted artist by its active and unreserved patronage.   [9]

JOHANN STRAUSS THE ELDER

And then there is Strauss, conducting his fine orchestra; and when the new waltzes he writes expressly for each fashionable ball turn out successful, the dancers stop to applaud him, the ladies approach the platform and throw him bouquets, and he is recalled at the end of the waltz. Thus there is no jealousy between dancing and music; each shares with the other in its pleasure and success. This is only fair, for Strauss is an artist. The influence he has already exercised over musical feeling throughout Europe in introducing cross-rhythms into waltzes is not sufficiently recognized. So piquant is the effect that the dancers themselves have already sought to imitate it by creating the *deux-temps* waltz, although the music itself has kept the triple rhythm. If, outside Germany, the public at large can be induced to understand the singular charm frequently resulting from contrary rhythms, it will be entirely owing to Strauss. Beethoven's marvels in this style are too far above them and act at present only upon exceptional hearers; Strauss has addressed himself to the masses, and his numerous imitators have been forced, by imitation, to second and support him.

The simultaneous employment of the various divisions of the bar and syncopated accentuations of the melody, even in regular and invariable form, is to simple rhythm what the harmonies of parts in motion are to plain chords, I might even say, what harmony itself is to the unison and the octave. [10]

SELF-EVALUATION

Generally speaking, my style is very bold, but it has not the slightest tendency to subvert any of the constituent elements of art. On the contrary, it is my endeavor to add to their number. I never dreamt of making music *without melody*, as so many in France are stupid enough to say. Such a school now exists in Germany, and I detest it. It is easy to see that, without confining myself to a short air for the theme of a piece, as the great masters often do, I have always taken care that my compositions be melodically rich. The value of the melodies, their distinction, novelty, and charm, may of course be disputed. It is not for me to give an estimate of them; but to deny their existence is unfair and absurd. As they are often on a very large scale, however, an immature or unappreciative mind cannot properly distinguish their forms; or they may be joined to other secondary melodies, which are invisible to that class of mind; and lastly, such melodies are so unlike the little absurdities to which that term is applied by the lower stratum of the musical world, that it finds it impossible to give the same name to both.

The prevailing characteristics of my music are passionate expression, intense ardor, rhythmical animation and unexpected turns. When I say passionate expression, I mean an expression determined to strengthen or underscore the inner meaning of its subject, even when that subject is the contrary of passion, and when the feeling to be expressed is but gentle and tender, or even profoundly calm. This is the sort of expression that has been discovered in the *Enfance du Christ*, the *Ciel* scene in the *Damnation of Faust* and in the *Sanctus* of the *Requiem*.

[11]

MICHAEL IVANOVITCH GLINKA

1804–1857

Oskar von Riesemann, in his *Monographien zur russischen Musik*, ably sums up the character of the nineteenth century, the period which saw the inception of Russian national music and its rise to international prominence. He says: "In the development of Russian music, dilettantism plays a noteworthy and highly significant role. One is tempted to advance the paradoxical assertion that the best Russian musicians were and are to be sought everywhere except among musicians themselves."

Though Glinka is usually considered the founder of the Russian national school, he was no reformer or revolutionary in the sense of the "Five" who followed him and regarded him as their musical god. His consciousness of a national art was much less definite than theirs. In fact, it was not even in Russia, but during a long sojourn (1830–34) in Italy that he began to realize that Italian music did not satisfy his artistic needs, and was seized with nostalgia for the Russian scene, an urge toward remembered Russian folk song.

Happily enough, his lack of an accomplished technic proved an asset. The then accredited German training might have hamstrung him, for folk song is not necessarily enriched by academic handling. Russian musical language had to grow from within in order to ripen. Glinka found new ways of employing it in his own art music. "His triumphs of artistic insight are lucky hits rather than the fruits of harnessed inspiration," says Gerald Abraham in his essay, "Glinka and his Achievement."

He did not so much use Russian folk tunes literally, as distill from them their feeling, their essence. In his operas, *A Life for the Czar* (1836) and *Russlan and Ludmilla* (1842), the irregular metrical rhythms of Russian folk song are found. He employs modality, related to Russian church music of which he made a profound study,[1] and the combining of leader and chorus which is the traditional manner of rendering a Russian folk tune.

Research into the folk music of one's own land is apt to lead to an

[1] See p. 221.

128

interest in the folk music of other countries. While visiting Spain (1845–47 and 1851), Glinka picked up a quantity of Spanish folk tunes which he later utilized in his effective orchestral works, *Summer Night in Madrid* and *Jota Aragonesa*.

Not only his background but lifelong illnesses, some real, others imaginary, and a natural indolence kept Glinka from pushing his progressive ideas. As Fouque says, in his *Glinka d'après ses mémoires et sa correspondance*: "It was only after his death that he became a reformer and innovator; in his lifetime his ambition was not so far-reaching."

JOHN FIELD'S PLAYING

Although I did not hear him very often, I still recall his playing, at once gentle and forceful and marked by an admirable precision. It was as if he did not strike the keyboard, but that his fingers, like great drops of rain, poured over the keys as pearls on velvet. I do not share —and here I believe myself in accord with all those who, loving music sincerely, might have heard Field play—I do not share the opinion of Liszt who told me one day that he found the master's playing "endormi." No, Field's playing was not sleepy; on the contrary, it was often daring, temperamental, unpredictable. It was just that he was careful not to lower his art to the level of charlatanism; pounding the ivories in the style of present-day fashionable pianists was never his ideal. [1]

LISZT'S PLAYING

Despite the general blind enthusiasm which I, too, partly shared, I can now render a complete account of the impressions which Liszt's playing made on me. He played Chopin Mazurkas, Nocturnes and Etudes, the entire brilliant modern school in particular, very beautifully, if somewhat à la française, that is to say, with exaggerations of nuance. His Bach, all of whose *Well-Tempered Clavier* he knew practically by heart, and his Beethoven Sonatas were, to my taste, not so satisfying. In classical music his playing had no real dignity; there was something "bangy" about his touch. In his performance of Hummel's *Septet*, one felt the carelessness of the grand seigneur. Hummel himself played the work incomparably better and more simply. On the whole, I would not place the entire manner in which Liszt handled the piano from the point of view of external finish, in the same class with the playing of Field, Charles Mayer or even Thalberg, particularly in scale passages.

[2]

RUSSIAN SONG

We inhabitants of the north feel differently. Life's experiences touch us either not at all or sink deep into our souls. With us, it is either mad boisterousness or bitter tears. Even love, that wondrous emotion which brightens the entire universe, is always bound up in us with a certain sadness. There is no doubt that our melancholy Russian songs are children of the north which we have, perhaps, taken over from the east. The songs of the orientals are just as melancholy, even in gay Andalusia.

[3]

MUSIC IN PARIS: BERLIOZ

From: Letter to Nestor Koukolnik, Paris, April 15, 1845

Chance has thrown me into the company of several pleasant people, and I have found some friends in Paris, just a few, to be sure, but sincere and full of talent. The most precious acquaintance I have made here is, without doubt, Hector Berlioz. Learning to know his works, so discredited by some, so admired by others, was one of the principal objects I had in mind in coming to Paris. Luck favored me. Not only have I heard some Berlioz music in concert and even in rehearsal, but I am now on intimate terms with this composer, to my mind the foremost of our time (and his genre, of course), and have become his friend, as far as is possible with a fellow as eccentric as he. This is my opinion of him:

In the realm of fantasy, no one has such colossal invention; and his musical combinations possess, among all their other merits, the quality of true novelty. Breadth in ensemble, abundance of detail, a compact harmonic tissue, powerful and until now unheard-of orchestration are the attributes of Berlioz' music. In the drama, carried away by his fantastic temperament, he is out of his element, lacks naturalness and gets on the wrong track. Among his pieces which I have heard, here are those which I prefer: the overture to the *Francs-Juges*, the Queen Mab scherzo from *Romeo and Juliet*, the march of the pilgrims from *Childe Harold*, and the "Dies Irae" and "Tuba Mirum," from the *Requiem*. All these pages have produced an indescribable impression on me. At the moment, I have at home several unpublished manuscripts by Berlioz which I am studying with unmixed pleasure.

I wrote Heindrich [1] my opinion of the Société des Concerts du Conservatoire; he must have conveyed it to you. The other day I heard

[1] Glinka's physician.

them do the *Pastoral Symphony*. It was good, too good to my way of thinking. The orchestra underlines every detail with such nicety and with such an affectation of nuances that the general effect is lessened. The posters and newspapers which I sent you have kept you abreast of my Paris beginnings. Here are some details:

At the third Berlioz concert, the "Spolie Tchistie" aria was much applauded. Soloieva began a little flat, but soon regained her pitch. My *Lesghinka*, which is written, as you know, for two orchestras, lost much of its effect arranged for only one, although, to tell the truth, the one was enormous. Was it the fault of the arrangement or was the performance not perfect? It was not a success for me nor for Berlioz who is very fond of the piece and had selected it himself.

At the fourth concert Soloieva sang much less well, and at the one which I gave at the Salle Herz she lost her head so completely in the middle of the duet from *Puritani* that she could not reappear in the following numbers. Marras saved the day by coming on and singing, unscheduled, the cavatina from *L'Elisir d'Amore*, which he did marvellously. The fifty-two musicians from the orchestra of the Théâtre Italien played very well. My pieces were well received, especially the *Scherzo in the form of a Waltz*. They are playing it everywhere; my song "Il Desiderio" is also being sung all over.

The attempts at translation having failed, I was reduced to programming these insignificant pieces myself. The concerts require music which can be understood at the first hearing but aside from this, I did not want to make my debut here with anything but pieces written in Russia for Russia.

I might say that the success I obtained as a bird of passage was very important for me. Berlioz, Herz and others read my scores. An enormous article by Berlioz appeared in the *Débats* which will prove to you that my *amour-propre* as a composer should be fully satisfied.

In short, I am very pleased with my trip. Paris is a marvellous city. The variety of intellectual pleasures is inexhaustible, and I cannot recall any period in my entire life which has been more enjoyable than these last months I have spent here.

From the artistic point of view, the study of Berlioz' compositions and acquaintance with the Paris public have led me to some important conclusions. I have resolved to enrich my repertoire with some concert pieces for orchestra which will take the form of picturesque fantasias and, health permitting, I shall write much. Up to now, instrumental music has been divided into two opposing categories: quartets or symphonies which, appreciated by a minority, frighten the mass of the public by their complexity, and concertos, variations, etc., which tire the ear by their incoherence, thus giving the listener the feeling that they are difficult for the performer. It seems to me that one can succeed in reconciling the demands of art with the needs of our time and, in turning to account the improvements brought to the manufacture of instruments and to musical execution, one should be able to write pieces which are equally agreeable to connoisseurs and to the general public.

I have already set to work. I am writing a coda for my Tchernomor [1] march. This fragment has been well liked here, but it needs a coda.

In Spain, the originality of the folk melodies will be a great help to me for the fantasias I have in mind. I shall see on the spot if it is possible to compose an opera in the Spanish style. At all events, I shall strive to translate my impressions into music.   [4]

[1] From *Russlan and Ludmilla.*

FELIX MENDELSSOHN

1809-1847

"I wish to be calm and collected and go through this affair with the cool-
ness I have always managed to preserve hitherto, when taking an important step in life."

The above excerpt from Mendelssohn's letter to his mother announcing his contemplated marriage condenses in a sentence his outstanding
qualities: reflection, order, good taste, manners. It is small wonder that
Mendelssohn grew into one of the most cultured musicians who ever
lived, coming as he did from a home of wealth and breeding, a home
where the élite of the diplomatic, artistic, literary and scientific worlds
assembled—where Goethe, the *summmum bonum* of intellectual and social prestige, was admired. Provided with the best tutors, supplied
with a private orchestra and any other facilities necessary to try out his
experiments in composition, he developed into a finished pianist, composer and conductor.

He has frequently been compared to Mozart, both of them having
been *Wunderkinder*. But whereas Mozart combined the Italian with the
German spirit, Mendelssohn's was essentially German, not in its reactionary but in its classical aspect. His curiosity and the encouragement
of his composition teacher, Zelter, led him to a profound study of Bach,
whose *St. Matthew Passion* he resurrected from oblivion. A nationalist,
he founded the Leipzig Conservatory to further German art and artists,
and included in its faculty a brilliant galaxy of teachers. As conductor of
the Gewandhaus orchestra in Leipzig, he elevated it into one of the most
polished organizations in Europe.

The acute letters from his *Wanderjahre* reflect the bigness as well as
the picayuneness of the German point of view. Here we find comments
on the importance of German musical decentralization in contrast to the
concentration of French music in Paris, a comparison of North and
South German musical appreciation and temperament, a penetrating
description of Holy Week in Rome side by side with a censure of Swiss
cowgirls for the perpetration of parallel fifths in their yodeling. He
was ill at ease with the bluntness—to Mendelssohn, the crudeness—and
passionate exhibitionism of a Berlioz. He shunned it.

SWISS YODELING

Letter to Zelter, Secheron, September 13, 1822

I want to tell you something about the singing of the Swiss.
First of all, the yodeling. I say "first of all" because it is familiar throughout Switzerland and every Swiss knows how to yodel. It consists of notes which are produced from the throat and generally they are ascending sixths, for instance:

Certainly this kind of singing sounds harsh and unpleasant when it is heard near by or in a room. But it sounds beautiful when you hear it with mingling or answering echoes, in the valleys, on the mountains or in the woods, and there, such shouting and yelling seem truly to express the enthusiasm of the Swiss people for their country. When one stands on a crest early in the morning, with a clear sky overhead, and hears the singing accompanied, now loudly, now softly, by the jingling of cowbells from the pasture below, then it sounds lovely; indeed, it fits perfectly into the picture of a Swiss landscape as I had imagined it.

Second, there is the highly praised singing of the Swiss girls, which is especially indigenous in the Bernese Overland. Unfortunately I cannot say much about it that is favorable. True, they mostly sing in four parts, but everything is spoiled by one voice which they use like a *flauto piccolo*. For this girl never sings a melody; she produces certain high notes—I believe purely at her discretion—and thus, at times, horrible fifths turn up. For instance, I heard:

This should evidently be:

without the top voice.

Apart from this, they could be good singers, because they prove the saying: "Cantores amant humores" completely. Four of them put away twenty-four bottles of wine!   [1]

SCHOLARLY VERSUS "PEOPLE'S" MUSIC

Letter to Zelter, Munich, June 22, 1830

The organist [in Weimar] offered me the choice of hearing something "scholarly," or something for "the people" (because he said that, for people in general, one must compose only easy and bad music). I asked him for something scholarly, but it was not much to be proud of; he modulated around enough to make one giddy, but nothing unusual came of it; he made a number of entries, but no fugue was forthcoming. When my turn came to play to him, I started with the "D minor Toccata" of Sebastian and remarked that this was both scholarly and something for "the people" too, at least for some of them; but mind, hardly had I begun to play when the superintendent dispatched his valet upstairs with the message that this playing must stop right away because it was a weekday and he could not study with that much noise going on. . . .

Here, in Munich, the musicians behave exactly like that organist; they believe that good music may be considered a heaven-sent gift, but in the abstract only; for, as soon as they sit down to play, they produce the stupidest, silliest stuff imaginable, and when people do not like it they pretend that is because it is still too highbrow. Even the best pianists have no idea that Mozart and Haydn also composed for the piano; they have only the vaguest notions of Beethoven, and consider the music of Kalkbrenner, Field and Hummel classical and scholarly. On the other hand, having played myself several times, I found the audience so receptive and open-minded that I was doubly vexed by these frivolities. Recently, at a soirée given by a countess who is supposed to be a leader of fashion, I had an outburst. The young ladies, quite able to perform adequate pieces very nicely, tried to break their fingers with juggler's tricks and rope dancer's feats by Herz. When I was asked to play, I thought: "Well, if you get bored, it serves you right," and started right out with the "C-sharp minor Sonata" of Beethoven. When I finished, I noticed that the impression had been enormous; the ladies were weeping, the gentlemen hotly discussing the importance of the work. I had to write down a number of Beethoven sonatas for the female pianists who wanted to study them. Next morning the countess summoned her piano teacher and asked him for an edition of good, really good, music by Mozart, Beethoven and Weber. This story went around Munich, and the good-natured musicians were very pleased that I had set myself up as a preacher in the desert. Subsequently I gave the leading pianist a long sermon and reproached her for having contributed nothing here to the knowledge and appreciation of the works of the great masters and for having followed the popular trend, instead of guiding the taste of the public. She vowed she would do better.   [2]

HOLY WEEK IN ROME

From a letter to his family, April 4, 1831

People have often zealously praised or hotly censured the ceremonies of Holy Week, and yet omitted comment on the main point, namely, the total effect. My father will probably remember the description of Mlle. de R.—who, after all, only expressed what most people do who write or talk about music and art—when, in a hoarse, common voice, she attempted at dinner to give us some idea of the fine, clear Papal choir. Many others have taken just the music and found fault with it, because the external adjuncts required to produce the full effect were lacking. These people may be right; still, so long as these indispensable externals are there, and especially in such perfection, just so long will the music produce its effect. And the more convinced I am that place, time, order, and the vast crowd of human beings awaiting in the most profound silence the moment for the music to begin, contribute largely to the total effect, the more odious I find it to have any part deliberately singled out from what is indivisible in order to depreciate it. That man must be unhappy, indeed, in whom the devotion and reverence of a vast assemblage does not arouse similar feelings of devotion and reverence, even if the congregation is worshipping the Golden Calf; he alone may destroy this who can replace it with something better.

Whether one person's reaction echoes that of another, whether it is due to the great reputation of the service or is merely the product of imagination, is all one. The fact is that we have a perfect totality which has exercised the most powerful influence for centuries past, and still exercises it. Therefore I reverence it as I do every species of real perfection. Thus you must not expect from me a formal criticism of the singing, as to whether they intoned correctly or incorrectly, in tune or out of tune, or whether the compositions are good. I would rather try to show you that the affair as a whole makes a great impression, and that everything contributes to this end. . . .

The first ceremony was on Palm Sunday. The press of people was so great that I could not reach my usual place on what is called the Prelate's Bench, but was forced to stand among the Guard of Honor. There, although I had a good view of the solemnities, I could not follow the singing properly, as they pronounced the words very indistinctly, and I had still no book. The result was that, on this first day, the various antiphonies, gospels, and psalms, and the custom of chanting which is followed here, made the most confused and singular impression on me. I had no clear conception of what rule was being followed in the various cadences. I took particular pains to discover that rule and succeeded so well, that at the end of Holy Week I could have sung with them. Thus I also avoided the boredom universally complained of during the endless psalms before the "Miserere"; for I caught the variety in the monotony and, when perfectly certain of any particular cadence, I instantly wrote it down. Thus, by degrees, I made out the melodies of eight psalms correctly. I also noted down the antiphonies, etc., and was thus constantly occupied and interested.

The first Sunday, however, as I have told you, I could not make it all out satisfactorily; I only knew that they sang the chorus "Hosanna in Excelsis" and intoned various hymns, whilst twisted palms were offered to the Pope, which he distributed among the Cardinals. These palms are long staffs, decorated with many ornaments (buttons, crosses and crowns), all made entirely of dried palm leaves, which look like gold. The Cardinals, who are seated in the chapel in a square, with the abbots at their feet, now advance, each in turn, to receive their palms, with which they return to their places. Then come the bishops, monks, abbots and the rest of the ecclesiastics, the papal singers, the knights, and others, who receive olive branches entwined with palm leaves. This makes a long procession, during which the choir continues to sing uninterruptedly. The abbots, who have held the long palms of their Cardinals like sentinels' lances, lay them on the ground before them, and at this moment there is a brilliance of color in the chapel such as I have never seen at any ceremony. There were the Cardinals in their gold embroidered robes and red caps, and the purple abbots in front of them with golden palms in their hands; then there were the gaudy servants of the Pope, the Greek priests and the Greek patriarchs in the most gorgeous attire; the Capuchins with long white beards and all the other monks; then, again, the Swiss in their popinjay uniforms, all carrying green olive branches; and all this time the singing is going on. It is, of course, hardly possible to distinguish what is being sung; one just enjoys the sound.

Then they carry in the Pope's throne, on which he is elevated in all processions. The Cardinals, two by two, with their palms, head the procession and, the folding doors of the chapel being thrown open, they slowly file through. The singing, which up to now has enveloped one like an element, becomes fainter and fainter, for the singers also walk in procession, and at length it is only heard softly from a distance. Then the choir in the chapel bursts forth very loudly with a query, to which the distant choir responds, and so it goes on for a time, till the procession again draws near and the choirs reunite. Whatever they may be singing, it produces a marvellous effect; and though it is true that the hymns, sung in unison, are monotonous and even formless, that they are without any proper connection and are sung fortissimo throughout, I still base my appeal on the impression which the whole must make on everyone. After the procession, the gospel is chanted in the most unusual tone, and is succeeded by the "Mass." I must also mention my favorite moment, the "Credo." The priest takes his place for the first time in the center, before the altar, and after a short pause intones in his hoarse, old voice the Credo of Sebastian Bach. When he has finished, the priests stand up and the Cardinals leave their seats and advance into the middle of the chapel, form a circle and all repeat the responses in loud voices, "Patrem omnipotentem," etc. The choir then chimes in, singing the same words. When I heard my well-known

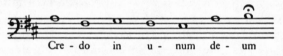

Cre - do   in   u - num   de - um

for the first time, and all the grave monks around me began to recite in loud, eager tones, it gave me quite a start; this is the moment I still like best of all. . . . The "Stabat Mater," which succeeds the "Credo," created the least effect. They sang it poorly, out of tune and abridged. The Singakadamie does it infinitely better.

There was nothing on Monday or Tuesday; but on Wednesday, at half-past four, vespers began. The psalms are sung in alternate verses by two choirs, although invariably by one voice group, bass or tenor. For an hour and a half, therefore, nothing but the most monotonous music is heard; the psalms are only interrupted once by the lamentations, and this is the first moment when, after a long time, a full chord is heard. This chord is very softly intoned, and the whole piece is sung *pianissimo*, whilst the psalms are shouted as loudly as possible, and always on one note, on which the words are uttered with the utmost rapidity. A cadenza occurs at the end of each verse, which defines the different characteristics of the various melodies. It is not surprising, therefore, that the mere softness of the sound in the first lamentation should produce so touching an effect. Then it goes on again in a monotone. A wax light is extinguished at the end of each psalm, so that in the course of an hour and a half, the fifteen lights around the altar are all out. Six large-size candles still burn in the vestibule high over the

entrance. The whole strength of the choir with altos, sopranos, etc.
intones (fortissimo and in unison) a new melody, the "canticum Zacha-
riae," singing it very slowly and solemnly in the twilight; the last remaining candles are then extinguished. The Pope leaves his throne and
falls on his knees before the altar, and all around do the same, repeating
a Paternoster *sub silentio;* that is, a pause follows, during which you
know that each Catholic present is saying the Lord's prayer, and immediately afterwards the "Miserere" begins pianissimo thus:

To me this is the most sublime moment of the whole ceremony. You can
easily picture to yourself what will follow, but not this beginning. The
continuation, which is the "Miserere" by Allegri, is a simple sequence
of chords on which embellishments have been superimposed. This is
either traditional or—what seems to me far more probable—the work
of some clever maestro who had a few fine voices at his disposal, and in
particular a very high soprano. These embellishments always recur on
the same chords and, as they are cleverly devised and beautifully adapted
to the voice, one always enjoys hearing them. I could not detect anything unearthly or mysterious in the music; indeed I am perfectly contented to have its beauty earthly and comprehensible.   [3]

THE MEANING OF MUSIC

From: Letter to Marc-André Souchay,[1] Berlin,
October 15, 1842

There is so much talk about music, and yet so little is said. For my
part, I believe that words do not suffice for such a purpose, and if I
found they did suffice I would finally have nothing more to do with
music. People often complain that music is too ambiguous, that what
they should be thinking as they hear it is unclear, whereas everyone
understands words. With me it is exactly the reverse, and not only with
regard to an entire speech, but also with individual words. These,
too, seem to me so ambiguous, so vague, so easily misunderstood in

[1] Souchay had asked Mendelssohn the meanings of some of his *Songs Without
Words.*

comparison to genuine music which fills the soul with a thousand things better than words. The thoughts which are expressed to me by music that I love are not too indefinite to be put into words, but on the contrary, too definite. And so I find in every effort to express such thoughts, that something is right but at the same time, that something is lacking in all of them. . . . If you ask me what I was thinking of when I wrote it, I would say: just the song as it stands. And if I happen to have had certain words in mind for one or another of these songs, I would never want to tell them to anyone, because the same words never mean the same things to different people. Only the song can say the same thing, can arouse the same feelings in one person as in another, a feeling which is not expressed, however, by the same words.   [4]

A PLEA FOR NEW MUSIC

From: Letter to Ferdinand Hiller, Berlin, July 15, 1838

You will have heard that I was at Cologne for the Festival. It all went well; the organ was splendidly effective in Handel and still more so in Bach—it was some newly discovered music of his, which you don't yet know, with a pompous double chorus. But despite this the interest one feels in something new and untried was lacking, to my mind at least. I like it so much when there is that kind of uncertainty which leaves room for me and the public to have an opinion. In Beethoven, Handel and Bach one knows beforehand what is coming and always must come, and a great deal more besides. You are quite right in saying that it is better in Italy, where people have new music every year, and must also have a new opinion every year. If only music and opinion were a little bit better!   [5]

ROSSINI

Letter to his mother and sister, Rebecca,
Frankfurt, July 14, 1836

Early yesterday I went to see him [Ferdinand Hiller], and whom should I find sitting there? Rossini, big, fat, and in the sunniest frame of mind. I really know few men who can be so amusing and witty as he, when he chooses; he kept us laughing the whole time. I promised that the Cecilia Association would sing the B-minor Mass for him and several other works of Sebastian Bach. It will be quite too much fun to see Rossini obliged to admire Bach. He thinks, however, "different countries, different customs," and is resolved to howl with the wolves. He says he is fascinated by Germany, and when he once gets the list of wines at the Rhine Hotel in the evening, the waiter is obliged to show him the way to his room, or he could never manage to find it. He tells the most laughable tales about Paris and all the musicians there, as well as about himself and his compositions, and how he entertains the deepest respect for all the men of the present day—so that you might really believe him, if you had no eyes to see his clever face. Intellect, animation and wit sparkle in all his features and in every word, and whoever does not consider him a genius ought to hear him expatiating in this way, in order to change his opinion. [6]

BERLIOZ

From: Letter to his mother, Rome, March 15, 1831

But now you shall hear about Berlioz and his music. He makes me sad, because he is really a cultured, agreeable man and yet composes so very badly.

The day after tomorrow he is going back to Paris. He seems terribly in love, and this has been the inspiration for a symphony which he calls *Episode de la vie d'un artiste*. When it was performed, 2000 copies of explanatory notes were distributed. In them he says that the composer has imagined the theme of the first movement as depicting a charming young lady who has fascinated the artist, and that his rage, jealousy, tenderness and tears are pictured in it. The second movement describes a ball where everything seems empty to him because she is missing. The third is called *scène aux champs;* the cowherds play a *ranz de vaches,* the instruments imitating the rustle of the leaves (all this in the printed program). Fear and hope are mixed in the artist's soul. Before the fourth movement (so continues the program), the artist, having poisoned himself with opium but misjudged the quantity, instead of dying has the most horrible visions. The fourth movement is just such a vision where he is present at his own execution; it is called *marche au supplice*. The fifth and last is called *songe d'une nuit*, in which he sees the witches dancing on the Blocksberg, his beloved among them. At the same time he hears the distorted *cantus firmus* of the "Dies Irae," to which the witches are dancing.

How utterly loathsome all this is to me, I don't have to tell you. To see one's most cherished ideas debased and expressed in perverted caricatures would enrage anyone. And yet this is only the program. The execution is still more miserable: nowhere a spark, no warmth, utter foolishness, contrived passion represented through every possible exaggerated orchestral means: four tympani, two pianos for four hands, which are supposed to imitate bells, two harps, many big drums, violins divided into eight parts, two parts for the double basses which play solo passages, and all these means (to which I would not object if they were properly employed) used to express nothing but indifferent drivel, mere grunting, shouting, screaming back and forth. And when you see the composer himself, that friendly, quiet, meditative person, calmly and assuredly going his way, never for a moment in doubt of his vocation, unable to listen to any outside voice, since he wishes to follow only his inner inspiration, when you see how keenly and correctly he evaluates and recognizes everything, yet is in complete darkness about himself —it is unspeakably dreadful, and I cannot express how deeply the sight of him depresses me. I have not been able to work for two days.   [7]

THE NIBELUNGEN POEM AS A POSSIBLE OPERA SUBJECT

From: Letter to his sister, Fanny,
Leipzig, November 14, 1840

Do you know that your suggestion as to the "Nibelungen" seems most interesting to me? It has been constantly in my head ever since, and I mean to spend my first day of leisure reading the poem, for I have forgotten the details and can only recall the outlines and the general coloring which seem to me gloriously dramatic. Will you kindly give me your more specific ideas on the subject? Evidently the poem is more present in your memory than in mine. I scarcely remember what your allusion to the "sinking into the Rhine" refers to. Could you point out to me the various passages which struck you as particularly dramatic when the idea first occurred to you? And above all, say something more definite on the subject; the whole tone, the pictorial qualities and the characteristic features impress my imagination strongly.   [8]

FRÉDÉRIC FRANCOIS CHOPIN
1810–1849

Whether for career purposes, through natural inclination, or both, Chopin leaned toward aristocrats and aristocratic ways. Most of his letters reflect this; they offer far fewer reflections of primarily musical interest. He was not a great reader, not an intellectual in the sense of Mendelssohn or Schumann, his two outstanding romantic contemporaries. For all his moving in the company of the literary and musical luminaries of his day, despite his affair with George Sand, he remained an intellectual amateur. History has completely reversed his opinions on the artists of his time: posterity has practically forgotten Kalkbrenner whom he placed above Liszt as a pianist, and the glamor of Meyerbeer is no more.

Schumann's famous and generous, "Hats off, gentlemen, a genius!" is tempered elsewhere by his comments on Chopin's limitations, the weakness of his orchestral and chamber music technique, his one-sidedness in composing for the piano only. Yet he was probably the greatest composer for the piano who ever lived, indeed created a piano literature of his own. Liszt and Wagner owe much to his exquisite chromaticism, and later piano composers have leaned heavily on his style and sonorities.

MUSICAL LIFE IN VIENNA, 1830

From: Letter to his family, Vienna, Wednesday
before Christmas, 1830

Among the numerous pleasures of Vienna, the hotel evenings are famous. During supper, Strauss or Lanner play waltzes; they are the local Swiesewscy. After every waltz, they get huge applause; if they play a *Quodlibet*, or jumble of opera, song and dance, the hearers are so overjoyed that they don't know what to do with themselves. It shows the corrupt taste of the Viennese public. [1]

From: Letter to Jan Matuszýnski, Vienna,
December 26, 1830

As for Thalberg, he plays excellently, but he's not my man. Younger than I, he pleases the ladies, makes potpourris from the *Dumb Girl*, gets his piano effects by means of the pedal, not the hand, takes tenths as easily as I do octaves—has diamond shirt studs—does not admire Moscheles; so don't be surprised that only the *tutti* of my concerto pleased him. *He also writes a concerto.* [2]

MUSIC IN PARIS, 1831

From: Letter to Tytus Wojciechowski,
Paris, December 12, 1831

Paris is whatever you choose: you can amuse yourself, be bored, laugh, cry, do anything you like and nobody looks at you, because thousands of others are doing the same, and everyone goes his own way. I don't know where there can be so many pianists as in Paris, so many asses and so many virtuosi. . . . I have met Rossini, Cherubini, Baillot, etc., also Kalkbrenner. You would not believe how curious I was about Herz, Liszt, Hiller, etc. They are all zero beside Kalkbrenner. I confess that I have played like Herz, but would wish to play like Kalkbrenner. If Paganini is perfection, Kalkbrenner is his equal, but in quite another style. It is hard to describe to you his calm, his enchanting touch, his incomparable evenness, and the mastery that is displayed in every note; he is a giant walking over Herz and Czerny and all, and over me. What can I do about it? When I was introduced, he asked me to play something. I should have liked to hear him first; but knowing how Herz plays, I put my pride in my pocket and sat down. I astonished Kalkbrenner, who at once asked me, was I not a pupil of Field, because I have Cramer's method and Field's touch. (That delighted me.) I was still more pleased when Kalkbrenner, sitting down to the piano and wanting to do his best before me, made a mistake and had to break off! But you should have heard it when he started again; I had not dreamed of anything like it. Since then we meet daily; either he comes to me or I go to him; and on closer acquaintance he has made me an offer: that I study with him for three years, and he will make something really—really out of me. I answered that I know how much I lack, but that I cannot exploit him, and three years are too long. But he convinced me that I can play admirably when I am in the mood, and badly when I am not, a thing which never happens to him. After close examination, he told me that I have no school, that I am on an excellent road, but can slip off the track. He says that after his death, or when he finally stops playing, there will be no representative of the great pianoforte school, and that, even if I wish it, I cannot build up a new school without knowing the old, in a word, that I am not a perfected machine and that this hampers the flow of my thoughts. He concedes that I have a mark in composition, and that it would be a pity not to become what I have the promise of being—and so on, and so on.

I don't know whether there has ever been such magnificence in a theater, whether it has ever before achieved the pomp of the new five-act opera, *Robert le Diable*, by Meyerbeer, who wrote *Il Crociato*. It is a masterpiece of the new school, in which devils (huge choirs) sing through speaking-trumpets, and souls rise from graves (but not as in *The Charlatan*,[1] just in groups of fifty or sixty). There is a diorama in the theater against which, at the end, you see the interior of a church, a whole church, at Christmas or Easter, lighted up, with monks, and all the congregation on the benches, and censers—there is even the organ the sound of which, on stage, is enchanting and amazing (incidentally, it nearly drowns out the orchestra); nothing of the sort could be put on anywhere else. Meyerbeer has immortalized himself.   [3]

MUSIC IN ENGLAND, 1848

From: Letter to Wojiech Grzymala,
London, October 21, 1848

Art here means painting, sculpture and architecture. Music is not an art, and is not called art; if you say "an artist," an Englishman understands the word as meaning a painter, architect or sculptor. Music is a profession, not an art, and no one speaks or writes of any musician as an artist, for in their language and customs it is something else; it is a *profession*. Ask any Englishman, and he will tell you so, and Neukomm assured me of it, too. No doubt it is the fault of the musicians, but try to correct such things! These queer folk play for the sake of beauty, but to teach them *decent* things is a joke; Lady ——, one of the most highly regarded great ladies here in whose castle I spent a few days, is considered a great musician. One day, after my piano playing, and after various songs by other Scottish ladies, they brought a kind of accordion, and she began with the utmost gravity to play on it the most atrocious

[1] Polish opera by Kurpinsky.

tunes. How about that? Every creature here seems to have a screw loose. Another lady, showing me her album, said to me: "La reine a regardé dedans et j'ai été à côté d'elle." A third, that she is "la treizième cousine de Marie Stuart." Another sang a French-English romance, standing up for the sake of originality, and accompanying herself on the piano: J'aie aiiemaiie (j'ai aimé!!!). The Princess of Parma told me that one lady whistled for her to a guitar accompaniment. Those who know my compositions ask me:—Jouez-moi votre second soupir— j'aime beaucoup vos cloches." And every observation ends with, "leik water [sic]," meaning that it flows like water. I have not yet played to any Englishwoman without her saying to me, "Leik water!!!" They all look at their hands, and play the wrong notes with much feeling. Eccentric people, God help them. [4]

ROBERT SCHUMANN

1810–1856

The nineteenth century saw the rise of the professional music journalist and critic. Previously, the practicing musician had written letters concerning his art, prefaces to his works defending his point of view or the works themselves, dedications to patrons and critical essays. The paid reviewer writing for magazines and newspapers was at first recruited from among the composers. Weber spent considerable time reviewing concerts and operas, Berlioz was a regular contributor to the *Journal des Débats* in Paris, and in his time Schumann was considered even more a journalist than composer.

He himself tells us in the foreword to his collected articles that, at the close of 1833, a group of young musicians used to meet at the Café Kaffeebaum in Leipzig almost every evening for companionship and shop talk. German music was in a none too healthy state. Rossini reigned over the stage, and the piano giants were Herz and Hünten, both all but forgotten today. Beethoven, Weber and Schubert had died a few years back. Mendelssohn's star was in the ascendant, wonderful rumors were circulating about Chopin, but neither could as yet lay claim to the fame they were later to achieve. During this interregnum, the Leipzig group's lively exchange of ideas resulted in the organization of the *Zeitschrift für Musik*. The actual running and editing of the influential journal fell to Schumann, and for ten years he continued the paper almost single-handed, during which period his musical composition took second place.

The motto of the *Zeitschrift* was a quotation from the prologue of Shakespeare's *Henry VIII* which expresses scorn for the commonplace and the determination to fight inferior art and to uphold the dignity of great art:

> . . . Only they
> That come to hear a merry bawdy play,
> A noise of targets, or to see a fellow
> In a long motley coat guarded with yellow,
> Will be deceiv'd . . .

Schumann practically idolized Mendelssohn, whom he considered the best musician of his time; Mendelssohn did not return the compliment and persisted in regarding Schumann as critic rather than composer. Schumann also championed Chopin who, according to certain reported conversations, became somewhat restive under his exaggerated admiration. And it is true that Schumann's literary work is the bastion of the romantic, of youthful idealism. Yet some of his essays are in the nature of prophecy later to be fulfilled.

HOUSE RULES AND MAXIMS FOR YOUNG MUSICIANS (1848)

The cultivation of the ear is of the greatest importance. Endeavor, in good time, to distinguish tones and keys. The bell, the window pane, the cuckoo—seek to discover what tones they produce.

You must practice scales and other finger exercises industriously. However, there are people who think they may achieve great ends by doing this alone; up to an advanced age, they practice mechanical exercises for many hours daily. That is as reasonable as trying to recite the alphabet faster and faster every day. Find a better use for your time.

"Dumb keyboards" have been invented; practice on them for awhile in order to see that they are worthless. Dumb people cannot teach us to speak.

It is not enough that your fingers know your pieces; you should be able to hum them to yourself, away from the pianoforte. Sharpen your powers of imagination so that you may be able to remember correctly not only the melody of a composition, but its proper harmonies as well.

As you grow older, converse more frequently with scores than with virtuosi.
Industriously practice the fugues of good masters; above all those of J. S. Bach. Let the *Well-Tempered Clavier* be your daily meat. Then you will certainly become an able musician.   [1]

Master Raro's, Florestan's and Eusebius'
Journal of Poetry and Thought

READING SCORES IN CONCERTS

As Eusebius observed a young student of music diligently following a rehearsal of Beethoven's *Eighth Symphony*, score in hand, he remarked: "*There* is a good musician!"—"By no means," said Florestan. "He is a good musician who understands the music without the score, and the score without the music. The ear should not need the eye, the eye should not need the (outer) ear."—"A lofty standard," concluded Master Raro, "but how I agree with you, Florestan!"

The anti-chromatic school should remember that, once upon a time, the seventh startled just as much as the diminished octave now does and that, through the development of harmony, passion received finer nuances by means of which music has been placed among those high mediums of art which have language and symbols for all spiritual states.

The cultivated musician may study a Madonna by Raphael, the painter a symphony by Mozart, with equal advantage. Yet more: in sculpture, the actor's art becomes fixed; the actor in turn transforms the sculptor's work into living forms; the painter turns a poem into a painting; the musician sets a picture to music. [2]

CHARACTERIZATION OF THE KEYS

*A study based on an article contributed
to a general dictionary in 1834.*

This has been advocated and opposed. Reason, as usual, lies in the middle. It is as inadmissible to say that this or that feeling, in order to be correctly expressed in music, must be translated in this or that key (anger, for example, in C-sharp minor) as to agree with Zelter who declares that any feeling may be expressed in any key. The analysis of this question was already begun in the last century; the poet Schubart especially professed to have found in some keys the characteristic expression of definite feelings. Though a great deal of poetic tenderness is to be found in his characterization, though he was the first to signalize the great differences that exist between the major and the minor scales, he piles up too many adjectives, epithets, and specifications in his work. However, this would not be of great concern had they all been correctly applied. For instance, he calls E minor a girl dressed in white, with a rose-colored bow at her bosom! In G minor he finds discontent, discomfort, worried anxiety over an unsuccessful plan, ill-tempered chewing of the lips. Now compare this idea with Mozart's Symphony in G minor, full of Hellenic grace! . . . No one will deny that a composition, transposed from its original key into another, produces a different effect or that this alteration is produced by a difference in the character of the keys; only try the *Désir* Waltz [1] in A major,

[1] In A-flat major; attributed to Beethoven, but actually a combination of Schubert's *Trauer-Walzer* and Himmel's *Favorite-Walzer*.

or the "Bridal Chorus" [1] in B major! The new key seems contradictory
to the feeling; the normal state of mind in which these compositions
were written has been carried into a foreign sphere. The process by
means of which the composer selects this or that principal key for the
expression of his feelings is as little explicable as the creative process
of genius itself, which selects a certain form as the mould which most
accurately embodies the thought. The composer selects the correct key
with no greater reflection than does the painter in selecting his colors.
It would be a good idea—had we space for it—to compare the predominant character of classic masterworks set in the same keys, to discover whether or not certain moods, in the course of time, had not
conventionally referred themselves to certain keys. The difference
between major and minor must be allowed beforehand. The former is
the active, virile principle; the latter, the passive, the feminine. Simple
feelings demand simple keys; the more complicated ones require those
which are less frequently heard. Thus one might observe the rising
and falling [of the temperature of feeling] in the interwoven succession
of rising and falling fifths, and accept F-sharp—the middle point in the
octave, the so-called tritonus—as the highest point, which again descends through the flat keys to the simple, unadorned C major.   [3]

OBSERVATIONS

From miscellaneous reviews

Nature would burst should she attempt to produce nothing save
Beethovens.

Titles for pieces of music, since they again have come into favor in
our day, have been censured here and there, and it has been said that
"good music needs no sign-post." Certainly not, but neither does a title
rob it of its value; and the composer, in adding one, at least prevents
a complete misunderstanding of the character of his music. If the poet
is licensed to explain the whole meaning of his poem by its title, why
may not the composer do likewise? What is important is that such a
verbal heading should be significant and apt. It may be considered the
test of the general level of the composer's education.   [4]

[1] From Weber's *Freischütz*, in C major.

CHILD PRODIGIES

From a review

We love child prodigies. Whoever accomplishes extraordinary things in youth will, if he continues to learn, bring about in his age things even more extraordinary. Also certain technical abilities should be developed to the point of virtuosity as early as possible. But that to which our young artist especially owes his reputation we oppose as thoroughly false—we mean public improvisations during childhood and youth. We do not address ourselves to him, whose uncommon talent we recognize, but to his mentor, his teacher, or whoever he may be.

Who would seek again to close the bud that has once unfolded? It would be useless. It would be unnatural to repress a powerful, early-matured inclination. It is common enough to see some particular sense sooner developed in one person than in another. But the rare flowers of January should be patiently fostered and cherished in still seclusion before they are exhibited to the gaze of the cold world.

Our delightful young artist, if thoughtful and thoroughly musical, must feel that much is still lacking; even the correct use of his instrument; besides, the technical repose which betrays a perfected schooling; certain execution which is only attained by continuous study; and above all things a healthy tone, which no one can acquire instinctively. If we are not mistaken, a few years hence he will thank us for placing firmly before him the future, which is not to be jested with. But even if mistaken, we would be forced to say that in him a talent had been lost deserving of a better fate.

In any case, I would like to remind him of a significant old legend. Apollo once bestowed his friendship on a beautiful mortal who grew more and more god-like, more and more akin, in form and spirit, to his divine protector. But he betrayed his secret to men prematurely. The enraged god appeared to him no longer, and the youth, overwhelmed by grief, looked unceasingly into the eyes of the sun, his beloved friend, until he died. Betray not thy divine gifts to men until commanded by the Muse who bestowed them upon thee and of whom thou hast become worthy. For the artist, the beautiful mortal, the god transforms himself into imagination. *Eusebius* [5]

J. S. BACH

In the course of time the distance between sources diminishes. Beethoven, for instance, did not need to study all that Mozart studied —Mozart, not all that Handel—Handel, not all that Palestrina—because these had already absorbed the knowledge of their predecessors. But there is one source which inexhaustibly provides new ideas—Johann Sebastian Bach. *Florestan*   [6]

From: Letter to Keferstein, January 31, 1840

The whole so-called Romantic School (of course I am speaking of Germans) is far nearer to Bach in its music than Mozart ever was; indeed, it has a thorough knowledge of Bach. I myself make a daily confession of my sins to that mighty one, and endeavor to purify and strengthen myself through him. And then, however honest and delightful Kuhnau may be, one can hardly place him on a level with Bach. Even if Kuhnau had written *The Well-tempered Clavier*, he would still be but a hundredth part of him. In fact, to my mind Bach is unapproachable—he is unfathomable.   [7]

DOMENICO SCARLATTI

Scarlatti possesses many excellent qualities which distinguish him from his contemporaries. The order of the ideas—armored, as it were—such as we find in Bach, is missing; he is much less substantial, more ephemeral, rhapsodic. One has difficulty in always following his music, because he quickly knots and then unties again the musical threads. Compared to that of his contemporaries, his style is brief, pleasing, and piquant. His works certainly take an important place in piano literature —by continuing much that was new at the time; by the many-sided use they made of the instrument; and in particular by a more independent use of the left hand—but we confess that much in this music no longer pleases us nor ought to please us.

How can any of these compositions be compared with those by our better composers! How clumsy is the form, how rudimentary the melody, how limited the modulation! Especially in comparison with Bach! As one spirited composer [Mendelssohn] once said about Ph. Em. and J. Seb. Bach—their relation equals that of a dwarf and a giant. However, the true pianist, if he wants to be an artist, should become acquainted with the leaders of all different schools, and particularly with Scarlatti, who obviously raised the art of piano playing to a higher level. Yet one should not play too many of these pieces in succession, because they are very similar in movement and character. If presented in one measure and due time, they will continue to sound fresh and new to the listener.   [8]

BEETHOVEN: THE FOUR OVERTURES TO *FIDELIO*

It should be written in golden letters that last Thursday the Leipzig Orchestra performed—*the four overtures to "Fidelio," one after another.* Thanks to you, Viennese of 1805, that the first did not please you and that Beethoven in divine rage therefore poured forth the three others. If he ever appeared powerful to me, he did so on that evening, when, better than ever, we were able to listen to him, forming, rejecting, altering in his own workshop, and glowing with inspiration. He was most gigantic in his second start. The first overture was not effective; stop! thought he, the second shall rob you of all thought—and so he set himself to work anew and allowed the thrilling drama to pass before him, again singing the joys and sorrows of his heroine. This second overture is demonic in its boldness—even bolder, in certain details, than the third, the well-known great one in C major. But it did not satisfy him; he laid this one aside also, merely retaining certain passages from which, already more certain and conscious, he formed the third. Afterwards there followed the lighter and more popular one in E major, which is generally heard in the theater as the prelude.

Such is the great four-overture work. Formed after the manner of Nature, we first find in it the roots from which, in the second, the giant trunk arises, stretching its arms right and left, and finally completed by its leafy crown. *Florestan* [9]

WEBER'S *EURYANTHE*

Review, September 23, 1847

We raved over this as we had not done about anything for a long time. This music is too little known and appreciated. It is heart's blood, the noblest that he had; and this opera certainly cost him a part of his life—but he is also immortal because of it. It is a chain of sparkling jewels from beginning to end—all brilliant and flawless. How splendid the characterization of certain figures, such as Eglantine and Euryanthe —and how the instruments sound! They speak to us from the innermost depths. We were full of it—talked long of it. I think the most inspired number of the opera is the duet between Lysiart and Eglantine in the second act. The march in the third act is also admirable. However, the crown must be awarded to the entire work and not to separate passages.
[10]

SCHUBERT'S LAST COMPOSITIONS [1]

If fertility be a distinctive mark of genius, then Franz Schubert is a genius of the highest order. Not much over thirty when he died, he wrote in such abundance that but half of his compositions have as yet been published; another part will soon follow, while a still greater part will never, or not for a long time be given to the public. Among his first-mentioned works his songs obtained the quickest and widest popularity; gradually he would have set all German literature to music; he would have been the man for Telemann, who claimed that "a good composer should be able to set public notices to music." Whatever he felt, he poured forth in music; Aeschylus, Klopstock, so difficult to set to music, yielded to his hand, while he drew the most profound meaning from the lighter verses of Müller and others. And what a multitude of instrumental works of every form and kind!—Trios, quartets, sonatas, rondos, dances, variations, for two and four hands, large and small, full of the strangest things, and of the rarest beauties, which our journal has elsewhere characterized. Among the works that await publication, masses, quartets, a great number of songs, etc., have been mentioned to us. The last section comprises his larger compositions, several operas, sacred music, several symphonies and overtures, etc., now in the possession of his heirs.

The last of Schubert's compositions which have appeared are entitled "Grand Duo for Pianoforte for Four Hands," opus 140, and "F. Schubert's Last Composition, Three Grand Sonatas for Pianoforte." [C minor, A major, B-flat major, opus posth.]

There was a time when I was loath to mention Schubert, and would only at night speak of him to the trees and stars. Who of us does not rave at some time? Enraptured with this new mind, whose wealth seemed to me boundless and incommensurable, deaf to everything that could bear witness against him, I thought of nothing but of him. With increasing years, with increasing demands, the circle of our favorites grows smaller and smaller. The cause of this is in ourselves as well as in them. Who is the master of whom one holds the same opinion all one's life? Experiences which youth has not yet achieved are necessary to the evaluation of Bach; it even underestimates Mozart's greatness. Mere musical studies are not enough to enable us to understand Beethoven, just as in certain years he inspires us with one work rather than with

[1] Schumann made a mistake here: the *Lieder* of the *Schwanengesang* and the String Quintet in C major, opus 163—both of which he apparently did not know— were written after the compositions reviewed in this article.—Konrad Wolff.

another. It is certain that equal ages exert a reciprocal attraction upon
each other, that youthful enthusiasm is best understood by youth, and
the power of the mature master by the full-grown man. So Schubert
will always remain the favorite of youth. He gives what youth desires
—an overflowing heart, daring thoughts, and swift deeds; he tells them
what they most love, romantic stories of knights, maidens, and adventures; he intermingles a little wit and humor, but not so much that the
basic softness of the mood is thereby troubled. Moreover he gives wings
to the performer's own imagination like no other composer save Beethoven. His easily followed peculiarities tempt one to imitate them; we
would like to carry out a thousand ideas suggested by him. Thus is it
that he has a great future.   [11]

CHOPIN

Chopin might now publish anything without his name; one would
nevertheless immediately recognize him. This remark includes praise
and blame; praise for his gifts; blame for his endeavor. He possesses
such remarkable original power that, whenever it displays itself, it is
impossible for a moment to be uncertain as to its source; and he adds to
this an abundance of novel forms that compel our admiration for both
their tenderness and boldness. But, though ever new and inventive in the
outward forms of his compositions, he remains in special instrumental
effects intrinsically the same, and we almost fear that he will not rise
any higher than he has already risen. And although this is high enough
to render his name immortal in the history of modern art, he limits
himself to the narrow sphere of piano music, whereas with his powers
he might climb to far greater heights, whence to exercise an immense
influence on the general development of our art. Let us, however, be
content. He has already created so much that is beautiful, continues
to give us so much, that we ought to be satisfied, for we should certainly congratulate any artist who has accomplished merely half as
much as he. To deserve the name of poet it is not necessary to write
thick volumes; one or two true poems are enough for that, and Chopin
has written such. The above-named nocturnes are also poems; they distinguish themselves essentially from his earlier ones through simpler
ornamentation and a more modest grace. We know how Chopin formerly comported himself, as though overstrewn with spangles, gold
trinkets, and pearls. He has altered and grown older; he still loves
jewelry, but of a more distinguished kind, through which the loftiness
of poetry gleams all the lovelier. Indeed, one must grant him taste, and

of the finest, though of a kind not meant for specialists of thorough-bass on the lookout for consecutive fifths and infuriated by every one they detect. Yet they might learn much from Chopin, above all, how to write fifths. We must direct attention to the ballade as a most remarkable work. Chopin has already written one composition of the same name [in G minor]—one of his wildest and most original compositions; the new one is different—as a work of art inferior to the first, but equally fantastic and inventive. Its impassioned episodes seem to have been inserted afterwards. I recollect very well that when Chopin played the ballade here, it ended in F major; now it closes in A minor. At that time he also mentioned that certain poems of Mickiewicz had suggested his ballade to him. On the other hand, a poet might easily be inspired to find words to his music; it stirs one profoundly. The waltz finally is, like his earlier ones, a salon piece of the noblest sort; if it were played for dancers, Florestan thinks at least half of the ladies should be young countesses. And he is right, for Chopin's waltz is thoroughly aristocratic.   [12]

LISZT

I had heard him [Liszt] before; but it is one thing when the artist is playing before a public, and another, when he is playing before a small group—even the artist himself changes. The beautiful illuminated hall, the glow of candlelight, the handsomely dressed audience—all this tends to elevate the frame of mind of the giver as well as that of the receiver. And now the daemon began to stir in him; first he played with the public as if to try it, then gave it something more profound, until he had enmeshed every member of the audience with his art and did with them as he willed. With the exception of Paganini no artist to a like degree possesses this power of subjecting the public, of lifting it, sustaining it, and letting it fall again. A Viennese writer has composed a poem on Liszt, consisting of nothing but adjectives attached to the single letters of his name. Intrinsically of bad taste, the poem nevertheless is applicable, for just as letters and concepts rise before us when turning the pages of a dictionary, so here there arise tones and emotions. Within a few seconds tenderness, boldness, exquisiteness, wildness succeed one another; the instrument glows and flashes under the master's hands. All this has already been described a hundred times, and the Viennese, especially, have tried to catch the eagle in every way— through pursuits, snares, pitchforks, and poems. But he must be heard —and also seen; for if Liszt played behind the screen, a great deal of poetry would be lost.   [13]

But what is most difficult is, precisely, to talk about this art. It is no longer pianoforte playing of this kind or that; instead, it is generally the outward expression of a daring character whom Fortune has permitted to dominate and to triumph not with dangerous implements, but with the peaceful means of art. No matter how many important artists have passed before us in the last years; no matter how many artists equaling Liszt in many respects we ourselves possess, not one can match him in point of energy and boldness. People have been fond of placing Thalberg in the rank beside him and then drawing comparisons. But a look at both heads decides the question. I remember the remark of a Viennese draftsman who said not inaptly of his countryman's head that it resembled "that of a handsome young countess with a man's nose"; while of Liszt he observed that "he might sit to any painter as a Greek god." There is a similar difference in their art. Chopin stands nearer to Liszt as a player, for at least he loses nothing beside him in magic tenderness and grace; Paganini, nearest of all, and among women, Madame Malibran; [1] from the latter two Liszt himself acknowledges that he has learned the most. [14]

LISZT'S RECITAL AT LEIPZIG, MARCH 17, 1840

He began with the scherzo and finale of Beethoven's *Pastoral* Symphony. The selection was capricious enough, and for many reasons unfortunate. At home, in a *tête-à-tête*, this extremely careful transcription might lead one almost to forget the orchestra. But in a large hall, in the place where we have been accustomed to hear the symphony itself performed frequently and perfectly by the orchestra, the weakness of the pianoforte was all the more striking; particularly since the transcription attempts to reproduce the masses in all their fullness.

A simpler arrangement, a mere indication, would perhaps have been much more effective here. Of course one could nevertheless recognize the master of the instrument. People were satisfied; they had at least seen him shake his mane. To sustain the figure, the lion presently began to show his power. This was in a fantasy on themes by Pacini, which he played in a most remarkable fashion. But I would sacrifice all the astonishing, audacious *bravura* that he displayed here for the sake of the magical tenderness that he expressed in the following étude. With the sole exception of Chopin, as I have already said, I know no one who could equal it. He closed with the well-known *Chromatic Galop;* and as the clapping refused to cease, he added his famous *Bravura Waltz.* [15]

[1] Famous operatic contralto.

BERLIOZ

From: Review of *Symphonie Fantastique*, 1835

Berlioz does not try to be pleasing and elegant; what he hates, he grasps fiercely by the hair; what he loves, he almost crushes in his fervor.   [16]

He does not squeeze out his themes to the last drop, nor does he sour our pleasure in a good idea by tiresome thematic treatment, as do so many others. In fact, he indicates that he might have worked things out more rigorously, had he so chosen and had it been fitting—sketches in the concise, sparkling manner of Beethoven. He often expresses his loveliest thoughts only once, *en passant*, as it were.   [17]

His melodies are distinguished by such intensity of almost every tone that, like some old folk songs, they will scarcely bear any harmonic accompaniment; indeed they would even lose fullness of tone through it. On this account, Berlioz generally harmonizes them with a sustained ground bass or with the chords of the surrounding upper and lower fifths. To be sure, his melodies are not to be listened to with the ears alone, else they will remain unheeded by those who do not know how to round them out from within, that is to say, not with half a voice but wholeheartedly. For those who do, however, they will take on a significance which appears to root itself ever deeper the oftener they repeat them.   [18]

Born a virtuoso in respect to the orchestra, Berlioz demands inordinate things both of the individual executants and of the ensemble— more than did Beethoven, more than all others. But it is not greater technical proficiency that he asks of the instrumentalist. He demands sympathy, study, love. The individual must subordinate himself to serve the whole, and this in turn must subject itself to the will of the leader.   [19]

TANNHÄUSER

From: Letter to Mendelssohn, October 22, 1845

Wagner, though certainly a brilliant fellow and full of original, audacious ideas, can hardly set down (and think out) a four measure phrase beautifully or even correctly. He is one of those people who have not learned their harmony lessons, nor learned how to write four-part chorales, and this their work makes plain. Now that the whole score is before our eyes, nicely printed, with its parallel fifths and octaves, he would probably like to correct and to erase—too late! But enough! The music is not a bit better than *Rienzi;* if anything, more pallid and forced. But should you say this to people, they should suspect you of jealousy, so I say it only to you, since you know it all anyway. . . . [After seeing the performance, however, Schumann, in a letter dated November 12, somewhat amends this view as follows:]

I hope soon to be able to talk to you about *Tannhäuser*. I have taken back some of the things I wrote you after reading the score: from the stage, everything strikes one very differently. I was quite moved by many parts of it.   [20]

BRAHMS

From: Schumann's last article, "New Roads," 1853

Many new and significant talents have arisen; a new power in music seems to announce itself; the intimation has been proven true by many aspiring artists of the last years, even though their work may be known only in comparatively limited circles. To me, who followed the progress of these chosen ones with the greatest sympathy, it seemed that under these circumstances a musician must inevitably appear, called to give expression to his times in ideal fashion; a musician who would reveal his mastery not in a gradual evolution but one who, like Athene, would spring fully armed from the head of Zeus. And such a one *has* appeared; a young man over whose cradle Graces and Heroes have stood watch. His name is Johannes Brahms, and he comes from Hamburg, where he has been working in quiet obscurity, though instructed in the most difficult statutes of his art by an excellent and enthusiastically devoted teacher [Eduard Marxsen in Hamburg]. A well-known and honored master recently recommended him to me. Even outwardly he bore the signs which proclaimed "This is a chosen one." Sitting at the piano, he began to disclose wonderful regions to us. We were drawn into ever more enchanting spheres. Besides, he is a performer of genius who can make of the piano an orchestra of lamenting and loudly jubilant voices. There were sonatas—veiled symphonies rather; songs, the poetry of which would be understood even without words, although a profound vocal melody runs through them all; single piano pieces, some of them turbulent in spirit while graceful in form; again sonatas for violin and piano, string quartets, every work so different from the others that they seemed to stream from their own individual source. And then it was as though, like a rushing torrent, they were all united by him into a single waterfall, the cascades of which were overarched by a peaceful rainbow while butterflies played about its borders and it was accompanied by the voices of nightingales.

Should he direct his magic wand where the massed power in chorus and orchestra may lend him their force, we can look forward to even more wondrous glimpses of the secret world of spirits. May the highest genius strengthen him to this end! Since he possesses yet another facet of genius—modesty—we may surmise that it will come to pass. His fellow musicians hail him on his first steps into a world where perhaps wounds await him. But there will be also palms and laurels. In him, we welcome a strong champion.   [21]

IV

LISZT
DARGOMIJSKY
WAGNER
VERDI

FRANZ LISZT

1811–1886

Liszt's letters and critical writings, which fill many volumes and reflect his vast erudition, are perhaps no less an index to his importance as man and musical personality than is his music. To be sure, the invention of the symphonic poem patently influenced Saint-Saëns, Richard Strauss, and a host of other late nineteenth century composers, but it was Liszt's literary work which brought to the fore most of the important music of his contemporaries.

Scarcely any young composer of worth who came to his notice —and few failed to—was not encouraged, and his music keenly analyzed and criticized. What is more, it was brought to performance and helped toward publication through Liszt's immense influence. Similarly, performers were helped forward in their careers. Liszt offered them his invaluable, free instruction and undertook to procure them engagements on an almost wholesale basis, acting as agent or manager in the best sense of the word. He drew a clear line of demarcation between genius and talent: men like Wagner, Berlioz and Schumann he accepted as they were; he tried to improve, through suggestion and advice, the creation of lesser composers; the truly bad was never cut to pieces—it was correctly ignored.

The wide scope of Liszt's literary output, both in French and German, includes a prodigious volume on Hungarian gypsy music, on the music of the Jews and other nations, on concert and theater music, and music contemporary, ancient and of the future.

HOLIDAY SYNAGOGUE SERVICE IN VIENNA

From: *Die Israeliten,* no date

Only once have we had the awesome experience of seeing and hearing what can happen in Jewish art when, in new art forms created by their Oriental genius, the Israelites pour out the full splendor of their fantasies and dreams, the full intensity of their feelings and stifled passions, and reveal the glow of that burning fire which they most often cautiously cover with ashes that it may seem cold to us.

In Vienna we were acquainted with the famous tenor Sulzer, who, as cantor of the synagogue, had acquired a distinguished reputation among a circle of true connoisseurs. . . . To hear him we went to the synagogue where he both directs and assumes the chief rôle in the music.

Rarely have we been so deeply stirred, so affected that our spirit surrendered unresistingly to sympathy and devotion as on that evening when, in the light of a thousand candles like stars on a far horizon, a strange chorus of muffled, hollow voices resounded about us. Every breast seemed a dungeon, from the depths of which an inscrutable being strove to break forth in order to glorify, in the midst of sorrow and slavery, the God of the Covenant, to cry to Him with devout and steadfast faith that He one day deliver them from this endless imprisonment, lead them from this despised ground, from these strange rivers, from this new Babylon, the great whore, and unite them again with incomparable glory in their own realm before which the nations tremble.

While the imagination of a Christian must feel itself overwhelmed by the burden of so many reminders which emerge before the altar without sacrifices or sacrificers, and before the holy parchments which, as in the time of Caiaphas, are encased in silk and brocade,—before this holy writ which, in its red sheath, surrounded by an abundance of mystic hanging lamps resembling heaped-up, glowing coals every single one of which seems to have been gathered here so that on the day of the heavenly judgment they might fall back on the guilt-laden heads,—they, on the contrary, who in place of a burnt-offering brought themselves to the sacrifice, who instead of the High Priest became the sacrificers, who put the seal of their faith on the holy, fervently prayed-for revenge through a life of ample mortification, a life grappling with death under abuse, they preserved under an impenetrable disguise their untroubled, undecipherable facial expression betraying neither entreaty nor ecstasy, while their voices confidently affirmed the fearful threefold thought: *Adonai! Elohim! Jehovah!* [1]

THE GYPSY ORCHESTRA

From: *Des Bohémiens et de leur musique en Hongrie*, 1859

The Hungarian gypsy orchestra consists today of several instruments, variously combined ad libitum. Its basis has always been the violin and the cembalon, the latter a long rectangular strung board in the style of a square piano, which is struck with mallets and gives a warm, lightly echoing tone. The cembalon, to judge by the stringed instruments which hail from the East, is evidently of oriental origin. In Hungary only the gypsies play it. The oldest accounts of this stranger in the land—it was mentioned as early as the fifteenth century—give a precise description which agrees perfectly with the present cembalon. It is still widely found among the peasants of Little Russia who generally hang it about their necks by a long, flexible leather strap. They can thus play it without laying it on a table, which increases its sonority and metallic vibrations. Like the violin, the cembalon lends itself to embellishments of small notes, trills and runs to every organ point.

The entire instrumental ensemble in a gypsy orchestra serves practically only to double the harmony, mark the rhythm and provide the accompaniment. Flutes, clarinets, a few brass instruments, a violoncello, contrabass and numerous violins—these are the usual instruments. The violins and cembalon are given the main parts; they carry the grand roles in the musical arrangement to be played off, like the *primo uomo* and *prima donna* in the old Italian opera. They are, in the musical jargon of civilized *Bohême*, the "stars" of the band.

The first violin spins out all the twists of fancy and moods of the virtuoso, whose technique often in no way resembles ours. The cembalonist must follow this course, provide a rhythm for it, set off the accelerations and retards, the strength or slackening of the beat. With the dexterity and agility of a juggler, he races the little wooden mallets across the brass and steel strings which, in this primitive design, take the place of the complicated piano mechanism we set in motion by means of ivory, mother-of-pearl and tortoise-shell keys.

The cembalon player, like the first violinist, has the right to develop certain passages and to improvise endless variations at his pleasure . . . He forces the others to surround, assist, yes, even to follow him blindly, whether he fancies a funeral hymn or a mad gay song. Now and then a good violoncello or clarinet will compete with them and claim the right of uninhibited improvisation. Several such virtuosi have even created a name for themselves in this genre, but they remain exceptions.   [2]

CONDUCTING MODERN MUSIC

From: "A Letter on Conducting," 1853

The works for which I openly confess my admiration and predilection are for the most part those which the more or less famous conductors—especially the so-called *tüchtige Kapellmeister* (efficient band leaders)—have rarely honored with their personal favor, and have as rarely performed. To my way of thinking, these works, beginning with those commonly identified as belonging to the *last period* of Beethoven —excused until not so long ago by Beethoven's deafness and mental derangement—exact from performers and conductors an *advance* which is being carried out at the moment—though it is far from being realized everywhere—in the accentuation, rhythm, manner of phrasing and declamation of certain passages, and in bringing out light and shade: in a word, an *advance* in the style of performance itself. It establishes between players and conductor a different kind of bond from that which is cemented by the imperturbable beating of time. Often the vulgar maintenance of the beat and of each bass note of the measure | 1, 2, 3, 4, | 1, 2, 3, 4, | clashes with both sense and expression. There, as elsewhere, *the letter kills the spirit,* and to this I could never subscribe, however plausible might be the hypocritically impartial attacks to which I am exposed.

For the works of Beethoven, Berlioz, Wagner, etc. I see fewer advantages than elsewhere (and even elsewhere I would contest them) in the conductor's functioning like a windmill, sweating profusely, the better to communicate warmth to his personnel. In these works, above all, where it is a question of understanding and feeling, a question of addressing the intelligence and of firing hearts in a communion with the beautiful, the great and the true in art and in poetry, the capacity and the ancient routine of the average *maître de chapelle* are no longer *adequate,* indeed are contrary to the dignity and sublime freedom of art. Though it displease my complacent critics, I shall . . . never accommodate myself to the role of "professor" of time-beating, for which my twenty-five years of experience, study and sincere passion for art have in no way prepared me.

Whatever esteem I profess for many of my colleagues, and no matter how freely I am pleased to acknowledge the good services they have performed and continue to perform for art, I do not feel obliged to follow their example in every instance, whether in the choice of works to be performed or the manner of conceiving and directing them. The real task of the conductor consists, in my opinion, in making himself ostensibly quasi-useless. We are pilots, not drillmasters. Even though this idea in particular will meet still more opposition, I can not change it, since I hold it to be just. Put into practice with the orchestra at Weimar, it has led to excellent results which my critics themselves have praised. I shall continue therefore, without discouragement or false modesty, to serve art in the best way I understand it, which I hope will be the *best* way.   [3]

From: "On Beethoven's Music to *Egmont*," 1854

THE STANDING OF THE MODERN MUSICIAN

Little by little musicians . . . stopped living exclusively in their ideal world. They also reached the point of being considered intellectual people outside the special practice of their art, even by those with scant technical understanding of it. In our time we have not yet ceased viewing musicians as rare, curious phenomena, half-angels, half-donkeys, who bring heavenly songs to mortals, but who, at the same time, in their day-to-day life, are to be treated in the most ambiguous manner or with the most unambiguous scorn. We are *beginning* to recognize them now as people who, along with the rest of humanity, must comply with the moral duty of developing their minds and acquiring for themselves a general and varied culture; we agree that among them are some who are as skilful with words as with notes.

BEETHOVEN'S MUSIC TO *EGMONT*

When the time approaches which decrees a thoroughgoing change in art, induces the impulse for its greater progress and, with hitherto unsuspected vigor and drive, propels it onto new paths, the important moment announces itself generally through prophetic signs.

The world, however, seldom suspects the prophetic meaning of such signs when first revealed. . . . Only when the sun of a new day already stands high in the heavens does the world recognize that the scattered rays which, like the dawn, announced the light of a new morning, all emerge from one and the same focal point.

A performance the other day of Goethe's *Egmont* with Beethoven's music aroused such thoughts in us. In *Egmont* we discover one of the first examples in modern times of the great composer drawing his inspiration directly from the work of a great poet. As insecure and unsteady as Beethoven's steps may appear to us in this, his first attempt, so in his own time were they brave and significant.   [4]

THE STYLES OF BEETHOVEN

From: Letter to Wilhelm von Lenz [author of *Beethoven et ses trois styles*, 1852], Weimar, December 2, 1852

To us musicians the work of Beethoven parallels the pillars of smoke and fire which led the Israelites through the desert, a pillar of smoke to lead us by day, and a pillar of fire to light the night, so that we may march ahead both day and night. His darkness and his light equally

trace for us the road we must follow; both the one and the other are
a perpetual commandment, an infallible revelation. If it were up to me
to categorize the diverse states of thought of the great master as manifested in his sonatas, symphonies, quartets, I should hardly stop at the
division into *three styles* generally adopted today, and which you have
followed, but . . . would frankly weigh the big question which is the
crux of criticism and musical aesthetics to the point where Beethoven
has led us: that is, how much traditional, conventional form necessarily
determines organization of thought.

The solution of this question, as it is derived from Beethoven's works,
would lead me to divide his works, not into three styles or periods (*style*
and *period* being here only corollary, subordinate terms, of vague and
equivocal significance), but very logically into two categories: one in
which the traditional and conventional form contains and rules thought,
and the other in which thought recreates and fashions a form and style
appropriate to its needs and inspiration. Undoubtedly, in proceeding
thus, we shall encounter head-on those perennial problems of *authority*
and *freedom*. But why should that frighten us? In the liberal arts, fortunately, they entail none of the dangers and disasters which their fluc-
tuations occasion in the political and social world for, in the realm of
the Beautiful, genius alone is the authority, dualism disappears, and the
concepts of authority and liberty are restored to their original identity.
Manzoni, in defining genius as "a greater borrowing from God," has
eloquently expressed this truth.   [5]

MENDELSSOHN'S MUSIC TO *A MIDSUMMER-NIGHT'S DREAM*

From the essay of same title, 1854

Mendelssohn, with a sure touch, fixed upon those passages in the play
which music might strengthen and spice, thus heightening the charm
of the whole. He allowed his art a precisely measured share in the
piece. His overture is an organic blending of heterogeneous elements,
with its piquant originality, symmetry and pleasing sound, its grace
and freshness that rise to the heights of the poetry itself. One need only
recall the chords in the bass at the start and finish! Do they not resemble gently lowering and lifting eyelids that frame a gracious dream
world of the loveliest contrasts? In these contrasts the elements of
the sentimental, the fantastic and the comic meet, each masterly characterized and yet intertwined by delicate strands of beauty!

Mendelssohn's talent adapted itself fully to the happy, roguish, be-
witched and bewitching atmosphere in which this exceedingly witty

composition of Shakespeare moves. He had a real capacity for depicting these enchanted elves, for interpolating in their caressing, chirping song the bray of the donkey, without rubbing us the wrong way. . . . No musician was so equipped to translate into music the delicate yet, in certain externals, embarrassing sentimentality of the lovers as he did in the third entr'acte, in a kind of prettily orchestrated song without words; no one could paint as he the rainbow dust, the mother-of-pearl shimmer of these sprites, could capture the brilliant accent of a royal wedding feast.   [6]

CHOPIN

From: "Friedrich Chopin," 1850

To him we owe the extension of chords, broken as well as unbroken, and ornamented chord figures, chromatic and enharmonic progressions of which his works offer such astounding examples; little groups of passing tones which are scattered over the melodic figure like brightly shimmering dewdrops. He lent to this sort of embellishment, the prototype of which could be found only in the *fiorituras* of the great old Italian school of singing, the unexpected and the richly varied which reach beyond the capacity of the human voice. Until then these ornaments had been merely slavishly copied as monotonous and stereotyped trimmings on the piano. He discovered those remarkable harmonic progressions by means of which he impressed a serious character on pieces of music whose unimpressive themes did not seem to *demand* profound significance. Chopin did not content himself merely with a framework within which he could plan his sketches with complete freedom. At times it pleased him to establish his thoughts in classical forms. He wrote concertos and sonatas. Yet in these we readily discover more purposefulness than inspiration. His inspirations were powerful, fantastic, impulsive; his forms could be naught but free. He must have had to do violence to his genius, we believe, every time he sought to subject it to rules and regulations which were not his own and did not accord with the demands of his spirit. He belonged to those whose charm unfolds especially when they avoid the beaten path.   [7]

BERLIOZ' *ROMEO AND JULIET*

From: Letter to Gustav Schmidt,[1] Weimar, March 6, 1853

By this morning's mail I am sending you the score and parts of Berlioz' symphony, *Romeo and Juliet*, together with two pairs of antique cymbals which you will need for *Queen Mab*.

I think you will find it expedient to have the complete title of the second part printed in the program just as it appears on Berlioz' score: *Deuxième partie—Roméo seul—Concert et Bal. Grande Fête chez Capulet*. Also, I think it would not be at all amiss if you were to have the German text of the story of Queen Mab—or, better still, the quotation from Shakespeare—printed as a program note. Again I urge you to rehearse the string and wind sections separately. *Queen Mab*, especially, is a difficult piece. When I conduct it, I like occasionally to use Beethoven's method of beating four measures as four quarters, as if it were in 4/4 time (*ritmo di quattro battute*, as in the "Scherzo" of the *Ninth Symphony*), thus securing more repose without affecting your precision in any way. Try it some time; I think you will agree that I am right. I advise you to keep the antique cymbals near your stand—and as a rule, Berlioz prefers to have the fermatas *very long*.   [8]

---

[1] Conductor (1816–82) of opera orchestra in Frankfurt a/M (1851–61).

ALEXANDER SERGEIVITCH DARGOMIJSKY

1813–1869

"Glinka's work," says Gogol, "was a happy beginning," but the Italian-bred Russian musical public accepted Glinka primarily as an exotic and his Russian folk song ideas as a kind of musical tidbit. Dargomijsky, following close on Glinka in years and theories, found acceptance even more difficult.

A skillful pianist and violinist, Dargomijsky was also a well-trained singer and vocal coach, these last exercising a beneficial effect on his composition, the bulk of which embodied opera and song. He achieved his initial success with *Russalka* (1856), an opera based on Pushkin's text which the composer followed almost literally. Since Pushkin had not conceived the work as a libretto with set arias, ensembles and choruses, Dargomijsky was obliged to contrive the short phrase of melodic recitative which he developed and perfected in *Russalka* and in his last major work, *The Stone Guest* (1872), based on the Don Juan legend. His operas exhibit a perfect union between text and music; one could hardly separate the one from the other. From melodic recitative, characteristic of the individual personages in an opera, it is but a step to the leitmotiv later employed by Wagner in his music dramas.

ARTISTIC EFFECT AND ARTISTIC IMPRESSION

From: Letter to Mme Karmalina, no date

Now concerning "effects," I shall try to explain my ideas to you as clearly as possible.

Perhaps it is suitable that a performing talent think about external effects from time to time. Charlatanism works on the masses. The creative talent, on the contrary, must never subordinate inspiration to external effect. I admit that the ability to produce effect proves the existence of the gift of observation, understanding, a certain degree of fantasy and perhaps even talent. Yet forced effects dazzle at the start, only to appear the more dull later. On the other hand, the artist's genuine inspiration minus extraneous means not only makes a strong impression on the chosen few among his listeners in the beginning, but also stimulates in them later a crescendo of lofty and noble enjoyment. You see that I differentiate between two kinds of artistic results: effect and impression.   [1]

OFFICIAL CONCERT LIFE

From: Letter to Mme Karmalina, November 1859

I have little liking for concerts . . . they interest me practically not at all. Compared to theater, to dramatic music, they bore me exceedingly. Besides, I don't like all the charlatanism, the pedantic squabbles of the "connoisseurs," the unsuccessful composers and journalists. All this prevails in the concert world in a horrible way, and woe to the artist who takes it into his head to become a part of these cerebral fistfights. If you only knew how peacefully and pleasantly I pass the time at home in a circle of friends, not numerous, but among whom genuinely friendly relations, based on true reciprocity and a real devotion to art, prevail. This circle consists of several of my women students and a number of talented people who love to sing. Here we sing Russian music simply, properly, and without straining after artificial effects, just as our late friend, Mikhail Ivanovitch [Glinka] loved it. In former years my evenings were darkened by the presence of various quarrelsome and glory-seeking "connoisseurs." This winter they have all stayed away, and my singers couldn't be more delighted with our solitude. Altogether my musical life runs along most agreeably. First, the theater directorate: it doesn't exactly encourage me, but it also doesn't persecute me, as formerly. Second, the noisy "polite society," the learned music world and the journalistic whirl have seemingly forgotten my existence, so that I can enjoy my art alone and in peace, and can compose for the few. I hope that I may always have these few; to write for them is my heart's desire.   [2]

THE RESOURCES OF FOLK MUSIC

From: Letter to Count Odojewski, Summer 1853

The more I study the elements of our national music, the more diverse riches do I discover in it. Until now only Glinka has given a great place to folk music in Russian art music, though in my opinion, he has touched but one of its aspects, the lyric. His drama is inclined to be too tearful; his treatment of the comic loses its native drive. I speak of the character of his music, since its mechanics are always admirable. Within the limits of my powers and abilities, I am working in *Russalka* on the development of our dramatic (musical) elements. I shall be happy if I can achieve in this direction the half of what Mikhail Ivanovitch reached in his sphere.   [3]

CONFESSIONS

From: *Autobiography*

Were there no women in the world, no women singers, I would never have become a composer. They have been my inspiration my whole life long.   [4]

From a letter, no date

Mediocrity seeks out melodies which flatter the ear. I do not chase such. I want music strictly to express the word. I want truth.   [5]

RICHARD WAGNER

1813–1883

Given his towering compulsion to uproot and re-form the world and its art concepts in his own image, it is no wonder that Wagner's writing is dominated by a perpetual aggressiveness and combativeness, by a riveting-like repetition of the first person singular. His *Autobiographic Sketch* and *A Communication to My Friends* ("friends" were those who "understood" him, that is, bent their every thought and action in his behalf and to his every wish) are replete with self-pity and even a persecution mania with its accompanying conceit.

A man of monstrous energy, Wagner not only composed the music and librettos for his colossal operas, but, to defend and explain his creative works, he indulged in a vast amount of turgid, verbose polemical writing. His two most extensive and important literary works, *Opera and Drama* and *The Art-Work of the Future*, expound in endless variation his theory of the blending of poet and musician, poetry and music, to create the perfect drama. As a poet, he himself was rather inadequate, as Hanslick shows in his brilliant essay on *Tristan and Isolde*, in which he quotes some of its lines—fair examples of the whole—with their often monotonous, sometimes grotesque alliterations. And Wagner's obsession with an idea, which we note in his writings, has a parallel in his music, great as it is; specifically, in the sledge-hammer insistence with which he uses a leitmotiv to depict character and situation. Again to cite Hanslick, who had a keener appreciation of Wagner than most Wagnerites or anti-Wagnerites, the "Prelude" to *Tristan* with its infinite iteration of gnawing themes reminded him of nothing so much as a primitive painting in which the entrails of an early martyr are endlessly drawn out on a reel. It is a well-known fact, of course, that all his life Hanslick was an outspoken opponent of Wagner.

Wagner's success and influence were unequalled. He lived to see a theater devoted to his work exclusively, to which flocked all the intellectuals, musicians, the great and the small of the world. His own literary output was outdistanced by the miles of literature about him

174

and his theories, and his gigantic musical talent was imitated, in style if not in content, by practically every composer who followed him. It has taken two world cataclysms to bring the musical world back to objectivity and a road that is not overlaid with his dicta.

OPERA AND DRAMA

From: *Opera and Drama*, 1851

There lies before me, in Brockhaus' *Gegenwart*, a lengthy article entitled "Modern Opera," the work of an able and experienced art critic. The author ranges side by side all the notable phenomena of modern opera, in most instructive fashion, and quite plainly teaches by them the whole history of the error. He almost lays his finger on this error, almost unveils it before our eyes, but then he feels unable to speak out boldly . . . so that, in a measure, he again clouds the mirror which had begun to reflect a brighter and yet brighter light. He *knows* that opera has no historical—or more correctly, natural—origin; that it has not arisen from the folk-, but from an art-caprice; he correctly *divines* the noxious character of this caprice, when he calls it an arrant blunder of most living French and German opera composers "that they strive on the path of *musical* characteristique for effects that one can reach alone by the *sharp-cut, intellectual word of dramatic poetry*"; he gets as far as the well-grounded doubt, whether opera is not after all a quite self-contradictory, unnatural genre of art; he shows in the works of Meyerbeer—here, to be sure, almost unconsciously—this un-nature driven to its most vicious pitch; but instead of coming out roundly with the needful thing, already on the tongue of every one, he suddenly veers round, to insure an everlasting life for criticism, and heaves a sigh that Mendelssohn's too early death should have hindered, i.e., staved off, the *solution* of the riddle!

What does this critic mean by his regret? Is it merely the assumption that Mendelssohn, with his fine intelligence and unusual musical gifts, would have been in the position to write an opera in which the evident contradictions of this art form should be brilliantly set right and reconciled? Or, supposing that, despite those gifts and that intelligence, he were unable to effect this, would he thereby have certified these contradictions for good and all, and proved the genre unnatural and null? Did the critic, then, imagine he could make this proof dependent on one peculiarly gifted musical personality? Was Mozart a lesser musician? Is it possible to find anything more perfect than every piece of his *Don Juan?* What could Mendelssohn, in the happiest event, have done beyond delivering, number for number, pieces that should equal Mozart's in their perfection? Or does the critic wish for something else, something more than Mozart ever made? There we have it: *he demands the great one-centered fabric of the drama's whole; he demands—between the lines—the drama in its highest fill and potency.*

But to whom does he address this claim? *To the Musician!* The harvest of his exhaustive survey of opera's accomplished facts, the solid knot into which he had bound each thread of knowledge in his skilful hand, he lets slip and casts the whole thing back again into its ancient chaos! He wants a house built for him and turns to the carver or upholsterer; the *architect,* who includes within himself the carver, the upholsterer and all the other needful aids for decking-out the house, since he gives their endeavours aim and order—he never thinks of *him.* He had solved the riddle; yet its solution brought him, not the light of day, but only a lightning flash in pitch-dark night, after whose vanishing the pathway suddenly becomes but still more indiscernible.

The solution of the riddle lies before our eyes, it speaks aloud from the very surface of the show; that critics and artists alike can still turn their heads from its acknowledgment is the veritable woe of our art-epoch. Let us be ever so honestly concerned with art's true substance, let us be ever so righteously wroth in our campaign against the lie: yet we deceive ourselves about that substance, and with all the power-lessness of such deception, we fight against that lie, the while, anent the essence of the most puissant art form in which music greets the public ear, we persistently abide in the selfsame error from which that art form sprang all unawares, and to which alone is to be ascribed its open shattering, the exposure of its nullity.

It almost seems to me as though ye required a mighty courage, an uncommonly bold resolve, to acknowledge and proclaim that error. It is as though ye felt the ground would slip away from all your present musical producings, if once ye made that necessary avowal, and that it therefore needs an unparalleled self-sacrifice to bring yourselves to do it. But yet, meseems, it calls for no excess of strength or trouble, and least of all, of pluck or daring: it is nothing but a question of simply, and without any outlay upon wonder and amaze-ment, acknowledging a patent fact, long felt but now grown past denial. I almost blush to speak with *lifted* voice the brief formula that bares the error, for I well might be ashamed to give the air of weighty

novelty to something so clear, so simple, and so certain, that I should
fancy all the world must long ago have got the thing by heart. If I do
pronounce this formula with stronger accent, if I declare aloud that
the error in the art-genre of opera consists herein:

THAT A MEANS OF EXPRESSION (MUSIC) HAS BEEN MADE
THE END, WHILE THE END OF EXPRESSION (THE DRAMA)
HAS BEEN MADE A MEANS,

I do it nowise in the idle dream of having discovered something new,
but with the object of posting the error so plain that every one may
see it, and of thus taking the field against that miserable half-heartedness
which has spread its pall above our art and criticism. . . .

Can it possibly be doubted that in opera music has actually been
taken as the end, the drama merely as the means? Surely not. The
briefest survey of the historic evolution of opera teaches us this quite
past disputing; everyone who has busied himself with the account of
that development has, simply by his historical research, unwillingly
laid bare the truth. Not from the medieval folk plays, in which we
find the traces of a natural coöperation of the art of tone with that
of drama, did opera arise, but at the luxurious courts of Italy—notably
enough, the only great land, of European culture in which the drama
never developed to any significance—it occurred to certain distinguished persons, who found Palestrina's church music no longer to
their liking, to employ the singers, engaged to entertain them at their
festivals, on singing *arias*, i.e., folk tunes stripped of their naïveté and
truth, to which "texts" thrown together into a semblance of dramatic
cohesion were added waywardly as underlay.

This *dramatic cantata*, whose contents aimed at anything but drama,
is the mother of our opera; nay more, it is that opera itself. The more
it developed from this, its point of origin, the more consistently the
purely musical aria, the only vestige of remaining form, became the
platform for the dexterity of the singer's throat; the more plainly did
it become the office of the *poet*, called in to give a helping hand to
their musical diversions, to carpenter a poetic form which should
serve for nothing further than to supply the needs both of the singer
and of the musical aria form with their verse requirements. Metastasio's
great fame consisted in this, that he never gave the musician the
slightest harass, never advanced an unwonted claim from the purely
dramatic standpoint, and was thus the most obedient and obliging
servant of the musician.

Has this relation of the poet to the musician altered by one hair's-
breadth, to our present day? To be sure, in one respect: that which,

according to purely musical canons, is now held to be dramatic, and which certainly differs widely from the old Italian opera. But the chief characteristic of the situation remains unchanged. Today, as one hundred fifty years ago, the poet must take his inspiration from the musician, he must listen for the whims of music, accommodate himself to the muscian's bent, choose his stuff by the latter's taste, mould his characters by the timbres expedient for the purely musical combinations, provide dramatic bases for certain forms of vocal numbers in which the musician may wander at his ease,—in short, in his subordination to the musician, he must construct his drama with a single eye to the specifically musical intentions of the composer,—or else, if he will not or cannot do all this, he must be content to be looked on as unserviceable for the post of opera librettist. Is this true, or not? I doubt that any can advance one jot of argument against it.

The aim of opera has thus ever been, and still is today, confined to music. Merely so as to afford music with a colourable pretext for her own *excursions,* is the purpose of drama *dragged on*—naturally, not to curtail the ends of music, but rather to serve her simply as a *means* . . . No one attempts to deny this position of drama toward music, of the poet toward the tone-artist; only, in view of the uncommon spread and effectiveness of opera, people have believed that they must make friends with a monstrosity, nay, must even credit its unnatural agency with the possibility of doing something altogether new, unheard, and hitherto undreamt: namely, of erecting the genuine drama on the basis of absolute music.

I have made it the goal of this book to prove that by the collaboration of precisely *our* music with dramatic poetry a heretofore undreamt significance not only can, but *must* be given to drama: to reach that goal, I must begin with a complete exposure of the incredible error in which those are involved who believe they may await the higher fashioning of drama from the essence of our *modern opera,* i.e., from the placing of poetry in a contra-minded position toward music.

Let us, therefore, first turn our attention exclusively to the nature of opera!   [1]

OPERA AND THE NATURE OF MUSIC

From: *Opera and Drama,* 1851

Everything lives and lasts by the inner necessity of its being, by its own nature's need. It lay in the nature of the art of tone to evolve and become capable of the most definite and manifold expression; which capability, albeit the need thereof lay hid within her soul, she would never have attained, had she not been thrust into a position vis-a-vis the art of poetry where she saw herself compelled to answer claims upon her utmost powers, even though those claims asked the impossible of her.

Only in its form can a being express itself; the art of tone owed all her forms to dance and song. To the *word-poet*, who merely wished to make use of music to heighten his own mode of expression in drama, she appeared solely in that narrowed form of song-and-dance; here she could not possibly reveal to him the wealth of utterance whereof, in truth, she still was capable. Had the art of tone remained once and for all in a position toward the word-poet such as the latter now occupies towards herself in opera, then she could only have been employed by him in her meanest powers, nor would she ever have evolved as the supremely mighty organ of expression that she is today. Music was therefore fated to credit herself with possibilities which, in very truth, were doomed to stay impossibilities for her; herself a sheer organ of expression, she must rush into the error of desiring plainly to outline the thing to be expressed; she must venture on the boastful attempt to issue orders and articulate aims *there* where, in truth, she can only subordinate herself to an aim *her* essence cannot even formulate, but to whose realization she gives, by her subordination, its only true enablement.

Music has developed along two lines in that art genre which she dominates, the opera: along an *earnest* line—with all the tone-poets who felt lying on their shoulders the burthen of responsibility that fell to music when she took upon herself alone the aim of drama; along a *frivolous* line—with all the musicians who, as though driven by an instinctive sense of the impossibility of achieving an unnatural task, have turned their backs upon it and, heedful only of the profit which opera had won from an uncommonly widespread popularity, have given themselves over to an unmixed musical empiricism. It is necessary that we should commence by fixing our gaze upon the first, the *earnest* line.

The musical basis of opera was, as we know, nothing other than the *aria;* this aria, again, was merely the folk song as rendered by the art singer before the world of rank and quality, but with its word-poem left out and replaced by the product of the art poet commissioned to that end. The conversion of the folk tune into the operatic aria was primarily the work of that art singer, whose concern was no longer for the right delivery of the tune, but for the exhibition of his vocal dexterity. It was he who parcelled out the resting-points he needed, the alternation of more lively with more placid phrasing, the passages where, free from any rhythmic or melodic curb, he might bring his skill to bear as it pleased him best. The composer merely furnished the singer, the poet in his turn the composer, with the material for their virtuosity.

The natural relation of the artistic factors of drama was, at bottom, as yet not quite upheaved: it was merely distorted, inasmuch as the performer, the most necessary condition for drama's possibility, represented but one solitary talent—that of absolute song-dexterity—and nowise all the conjoint faculties of artist man. This one distortion of the character of the performer, however, sufficed to bring about the ultimate perversion of the natural relation of those factors: to wit, the absolute preferment of the musician before the poet. Had that singer been a true, sound and whole dramatic performer, then had the composer come necessarily into his proper relation with the poet; the latter would then have firmly spoken out the dramatic aim, the measure for all else, and ruled its realizing. But the man who stood nearest that singer was the composer,—the composer who merely helped the singer to attain his aim; while this aim, cut loose from every vestige of dramatic, nay even poetic bearing, was nothing other, through and through, than to show off his own specific song-dexterity. . . .

Into the dramatic cantata, to satisfy the luxurious craving of these eminent sirs for change in their amusements, there was dovetailed next the ballet. Dance and dance tune, borrowed just as waywardly from the folk dance and its tune as was the operatic aria from the folk song, joined forces with the singer, in all the sterile immiscibility of unnatural things; while it naturally became the poet's task, midst such a heaping-up of inwardly incongruous matter, to bind the samples of the diverse art dexterities laid before him into some kind of patchwork harmony. Thus, with the poet's aid, an ever more obviously imperative dramatic cohesion was thrust on *that* which, in its actual self, was crying for no cohesion whatever; so that the aim of drama, forced on by outward want, was merely lodged, by no means housed. Song tune and dance tune stood side by side in fullest, chillest loneliness, for exhibition of the agility of singer or of dancer; and only in that which was to make shift to bind them, to wit the musically recited dialogue, did the poet ply his lowly calling, did the drama peep out here and there.

Neither was recitative itself, by any means, some new invention proceeding from a genuine urgence of opera towards the drama. Long before this mode of intoning was introduced into opera, the Christian Church had used it in her services, for the recitation of biblical passages. The banal singsong of these recitals, with its more listlessly melodic than rhetorically expressive incidence of tone, had been early fixed by ritualistic prescript into an arid semblance of speech, but without its reality; and this it was that, merely moulded and varied by musical caprice, passed over into the opera. So that, what with aria, dance tune and recitative, the whole apparatus of musical drama—unchanged in essence down to our very latest opera—was settled once for all. Further, the dramatic groundplans laid beneath this apparatus soon won a kindred stereotyped persistence. Mostly taken from an entirely misconstrued Greek mythology, they formed a theatric scaffolding from which all capability of rousing warmth of human interest was altogether absent, but which, on the other hand, possessed the merit of lending itself to the good pleasure of every composer in his turn; in effect, the majority of these texts were composed over and over again by the most diverse of musicians.

The so famous revolution of Gluck, which has come to the ears of many ignoramuses as a complete reversal of the views previously current as to opera's essence, in truth consisted merely in this: the musical composer revolted against the wilfulness of the singer. The composer, who, next to the singer, had drawn the special notice of the public to himself—since it was *he* who provided the singer with fresh supplies of stuff for his dexterity—felt his province encroached upon by the operations of the latter; he busied himself to shape the stuff according to his own inventive fancy and thus secure that *his* work also, and perchance at last *only* his work, might catch the ear of the audience. To reach his ambitious goal *two* ways stood open to the composer: either, by use of all the musical aids already at his disposal or others yet to be discovered, to unfold the purely sensuous contents of the aria to their highest, rankest pitch; or—and this is the more earnest path, with which we are concerned at present—to put shackles on a capricious execution of that aria, by endeavouring to give the tune, before its execution, an expression answering to the underlying word text. . . . Gluck was not the first who indited feeling airs, nor his singers the first who delivered them with fit expression. But he *bespoke with consciousness and firm conviction* the fitness and necessity of an expression answering to the text substratum, in aria and recitative; this makes him the departure point of a thorough change in the quondam situation of the artistic factors of opera toward one another. Henceforth the sceptre of opera passes definitely over to the composer: the singer becomes the *agent of the composer's aim*, and this aim is consciously declared to be the matching of the dramatic contents of the text substratum with a true and suitable expression. Thus, a halt was cried only to the unbecoming, heartless vanity of the singing virtuoso, but all the rest of opera's unnatural organism remained unaltered. Fenced off each from each, aria, recitative and dance piece stand side by side, as unaccommodated in the operas of Gluck as before him, and as, with scarcely an exception, they still stand today.

In the situation of the *poet* toward the composer not one jot was altered; rather had the composer grown more dictatorial, since, with his declared consciousness of a higher mission—made good against the virtuoso singer—he set to work with more deliberate zeal at the arrangement of opera's framework. To the poet it never occurred to meddle with these arrangements; he could not so much as dream of music, to which the opera had owed its origin, in any other form than those narrow, close-ruled forms he found set down before him, as binding even upon the musician himself. To tamper with these forms by advancing claims of dramatic necessity . . . would have seemed unthinkable to him, since it was precisely in these forms alone—inviolable even for the musician—that he could conceive of music's essence. Wherefore, once engaged in the penning of an opera text, he must needs pay even more painful heed than the musician himself to the observance of these forms; at utmost leave it to that musician, in his own familiar field, to carry out enlargements and developments, in which he could lend a helping hand but never take the initiative. Thus the poet, who looked up to the composer with a certain holy awe, rather confirmed the latter's dictatorship in opera, than set up rival claims thereto; for he was witness to the earnest zeal the musician brought to his task.

It was Gluck's successors who first bethought them to draw profit from their situation for the actual widening of the forms at hand. These followers, among whom we must class the composers of Italian and French descent who wrote for the Paris opera stage at the close of the past and beginning of the present century, gave to their vocal pieces not only more warmth and straightforwardness of expression, but a more extended formal basis. The traditional divisions of the aria, though still substantially preserved, were given a wider play of motive; modulations and connecting phrases were drawn into the sphere of expression; the recitative joined on to the aria more smoothly and less waywardly and, as a necessary mode of expression, stepped into that aria itself. Another notable expansion was given to the aria in that, obedient to the dramatic need, more than *one* person now shared in its delivery, and thus the essential monody of earlier opera was beneficially lost. Pieces such as duets and terzets were indeed known long before; but the fact that two or three people sang in one piece had not made the slightest essential difference in the character of the aria: once started, this had remained exactly the same in melodic plan and insistence on the tonality—which bore no reference to any individual expression, but solely to a general, specifically musical mood—and not a jot of it was really altered, no matter whether delivered as a monologue or duet, excepting at the utmost quite materialistic details: namely, its musical phrases were either sung alternately by different voices, or in concert through the harmonic device of combining two, three, or more voices at once. To apply that specifically musical factor in such a way that it should be susceptible of a lively change of individual expression, was the object and the work of these composers, as shown in their handling of the so-called *dramatic musical ensemble*. The essential musical substance of this ensemble was still, indeed, composed of aria, recitative and dance tune; only, when once a vocal expression in accord with the text substratum had been recognized as a becoming claim to make on aria and recitative, the truthfulness of such expression must logically be extended to everything else in the text that betrayed a particle of dramatic coherence. From the honest endeavor to observe this logical consistency arose that broadening of the older musical forms in opera which we meet in the serious operas of Cherubini, Méhul and Spontini. We may say that in these works there is fulfilled all that Gluck desired, or could desire; nay, in them is once for all attained the acme of all natural, i.e., in the *best* sense, consequential evolution on the original lines of opera.

Now how did the poet respond to all this? . . . With all the maturing of opera's musical form, with all the development of its innate powers of expression, the position of the poet had not altered in the slightest. He still remained the platform-dresser for the altogether independent experiments of the composer. When the latter, by attained success, felt his power of freer motion growing within those forms of his, he simply bade the poet serve him his material with less fear and trembling. . . . The poet certainly won an access of importance, but only as the musician mounted upwards in advance and bade him merely follow. The strictly musical possibilities, as pointed out by the composer, the poet had to keep in mind as the only measure for all his orderings and shapings, nay even for his choice of stuff; and thus, for all the fame that *he* began to reap also, he remained but the skillful servant who was so handy at waiting on the "dramatic" composer.

Mere stereotyped rhetoric phrases were the prime requirement from the poet, for on this soil alone could the musician gain room for the expansion that he needed. . . . To have allowed his heroes to speak in brief and definite terms, surcharged with meaning, would have only drawn upon the poet the charge of turning out wares impracticable for the composer. Since, then, the poet felt constrained to put trite and meaningless phrases in the mouth of his heroes, even the best will in the world could not have enabled him either to infuse a real character into persons who talked like that, or to stamp the sum total of their actions with the seal of full dramatic truth. His drama was forever a mere *make-believe* of drama; to pursue a *real dramatic aim* to its legitimate conclusions could not so much as occur to him. Therefore, strictly speaking, he only translated drama into the language of opera, and, as a matter of fact, mostly adapted long familiar dramas already played to death upon the acting stage, as was notably the case in Paris with the tragedies of the Théâtre Français. The dramatic aim, thus bare within and hollow, passed manifestly over into the mere intentions of the composer; from him was that awaited which the poet gave up from the first. To him alone—to the composer—must it therefore fall to clothe this inner void and nullity of the whole, so soon as ever he perceived it; and thus he found himself saddled with the unnatural task of . . . imagining and calling into life . . . of virtually penning the drama, of making his music not merely its expression but its *content;* and yet this content, by the very nature of things, was to be none other than the drama's self!

It is here that the predicate "dramatic" most palpably begins to work a strange confusion in men's notions of the nature of music. Music, as an art of *expression*, can in its utmost wealth of such expression be nothing more than *true;* it has, conformably therewith, to concern itself only with *what* it should express. In opera this is unmistakably the feeling of the characters conversing on the stage, and a music which fulfills this task with the most convincing effect is all that it ever can be. . . . With all its perverse efforts, music, or at least effective music, has actually remained naught other than expression. But from those efforts to make it in itself a content—and the content of a drama, forsooth—has issued what we must recognize as the consequential downfall of opera and an open demonstration of the radical un-nature of that genre of art.   [2]

GIUSEPPE VERDI

1813-1901

Few composers have been so utterly realistic about the worth of their work as Verdi. Few as were his limitations, he was aware of them and never attacked any musical problem which he could not solve to his own satisfaction. To the student of his operas those tunes, which seem commonplace, sometimes even trite, out of context, assume a strong character and dramatic intensity in their right setting, for Verdi was not only a gifted composer but a powerfully dramatic one. The quartet from *Rigoletto* is musically brilliant; it is also a keen study in characterization. *Trovatore, Traviata,* as well as *Rigoletto* and others have survived thousands of performances for almost a hundred years because of their dramatic as well as their musical impact. In his last works, *Otello* and *Falstaff,* he reached new heights of dramatic power; and in the latter, composed at the age of eighty, he introduced for the first time an element of humor.

His operas originally derived their popularity from their patriotic as well as their musical merits. The stirring "Va, pensiero, sull'ali dorate" from his *Nabucco* inspired the youth of Italy in their anti-Austrian struggle, and become practically a national hymn. Verdi himself was an ardent patriot. When, after the liberation of Italy, there was widespread depression and poverty in his native land, he drew on his substantial fortune to help his countrymen and used his estate at Sant' Agata to give employment to the people of his village, boasting in his letters that "his" villagers did not have to emigrate to the United States in order to survive.

Verdi was painstakingly careful about the production of his operas; he always included in his contracts a clause which allowed him to withdraw a work up to its dress rehearsal, if the production displeased him. He was totally oblivious to critics, once the works had been mounted. To quote one of his letters: "As for the newspapers, does anybody force you to read them? And as to the public, when your conscience tells you that you have written something good, never mind if it is abused (sometimes it's a good sign). The day of justice will come, and it is a great pleasure for the artist, a supreme pleasure, to be able to say: 'Imbeciles, you were wrong.' "

OPERA

From a contract with Ricordi Publishers
Florence, May 20, 1847

In order to prevent changes which theaters make in musical works, it is forbidden to insert anything into the above-mentioned score, to make cuts, raise or lower a key, or in general make any alteration which would entail the slightest change in instrumentation, on pain of 1000 francs fine, which I shall demand of you for every theater where a change is made in the score.   [1]

From: Letter to Cammarano, Paris, November 23, 1848

I know you are rehearsing *Macbeth*,[1] and since it is an opera which interests me more than all the others, you will permit me to say a few words about it. They gave the rôle of Lady Macbeth to Tadolini, and I am very surprised that she consented to do the part. You know how much I admire Tadolini, and she knows it herself; but in our common interest I think we should stop and consider. Tadolini has too great qualities for this rôle! Perhaps you think that a contradiction! Tadolini's appearance is good and beautiful, and I would like Lady Macbeth twisted and ugly. Tadolini sings to perfection, and I don't wish Lady Macbeth really to sing at all. Tadolini has a marvellous, brilliant, clear, powerful voice, and for Lady Macbeth I should like a raw, choked, hollow voice. Tadolini's voice has something angelic. Lady Macbeth's voice should have something devilish. Pass on these reflections to the management and Maestro Mercadante: more than anyone else, he will approve my ideas. Pass them on to Tadolini herself, and then do what you think best, according to your lights.

Tell them that the most important numbers of the opera are the duet between Lady Macbeth and her husband and the sleep walking scene. If these two numbers are lost, then the opera falls flat. And these two numbers absolutely must not be sung:

> They must be acted and declaimed
> With very hollow voice,
> Veiled: otherwise it will
> make no effect.
> The orchestra *con sordini*.

The stage extremely dark. In the third act, the apparitions of the kings (I have seen this in London) must take place behind a special opening at the back with a thin, *ashen-colored* veil before it. The

1 First version.

kings must not be dolls, but eight men of flesh and blood. The place they pass over must be like a mound, and you must be able clearly to see them ascend and descend. The stage must be completely dark, especially when the cauldron disappears, with light only where the kings appear. The music underneath the stage must be reinforced for the big San Carlo house. But take care there are no trumpets or trombones. The sound must seem far away, muffled, therefore it must be composed of bass clarinets, bassoons, contrabassoons, and nothing else.

[2]

From: Letter to Cesare De Sanctis, Busseto, March 12, 1853

I adore *Faust*, but I shouldn't like to treat it. I've studied it a thousand times, but I don't find Faust's character musical—musical (understand me well) in the way I feel music.   [3]

From: Letter to Cesare De Sanctis,
Sant' Agata, April 22, 1853

My long experience has confirmed me in the beliefs I've always held concerning dramatic effect, though in my youth I didn't have the courage to put them wholly into practice. (For instance, ten years ago I wouldn't have risked composing *Rigoletto*.) To me our opera nowadays sins in the direction of too great monotony, so much so that I should refuse to write on such subjects as *Nabucco, Foscari,* etc. They offer extremely interesting dramatic situations, but they lack variety. They have but one burden to their song; elevated, if you like, but always the same.

To be more explicit: Tasso's work may be better, but I prefer Ariosto a thousand times. For the same reason I prefer Shakespeare to all other dramatists, including the Greeks. As far as dramatic effectiveness is concerned, it seems to me that the best material I have yet put to music (I'm not speaking of literary or poetic worth) is *Rigoletto*. It has the most powerful dramatic situations, it has variety, vitality, pathos; all the dramatic developments result from the frivolous, licentious character of the Duke. Hence Rigoletto's fears, Gilda's passion, etc., which give rise to many dramatic situations, including the scene of the quartet which, so far as effect is concerned, will always be one of the finest our theater can boast. Many operas have been written on "Ruy Blas," eliminating the character of Don Cesare. But if I were to put that subject to music, I should be attracted above all by the contrast which that most original character produces. Now you will have understood what my feelings and thoughts are, and since I know I'm writing to a man of sincere, frank character, I take the liberty of telling you that though the subjects you propose are eminently dramatic, I don't find in them all the variety my crazy brain desires. You say that you can insert in *Sordello* some festivity, a banquet, or even a tournament, but even so the characters would still produce the same impression of gravity and austerity.   [4]

From: Letter to Antonio Somma,
Paris, May 17, 1854

I would be willing to set even a newspaper or a letter, etc. to music, but in the theater the public will stand for anything except boredom.
                                                                    [5]

From: Letter to Léon Escudier,
Genoa, June 11, 1867

Two things will always be wanting at the Opéra [at Paris]—rhythm and enthusiasm. They may do many things well, but they will never exhibit the fire that transports and carries one away, or at any rate not until they teach singing better at the Conservatoire. . . . But it is also a little the fault of you French, putting stumbling blocks in the ways of your artists with your *bon goût, comme il faut*, etc. . . . You should leave the arts in complete liberty and tolerate defects in matters of inspiration. If you terrify the man of genius with your wretched measured criticism, he will never let himself go, and you will rob him of his naturalness and enthusiasm. But if you are content as things are, and if the Opéra likes losing several hundred thousand francs and eight or ten months' time in producing an opera, then go on doing it—I don't mind.   [6]

From: Letter to Giulio Ricordi,
Sant' Agata, July 10, 1871

So-called vocal perfection concerns me little; I like to have rôles sung as I wish, but I am unable to provide the voice, the soul, that certain something which should be called the spark—it is usually described by the Italian phrase "to have the Devil on your back."   [7]

From: Letter to Clarina Maffei,
Sant' Agata, October 20, 1876

It may be a good thing to copy reality; but to invent reality is much, much better.

These three words "to invent reality," may look like a contradiction, but ask Papa [Shakespeare]! Falstaff he may have found as he was, but he can hardly have found a villain as villainous as Iago, and never, never such angels as Cordelia, Imogene, Desdemona, etc., etc. And yet they are so very real! It's a fine thing to imitate reality, but it is photography, not painting.   [8]

Letter to Clarina Maffei, April 20, 1878

We are all working, without meaning to, for the downfall of our theater. Perhaps I myself, perhaps you and the others, are at it, too. And if I wanted to say something that sounds foolish, I should say that the Italian Quartet Societies were the first cause; and that a more recent cause was the success of the performances (not the works) given by the Scala orchestra in Paris. I've said it—don't stone me! To give all the reasons would take up too much time. But why, in the name of all that's holy, must we do German art if we are living in Italy? Twelve or fifteen years ago I was elected president of a concert society, I don't remember whether in Milan or elsewhere. I refused, and I asked: "Why not form a society for vocal music? That's alive in Italy—the rest is an art for Germans." Perhaps that sounded as foolish then as it does now; but a society for vocal music, which would let us hear Palestrina, the best of his contemporaries, Marcello, and such people, would have preserved for us our love of song, as it is expressed in opera. Now everything is supposed to be based on orchestration, on harmony. The alpha and omega is Beethoven's *Ninth Symphony*, marvellous in the first three movements, very badly set in the last. No one will ever approach the sublimity of the first movement, but it will be an easy task to write as badly for voices as is done in the last movement. And supported by the authority of Beethoven, they will all shout: "That's the way to do it. . . ."

Never mind! Let them go on as they have begun. It may even be better; but it's a "better" that undoubtedly means the end of opera. Art belongs to all nations—nobody believes that more firmly than I. But it is practiced by individuals; and since the Germans have other artistic methods than we have, their art is basically different from ours. We cannot compose like the Germans, or at least we ought not to; nor they like us. Let the Germans assimilate our artistic substance, as Haydn and Mozart did in their time; yet they are predominantly symphonic musicians. And it is perfectly proper for Rossini to have taken over certain formal elements from Mozart; he is still a melodist for all that. But if we let fashion, love of innovation, and an alleged scientific spirit tempt us to surrender the native quality of our own art, the free natural certainty of our work and perception, our bright golden light, then we are simply being stupid and senseless.

[9]

From: Letter to Piroli, Genoa, February 2, 1883

Our music differs from German music. Their symphonies can live in halls; their chamber music can live in the home. Our music, I say, resides principally in the theater. Now the theaters can no longer exist without government subsidy.   [10]

ON CONDUCTORS

From: Letter to Giulio Ricordi, Genoa, April 11, 1871

As to conductors' inspiration . . . and to "creative activity in every performance" . . . that is a principle which inevitably leads to the baroque and untrue. It is precisely the path that led music to the baroque and untrue at the end of the last century and in the first years of this, when singers made bold to "create" (as the French say) their parts and in consequence made a complete hash and contradiction of sense out of them. No; I want only one single creator, and I shall be quite satisfied if they perform simply and exactly what he has written. The trouble is that they do not confine themselves to what he has written. I often read in the papers about effects that the composer never could have thought of, but for my part, I have never found such a thing. I understand everything you say about Mariani; [1] we are all agreed on his merit. But it is not a question of a single person, were he ever so eminent; it is a question of art itself. I deny that either singers or conductors can "create" or work creatively— this, as I have always said, is a conception that leads to the abyss. . . . Shall I give you an example? You spoke to me recently in praise of an effect that Mariani achieved in the overture to *La Forza del Destino* by having the brass enter fortissimo on G. Now then, I disapprove of

[1] Angelo Mariani (1822–73), Italian conductor, introduced *Lohengrin* to Italy, at Bologna, 1871.

this effect. These brasses, intended to be mezza voce, could not express anything but the Friar's song. Mariani's fortissimo completely changes the character of the passage and turns it into a warlike fanfare. It has nothing to do with the subject of the drama, in which all warlike matters are mere episodes. And there we are again on the path to the baroque and untrue.   [11]

MUSICAL EDUCATION

From: Letter to Giuseppe Piroli,
Genoa, February 20, 1871

In view of the musical conditions and tendencies of our day, the guiding principles which should be adopted by a commission for the reorganization of musical instruction are, in my opinion, as follows:

For young composers I should wish a long and thorough course of counterpoint in all its ramifications. Study of old music, both sacred and profane. But it must be kept in mind that not all old music is beautiful, either, and therefore it is necessary to choose.

No study of the moderns! Many people will think this strange. But today, when I hear and see so many works put together the way a bad tailor puts clothes together on a standard model, I cannot budge in my opinions. I know, of course, that many modern works could be cited which are as good as the old, but what of that!

When a young man has gone through a severe course of training, when he has achieved his own style, then, if he sees fit, he can study these works, and he will no longer be in danger of turning into a mere imitator. It may be objected: 'But who will teach him instrumentation? Who will teach him the theoretical aspects of composition?'— His own head and heart, if he has any.

For singers, I should want a broad knowledge of music, exercises in voice production, long courses in *solfège*, as in the past, exercises in clear diction both in speaking and singing. Then, without having any finishing master teach him embellishments or style, let the young man, who by now is solidly grounded in music and has a practiced, subtle voice, sing with his own feelings as his only guide. The result will not be singing according to any specific school, but according to inspiration. The artist will be an individuality; he will be *himself;* or better yet, he will be the character he has to portray in the opera.

I need not add that these musical studies should be combined with a broad literary education.   [12]

LIBERALISM IN MUSIC

From: Letter to Opprandino Arrivabene,
Genoa, March 17, 1882

In the matter of musical opinions we must be broad-minded, and for my part I am very tolerant indeed. I am willing to admit the melodists, the harmonists, the bores—those who want to be boring at all costs, as is smart—I appreciate the past, the present, and I would appreciate the future, too, if I knew anything about it and liked it. In a word, melody, harmony, coloratura, declamation, instrumentation, local color (a word so frequently used, in most cases only to hide the absence of thought): all these are only means. Make good music with these means, and I will accept everything, and every genre. In the *Barber*, for example, the phrase, *Signor, giudizio per carità*, is neither melody nor harmony. It is simply good, truthful declamation, and it is music. . . . Amen. [13]

PALESTRINA

From: Letter to Giuseppe Gallignani,
Milan, November 15, 1891

I am particularly glad for the performance of Palestrina's music: he is the real king of sacred music, and the Eternal Father of Italian music.

Palestrina cannot compete with the bold harmonic innovations of modern music, but if he were better known and studied, we would write in a more Italian spirit, and we would be better patriots (in music, I mean). [14]

ROSSINI AND BELLINI

From: Letter to Camille Bellaigue, Milan, May 2, 1898

I can't help thinking that, for abundance of real musical ideas, for comic verve, and truthful declamation, the *Barber of Seville* is the finest *opera buffa* in existence. Like you, I admire *William Tell*, but how many other magnificent, sublime things are in various of Rossini's other operas.

Bellini is weak instrumentally and harmonically, it's true; but he is rich in feeling and in a certain personal melancholy, which is completely his own. Even in his less well-known operas like *La Straniera*

and *Il Pirata*, there are long, long, long spun-out melodies, like nothing
that had been written before.   [15]

BERLIOZ

From: Letter to Opprandino Arrivabene, June 5, 1882

Berlioz was a poor, sick man who raged at everyone, was bitter and
malicious. He was greatly and subtly gifted. He had a real feeling for
instrumentation, anticipated Wagner in many instrumental effects.
(The Wagnerites won't admit it, but it is true.) He had no moderation.
He lacked the calm and what I may call the balance that produces
complete works of art. He always went to extremes, even when he
was doing admirable things.   [16]

WAGNER

From: Letter to Giulio Ricordi, February 14, 1883

Sad, sad, sad.
Wagner is dead!
When I read the news yesterday, I may truly say that I was completely crushed. Let us not discuss it. It is a great personality that
has disappeared. A name which leaves a mighty imprint upon the
history of art.   [17]

GOUNOD

From: Letter to Opprandino Arrivabene,
Sant' Agata, October 14, 1878

I know little about Gounod's success. But we mustn't delude ourselves. We must consider men as they are. Gounod is a great musician,
a great talent, who composes excellent chamber and instrumental music
in a manner all his own. But he isn't an artist of dramatic fiber. *Faust*
itself, though successful, has become small in his hands. *Romeo and
Juliet* and this *Poliuto* will be the same. In a word, he always does
the intimate piece well; but his treatment of situations is weak and
his characterization is bad.   [18]

PUCCINI

From: Letter to Opprandino Arrivabene, June 10, 1884

I have heard the composer Puccini well spoken of. I have seen a letter, too, reporting all kinds of good things about him. He follows the new tendencies, which is only natural, but he keeps strictly to melody, and that is neither new nor old. But it seems that he is predominantly a symphonist; no harm in that. Only here one must be careful. Opera is opera, symphony, symphony; I don't think it is a good idea to insert a symphonic piece into an opera just for the pleasure of letting the orchestra cut loose once in a while.   [19]

ON HIMSELF

From: Letter to Signor Filippi, March 4, 1869

Please don't think that when I speak of *my extreme musical ignorance* I'm merely indulging in a little *blague*. It's the truth, pure and simple. In my home there is almost no music, I've never gone to a music library, or to a publisher, to look at a piece of music. I keep up with a few of the best operas of our day, not by studying them, but only by hearing them now and then in the theater. In all this I have a purpose that you will understand. So I repeat to you: of all past or present composers, I am the least erudite. Let's understand each other— I tell you again that this is no *blague* with me: I'm talking about *erudition*, not about musical *knowledge*. I should be lying if I denied that in my youth I studied long and hard. That is why my hand is strong enough to shape the sounds as I want them, and sure enough for me generally to succeed in making the effect I have in mind. And when I write something that doesn't conform to the rules, I do it because, in that case, the strict rule doesn't give me what I need, and because I don't really believe all the rules that have been taught up to now are good. The schoolbooks of counterpoint must be revised.

[20]

V

GOUNOD
LALO
SMETANA
BRAHMS
BORODIN
CUI
SAINT-SAËNS
BALAKIREV
BIZET

CHARLES FRANÇOIS GOUNOD

1818–1893

Two outstanding traits, his profound religious feeling and his deep
filial love, show forth markedly in Gounod's *Mémoires d'un artiste*.
The tenderest recollections of his mother, who was his first teacher
and guiding spirit, whose perseverance and hard work aided him im-
measurably in developing his career, weave their way through the
entire book. His first hearing of *Don Giovanni* at her side is one of
his most touching memories.

Gounod studied for the priesthood, but at the last moment abandoned
the call to give himself entirely to composition. Primarily a theater
composer, he still wrote many religious works, the best known of
which are *The Redemption* and *Mors et Vita*, composed during his
five years' stay (1870–5) in England, and first performed there. Earlier,
while living in Rome as *Prix de Rome* winner, he had made a thorough
study of the old church composers, whence his adoration for Palestrina
whose music is to him as integral a part of the Sistine Chapel as
Michelangelo's murals.

Essentially Gounod is a lyric composer. Even his stage works are
more lyric than dramatic. *Faust*, though musically effective, cannot
approach Goethe's play dramatically—but what musical setting of
Faust has? Nor does his *Romeo and Juliet* fully express the emotional
content of Shakespeare's original. It is their lyricism which has kept
both of these operas alive for the better part of a century.

From: *Mémoires d'un artiste*

PALESTRINA AND MICHELANGELO

There are works which must be seen or heard on the spot for
which they were created. The Sistine Chapel is one such special spot:
it is unique of its kind. The colossal genius who decorated its vaulted
ceiling and altar wall with his incomparable conceptions of Genesis
and the Last Judgment, that painter of the Prophets, with whom he
seems to stand on the same level, will doubtless never find his equal,

any more than will Homer or Phidias. Men of this stamp and stature are not seen twice; they are syntheses; they embrace the world, they exhaust and complete it, and what they have said no one can repeat after them. To me, Palestrina's music appears like a translation into song of Michelangelo's vast poetry, and I am inclined to believe that these two masters mutually clarify and illustrate each other. The spectator becomes the listener, and conversely, so that after a bit he is tempted to ask whether the Sistine Chapel—painting and music—is not the product of one and the same inspiration. The music and the painting permeate each other and form such a perfect and sublime unity, that it would seem the whole were the twofold expression of one and the same thought, the double voice of one and the same hymn. It might be said that what one hears is the echo of what one sees.

There is, in fact, so strong an analogy between the work of Michelangelo and Palestrina, such a relation of effect, that it is very difficult not to conclude that these two privileged spirits were possessed of the same combination of qualities, and I might even say, of virtues. In both the same simplicity, the same humility in the use of means, the same absence of preoccupation with effect, the same disdain of the seductive! One senses that the technique of the executing hand no longer counts, and that the soul alone, immutably fixed upon a nobler world, endeavors to express in obedient and modest form the sublimity of its contemplation. Even the general uniform tone which characterizes both the painting and the music seems to have its basis in the voluntary renunciation of all color. The art of both these men is, so to speak, a sacrament, where the visible symbol is no more than a veil thrown over the divine and living reality. Consequently, neither of these two great masters fascinates one at first glance. As a rule, one is attracted by the external gloss of things. Here it is not so; here the eye must look beyond the visible and the sensual. What you experience upon hearing a work of Palestrina is something akin to what you feel upon reading one of the splendid writings of Bossuet. You are struck by nothing as you go along, but at the end of the road you find that you have climbed prodigious heights. The word, that docile and faithful servant of thought, has neither sidetracked nor held you up in its own interest. Thus you have reached the summit without shock, without missing anything, without being diverted, without emotional strain, conducted by an unobtrusive guide who has concealed from you his tracks and his methods. It is this absence of worldly artifice, of vain coquetry, that renders the noblest works inimitable. To attain to their perfection requires the same spirit which created them and the same rapture out of which they arose.   [1]

DON GIOVANNI

Before describing the emotions that this incomparable masterpiece stirred in me, I ask myself if my pen can ever translate them—I do not say faithfully, since that seems to me impossible—but at least in such a way as to give some idea of what went on in me during those unparalleled hours, the charm of which has dominated my life like a luminous apparition, a kind of revelatory vision.

From the start of the overture I felt myself transported into an absolutely new world by the solemn and majestic chords of the Commandant's final scene. I was seized by a terror which froze me, and as the menacing progression began, with those descending and ascending scales unrolling above it, merciless and implacable as a death sentence, I was overcome by such dread that I buried my face in my mother's shoulder, and enveloped in the twofold embrace of the beautiful and the terrible, I whispered:

"Oh, mama, what music! this is truly music!"

Hearing Rossini's *Otello* had stirred the fibers of my musical instinct, but the impression which I got from *Don Giovanni* was of an altogether different significance and of quite another dimension. It seems to me that both impressions might be compared to those experienced by a painter who turns suddenly from the Venetian masters to Raphael, Leonardo da Vinci and Michelangelo. Rossini introduced me to purely musical delight; he charmed and fascinated my ear. Mozart did more; to the gratification deriving from the exclusively musical and sensuous, he added the profound and penetrating influence of truth of expression combined with perfect beauty. From beginning to end, the score was a long and inexpressible rapture— the pathetic tones of the trio at the Commandant's death, Donna Anna's lament over the body of her father, the grace of Zerlina and the consummate, masterful elegance of the trio of Maskers, the trio which starts the second act under Elvira's balcony; in a word, everything (for in this deathless work everything may be quoted) put me into that blessed state which one feels only before beautiful things to which the centuries must pay homage, things which are the yardstick of the aesthetic level of the arts. This performance counts as the loveliest experience of my childhood, and when, in 1839, I was awarded the *prix de Rome* my poor dear mother gave me the full score of *Don Giovanni* as a reward. [2]

BERLIOZ

Berlioz was a man all of a piece, a whole man who admitted neither to concessions nor transactions. He belonged to the race of Alcestis; hence, the race of Orontes [1] was naturally against him, and of Orontes there are, God knows, quite a few! People found him ill-tempered, sullen, biting, and what not! But along with his sensitivity, heightened to the point of irascibility, we must consider all the irritating, embittering experiences, all the personal misfortunes and the thousand and one setbacks and rejections endured by this proud spirit, incapable of any base desire to please or of cowardly, low fawning.

If his criticisms seemed all too severe to those whom they touched, at least it could never be said that his motive was jealousy, so incompatible with his noble, generous and loyal nature.

The trials Berlioz had to undergo as a contestant for the *grand prix de Rome* were the prophetic prelude to those he had to meet throughout the rest of his career. He competed four times and obtained the prize only at the age of twenty-seven, in 1830, by dint of perseverance and in spite of all sorts of obstacles which he had to surmount. In the very same year that he carried off the prize with his cantata, *Sardanapale*, he had a work performed which showed how far his artistry had developed from the standpoint of conception, color and technical mastery. His *Symphonie fantastique (An Episode in the Life of an Artist)* was a veritable musical event, the importance of which may be gauged by the fanatic adherence of some and the violent opposition of others. However, no matter how much one might argue about such a composition, it reveals, in the young man who produced it, the very highest faculties of invention and a powerful poetic feeling which one rediscovers in all his works. Berlioz hurled into musical circulation a multitude of effects and orchestral combinations unknown before him and which even the most illustrious musicians have not hesitated to make their own. He revolutionized the domain of instrumentation, and in this respect at least, he can be said to have created a "school." And yet, despite the brilliant triumphs, in France as well as abroad, Berlioz was under attack all his life. Although his personal direction as an eminent orchestral conductor and his indefatigable energy added so many elements of clarity and chances for success to performances, he never had more than a limited and restrained public. He lacked the "public," that "everybody" which makes success *popular*. His *Les Troyens*, which he had foreseen as being the source of all his sorrows,

[1] A figure in Molière's *Misanthrope*.

truly finished him. It can be said of him, as of his heroic namesake, Hector, that he perished under the walls of Troy.

With Berlioz all impressions, all sensations—whether joyful or sad —are expressed in extremes, at the point of delirium. As he himself says, he is a "volcano." Our sensitivity carries us equally far in sorrow and joy: Tabor and Golgotha are related. Happiness does not consist of the absence of suffering, any more than genius consists of the absence of faults.

The great geniuses suffer and must suffer, but they need not complain; they have known intoxication unknown to the rest of men and, if they have wept tears of sadness, they have poured tears of ineffable joy. That in itself is a heaven for which one never pays what it is worth. [3]

EDOUARD LALO

1823–1892

Lalo's *Symphonie Espagnole* is practically his only work—a few songs excepted—which is played frequently today. The piece comes by its authentic Spanish flavor legitimately, Lalo being a descendant of a family of pure Spanish origin which established itself in Flanders at the time of the Spanish Conquest. However, he was born in Lille, and belonged to the school of Saint-Saëns which composed French-flavored romantic music in German classic form.

In his letters to the renowned violinist Sarasate—who, incidentally, introduced Lalo's *Violin Concerto in F* and the *Symphonie Espagnole* —he expresses his particular reverence for Beethoven, Schubert and Schumann in contrast to his distaste for Brahms who, he felt, was highly overrated in Germany and whom he considered merely the shadow of his German predecessors.

His *Le Roi d'Ys*, an opera of which only the overture is sometimes performed, was his first and most brilliant success.

TITLES OF COMPOSITIONS

From: Letter to Otto Goldschmidt,[1]
Paris, August 20, 1879

I absolutely reject the title *Suite* for my last piece [*Concerto Russo*]; the Suites of Massenet, Godard, Guiraud, Ries, Raff, Hoffman, Holstein, etc., etc. have made the word repellent to me; it's a worn-out tag, one must find another. Artistically, a title means nothing and the work itself is everything; this is an absolute principle; but *commercially*, a tainted, discredited title is never a good thing. I kept the title *Symphonie Espagnole* contrary to and in spite of everybody, first, because it conveyed my thought—that is to say, a violin solo soaring above the rigid *form* of an old symphony—and then because the title was less banal than those which were proposed to me. The cries and criticisms have died or will die down; the title will remain, and in a

---

[1] The accompanist of Sarasate.

letter of congratulation Bülow wrote me that this *happy* title placed the piece beyond all the others.

Another example: that shapeless thing which calls itself the *Second Concerto* of Bruch (a concerto which has no first movement, which begins with the second, passes through an Intermezzo in recitative form and concludes with a poor finale) raised a clamor among the scholastics. Strictly, it is nothing but a suite, but Bruch kept the title, and did quite well *commercially;* it is classed as a concerto, and violinists who play the magnificent *First Concerto* want to play the *Second.* With this title, it is given as the main number in a program; with the *real* title, *Suite,* another concerto would have to be given first. So you see, *commercially* a title is of great importance. There is no hurry about my last piece, but don't announce it as a Suite; upon reflection, I do not want that dull title. The shouts and the criticisms are of little importance; I would like to add an imaginative and characteristic word to the title Concerto; find it for me; you will be doing me a great favor. I shall also search for one on my own.   [1]

BRAHMS

Letter to Pablo Sarasate, Paris, August 28, 1878

My dear friend: I am writing you today in a state of inexpressible stupefaction! The cause is the *Second Symphony in D* of Brahms. I read it yesterday morning, and heard it the same day at the Concert Populaire. So this is the gentleman some place above, and others at the side of, Schumann!! Schumann, the great poet, powerful, inspired, whose every note is *individual,* and the composer of the *Second Symphony in D* judged on the same scale! It is grotesque!

Brahms is an inferior spirit whose pickax has probed every nook of counterpoint and modern harmony. This is his only recommendation. He is not a born musician; his inventiveness is always insignificant and imitative; in his latest symphony, the imitativeness is especially flagrant. I have conscientiously followed his chamber music work: It holds up because it is based on deep study, but as for invention, it is faltering, and one senses that here is a man who looks right and left for what he can not find within himself. Furthermore, on the pretext of increasing the sonorities, he abuses unison writing unbearably. (Beethoven knew enough about harmony to be aware of unisons but his power over sonority needed no such ridiculous means to achieve it.) And lastly, the piano quintet: There is in the ensemble of this work an explosive quality which gives one the hope that the composer has definitely found his groove. Alas! the works that follow flounder in a quagmire of exercises and are absolutely insignificant from the point of view of invention. Since his last chamber music works I have not read anything of this composer, and before the concert I had never heard any of his orchestral compositions. You will tell me the Pasdeloup performance is not good. So be it. But that goes for everything, and Pasdeloup had rehearsed the new symphony, which moreover, is not difficult. On the same program they played Mozart's *Symphony in G* which, when it elbows an orchestral page of Beethoven, seems a dwarf, but which appeared a colossus beside the Brahms. The first and last movements are of a shabby, old-fashioned invention, and constantly imitate Mendelssohn and Beethoven in all the themes which serve as the basis for the developments. The andante forms a contrast to these two puerile movements, but is no less boring; it reminds me of a gentleman who puts on a profound and ominous air to iterate and re-iterate in a cavernous voice: "This sword is the most beautiful day of my life!"—"The ship of state sails on a volcano!" The scherzo is a pretty little genre piece.

As for Brahms's orchestra, that is to me the most stupefying thing of all. He understands nothing about choice of timbres, he orchestrates like a pianist; if one of us were to perpetrate anything so mediocre as professional orchestrators, we would say: My dear friend, you have talent—but hurry back to school.

To sum it up: the quintet I had believed the point of departure for a vigorous fellow who had finally mastered his own resources and would produce a series of remarkable works; the quartet, on the contrary, is the apogee of a composer who has only gone from bad to worse; and this latest symphony ranks below his least quartet.

A stupid scene occurred at the concert: the public booed and hissed; it was the same idiots who had just encored an absurd guitar trifle of Taubert.[1] So I applauded to the hilt for the sole reason that extremes call forth extremes, and because I find it monstrous for imbeciles to hiss an artist whose worth I dispute because his partisans have placed him too high, but who is nevertheless of incontestable significance. As for his symphony, I repeat, it merits neither applause nor hisses.

I met Saint-Saëns that same evening, and his opinion of the symphony was identical.

Here you have a long letter, but it will prove to you the esteem in which musicians held Brahms and his reputation from across the Rhine, for everybody put himself out to go and admire the Mountain ad-

[1] Karl Gottfried Taubert, 1811–91, an astonishingly prolific composer, considered quite good in his day.

vertised to them and it is not their fault that the Mountain birthed only
a Mouse.   [2]

BRAHMS'S *PIANO CONCERTO IN D MINOR*

From: Letter to Pablo Sarasate, Paris, August 27, 1879

This is the fifth time I have heard this *Concerto*, and I have retained
the same impression each time: It is always very interesting, the first
movement is very beautiful, but I maintain that when a soloist is set
on the stage, he must be given the main rôle, and not be treated as a
simple instrument in the orchestra. If the *solo* genre displeases the
composer, let him write symphonies, or something else for the orchestra
alone, but don't let him bore me with fragments of solos constantly
interrupted by the orchestra, and naturally much less interesting than
what the orchestra has just said. The Brahms *Concerto* is a great
orchestral piece, but when the piano interrupts the orchestra, it ir-
ritates me. The Beethoven and Mendelssohn *Concertos* are as symphonically written as this one of Brahms, but in the former two the
lady or gentleman soloist interests me, whereas in the last he annoys me.

[3]

BEDŘICH (FRIEDRICH) SMETANA

1824–1884

As composer, conductor, pianist and critic, Smetana devoted himself to establishing and developing Czech national art. His schooling had been German, as was the custom in Czech communities at that time. He spent a number of years concertizing in Germany and Holland. In Sweden, he gave piano recitals and also conducted the Göteborg Philharmonic for three years. With the Bohemian national renaissance, however, Smetana's interests became one with those of his own country. He returned to Prague, where he became one of the leaders of Czech intellectual life.

As director of the National Opera House, he promoted native opera in the native language (performance of opera in Prague had vacillated between the German and Czech languages for years, the German dominating). With the financial aid of Liszt, he established a music school in Prague. His musical ideas and plans, propagated in newspaper articles and reviews, greatly influenced the musical development of the period.

The Bartered Bride, firmly established in the repertoire of almost every opera company the world over, skillfully translated Bohemian folk song into a higher form. The Czech idiom is also incorporated in his other operas, scarcely known and practically never performed outside his native land. In *My Country*, a collection of six symphonic poems of which *The Moldau* is the most played, Smetana painted the history and landscape of his country through its own folk music.

The last ten years of his life were marred by total deafness. Despite this affliction, he composed, among other things, one of his most important works, the string quartet *Aus meinem Leben* (1876).

ABSOLUTE MUSIC

Absolute music is impossible for me in any genre.

My compositions do not belong to the realm of absolute music, where one can get along well enough with musical signs and a metronome.

My quartet, *From My Life* (*Aus meinem Leben*), does not consist merely of a formal game of tones and motives, by means of which the composer exhibits his skill. On the contrary, my aim was to present to the listener scenes from my life.

I am no enemy of old forms in old music, but I am against imitating them today. I came to the conclusion myself—no one pointed it out to me—that hitherto existing forms are finished.   [1]

OPERA

Opera must not be a musical production in which one sings for the sake of singing, where everything moves along according to the beat . . . where the baton is of principal importance. Opera must be lifted to the realm of drama where one forgets the external workings of the machinery.   [2]

When the public understands nothing of the text, it contents itself with a pretty melody. The situation is quite different in the case of truly dramatic operas where both words and music must be given due expression. Here one must sing exclusively in the language of the public.   [3]

I am no friend of overtures. On first hearing, when they are entirely unfamiliar, the audience cannot even understand them. Here the overture is nothing but a game of tones. I was pressed into writing my overtures, those to *The Kiss* and *The Secret*, for example, by several friends. My overtures do not please me. I have written none to my serious operas, just a short introduction to the first scene. In the case of *Libussa*, it was different. Its festive character demanded a rather long prelude. But also in comic operas, an overture belongs only when one can write a grand allegro, as in *The Bartered Bride*.

[4]

MUSIC IN SWEDEN

Letter to Liszt, Göteborg, April 10, 1857

Honored Master and Friend!

Allow me to use this salutation. Your many examples of friendly affection give me that right, I hope. Though I am not one of those lucky ones who can actually call themselves your students, you are nevertheless my Master, and I am grateful to you for everything.

Since those memorable, to-me-unforgettable days of your last year's stay in Prague, my material situation has somewhat altered. A short time after your departure, I also left. Following Dreyschock's advice that I move to Sweden, namely to Göteborg, I arrived here in mid-October of last year. The result of two concerts was the repeated invitation by the musical contingent that I take up permanent residence. Economically I am in a much better position than in Prague, as I am literally inundated with lessons; but musically I am completely isolated, not only because of a dearth of musical communication, but also because of a lack of direction. The people here are still solidly fixed in an antediluvian artistic point of view. Mozart is their idol, though he is not really understood, Beethoven is feared, Mendelssohn declared unpalatable, and the moderns are unknown. I performed Schumann's works here for the first time. However, it is fruitless to continue to talk about the conditions prevailing here.

What primarily induced me to remain is the possible large sphere of activity in my art. Out of the tragic remains of the old Mozart Society, a new Society has been formed under the name "The Society for Old and New Classic Music" which appointed me its director at a monthly salary of 100 Swedish thalers. They meet weekly and study large-scale works, the choice of which is left to me. Thus I have the best opportunity to further the progress and taste of the people. For our first effort I chose Mendelssohn's *Elijah*, in order to win increasing acceptance and understanding of the modern masters. I was also very fortunate in that we could perform this work publicly. What it means, however, to prepare such a work with untrained singers—soloists included—and an orchestra composed partly of the military and partly of undisciplined dilettantes, you can scarcely imagine. Nevertheless, the performance was successful enough to elicit a general demand for the repetition of the same work at Easter—this week—at one of the churches in town. At the same time, I have rehearsed the group in Schumann's *Paradise and the Peri* with piano, and what do you think? They liked it so much that they decided on its performance for the next winter season. In my last concert I shall also do Gade's *Erlking's Daughter*, a fairly light and easily understood work which will also serve to smooth the path for one of the greatest of contemporary masters as yet unknown here.

So you see, my honored friend, here I am effective as I could never have been in Prague, and since I have found fertile soil for good works, I can hope to give a most gratifying direction to art in a short time. Besides, I have introduced Wagner, Schumann and yourself to smaller circles and found what I was looking for, receptivity. The Göteborg inhabitants, left to themselves until now, did not know what art is all about. They are mainly wealthy merchants who *carry on* (if I might use the expression) this very superfluous art insofar as it affords them a bit of passing entertainment. Yet now they are really demanding more, and my energy as well as my ruthless promotion of contemporary masters, seems to please them. Next season I hope to achieve even better and greater results. [5]

JOHANNES BRAHMS

1833–1897

It is hard to understand why Brahms's works were at first considered dry. Actually, they are at times lushly romantic, often full of good humor, yet always within the bounds of good taste. His culture was too great to allow any lapses.

He was no virtuoso composer, but his works are difficult all the same, their virtuosity stemming from their ideas, from the actual content of the music rather than from mere effects. He was a master of technique; hence his intricate polyphony, his involved cross-rhythms and the fluency of his developments.

It is interesting that in his letters, even those in which technical problems are discussed, he is always shorter than his correspondents. He lacked either the inclination or the time to write at length. His extended letter to Eduard Hanslick—his admirer and champion— quoted below, concerning the two early cantatas of Beethoven, is therefore of special interest. It was probably intended for publication, and Hanslick included it in his *Am Ende des Jahrhunderts*.

Brahms's friendship with Clara Schumann was life-long, beginning with her husband's recognition [1] of Brahms as a "genius" in his early manhood, and extended with but a brief hiatus to her death. He made an arrangement of the Bach *Chaconne* for the left hand alone at the time Clara Schumann had hurt her right hand. Curiously enough, he was unaware of her injury when he sent her the manuscript and accompanying letter.

INSPIRATION

From: Letter to Clara Schumann, Hanover,
February 22, 1856

It always saddens me to think that after all I am not yet a proper musician; still, I have more aptitude for the calling than probably

---

[1] See p. 159.

many of the younger generation. It gets knocked out of me. Boys should be allowed to indulge in jolly music; the serious kind comes of its own accord, although the lovesick does not. How lucky is the man who, like Mozart and others, goes to the tavern of an evening and writes some fresh music. For he lives while he is creating, though he does what he likes.   [1]

VARIATIONS

Letter to Joseph Joachim, Düsseldorf, June, 1856

At times I reflect on the Variation form and I come to the conclusion that variations should be kept purer, more strict.

The older composers adhered strictly to the bass of their theme—the bass is the actual theme—throughout.

Beethoven varies his melody, harmony and rhythm so beautifully.

However, I am sometimes inclined to think that the moderns (we both!) rummage about too much with the theme. We anxiously hang on to the melody, but don't treat it freely. We create nothing new out of it; we merely overload it, and hence the melody is rendered unrecognizable.   [2]

BACH'S *CHACONNE*

From: Letter to Clara Schumann, Pörtschach, June, 1877

The *Chaconne* is, in my opinion, one of the most wonderful and most incomprehensible pieces of music. Using the technique adapted to a small instrument, the man writes a whole world of the deepest thoughts and most powerful feelings. If I could picture myself writing, or even conceiving, such a piece, I am sure that the extreme excitement and emotional tension would have driven me mad. If one has no supremely great violinist at hand, the most exquisite of joys is probably simply to let the *Chaconne* ring in one's mind. But the piece certainly inspires one to occupy oneself with it somehow. One does not always want to hear music actually played, and in any case Joachim is not always there, so one tries it otherwise. But whether I try it with an orchestra or piano, the pleasure is always spoiled for me. There is only one way in which I can secure undiluted joy from the piece, though on a small and only approximate scale, and that is when I play it with the left hand alone. . . . The same difficulty, the nature of the technique, the rendering of the arpeggios, everything conspires to make me feel like a violinist.

You try it yourself. I only wrote it for you. But do not overstrain your hand; it requires so much resonance and strength. Play it for a while mezza voce. Also make the fingering easy and convenient. If it does not exert you too much—which is what I am afraid of—you ought to get great fun out of it.   [3]

SCHUMANN

Letter to Heinrich von Herzogenberg,
Vienna, October, 1886

I think you and Joachim will derive considerable pleasure and interest from the enclosed.

It is an exact compilation of the printed score and the original concept of Schumann's *D Minor symphony*, modestly and, I think, unjustly described by the composer in his introduction as a rough sketch. You are, of course, familiar with the state of affairs, which is quite simple.

Schumann was so upset by a first rehearsal, which went off badly, that he subsequently instrumentated the symphony afresh at Düsseldorf, where he was used to a bad and incomplete orchestra.

The original scoring has always delighted me. It is a real pleasure to see anything so bright and spontaneous expressed with corresponding ease and grace. It reminds me (without comparing it in other respects) of Mozart's *G minor*, the autograph of which I also possess. Everything is so absolutely natural that you cannot imagine it different; there are no harsh colors, no forced effects, and so on. On the other hand, you will no doubt agree that one's enjoyment of the revised form is not unmixed; eye and ear seem to contradict each other.   [4]

THE *MEISTERSINGER*

From: Letter to Clara Schumann, Vienna,
March 20, 1870

The *Meistersinger* had to be put on the program five times and taken off again, and now the repeat performances are causing just as much bother. This alone is enough to prevent the public from working up any enthusiasm, and a certain amount of *go* is necessary for that. I think the public is much less interested than I expected. I am not enthusiastic, either, about this work or about Wagner in general, but I listen as attentively as possible—and as often—as I can stand it. I confess it provokes one to discussion. But I am glad it is not necessary to say all that I feel about it plainly and aloud, etc. This I do know: In everything else I attempt, I step on the heels of my predecessors who embarrass me. But Wagner would not hinder me at all from proceeding with the greatest pleasure to the writing of an opera.

[5]

THE YOUNG BEETHOVEN; COLLECTED EDITIONS

Letter to Eduard Hanslick, Vienna, May, 1884

Dear friend: You went away and left me a treasure without having looked it over yourself. Hence, I must write you a few words of thanks so that you may know just how valuable a treasure it is. There is no doubt whatsoever that in it the two cantatas which Beethoven wrote in Bonn—on the death of Joseph II and the accession of Leopold II —have been discovered. Thus we now have two large-scale works for chorus and orchestra from a period in which no compositions to which we could attach any particular significance existed, as far as we knew. If they did not bear the date (February, 1790), we would guess them to be of a later period, since we know nothing of that period! However, even if there were no name on the title page, there would still be no doubt concerning the composer—throughout it is altogether Beethoven! Here are the beautiful, noble pathos, the great sensitivity and imagination, the power as well as violence of expression, added to the special quality of the voice leading and declamation at which we marvel in his later works!

Naturally the cantata on the death of Joseph II interests us chiefly. For such an historical event one doesn't write merely a *pièce d'occasion!* Were we to commemorate this unforgettable, irreplaceable man today, we would be as impassioned about it as Beethoven and everyone else at the time. Nor did Beethoven merely write a *pièce d'occasion.* We have only to observe how this artist never fails to fashion artistically, to exert his greatest efforts, and this is more easily seen in a young man than in the master. In the very first mourning chorus, we get the picture of Joseph himself. Not a word or note would leave you in doubt. A recitative, uncommonly vigorous, follows: "A mighty one, his name, Fanaticism, rose from the depths of Hell" (later crushed by Joseph, in an aria). I cannot help thinking back on that time when—as the vehement words demonstrate—the entire world understood what it had lost in Joseph. The young Beethoven also understood that he had something great to say, and as was right, said it forcefully right at the start, in the powerful Overture. To the words: "The people came forth into the light," we hear the magnificent F-major movement from the finale of *Fidelio*. Here, as there, the beautiful, moving melody in the oboe. We find many examples where the great masters use the same thought in several places. I find it particularly good here. How deeply Beethoven must have felt the melody in the cantata, as deeply and beautifully as later, when he sang the noble song of the love of a woman—a song of liberation as well—to its conclusion. After further arias and recitatives, the work closes with a repetition of the opening chorus. But I don't want to describe it any further just now. Nor will I go into the second cantata. . . .

Now then, my dear friend, I already hear you asking when the cantatas will be performed and when published. And right there my pleasure stops. Publishing has become so fashionable, that is, the publishing of things which do not at all deserve it. You know it has always been my heart's desire that the so-called collected works of our masters should not be published so "collectively," but be made available, completely, yet singly, in good copies in our larger libraries. You know how zealously I have sought to become acquainted with their unprinted works. But I do not want to own all the printed works of even some of our most beloved masters. I find it neither fitting nor healthy that amateurs or young artists be misled into overloading their libraries or their brains with "collected works" and into confusing their sense of values.

Our Haydn has not yet had the honor of a complete edition. A truly complete edition of his works would be as impossible as it would be impractical. Yet how desirable a manuscript collection of the same, and a number of facsimiles for public libraries would be. How little is done to bring out new editions of certain works which it would be so desirable to study and circulate—for example, old vocal music of every genre. You will perhaps say that they are never made use of. But they should be; and no doubt they are being used more and more. . . .

But these are long-winded themes, and I don't want to improvise any further variations on them for you. They also tend too exclusively toward the *minor* and I know that some *major* ones are possible and necessary.

Come back soon and share with me the quite special feeling and pleasure of being the only one in the world who is aware of these deeds of a hero.   [6]

ALEXANDER BORODIN

1833–1887

Whereas his colleagues in the "Koochka" earned their livelihood at jobs of secondary importance to their music, Borodin served two professions with equal devotion. He was both chemist-doctor and composer; his scientific papers and books were as valid as his musical compositions. He devoted his energies also to the organization of musical education, especially for women.

Though most of his music is based on Russian folksong, he leaned strongly, like his mentor Balakirev, toward the oriental, witness the barbaric eastern splendor of *Prince Igor* (1869–87) and *On the Steppes of Central Asia* (1880). He was a long time in composing the former, which he did not complete due to lack of time and an imperfect technique. Nor did he neglect "absolute" music; he wrote two symphonies, three string quartets and various other pieces of chamber music.

A keen sense of humor is manifest in both his letters and his music. An early work, *The Bogatyrs* (1867) parodies the styles of Meyerbeer, Rossini and others, and the letter on the *Paraphrases* quoted here has its delightfully funny aspects. His correspondence with his wife while he was away on a scientific-musical trip in western Europe is whimsical and full of characteristic high spirits. His comments on Liszt whom he met in Jena and Weimar are apt and penetrating.

As he was more objective than Rimski-Korsakov in his relations with Balakirev, his letter describing the leader's desertion of the group to embrace mysticism and pietism is all the more poignant.

LISZT'S PIANO CLASSES

From: Letter to Mme Borodin, Jena, July 12, 1877

Liszt never assigns any pieces to his students; he allows them freedom of choice. However, he gives them general advice in order to avoid their being stopped after a few measures with a remark of this kind: "What odd taste to play such an ineptitude!"

He pays little attention to technique, to fingering, but concerns himself primarily with interpretation and expression. But, except in rare cases, his students possess excellent techniques, although they stem from very different schools.

Above all Liszt impressed me with his personality.   [1]

BALAKIREV

From: Letter to Mme Borodin, October 24–25, 1871

I don't understand why Balakirev turns away so stubbornly from our circle and obviously avoids any encounter with us. I fear that his mind is not quite in order, but perhaps it's only his conceit gnawing at him. He is so despotic by nature that he demands complete subordination to his wishes, even in the most trifling matters. It doesn't seem possible for him to understand and acknowledge freedom and equality. He cannot endure the slightest opposition to his tastes, even to his whims. He wants to impose his yoke upon everyone and everything. Yet he is quite aware that we all have already grown up, that we stand firmly on our feet, and no longer require braces. This evidently irks him. More than once he has said to Ludma: [1] "Why should I hear their things, they are all so mature now that I've become unnecessary to them, they can do without me, etc." His nature is such that it positively requires minors, over whom he can fuss like a nurse over a child. So he draws around him Miladorevitch, Pomazansky and even, so they say, that "perfume bottle," i.e. Shcherbachov,[2] although he must know there's nothing that can come from this last one. He has run Pomazansky quite breathless, forcing him to write a Russian overture, nine-tenths of which has been composed by Mili himself, for he doesn't give Pomazansky the slightest freedom to act according to his own wishes. However, the overture is very good, interesting in its themes and development, beautifully orchestrated, and so on. But all this is Mili, Mili, and Mili, while Pomazansky as a personality doesn't exist. Meanwhile the alienation of Mili, his obvious turning away from the circle, his sharp remarks about many, especially Modeste (Moussorgsky), have considerably cooled the group's sympathies. If he goes on like this, he may easily isolate himself and, in his situation, this would amount to spiritual death. I, and not I alone, but the others too, feel very sorry for Mili; but what's to be done? Even Ludma, who used to be able to pacify him, has lost all influence over him. There may also be a reason for his estrangement in his strange and unexpected

[1] Glinka's sister, friend and champion of the Five, especially of Moussorgsky.
[2] These three were Balakirev's satellites.

switch to pietism of the most fanatic and most naïve sort. For instance, Mili doesn't miss a single morning mass, breaks a piece from his holy wafer, fervently crosses himself before each church, etc. It's quite possible that, in these circumstances, it's unpleasant for him to meet people who are unsympathetic to all this; he may even be afraid of the tactless and coarse barrage of reproaches from Vladimir Stasov [1] who, whenever he meets him, starts forthwith "demonstrating" to him that all this is nonsense, that he "cannot understand" how an intelligent man like Mili, and so on, and so on. Moreover, most of the reproaches concern his apathy to musical matters, especially during the last year. . . . Modinka (Moussorgsky) is offended by Mili's unjust, high-handed remarks about *Boris*, expressed tactlessly and sharply in the presence of people who on no account ought to have heard them. Korsinka (Rimski-Korsakov) resents his indifference to *Pskovityanka* and is pained by Mili's behavior.

Cui also is indignant about Mili's apathy and his lack of interest in what happens in our musical circle. Before, Mili used to be concerned with the slightest novelty, even in embryo. There is no denying that the abyss between him and us grows wider and wider. This is terribly painful and pitiful. Painful chiefly because the victim of all this will be Mili himself. The other members of the circle now live more peacefully than ever before. Modinka and Korsinka particularly, since they began to share a room, have both greatly developed. They are diametrically opposed in musical qualities and methods; one seems to complement the other. Their influence on each other has been extremely helpful. Modeste has improved the recitative and declamatory sides of Korsinka who has, in his turn, wiped out Modeste's tendency towards awkward originality, and has smoothed all his rough harmonic edges, his pretentiousness in orchestration, his lack of logic in the construction of musical form—in a word, he has made Modeste's things incomparably more musical. And in all the relations within our circle there's not a shadow of envy, conceit or selfishness; each is made sincerely happy by the smallest success of another. . . . Mili alone shuns this *family* equality. [2]

LISZT ON BORODIN'S *FIRST SYMPHONY*

From: Letter to Mme Borodin, Jena, July 12, 1877

He [Liszt] told me that he had presented my modulations as models to his students. Pointing out several, he remarked that nothing similar could be found in Beethoven, Bach, or anywhere else, for that matter,

---

[1] Art and music critic, champion and sponsor of the "Five."

and that despite its novelty and originality, the work could not be cavilled with since it was so polished, definitive and full of attractive qualities. He regarded the first movement very highly; its pedal points, particularly the one in C, pleased him enormously.

He said nothing special about the other movements, but gave me some practical advice in case I were to publish a second piano version, namely, that of writing certain passages an octave higher or lower to facilitate reading.   [3]

THE *PARAPHRASES*

From: Letter to M. and Mme G. Huberti,
December 14, 1886

[Borodin collaborated with Rimski-Korsakov, Liadov and Cui on a humorous (really serious) set of 24 variations and 14 little piano pieces called "Paraphrases" on an obbligato theme akin to our "Chopsticks," "dedicated to little pianists who can play the tune with one finger of each hand."]

I take the liberty of sending you, for your little girls, my—or rather our—"Paraphrases," twenty-four variations, and fourteen little pieces for piano on the favorite theme of the "Koteletten [Chop] Polka":

which is so popular with the little ones in Russia. It is played with one finger of each hand. The origin of this work is very funny. One day, Gania (one of my adopted daughters) asked me to play a duet with her.

"Well, but you do not know how to play, my child."

"Yes, indeed, I can play this":—

I had to yield to the child's request, and so I improvised the polka which you will find in this collection. The four keys, C major, G major, F minor and A minor, of the four parts of the polka in which the unchanging theme of the "Koteletten Polka" makes a kind of *cantus firmus* or counterpoint, caused much laughter among my friends, afterwards joint-authors of the "Paraphrases." They were amused. First one and then another wanted to try his hand at a piece in this style. The joke was well received by our friends. We amused ourselves by performing these things with people who could not play the piano. Finally we were requested to publish this work. Rahter became the proprietor and publisher. This music fell into Liszt's hands, who was delighted with it. He wrote a charming letter about it to one of his friends in St. Petersburg; the letter was very flattering to the author of the "Paraphrases." One day the friend of Liszt's who had received this letter mentioned it in a musical article. The critics, our enemies, were infuriated, and said that Liszt could not have approved of such a work, that he never wrote the letter, that the whole thing was a falsehood, and finally that we composers had compromised ourselves by the publication of such a work.

When Liszt heard all this, he laughed heartily. He wrote to us: "If this work is considered *compromising*, let me *compromise* myself with you." It was then that he sent the scrap of music that serves as an introduction to my polka, requesting Rahter to print it in the second edition of the "Paraphrases" already on the press. In view of Liszt's great authority, Rahter thought well to engrave the facsimile of the leaflet sent by the great master. The reproduction of this leaflet was printed and added to the music of the first edition. Our enemies were silenced. Liszt was very fond of this humorous work, and it always amused him to play it with his pupils.

The page added by Liszt bore the title: "Variation for the second edition of the *marvellous* work of Borodin, César Cui, Liadov and Rimski-Korsakov, by their devoted Franz Liszt, Weimar, July 28th, 1880. To be placed between pages 9 and 10 of the early edition, after the finale of C. Cui, and as prelude to the polka by Borodin." [4]

CÉSAR CUI

1835–1918

The name César Cui usually calls to mind an exotic tidbit which has been arranged for almost every conceivable musical combination, and was especially popularized by Fritz Kreisler's wide-selling recording "Orientale," from the *Kaleidoscope Suite*. Yet Cui was the composer of numerous songs, choruses, symphonic works and four operas which had considerable vogue in Russia during the late nineteenth century. With Balakirev, he founded the new Russian school, known as the "Big Five" or "Koochka," a group which gave tremendous impetus to Russian national music.

By profession he was a military man; he attained the rank of general, became professor at the Military Academy in St. Petersburg, and, as an authority on fortifications, wrote several books on the subject. Like most of his colleagues, he practiced music as an avocation. As he so often says in his book of essays, *La Musique en Russie:* "Musical composition does not feed a man in Russia."

Of his earlier compositions, including the operas *The Prisoner of the Caucasus* and *The Mandarin's Son*, most are written in the West European idiom of his time; his last two musical dramas, *William Ratcliffe* and *Angelo*, considered his most powerful works, were composed along the lines of the credo laid down by the "Five."

For years a critic on one of the most influential musical journals in St. Petersburg, he used his sharp and witty pen to defend the aesthetic and to further the works of the new Russian school.

RUSSIAN FOLK MUSIC

From: Article in the *Revue et gazette musicale*, Paris, 1878–79

One of the principal elements in the structure of Russian song is the complete freedom of rhythm, carried to the point of caprice. Not only may the musical phrases be composed of an unequal number of measures, but even in the same song the rhythm of the measures may change several times. Here is an example:

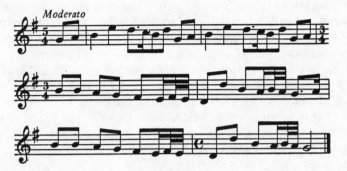

This song starts with two measures of 5/4, followed by three measures of 3/4, and the motive finishes with one measure of 4/4. One finds measures of seven beats as well as five; yet, in spite of the daring of such license, the musical phrase never loses its naturalness, for it adapts itself perfectly to the text; everything turns out correctly pronounced and accented. The Russian people have ever felt the need to subordinate the music to the prosodic exigencies of the text—an indication of real superiority of artistic instinct. These changing rhythms are, above all, *right*, since they are supremely expressive. At the same time, they utterly exclude the impression of banality and monotony which sometimes results from the prolonged use of a uniform and overworked rhythm.

But their very variety is such that an unpracticed ear does not grasp certain Russian songs clearly, as long as the musical phrases are not divided and established into precise measures. Another notable fact in the whole of vocal music of the Russian people is that, very often, the theme is not constructed on the current European scale, but on old Greek modes, the origin of church music. The *Lydian* mode (the scale of F without the B flat) and the *Dorian* mode (the scale of D without C sharp and F sharp), especially the latter, are most frequently used in Russian folk songs.

The use of the Greek modes furnishes proof of the antiquity of Russian folk songs; it has the further advantages of making their contours more individual, by communicating to even the most ordinary melodies a certain originality of appeal, and above all a great diversity because, in Greek music, the position of the half steps varies with each mode, while in European music it is fixed.

Couldn't the composer in quest of new effects, tired of the uniformity of our harmonic and melodic constructions, exploit this fertile mine? Must not the new, in a certain measure, come out of the old, and isn't there the germ of flourishing youth in what we call decay? More than once have the potent masters had recourse to the old modes; let us cite only Beethoven, who, in his *Quartet Opus 132*, wrote an Adagio in the Lydian mode; it is one of the most admirable productions in musical art.

The Russian folk song imperiously demands an original harmonization and a very special art of modulation. First, it is rare to come on a song the melody of which can be treated entirely in one of the two modes, major or minor; most often, even if it spans but a few measures, it passes from the minor to its relative major and vice versa. These changes, generally unexpected, are almost always of a striking and sympathetic effect.

Here again is a happy example of a modulation from the major to the minor, by descending one tone:

It also happens that the harmony of a single chord remains stationary throughout an entire song, which lends it an overall quality of vague melancholy, a complexion of deliberate monotony.

Russian folk tunes are ordinarily confined within a very restricted note-span, only rarely exceeding the interval of a *fifth* or *sixth*. And the older the song, the smaller the compass of its note-span. The theme is always short; some are limited to two measures, but these measures are repeated as many times as the scope of the text demands. [1]

THE CREDO OF THE "BIG FIVE"

From: Article in the *Revue et gazette musicale*, Paris, 1878–79

The new Russian school has undertaken to bring to light certain principles of the highest importance, the first of which is the following: *Dramatic music must always have an intrinsic worth, as absolute music, independent of the text.* This principle has been too long neglected; even today it is far from being strictly observed. Because composers have been mainly preoccupied with pure melody and vocal virtuosity, guarantees of success, the most astounding and naïve banalities have been justified and accepted. What would have been discarded with justifiable disdain in a symphonic composition, found its way naturally into opera. In this business, the Italians are masters beyond compare. Content with facile successes, based on florid passages and on high B flats and C sharps, keeping step with and sustaining the public's bad taste, they not only resort to using the most banal themes, but they parade these horrors in all their nakedness, never so much as attempting to mitigate them with even slightly elegant harmonies. The best among these musicians either repeat each other or repeat themselves, in style, themes and harmonies. In this way they have managed to make their operas a series of degenerate twins which bear a distressing resemblance to each other. To be convinced, one has merely to glance at the thirty-odd Italian operas of Rossini, at the seventy and more of Donizetti.[1] Both offer two or three typical works, of which the rest of their output is only a more or less feeble and pallid reproduction. And even in their masterpieces, what commonplaces, what insignificant and stale pages!

In the case of a great number of non-Italian composers, the results are just about the same: they write too much, too often they speculate on the fortunate abilities of the performers, on the beautiful and irresistible effect of the *décor*, on the ever certain charm of the ballet scenes. Would Meyerbeer himself, one of the greatest dramatic composers, not gain a great deal if he suppressed the princesses and queens with their roulades in his operas?

The new Russian school envisages the question from an absolutely different point of view. According to its principles, nothing must deflect opera music from being in itself *true and beautiful music;* everything that is most seductive in musical art must relate to it; the

[1] Donizetti wrote sixty-two operas.

charm of harmony, the science of counterpoint, polyphony and orchestral color must be equal. Such a precept might not appear practical
or applicable. It might seem that a pause here and there, to make room
for more or less prolonged trivialities, would serve the audience well,
would spare it the fatigue of too long sustained attention. Not at all!
The Russian school is unwilling to reap profit from such combinations,
advantageous as they may seem, or to make any such concessions. It
will not alter its position in this regard for any price. It advances
surely and proudly toward the ideal which beckons it—this lively
source of intellect, honesty and eternal poetry—without troubling
over success or lack of it.

*Vocal music must be in perfect agreement with the sense of the
words.* Again a clear and simple truth, good to repeat, and the application of which is all too frequently neglected. The text does not serve
exclusively to facilitate vocal gymnastics; if such were its object, a
text could be chosen at random and joined to no matter what music.
Since texts vary, since each has its particular meaning, it is absolutely
necessary that the musical part be intelligently adapted to it. Each
phrase of the text must have its equivalent in a correct musical
declamation. It is from the sense of the text that the musical phrase
must emerge, the tones being intended to complete the effect of the
word. Psychological feeling can often be expressed with more depth
and power in music than ever by words. One of the chief properties
of music is that of depicting in vital and expressive colors the movements of the spirit, of the emotions, of communicating directly and
fully with the most profound sensibilities of the human heart; language,
on the other hand, creates for it a definite meaning, defines in some
fashion all its aspirations.

These convictions, solidly established on the absolute union of text
and music, make for the fact that the Russian school does not treat
the question of poetry lightly; the musicians who represent this school
resort, by preference, to the productions of the great poets. They seek
out art in the subject itself, and aspire, with their chosen text, to give
birth to a new creation which should be a work of art in two senses,
the poetic and musical.

For music as well as for libretto, *the structure of the scenes composing an opera must depend entirely on the relation of the characters,
and on the general movement of the play.* Here is an elementary logic
which the greatest composers sometimes overlook. In how many operas
one finds that a chorus or ensemble ignores the meaning of the words,
wastes an enormous amount of time on stage singing some *corriam* or
fuggiam, before they finally stir a step. Or, and here we have an em-

barrassment of riches, there is a catastrophe, some grave dramatic disaster; this is the signal for the cast to line up before the footlights, with the chorus ranged in rows at their heels, and break into a long piece to broad and slow movements; when this is finished, the applause and recalls done with, the catastrophe resumes its course. In defiance of good sense, opera music has taken certain arbitrary turns and bizarre shapes. One rarely finds opera pieces built otherwise than on two or three sections held together by colorless recitatives. Watch this hero of the lyric stage, tenor or baritone, as he comes forward to the prompter's box. He is going to sing his big aria. First, he must exhibit his declamatory talent, and so he commences with several phrases of recitative. Then, to prove his aptitude for broad singing, he attacks an andante cantabile; but he also excels, thank God, in bravura airs, adorned with fioriture, so along must come an allegro, at the end of which an almost impossible note, either high or low, bursts forth, held interminably over a fermata . . . As for the duos, trios, quartets, etc., they are, for the most part, tailored to the same pattern.

The Russian school understands all the falsity of these immutable, stereotyped forms. It is convinced that the musical development of an opera demands a complete independence of forms, and is governed only by the text and the dramatic situation. A certain regularity of form, clever architectural workmanship, embellished with liberties in good taste, are admissible in opera, provided they are well motivated; for instance, they can admit of a march, characteristic dances, an overture or entr'actes, essentially symphonic pieces. But these regular forms, culled from the realm of pure instrumental music, can not reasonably square with dramatic and ever-changing scenes, where the themes and rhythms might be impaired, where recapitulations and repeats might be contrary to the inner meaning of the action. Motives of great breadth or a sustained melody such as a cantilena, are always good in the right place, for example, in expressing lyric movements. But one can also modify them, making them reappear as fragments, recasting them in different ways; one can reduce them to short phrases of melodic recitative. All depends on the action in the scene; the music must never take a separate road and isolate itself from the text. A model of melodic form, no matter how successful, can never serve as the basis for several pieces in the same opera, for the reason that ordinarily two completely similar situations with analogous texts do not occur in the same lyric work.

The new Russian school does not reject ensembles or choruses, but it insists that scenes of this genre be seriously motivated; the pace of the drama must not be slowed down. Choruses represent the crowd, the people, and not merely the choristers; they must have a definite purpose, portray a mob, a riot, etc., and not be interspersed among other pieces for the sake of contrast only, or to allow the soloists a rest.

Furthermore, the new Russian school is striving musically to project the character and type of the dramatis personae as clearly as possible, to model each phrase of a rôle to an individual and not a general pattern, and lastly, to portray truthfully the historical epoch of the drama, and to depict the local color, the descriptive as well as the picturesque aspects of the action in its poetic as well as exact sense.

Doubtless all these principles have considerable affinity with Wagnerian ideas; but the methods of attaining the same end differ essentially between the two schools. Wagner concentrates all his musical interest on the orchestra, to the point of granting only secondary importance to the vocal part. While he is stating the theme in the orchestra, the characters in his operas deliver only fragments of recitatives which, taken separately, have neither intrinsic worth nor precise meaning. It is a completely false procedure. The personages in an opera hold the stage, they are not restricted to complementing the orchestra; they pronounce the words of the text, which of necessity dictate the music; it is through them that the action occurs; the public looks at them and listens to them; consequently, it is on them and not on the orchestra that the principal musical rôle must devolve. Thanks to the manner in which Wagner treats—or rather, mistreats—the question, the interest of the background comes to the fore; furthermore, in his work, orchestra and singing collide, battle one another, until the orchestra ends by killing the singing. Wagner seems to lend all his efforts to minimize the musical rôle of the characters in his works. On the contrary, the Russian musicians reserve musical supremacy, all the important phrases of the score (with rare exceptions) for the singers. For them the singers are the true interpreters of the musical ideas of the composer. In this one clearly sees that the new Russian school derives from Glinka and Dargomijsky.

To denote the character of each personage Wagner adopts the following procedure: in one fashion or another, he clothes his singer in a musical phrase, as with a costume, which he "wears" everywhere, and which announces each of his stage entrances. This device, simple and appropriate as its purpose may seem, does little honor to Wagnerian heroes: why are they condemned in perpetuity to one motive? Why are they denied announcing themselves in various ways? It recalls, as some have remarked, the naïve legends issuing from the mouths of people in colored medieval prints. The Russian composer is not so stingy with themes for his characters; he gives them as many as the situations seem to him to demand. It is true that he reserves the right to handle these themes in different ways (changing rhythm, color, harmony, etc.); in being developed and varied, they will lose none of their unity but will depict the character of the personages with all desired flexibility. Besides using orchestral fragments of phrases to symbolize a person, Wagner also uses them to express an *idea*, for example, vengeance, or even an inanimate object, a sword; the slightest reference to the idea, the most fleeting reminiscence of the object is enough for the phrase to reappear immediately like a jack-in-the-box. As if a person could not have a completely different opinion or quite another feeling on seeing the same object! It goes without saying that the Russian school is not given to similar errors.   [2]

CAMILLE SAINT-SAËNS

1835–1921

Pianist, organist, composer, conductor, critic, essayist, poet and drama-tist, versatile Saint-Saëns also represents all that is elegant in French culture. His music is rarely inspired in content, yet it possesses great technical facility and impeccable form. Similarly, his writings exhibit a stylistic fluency and clarity of which he was admittedly proud.

In 1871 Saint-Saëns and Roman Bussine founded the Societé Na-tionale de Musique, which they created in order to encourage the performance of French instrumental music. The Societé advanced the works of Franck, Chausson, Lalo, D'Indy and Fauré, among others. Saint-Saëns' own symphonic poems received performances through this organization. Two of his best efforts in this genre, the *Danse Macabre* and *Le Rouet d'Omphale*, are today the most frequently played pieces from his immense output. His showy piano concertos, once very popular with virtuosos, have been eased out of the repertoire because of their slim musical content.

PARIS CONSERVATORY

From: *Portraits et souvenirs,* 1899

I loved its antiquity, the utter absence of any modern note, its atmosphere of other days. I loved that absurd court with the wailing notes of sopranos and tenors, the rattling of pianos, the blasts of trum-pets and trombones, the arpeggios of clarinets, all uniting to form that ultra-polyphony which some of our composers have tried to attain— but without success. [1]

SIMPLICITY

From: *École buissonnière,* 1913

He who does not take a thorough pleasure in a simple chord progres-sion, well constructed, beautiful in its arrangement, does not love music; he who does not prefer the first "Prelude" in the *Well-Tempered*

Clavier played without nuances as the composer wrote it for the instrument, to the same prelude embellished with a passionate melody, does not love music; he who does not prefer a folk tune of a lovely character, or a Gregorian chant without any accompaniment to a series of dissonant and pretentious chords does not love music.   [2]

EMBELLISHMENTS

From: *Au courant de la vie*, 1914

Nowadays music is written pretty nearly as it should be executed; in the old days it was otherwise, and conventional signs were used which had to be translated. Performing old music as it is written is comparable to spelling a foreign language one does not know how to pronounce. The greatest difficulty, apparently, is the appoggiatura which is no longer in use in our time. Everybody interprets it in his own fashion according to his taste: now, this is not a matter of taste, but of erudition. It is not a question of knowing what one prefers, but what the composers intended to write.

Lastly, there is a multitude of signs the interpretation of which is sometimes impossible, all the textbooks of the period telling us that they can not be described, that one must have heard a teacher sing them. Happily, there is a great probability that these ornaments are not indispensable, their profusion being due to the bad taste of the period, and their omission is not at all regrettable.   [3]

OPERA SUBJECTS

From: *Portraits et souvenirs*, 1899

Oceans of ink have been spilled in discussing the question of whether the subjects of operas should be taken from history or mythology, and the question is still a moot one. To my mind it would have been better if the question had never been raised, for it is of little consequence what the answer is. The only worthwhile considerations are whether the music is good and the work interesting. But *Tannhäuser*, *Lohengrin*, *Tristan* and *Siegfried* appeared, and the question sprang up. The heroes of mythology, we are told, are invested with a prestige which historical characters can never have. Their deeds lose significance, and in their place we have their feelings, their emotions, to the great benefit of the operas. After these works, however, Hans Sachs (*Die Meistersinger*) appeared, and although he is not mythical at all, he is nevertheless a fine figure. But in this case the plot is of little account, for the interest lies mainly in the emotions—the only thing, it appears, which music with its divine language ought to express.

It is true that music makes it possible to simplify dramatic action, and it gives a chance, as well, for the free expression and play of sentiments, emotions and passions. In addition, music makes possible pantomimic scenes which could not otherwise be done, and the music itself flows more easily under such conditions. But that does not mean that such conditions are indispensable for music. Music in its flexibility and its adaptability offers inexhaustible resources. Give Mozart a fairy tale, and he creates without effort an immortal masterpiece.

Now, the supernatural lends itself admirably to expression in music and music finds in the supernatural a wealth of resources. But the resources are by no means indispensable. What music must have above all are emotions and passions, laid bare and set in action by what we term the situation. And where can one find more or better situations than in history?

From the time of Lulli until the end of the eighteenth century, French opera was legendary, that is to say, it was mythological in character and [so offered] material for a spectacle. Tragedy, as we know, does not do this, for it can be developed only with considerable difficulty when the stage is crowded with actors. Opera, on the contrary, which is free in its movements and can fill a vast stage, seeks for pomp, display, for halos in which gods and goddesses may appear, in fact, for anything that can be staged. If local color was not used, it was because local color had not been invented. Finally, as we all get tired of everything, so they tired of mythology. Then the historical work was adopted and appeared on the stage with success, as is well known. The historical method had no rival until *Robert le Diable* rather timidly brought back the legendary element which triumphed later in the work of Richard Wagner. From the point of view of opera, mythology supplies one advantage in the use of the miraculous. But the rest of the mythical element rather offers difficulties. Characters who never existed and in whom no one believes cannot be made interesting in themselves. They do not sustain, as is sometimes supposed, the music and poetry. On the contrary, the music and poetry give them such reality as they possess. We could not endure the interminable utterances of the mournful Wotan, if it were not for the wonderful music that accompanies them. Orpheus weeping over Euridice would not move us greatly, if Gluck had not known how to captivate us by his first notes. If it were not for Mozart's music, the puppets of the *Magic Flute* would amount to nothing.   [4]

BACH AND MOZART

From: Letter to Camille Bellaigue, Cairo, February 4, 1907

What gives Sebastian Bach and Mozart a place apart is that these two great expressive composers never sacrificed form to expression. As high as their expression may soar, their musical form remains supreme and all-sufficient.   [5]

COLOR IN BEETHOVEN AND HANDEL

From: Letter to Camille Bellaigue, Las Palmas,
January 23, 1897

First, concerning the famous "Chorus of Dervishes": Since you, just as I, have witnessed those mystical "spinning tops" whirling in Cairo, how is it that you have never noticed the identity of the triplets played by the flutes which accompany them with those in the chorus of the *Ruins of Athens?* In my opinion, it is impossible that Beethoven, through the simple intuition of genius, could have thought it up; he must have had an authentic document at his disposal. Obviously, the effect is much more beautiful in his work than in its "natural" state, but that is not the important point.

Then, on the subject of Handel: I have studied Handel considerably and, besides, having had the good fortune of browsing in the Queen's Library at Buckingham Palace, I was curious to see what the contemporaries and the predecessors of the great master wrote, and to discover why and in what way he had eclipsed them. I finally came to the odd conclusion that he had achieved his astonishing popularity through his use of the picturesque and the descriptive, something new and unheard-of at the time. Others besides him possessed the sovereign gift of writing choruses, handling fugues. What he added was color, that modern element which we no longer notice for good and sufficient reasons.

Here it cannot be a question of the exotic. Take a look at *Alexander's Feast, Israel in Egypt* and particularly *L'Allegro ed il Penseroso* with this point of view in mind, and try to forget all that has been done since. At every turn you will find the pursuit of the picturesque, the effects of imitation. It is real and very intense for the milieu in which it was produced, and where it seems to have been unknown up to then. [6]

THE WAGNER LITERATURE

From: Early Draft of the article "L'illusion wagnérienne,"
Revue de Paris, 1899

For forty years and more, newspaper and magazine articles, brochures and books have been accumulating on Richard Wagner, his works and his theories; for twenty-five years they have been swarming in every language. A library could be built with them. And each day appear still new articles, new brochures, and new books. One would think that after all of Wagner's own writings and the illuminating tract by Liszt on *Tannhäuser* and *Lohengrin* there would be little left to say about the theories, let alone anything else. Such an excess is really amazing.

But there is something still more surprising.

So long as these studies limit themselves to analysis of the works, all is well, except that it is perforce ever the same thing, and it is hard to see the need for the perpetual reiteration; but as soon as they approach the core of the question and venture into the heart of things, as soon as they try to explain wherein the new art differs *essentially* from the old, why music drama must be mythological, how the old and new art are separated by an insuperable abyss, and other similar questions, a thick fog descends on their style; their words conflict, become strange and incoherent, they talk gibberish, and finally sheer nonsense. Observe that though there are some madmen and imbeciles among these commentators, there are others, on the contrary, whose names are synonymous with intelligence and talent, yet they do not escape this fatal tendency.

For a long time I told myself: it is not the light which is lacking, it is my eye which is weak, and I forced myself to see. I made the most sincere and the most useless efforts to understand. Finally, not a little weary, I wrote one day to a critic noted for his clarity, in order to obtain, if possible, new light. He published my letter and responded with an article full of wit—he couldn't do otherwise—but which shed no new light whatsoever.

I had to renounce trying to understand, and then some lines hidden in the depths of my memory turned up and murmured very low in my ear:

Ce qui se conçoit bien s'énonce clairement
Et les mots pour le dire arrivent aisément.[1]

If all these notoriously intelligent people make themselves so badly
understood, I asked myself, can it be that they do not understand
themselves too well? What, so much mumbo jumbo, so much ambiguity
in order to explain to people how operas are hereafter to be written?
I understand all right, but you are wasting your breath. As long as the
public sees a stage with characters who express themselves in song,
they will call it opera. Why, because one has discovered a new form of
musico-dramatic presentation, is it necessary in discussing it, to use
abstruse and mystic phraseology such as one employs in the study of
the highest speculations of metaphysics and philosophy!   [7]

OVERCOLORATION IN MUSIC

From: Letter to Bellaigue, Cairo, January 30, 1907

In my opinion, the desire to push works of art beyond the realm of
art means simply to drive them into the realm of folly. Richard Strauss
is in the process of showing us the road.   [8]

[1] What is well conceived is clearly said, and the words to say it come easily
(Boileau, *L'art poétique*).

MILI ALEXEIVITCH BALAKIREV
1837–1910

The impetus towards nationalism in Russian music derived from Glinka and Dargomijsky, but leadership in the nationalist movement fell to Balakirev, the stronger, more dominating personality. The group of composers which he gathered around him was completely under his influence. He not only set the direction of their work, but minutely criticized and practically wrote their compositions. When they had achieved musical maturity and launched out on their own, their artistic independence was to him tantamount to repudiation. His resentment took the form of retiring from musical activity into a preoccupation with religion and mysticism, from which he rarely emerged—and then almost only to influence new and younger talents, for the most part less important than the initial group of Cui, Rimski-Korsakov, Moussorgsky and Borodin.

Self-taught both as composer and conductor, Balakirev was vehemently opposed to formal theoretical study, which he considered pedantry, inimical to genuine creativity. This lack of formal technical training and consequent slow pace in composition, as well as the time he spent in working on other people's creations, limited his own output. The two works which survive in occasional contemporary programs are the Oriental fantasy for piano, *Islamey*, and the symphonic poem, *Thamar*.

TCHAIKOVSKY'S *FATUM*

From: Letter to P. I. Tchaikovsky, St. Petersburg,
March 18, 1869

Laroche advises you to study examples of the classics. I don't advise this at all. You know these samples of the classics all too well as it is, and you also know that command of form and variety of forms have advanced considerably since then. In studying the classics you would learn again only the things you used to hear back in the days when Zaremba lectured you on the theory of the form of the rondo in connection with the fall of Adam and Eve. Better turn to Liszt in whose "Les Preludes," for instance, you will find precisely the form you would have needed for your *Fatum*, and you will see how wonderfully everything is motivated. There you will see neither a pieced together effect nor needless embroidery. True, there is some cheap, empty decoration . . . but this goes on for only a short while . . . and after a bit the music again comes into its own. He squeezes practically all the juice out of his themes . . . Unfortunately the Italian theme is very bad, but look what organized correlation between the parts.

You can see the same thing, for instance, in *A Night in Madrid*. I remind you of the latter because I am pleased to note that Glinka finds great favor with you—in the *Fatum* I could see that the chorus of "It will perish" had made a strong impression on you, one you can not get rid of. [1]

TCHAIKOVSKY'S OVERTURE *ROMEO AND JULIET*

From: Letter to P. I. Tchaikovsky, Berlin,
December 13, 1869

I rejoiced at last to receive your sketches from the new Overture. As you have already finished it and it even will be performed soon . . . I am telling you frankly my opinion of the themes you sent. The first theme is not at all to my liking. It is possible that in being worked out, it will achieve meaningful beauty, but written out naked, as you sent it to me, it does not present either beauty or strength and does not paint fittingly the character of Friar Lawrence. Here must be something in the manner of the Liszt chorales (*Der nächtliche Zug, Hunnenschlacht* and *St. Elizabeth*) with ancient Catholic character, resembling orthodoxy, while your theme has an entirely different character—the character of a quartet theme by Haydn, the genius of burgher music, awakening a strong thirst for beer. Here there is neither the ancient nor the Catholic; I rather see, in the manner of Gogol, comrade Kunz who wanted to cut off his nose to avoid the expense of snuff. However, it may be that in the treatment your theme achieves an entirely different character, and in that case, I retract my words.

Concerning the theme in B minor, this is not a theme, but a very beautiful introduction to a theme and after the C major running passage there certainly must be a strong, energetic, melodious design. I suppose that is the way it is, only you were too lazy to write it out for me.

The first D flat theme is very beautiful, although somewhat decadent, and the second D flat major is simply enchanting. I often play it and have a great wish to kiss you for it. Here there is delight and the sweetness of love and, in general, much which must be to the liking of the perverse German Albrecht. When I play

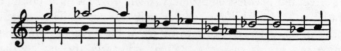

it appears to me that you are lying in the bath and that Artiha Padilla herself is rubbing your tummy with the hot fragrant suds. But one thing I will say against this theme: there is little inner spiritual love, but only physical, passionate torment with even a hint of the Italian. Romeo and Juliet are certainly not Persian lovers, but European. I do not know whether you will understand what I mean. I always feel I lack the gift of words when I enter into musical criticism and so try to some degree to clarify by example. I cite the first theme I come across in which, in my opinion, the love is more deeply felt: the second theme in Schumann's overture, *The Bride of Messina*. The theme has its defects—sickly towards the end and a bit sentimental—but the basic feeling of which it is full is true. In conclusion, I say to you that I impatiently desire to receive your score in order to have at last a full understanding of this brilliant Overture which I consider the best of your compositions, and the dedication of it to me is extremely agreeable.

It is your first composition which draws itself to one in its total beauty.   [2]

GEORGES BIZET

1838–1875

Bizet's correspondence with his two students, Edmond Galabert and Paul Lacombe, consists mainly of technical discussions, but it is also enlivened with keen evaluations of his musical contemporaries. To Mme Halévy, his mother-in-law, he writes enthusiastically of Wagner, but at the same time recognizes the German's human and musical weaknesses. In a letter to his mother from Rome, where he spent three years as a *Prix de Rome* winner, Bizet can speak as objectively of his own melodic gift, a talent which he considers essential to popular success.

Certainly his works contained enough beautiful melodies and brilliant effects to have won him acclaim during his lifetime, but unfortunately they gave him for the most part posthumous fame. Today his *Carmen* is frequently referred to as the "perfect" opera, yet it was received rather coldly when first staged—Bizet is said to have left the theater before the end of the première. He had never been to Spain before writing the work, yet it is considered a genuine reflection of Spanish life, though only outside Spain, and has served as a model for the Italian *verismo* school of operatic composers.

LETTERS FROM ROME

GENIUS

To Hector Gruyer, December 31, 1858

There are two kinds of genius: natural genius and rational genius. Though I admire the latter immensely, I will not hide the fact that the former has all my sympathies. Yes, I have the courage to prefer Raphael to Michelangelo, Mozart to Beethoven, and Rossini to Meyerbeer, which is equivalent to saying that if I had heard Rubini,[1] I would have preferred him to Duprez.[1] I do not place the one group in second rank in order to put the other in first; that would be absurd. It is just a matter of taste. One sort of idea exerts a stronger attraction on me than the other. When I see the *Last Judgment*, when I hear the *Eroica*

[1] Rubini and Duprez were famous tenors.

or the fourth act of the *Huguenots,* I am moved and surprised, and my eyes, ears and intelligence are inadequate to admire them enough. But when I hear the *Marriage of Figaro* or the second act of *William Tell,* I am altogether happy, I experience a feeling of well-being, a complete satisfaction, I forget everything. Ah, how fortunate they are who are thus gifted!   [1]

FACILITY IN ART

To his mother, January 22, 1859

Facility in art is almost indispensable, yet only when the man and the artist are mature does it cease to be a threat. I don't want to do anything that is merely stylish; I want to have ideas before beginning a piece.   [2]

VERDI

To his mother, February 19, 1859

Verdi is a man of great talent who lacks the essential quality which makes the great masters: style. But he has bursts of marvellous passion. His passion is brutal, it is true, but it is better to be impassioned in this way than not at all. His music is at times exasperating, but it is never boring. In short, I do not understand the fanatics or the detractors he has excited. In my opinion, he merits neither the one nor the other.

[3]

THE MELODIC GIFT

To his mother, March 19, 1859

You attribute the series of failures of which our better composers have been the victims for several years to the weakness of their libretti. You are right, but there is another reason: these composers haven't a complete talent. Some—Massé, for example—lack style, a broad conception. Others—David (Félicien), I suppose—lack musical experience and understanding, soul. Even the strongest lack the one means which the composer must have to make himself comprehensible to the public today: the melodic gift, which is quite wrongly called the "idea." One can be a great artist without having it, but then one must renounce money and popular success. But one may also be a superior person and possess this precious gift, witness Rossini. Rossini is the greatest of all because he has, like Mozart, all the qualities: loftiness, style and finally . . . the melodic sense. I am utterly convinced of what I am telling you, and that is why I have hope. I know my business well, I orchestrate very well, I am never ordinary, and I have finally discovered this eagerly sought open sesame. I have a dozen good melodies in my opera [*Les Pêcheurs de perles*], real ones, rhythmic and easily remembered, and yet I have made no concessions in my taste. I would like you to hear it all. You would see that I have already found a little of what I lacked so completely. Next year I shall try for real melodic line in grand opera. That is much more difficult, but it is already something to have found it in opéra comique.   [4]

ITALIAN MUSIC

From: Letter to Paul Lacombe, [?], March 11, 1867

I lived in Italy for three years and wanted no part of the country's disreputable way of life, though I was taken with the temperament of some of its composers. Moreover, my sensuous nature allowed itself to be carried away by this music, at once facile, lazy, amorous, sensual and passionate. I am by conviction, heart and soul, German. But sometimes I lose myself in low artistic places. And I must confess to you in a whisper that I get infinite pleasure from it. In a word, I love Italian music as one loves a mistress, but she must be charming. And when we have cited two thirds of *Norma*, four pieces from *Puritani*, three from *Somnambula*, two acts of *Rigoletto*, an act of *Trovatore* and just about half of *Traviata*—add *Don Pasquale*—we can throw the rest away anywhere you please. As for Rossini, he has his *William Tell*—his sun— *Count Ory*, the *Barber* and one act of *Otello*—his planets. Because of these we may pardon the terrible *Semiramide* and all his other sins. [5]

SOME CLASSICAL COMPOSERS

From: Letter to Paul Lacombe, [?], December, 1867

I place Beethoven above the greatest, the most famous. The *Choral Symphony* is for me the culminating point of our art. . . . Neither Mozart with his divine form, nor Weber with his powerful, colossal originality, nor Meyerbeer with his thundering dramatic genius can, in my opinion, dispute the crown of this Titan, this Prometheus of music. He is overwhelming.

Only one man knew how to compose quasi-improvised music, or at least, what seems such. That is Chopin. Here is a charming personality, strange, unique, inimitable.

To my mind, the repeating of expositions has become old-fashioned; most of Beethoven's and Mendelssohn's symphonies (and of course, Mozart's) would gain by being performed without repeats.   [6]

WAGNER'S *RIENZI*

From: Letter to Edmond Galabert, [?], April, 1869

Yesterday I attended the dress rehearsal of *Rienzi* at the Théâtre Lyrique. It began at 8 o'clock and finished at 2. Eighty musicians in the orchestra, thirty on the stage, a hundred and thirty in the chorus, a hundred and fifty supers. A badly constructed piece. A single rôle— Rienzi. A racket that cannot be described; a jumble of Italian motives; a bizarre and bad style; music of decadence rather than of the future. Wretched numbers! Admirable numbers! all in all, an astounding work, terrifically *alive:* a grandeur, an Olympian breath! Genius, immoderate, disorderly, but genius! Will it be a success? I don't know! The hall was filled, and no claque! Prodigious effects! Disastrous effects! Enthusiastic cries! then half-hour gloomy silences! Some maintained: "It's bad Verdi!" others: "It's good Wagner!" It is sublime! It's frightful! It's mediocre! It isn't bad! The audience is perplexed! It is very amusing. Few people have the courage to persist in their hatred of Wagner.   [7]

From: Letter to Mme Halévy, [?], May 29, 1871

WAGNER

It is the fate of great geniuses to be misunderstood by their contemporaries. Wagner is no friend of mine and I am fairly indifferent to him, yet I cannot forget the immeasurable enjoyment which I owe to this original genius. The charm of his music is inexpressible. Here are voluptuousness, tenderness, love.

If I played you some of it for a week, you would become passionately fond of it. Moreover, the Germans, who, alas, are just as good as we are musically, have understood that Wagner is one of their most solid pillars. This man is the nineteenth century German spirit incarnate.

You know very well how painful disdain can be to a great artist. Fortunately for Wagner, he is endowed with such insolent conceit that criticism can't touch his heart—admitting that he has a heart, which I doubt.

I will not go so far as you and I will not pronounce Beethoven's name alongside Wagner's. Beethoven is not a man, he is a god, like Shakespeare, like Homer, like Michelangelo! Well, take the most intelligent audience and play the greatest pages which our art possesses for them —the *Choral Symphony*. They will understand nothing, absolutely nothing. We have had this experience; we repeat it every year with the same result. It is only that Beethoven is fifty years dead and it is the fashion to find his music beautiful.

Judge for yourself, forgetting everything that you have heard said, forgetting the foolish and malicious articles and the most spiteful book published by Wagner [a book tearing down the French and French music], and you will see. It is not the music of the future—that means nothing—but it is, as you have said so well, the music of all times. . . .

Of course, in spite of my admiration, if I thought I were imitating Wagner, I would never write another note. A fool imitates. It is better to do inferior work of one's own than to copy someone else's. And besides, the more beautiful the model, the more ridiculous the imitation. Michelangelo, Shakespeare and Beethoven have been imitated. Heaven knows what horrors this rage for imitation has thrust on us.   [8]

SUCCESS IN ART

In art (music, painting, above all, sculpture) as in letters, what makes success is talent, and not ideas. The public (and I speak of intelligent people, the rest don't count: that's my democracy for you)—the public understands the idea *later*. To achieve this *later*, the artist's talent must manifest itself in an agreeable form and so ease the road for the public, not repel it from the outset.

Thus Auber, who had so much talent and few ideas, was almost always understood, while Berlioz, who had genius but no talent at all, was almost never understood.   [9]

VI

MOUSSORGSKY
TCHAIKOVSKY
DVOŘÁK
GRIEG
RIMSKI-KORSAKOV
FAURÉ
D'INDY
PUCCINI

MODESTE PETROVITCH MOUSSORGSKY

1839–1881

The most original, most vital of the "Big Five" was Moussorgsky; one might even call him the genius of the group. He was also one of the most national of all the Russian composers. In his music, which is primarily vocal, Russian folk song, with its melodic, rhythmic and harmonic idiom and its irregularities, played a tremendous role.

He speaks constantly in his letters of his search for realism and truth, both in speech and action. All his efforts are bent toward finding the exact combination of everyday speech and song. Each word must discover its *ton juste,* and the composer must be able to write to ordinary prose as well as poetry. Actually, his work is highly lyrical, but simple, direct, spare, and unmarred by undue ornamentation.

The complete fulfillment of his great gifts was aborted by a lack of solid technique and an addiction to drink—Rimski-Korsakov once remarked that Moussorgsky would "trans-cognac" himself. The awkward way in which he manipulated his abundant individual ideas and harmonies accounted for Rimski-Korsakov's revisions of his work. The many later arguments over the quality of the originals vs. revisions gave rise to a movement to reinstate the former. Even critics who prefer the revisions have to admit that they cancel out those features to which Moussorgsky owed his power. As Liadov observed: "It seems easy enough to correct Moussorgsky's defects; but when this is done, it is impossible not to feel that the result is no longer Moussorgsky."

TEXT AND MUSIC IN *THE MARRIAGE*

From: Letter to Ludmila Shestakova,
[Shilovo], July 30, [1868]

This is what I would like: my stage people should speak like living people; but besides this, their character and power of intonation, supported by the orchestra, which forms the musical pattern of their speech, must achieve their aim directly, that is, my music must be an artistic reproduction of human speech in all its finest shades. . . . That is the ideal toward which I strive.

Now I am working on Gogol's *Marriage*. The success of Gogol's speech depends on the actor, on his true intonation. I want to give Gogol his place and the actor his also; in other words, I want to speak musically as the characters of Gogol would wish to speak, and in such a way that no one could say it in any other way. In *Marriage* I am crossing the Rubicon. This is living prose in music. The scorn of musician-poets for common human speech, stripped of all heroic robes will not be found here; instead there is reverence toward the language of mankind; this is a reproduction of simple human speech. [1]

THE GERMANS AS VOCAL COMPOSERS

From: Letter tc Alexandra and Nadeshda Purgold,
Petrograd, June 20, 1870

The greatest German geniuses, Beethoven, Weber and Schumann (each in his own way) were poor vocal composers. . . . The Germans sing as they speak, but they speak *à faire tonner le gosier*, but when they compose for singing, then they do not think of the *gosier*, forcibly cramming human thought into the frame of a preconceived musical phrase.—As a people they are theoretical in music, too, and at every other step fall into abstraction. Educated on the Russian soil of realism, you will not (I hope) like the German roosters' *Sehnsucht*. [2]

TECHNIQUE

From: Letter to V. V. Stasov, Petrograd, July 13, 1872

Maybe I'm afraid of technique, because I'm poor at it? However, there are some who will stand up for me in art, and in this respect as well. For example, I cannot bear it when a hostess serves a good pie she has prepared and, while we are eating, says: "A million *puds* of butter, five hundred eggs, a whole bed of cabbages, 150¼ fish. . . ." You are eating the pie and it tastes good, then you hear all about the kitchen, and at once you can imagine the cook, always dirty, a chopped-off chicken head lying on a bench, gutted fish on another . . . and well, the pie grows less tasty. There is in ripe artistic productions that side of chaste purity, that when touched by dirty paws, grows loathsome.

In truth, until the artist musician rids himself of his diapers, his braces, straps, so long will the *symphonic* priests rule, setting up their Talmud "of the 1st and 2nd editions," as the alpha and omega in the life of art. The little brains sense that their Talmud cannot be used in living art; where there are people and life, there is no place for prejudicial paragraphs and articles. And so they cry: "Drama, the stage, they cramp us—give us space!" And here they go giving free rein to their brains: "The world of sounds is unlimited!" Yes, but their brains are limited, so what use is this sound of worlds, or rather world of sounds! One gets as much space when lying on "the lawn and following the flight of the heavenly clouds": there's a fleecy lamb, there's an old granddad, there's simply nothing at all, then suddenly, a Prussian soldier. I can't blame Polonius for agreeing with Hamlet about the clouds. The esteemed cloud is very changeable and in the wave of the hand, may turn from a camel to, perhaps, a Laroche.[1] It isn't the symphonies I object to, but symphonists—incorrigible conservatives. So do not tell me why our musicians chatter more often about technique than about aims and historical tasks—because, this derives *from that*.   [3]

MUSICAL GIANTS

From: Letter to V. V. Stasov, St. Petersburg,
October 18, 1872

In poetry there are two giants: coarse Homer and refined Shakespeare. In music there are two giants: the thinker Beethoven, and the super-thinker Berlioz. When around these four we gather all their generals and aides-de-camp, we have a pleasant company; but what has this company of subalterns achieved? Skipping and dancing along in the paths marked out by the giants—but to dare to "go very far ahead," this is terrifying!   [4]

OPERA

From: Letter to Arseni Golenishchev-Kutuzov,
Tsarskoye-Selo, August 15, 1877

Pushkin wrote Boris in dramatic form, but not for the stage; Gogol wrote *The Fair at Sorochintzi* in the form of a story—and, of course, not for the stage. But both giants with their creative power projected so subtly the contours of scenic action that all one has to do is to apply the colors. But woe to him whose whim it is to use Pushkin or Gogol for his only text. . . . As only the *genuine, sensitive* nature of an artist can create in the realm of the word, the musician must maintain a very "polite" attitude towards the creation, in order to penetrate into its very substance, into the very *essence* of that which the musician

[1] Music critic in St. Petersburg.

intends to embody in musical form. The genuine, *truly artistic* cannot be anything but capricious, because *independently* it cannot easily be embodied in another artistic form, because it is *independent* and demands profound study and sacred love. But when artistic kinship between workers in different fields of art does work out—it's a fine trip!   [5]

SELF-EVALUATION

Prepared for Riemann's *Musik-Lexikon*, June 1880

Moussorgsky cannot be classed with any existing group of musicians, either by the character of his compositions or by his musical views. The formula of his artistic *profession de foi* may be explained by his view, as a composer, of the task of art: art is a means of communicating with people, not an aim in itself. This guiding principle has defined the whole of his creative activity. Proceeding from the conviction that human speech is strictly controlled by musical laws, he considers the task of musical art to be the reproduction in musical sounds not merely of the mood of a feeling, but chiefly of the mood of human speech. Acknowledging that in the realm of art only artist-reformers such as Palestrina, Bach, Gluck, Beethoven, Berlioz and Liszt have created the laws of art, he considers these laws as not immutable but liable to change and progress, like the entire spiritual world of man.   [6]

PETER ILYITCH TCHAIKOVSKY

1840-1893

The letters to his patron, Nadezhda von Meck, reflect one almost complete, if somewhat romanticized aspect of Tchaikovsky's career—and his was the first truly professional career in Russian musical history. He took up music only in his twenties—previously he had worked as a government clerk—but he devoted the rest of his life to it entirely.

Tchaikovsky was less vehemently national than the members of the "Five." He employed Russian folk themes in his compositions, but not to the extent that they did, nor with the same passion. He chose Russian subjects for his operas, but his treatment of them was not necessarily Russian, for his study with Rubinstein and his travels outside Russia gave him a West European outlook. Yet he was neither indifferent nor antagonistic to the "Five," as general opinion would have it. There is a volume of correspondence between him and Balakirev in which the works Tchaikovsky submitted to the latter are thoroughly criticized, and suggestions for improvement freely offered and accepted. He had a healthy respect for Rimski-Korsakov and for his efforts to fortify his academic background, and a sympathetic insight into the genius of Moussorgsky.

Like so many cultivated and travelled Russians, he was strongly Francophile. His admiration for Bizet was boundless. The German mind, on the other hand, was antipathetic to him. His revulsion against Brahms seemed almost physical; he admired some of Wagner's music, if not his ideas or his longwindedness. He once wrote Mme von Meck that he felt Wagner was a symphonist rather than an opera composer, great rather than good.

THE "BIG FIVE"

From: Letter to Mme von Meck, San Remo,
December 24, 1877 (January 5, 1878)

The young Petersburg composers are very gifted, but they are all impregnated with the most horrible presumptuousness and a purely amateur conviction of their superiority to all other musicians in the universe. The one exception, in latter days, has been Rimski-Korsakov. He was an "auto-dictator," like the rest, but recently he has undergone a complete change. By nature he is very earnest, honorable, and conscientious. As a young man he dropped into a set which first solemnly assured him he was a genius, and then proceeded to convince him that he had no need to study, that academies were destructive to all inspiration and dried up creative activity. At first he believed all this. His earliest compositions bear the stamp of striking ability and a lack of theoretical training. The circle to which he belonged was a mutual admiration society. Each member was striving to imitate the work of another, after proclaiming it as something very wonderful. Consequently the whole set suffered from one-sidedness, lack of individuality, and mannerisms. Rimski-Korsakov is the only one among them who discovered, five years ago, that the doctrines preached by this circle had no sound basis, that their mockery of the schools and the classical masters, their denial of authority and of the masterpieces, was nothing but ignorance. I possess a letter dating from that time which moved me very deeply. Rimski-Korsakov was overcome by despair when he realized how many unprofitable years he had wasted, and that he was following a road which led nowhere. He began to study with such zeal that the theory of the schools soon became to him an indispensable atmosphere. During one summer he completed innumerable exercises in counterpoint and sixty-four fugues, ten of which he sent me for inspection. From contempt for the schools, Rimski-Korsakov suddenly went over to the cult of musical technique. Shortly after this, his symphony and also his quartet appeared. Both works are full of obscurities and —as you will justly observe—bear the stamp of dry pedantry. At present he appears to be passing through a crisis, and it is hard to predict how it will end. Either he will turn out a great master, or be lost in contrapuntal intricacies.

Cui is a gifted amateur. His music is not original, but graceful and elegant; it is too coquettish, "made-up"—so to speak. At first it pleases, but soon satiates us. That is because Cui's specialty is not music, but fortification, about which he has to give a number of lectures in the various military schools in St. Petersburg. He himself once told me he could only compose by picking out his melodies and harmonies as he sat at the piano. When he hit upon some pretty idea, he worked it up in every detail, and this process was very lengthy, so that his opera, *Ratcliff*, for instance, took him ten years to complete. But, as I have said, we cannot deny that he has talent of a kind—and at least taste and instinct.

Borodin—aged fifty—Professor of Chemistry at the Academy of

Medicine, also possesses talent, a very great talent, which, however, has come to nothing for want of instruction, and because blind fate has led him into the science laboratories instead of a vital musical existence. He has less taste than Cui, and his technique is so poor that he cannot write a bar without assistance.

With regard to Moussorgsky, as you very justly remark, he is "used up." His gifts are perhaps the most remarkable of all, but his nature is narrow, and he has no aspirations towards self-perfection. He has been too easily led astray by the absurd theories of his set and the belief in his own genius. Besides which, his nature is not of the finest quality; he likes what is coarse, unpolished, and ugly. He is the exact opposite of the distinguished and elegant Cui.

Moussorgsky plays with his lack of polish; he even seems proud of his want of skill, writing just as it comes to him, believing blindly in the infallibility of his genius. As a matter of fact, his very original talent flashes forth now and then.

Balakirev is the greatest personality of the entire circle. But he lapsed into silence before he accomplished much. He possesses a wonderful talent which various fatal hindrances have helped to extinguish. After having proclaimed his agnosticism rather widely, he suddenly became "pious." Now he spends all his time in church, fasts, kisses the relics—and does very little else. In spite of his great gifts, he has done a great deal of harm. For instance, it was he who ruined Korsakov's early career by assuring him he had no need to study. He is the inventor of all the theories of this remarkable circle which unites so many undeveloped, falsely developed, or prematurely decayed talents.

These are my frank opinions of these gentlemen. What a sad phenomenon! So many talents from which—with the exception of Rimski-Korsakov—we can scarcely hope for anything serious. But this is always our case in Russia: vast forces which are impeded by the fatal shadow of a Plevna from taking the open field and fighting as they should. But all the same, these forces exist. This Moussorgsky, with all his ugliness, speaks a new idiom. Beautiful it may not be, but it is new. We may reasonably hope that Russia will one day produce a whole school of strong men who will open up new paths of art.   [1]

RICHARD WAGNER AND THE *RING*

From: Letter to Mme von Meck, Vienna,
November 26 (December 8), 1877

What a Don Quixote is Wagner! He expends all his strength in pursuing the impossible, and all the time, if he would but follow the natural bent of his extraordinary gift, he might evoke a whole world of musical beauties. In my opinion Wagner is a symphonist by nature. He is gifted with genius which has wrecked itself upon his tendencies; his inspiration is paralyzed by theories which he has invented, and, *nolens volens*, wants to put into practice. In his efforts to attain "reality," "truth" and "rationalism," he lets *music* slip quite out of sight, so that in his four latest operas it is more often than not conspicuous by its absence. I cannot call music that which consists of kaleidoscopic, shifting phrases which succeed each other without a break and never come to a close, that is to say, never give the ear the least chance to rest upon musical form. Not a single broad, rounded melody, nor yet one moment of repose for the singer! The latter must always pursue the orchestra and be careful never to lose his note, which has no more importance in the score than some note in the fourth horn. But there is no doubt Wagner is a great symphonist. I will prove to you by one example how far the symphonic prevails over the operatic style in his operas. You have probably heard his celebrated "Ride of the Valkyries?" What a great and marvellous picture! How we actually seem to see these fierce heroines flying on their magic steeds amid thunder and lightning! In the concert room this piece makes an extraordinary impression. On the stage, in view of the cardboard rocks, the canvas clouds, and the soldiers running about awkwardly in the background—in a word, seen in this very inadequate theatrical heaven, which makes a poor pretence of recreating the illimitable realms above—the music loses all power of expression. Here the stage does not enhance the effect, but acts rather like a wet blanket. Finally, I cannot understand, and never shall, why the *Nibelungen* should be considered a literary masterpiece. As a national saga, perhaps, but as a libretto—distinctly not!

Wotan, Brünnhilde, Fricka, and the rest are all so impossible, so little human, that it is very difficult to feel any sympathy with their destinies. And how little life! For three whole hours Wotan lectures Brünnhilde upon her disobedience. How wearisome! And with it all, there are many fine and beautiful episodes of purely symphonic description.   [2]

BRAHMS AND HIS *CONCERTO FOR VIOLIN*

From: Letter to Mme von Meck, Rome,
February 18 (March 1), 1880

The *Concerto* of Brahms does not please me better than any of his other works. He is certainly a great musician, even a Master, but his mastery overwhelms his inspiration. So many preparations and circum-

locutions for something which ought to come and charm us at once—
and nothing does come but boredom. His music is not warmed by any
genuine emotion. It lacks poetry, but makes great pretensions to profundity. These depths contain nothing; they are void. Take the opening
of the *Concerto*, for instance. It is an introduction, a preparation for
something fine; an admirable pedestal for a statue; but the statue is
lacking, we only get a second pedestal piled upon the first. I do not
know whether I have properly expressed the thoughts, or rather feelings,
which Brahms's music awakens in me. I mean to say that he never expresses anything, or, when he does, he fails to express it fully. His music
is made up of fragments of some indefinable *something*, skillfully welded
together. The design lacks definite contour, color, life.

But I must simply confess that, independent of any definite reproach,
Brahms, as a musical personality, is antipathetic to me. I cannot abide
him. Whatever he does—I remain unmoved and cold. It is a purely instinctive feeling.   [3]

BIZET'S *CARMEN*

From: Letter to Mme von Meck, Simski,
July 18 (30), 1880

Yesterday evening—to take a rest from my own work—I played
through Bizet's *Carmen* from cover to cover. I consider it a *chef-
d'oeuvre* in the fullest sense of the word: one of those rare compositions
which seems to reflect most strongly in itself the musical tendencies of
a whole generation. It seems to me that our period differs from earlier
ones in this one characteristic: contemporary composers *are engaged in
the pursuit of charming and piquant effects,* unlike Mozart, Beethoven,
Schubert, and Schumann. What is the so-called New Russian School but
the cult of varied and pungent harmonies, of original orchestral combinations and every kind of purely external effect? Musical ideas give
place to this or that union of sounds. Formerly there was *composition,
creation;* now (with few exceptions) there is only research and invention. This development of musical thought is by nature purely intellectual, consequently contemporary music is clever, piquant, and eccentric, but cold and lacking the glow of true emotion. And behold,
a Frenchman comes on the scene, in whom these qualities of piquancy
and pungency are not the outcome of effort and reflection, but flow
from his pen as in a free stream, flattering the ear, but touching us also.
It is as though he said to us: "You ask nothing great, superb, or grandiose
—you want something *pretty*, here is a *pretty opera*"; and truly I know

of nothing in music which is more representative of that element which I call *the pretty* (le joli). . . . I cannot play the last scene without tears in my eyes; the gross rejoicings of the crowd who look on at the bullfight, and, side by side with this, the poignant tragedy and death of the two principal characters, pursued by an evil fate, who come to their inevitable end through a long series of sufferings.

I am convinced that ten years hence *Carmen* will be the most popular opera in the world. But no one is a prophet in his own land. In Paris *Carmen* has had no real success.   [4]

COMPOSITION

From: Letter to Mme von Meck, Kamenka, June 24 (July 6), 1878

You want to know my methods of composing . . . it is very difficult to give a satisfactory answer to your question, because the circumstances under which a new work comes into the world vary considerably in each case.

(1) Works which I compose on my own initiative—that is to say, from an invincible inward impulse.

(2) Works which are inspired by external circumstances: the wish of a friend, or publisher, and *commissioned* works.

Here I should add that experience has taught me that the intrinsic value of a work has nothing to do with its place in one or the other of these categories. It frequently happens that a composition which owes its existence to external influences proves very successful, while one that proceeds entirely from my own initiative may, for various indirect reasons, turn out far less well. These indirect circumstances, upon which depends the mood in which a work is written, are of the greatest importance. During the actual time of creative activity, complete quiet is absolutely necessary to the artist. In this sense every work of art, even a musical composition, is *objective*. Those who imagine that a creative artist can—through the medium of his art—express his feelings at the moment when he is *moved*, make the greatest mistake. Emotions—sad or joyful—can only be expressed *retrospectively*, so to speak. Without any special reason for rejoicing, I may be moved by the most cheerful creative mood, and vice versa, a work composed in the happiest surroundings may be touched with dark and gloomy colors.

In a word, an artist lives a double life: an everyday human life and an artistic life, and the two do not always go hand in hand.

In any case, it is absolutely necessary for a composer to shake off all the cares of daily existence, at least for a time, and give himself up entirely to his art-life. Works belonging to the first category do not require the least effort of will. It is only necessary to obey our inward promptings, and if our material life does not crush our artistic life under its weight of depressing circumstances, the work progresses with inconceivable rapidity. Everything else is forgotten, the soul throbs with an incomprehensible and indescribable excitement, so that, almost before we can follow this swift flight of inspiration, time passes literally unreckoned and unobserved.

There is something *somnambulistic* about this condition. *On ne s'entend pas vivre*. It is impossible to describe such moments. Everything that flows from one's pen, or merely passes through one's brain (for such moments often come at a time when writing is an impossibility) under these circumstances is *invariably good*, and if no external obstacle comes to hinder the creative glow, the result will be an artist's best and most perfect work. Unfortunately, such external hindrances are inevitable. A duty has to be performed, dinner is announced, a letter arrives, and so on. This is the reason why there exist so few compositions which are of equal quality throughout. Hence the *joins, patches, inequalities and discrepancies*.

For the works in my second category, it is necessary to *get into the mood*. To do so, we are often obliged to fight indolence and disinclination. Besides this, there are many other fortuitous circumstances. Sometimes the victory is easily gained. At other times inspiration eludes us, and cannot be recaptured. I consider it, however, the *duty* of an artist not to be conquered by circumstances. He must not wait. Inspiration is a guest who does not care to visit those who are indolent.

I may say that, under normal conditions, there is no hour of the day in which I cannot compose. Sometimes I observe with curiosity that an uninterrupted activity—independent of the subject of the conversation I may be carrying on—continues its course in that department of my brain which is devoted to music. Sometimes it takes a preparatory form, that is, the consideration of all details that concern the elaboration of some projected work; another time it may be an entirely new and independent musical idea, and I make an effort to hold it fast in my memory.

Now I will try to describe my actual procedure in composition.

I usually write my sketches on the first piece of paper to hand. I jot them down in the most abbreviated form. A melody never stands alone, but invariably with the harmonies which belong to it. These two elements of music, together with the rhythm, must never be separated; every melodic idea brings its own inevitable harmony and its suitable rhythm. If the harmony is very intricate, I set down in the sketch a few details on the working out of the parts; when the harmony is quite simple, I put in only the bass, or a figured bass, and sometimes not even this. If the sketch is intended for an orchestral work, the ideas appear ready-colored by some special instrumental combination. The original plan or instrumentation often undergoes some modification.

The text must *never* be written after the music, for if music is written to given words only, these words invoke a suitable musical expression. It is quite possible to fit words to a short melody, but in treating a serious work such adaptation is not permissible. It is equally impossible to compose a symphonic work and afterwards to attach to it a programme, since every episode of the chosen programme should evoke its corresponding musical presentment. This stage of composition—the sketch—is remarkably pleasant and interesting. It brings an indescribable delight, accompanied, however, by a kind of unrest and nervous agitation. Sleep is disturbed and meals forgotten. Nevertheless, the development of the project proceeds tranquilly. The instrumentation of a work which is completely thought out and matured is a most enjoyable task.

The same does not apply to the bare sketch of a work for pianoforte or voice, or little pieces in general, which are sometimes very tiresome.

You ask: Do I confine myself to established forms? Yes and no. Some compositions imply the use of traditional forms, but only as regards their general features, the sequence of the movements. The details permit of considerable freedom of treatment, if the development of the ideas requires it.

You ask me about melodies built upon the notes of the harmony. I can assure you, and prove it by many examples, that it is quite possible, by means of rhythm and the transposition of the notes, to evolve millions of new and beautiful melodic combinations. But this applies only to homophonic music. With polyphonic music such a method of building up a melody would interfere with the independence of the parts. In the music of Beethoven, Weber, Schumann, Mendelssohn, and especially Wagner, we frequently find melodies which consist of the notes of the common chord; a gifted musician will always be able to invent a new and interesting fanfare. [5]

From: Letter to Mme von Meck, Kamenka,
June 25 (July 7), 1878

Yesterday, when I wrote you about my methods of composing, I did not sufficiently enter into that phase which related to the working out of the sketch. This phase is of primary importance. What has been set down in a moment of ardor must now be critically examined, improved, extended, or condensed, as the form requires. Sometimes one must do oneself violence, must sternly and pitilessly take part against oneself, before one can mercilessly erase things thought out with love and enthusiasm. I cannot complain of poverty of imagination, or lack of inventive power; but on the other hand, I have always suffered from my want of skill in the management of form. Only after strenuous labor have I at last succeeded in making the form of my compositions correspond, more or less, with their contents. Formerly I was careless and did not give sufficient attention to the critical overhauling of my sketches. Consequently my "seams" showed, there was no organic union between my individual episodes. This was a very serious defect, and I only improved gradually as time went on; but the form of my works will never be *exemplary*, because, although I can modify, I cannot radically alter the essential qualities of my musical temperament.   [6]

INSTRUMENTATION

From: Letter to Mme von Meck, Clarens,
March 5 (17), 1878

You ask how I manage my instrumentation. I never compose in the abstract; that is to say, the musical thought never appears otherwise than in a suitable external form. In this way I invent the musical idea and the instrumentation simultaneously. Thus I thought out the scherzo of our symphony [*Fourth Symphony*] at the moment of its composition —exactly as you heard it. It is inconceivable except as pizzicato. Were it played with the bow, it would lose all its charm and be a mere body without a soul.

As regards the Russian element in my works, I may tell you that not infrequently I begin a composition with the intention of introducing some folk melody into it. Sometimes it comes of its own accord, unbidden (as in the finale of our symphony). As to this national element in my work, its affinity with the folk songs in some of my melodies and harmonies comes from my having spent my childhood in the country, and, from my earliest years, having been impregnated with the characteristic beauty of our Russian folk music. I am passionately fond of the national element in all its varied expressions. In a word, I am Russian in the fullest sense of the word.   [7]

ANTONIN DVOŘÁK

1841–1904

Influenced from his childhood by his native music, Dvořák incorporated Bohemian folk song or its spirit in a major part of his composition. It is natural, then, that when he came to the United States in 1892 to act as director of the National Conservatory of Music in New York, he should have evinced a strong interest in American folk music, the Negro element of which particularly attracted him. Among the fruits of his two years' stay in this country were the *American* quartet (Op. 96) and the symphony *From the New World*, both based on the American folk idiom. The symphony was orchestrated in Spillville, Iowa, a colony of Bohemian immigrants, where he spent his summers. The similarity between one of its principal subjects and "Swing Low, Sweet Chariot" has often been commented upon, although Dvořák repeatedly maintained that he never quoted actual themes.

The following article, a summary of his impressions of music in America, written in 1895 with the coöperation of Edwin Emerson, Jr., at the request of *Harper's Magazine*, has such a contemporaneous ring that it might have appeared yesterday. Most of the problems he discusses still burden the American musical scene.

With the establishment of music schools such as Eastman in Rochester (1918), Juilliard in New York (1919), Curtis in Philadelphia (1924), not to mention numerous other institutions functioning throughout the country, the opportunities for study available to the talented student are not so tragically limited as they were in his day. However, the position of the professional composer and performer is just about as uncertain as it was then. Now as then there exists only one major opera company, fairly inaccessible to the average audience. There are certainly more orchestras dotting the country today than in Dvořák's time; their personnel is perhaps predominantly American, but the actual situation has not been alleviated, since practically none is self-supporting. The questions of opera in English, of native operas cast with native singers, the creation of repertory theaters as well as orchestras in all of our large cities and their partial support through government, state or municipal subsidy are still current topics of discussion.

MUSIC IN AMERICA

From: Article in *Harper's Magazine*, February, 1895

The two American traits which must impress the foreign observer, I find, are the unbounded patriotism and capacity for enthusiasm of most Americans. Unlike the more diffident inhabitants of other countries, who do not "wear their hearts upon their sleeves," the citizens of America are always patriotic, and no occasion seems to be too serious or too slight for them to give expression to this feeling. Thus nothing better pleases the average American, especially the American youth, than to be able to say that this or that building, this or that new patent appliance, is the finest or the grandest in the world. This, of course, is due to that other trait—enthusiasm. The enthusiasm of most Americans for all things new is apparently without limit. It is the essence of what is called "push"—American push. Every day I meet with this quality in my pupils. They are unwilling to stop at anything. In the matters relating to their art they are inquisitive to a degree that they want to go to the bottom of all things at once. It is as if a boy wished to dive before he could swim.

At first, when my American pupils were new to me, this trait annoyed me, and I wished them to give more attention to the one matter in hand rather than to everything at once. But now I like it, for I have come to the conclusion that this youthful enthusiasm and eagerness to take up everything is the best promise for music in America. The same opinion, I remember, was expressed by the director of the conservatory in Berlin,[1] who, from his experience with American students of music, predicted that America within twenty or thirty years would become the first musical country.

Only when the people in general, however, begin to take as lively an interest in music and art as they now take in more material matters will the arts come into their own. Let the enthusiasm of the people once be excited, and patriotic gifts and bequests must surely follow.

It is a matter of surprise to me that all this has not come long ago. When I see how much is done in every other field by public-spirited men in America—how schools, universities, libraries, museums, hospitals, and parks spring up out of the ground and are maintained by generous gifts—I can only marvel that so little has been done for music. After two hundred years of almost unbroken prosperity and expansion, the net results for music are a number of public concert halls of most recent growth, several musical societies with orchestras of noted excellence, such as the Philharmonic Society in New York, the orchestras of Mr.

[1] Probably Joseph Joachim, director of the Hochschule für Musik.

Thomas[1] and Mr. Seidl,[2] and the superb orchestra supported by a public-spirited citizen [3] of Boston; one opera company, which only the upper classes can hear or understand, and a national conservatory which owes its existence to the generous forethought of one indefatigable woman.[4]

It is true that music is the youngest of the arts, and must therefore be expected to be treated as Cinderella, but is it not time that she were lifted from the ashes and given a seat among the equally youthful sister arts in this land of youth until the coming of the fairy godmother and the prince of the crystal slipper?

Art, of course, must always go a-begging, but why should this country alone, which is so justly famed for the generosity and public spirit of its citizens, close its door to the poor beggar? In the Old World this is not so. Since the days of Palestrina . . . princes and prelates have vied with each other in extending a generous hand to music. Since the days of Pope Gregory the Church has made music one of her own chosen arts. In Germany and Austria, princes like Esterházy, Lobkowitz, and Harrach, who supported Haydn and Beethoven, or the king of Bavaria, who did so much for Wagner, with many others, have helped create a demand for good music, which has since become universal, while in France all governments, be they monarchies, empires or republics, have done their best to carry on the noble work that was begun by Louis XIV. Even the little republic of Switzerland annually sets aside a budget for the furtherance of music, literature and the arts.

The great American republic alone, in its national government as well as in the several governments of the States, suffers art and music to go without encouragement. Trades and commerce are protected, funds are voted away for the unemployed, schools and colleges are endowed, but music must go unaided, and be content if she can get the support of a few private individuals like Mrs. Jeannette M. Thurber and Mr. H. L. Higginson.

Not long ago a young man came to me and showed me his compositions. His talent seemed so promising that I at once offered him a

[1] Theodore Thomas (1835–1905), conductor of the Chicago Orchestra from its inception in 1891.

[2] Anton Seidl (1850–98), succeeded Thomas as conductor of the New York Philharmonic Society in 1891; he performed Dvořák's Symphony "From the New World" in 1893.

[3] Henry Lee Higginson (1834–1919) established the Boston Symphony Orchestra in 1881 with an endowment of $1,000,000.

[4] The National Conservatory of Music of America was founded in New York City in 1881 by Mrs. Jeannette M. Thurber; Dvořák was its director from 1892–5.

scholarship in our school, but he sorrowfully confessed that he could not afford to become my pupil because he had to earn his living by keeping books in Brooklyn. Even if he came just two afternoons in the week, or on Saturday afternoon only, he said, he would lose his employment, on which he and others had to depend. I urged him to arrange the matter with his employer, but he only received the answer: "If you want to play, you can't keep books. You will have to drop one or the other." He dropped his music.

In any other country, the State would have made some provision for such a deserving scholar, so that he could have pursued his natural calling without having to starve. With us in Bohemia, the Diet each year votes a special sum of money for just such purposes, and the imperial government in Vienna on occasion furnishes other funds for talented artists. Had it not been for such support I should not have been able to pursue my studies when I was a young man. Owing to the fact that, upon the kind recommendation of such men as Brahms, Hanslick and Herbeck,[1] the Minister of Public Education in Vienna on five successive years sent me sums ranging from four to six hundred florins, I could pursue my work and get my compositions published, so that at the end of that time I was able to stand on my own feet. This has filled me with lasting gratitude towards my country.

Such an attitude of the State towards deserving artists is not only kind but wise. For it cannot be emphasized too strongly that art, as such does not "pay," to use an American expression—at least, not in the beginning—and that the art that has to pay its own way is apt to become vitiated and cheap.

Just as the State here provides for its poor, industrial scholars and university students, so should it help the would-be students of music and art. As it is now, the poor musician not only cannot get his necessary instruction in the first place, but if by any chance he has acquired it, he has small prospects of making his chosen calling support him in the end. Why is this? Simply because the orchestras in which first-class players could find a place in this country can be counted on one hand; while of opera companies where native singers can be heard, and where the English tongue is sung, there is none at all. Another thing which discourages the student of music is the unwillingness of publishers to take anything but light and trashy music. European publishers are bad enough in that respect, but the American publishers are worse. Thus,

[1] Johann Herbeck (1831–77), conductor in Vienna, like Brahms and Hanslick a member of the Austrian Commission for the State Music Prize.

when one of my pupils last year produced a very creditable work, and a thoroughly American composition at that, he could not get it published in America, but had to send it to Germany, where it was at once accepted. The same is true of my own compositions on American subjects, each of which has had to be published abroad.

No wonder American composers and musicians grow discouraged, and regard the more promising conditions of music in other countries with envy! Such a state of affairs should be a source of mortification to all truly patriotic Americans. Yet it can be easily remedied. . . .

Our musical conservatory in Prague was founded but three generations ago, when a few nobles and patrons of music subscribed five thousand florins which was then the annual cost of maintaining the school. Yet that little school flourished and grew, so that now more than sixfold that amount is annually expended. Only lately a school for organ music has been added to the conservatory, so that the organists of our churches can learn to play their instruments at home, without having to go to other cities. Thus a school benefits the community in which it is. . . .

If a school of art can grow so in a country of but six million inhabitants, what much brighter prospects should it not have in a land of seventy millions? The important thing is to make a beginning, and in this the State should set an example.

They tell me that this cannot be done. I ask, why can't it be done? If the old commonwealths of Greece and Italy, and the modern republics of France and Switzerland, have been able to do this, why cannot America follow their example? The money certainly is not lacking. Constantly we see great sums of money spent for the material pleasures of the few, which, if devoted to the purposes of art, might give pleasure to thousands. If schools, art museums and libraries can be maintained at the public expense, why should not musical conservatories and playhouses? The function of the drama, with or without music, is not only to amuse, but to elevate and instruct while giving pleasure. Is it not in the interest of the State that this should be done in the most approved manner, so as to benefit all of the citizens? Let the owners of private playhouses give their performances for diversion only, let those who may, import singers who sing in foreign tongues, but let there be at least one intelligent power that will see to it that the people can hear and see what is best, and what can be understood by them, no matter how small the demand.

That such a system of performing classic plays and operas pleases the people was shown by the attitude of the populace in Prague. There the people collected money and raised subscriptions for over fifty years

to build a national playhouse. In 1880 they at last had a sufficient amount
and the "National Theatre" was accordingly built. It had scarcely been
built when it was burned to the ground. But the people were not to be
discouraged. Everybody helped, and before a fortnight was over more
than a million had been collected, and the house was at once built up
again, more magnificent than it was before.

In answer to such arguments I am told that there is no popular demand
for good music in America. That is not so. Every concert in New York,
Boston, Philadelphia, Chicago or Washington, and most other cities, no
doubt, disproves such a statement. American concert halls are as well
filled as those of Europe, and, as a rule, the listeners—to judge them by
their attentive conduct and subsequent expression of pleasure—are not
a whit less appreciative. How it would be with opera I cannot judge,
since American opera audiences, as the opera is conducted at present,
are in no sense representative of the people at large. I have no doubt,
however, that if the Americans had a chance to hear grand opera sung
in their own language they would enjoy it as well and appreciate it
as highly as the opera-goers of Vienna, Paris, or Munich enjoy theirs.
The change from Italian and French to English will scarcely have an
injurious effect on the present good voices of the singers, while it may
have the effect of improving the voices of American singers, bringing
out more clearly the beauty and strength of the timbre, while giving
an intelligent conception of the work that enables singers to use pure
diction, which cannot be obtained in a foreign tongue.

The American voice, so far as I can judge, is a good one. When I
first arrived in this country, I was startled by the strength and the depth
of the voices in the boys who sell papers on the street, and I am still
constantly amazed at its penetrating quality.

In a sense, of course, it is true that there is less of a demand for music
in America than in certain other countries. Our common folk in Bohemia know this. When they come here, they leave their fiddles and
other instruments at home, and none of the itinerant musicians with
whom our country abounds would ever think of trying their luck over
here. Occasionally, when I have met one of my countrymen whom I
knew to be musical in this city of New York or in the West, and have
asked him why he did not become a professional musician, I have
usually received the answer, "Oh, music is not wanted in this land." This
I can scarcely believe. Music is wanted wherever good people are, as
the German poet has sung. It only rests with the leaders of the people
to make a right beginning.

When this beginning is made, and when those who have musical talent
find it worth their while to stay in America and to study and exercise

their art as the business of their life, the music of America will soon become more national in its character. This my conviction, I know, is not shared by many who can justly claim to know this country better than I do. Because the population of the United States is composed of many different races, in which the Teutonic element predominates, and because, owing to the improved method of transmission of the present day, the music of all the world is quickly absorbed in this country, they argue that nothing specially original or national can come forth. According to that view, all other countries which are but the results of a conglomeration of peoples and races, as, for instance, Italy, could not have produced a national literature or a national music.

A while ago I suggested that inspiration for truly national music might be derived from the Negro melodies or Indian chants. I was led to take this view partly by the fact that the so-called plantation songs are indeed the most striking and appealing melodies that have yet been found on this side of the water, but largely by the observation that this seems to be recognized, though often unconsciously, by most Americans. All races have their distinctively national songs, which they at once recognize as their own, even if they have never heard them before. . . .

What songs, then, belong to the American and appeal more strongly to him than any others? What melody could stop him on the street if he were in a strange land and make the home feeling well up within him, no matter how hardened he might be or how wretchedly the tune were played? Their number, to be sure, seems to be limited. The most potent as well as the most beautiful among them, according to my estimation, are certain of the so-called plantation melodies and slave songs, all of which are distinguished by unusual and subtle harmonies, the like of which I have found in no other songs but those of old Scotland and Ireland. The point has been urged that many of these touching songs, like those of Foster, have not been composed by the Negroes themselves, but are the work of white men, while others did not originate on the plantations, but were imported from Africa. It seems to me that this matters but little. . . . The important thing is that the inspiration for such music should come from the right source, and that the music itself should be a true expression of the people's real feelings. To read the right meaning the composer need not necessarily be of the same blood, though that, of course, makes it easier for him. The white composers who wrote the touching Negro songs which dimmed Thackeray's spectacles so that he exclaimed, "Behold, a vagabond with a corked face and a banjo sings a little song, strikes a wild note, which sets the whole heart thrilling with happy pity!" had a . . . sympathetic comprehension of the deep pathos of slave life. If, as I have been informed they were, these songs were adopted by the Negroes on the plantations, they thus became true Negro songs. Whether the original songs which must have inspired the composers came from Africa or originated on the plantations matters as little as whether Shakespeare invented his own plots or borrowed them from others. The thing to rejoice over is that such lovely songs exist and are sung at the present day. I, for one, am delighted by them. Just so it matters little whether the inspiration for the coming folk songs of America is derived from the Negro melodies, the songs of the creoles, the red man's chant, or the plaintive ditties of the homesick German or Norwegian. Undoubtedly the germs for the best in music lie hidden among all the races that are commingled in this great country. The music of the people is like a rare and lovely flower growing amidst encroaching weeds. Thousands pass it, while others trample it under foot, and thus the chances are that it will perish before it is seen by the one discriminating spirit who will prize it above all else. The fact that no one has as yet arisen to make the most of it does not prove that nothing is there.

Not so many years ago Slavic music was not known to the men of other races. A few men like Chopin, Glinka, Moniuszko, Smetana, Rubinstein, and Tchaikovsky, with a few others, were able to create a Slavic school of music. Chopin alone caused the music of Poland to be known and prized by all lovers of music. Smetana did the same for us Bohemians. Such national music, I repeat, is not created out of nothing. It is discovered and clothed in new beauty, just as the myths and the legends of a people are brought to light and crystallized in undying verse by the master poets. All that is needed is a delicate ear, a retentive memory, and the power to weld the fragments of former ages together in one harmonious whole . . . The music of the people, sooner or later, will command attention and creep into the books of composers.

An American reporter once told me that the most valuable talent a journalist could possess was a "nose for news." Just so the musician must prick his ear for music. Nothing must be too low or too insignificant for the musician. When he walks he should listen to every whistling boy, every street singer or blind organ-grinder. I myself am often so fascinated by these people that I can scarcely tear myself away, for every now and then I catch a strain or hear the fragments of a recurring melodic theme that sound like the voice of the people. These things are worth preserving, and no one should be above making a lavish use of all such suggestions. It is a sign of barrenness, indeed, when such characteristic bits of music exist and are not heeded by the learned musicians of the age.

I know that it is still an open question whether the inspiration derived from a few scattered melodies and folk songs can be sufficient to give a national character to higher forms of music, just as it is an open question whether national music, as such, is preferable. I myself, as I have always declared, believe firmly that the music that is most characteristic of the nation whence it springs is entitled to the highest consideration.

———————

Of course, as I have indicated before, it is possible for certain composers to project their spirit into that of another race and country. Verdi partially succeeded in striking Oriental chords in his *Aida*, while Bizet was able to produce so thoroughly Spanish strains and measures as those of *Carmen*. Thus inspiration can be drawn from the depths as well as from the heights, although that is not my conception of the true mission of music. Our mission should be to give pure pleasure, and to uphold the ideals of our race. Our missions as teachers is to show the right way to those who come after us.

My own duty as a teacher, I conceive, is not so much to interpret Beethoven, Wagner, or other masters of the past, but to give what encouragement I can to the young musicians of America. I must give full expression to my firm conviction, and to the hope that just as this nation has already surpassed so many others in marvellous inventions and feats of engineering and commerce, and has made an honorable place for itself in literature in one short century, so it must assert itself in the other arts, and especially in the art of music. Already there are enough public-spirited lovers of music striving for the advancement of this their chosen art to give rise to the hope that the United States of America will soon emulate the older countries in smoothing the thorny path of the artist and musician. When that beginning has been made, when no large city is without its public opera house and concert hall, and without its school of music and endowed orchestra, where native musicians can be heard and judged, then those who hitherto have had no opportunity to reveal their talent will come forth and compete with one another, till a real genius emerges from their number, who will be as thoroughly representative of his country as Wagner and Weber are of Germany, or Chopin of Poland.

To bring about this result we must trust to the ever youthful enthusiasm and patriotism of this country. When it is accomplished, and when music has been established as one of the reigning arts of the land, another wreath of fame and glory will be added to this country which earned its name, the "Land of Freedom," by unshackling her slaves at the price of her own blood. [1]

EDVARD HAGERUP GRIEG

1843–1907

Grieg's unusual juxtaposition of Mozart and Wagner, his canny penetration into the essential differences between Schubert and Mendelssohn mark the knowledgeable musician. Stylistically an exponent of the German Romantic school—Schumann and Wagner were his favorite Romantic composers—Grieg adopted Norwegian folk song and dance rhythms as the basis of his compositions. As he says, he "dipped into the rich treasures of native folk song and sought to create a national art out of this hitherto unexploited expression of the folk soul of Norway."

He was a song writer of considerable stature and his *I Love You*, *A Swan* and *To a Waterlily* still maintain a place in the active repertoire. Hence the validity of his article on the songs of Schumann. Only a perceptive composer of songs could so well understand the Schumann *Lied*, its virtues and faults.

Although his large works, the piano concerto and the violin and piano sonatas, are still very popular—they are strong and well-knit works—it is through his beautiful piano miniatures that he is best known. His lyric rather than epic talent is best summed up in these autobiographical remarks: "Artists like Bach and Beethoven erected churches and temples on the heights. I wanted, as Ibsen expresses it in one of his last dramas, to build dwellings for men in which they might feel at home and happy."

MOZART AND WAGNER

From: Article in *The Century Magazine*, November, 1897

"What kind of face would Bach, Handel, Haydn and Mozart make after hearing an opera by Wagner?" asks an English writer. I shall not attempt to answer for the first three, but it is safe to say that Mozart, the universal genius whose mind was free from Philistinism and one-sidedness, would not only open his eyes wide, but would be as delighted as a child with all the new acquisitions in the departments of drama and orchestra. In this light must Mozart be viewed. . . . Where he is greatest, he embraces all times.

In Bach, Beethoven and Wagner we admire principally the depth and energy of the human mind; in Mozart, the divine instinct. His highest inspirations seem untouched by human labor. Unlike the masters cited, no trace of struggle remains in the forms in which he molded his material. Mozart has the childish, happy, Aladdin nature which overcomes all difficulties as in play. He creates like a god, without pain. . . .

His early and perfect mastery of the technic of composition suggests an interesting comparison with Wagner. Both of these masters won immortality with their operas. Both threw themselves with all the enthusiasm of youth into this branch of art. Wagner's experience, acquired by early activity as a conductor, has its counterpart in the strict training Mozart received through his travels, begun in childhood as a musician. The result in each case is clearness. Both these musicians are from the outset complete masters of the complicated apparatus required for the writing of an opera—an apparatus most composers learn to control only by long and laborious effort, with hard struggles and disappointments. Let us place the two juvenile masterworks, *The Abduction from the Seraglio* and *Tannhäuser* side by side. There is no wavering in either, but perfect certainty in aim and in choice of means. On the basis of this technical mastership the individuality of each master develops with wonderful rapidity. The step from *Tannhäuser* to *Lohengrin* is just as great as that from the *Abduction* to *Figaro. Lohengrin* and *Figaro!* The warm light of fully conscious personality is diffused from every bar of these two masterworks. If we review further the creative activity of their composers, what melancholy seizes us in contemplating Mozart's fate! All the principal works of Wagner were yet to be written; also it is true, the two greatest of Mozart's— *Don Giovanni* and *The Magic Flute;* but after these his life was cut short at the beginning of his manhood. The death of Mozart before he had passed his thirty-fifth year is perhaps the greatest loss the musical world has ever suffered. . . . To his last hour his genius continued to develop. In *The Magic Flute* and the *Requiem* we have a presentiment that new hidden springs are on the point of bursting forth. That Mozart learned to know and love Bach so late in his life must be regarded as a leading circumstance in connection with this fact. With what deep fervor he allowed this man to strike root in his own personality, we see, among other things, in the delightful fugued choral in the last act of *The Magic Flute.* It was Wagner's polyphonic power that secured him his later triumphs; and this same power would have led Mozart to new victories if he could have been permitted to live longer. For it was this power which, notwithstanding the influence of the Italian school, lay in the depth of his German soul, and which Bach first helped him to find in the privacy of his own personality.

When we compare Mozart and Wagner, the truth of the proverb that "extremes meet" forces itself upon us. That these two masters represented the "extremes" is easily understood by any lover of music, but it may perhaps be necessary to indicate where they "meet." Truly Weber may be regarded as Wagner's predecessor; but if Gluck is named, and not improperly, as the man on whose shoulders Wagner stands, then we must not forget how much he owes to Mozart. For the greatness of Mozart lies in the fact that his influence in the dramatic part of music extends to our time. I have in mind, for example, the developed recitative where Mozart more and more trod paths which it remained for Wagner to develop in his dialogue still further for the modern music drama. Certain recitatives of Donna Anna and Elvira in *Don Giovanni* are the originals after which our whole conception of the recitative has been molded.   [1]

SCHUMANN AND MENDELSSOHN

From: Article in *The Century Magazine*, January 1894

The influence which Schumann's art has exercised and is exercising in modern music cannot be overestimated. In conjunction with Chopin and Liszt, he dominates at this time the whole literature of the piano, while the piano compositions of his great contemporary Mendelssohn, which were once exalted at Schumann's expense, would seem to be vanishing from the concert program. . . . In orchestral compositions Mendelssohn still maintains his position, while Schumann has taken a place at his side as his equal. I say his equal, for surely no significance can be attached to the circumstance that a certain part of the younger generation (Wagnerians chiefly) have fallen into the habit of treating Schumann, as an orchestral composer, *de haut en bas*. These enthusiasts, equipped with an excess of self-esteem, and holding it to be their duty to level everything which, according to their opinion, interferes with the free view of the Bayreuth master, venture to shrug their shoulders at Schumann's instrumentation, to deny his symphonic sense, to attack the structure of his periods and his plastic faculty. They do not even hesitate to characterize his entire orchestral composition as a failure; and in order to justify this indictment, they propound the frank declaration that his orchestral works are only instrumentalized piano music. The fact that Schumann did not occupy himself with Mendelssohn's formally piquant effects, and was not an orchestral virtuoso in the style of Wagner, is turned upside-down in the effort totally to deny him both the plastic sense and the faculty of instrumentation. At the same time they refrain from recognizing all the ideal advantages that primarily make Schumann the world-conquering force he has now virtually become. . . .

It is not to be denied that in his tone-blending of piano and stringed instruments he never attained the height which Mendelssohn and Schubert reached. It has also been affirmed that he neglects absolute harmony, that his stringed instruments, carrying the melody, do not always enter in the most appropriate places, etc. But such things are trifles which an intelligent conception and careful study will easily remedy. The principal thing—the splendid impulse and illusion—is rarely wanting. Minor impracticabilities, which hundreds of smaller spirits easily avoid, are, strange to say, to be met with in Schumann. . . .

The three quartets for stringed instruments (Opus 41) are conceived with as much originality as love. Schumann, to be sure, often ignores that traditional notion that the character of the quartet for stringed instruments is only polyphonic. Hence, the complaint of want of style in his quartets, as well as the charge that the instruments do not attain their full musical value. . . . It is related by reliable contemporaries that these quartets did not find favor in Mendelssohn's eyes. It was during the intercourse of both masters in Leipzig that Schumann one day confided to Mendelssohn that he had suddenly been seized with a desire to write quartets for stringed instruments, but that he had just taken steps to carry out a long-cherished plan to visit Italy and was therefore in a dilemma.

"Remain here and write the quartets," was Mendelssohn's counsel, which Schumann accepted. He remained in Leipzig, and concentrated the whole strength of his soul upon the completion of the task which he had set himself. When Mendelssohn, however, received the quartets, he is reported to have said: "I rather wish now that Schumann had gone to Italy."

We ought not to wonder at this. Mendelssohn never, or at least, very rarely, departed in his works for stringed instruments from the severest principles of polyphony, as practiced by Haydn, Mozart and by Beethoven in his earlier works. Schumann had his roots rather in the later works of Beethoven, where—as is also the case with Schubert —he is not afraid of applying homophony, or even symphonic orchestral style, in quartets for string instruments. Upon this fact, in part, rests the opinion that Mendelssohn and Schumann, though they may be named as contemporaries, are yet far apart, the former closing a great artistic period, the classic, and the latter preparing and introducing a no less great one, the romantic. Both masters met, as it were, upon the same threshold. But they certainly did not pass each other coldly by. On the contrary, they paused to exchange many a winged word. It is not to be denied, however, that it would have been better for Schumann if he had listened less to Mendelssohn's maxims and set more store by his own. His admiration for Mendelssohn is beautiful, but there is in this beauty a certain weakness, and this is perhaps closely connected with his later tragic fate.

A survey of Schumann's art will disclose the fact that, having emerged from his youth and early manhood, he was no longer able, as it were, to think his own thoughts with full consistency to the end. He was afraid of himself. It was as if he did not dare acknowledge the results of the enthusiasm of his youth. Thus it happened that he frequently sought shelter in the world of Mendelssohn's ideas. From the moment he did this, he passed his zenith; his soul was sick; he was doomed long before the visible symptoms of insanity set in.

Much is whispered in corners about the attitude of Schumann and Mendelssohn toward each other. One thing is, however, likely to impress the unprejudiced observer as curious, viz., that Schumann's writings furnish numerous and striking evidences of his boundless admiration for Mendelssohn, while the latter in his many letters does not once mention Schumann or his art. This cannot be due to accident. Whether Mendelssohn was really silent, or whether the editor of his letters, out of regard for his memory, has chosen to omit all references to Schumann, is of slight consequence. This, however, is beyond dispute: his silence speaks, and we of posterity have the right to draw the clue to a judgment of the opinions which the two masters entertained of each other. Of petty envy on Mendelssohn's part there can be no suspicion. He was of too pure and noble a character to be animated by such a sentiment; and, moreover, his fame was too great and too well established in comparison with Schumann's. But his horizon was too contracted to enable him to see Schumann as the man he was. How perfectly comprehensible! He had his forte in clear delineation, in classical harmony; and where Schumann fell short of his requirements in this respect, his honesty forbade him to feign a recognition he could not candidly grant.   [2]

SCHUMANN'S SONGS

From: Article in *The Century Magazine*, January 1894

If there is anything at all that Schumann has written which has become, and has deserved to become, world literature, it is surely his songs. All civilized nations have made them their own. And there is probably in our own day scarcely a youth interested in music to whom they are not, in one way or another, interwoven with his most intimate ideals. Schumann is the *poet*, contrasting in this respect with his greatest successor, Brahms, who is primarily *musician*, even in his songs.

With Schumann the poetic conception plays the leading part to such an extent that technically important musical considerations are subordinated, if not entirely neglected. For all that, even those of his songs of which this is true exert the same magic fascination. What I particularly have in mind is his great demand upon the compass of the voice. It is often no easy thing to determine whether the song is intended for a soprano or an alto, for he ranges frequently in the same song from the lowest to the highest register. Several of his most glorious songs begin in the deepest pitch and gradually rise to the highest, so that the same singer can rarely master both. Schumann, to be sure, occasionally tries to obviate this difficulty by adding a melody of lower pitch, which he then indicates by smaller notes placed under the melody of his original conception. But how often he thereby spoils his most beautiful flights, his most inspired climaxes. Two instances among many occur to me—"Ich grolle nicht" and "Stille Tränen"—for which one will scarcely ever find an interpreter who can do equal justice to the beginning and the end. But if, on the other hand, a singer has a voice at his command capable of such a feat, he will produce the greater effect. . . .

It cannot be maintained that Schumann was the first to accord a conspicuous role to the accompaniment of his songs. Schubert had anticipated him as no other of his predecessors had done, in making the piano depict the mood. But what Schubert began, Schumann further developed; woe to the singer who tries to render Schumann without keeping a close watch over what the piano is doing, even to the minutest shades of sound. I have no faith in a renderer of Schumann's songs who lacks appreciation of the fact that the piano has fully as great a claim upon interest and study as the voice of the singer. Nay, I would venture to assert that, up to a certain point, he who cannot play Schumann, cannot sing him either. In his treatment of the piano, Schumann was, furthermore, the first who, in a modern spirit, utilized the relation between song and accompaniment which Wagner has later developed to a degree that fully proves what importance he attached to it. I refer to the carrying of the melody by the piano, or the orchestra, while the voice is engaged in the recitative. Heaven preserve me, however, from insinuating that Wagner consciously could have received an impulse from Schumann! A dyed-in-the-wool Wagnerian would, of course, regard even a hint of such a possibility as an outrageous want of respect for the master of Bayreuth which would amount almost to an insult. But, for all that, it is a fact that contemporaries influence each other whether they want to or not. That is one of nature's eternal laws, to which we are all subject. You will perhaps ask: Where, then, is the mutual influence of Rossini, Beethoven and Weber? And my response is: It is of a negative character, and accordingly still present. But in the above-mentioned particular case—that of Schumann and Wagner—it is absolutely positive. It is, however, true that Schumann only hints at the things out of which Wagner constructs a perfect system. But there is this to be said: Schumann is here the foreseeing spirit who planted the tree which later, in the modern music drama, was to bear such a glorious fruit. [3]

NIKOLAI ANDREYEVITCH RIMSKI-KORSAKOV

1844–1908

Like his colleagues in the "Big Five," Rimski-Korsakov was a musician by avocation, at least at the inception of his composing career. By profession he was a naval officer, following in the tradition of his family. His first large scale work, a *Symphony in E flat minor* (Opus 1), was composed under Balakirev's influence and guidance, while he was still ignorant of even the names of chords and the elementary rules of part writing.

Unlike his colleagues, he devoted himself assiduously to the formal study of harmony, counterpoint and form, study which aroused cynicism in Moussorgsky (who dubbed it "routine, lifeless and reactionary") and scepticism in Tchaikovsky (who spoke of "contrapuntal intricacies"—see p. 250). Nevertheless, it was this study which enabled him to revise and polish Moussorgsky's at times awkwardly written and often unfinished works after the latter's death, to orchestrate Dargomijsky's *Stone Guest* and with the aid of his pupil, Glazounov, to finish and orchestrate Borodin's *Prince Igor.*

He acquired the principles of musical theory while teaching them at the St. Petersburg Conservatory, certainly as effective a way of learning as possible—and his profound knowledge of wind instruments as inspector of naval bands. His great skill as an orchestrator stemmed from the same practical experience, the reading of Berlioz' *Traité d'Instrumentation,* and the absorption of Glinka's scores.

Numbered among his many gifted students were Glazounov, Ippolitov-Ivanov, and Stravinsky.

His treatise, *Principles of Orchestration,* with many examples culled from his compositions, is an invaluable contribution to the subject. His slim volume on harmony is still valid, and his autobiography, *My Musical Life,* is in effect a history of Russian music from the middle nineteenth through the early twentieth century. If it is not altogether reliable, that is because much of it was written years after the events described and was colored by distance.

ORCHESTRATION

From: Preface to *Principles of Orchestration*, 1896–1908

Our post-Wagnerian epoch is the age of brilliance and imaginative quality in orchestral tone-coloring. Berlioz, Glinka, Liszt, Wagner, modern French composers—Delibes, Bizet and others; those of the new Russian school—Borodin, Balakirev, Glazounov and Tchaikovsky —have brought this side of musical art to its zenith; they have eclipsed, as colorists, their predecessors, Weber, Meyerbeer and Mendelssohn, to whose genius they are nevertheless indebted for their own progress. In writing this book my chief aim has been to provide the well-informed reader with the fundamental principles of modern orchestration from the standpoint of brilliance and imagination, and I have devoted considerable space to the study of tonal resonance and orchestral combination.

I have tried to show the student how to obtain a certain quality of tone, how to acquire uniformity of structure and requisite power. I have specified the character of certain melodic figures and designs peculiar to each instrument or orchestral group, and reduced these questions briefly and clearly to general principles; in short, I have endeavored to furnish the pupil with matter and material as carefully and minutely studied as possible. Nevertheless, I do not claim to instruct him as to how such information should be put to artistic use, nor to establish my examples in their rightful place in the poetic language of music. For, just as a handbook of harmony, counterpoint, or form presents the student with harmonic or polyphonic matter, principles of construction, formal arrangement, and sound technical methods, but will never endow him with the talent for composition, so a treatise on orchestration can demonstrate how to produce a well-sounding chord of certain tone quality, uniformly distributed, how to detach a melody from its harmonic setting, correct progression of parts, and solve all such problems, but will never be able to teach the art of poetic orchestration. To orchestrate is to create, and this is something that cannot be taught.

It is a great mistake to say: this composer scores well, or that composition is well orchestrated, for orchestration is *part of the very soul of the work*. A work is thought out in terms of the orchestra, certain tone colors being inseparable from it in the mind of its creator and native to it from the hour of its birth. Could the essence of Wagner's music be divorced from its orchestration? One might as well say that a picture is well *drawn* in colors.

More than one classical and modern composer has lacked the capacity to orchestrate with imagination and power; the secret of color has remained outside the range of his creative faculty. Does it follow that these composers do not *know how* to orchestrate? Many among them have had greater knowledge of the subject than the mere colorist. Was Brahms ignorant of orchestration? And yet, nowhere in his works do we find evidence of brilliant tone or picturesque fancy. The truth is that his thoughts did not turn towards color; his mind did not exact it.

The power of subtle orchestration is a secret impossible to transmit, and the composer who possesses this secret should value it highly, and never debase it to the level of a mere collection of formulae learned by heart.

Here I may mention the case of works scored by others from the composer's rough directions. He who undertakes such work should enter as deeply as he may into the spirit of the composer, try to realize his intentions, and develop them in all their essential features.

Though one's own personality be subordinated to that of another, such orchestration is nevertheless creative work. But on the other hand, to score a composition never intended for the orchestra, is an undesirable practice. Many musicians have made this mistake and persist in it. In any case this is the lowest form of instrumentation, akin to tinted photographs, though of course the process may be well or badly done.

As regards orchestration, it has been my good fortune to belong to a first-rate school, and I have acquired the most varied experience. In the first place, I have had the opportunity to hear all my works performed by the excellent orchestra of the St. Petersburg Opera. Secondly, from an impulse to experiment, I have scored for orchestras of different sizes, beginning with simple combinations (my opera *May Night* is written for natural horns and trumpets), and ending with the most advanced. In the third place, I conducted the choir of the Military Marine for several years and was therefore able to study wind instruments. Finally, I formed an orchestra of very young pupils and succeeded in teaching them to play, quite competently, the works of Beethoven, Mendelssohn, Glinka, etc. All this has enabled me to present this work to the public as the result of long experience.

As a starting point I lay down the following fundamental axioms:

I. *In the orchestra there is no such thing as ugly quality of tone.*

II. *Orchestral writing should be easy to play;* a composer's work stands the best chance when the parts are well written.[1]

[1] A. Glazounov has well expressed the various degrees of excellence in scoring, which he divides into three classes: (1) When the orchestra sounds well, playing

III. *A work should be written for the size of orchestra that is to perform it*, not for some imaginary body; many composers persist in doing so, introducing brass instruments in unusual keys upon which the music is impracticable because it is not played in the key the composers intends.

It is difficult to devise any method of learning orchestration without a master. As a general rule it is best to advance by degrees from the simplest scoring to the most complicated.

The student will probably pass through the following phases: (1) The phase during which he puts his entire faith in percussion instruments, believing that beauty of sound emanates entirely from this branch of the orchestra—this is the earliest stage; (2) The period when he acquires a passion for the harp, using it in every possible chord; (3) The stage during which he adores the wood winds and horns, using stopped notes in conjunction with strings, muted or pizzicato; (4) The more advanced period, when he has come to recognize that the string group is the richest and most expressive of all.

When the student works alone, he must try to avoid the pitfalls of the first three phases. The best plan is to study full scores and listen to an orchestra, score in hand. But it is difficult to decide what music should be studied and heard. Music of all ages, certainly, but principally the fairly modern. This music will teach the student how to score; classical music will prove of negative value to him. Weber, Mendelssohn, Meyerbeer (*The Prophet*), Berlioz, Glinka, Wagner, Liszt, and modern French and Russian composers—these will prove his best guides. It is useless for a Berlioz or a Gevaert to quote examples from the works of Gluck. The musical idiom is too old-fashioned and strange to modern ears; such examples are of no further use today. The same may be said of Mozart and of Haydn, the father of modern orchestration.

The gigantic figure of Beethoven stands apart. His music abounds in countless leonine leaps of orchestral imagination, but his technique, viewed in detail, remains much inferior to his titanic conception. The use of the trumpets, standing out above the rest of the orchestra, the difficult and unhappy intervals he gives to the horns, the distinctive features of the string parts and his often highly-colored manner of employing the wood winds are features that will cause the student

---

from sight; magnificent after a few rehearsals; (2) When effects cannot be brought off except with the greatest care and attention on the part of conductors and players; (3) When the orchestra never sounds well. Evidently the chief aim of orchestration is to obtain the first of these results. [Author's note.]

of Beethoven to stumble upon a thousand and one points of contradiction.

It is a mistake to think that the beginner will light upon no simple and instructive examples in modern music, in Wagner and others. On the contrary, clearer, and better examples are to be found amongst modern composers than in what is called the range of classical music.

[1]

FORMAL STUDY

From: Letter to Semyon Kruglikov, November 9, 1880

One can learn by oneself; sometimes one needs advice, but one has also to learn, that is, one must not neglect harmony and counterpoint and the development of a good technique and a clean leading subject. All of us, myself and Borodin and Balakirev, but especially Cui and Moussorgsky, neglected this. I consider that I caught myself in time and made myself get down to work. Owing to such deficiencies in technique Balakirev writes little; Borodin, with difficulty; Cui, sloppily; Moussorgsky, messily and often nonsensically; and all this constitutes the very regrettable specialty of the Russian school.   [2]

GABRIEL FAURÉ

1845–1924

As a rule, the composer-journalist tends to be violent in his likes and dislikes. He is often unconsciously biased, fights opposing schools, defends his own disciples who, in turn, rally around him.

In Fauré we find the dispassionate critic. His writing was considered and balanced. No work was completely bad to him, even if he disagreed altogether with its artistic tenets. He tried to discover its good and bad points and gave the reasons for his opinions. An enemy of pedantry and scholasticism, but also of uncontrolled, senseless innovation, he believed in order, good taste, real emotion, lyricism without grandiloquence, simplicity and honesty. How different from Berlioz who, though more sparkling and more literary, is almost always mordant and sarcastic!

Fauré spent years as a reviewer, yet he maintained that the musician should write only music. His own music is of a piece with his literary work, original, tasteful, never deliberately defiant of the rich musical past.

Most of the present quotations are taken from his *Opinions musicales*, a selection from the more than three hundred reviews he wrote during his many years as music critic for the newspaper *Figaro*. Many of these articles have only a topical interest, written as they were about the performances of the previous evening, or concerning then contemporary works, many of which are no longer known today. But one can cull important points of view and studied wisdom about music. His critique on the first performance of Strauss's *Salomé* in Paris, for example, is deeply penetrating and still valid.

GLUCK

From a review, April 13, 1905

If it were necessary to demonstrate once again how, in musical matters, we French still denigrate ourselves, how we unjustly persist in paying attention only to events which happen beyond our frontiers, in giving credit to opinions which come to us from abroad, I would only need recall the case of Gluck. Under the influence of Lully, Handel, Rameau, and even more, on the irresistible impulse of his own genius, Gluck abandoned Italian art, "that titillator of the ear," resolved instead to penetrate the spirit and to move the heart, and so conceived that powerful and expressive art, each manifestation of which always moves us so profoundly. And it was when Gluck, with *Orpheus* and *Alceste*, became the great Gluck, that his compatriots ceased to comprehend him.

The celebrated artist then turned his gaze towards Paris. Paris welcomed him; in spite of the enraged Piccinists, Paris acclaimed *Orpheus, Iphigenia in Aulis, Alceste, Armide, Iphigenia in Tauris;* and it was Paris, finally, which confirmed that glory which neither the years, nor the currents of new conceptions, nor the fickleness of taste and opinion have been able to diminish. And are we not right in maintaining that Gluck belongs to us a little? For Lully and Rameau, the masters who pointed out to him the road he was to travel so gloriously, were ours; Paris was the principal theater of his triumph; also, Quinault furnished him *Armide*, and Racine the two *Iphigenias*, and thus, three times his musical genius was inspired by our literary genius.

We must rejoice that the public has been able to draw closer in these last years to the masterpieces of Gluck; that it has been able to appreciate, with theatrical performances, this art so highly suited to the feelings he translates with a strength of expression which has never been surpassed.

And what feelings could be nobler, more powerful, more touching than those which motivate Orpheus, or Alceste, or Iphigenia?   [1]

MOZART

From a review, June 1, 1909

Mozart's music is particularly difficult to perform. His admirable clarity exacts absolute cleanness; the slightest incorrectness in it stands out like black on white. As I heard Saint-Saëns say lately: "It is music in which all the notes must be heard." Essentially simple, natural, it demands a simple, natural expression as well; in other words, that to which its interpreters, even the best-intentioned, have least accustomed us.   [2]

SAINT-SAËNS AS TEACHER

From an article, 1922

It was not enough for him to initiate us [1] into Schumann, Liszt and Wagner, and thus to open new horizons to us: he also wished to be kept informed about our works in composition. He read them with an interest and care which only masterpieces would merit. He then handed out praise or blame, always with examples and advice which impressed us, made us marvel, filled us with courage. And because he did not hesitate to make us the confidants of his own works as they progressed, we imbibed at its very source the most fruitful instruction that could be given.   [3]

CARMEN

From a review, December 24, 1904

That Merimée's novelette, transported onto the stage of the Favart Théâtre in 1875, could have surprised and disconcerted the public, that it should have seemed scarcely to conform to the traditions of the Opéra Comique is understandable. What is not understandable is that Bizet's music, so utterly clear, so sincere, so colorful, sensitive and charming should not have conquered the public from the outset; dramatic eloquence of such pathos, so vigorous and direct, should immediately have moved the audience.

This music had to achieve the extraordinary reputation it acquired abroad, before our ears, our spirits and our hearts finally opened to it. It was necessary for time to intervene here.

Fortunately time could accomplish its task of justice without the admirable qualities in Bizet's score being altered an iota. The youth, joy, passion and life which it contains remain as overflowing as they are unalterable. And the indifference and hostility of yesteryear have given way to the most brilliant, most universal favor.

This does not mean, however, that the lesson has proved profitable. The injustice of which Bizet was victim will crop up anew along the road of other artists, until the end of time.   [4]

[1] Fauré, at the age of fifteen, studied with Saint-Saëns, who was then twenty-five, at the École Niedermeyer in Paris.

WHAT IS RELIGIOUS MUSIC—FRANCK AND GOUNOD

From an article, 1922

The music heard daily in churches often invites severe criticism. On the other hand, some Paris and provincial choirmasters distinguish themselves in the choice and execution of works truly worthy of their purpose. There is, however, no conclusive standard of excellence. Such and such a composition, nobly conceived and purely written, might seem overadorned or wanting in religious character to some minds. What music is religious? What music is not? To try to resolve the question is quite hazardous, since no matter how deeply sincere a musician's religious feeling may be, it is through his personal taste that he expresses it and not according to rules one can fix. Every classification in this field of ideas has always seemed arbitrary to me. Can one maintain, for example, that among those religious compositions of César Franck which reach the loftiest heights (up to the very quiver of angels' wings), there might not be a few which, because of their very smoothness, are not absolutely free of sensuality? On the other hand, doesn't that child voice which soars alone to sing *Gloria in excelsis Deo* in the *Messe Solennelle* of Gounod create an effect of exquisite purity? And because the text of the *Agnus Dei* inspired him to accents of ineffable tenderness, can one say that Gounod profaned the text? I cite these two musicians because the religious style of the one has so often been contrasted with the religious style of the other, and because I am trying to show that in the realm of truly musical and beautiful works, it is almost impossible to draw a line of demarcation between those which are religious and those that "savor of heresy."   [5]

PUCCINI

From a review, December 29, 1906

Puccini is the most famous of the musicians who today represent the Italian school; he is one of the most gifted, certainly the best equipped and the most experienced. Though he translates moving situations by means one may find too uniform, though accents, emphatic and often wanting in invention, take too important a place in his works, on the other hand, he excels in scenes of movement; his verve, his taste for harmonic and orchestral quests, his manner of adorning the most slender ideas with charming details, present a feast of pleasure to the listener.   [6]

SALOMÉ

From a review, May 9, 1907

Without questioning the interest which the appearance of a new work by Mr. Richard Strauss arouses, isn't it permissible to believe that a great part of the emotion which the presentations of *Salomé* have stirred up, wherever they have taken place, is due to the extraordinary strangeness of the work?

If the subject lent itself to the least levity, one might add that, coinciding with the projected abolition of capital punishment in our country, a decapitated head offers a singular spectacle. But this is no occasion for pleasantry, for here we are concerned with a biblical legend, with a doomed poet, and a foreign musician whose personality and talent enjoy a highly justified and universally established reputation.

The novelty which primarily distinguishes the score of *Salomé* is that Mr. Richard Strauss carries over into it the particular aesthetic which his symphonic poems embody; that is, the principles of musical description and analysis forced to their extreme limits. *Salomé* is a symphonic poem with vocal parts added. Here there is not a character whose physical individuality, whose morality (or immorality), whose thoughts and acts are not minutely translated, almost to the point of naïveté. Atmosphere and color are portrayed in their finest nuances, all by means of mediocre themes, it is true, but developed, worked, interwoven with such marvellous skill that their intrinsic interest is exceeded by the magic of an orchestral technique of real genius, until these themes—mediocre, as I said—end by acquiring character, power, and almost emotion.

This cleverness, this prodigious facility, has its drawbacks. The instability of the music, the fleeting changes of orchestral effects, always new, always arresting, scarcely absorbed before replaced by others, end by creating a perpetual dazzle which tires not only the spirit, but—does this seem absurd?—even the eyes. Besides, is it because of the particularly brutal character of the subject, or is it solely to shock that Mr. Strauss has introduced so many cruel dissonances which defy all explanation? Is it to parallel Good and Evil, which run side by side in the drama, that he has juxtaposed the least reconcilable tonalities in his music? It will be said that his bewitching orchestra makes everything permissible, which is often true; I could not help thinking so in suffering certain terrible discords, while Salomé, kissing the lips of the beheaded prophet says: "There is a bitter taste on thy mouth."

Nevertheless, as far as I am concerned, these criticisms do not denote weaknesses, but only musical means with which I cannot sympathize, in a work vigorously conceived, executed with skill and virtuosity of the first order, and which contains some very impressive pages: for example, the first appearance of Jochanaan from the cistern, Salomé's dance—a veritable little drama in a big drama—the extraordinary and comic discussion of the five Jews, and especially the final scene, one of genuine beauty. [7]

VINCENT D'INDY

1851–1931

Devoutly religious and inclined toward mysticism, D'Indy conceived of art as based on faith and love. Ideologically, he was a disciple of his master, César Franck; musically, he inherited from him the "cyclic" idiom.

Like so many nineteenth century French musicians, he was also strongly influenced by Wagner, and added many pages to the literature promulgating the German composer's ideas. He attended the first performances at Bayreuth in 1876, and continued an avid visitor for many years thereafter. Yet his own most important pieces, notably the *Symphonie sur un chant montagnard français*, employed French material and idiom. He also published collections of French folk music. However, it took the post-d'Indyan generation to release completely the Wagnerian stranglehold on French music.

Keenly analytical and highly erudite, D'Indy was deeply interested in education. He tried unsuccessfully to promote a governmental reappraisal of studies at the Paris Conservatoire, later had the opportunity to put his ideas into practice by helping to form the Schola Cantorum, a school whose motto read "Une école de musique répondant aux besoins modernes." A number of well-known French and foreign composers received their training at the Schola Cantorum, among them Satie, Auric, Canteloube, Turina and Daniel Gregory Mason.

From his experience of many years as teacher in the school D'Indy wrote his *Cours de composition musicale*, a valuable textbook analyzing musical forms.

METHODS OF WORK

From: *César Franck*, 1906

The creation of any work of art, plastic or phonetic, demands, if the artist is really anxious to express his thoughts sincerely, three distinct periods of work: the *conception*, the *planning*, and the *execution*. The first . . . is subdivided into two operations: the *synthetic* and the *analytic* conception. That signifies for the symphonist the laying down of the broad lines, the general plan of the work, and the determination of its constituent elements, i.e., the themes, or musical ideas, which will become the essential points of this plan.

These two undertakings generally succeed each other, but are nevertheless connected, and may modify each other in the sense that the nature of the *idea* (the personal element) may lead the creative artist to change the order of his preconceived plan; while, on the other hand, the nature of the *plan* (the element of generality) may invoke certain types of musical ideas to the exclusion of others. But whether it be synthetic or analytic, the *conception* is always independent of time, place, or surroundings—I had almost added, of the artist's will; he must, in fact, wait until the materials from which his work will be built—materials which will account for the form while they are also influenced by it—present themselves to his mind in a completely satisfactory way.

This mysterious period of conception is sometimes of long duration, especially with the great composers (look at Beethoven's sketchbooks), for their artistic consciences compel them to exercise extreme severity in the choice of their utterances, whereas it is characteristic of second-rate musicians, or those who are infatuated with their own merits, to be satisfied with the first matter which comes to hand, although its inferior quality can only build a fragile, transient edifice.

The second period in the creation of a work, which we call the planning or ordering, is that in which the artist, utilizing the elements previously conceived, decides upon the definite disposition of his work as a whole and in its minutest details.

This phase, which still necessitates a certain amount of invention, is sometimes accompanied by long moments of hesitation and cruel uncertainties. It is the time when a composer undoes one day what it has cost him so much trouble to build up the day before, but it also brings him the full delight of feeling himself in intimate communion with the beautiful.

Finally, when heart and imagination have conceived, when intelligence has ordered the work, there comes the last stage of *execution*, which is mere play to a musician who knows his business thoroughly; this includes the actual writing, the instrumentation, if required, and the plastic presentation on paper of the finished work.

If, as regards the general planning and execution of the work, the procedure is more or less identical with all composers, it is far from uniform in all that concerns the thematic conception and the disposition of the various elements. One musician must patiently await the blossoming of his ideas; another will endeavor to force their coming with violence and excitation; a third—like Beethoven—will write in feverish haste an incredible number of different sketches of a single musical thought; a fourth—Bach, for instance—will not give his theme plastic shape until it is absolutely established in his own mind. [1]

ORCHESTRATION

From: "Concerts Lamoureux," Review in *La Revue S.I.M.*, March 1, 1914

I do not deny that orchestral facility constitutes a precious quality, but I consider it a quality of second rank in comparison with musical inventiveness. What difference does it make to us that such and such a piece is indifferently orchestrated, if it has superior musical significance. The faults in certain passages of Beethoven which must be *interpreted* in order to bring out their melodic design do not alter in any way the harmonious unity of the masterpieces of the titan and the clumsiness in the instrumentation will never prevent the *Rhenish Symphony* of Schumann from remaining one of the beautiful manifestations of the human spirit in music.

Obviously it were preferable that every composer combine both qualities: beauty of content and orchestral competency, but it is certain that an artist like Schumann who has *music* on his side is infinitely superior to one who has only instrumentation to his credit, and *a fortiori*, to one like Grieg, for example, who possesses neither one nor the other. [2]

THE STRING QUARTET

From: *César Franck*, 1906

The form of composition known as the string quartet must be a work of maturity, if it is to have real artistic significance.

Do not suppose that I intend to lay down a dogmatic law. Heaven forbid! The assertion, however, is proved by experience and corroborated by historical observation.

Even among musicians of genius, there is no example of a really *good* string quartet which dates from a youthful period. Mozart's finest quartets date from 1789–90, when the composer was thirty-three— almost the equivalent of old age in this particular instance.

Beethoven waited until he was thirty before he ventured to handle this form of composition, having refused at twenty-seven the tempting offers made to him by Count Apponyi; and it was not until nine years later, with the seventh quartet, in F, that he began to realize all that this form was capable of becoming. The first ten or eleven of his works in this field are merely essays, and the era of the true Beethoven quartet—of those which created a new art of music with the help of four instruments—only dates from 1822, when the musician was in his fifty-third year.

Edvard Grieg, in a sensational article upon his own early studies, written for an American paper,[1] relates that on his entrance to the Leipzig Conservatory, Reinecke, as might be expected from a worthy German pedagogue, directed him to write a string quartet. The work was bad, as the composer himself frankly owns, but the results of this early educational mistake remained with Grieg who, while he was a charming improviser of more or less national songs, was no symphonist, and never succeeded in becoming one.

But, it may be objected, those who can write for orchestra must *a fortiori* be able to compose a quartet. This opinion is quite erroneous, and could only proceed from persons of superficial judgment.

There is scarcely any connection between the two methods of realizing an idea by means of the string quartet of the orchestra and realizing it in the form of chamber music. The basis, the form, the style of writing are in the latter case almost the opposite of what they would be in an orchestral symphony. Thus it comes about that youthful quartets—those written too early in life—though they may present certain seductive and ear-tickling qualities, soon grow old and perish for lack of solidity and structure.   [3]

CÉSAR FRANCK

From: *César Franck*, 1906

Franck was the exact opposite of a disciple of the Renaissance. Far from regarding form as an end in itself, as did most painters and architects of that period, thus creating a *conventional* type of beauty injurious to the normal development of the art, still more remote from the system of certain modern "renaissants" who tend to do away with all forms because they are incapable of creating them efficiently, Franck never considered that manifestation of a work which we call *form* as anything but the *corporeal* part of the entity of an art work ("l'être oeuvre d'art"), destined to serve as the visible outer covering

[1] "My First Success," *The Independent* (1905).

of the *idea*, while still remaining firmly based upon those great foundations which constitute the natural traditions of all art.

Although Franck owed nothing to the Renaissance, he had, on the other hand, much greater affinity, through his qualities of clearness, luminosity and vitality, with the great Italian painters of the fourteenth and fifteenth centuries. His ancestors were Gaddi, Bartolo Fredi, and Lippi rather than the artists of the later periods. Even Perugino's angels, with their somewhat affected attitudes, have already scarcely anything in common with the angels of *Redemption;* and if we may rediscover the Virgin of *The Beatitudes* in some fresco by Sano di Pietro, it would never enter our heads to invoke Franck's presentment of her while looking at La Fornarina, who served Sanzio for model, or even at some cleverly grouped Pietà by Van Dyck, or Rubens.

Franck's art, then, like that of the primitive Siennese and Umbrian painters, was an art of clear truth and luminous serenity. His light was entirely spiritual, excluding the least touch of violent color; for although Franck was an "expressive" artist, he was never a colorist in the true sense of the word; we must acknowledge this defect in him; and in this respect, again, it is impossible to associate him with the Dutch or Flemish schools.

But continuing our researches into the question of his atavistic links, we shall discover another line of artists to whom he is closely related— those modest and admirable craftsmen to whom we owe the wonderful typical beauty and eurythmy of our French cathedrals. As will be seen from the picture which I have endeavored to draw of Franck's moral nature, he shares not only the modesty, simplicity, and self-abnegation of our gentle "imagers" and builders of the thirteenth century, but also their absolute sincerity of inspiration and naïve conscientiousness in the execution of a work. [4]

GIACOMO PUCCINI

1858–1924

In everything he wrote, including even his letters, Puccini was entirely a man of the theater. When he was at work on an opera, he was constantly badgering his librettists directly, or indirectly through his publisher, for more and more material, for changes in the material at hand, until he felt that the very best, the most theatrical had been squeezed from them. When a work was finished, he set out relentlessly to pursue new libretti, avidly grasping one and then another, and just as brusquely discarding them when they did not completely meet his rigorous demands.

It is interesting that Puccini considered *The Girl of the Golden West* (1910) a greater piece than *La Bohème* (1896). Actually the former was a tremendous success at its première, and *La Bohème* opened to failure, but its charm, bittersweet gaiety and humanity have made it one of the most popular operas in the repertoire. *Madame Butterfly* (1904) was also received with hostility, only to become, after some revamping, another of Puccini's most successful works.

His first opera, *Le villi* (1884), written for a competition sponsored by the Italian publisher Sonzogno, did not win the prize, but brought him to the attention of Giulio Ricordi who commissioned his next opera, *Edgar* (1889), and attached him permanently to his publishing house. As advisor, agent and publisher, Ricordi did much to help Puccini become one of the mainstays of universal operatic literature.

DEBUSSY'S *PELLÉAS ET MÉLISANDE*

From: Letter to Giulio Ricordi, Paris, November 15, 1906

Debussy's *Pelléas et Mélisande* has extraordinary harmonic qualities and the most delicate instrumental effects. It is very interesting, in spite of its coloring, which is sombre and unrelieved like a Franciscan's habit. [1]

STRAUSS'S *SALOMÉ*

From: Letter to Giulio Ricordi, Naples, February 2, 1908

Last night I was able to go to the *première* of *Salomé*, conducted by Strauss, and sung (?) by Bellincioni, whose dancing is marvellous. It was a success . . . but there must be many who doubt the verdict. The playing of the orchestra was like a badly mixed Russian salad. But the composer was there, and everybody says that it was perfect.

At the rehearsals when Strauss was trying to work up his orchestra to a rough and tempestuous kind of execution, he said: "Gentlemen, this is not a question of music, but of a menagerie. Make a noise! Blow into your instruments!" What do you think of that?   [2]

STRAVINSKY'S *SACRE DU PRINTEMPS*

From: Letter to Tito Ricordi, Paris, no date

I went to hear the *Sacre du Printemps:* the choreography is ridiculous, the music sheer cacophony. There is some originality, however, and a certain amount of talent. But taken altogether, it might be the creation of a madman. The public hissed, laughed, and—applauded. [3]

LA BOHÈME

From: Letter to Giulio Ricordi, Torre del Lago, September 7, 1894

There is no doubt about its being an original work! And such a one! The last act is most beautiful. So is that of the Quartier Latin, but very difficult. . . . It would be a good thing if you would glance through it, too, and rid it of certain extravagances which are really quite unessential. For example: "The horse is the king of animals," and "Rivers are wines made of water," and many other such lines which Illica [the librettist] loves like his own sons (if he had any). What must be shortened—and very much—is the second act, at the Barrière d'Enfer. This, in my opinion, is the weak act. Shall I be proved wrong? All the better! But the one which I think particularly successful is the last. The death of Mimi, with all that leads up to it, is very moving. [4]

From letter to the same, no date

You will have the copy of Act IV at hand. Will you be so good as to open it at the point where they give Mimi the muff? Don't you think

it rather poor at the moment of her death? Just an extra phrase, a word
of affection to Rudolph, would be enough. No doubt it is a fancy of
mine, but when this girl, for whom I have worked so hard, dies, I
should like her to leave the world less for herself and a little more for
him who loved her.   [5]

TOSCA

From: Letter to Giulio Ricordi, Torre del Lago,
October 12, 1899

Your letter was an extraordinary surprise to me! I am still under the
unpleasant impression. Nevertheless I am quite convinced that if you
read the act [III] through again, you will change your opinion! This
is not vanity on my part. It is the conviction of having colored to the
best of my ability the drama which was before me. You know how
scrupulous I am in interpreting the situation or the words and all
that is of importance, before putting anything down on paper. The
detail of my having used a fragment of *Edgar* can be criticized by
you and the few who can recognize it, and may be taken as a labor-
saving device, if you like. As it stands, if one rids oneself of the idea
that it belongs to another work, if one wipes out *Edgar*, Act IV, it
seems to me full of the poetry which emanates from the words. Oh, I
am sure of this and you will be convinced when you hear it in its
place, in the theater. As for its being fragmentary, I wanted it so. It
cannot be a uniform and tranquil situation such as one connects with
other love duets. Tosca's thoughts continually return to the necessity
of a well-acted fall on Mario's part and a natural bearing in face of the
firing squad.   [6]

From: Letter to Don Pietro Panichelli, no date or place

At the end of the first act in the Church of Sant' Andrea della Valle
there is sung a solemn *Te Deum* of rejoicing for a victory. Now, I
want to know the words of the priests as they pass in procession from
the sacristy to the altar. Afterwards, in order to accentuate the contrast between the filthy desires of Scarpia and the mysterious atmosphere of the place, there should be a great *Te Deum*. Now please
let me know the exact tone of the church bells in the neighborhood of
Castel Sant' Angelo and the exact tone of the big bell at St. Peter's. [7]

MADAME BUTTERFLY

From: Letter to Giulio Ricordi, Torre del Lago,
April 23, 1902

For my part, I am laying stone on stone and doing my best to make Mr. F. B. Pinkerton sing like an American. [8]

From: Letter to the same, Torre del Lago, no date

I have had a visit today from Mme Ohyama, wife of the Japanese Ambassador. She told me a great many interesting things and sang some native songs to me. She has promised to send me some native Japanese music. I sketched the story of the libretto for her, and she liked it, especially as just such a story as Butterfly's is known to her as having happened in real life. [9]

THE GIRL OF THE GOLDEN WEST

From: Letter to Tito Ricordi, New York,
February 18, 1907

The world is expecting an opera from me, and it is high time it were ready. We've had enough now of *Bohème*, *Butterfly* and Co.! Even I am sick of them! But I really am greatly worried! I am tormented not for myself alone, but for you, for Signor Giulio, and for the house of Ricordi to whom I wish to give and must give an opera that is sure to be good.

Here, too, I have been on the lookout for subjects, but there is nothing possible, or rather, complete enough. I have found some good ideas in Belasco, but nothing definite, solid, or complete.

The "West" attracts me as a background, but in all the plays which I have seen, I have found only some scenes here and there that are good. There is never a clear, simple line of development; just a hodge-podge and sometimes in very bad taste and very *vieux jeu*. [10]

From: Letter to Giulio Ricordi, Boscolungo, no date

The *Girl* promises to become a second *Bohème*, but more vigorous, more daring, and on an altogether larger scale. I have in mind a magnificent scenario, a clearing in the great Californian forest, with some colossal trees. But we shall need eight or ten horses on the stage. [11]

From: Letter to Sybil Seligman, Torre del
Lago, July 12, 1907

Have you any means of obtaining in America or in London itself,
some early American music and some modern music too? I'm writing
on my own account, but I need as much as possible in order to *get
the atmosphere.*   [12]

IL TRITTICO (IL TABARRO, GIANNI SCHICCHI, SUOR ANGELICA)

From: Letter to Sybil Seligman, Vienna, October 17, 1920

The *Trittico* is coming on next Wednesday at the former Imperial
Opera House. I think it will be a magnificent success. Jeritza is
really an original artiste—perhaps the most original I have ever known.
She has all the gifts necessary to make a real impression. I heard her
in *Tosca* and in the second act she does certain things simply marvellously. She is a magnificent Giorgette in the *Tabarro.*

There is another artiste, Lehmann, who sings Angelica. She's a first-
class singer and she too would be very much liked in London.   [13]

TURANDOT

From: Letter to Giuseppe Adami, no date

If I touch the piano, my hands get covered with dust. My desk is
piled up with letters—there isn't a trace of music. Music? Useless, if I
have no libretto. I have the great weakness of being able to write only
when my puppet executioners are moving on the scene. If only I could
be a purely symphonic writer! I should then at least cheat time—and
my public. But that was not for *me.* I was born so many years ago—
oh, so many, too many, almost a century—and Almighty God touched
me with His little finger and said: "Write for the theater—mind, only
for the theater." And I have obeyed the supreme command. Had He
marked me out for some other task perhaps I should not be, as now,
without material. . . . I get such nice, encouraging letters, but if, instead of these, one act were to arrive of our glittering Princess
[Turandot], don't you think it would be better? You would give me
back my calm and my confidence, and the dust would not settle on
my piano any more, so much banging would I do, and my desk would
have its brave array of scoring sheets again.   [14]

From: Letter to the same, Torre del
Lago, November 10, 1920

I am afraid that *Turandot* will never be finished. It is impossible to work like this. When fever abates, it ends by disappearing, and without fever there is no creation; because emotional art is a kind of malady, an exceptional state of mind, over-excitation of every fibre and every atom of one's being, and so on, *ad aeternam*.

For me the libretto is nothing to trifle with. It is not a question of finishing it. It is a question of giving life that will endure to a thing which must be alive before it can be born, and so on till we make a masterpiece.   [15]

VII

WOLF
MAHLER
MACDOWELL
DELIUS
DEBUSSY
STRAUSS
DUKAS
BUSONI

HUGO WOLF

1860–1903

During his three years as music critic of the *Salonblatt* in Vienna, Hugo Wolf managed, by his violent attacks, open and covert, on many of his contemporaries, particularly Brahms, to create many enemies. His fanatical espousal of Wagner in the Vienna of his time also conspired to make him cordially disliked by the powerful Brahms contingent ruling Viennese musical life. Nor did his admiration of Bruckner—considered by the musical élite of Vienna a stupid, long-winded, peasant composer—gather him many friends.

Constantly struggling with poverty, Wolf led a hard, bitter life, and his writings reflect his bitterness. But he was uncompromising with truth as he saw it, and his sincerity lends validity and vigor to his reviews.

He was one of the greatest of song writers; his *Lieder*, which express every shade of emotion, owe much of their strength to his keen perception of the *word* in relation to music. However, he possessed no real dramatic or theater sense, and his operas, although full of exquisite music, do not stand up under theatrical production. Mahler's rejection, or what Wolf thought was a rejection, of his opera *Der Corregidor* hastened a mental collapse toward which he had been heading for a long time. A manifestation of his insanity was his delusion that he had been named director of the Vienna Opera, that he was dismissing Mahler, and was "commanding" the production of his opera.

REVIEWS FROM THE *SALONBLATT*

MODERN CHAMBER AND SYMPHONIC MUSIC

February 8, 1884

A first-rate painter once assured me that it is easier to turn out a good picture in water color than in oils. Could one not compare the four string instruments with the paleness of aquarelle, and the glowing color of the orchestra with the warm tones of oils? We can answer the question quite well from the musical point of view also. It is the adroit manipulation of technique, not the need to express a musical thought, which induces our modern composers to write chamber music. Hence their adagios—movements in which Beethoven's heart expands into an immeasurable world, a world which encloses within itself every human heart, so that all may share in the superhuman raptures one heart alone cannot bear—hence their adagios are dull, artificial, tortured, and their poverty of thought with its mask of boredom grimaces at us over and over again through no matter what clever piquancy. The modern composer still feels himself most secure in the scherzo and the finale. He need merely be a clever contrapuntalist, need merely juggle the voices gaily to give himself the air of actually accomplishing something. Intricate inversions, strettos according to the rules, perhaps a witty fugato, or even a fugue! This fills the public with fear and respect. Two, three or four themes when all else fails—piled one on another, torn asunder, attacked again, and hunted down afresh—a small skirmish, but without the thunder of cannon, without battle cries, with little powder, but with all the more flashing cavalry charges, a troupe of make-believe gypsies, Czardas, etc. Truly a charming hash and quite amusing! But for a time at least, the boredom which has crept up on us while we were hearing the adagios is banished, and therefore we find the chamber music of modern composers (andantes and adagios excepted) still bearable.   [1]

ITALIAN OPERA SINGERS

March 30, 1884

In Italy, where only Italian music is fostered, one may be delighted with the grotesque operatic singing style, with the exaggerated gestures of the singers. There it pays less to sing beautifully than effectively, just as the gestures do not so much underline the word as the melodic line. So an Italian singer will sing the news of a shocking occurrence with unparalleled calm, as long as no high B or C looms before him, whereas the most casual circumstance, provided the singer's throat has been adequately considered by the composer, can throw him into an excitement and mobility which, in terms of vocal effects, falls more or less into the farcical. The most arrant scoundrel in the most horrible revenge aria bowls over the Italian rabble no less than the most sentimental lover in his tenderest lyrical outpourings. The high notes are the deciding factor. The Italian *eo ipso* does not bother about the action onstage; even the single musical numbers and recitatives exist for him only insofar as the vocal wrinkles in them have been duly taken care of. The singer wishes to roar or whisper, and the public wishes to be roared at or fluted to. These people understand one another, and therefore any intimacy between singer and audience, be it ever so vulgar, need not astonish us. Thus, for instance, the slain victim of an onstage duel, resurrected through the miracle of applause, takes the arm of his deadly foe, steps before the footlights, and together they politely thank the audience. Thereupon, immediately after the interjected peace, he madly attacks his newly won friend just as quickly, and as happily slays him; whereupon the mutual love-making between the singer and the audience begins anew, to last as long as it amuses both.   [2]

VISITING AND RESIDENT CONDUCTORS

November 9, 1884

One can be an excellent conductor and yet not be at one with an orchestra not one's own, as, for instance, a virtuoso is with any instrument. This is natural. The instrument is a soulless machine, the orchestra an organic body, consisting of the most heterogeneous individuals. To the piano virtuoso it is of no moment whether he plays on a Bösendorfer, Blüthner, Bechstein or a Steinway, as long as the instrument itself is good. Also it is a matter of indifference to X if Y played on it the day before, etc. In this respect the orchestra is quite different. The latter gets used to its conductor in time, refractory as it might be at the start. It is a wild horse, which resists bridle and rider at first, but finally accustoms itself to both. Let a strange rider mount it, and though the reins be handled precisely as by the original rider, you will see a sorry picture. The relation between the orchestra and its conductor is exactly the same. Tradition is mighty. Habit is perhaps the strongest of all passions. An orchestra upon which its conductor (Mr. A) has impressed the seal of his individuality in certain characteristics of rhythm, melody, in solo and ensemble playing, in the diverse balances of wood, brass and string instruments, in the constantly changing accents, nuances from *ppp* to *fff*, and a thousand other finesses, cannot, in a few rehearsals, be brought to the point where it interprets satisfactorily the intentions of another conductor (Mr. B), when it took years of effort on the part of conductor A to accustom it to himself. To God alone are all things possible.   [3]

BRAHMS'S *THIRD SYMPHONY*

November 1884

As a symphony of Herr Dr. Johannes Brahms, it is to some extent a capable, meritorious work; as a symphony of a second Beethoven it is a complete failure, since one must ask of a second Beethoven all that which is lacking in a Dr. Johannes Brahms—originality. Brahms is the epigone of Schumann and Mendelssohn and as such exercises about as much influence on the course of the history of art as the late Robert Volkmann, that is, he has for the history of art just as *little* importance as Volkmann, which is to say *no* influence at all. He (Brahms) is a proficient musician who knows his counterpoint, to whom occur ideas now and then good, occasionally excellent, now and then bad, here and there familiar, and frequently no ideas at all. . . .

Schumann, Chopin, Berlioz, Liszt, the leaders of the revolutionary movement in music since Beethoven (in which period Schumann himself hoped for a Messiah and in the person of—Brahms!) have passed by our symphonist without trace. He was, or pretended to be, blind, as the eyes of astonished mankind opened and overflowed before the radiant genius of Wagner, as Wagner, like Napoleon, borne on the waves of the Revolution, led them into new channels by his despotic power, created order, and performed deeds that will live on eternally in the memory of mankind. But the man who has written three symphonies and apparently intends to allow a further six to follow these three cannot be affected by such a phenomenon, for he is only a relic from primeval ages and no vital part of the great stream of time.

As in those days people danced minuets, i.e. wrote symphonies, so Herr Brahms also writes symphonies, whatever may have happened meanwhile. He comes, like a departed spirit back to his home, staggers up the rickety staircase, turns with much difficulty the rusty key which creakingly opens the cracked door of his deserted dwelling, and sees with absentminded gaze the cobwebs pursuing their airy constructions and the ivy staring in at the gloomy windows. A bundle of faded manuscript paper, a dusty inkpot, a rusty pen arouse his attention. As though in a dream he totters to an antediluvian armchair and broods and broods and can't rightly recollect anything at all. At length his mind begins to clear; he thinks of good old Father Time, whose teeth have all fallen out, who has become shaky and wrinkled and who cackles and chatters like an old woman. He listens long to this voice, to these sounds—so long that at length it seems to him as if they had shaped themselves into musical motives. With an effort he reaches out for the pen, and what he writes down are notes, to be sure, whole hosts of notes. These notes are now stuffed into the good old form according to the rules and the result is—a symphony!   [4]

BRUCKNER

December 28, 1884

I mentioned Mr. Bruckner before as a titan at battle with the gods. Truthfully I could scarcely think of a more suitable metaphor with which to describe the peculiarities of this composer. Praise as well as blame are equally divided in this description. . . . An extraordinary artistic natural power, freshness, and naïveté at war with musical consciousness, intelligence out of step with the educational heights achieved by our time, these are the principal characteristics in the creative work of this artist, which unfortunately find themselves in conflict with one another. Had the composer been able to reconcile these conflicts, he would doubtless have grown into one of what Liszt terms the "all-embracing great." The lack of intelligence is what makes the Bruckner symphonies, for all their originality, greatness, strength, fantasy and invention, so hard for us to understand. Everywhere will, colossal strivings, but no gratification, no artistic resolution. From this stems the formlessness of his works, the apparent exaggeration of his expression. Bruckner wrestles bravely with the idea, but hasn't the courage to place it foremost, and thus to write with a clear conscious-ness. Thus he wavers, half in Beethoven, half in the new discoveries, as in Liszt's symphonic poems, where they have found their most complete expression, sending out roots between the two, without being able to decide on either. That is his misfortune. Nevertheless I do not hesitate to designate the symphonies of Bruckner as the most significant symphonic creations that have been written since Beethoven.   [5]

HAYDN'S *CREATION*

November 15, 1885

The Creation of Haydn! What a devout, childlike spirit speaks from the heavenly clear tones of Haydn's muse! What naturalness, sim-plicity, what perception and sensitivity! What a great artist Haydn is: listening to his works, one is not struck by their ingenuity, and yet what an abundance of ingenious forms surround his graceful tone pictures! His extraordinarily fine artistic sense is evidenced especially in what has been assiduously exercised of late, but at the same time has fallen into disrepute—tone painting. In fact, we should shudder to think of a subject like *The Creation* or *The Seasons*, which give so much opportunity for tone painting, being handled or, more aptly, mishandled by a modern composer. We would not, for sheer imagery, get to hear any music. Should a modern composer wish to illustrate Chaos musically, we should certainly find no triad there, unless it were an occasional augmented one; but in all probability the duty would fall to open fifths to defray the musical costs of such a presentation.

If one takes for granted that at the sight of Chaos progressions of fifths sounded in the ears of God, then it must have been righteous self-defense and not wantonness or even malevolence, as certain philosophers suppose, that brought Him to the desperate resolve to inflict so much misfortune on the world in the ridiculously short period of seven days.

However, it would be all right if it stopped with these devilish resources, but nowadays dissonances and glaring instrumental effects fall like hailstones, and one might believe that Chaos had become a wild animal suffering from toothache, so groans and moans the orchestra. If the composer hereby intended to portray the tumbling of hostile air waves one over another, or the hiss of a fiery rocket, or some other elemental occurrence, he may have meant well, but he achieved nothing, and we form a bad opinion of his ability.

However, confusion can so far obtain, when the purely external predominates in tone painting, that thanks to sheer atmosphere, no atmosphere, thanks to sheer characterization, no character is achieved, but always a disjointed elaboration, never an effective whole. How different Haydn is! Observe Chaos in his *Creation*. The very first measures with the muted violins inspire in us the sensation of standing before a mysterious presence. A magician, he conjures up the dark image of Chaos. Gray cloud masses illuminated by strange iridescent lights revolve slowly in a confused ferment. Listen! what were those voices? such distressed, wailing sounds—such gently serious songs? They mingle, dissolve, fall silent—another vision, radiant with magic beauty emerges from the darkness. The soul is filled with awe at sight of this magical apparition. Quietly moving, it wanders along its course. It soars aloft; it colors the air with crimson, it falters, falls—a flash from the black depths—and the apparition has vanished. Seas of clouds envelop the richly colored scene again. The tone poet has awakened from his dream. This is, to be sure, but a meager sketch compared to the fantastic world which the composer envisions in his waking dream. But had Haydn wished to set to music exactly what he saw, we may be certain that Chaos would have remained all the more incomprehensible to us, whereas now it speaks to us all the more vividly. Why? Because the composer translated through his musical feeling not the face but the impression of the face.   [6]

BERLIOZ' *DAMNATION OF FAUST*

March 1886

Berlioz was incapable of creating an organic work of art, congruent in form and content, like the two compositions of Wagner and Liszt (the *Faust* overture and *Faust* symphony). His *Faust* is a fragmentary mosaic, a building without plan, full of the most beautiful detail but without a conscious aim. The Faust theme, in its purely human features an inexhaustible spring of artistic ideals, disintegrates with Berlioz into the idle play of arbitrary fancies, which, though admirable in themselves and full of genius, shatter the poetic intention and do not allow complete enjoyment of the whole work. This reproach applies also to Schumann's *Faust*. An inner instability is common to both, and if Schumann's *Faust* follows with finer feeling Goethe's original, Berlioz' work surpasses it in musical content. But whatever one may think of Berlioz' conception of the Faust idea, one thing is certain—that almost every number in this work invites our most ardent admiration.   [7]

GUSTAV MAHLER

1860–1911

In the introduction to her collection of Mahler's letters, Alma Mahler comments on the laconic, sparse quality of his later letters, ascribing his terseness to the taciturnity of the creative musician. It is true that Bach, Beethoven and Handel were very sparing in their remarks about music, most of their letters dealing with everyday business and domestic problems. A goodly number of Mahler's letters, however, do dilate on his opinions, his musical and artistic credos. His later correspondence voices his own tremendous efforts to achieve financial security through his conducting so that he might devote himself more fully to composing—his first love. Most of his composing was done perforce between operatic and concert seasons.

A man of intense concentration, his absorption in his work often put him into an almost hypnotic condition. His constant search for perfection as composer and conductor was his undoing. Perfection demands tyranny, and tyranny breeds enemies. Of the latter Mahler had plenty.

He was a great admirer of Wagner, and an advocate of the immense Wagner orchestra. (A youthful Mahler opera demanded a full orchestra offstage.) Though temperamentally different from Richard Strauss, he respected his work, and was grateful that, in the face of strong opposition, Strauss performed his *First Symphony* and gave his *Second* ("The Resurrection") its first hearing. Unlike Strauss, he scorned the prearranged program in music, using words in his scores only to give final illumination to his work. *Das Lied von der Erde* is the superlative example of the combination of the symphony and the word.

PROGRAM NOTES

From: Letter to an unknown addressee, May 15, 1894

Please accept my thanks for your kind offer. However, it is hardly my intention to confuse the audience at a musical performance with technical remarks,—and in my opinion it amounts to nothing else when one stuffs a "program booklet" into the audience's hands, thereby forcing it to see rather than to hear!

Certainly I consider it necessary that the web of motives be clear to every listener. But do you really believe that in a modern work the singling out of several themes is sufficient for this? One must achieve the cognition and recognition of a musical work through exhaustive study, and the more profound a work, the harder it is, and the longer its study takes. At a first performance, however, the principal thing is to give oneself with pleasure or displeasure to the work, to allow the human-poetic in general to affect one, and if one then feels drawn to it, to occupy oneself with it more thoroughly. How does one do when one meets a person, who is certainly much more profound and better than his work? Where is the program booklet here? Here also it means sedulously cultivating him and zealously studying him. Of course, he grows and changes, whereas the work always remains the same. But at some point or other, comparisons always limp. [1]

PROGRAM MUSIC

From: Letter to Max Kalbeck, Meiernigg, no date

Beginning with Beethoven there exists no modern music which hasn't its inner program. But no music is worth anything when the listener has to be instructed as to what is experienced in it—in other words, what he is expected to experience. And so again: *pereat*—every program! One must bring along one's ears and heart and, not least, surrender willingly to the rhapsodist. A bit of mystery always remains— even for the creator! [2]

THE WORD AND MUSIC

Letter to Max Marschalk,[1] Hamburg, March 26, 1896

For myself I know that so long as I can sum up my experience in words, I can certainly not create music about it. My need to express myself in music symphonically begins precisely where dark feelings hold sway, at the gate which leads into the "other world," the world in which things no longer are divided by time and space.

So, just as I find it insipid to invent music to a program, so I view it as unsatisfactory and unfruitful to wish to give a program to a piece

---

1 (1863–1940). Critic, teacher, and composer, who had written program notes for Mahler's *First Symphony*.

of music. That does not alter the fact that the motive for a musical picture is certainly an experience of the author's, indeed an actual one, which might after all be concrete enough to be clothed in words. We stand now—of that I am certain—at the great crossroads which divides forever the diverging paths of symphonic and dramatic music so easily visible to the eye of him who is clear about the direction of music. Even now, should you hold up a Beethoven symphony against the tone pictures of Wagner, you will easily recognize the essence of the difference between them. Indeed, Wagner made the means of expression of symphonic music his own, just as now the symphonist fully qualified in and completely conscious of his medium, will take over from the wealth of expression which music gained through Wagner's efforts. In this sense, all the arts, yes, even art and nature hang together. However, this has not been thought about enough as yet, because up to now not enough perspective has been gained on the subject. I have not concocted this "system" and then adapted my creation to it either; but only after writing several symphonies (with real birth pangs), and forever coming up against the same misunderstandings and questions, did I finally—for me at least—gain this insight into things.

In spite of everything, it is therefore good that at the beginning, when my style is still foreign to him, the listener be provided with a few signposts and milestones along his journey, or shall we say: a map of the stars to comprehend the night sky with its shining worlds. But such an exposition cannot offer more. A person must fasten upon something he knows, or he gets lost. Consequently I shall be grateful to you if you publish your essay. I like it better than anything else which has been said of me up to now.   [3]

ADVICE TO A COMPOSER

From: Letter to Max Marschalk,
Hamburg, April 12, 1896

You still go out primarily for "tone and color"! It is the fault of all gifted beginners who create today. I could show you similar things in my own development. Mood music is a dangerous foundation. Believe me, it rests principally on the old tried and true: Themes, clear and plastic, distinctly recognizable in every transformation and further development; then a varied and, above all, arresting execution through the logical development of the inner idea, and conversely, through the genuine contrasting of themes pitted one against another. . . .

You must get rid of the pianist in you. This is no orchestral movement; it is conceived for piano and then fairly slavishly translated in the spirit of that instrument for orchestra. . . .

I have suffered from this also. We of today all proceed from the piano, whereas the old masters stem from the violin and the voice. . . .

You frequently carry through long stretches in the same rhythm and even with the same orchestration. This makes for monotony. Change and contrast! This is and remains the secret of effectiveness! In this manner even blockheads manage for a time to hide lack of content.   [4]

COMPOSING FOR THEATER AND CONCERT HALL

From: Letter to Guido Adler, New York, January 1, 1910

The technique of the theater is altogether different, and I am convinced that a host of my inadequacies in instrumentation up to now rests on the fact that I am accustomed to listening under the completely different acoustical conditions of the theater.   [5]

TEMPO IN CONDUCTING

From: A statement, no date

A tempo is correct when everything can still be heard. When a figure can no longer be understood because the tones run into one another, then the tempo is too fast.

In a Presto the extreme limit of distinctness is the correct tempo; beyond this it loses its effectiveness.   [6]

BRAHMS AND BRUCKNER

From: Letter to Alma Mahler, Meiernigg, 1904

I have now gone through practically all of Brahms. Well, I must say, he is really a little man with a narrow chest. Heavens, when one has at the same time been buffeted by the blast from Richard Wagner's lungs! How Brahms in his poverty must economize in order to get along! Whereby I do not mean to insult him. Where he gets stuck—you will be astonished when I say this to you—is in his so-called "developments." Only in the rarest cases does he know what to do with his frequently lovely themes. Only Beethoven and Wagner *knew*.

After I had gone through all of Brahms, I turned again to Bruckner. Singularly average people! The former remained "im Löffel" [in the crucible] too long, the latter must now be poured into it. Now I am on Beethoven. There are only *he* and *Richard*—and otherwise nothing!

[7]

RICHARD STRAUSS

From: Letter to Alma Mahler, Salzburg, July 16, 1906

Strauss is now also here, and especially charming, as he always is when we are alone together. However, his nature will always remain foreign to me. His manner of thinking and feeling is worlds apart from mine. I wonder if we two will ever meet on the same planet. [8]

SALOMÉ

From: Letter to Alma Mahler, Berlin, January, 1907

It is truly a work of genius, a very strong work, which definitely belongs among the most significant which our age has brought forth. It seethes under a mass of lava, a volcano, a subterranean fire—not merely fireworks. It is the same with Strauss's entire personality. At the same time it is so difficult to separate the wheat from the chaff in him. But I have achieved a tremendous respect for the entire phenomenon and confirmed it anew. I am very happy about it! Here I can go along all the way! [9]

THE *SECOND SYMPHONY*

Letter to Anton Seidl, Hamburg, February 17, 1897

You have given me great joy and a powerful stimulation with your kind and thoughtful letter. It is curious how, in a certain sense, you have clarified me to myself. You have quite decisively characterized my aims, in contrast to those of Strauss. You say correctly that my "music finally arrives at its program as a last ideal elucidation, whereas in Strauss the program is present as a given curriculum." I believe that with this you have particularly hit on the great enigmas of our time, and have at the same time pointedly expressed the either-or. When I conceive a large musical structure, I always come to the point where I must bring in the word as the bearer of my musical idea. Something similar must have happened to Beethoven in his *Ninth*, only that his own time could not yet furnish him with the material suitable for this.

For basically the Schiller poem is not capable of formulating the fantastic which he had in mind. Incidentally, I recall that Richard Wagner at some point expresses this quite plainly. In the last movement of my second symphony it so happened to me, that I actually searched through the entire world literature back to the Bible to find the redeeming word—and finally was forced to lend words myself to my feelings and thoughts.

How I got the inspiration for this is profoundly significant for the nature of artistic creation.

For a long time I turned over in my mind the inclusion of a chorus in the last movement, and only the fear that this might be considered a superficial imitation of Beethoven made me hesitate again and again. At this time Bülow died, and I was present at his memorial. The mood in which I sat there and thought of him who had passed away was exactly the spirit of the work which I was then mulling over. Then the chorus from the organ loft intoned the Klopstock chorale "Resurrection"! This struck me like a flash of lightning and everything appeared quite clear and distinct within me! The creator waits for this flash; this is the "holy conception!"

What I experienced at that moment, I had now to create in sound. And yet, had I not already borne this work within me, how could I have had such an experience? After all, thousands sat with me in the church at that moment! So it always is with me: only when I experience, do I compose—only when I compose, do I experience! I know that you understand me without my elaborating upon this any further. A musician's nature can hardly be expressed in words. It would be easier to explain how he is different from others. What it is, however, perhaps he least of all would be able to explain. It is the same with his goals, too. Like a somnambulist he wanders toward them—he doesn't know which road he is following (it may skirt dizzy abysses) but he walks toward the distant light, whether this be the eternally shining stars or an enticing will-o'-the-wisp.   [10]

THE *THIRD SYMPHONY*

From: Letter to Anna Bahr-Mildenburg,
Steinbach am Attersee, July 18, 1896

But I have surely written you that I am at work on a large composition. You cannot believe how this claims one's entire being, and how one is often so deep in it that for the outer world one is as if dead. Try to conceive a work so vast, that in it the entire world is mirrored

—one is, so to speak, only an instrument on which the whole universe plays. (I have explained this to you often, and you must accept it, if you really wish to understand me. Everyone who wishes to live with me must learn this. In such moments I no longer belong to myself.) . . . These are fearful birth pains which the creator of such a work suffers, and before all this organizes itself, builds itself up, and ferments in his brain, it must be preceded by much preoccupation, engrossment with self, a being-dead to the outer world. My symphony will be something which the world has not as yet heard! In it all nature becomes a voice and reveals profound mysteries as one has perhaps surmised only in dreams. I tell you that at certain points I become uneasy, and it seems to me as if I myself had not done it at all. If only I can fulfill everything as I project it to myself! [11]

EDWARD ALEXANDER MACDOWELL
1861–1908

The music of MacDowell is practically never heard today, apart from conservatory performance. Yet, among the few American composers of his time, he was the most important, exerting a strong influence over the American musical scene at the turn of the century. Though he availed himself of American Indian themes in some of his pieces, he can scarcely be termed a composer of American music. His roots were planted in German Romanticism, and he was somewhat influenced by French Impressionism—he lived and studied in Paris for a while, and was a fellow-student of Debussy's at the Conservatoire. In Frankfurt and Stuttgart he completed his studies and began his professional life.

He has often been compared with Grieg; they are both at their best in their programmatic miniatures. A mutual admiration existed between them, MacDowell having dedicated two of his piano sonatas to his Norwegian contemporary, while Grieg is quoted as having remarked, "I consider MacDowell the ideally endowed composer."

In 1896 MacDowell was appointed head of Columbia University's music department, an unhappy connection which ended badly, since he and the authorities differed widely on methods of pedagogy. Chosen from among his university lectures, his *Critical and Historical Essays* (1912), parts of which are quoted here, form a short history of music punctuated by his own ideas. Though many of his statements and conclusions have not withstood the passing of time, his basic ideas on opera, folk music, national music, the very components of music, retain a kernel of validity and a contemporary interest.

From: *Critical and Historical Essays*

EMBELLISHMENTS

The elaboration of detail and the addition of passing and ornamental notes to every melody is distinctly an Oriental trait, which finds vent not only in music but also in architecture, designing, carving, etc. It is considered by many an element of weakness, seeking to cover a poverty of thought by rich vestments. And yet, to my mind, nothing can be more misleading. In spite of Sir Hubert Parry and other writers, I cannot think that the Moors in Spain, for instance, covered poverty of thought beneath superficial ingenuity of design. The Alhambra outdoes in "passage work," in virtuoso arabesques, all that an army of Liszts could do in piano literature; and yet the Arabs were the saviors of science, and promoted the greatest learning and depth of thought known in Europe in their time. As for Liszt, there is such an astounding wealth of poetry and deep feeling beneath the somewhat "flashy," bombastic trick of speech he inherited, that the true lover of music can no more allow his feelings to be led astray by such externals than one would judge a man's mind by the cut of his coat or the hat he wears. [1]

RHYTHM AND MELODY

We may regard rhythm as the intellectual side of music, melody as its sensuous side. The pipe is the one instrument that seems to affect animals—hooded cobras, lizards, fish, etc. Animals' natures are purely sensuous, therefore the pipe, or to put it more broadly, melody, affects them. To rhythm, on the other hand, they are indifferent; it appeals to the intellect, and therefore only to man.

This theory would certainly account for much of the potency of what we moderns call music. All that aims to be dramatic, tragic, supernatural in our modern music, derives its impressiveness from rhythm [1]. . . . All through Wagner's music dramas this powerful effect is employed, from The Flying Dutchman to Parsifal. Every composer from Beethoven to Nicodé [2] has used the same means to express the same emotions; it is the medium that prehistoric man first knew; it produced the same sensation of fear in him that it does in us at the present day.

Rhythm denotes a thought; it is the expression of a purpose. There is will behind it; its vital part is intention, power; it is an act. Melody, on the other hand, is an almost unconscious expression of the senses; it translates feeling into sound. It is the natural outlet for sensation. In anger we raise the voice; in sadness we lower it. In talking we give expression to the emotions in sound. In a sentence in which fury

---

[1] The strength of the "Fate" motive in Beethoven's Fifth Symphony undoubtedly lies in the succession of the four notes at equal intervals of time. Beethoven himself marked it So pocht das Schicksal an die Pforte.

[2] Jean-Louis Nicodé (1853–1919), pianist and conductor, composed four symphonic poems.

alternates with sorrow, we have the limits of the melody of speech. Add to this rhythm, and the very height of expression is reached; for by it the intellect will dominate the sensuous.   [2]

FOLK SONG AND HARMONY

One point must be very distinctly understood, namely, that what we call harmonization of a melody cannot be admitted as forming any part of folk song. Folk melodies are, without exception, homophonous. This being the case, perhaps my statement that the vital principle of folk music in its best state has nothing in common with nationalism (considered in the usual sense of the word) will be better understood. And this will be the proof that nationalism, so-called, is merely an extraneous thing that has no part in pure art. For if we take any melody, even of the most pronounced national type, and merely eliminate the characteristic turns, affectations, or mannerisms, the theme becomes simply music, and retains no touch of nationality. We may even go further; for if we retain the characteristic mannerisms of dress, we may harmonize a folk song in such a manner that it will belie its origin; and by means of this powerful factor (an essentially modern invention) we may even transform a Scotch song with all its "snap" and character into a Chinese song, or give it an Arabian flavor. This, to be sure, is possible only to a limited degree; enough, however, to prove to us the power of harmony; and harmony, as I have said, has no part in folk song.

To define the rôle of harmony in music is no easy matter. Just as speech has its shadow languages, gesture and expression; just as man is a duality of idealism and materialism; just as music itself is a union of the emotional and the intellectual, so harmony is the shadow language of melody; and just as in speech this shadow language overwhelms the spoken word, so in music harmony controls the melody. . . .

Melody, therefore, may be classed as the gift of folk song to music; and harmony is its shadow language.   [3]

CRITICISM

My reason for insisting on the importance of all lovers of art being able to form their own opinions is obvious, when we consider that our musical public is obliged to take everything on trust. For instance, if we read on one page of some history (every history of music has such a page) that Mozart's sonatas are sublime, that they do not contain one note of mere filigree work, and that they far transcend anything written for the harpsichord or clavichord by Haydn or his contemporaries, we echo that saying, and, if necessary, quote the "authorities." Now if one had occasion to read over some of the clavichord music of the period, possibly it might seem strange that Mozart's sonatas did not impress with their magnificence. One might even harbor a lurking doubt as to the value of the many seemingly bare runs and unmeaning passages. Then one would probably turn back to the authorities for an explanation and find perhaps the following: "The inexpressible charm of Mozart's music leads us to forget the marvellous learning bestowed upon its construction. Later composers have sought to conceal the constructional points of the sonata which Mozart never cared to disguise, so that incautious students have sometimes failed to discern in them the veritable 'pillars of the house,' and have accused Mozart of poverty of style because he left them boldly exposed to view, as a great architect delights to expose the piers upon which the tower of his cathedral depends for its support." (Rockstro, *History of Music*, p. 269.) Now this is all very fine, but it is nonsense, for Mozart's sonatas are anything but cathedrals. It is time to cast aside this shibboleth of printer's ink and paper and look the thing itself straight in the face. It is a fact that Mozart's sonatas are compositions entirely unworthy of the author of the *Magic Flute*, or of any composer with pretensions to anything beyond mediocrity. They are written in a style of flashy harpsichord virtuosity such as Liszt never descended to, even in those of his works at which so many persons are accustomed to sneer.   [4]

SUGGESTION IN MUSIC

I believe that music can suggest forcibly certain things and ideas as well as vague emotions encased in the so-called "form" and "science" of music.

If we wish to begin with the most primitive form of suggestion in music, we shall find it in the direct imitation of sounds in nature. We remember that Helmholtz, Hanslick, and their followers denied to music the power to suggest things in nature; but it was somewhat grudgingly admitted that music might express the emotions caused by them. In the face of this, to quote a well-known instance, we have the *Pastoral Symphony* of Beethoven, with the thrush, cuckoo, and thunderstorm. The birds and the storm are very plainly indicated; but it is not possible for the music to be an expression of the emotions caused by them, for the very simple reason that no emotions are caused by the cuckoo and thrush, and those caused by thunderstorms range all the way from depression and fear to exhilaration, according to the personality of individuals.

That music may imitate any rhythmic sounds or melodic figure occurring in nature, hardly needs affirmation. Such devices may be accepted almost as quotations, and not be further considered here. The songs of birds, the sound made by galloping horses' feet, the moaning of the wind, etc., are all things which are part and parcel of the musical vocabulary, intelligible alike to people of every nationality. I need hardly say that increasing intensity of sound will suggest vehemence, approach, and its visual synonym, growth, as well as that decreasing intensity will suggest withdrawal, dwindling, and placidity.

The suggestion brought about by pattern is very familiar. It was one of the first signs of the breaking away from the conventional trammels of the contrapuntal style of the sixteenth and seventeenth centuries. The first madrigal of Thomas Weelkes (1590) begins with the words, "Sit down," and the musical pattern falls a fifth. The suggestion was crude, but it was caused by the same impulse as that which supplied the material for Wagner's "Waldweben," Mendelssohn's "Lovely Melusina," and a host of other works.

The fact that the pattern of a musical phrase can suggest kinds of motion may seem strange; but could we, for example, imagine a spinning song with broken arpeggios? Should we see a spear thrown or an arrow shot on the stage and hear the orchestra playing a phrase of an undulating pattern, we should at once realize the contradiction. Mendelssohn, Schumann, Wagner, Liszt, and practically everyone who has written a spinning song, has used the same pattern to suggest the turning of a wheel. That such widely different men as Wagner and Mendelssohn should both have adopted the same pattern to suggest undulating waves is not a mere chance, but clearly shows the potency of the suggestion.

The suggestion conveyed by means of pitch is one of the strongest in music. Vibrations increasing beyond two hundred and fifty trillions of a second become luminous. It is a curious coincidence that our highest vibrating musical sounds bring with them a well-defined suggestion of light, and that as the pitch is lowered we get the impression of ever increasing obscurity. To illustrate this, I have but to refer you to the Prelude to *Lohengrin*. Had we no inkling as to its meaning, we should still receive the suggestion of glittering shapes in the blue ether.

The upward tendency of a musical phrase can suggest exaltation, and a downward trend may suggest depression, the intensity of which will depend upon the intervals used. As an instance we may quote the *Faust Overture* of Wagner, in which the pitch is used emotionally as well as descriptively. If the meaning I have found in this phrase seems to you farfetched, we have but to give a higher pitch to the motive to render the idea absolutely impossible.

The suggestion offered by movement is very obvious, for music admittedly may be stately, deliberate, hasty, or furious, it may march or dance, it may be grave or flippant.

Last of all I wish to speak of the suggestion conveyed by means of tone-tint, the blending of timbre and pitch. It is essentially a modern element in music, and in our delight in this marvellous and potent aid to expression we have carried it to a point of development at which it threatens to dethrone what has hitherto been our musical speech, melody, in favor of what corresponds to the shadow languages of speech, namely, gesture and facial expression. Just as these shadow languages of speech may distort or even absolutely reverse the meaning of the spoken word, so can tone color and harmony change the meaning of a musical phrase. This is at once the glory and the danger of our modern music. Overwhelmed by the new-found powers of suggestion in tonal tint and the riot of hitherto undreamed of orchestral combinations, we are forgetting that permanence in music depends upon melodic speech.

In my opinion, it is the line, not the color, that will last. That harmony is a potent factor in suggestion may be seen for the fact that Cornelius was able to write an entire song pitched upon one note, the accompaniment being so varied in its harmonies that the listener is deceived into attributing to that one tone many shades of emotion.

[5]

FREDERICK DELIUS

1862–1934

In the upsurge of musical experimentation following the First World War, dissonance, atonality, polytonality and polyrhythm were the order of the day. To Delius, a retiring, sensitive composer steeped in German Romanticism, this ultra-modern music was anathema. Hence his diatribe, quoted below, against what he considered musical chaos, his scorn of the Diaghilev ballets set to the "cacophonies" of Stravinsky, Prokofiev and the new French school, and his contempt for what he felt were the perverse uses to which Isadora Duncan put the classics.

Delius had chosen the musical profession against the wishes of his parents. Even after he became famous, neither his father nor his mother ever listened to a note of his music. To escape them he emigrated to Florida, ostensibly to raise oranges. Once there, he forgot all about his orange plantation, devoting himself to music study, earning his living by playing the organ in a Jacksonville church, and teaching. When they discovered his neglect of business, his parents recalled him to England, and it was only through Grieg's intercession that he was finally allowed to go to Germany for further study. It was in Germany that his work was first performed and understood.

Aloof, living in a world of his own, Delius was scarcely known in his native England whose landscapes he described so effectively in *Brigg Fair, Summer Night on the River, On Hearing the First Cuckoo in Spring* and other similar works. Nor was he recognized in France, where he made his home for many years.

One of the few compatriots to recognize Delius' gifts was Sir Thomas Beecham, who in 1929 performed a festival of his works which Delius, by then sick, blind and old, attended. Beecham's admiration of Delius has lasted to this day. In 1953 he staged *Irmelin*, the first of six of Delius' neglected operas.

THE STATE OF MUSIC TODAY

From: "At the Crossroads," September 1920

The time has come when every musician of serious aims should declare, in the interest of the public, what is his attitude towards the current attempts on the part of Russian impresarios, Parisian decadents and their press agents, to degrade his art to the level of a side show at a fair.

There is room in the world for all kinds of music to suit all tastes, and there is no reason why the devotees of Dada should not enjoy the musically imbecile productions of their own little circle as much as the patrons of musical comedy enjoy *their* particular fare. But when I see the prophets of the latest clique doing their utmost to pervert the taste of the public and to implant a false set of values in the rising generation of music-lovers by sneering at the great masters of the past, in the hope of attracting greater attention to the *petits maîtres* of the present—then I say it is time to speak openly and protest.

In the end, of course, all art finds its own level and takes its due place in the estimation of the world; and everything that is shallow, catchpenny, sensational and insincere sinks into oblivion from which no propaganda can rescue it. But why, in the meanwhile, should a whole generation be confused and contaminated by the specious clap-trap and humbug of a crew of little men who have deliberately set out to make the worse appear the better cause? Genius is not a mushroom growth. Inspiration does not come without hard work any more than a crop of corn. There is no short cut to glory. No great work of art has ever come into the world save as the fruit of years of earnest, unremitting endeavor on the part of its creator; and no great artist ever blasphemed his ancestors.

Music is a cry of the soul. It is a revelation, a thing to be reverenced. Performances of a great musical work are for us what the rites and festivals of religion were to the ancients—an initiation into the mysteries of the human soul. . . .

How does music stand today? Is the world full of men of as much importance as Bach and Beethoven, Chopin and Wagner? If we are to believe some of the composers themselves, or rather, their trumpeters and tub-thumpers, we have amongst us not the equals but the superiors, the *superseders* even, of the old masters. After a thousand years of evolution, music is just beginning to become articulate! Already some music publishers have put up electric signs and others have had recourse to their literary equivalent. The average man of the present day is so accustomed to having his mind made up for him by advertisements, posters and illuminated signs at every street corner, that he comes to believe implicitly anything he reads often enough on the hoardings. If this is the case with patent medicines, it is also the case with art, and we find that propaganda and advertisement carry all before them.

This is an age of anarchy in art; there is no authority, no standard, no sense of proportion. Anybody can do anything and call it "art" in the certain expectation of making a crowd of idiots stand and stare at him in gaping astonishment and admiration. . . .

Great men must be denied and great achievements scoffed at in order that the little ones may become conspicuous. There must be a complete transvaluation of values. Art has been "serious" too long; now let us play the fool, in season and out of season, let us deny everything, turn all our values upside down.

On this principle, a beautiful face is no longer as "interesting" as a grimace; but the interest of a grimace is *purely negative;* it depends entirely on its relation to the natural face. It is only the incongruity of the grimace with the normal features of humankind that causes merriment—the exaggeration of certain traits to the exclusion of others —a false perspective, a wrong proportion. The musical concomitant of a grimace is necessarily negative; it is only a pretentious development of the time-honored tradition of the bang on the big drum when the clown falls down.

Music does not exist for the purpose of emphasizing or exaggerating something which happens outside its own sphere. Musical expression only begins to be significant where words and actions reach their uttermost limit of expression. Music should be concerned with the emotions, not with external events. To make music imitate some other thing is as futile as to try and make it say *Good morning* or *It's a fine day*. It is only that which cannot be expressed otherwise that is worth expressing in music.

Music that needs "explanation," that requires bolstering up with propaganda, always arouses the suspicion that if left to stand on its own merits, it would very quickly collapse and be no more heard of. The present Franco-Russian movement in music is entirely founded on denial, denial of harmony, of coherence, of intellectual lucidity and spiritual content, denial of music, in fact.

Of course I shall be told that people said exactly the same thing about Wagner, and that after thirty years of active musical life I am not sufficiently cultured and that my sensibility is not yet sufficiently developed to appreciate the subtleties and novelties of the latest clique of composers. Exactly the same defence might be put up in favor of the jumblings of a child of four at the piano. . . .

The chief reason for the degeneration of present-day music lies in the fact that people want to get physical sensations from music more than anything else. Emotion is out of date and intellect a bore. Appreciation of art which has been born of profound thought and intensity of experience necessitates an intellectual effort too exhausting for most people of the present day. They want to be amused; they would rather feel music with their bodies than understand it through their emotions. It seems as though a tarantula has bitten them —hence the dancing craze: Dixie, Dalcroze, Duncan and Diaghilev, they are all manifestations of the same thing. In an age of neurasthenics, music, like everything else, must be a stimulant, must be alcoholic, aphrodisiac, or it is no good. . . .

There is no longer any respect for music as such. It can only be tolerated, it seems, as an accompaniment to something else, a dinner or a dance or what not. An impresario, shrewd enough to see what the public wants and to give it to them at the right time, comes along with a resuscitation of the old Italian ballet from St. Petersburg, proclaiming a *new* form of art compared with which all past achievements are as nothing. Led by the nose, the public and, worse still, many of the young musicians flock around him, and the critics cannot find enough adjectives of adulation for his shows.

A ballet is all very well in its proper place, as a pleasant after-dinner entertainment; but we don't want ballets to everything, and to proclaim the ballet as a form of great art, the art form of the future, in fact, is sheer bunkum. But the English public seems to have an insatiable appetite for ballets, and the demand for such works having speedily exhausted the slender stock of living composers' ideas, the scores of long-dead musicians are pressed into service. No one is immune. Bach fugues are employed as exercises in muscular mathematics and Beethoven sonatas interpreted (! ! !) by every hysterical, nymphomaniacal old woman who can gull the public into seeing "a revival of the Greek spirit" or some other highfalutin vision in the writhings and contortions of her limbs.

What is the effect on young people who may perhaps hear some great work for the first time in such an environment? The music will inevitably become associated in their minds with hopping and prancing and jigging, and in the end they will themselves be unable to hear it without twitching and fidgeting.

There seems to be a very prevalent belief that any Tom, Dick, or Harry has the right to tamper with a work of art, even to the extent of altering it beyond recognition and forcing it to serve a purpose its composer never dreamed of.

In this direction irresponsible "editors," "adapters" and "transcribers" are as much to blame as the dancing cranks. It is time a law was passed to keep good music from violation.

By all means become dancing dervishes if you want to, and dance in a delirious *cortège* right into the lunatic asylum; but don't try to justify your procedure in the name of art, nor degrade the works of great artists in doing so. Above all, don't spoil works of art for other people who may not want to dance in the same direction. We do *not* all go the same way home. [1]

THE FUTURE OF OPERA

From: An interview with G. M. Stevensen Reece, 1919

The future of opera generally as an art form? Length and cumbrousness, in my opinion, will be the first features to disappear, and that is the end towards which I am working—brevity and conciseness. Long dialogues and wearisome narrations must go, and will be replaced by short, strong emotional impressions given in a series of terse scenes. Ninety minutes to two hours is long enough for any opera, and by reducing intervals, as I have done in my own work, to three minutes instead of the usual half-hour necessitated by ponderous realistic decoration, this limit can be easily preserved.

Every word must be cleanly heard, and the construction of the work itself should obviate any need of explanation. Suggestion will replace masses of detail in opera, as in modern painting. By these methods I believe it will be possible for opera to become the supreme vehicle for the expression of the finest and subtlest psychological ideas, and we shall achieve 'opera without tears'—other than those, that is to say, of pleasant emotion and genuine thankfulness. [2]

CLAUDE DEBUSSY

1862–1918

From 1901 to 1914 Debussy wrote articles and reviews for *La Revue Blanche, Gil Blas, La Revue S. I. M.* (the publication of the French section of the International Society of Music) and various other magazines. In 1921 a number of these pieces were collected into a volume called *Monsieur Croche—Dilettante Hater*. Through this alter ego Debussy expressed his witty, sometimes cynical opinions on an almost infinite variety of musical subjects. Written as daily reviews, they nevertheless form a brilliant and permanent contribution to musical criticism. His ironic, acid, even vituperative literary style forms a contrast to the controlled emotion in his music, except, perhaps, some of the last works.

He never analyzes a work; he gives his impressions of it which are often more graphic, more enlightening than any analysis might be. No phrase could sum up some of Grieg's pieces more aptly than Debussy's "a pink bonbon filled with snow."

Never over-enthusiastic, he was not overwhelmed by great names and does not hesitate to criticize Gluck, Beethoven and even Bach. During the First World War, Durand brought out an edition of those classics which could not be procured from Germany. Debussy was assigned to edit the violin and piano sonatas of Bach. His letter to Jacques Durand concerning these works shows his independent attitude.

BACH

From: Letter to Jacques Durand, Paris, April 15, 1917

Never edit the Sonatas for violin and piano of J. S. Bach on a rainy Sunday. I've just finished revising the above, and I feel the rain inside.

When the old Saxon cantor has no ideas, he sets off on anything and is truly merciless. In short, he is unbearable except when he is admirable. That's really something, you'll say.

However, had he had a friend—an editor, perhaps—who would have gently advised him not to write one day a week, for example, we might have been spared several hundred pages, in which we must wander through a thicket of joyless measures which unwind pitilessly, with ever the same little rascal of a "subject" and "countersubject." Sometimes, frequently even, the prodigious writing which is, after all, but another bit of gymnastics to the old master, does not succeed in filling the terrific void which grows greater from his insistence on turning to account any old idea, no matter what the price.   [1]

MOZART

From: Letter to Jacques Durand, Paris, February 15, 1916

It is correct to say that, nowadays, the symphonies of Mozart are played badly, because one feels obliged to overstress the nuances.   [2]

BEETHOVEN AND THE SYMPHONY

From: *Monsieur Croche, Antidilettante*

A fog of verbiage and criticism surrounds the *Ninth Symphony*. It is amazing that it has not been finally buried under the mass of prose which it has provoked. Wagner intended to complete the orchestration. Others fancied that they could explain and illustrate the theme by means of pictures. If we admit to a mystery in this symphony, we might clear it up; but is it worthwhile? There was not an ounce of literature in Beethoven, not at any rate in the accepted sense of the word. He had a great love of music, representing to him, as it did, the joy and passion piteously absent from his private life. Perhaps we ought in the *Choral Symphony* to look for nothing more than a magnificent gesture of musical pride. A little notebook with over two hundred different renderings of the dominant theme in the Finale of this symphony shows how persistently Beethoven pursued his search and how entirely musical his guiding motive was; Schiller's lines can have only been used for their appeal to the ear. Beethoven determined that his leading idea should be essentially self-developing and, while it is of extraordinary beauty in itself, it becomes sublime because of its perfect response to his purpose. It is the most triumphant example of the moulding of an idea to the preconceived form; at each leap forward there is a new delight, without either effort or appearance of repetition; the magical blossoming, so to speak, of a tree whose leaves burst forth simultaneously. Nothing is superfluous in this stupendous

work, not even the Andante, declared by modern aestheticism to be
over long; is it not a subtly conceived pause between the persistent
rhythm of the Scherzo and the instrumental flood that rolls the
voices irresistibly onward to the glory of the Finale? Beethoven had
already written eight symphonies and the figure nine seems to have had
for him an almost mystic significance. He determined to surpass himself. I can scarcely see how his success can be questioned. The flood
of human feeling which overflows the ordinary bounds of the symphony sprang from a soul drunk with liberty which, by an ironical
decree of fate, beat itself against the gilded bars within which the mis-
directed charity of the great had confined him. Beethoven must have
suffered cruelly in his ardent longing that humanity should find utterance through him; hence the call of this thousand-voiced genius to the
humblest and poorest of his brethren. Did they hear it? That is the
question. Recently the *Choral Symphony* was performed together with
several of Richard Wagner's highly-spiced masterpieces. Once again
Tannhäuser, Siegmund and Lohengrin voiced the claims of the leitmotiv! The stern and loyal mastery of our great Beethoven easily
triumphed over this vague and high-flown charlatanism.

It seems to me that the proof of the futility of the symphony has
been established since Beethoven. Indeed, Schumann and Mendelssohn
did no more than respectfully repeat the same forms with less power.
The *Ninth Symphony*, none the less, was a demonstration of genius,
a sublime desire to augment and to liberate the usual forms by giving
them the harmonious proportions of a fresco.

Beethoven's real teaching, then, was not to preserve the old forms,
still less to follow in his early steps. We must throw wide the windows
to the open sky; they seem to me to have only just escaped being
closed forever. The fact that here and there a genius succeeds in this
form is but a poor excuse for the laborious and stilted compositions
which we are accustomed to call symphonies.

The young Russian school has endeavored to give new life to the
symphony by borrowing ideas from popular melodies; it has succeeded
in cutting brilliant gems; but are not the themes entirely disproportion-
ate to the developments into which they have been forced? Yet the
fashion for popular airs has spread quickly throughout the musical
world: from east to west the tiniest villages have been ransacked, and
simple tunes, plucked from the mouths of hoary peasants, find themselves, to their consternation, trimmed with harmonic frills. This gives
them an appearance of pathetic discomfort, but a lordly counterpoint
ordains that they shall forget their peaceful origin.

Must we conclude that the symphony, in spite of so many attempted transformations, belongs to the past by virtue of its studied elegance, its formal elaboration and the philosophical and artificial attitude of its audience? Has it not, in truth, merely replaced its old tarnished frame of gold with the stubborn brass of modern instrumentation? A symphony is usually built up on a melody heard by the composer as a child. The first section is the customary presentation of a theme on which the composer proposes to work; then begins the necessary dismemberment; the second section seems to take place in an experimental laboratory; the third section cheers up a little in a quite childish way, interspersed with deeply sentimental phrases during which the melody recedes, as is more seemly; but it reappears and the dismemberment goes on; the professional gentlemen, obviously interested, mop their brows and the audience calls for the composer. But the composer does not appear. He is engaged in listening modestly to the voice of tradition which prevents him, it seems to me, from hearing the voice that speaks within him. [3]

PEDALING IN CHOPIN

From: Letter to Jacques Durand,
Pourville, September 1, 1915

What Saint-Saëns says about the use of the pedal in Chopin is not, despite my respect for his venerable age, altogether correct, for I have very precise recollections on the subject from Mme Manté de Fleurville. Chopin wished his works to be practiced without pedal, and with but very rare exceptions, he did not wish it used at all. This is, moreover, that art of making of the pedal a sort of breathing apparatus, which I observed in Liszt's playing, when I had the opportunity of hearing him in Rome.

The real truth is, perhaps, that the abuse of the pedal is only a means of hiding a lack of technique, also, a means of making a lot of noise in order to cover the music which is being butchered. Theoretically, one should find a graphic means of indicating this "breathing." . . . This is not impossible to find. [4]

WAGNER AND PARSIFAL

From: *Monsieur Croche, Antidilettante*

Wagner's art can never completely die. It will suffer that inevitable decay, the cruel brand of time on all beautiful things; yet noble ruins must remain, in the shadow of which our grandchildren will brood over the past splendor of this man who, had he been a little more human, would have been altogether great.

In *Parsifal*, the final effort of a genius which compels our homage, Wagner tried to drive his music on a looser rein and let it breathe more freely. We have no longer the distraught breathlessness that characterizes Tristan's morbid passion or Isolde's wild screams of frenzy; nor yet the grandiloquent commentary on the inhumanity of Wotan. Nowhere in Wagner's music is a more serene beauty attained than in the prelude to the third act of *Parsifal* and in the entire Good Friday episode, although it must be admitted that Wagner's peculiar conception of human nature is also shown in the attitude of certain characters in this drama. Look at Amfortas, that melancholy Knight of the Grail, who whines like a shop girl and whimpers like a baby. Good heavens! A Knight of the Grail, a king's son, would plunge his spear into his own body rather than parade a guilty wound in doleful melodies for three acts! As for Kundry, that ancient rose of hell, she has furnished much copy for Wagnerian literature; I confess I have but little affection for such a sentimental draggle-tail. Klingsor is the finest character in *Parsifal:* a quondam Knight of the Grail, sent packing from the Holy Place because of his too pronounced views on chastity. His bitter hatred is amazing; he knows the worth of men and scornfully weighs the strength of their vows of chastity in the balance. From this it is quite obvious that this crafty magician, this old gaolbird, is not merely the only human character but the only moral character in this drama, in which the falsest moral and religious ideas are set forth, ideas of which the youthful Parsifal is the heroic and insipid champion.

Here, in short, is a Christian drama in which nobody is willing to sacrifice himself, though sacrifice is one of the highest of the Christian virtues! If Parsifal recovers his miraculous spear, it is thanks to old Kundry, the only creature actually sacrificed in the story: a victim twice over, once to the diabolical intrigues of Klingsor and again to the sacred spleen of a Knight of the Grail. The atmosphere is certainly religious, but why have the incidental children's voices such sinister harmonies? Think for a moment of the childlike candor that would have been conveyed if the spirit of Palestrina had been able to dictate its expression.

The above remarks apply only to the poet, whom we are accustomed to admire in Wagner, and have nothing to do with the musical beauty of the opera, which is supreme. It is incomparable and bewildering, splendid and strong. *Parsifal* is one of the loveliest monuments of sound ever raised to the serene glory of music.   [5]

STRAVINSKY'S *FIREBIRD*

From: Letter to Jacques Durand, Paris, July 6, 1910

You haven't spoken to me about the *Firebird*. It is not a perfect piece, but from certain aspects, it is nevertheless very fine, for here the music is not the docile servant of the dance. And at times you hear altogether unusual combinations of rhythms!

Undoubtedly French dancers would never have consented to dance to such music. Hence, Diaghilev is a great man, and Nijinsky is his prophet, unless it be Calvocoressi.   [6]

PELLÉAS ET MÉLISANDE

Letter to Eugène Ysaye, October 13, 1896

I was most touched by your kind letter and your friendly anxiety for *Pelléas et Mélisande*. The poor little creatures are so difficult to introduce into the world, for with a godfather like you the world doesn't want to have anything to do with them.

Now I must humbly tell you why I am not of your opinion about a performance of *Pelléas* in part. Firstly, if this work has any merit, it is in the connection between the drama and the music. It is quite obvious that at a concert performance this connection would disappear, and no one could be blamed for seeing nothing in the "silences" with which this work is starred. Moreover, as the simplicity of the work gains significance only on the stage, at a concert performance they would throw in my face the American wealth of Wagner, and I'd be like some poor fellow who couldn't afford to pay for the "contra-bass tubas"! In my opinion Pelléas and Mélisande must be given as *they are*, and then it will be a matter of taking them or leaving them, and if we have to fight, it will be worthwhile.   [7]

LES RONDES DE PRINTEMPS, IMAGES

From: Letter to Jacques Durand,
Pourville, September 3, 1907

The *Images* will be ready if I manage to finish the *Rondes* to my satisfaction. The music of this piece has this about it: it is elusive, and consequently cannot be handled like a robust symphony which walks on all fours (sometimes on threes, but walks nevertheless).

Besides, I am more and more convinced that music is not, in essence, a thing which can be cast into a traditional and fixed form. It is made up of colors and rhythms.

The rest is a lot of humbug invented by frigid imbeciles riding the backs of the Masters who have almost always written music of their own time.

Bach alone divined eternal truth.

In any case, music is a very young art, from the point of technique as well as knowledge.   [8]

AMERICAN PRODIGIES

Letter to Jacques Durand, September 22, 1908

I couldn't come to see you last Saturday as I had promised, since I had made an appointment with Mlle E. F. B., an American lady journalist, who came to ask my advice on bringing up little American geniuses. For you are not unaware that all future discoveries in art must hail henceforth from America.

So in order not to waste time, one must decide on the genius of a child at the age of eight or ten. This is so ridiculous as to be touching! I declared to Mlle B. that her compatriots should invent a machine into which one can put any child, rendering him a complete artist in five minutes.   [9]

INSTINCT

From: Letter to Jacques Durand, Paris, March 21, 1917

It is curious how two "parasitic" measures can demolish the most solidly built edifice. This is just what has happened to me, and nothing can prevent it, neither long experience nor the most beautiful talent! It is instinct only—as old as the world—which can save you!   [10]

RICHARD STRAUSS
1864-1949

Throughout a long and prolific creative career, Richard Strauss veered from the classical to the romantic to the super-realistic and back again. In his correspondence with Hofmannsthal, which covers their more than twenty years' collaboration, we witness the almost day-to-day changes in his artistic credo. After the volcanic, expanded Wagner-Berlioz orchestra of *Electra* and *Salomé*, in the first of which it pained him—if anecdote be true—that Mme Schumann-Heink's voice could still be heard above the din at a rehearsal, we see him turn to the chamber orchestra. This, he maintained, was the orchestra of the future, the orchestra which does not smother the human voice. Gradually he leaned more and more toward the unaccompanied spoken word. He had an uncanny sense of the value of word and idea, witness the long, successful collaboration with Hofmannsthal, who was so fertile in ideas, so skillful with the word.

His *Betrachtungen und Erinnerungen* (1949) comprise a series of essays in which he expresses his mature reflections on the ideas only touched upon in the letters. *On Composers and Conductors* states that for the "younger" generation, his symphonic poems are no longer valid. As a matter of fact, the blown-up works are less and less played, and it is likely that his immortality will rest more on *Rosenkavalier, Ariadne,* and *Till Eulenspiegel.*

He was a brilliant conductor, a flawless orchestral colorist: his views on conducting should be bible to all professionals, his musical works in themselves a textbook on instrumentation.

TEN GOLDEN RULES INSCRIBED IN THE ALBUM
OF A YOUNG CONDUCTOR
[ca. 1925]

1. Bear in mind that you are not making music for your own pleasure, but for the pleasure of your audience.

2. You must not perspire while conducting; only the public must get warm.

3. Direct *Salomé* and *Electra* as if they had been written by Mendelssohn: Elfin music.

4. Never encourage the brass, except with a curt glance, in order to give an important entrance cue.

5. On the contrary, never let the horns and woodwinds out of your sight; if you can hear them at all, they are too loud.

6. If you think that the brass is not blowing loud enough, mute it by a couple of degrees.

7. It is not enough that you yourself understand the singer's every word, which you know from memory; the public must be able to follow without effort. If the audience does not understand the text, it falls asleep.

8. Always accompany the singer so that he can sing without strain.

9. When you think that you have reached the most extreme prestissimo, take the tempo again as fast.[1]

10. If you bear all this cheerfully in mind, you, with your beautiful talent and great knowledge, will ever be the untroubled delight of your listeners.   [1]

COMPOSING AND CONDUCTING

(1929)

It is simply not true that one can compose "everything," insofar as one understands "composing" as the translation of an expression of feeling or perception into the symbolic language of music. At the same time, it is just as true that one can paint in tones and sounds, particularly motives expressing action, but there always remains the imminent danger of relying too much on the music and falling into the trap of a boring imitation of nature. In this case, though the music be done with ever so much spirit and technical know-how, it will always remain second-rate music.

My conviction is that in the future the sole decisive medium for dramatic effectiveness will be the instrumentation for smaller orchestra, which does not smother the singing voice as the larger orchestra does. This has been recognized in part by many younger composers, who believe that the orchestra for the opera of the future is the chamber orchestra which, in its crystal clear underscoring of the stage action, is alone capable of conveying the intentions of the composer with complete distinctness and with consideration for the voices. After all, it is

[1] Might I alter the above today (1948): take the tempo half as fast. (For Mozart conductors!) [Strauss' note.]

not altogether unessential that the public not only hear tones, but be able to follow the text exactly.

Among other things my stick technique was cavilled with formerly, because it was felt that the tempi in my conception of Beethoven were inadequate. However, I ask: "Who will conclusively maintain today that Beethoven himself did or did not want this or that tempo precisely so and not otherwise (perhaps more or less according to my conception)? Is there at all an established tradition?"

There is not. Therefore I emphasize that the purely personal and strongly artistic conviction of the orchestral conductor alone must decide what is right or wrong. Just as I have allowed every work of Beethoven, Wagner and others to mellow inside me for many years, so I reproduce them now with the belief that it is the only true and correct interpretation.

Again and again I have wanted to return to symphonic literature which occupied and enchanted me a great deal in my youth, but until today no bright ideas have occurred to me. Program music also is only possible and is only raised to the level of the artistic when its creator is above all a musician possessing imagination and vision. Otherwise he is a charlatan, for even in program music, the first and most important question is ever that of the worth and strength of the musical idea.

It lies perhaps in the nature of the times, that our successors, our "younger generation," our "moderns," can no longer view my dramatic and symphonic works as a valid expression of that which permitted me to live in them musically and as a human being, but which no longer holds any musical or artistic problems for me, though these are just beginning for the "younger generation." We are all children of our time, and can never leap beyond its shadow. [2]

THE EQUIPMENT OF A CONDUCTOR

Preface to *An Orchestra Player on Conducting* by Hans
Diestel, Baden bei Wien, July 15, 1931

When, as Royal Musical Director at the Munich Court Theater during the years 1886–89, I conducted my first opera (there were so many nice things in those days, what with unlimited subventions and singers without contractual vacations), my sixty-five-year-old father still sat in fabulous loyalty to duty an hour before curtain time in his accustomed chair of forty-five years as first horn, and was nervous not only about his own ticklish solos in *Così fan tutte*, but also lest the "green" baton of his unroutined *filius* on the podium reveal any weaknesses.

Somewhat disdainfully the old Lachner partisan and enemy of Bülow remarked: "Oh, you conductors, you flatter yourselves about the miracle of your authority! When a man takes over—the way he ascends the podium, opens the score, before he has lifted his baton—we already know whether he is master or we are."

Setting up these words as a motto, so to speak, for their work, I should like to admonish my colleagues of the podium: Don't be too proud of your three recalls after the third *Leonore* overture! There below in the pit, among the first violins, there to the rear among the horns, or all the way at the other end among the drums, sit Argus-eyed watchers, who follow your quarters and eighths with critical glances, who groan when you "flail about" the *allabreves* from *Tristan* in four-quarters "under their very noses," when you celebrate the "Scene at the Brook" or the second variation in the Adagio of the *Ninth* with twelve precisely beat-out eighths. They rebel, when you continuously scream down to them "pst" and "piano, gentlemen" during the performance, while your right hand unceasingly conducts forte. They blink when, at the beginning of the rehearsal, you warn: "The woods are not in tune," and then you yourself cannot say which instrument is too sharp or too flat. While the big chief believes that they are hanging on his baton, they are faithfully playing on, without glancing at him as he misses a beat; they chalk every wrong tempo to his "individual conception," when he conducts a symphony, perhaps for the first time, which they have played a hundred times before under better conductors.

The solo violist of the Vienna Philharmonic once called over to me at a rehearsal when, my baton not being at hand, I was about to take another: "Not that one, Doctor—that one has no rhythm."

In short, the tales of conductors tripped up by members of the orchestra could fill volumes! And yet, this malicious horde which dawdles about in a chronic mezzo-forte, which maintains no precision in recitative chords when the right man is not sitting at the helm, with what enthusiasm do these musicians—so often tortured by unskillful bungling at rehearsal, dead tired from giving lessons—with what devotion even, do they rehearse when they have confidence in their director, if he doesn't harass them uselessly. How they follow his slightest gesture throughout the evening (particularly if he has made them a present of one rehearsal), if his right hand, in full control of conducting technique, is capable of conveying his intentions to the minutest degree, if his eye, at once stern and benevolent, watches over their playing, and his left hand does not clench itself into a fist at fortissimos, and he doesn't unnecessarily pester them at *pianos*.   [3]

TIMELY NOTES ON MUSIC EDUCATION

(1933)

About 2500 years ago the great Confucius anchored the principles of Chinese ethics in three fundamental sentences:

a) Cult of the ancestors: that is, the reverent preservation and study of the achievements of ancestors.

b) Cultivation of good manners; that is, the relation to one's fellow creatures.

c) Cultivation of music: that is, the development of inner harmony.

We no longer know how Chinese music, which this philosopher himself so zealously practiced, and to the cultivation of which he attached such great importance, sounded; we see, however, that the art of music from Johann Sebastian Bach to Richard Wagner conquered the hearts of the entire civilized world, and today, even in the dubious form of radio listening, though it may not delight the ears, it still helps bridge the boredom of vacant evenings.

In what, then, does the so-called enjoyment of art by these music listeners chiefly consist? In the purely sensuous, musical treat, unprejudiced by any intellectual effort? One person is excited by the pleasing sound of a high tenor voice, the other by the brio of a Beethoven stretta, another gasps at the vocal facility of a coloratura singer. He admires the power and velocity of a piano virtuoso. He experiences a subconscious pleasant reaction to the sound of a Stradivarius fiddle. He is happy when he can grasp a halfway intelligible melody from the otherwise unbearable purgatory of a classical symphony. He breathes freely when, after the dissonances of a four-hour *Tristan*, after the "Gedibbere, bis der Dampfer kommt," as a good Hamburg lady wailed at the climax of the "Liebestod" with its unbelievable, magic sound— the last measure is considered the most beautifully orchestrated cadence in music history—he leaves the theater with at least a feeling of halfway animal well-being. But when I ask dozens of concertgoers, carried away by the wonderful motions and transports of their beloved conductor, what they actually heard, I receive in nine cases out of ten this response: Oh, the *Ninth;* it was marvellous, but the solo quartet was not good. The *Jupiter* symphony with the "famous" fugue, the *Trout* quintet, the *Unfinished*, the *Surprise* symphony, etc. Or after *Meistersinger:* What did you like best? Well, "Am stillen Herd" (Walter's audition solo), the "Prize Song," possibly even the quintet and the pompous overture. After *Walküre:* "Winterstürme wichen dem Wonnemond" (Siegmund's solo) and "especially the *Magic Fire* music." What the dear public actually heard, wherein lay the great impression

of an *Eroica*, or a *C sharp minor* quartet, what it is that merited the
enthusiasm over a Mozart *Figaro* or *Così fan tutte* finale, listeners will
not be able to explain who do not possess at least some skill in piano
playing, or as practicing dilettantes, devote themselves to chamber
music—as is done even today in Vienna on Sunday afternoons—and
thereby, through pleasant habit, bring to absolute music a gradually
increasing understanding. In what the fullest and greatest value of the
master creations of our music—the latest art to have reached flowering
—consists, only he can judge who has worked through the discipline
of harmony, counterpoint and form; who, reading a Wagner or Berlioz
score, can hear it with his inner ear, so that all the values of a *Lohengrin* and *Walküre* woodwind treatment, the primeval mysteries of the
orchestra in Wotan's narration are really a source of the highest artistic
enjoyment to him.

Music is a language which the layman believes he understands
better than Turkish, for instance, because its few characters are more
quickly learned than those of the Koran, and because the naïve ear
can retain a simple eight bar melody more easily and fancies it better
sounding than a Chinese sentence. Every child from the age of two
on learns his mother tongue easily and by imitation. When it leaves
primary school, it can read every book. Through daily comparison
the eye has already trained itself to the point where a twelve-year-old
student at the Pinakothek [art museum in Munich] can differentiate
a Madonna from a St. Sebastian, and by dint of diligent reading does
not take the signature of a Ruisdael for a Corot, or a Titian for a
Rembrandt. But has he thereby a true understanding of wherein a real
work of art differs from the most ordinary, tawdry work done in
cheap and gaudy colors? Can he ascertain why a Sans Souci picture by
Menzel is better painting than a Versailles *Coronation* by Anton von
Werner? Though he experience the same deep, pious awe on entering
the St. Stefan cathedral in Vienna as he does on hearing the Kyrie from
the Bach *B minor Mass*, though he sink into a pleasant, comfortable
mood in which his fantasy allows him to glimpse ineffable visions, will
he, without further ado, be able to recognize and enjoy that Gothic
dome, the *Meistersinger* score, in its full significance as an art work?
Since he at least knows the language, since he has eyes in his head, the
Wallenstein trilogy or the Sistine Madonna will at any rate offer him
more aesthetic enjoyment than one of the last Beethoven quartets, the
brittle sound of which does not even arouse in him the same pleasant
sensation as listening to the magnificently orchestrated *Lohengrin* prelude with its instinctively thrilling, grandiose climax. Every layman,

on listening to a Schiller poem, knows at least what he has heard. With a Mozart quartet, this is simply not the case.

Our humanistic culture still bases itself on disciplines, the study of which was an indispensable condition of higher intellectual learning before the invention of our music. It is today still burdened with un-essential studies of higher mathematics, rudiments of chemistry and physics which we can certainly leave to those in the universities and technical schools who wish to dedicate themselves to these professions. The study of music in our high schools, till now altogether neglected, is a requisite of higher general education. This means the study of at least harmony, form, counterpoint up to the understanding of a Bach fugue, the study of scores to the full comprehension of the contrapun-tal soul struggle in the third act of *Tristan*, the architecture and thema-tic development of a Beethoven symphonic movement, the symphonic construction of an act of the *Nibelungen Ring*.

Were this course of study systematically carried out at least among all high school students who are not completely unmusical, and who possibly also play an instrument—the others could be shunted to the department of plastic arts for similar technical study—a source of the most beautiful art enjoyment would be opened to them in their col-leges. It would be an epoch-making gain to carry through a reform in the high school system along the lines I have indicated.   [4]

MELODIC INSPIRATION

(1940)

Melody, as it reveals itself in the most distinguished artistic creations of our classicists, and up to Richard Wagner, belongs to the noblest gifts which an invisible godhead has made to humanity.

Mozart's melodies, his *G minor String Quintet*, Beethoven's sym-phonies, sonatas, quartets (the A flat major Adagio from the *E flat major Quartet*, Op. 127), Schubert's songs, the second and third acts of *Tristan* (to mention just a few outstanding examples) are symbols which reveal the most exalted truths of the soul, which are not "in-vented," but are "lent in a dream" to those favored with them. Whence they come, nobody knows, not even their creator, the unconscious in-strument of the world spirit. The melodic idea, coming straight out of the ether, which suddenly overtakes me, which appears without any material stimulus or psychic emotion—the latter is also frequently a direct cause, as I myself have experienced it in excitement of a quite different, not necessarily artistic order—emerges from the imagination, immediate, unconscious, without benefit of the intelligence. It is the greatest of divine gifts, not to be compared with any other.

Poetic inspiration can still have a connection with the intelligence, because it must externalize itself through words—melodic inspiration is the absolute revelation of final mysteries. Therefore the famous remark of Goethe to Eckermann on May 6, 1827: "I received impressions in my inner being, impressions more sensuous, more vigorous, lovelier, more colorful in hundreds of ways than those which my active imagination offered me; and as a poet I had nothing to do but artistically to mature such observations and impressions within myself, and to reproduce them through so lively a representation that others might obtain the same impressions when they heard or read what I described," touches but one part (actually the mechanical) of poetic activity. Inspiration itself (and particularly musical inspiration, melody) is not at all touched by it. Goethe's words are merely a very modest formulation of poetical labor, not definitive, but probably intended only for Eckermann's limited powers of comprehension. They do not penetrate the core of the workings of the artistic imagination.

Also Goethe's expression: "I have always regarded all my efforts and achievements as only symbolic" is but a paraphrase of that unconscious creative power which manifests itself most clearly and most directly in melodic inspiration, insofar as it is truly "inspiration" without any further effort of the intelligence.

What is an inspiration? In general, a musical inspiration is known as a motive, a melody with which I am suddenly "inspired," unbidden by the intelligence, particularly in the morning immediately on awakening, or in a dream—Sachs in the *Meistersinger:* "Glaubt mir, des Menschen wahrster Wahn wird ihm im Träume aufgetan." [1] Did my imagination work independently at night, without my consciousness, without being bound to "recollection" (Plato)?

My own experience: What at night I am stuck at a certain point in my composition, and in spite of all my digging no further profitable work seems possible, I shut the piano or my sketchbook, go to bed, and when I wake up in the morning, the continuation is there. By means of which mental or physical process?

Or shall we, following current colloquial usage, term inspiration that which is so new, so thrilling, so compelling and which penetrates "into the very depths of the heart" (Leonore), that it can not be compared

[1] Believe me, man's truest fancy is disclosed in his dreams.

with anything that preceded it. Quality? Whence stem the indescribable melodies of our classicists (Haydn, Mozart, Beethoven, Schubert), for which no models exist? Even in Johann Sebastian Bach's Adagios and in the works of his son, Philipp Emanuel, we hardly find themes which can be compared with the soaring, endless melodies of Mozart —not only in the arias of his dramatic works, but also in his instrumental works (I am thinking particularly of his G minor String Quintet). What then is direct inspiration, primary invention, and what is the work of the intelligence in these divine forms? Where is the boundary between intellectual activity and imagination?

The question is especially difficult to decide among our classicists; the wealth of their melodies is so enormous, the melody itself so new, so original and at the same time so individually varied, that it is difficult to determine the line between the first immediate inspiration and its continuation, its extension to the finished, expanded singing phrase. Particularly in Mozart and Schubert who died so young, and at the same time created a lifework of such colossal scope! (My father always said: "What Mozart did, that is, composed up to his thirty-sixth year, the best copyist of today could not write down in the same amount of time.") It must have been prompted—as in the lovely concluding tableau in the first act of Pfitzner's Palestrina—by the flying pen of angels. For the kind of work which is to be seen in Beethoven's sketchbooks can hardly exist here. Here everything seems immediate inspiration.

It has been my own experience in creative activity that a motive or a two to four measure melodic phrase occurs to me suddenly. I put it down on paper and immediately extend it to an eight, sixteen, or thirty-two bar phrase, which naturally does not remain unaltered, but after a shorter or longer "maturing" is gradually worked out into its definitive form which holds its own against even the most severe, blasé self-criticism. This work now proceeds at a rate which depends primarily on my awaiting the moment at which my imagination is capable and ready to serve me further. But this readiness is mostly evoked and promoted by considerable leisure, after lengthy reflection, also through inner excitement (also anger and indignation). These mental processes pertain not only to innate talent, but to self-criticism and self-development. "Genie ist Fleiss" [Genius is industry], Goethe is supposed to have said. But industry and the desire to work are inborn, not merely acquired.

Only where content and form are clothed in the highest perfection, as among our truly great, is finished art achieved. Our music scholars —I speak of the two principal names, Friedrich von Hausegger (Music as Expression) and Eduard Hanslick (Music as Form in Tonal Motion)

—made formulations which have since been considered as inimical opposites. This is wrong. They are the two aspects of music which mutually complement each other. The points of departure of our contemporary music are of various kinds. "Form in tonal motion" has its source truly in the dance, "music as expression" in the cry of pain, in the necessity to give artistic form to religious prayer (Gregorian chant, Palestrina Masses and the chorales of J. S. Bach). At the same time, proceeding from Monteverdi, the recitative developed, then flowed into the aria and with it into contemporary opera.

We may designate as "form in tonal motion" most of the Bach and Handel instrumental works, in the slow movements of which deeper feeling struggles for expression, a feeling which later speaks to our hearts directly with form-perfected logic in all gradations of emotion in the works of Haydn, Mozart, Beethoven and Schubert. The so-called sonata form which, from Haydn to the late Beethoven, fused itself with the emotional content of the works, was not achieved again by any of the descendants of these heroes, Brahms or Bruckner, for instance, in whose compositions, excellent in themselves, the sonata form has become a conventional formula in the midst of which one often painfully senses arbitrary music-making, whereas one stands with eyes and ears open in delight before a Haydn quartet.

These instrumental works of the classicists may also be termed "forms in tonal motion," but they are, however, no longer rhythmically moving tonal play as in Bach and Handel, but happy or impassioned, vital expressions of noblest spirituality. In the variation form still popular today, and of late frequently dull (in my *Don Quixote* carried *ad absurdum* and tragi-comically travestied), is found united all the passage work invented and constantly enriched by the classicists. Finally, Richard Wagner combined all kinds of rich passage work with the most evocative melodies to serve dramatic expression. *Tristan, The Ring, Meistersinger* and *Parsifal* constitute the peak toward which all species of "form in tonal motion" and "musical expression" strive. In Wagner music reached its greatest capacity for expression.   [5]

MOZART

(1944)

It has become the custom to treat this most sublime of all tonal masters as a "rococo artist," to represent his work as the epitome of the ornamental and the playful. Though it is correct to say that he was one who solved all "problems" before they were even posed, that in him passion is divested of everything earthly and seems to be viewed from a bird's-eye perspective, it is equally true that his work contains —even when transfigured, spiritualized and liberated from reality— all phases of human experience from the monumental, dark grandeur of the Commandant's scene in *Don Giovanni* to the daintiness of the Zerlina arias, the heavenly frivolities of *Figaro*, and the deliberate ironies of *Così fan tutte*.

With less amplitude, but with no less abundance the entire gamut of human feeling is expressed in his non-dramatic creations. To set up a uniform Mozart style for the reproduction of this infinitely fine and richly organized soul-picture is as foolish as it is superficial.

In Susanna's garden aria, in Belmonte's and Ferrando's A major and Octavio's G major arias, Eros himself sings in Mozart's melody; Love in its most beautiful, purest forms speaks to our feelings. Zerlina's two arias are not merely the expression of an ordinary, betrayed peasant girl. In the slow section of Donna Anna's so-called "Letter" aria, in both arias of the Countess in *Figaro*, we have before us the creations of the Ideal, which I can only compare with Plato's "Ideas," the proto-types of visions projected into real life. Almost immediately on Bach follows the miracle of Mozart, with his perfection and absolute ideal-ization of the melody of human song—I might call it the Platonic Idea or Prototype—not to be recognized by the eye, not to be grasped by the understanding, but to be divined by consciousness as most godly, which the ear is permitted to "breathe in." Mozartean melody is de-tached from every earthly form—the "thing in itself," like Plato's Eros, poised between heaven and earth, between the mortal and the immortal—liberated from the "will," it embodies the deepest penetra-tion of artistic imagination, of the unconscious, into the final mysteries, into the realm of the "archetypes." [6]

LETTERS TO HUGO VON HOFMANNSTHAL

Garmisch, July 28, 1916

I share your view completely that the prelude to *Ariadne* takes pre-cisely the new path which must be followed, and I myself incline to-ward realistic comedy with genuine, interesting people, be it of lyric content as *Rosenkavalier* with its superb Marschallin, or burlesque, a parody of the Offenbach type. But to alter the style of *Die Frau ohne Schatten* to the one toward which you are so sympathetic and toward which we must both steer, is absolutely wrong. This has nothing to do with the music or text; this lies in the material itself, in its romanticism, in its symbolism. One cannot inject red corpuscles into figures like the King, the Queen and the Nurse as one can into a Marschallin, an Octavian or an Ochs. I may rack my brain endlessly, and I am tormenting myself no end, what with sifting and more sifting, but my heart is only half in it, and since my head must accomplish the greater half of the work, there must remain a breath of academic frigidity in it (what my wife so aptly calls "music crocheting") which no bellows can fan into a real fire.   [7]

Garmisch, early September, 1916

Your cry of distress against "music-making" à la Wagner has pierced my heart and has thrown open the door onto a completely new landscape, so that, guided by *Ariadne*, and particularly by its prelude, I hope to betake myself completely into the realm of un-Wagnerian theater, into opera of the heart and humanity. I see my way clearly before me, and I thank you for having prodded me, but for me to achieve this, you must create the necessary librettos, librettos à la *Black Domino, Maurer und Schlosser, Wildschütz, Zar und Zimmermann, Teufels Anteil,* à la Offenbach, but they must be filled with Hofmannsthalish people instead of puppets. An amusing, interesting plot, be it clothed in dialogue, arias, duets, ensembles, vitalized with real composable people like the Marschallin, Ochs or Batak! In whatever form you wish! I promise you that I have now definitely stripped myself of the Wagnerian musical armor.   [8]

Munich, July 17, 1917

Today I want to express my strongest doubts concerning the melodrama form. It is the most awkward, most stupid art form that I know. Since every kind of musical exercise in the melodrama form must be limited to the veriest minimum, as otherwise the text is understood even less than in opera, it offers the musician the least rewarding of tasks and as a consequence, a very frugal aural feast to the public.   [9]

Garmisch, October 10, 1923

Everything that you have indicated with the word "spoken" I should like—for the present—to have really spoken. I find the so-called Mozartean "secco recitative" (with piano accompaniment) a not too happy art form, and am again beginning more and more to prefer dialogue between set pieces which gain a freshness thereby. First, the purely spoken word is better understood, and precisely in such realistic dialogue as in the first Aithra scenes, the sung notes obliterate the characteristic cadence. I have the feeling that the solo scene between Helena and Aithra which you read to me will be more effective if much of it is spoken, and undue length will be avoided. [10]

Rotterdam, January 29, 1924

I have purposely not participated in any literary manifestos in honor of your fiftieth birthday [February 1, 1924] as I cannot help but feel that everything which I might say to you in words would be banal in comparison to what I, as a composer, have said in tones about your magnificent poetry. That it was your words which drew from me the most beautiful music I had to give should afford you the utmost gratification. And so may Chrysothemis, the Marschallin, Ariadne, Zerbinetta, the Queen and, last but not least, the "much admired and much inveighed against" Helena [1] thank you along with me for everything that you have dedicated to me from your life's work, for everything you have demanded of me and have awakened to life. [11]

[1] *Die Ägyptische Helena* was their latest operatic collaboration up to that time.

PAUL DUKAS

1865–1935

Perhaps more prolific as writer than as composer, Paul Dukas was equally polished and productive in both fields. His wide literary background shows itself in his choice of musical subject matter: the *King Lear* and *Götz von Berlichingen* overtures, the opera *Ariane et Barbe-Bleu* (1907), and the *Sorcerer's Apprentice* (1897), for which he is most popularly known. This last, a realistic musical portrayal of Goethe's ballad, is a masterpiece of comedy in music.

For many years a contributor to *La Revue hebdomadaire*, the *Chronique des Arts* and other periodicals, he wrote on an endless variety of subjects and people: "Music and Literature," "Interpretations of Lyric Drama," "The *Faust* of Goethe and the Music," Wagner, Liszt, Berlioz, Schumann and a host of other nineteenth century celebrities to twentieth century Stravinsky. This wealth of essays was collected after his death in a sizable volume, *Écrits sur la Musique*.

The Paris Conservatoire and the École Normale de Musique numbered him among its most brilliant teachers; his edition of Rameau's works is exemplary for its profound scholarship and good taste.

COMEDY IN MUSIC

From: *Revue hebdomadaire*, September 1894

The question of the pictorial in music has been much discussed, but the study of its potential for the comic has, on the contrary, been left almost completely in the shade; however, it would seem to us that this study might be of some interest, if it only served to show once more what certain combinations of sounds can accomplish. Schumann, one of the first to take into account the comic power of music, points out, in several places in his writings, a number of passages from the symphonies of Beethoven which seem to suggest to him what he calls *grotesque* relations. The word is unfortunate and conveys the meaning badly. Yet, on examination of the passages in question, one gets a clearer picture of Schumann's idea. Beyond doubt these melodic or harmonic caprices of Beethoven, which sometimes occur in the midst of the most serious passages, must have had in his mind a certain humoristic significance.

The comic intention, then, is manifest but veiled, and therefore remains a little unclear. Thus, in the finale of the *Eighth Symphony*, so sparkling, so animated, so tender, with its middle phrase of a distant farewell, what can that singular A flat signify as it surges abruptly into the middle of the whirlwind and suddenly stops it? The totally strange appearance of this unusual note immediately convinces the listener musical enough to grasp the false relation it presents with that which surrounds it, that here is a humorous passage. But, truthfully speaking, these sallies risk remaining unexplained in instrumental music, and they are hardly detected by the majority of listeners. Schumann picks out several, of which some are doubtful, at least to us. However, it is certain that there are in Beethoven's music certain deliberate anomalies which remain incomprehensible if one does not attach a humorous connotation to them, the sense of which inevitably goes beyond its purely musical significance. Far be it from us, however, to attribute to these whims more importance than they deserve.

But when the music depends on a given text, its comic power shows itself effectively in quite a different way. Here the association of ideas plays the principal rôle; the comic element, as we have said, results only from a surprise juxtaposition and a disproportion between two kinds of ideas or feelings. It is especially through the connection of text and music that it stands out most clearly, whether this connection be that of sombre music to very gay words or the contrary, or that the contour of the melody, appropriate rhythms or a special instrumentation highlight the particular comic quality in the scene.

In tracing very far back into the history of music, one finds even among the primitives songs whose waggish, frolicsome burden is a striking example of what music, reduced to the mere resources of four vocal parts, can be in the hands of a man of spirit. We have often spoken of the chansons of Orlando di Lasso, à propos of the performances given them by M. Charles Bordes,[1] those which begin with the words: *Si vous n'êtes pas en bon poinct, Fuyons tous d'amour le jeu, Chanter, danser, faire cent tours*, etc., are so many perfect examples of comic music in the sixteenth century.

Later, through the perfection of dramatic style and especially through combinations of instrumentation, music was able to enter the domain of comedy with even more confidence, and display itself at

[1] Charles Bordes: The French conductor and composer who researched widely into early French choral music, and performed it with his excellently trained chorus, Les Chanteurs de St Gervais.

its ease. Already Lully, in composing songs and entr'actes for the comedies of Molière, had essayed certain comic effects, a bit embryonic, one must confess. But when one passes from Lully to Rameau, one discovers enormous progress. Here, as everywhere else, the author of *Hippolyte et Aricie* shows himself a genius, full of happy inspirations and charming ideas.

Open the score, for example, of *Platée* or *Junon Jalouse*, called *comedy ballet*, and performed in 1749. The story can be told in a few words: To cure Juno of her jealousy, Jupiter, on the advice of Mercury, feigns to be smitten with a ridiculous nymph of the marshes, Plateé, and in effect wins his point at the end of the piece, when the infuriated Juno tears the veil from the unfortunate Platée and can't help bursting into laughter at her looks. This theme abounds in burlesque situations which Rameau has expressed with an inexhaustible verve and without ever allowing the music to lose its importance. First comes the languorous air of Platée:

> *Dis-moi, mon cœur, dis-moi, t'es-tu bien consulté?*
> *Tu t'agites, tu me quittes!*
> *Est-ce pour Cithéron, t'a-t-il bien mérité?*

where one already finds repetitions of syllables such as Offenbach fancied, on: *t'es-tu, t'es-tu,* and *t'a-t-il, t'a-t-il.* A little further on, the nymph evokes (*pindarising,* says the score) the frogs to witness her happiness, and we have here an outburst of *Quoi? Quoi?* syncopated above a continuous pattern in the orchestra that is most amusing in effect. One would have to cite everything in the score if one wished to analyze the many conceits which do honor to the wit of Rameau. When Platée appears, accompanied by Jupiter, the chorus intones a chorus in six-eight measure:

> *Qu'elle est aimable, qu'elle est belle!*

on a descending scale, in repeated notes, which makes the *ai* of *aimable* stand out sixteen times, and which stops sharply, to fall again after a pause on the *ble* on the accented part of the following measure. Then slowly he adds his: *Qu'elle est belle!* Well sung, this should be irresistibly comic. But let us stop our quotations here.

Another charming author, whose music is as full of wit as of feeling, is Monsigny. But with him as with Rameau, the comic intent is above all realized by the special twist in the vocal part, cleverly modelled on the words, and not through any devices drawn from the resources peculiar to music as an independent art. One can not say as much for Grétry, although the latter may be more on the right track, in that often in his works, the comic stems exclusively from the music.

One voice in the orchestra, here and there, sounds a note artfully matching a word or gesture; or again, there are amusing contrasts of intensity and gentleness, as in the famous chorus of the soldiers in *Richard Coeur de Lion:* "Voici monseigneur!" which the soldiers shout into the ears of the unhappy Blondel with all their might, and which all of a sudden fades to an imperceptible whisper when the redoubtable general appears.

Certainly, it is the masters of the French school from Monsigny to Boieldieu who have succeeded best in making music speak the language of delicate and gracious comedy. After Rossini, whose genius had a disastrous influence on our national school, this amiable and lively grace was finished. Without taking from the Italian his irrepressible verve and his dazzling chaff, they took hold of his facile formulas, his Italian redundancies, his brilliant but often coarse instrumental effects. Pale successors of opera-bouffe replaced French lyric comedy. It seems at present that this is an art forever lost; the last reflection of it glimmered in Massenet's *Manon.*

But for music to rise by virtue of its own power to the pitch of great comedy without ceasing to be in itself a complete and perfectly pure art, we must wait for Mozart to appear. His theater is no longer like that of the French masters, a simple adaptation of music to words. His music is, by itself, superiorly organized; where Grétry puts only words to music, Mozart sees only a situation which he forces himself to set to music envisaged as an absolute art. That is why the scores of the *Marriage of Figaro* or *Don Giovanni* seem harmoniously molded ensembles in which all the effects, serious or gay, spring effortlessly from the heart of the music itself. Comic passages abound in the works of Mozart; everyone knows them from memory, and there is no need to enumerate them. However, how can one fail to notice that only such an art could triumph over a situation as complex as the duet between Don Giovanni and Leporello before the statue of the Commandant, in which the burlesque and the pathetic mingle in such a marvellous manner? Such a situation could not have been met by the more simple and literary art of the masters of the French school.

Shall we recall, to conclude these brief comments on the comic power of music, what the great contemporary masters have achieved? Berlioz in the *Damnation of Faust*, in *Benvenuto*, in *Beatrice and Benedict*, Weber in *Oberon*, and Mendelssohn in *A Midsummer Night's Dream?* And the astonishing Mime, and the prodigious Beckmesser of Wagner? Do the résumés of all these characteristic forces not demonstrate triumphantly that be it laughter or tears, feverish passion or religious ecstasy, nothing, in the category of human feelings, is a stranger to music? [1]

FERRUCCIO BUSONI

1866–1924

Busoni's pianism, especially in his last years, was of the highest order. His colossal technique, the fruit of years of unremitting labor, was forgotten in his imaginative interpretations. A consummate use of the pedal and a wide variety of color and dynamics gave his playing its fantastic quality. When George Bernard Shaw heard him, he remarked that no man could play that well and still compose.

Yet Busoni was a prolific composer, numbering among his works several operas, symphonic and chamber works and piano pieces. They reflect his intellectual, contemplative, philosophic nature. Today his works are rarely performed, but his many transcriptions of Bach still retain their place in the repertoire of all pianists.

He devoted a number of years to piano teaching—in Helsingfors, at the New England Conservatory in Boston, where he was not too happy because most of his students did not measure up to his artistic standards, and in Weimar, where a closer relation with ardent, enthusiastic students gave him greater stimulus and gratification.

His extended concert engagements took him to America—his *Indian Fantasy* is based on American Indian themes—England and the whole of Western Europe. The letters written on tour contain penetrating observations on music, musical happenings and personalities. He favored the return from the bloated orchestra of the late nineteenth and early twentieth centuries to the smaller classical ensemble—*vide* his criticism of Strauss—and championed the cause of melody at a time when its importance was being negated by the "newer" composers. This tendency toward classicism or neo-classicism and the feeling for melody are perhaps traceable to his mixed German and Italian heritage.

THE PIANOFORTE

From: Letter to Hugo von Hofmannsthal, no date

Respect the pianoforte! Its disadvantages are evident, decided and unquestionable: the lack of sustained tone, and the pitiless, unyielding adjustment of the inalterable semitonic scale.

But its advantages and prerogatives approach the marvellous.

It gives a single man command over something complete; in its potentialities from softest to loudest in one and the same register, it excels all other instruments. The trumpet can blare, but not sigh; contrariwise the flute; the pianoforte can do both. Its range embraces the highest and deepest practicable tones. Respect the pianoforte!

Let doubters consider how the pianoforte was esteemed by Bach, Mozart, Beethoven, Liszt, who dedicated their choicest thoughts to it.

And the pianoforte has one possession wholly peculiar to itself, an inimitable device, a photograph of the sky, a ray of moonlight—the pedal.

The effects of the pedal are unexhausted, because they have remained even to this day the drudges of a narrow-souled and senseless harmonic theory; the treatment accorded them is like trying to mould air or water into geometric forms. Beethoven, who incontestably achieved the greatest progress on and for the pianoforte, divined the mysteries of the pedal, and to him we owe the first liberties.

The pedal is in ill repute. For this, absurd irregularities must bear the blame. Let us experiment with *sensible* irregularities.   [1]

RULES FOR PRACTICING THE PIANO

From: Letter to Woltersdorf, Berlin, July 20, 1898

1. Practice the passage with the most difficult fingering; when you have mastered that, play it with the easiest.

2. If a passage offers some particular technical difficulty, go through all similar passages you can remember in other places; in this way you will bring system into the kind of playing in question.

3. Always join technical practice with the study of the interpretation; the difficulty often does not lie in the notes, but in the dynamic shading prescribed.

4. Never be carried away by temperament, for that dissipates strength, and where it occurs there will always be a blemish, like a dirty spot which can never be washed out of a material.

5. Don't set your mind on overcoming the difficulties in pieces which have been unsuccessful because you have previously practiced them badly; it is generally a useless task. But if meanwhile you have quite changed your way of playing, then begin the study of the old piece from the beginning, as if you did not know it.

6. Study everything as if there were nothing more difficult; try to interpret studies for the young from the standpoint of the virtuoso;

you will be astonished to find how difficult it is to play a Czerny or Cramer, or even a Clementi.

7. Bach is the foundation of piano playing, Liszt the summit. The two make Beethoven possible.

8. Take it for granted from the beginning that everything is possible on the piano, even when it seems impossible to you, or really is so.

9. Attend to your technical apparatus so that you are prepared and armed for every possible event; then, when you study a new piece, you can turn all your power to the intellectual content; you will not be held up by the technical problems.

10. Never play carelessly, even when there is nobody listening, or the occasion seems unimportant.

11. Never leave a passage which has been unsuccessful without repeating it; if you cannot do it in the presence of others, then do it subsequently.

12. If possible, allow no day to pass without touching your piano.

[2]

TRANSCRIPTIONS

From: Letter to his wife, Berlin, July 22, 1913

Transcription occupies an important place in the literature of the piano, and looked at from the right point of view, every important piano piece is the reduction of a big thought to a practical instrument. But transcription has become an independent art, no matter whether the starting point of a composition is original or unoriginal. Bach, Beethoven, Liszt and Brahms were evidently all of the opinion that there is artistic value concealed in a pure transcription, for they all cultivated the art themselves, seriously and lovingly. In fact, the art of transcription has made it possible for the piano to take possession of the entire literature of music. Much that is inartistic, however, has got mixed up with this branch of the art. And it was because of the cheap, superficial estimation made of it by certain men, who had to hide their nakedness with a mantle of "being serious," that it sank to what was considered a low level.   [3]

From: *Sketch of a New Esthetic of Music,* 1906

KEYS

We teach twenty-four keys, twelve times the two series of Seven, but, in point of fact, we have at our command only two, the major and the minor key. The rest are merely transpositions. By means of the several transpositions we are supposed to get different characteristics of harmony; but this is an illusion. In England, under the reign of the high concert pitch, the most familiar works are played a semitone higher than they were written, without changing their effect. Singers transpose an aria to suit their convenience, leaving untransposed what precedes and follows. Song writers not infrequently publish their own compositions in three different pitches; in all three editions the pieces are precisely alike.

When a well-known face looks out of a window, it matters not whether it gazes down from the first story or the third.

Were it feasible to elevate or depress a landscape, as far as the eye can reach, by several hundred yards, the pictorial impression would neither gain nor lose by it.

Upon the two series of Seven, the major key and the minor key, the whole art of music has been established; one limitation brings on the other.

To each of these a definite character has been attributed; we have learned and have taught that they should be heard as contrasts, and they have gradually acquired the significance of symbols: Major and Minor, *Maggiore e Minore,* Contentment and Discontent, Joy and Sorrow, Light and Shade. The harmonic symbols have fenced in the expression of music, from Bach to Wagner and yet further on until today and the day after tomorrow.[1] Minor is employed with the same intention, and has the same effect upon us now, as two hundred years ago. Nowadays it is no longer possible to "compose" a funeral march, for it already exists, once for all. Even the least informed, non-professional knows what to expect when a funeral march —whichever you please—is to be played. Even the layman can anticipate the difference between a symphony in major and one in minor.

Strange, that one should feel major and minor as opposites. They both present the same face, now more joyous, now more serious; a mere touch of the brush suffices to turn the one into the other. The passage from one to the other is easy and imperceptible; when it occurs frequently and swiftly, the two begin to shimmer and coalesce indistinguishably. But when we recognize that major and minor form one whole with a double meaning, and the "twenty-four keys" are simply an elevenfold transposition of the original two, we easily arrive at a

[1] This was written in 1906. The intervening ten years have somewhat helped to educate our ear. [Busoni's note]

perception of the unity of our system of keys (tonality). The conceptions of "related" and "foreign" keys vanish, and with them the entire intricate theory of degrees and relations. We possess one single key. But it is of a very poor nature.　　　　　　　　　　　　[4]

RESTS

Within our present-day music, that which most nearly approaches the essential nature of the art, is the rest and the hold. Consummate players, improvisers, know how to employ these means of expression in loftier and ampler measure. The tense silence between two movements—in itself music, in this environment—leaves wider scope for divination than the more determinate, but therefore less elastic, sound.

[5]

MELODY

From: Letter to his wife, Los Angeles, March 15, 1911

It can be said—contradict it who may—that Wagner was the first to recognize melody as the supreme law, and not only theoretically. On the whole, the older art of composition suffers from neglect of melody. Unconsciously we feel another standard in the classical works, and we do not measure them so strictly.

The broad strokes of the brush found in the later symphonic compositions are missing in the pre-Wagner music. There the eight-bar phrase reigns supreme, which for our feeling, seems a short breath. The quality of the music, too, within these eight bars is more primitive than that of the symphonic music.

With Beethoven, this strikes one most forcibly in his second period, which is the weakest, and is exemplified in its principal compositions, the *Fifth Symphony*, the *Waldstein* and the *Appassionata*, and the three *Quartets*, Op. 59.

I should like to repeat—and let them contradict me again—that in Beethoven's first period, feeling conquers helplessness; in the third, feeling is overshadowed by symphonic breadth and symphonic brilliance. Beethoven, in his second period, exploits the forceful ideas contained in the first.

The heroically passionate defiance of the *Pathétique* continues to be the basis for all pieces similar in feeling (only more extended) in the following period, headed by the *Fifth Symphony*. But the melodic element does not keep step with this extension and gets lost in—what shall I call it?—a kind of table-land of modulatory and figurative eloquence. I am thinking, for example, of the working out in the first movement of the *Appassionata*, where the persistent rush and intensity of temperament take the place of what should be content.

In this case it is more as if the thrilling eloquence and infectious conviction of an orator were making the effect, rather than his theme or the wealth of his ideas. It makes an effect, accordingly, on larger masses of people and with a more direct impact. Temperament disguises not only the content, but the feeling too; although it may not appear to be like this.

The deepest feeling needs the fewest words and gestures. It is an historical commonplace, repeated like a continuous cinematograph performance, that as each new composition appears, it is accused of a lack of melody. I have read this kind of accusation in criticisms after the first performance of Mozart's *Don Giovanni*, Beethoven's *Violin Concerto*, and Wagner's operas. And it is always taken for granted that the increase in technical complications is the reason for the decrease in melodic invention.

It almost seems as if technical mastery makes its effect by being unusual, whereas melody is only perceived as such when it appears in commonplace and familiar ways.

But as a matter of fact Mozart, as a maker of melodies, was richer than his predecessors; Beethoven broader, more ingenious than Mozart, and Wagner more voluptuous than Beethoven (if perhaps less noble and original).

Beethoven himself in his third period—at times in the string quartets —dissolves the rigid symphonic mechanism into melody and psychology. Wagner was more material; and it is against this materialism that some living composers are trying to react.

Immaterialism is the true being of music; we are on the track of it; we wander through narrow underground corridors at the end of which a strange, distant, phosphorescent light gives us a glimpse of the passage leading out into a marvellous grotto.

When once we have reached the vaulted room in nature's mysterious palace, then our souls can learn to soar with speech; and it will sound forever, like a blossoming and exalted melody. [6]

RICHARD STRAUSS

From: Letter to his wife, Rochester, N.Y., March 21, 1904

Strauss is a person of decided talent and has rich gifts. Polyphony and movement are necessary elements to him.

An admirable facility for making things complicated and spreading out what is small. Strauss seems to write out the principal voices, then the principal middle voice, and afterwards cram everything there is still room for in between. One can go on and on with that, but he does not stop in time. He does not understand the mastery of the unfinished. [7]

From: Letter to his wife, Plymouth, April 2, 1904

His [Strauss's] orchestration—in spite of unusual virtuosity—is not "sonorous" because his style of composing is opposed to his orchestral writing. It branches out too much. I believe he has made a mistake in some of the proportions again. He has said to himself, "Wagner makes everything sound, but I am often unable to achieve this." That is because Wagner concentrates everything on the principal idea. Strauss really has twelve subordinate ideas, and they are in confusion; the chief idea lies more in the atmosphere than in the motive, but it is easily effaced by overloading. [8]

AN EARLY RECORDING SESSION

From: Letter to his wife, London, November 20, 1919

My suffering over the toil of making gramophone records came to an end yesterday after playing for three and a half hours! I feel rather battered today, but it is over. From the first day I have been as depressed as if I were expecting to have an operation. To do it is stupid and a strain. Here is an example of what happens: They wanted the *Faust* waltz (which lasts a good ten minutes) *but it was only to take four minutes!* That meant quickly cutting, patching and improvising, so that there should still be some sense left in it; watching the pedal (because it sounds bad); thinking of certain notes which had to be stronger or weaker in order to please this devilish machine; not letting oneself go for fear of inaccuracies and being conscious the whole time that every note was going to be there for eternity; how can there be any question of inspiration, freedom, swing, or poetry? Enough that yesterday, for nine pieces of four minutes each (half an hour in all), I worked for three and a half hours! Two of these pieces I played four or five times. Having to think so quickly at the same time was a severe effort. In the end, I felt the effects in my arms; after that, I had to sit for a photograph, and sign the discs. At last it was finished. [9]

VIII

SATIE
ROUSSEL
VAUGHAN WILLIAMS
REGER
RACHMANINOFF
SCHOENBERG
HOLST
IVES
RAVEL
FALLA
BLOCH

ERIK SATIE

1866–1925

Considered by many of his contemporaries and by historians as a dilet-tante, Erik Satie nevertheless exerted a potent influence on twentieth century French composers. Fairly prolific in the smaller genres, he never attempted any truly large scale work. However, Debussy thought enough of his *Gymnopédies* to orchestrate them, and Ravel practically quoted the theme of one of them in his *Valses nobles et sentimentales*. To his long stint as pianist in a Montmartre bar we owe also some charming music-hall ballads and down-to-earth tunes.

Though not actually an anti-Wagnerite, Satie helped to stem the Wagnerian flood that threatened to inundate French musical thought and composition. He was a precursor of Impressionism, yet he promptly turned his knife-edged wit on the movement when he felt it was growing too atmospheric, too rarefied and affected. His satiric humor shows itself in the titles for some of his works—*Trois morceaux en forme de poire* (Three pieces in the form of a pear), *Pièces froides* (Chilly pieces), *Choses vues à droite et à gauche, sans lunettes* (Things seen right and left, without glasses), also in his expression marks: *en clignant l'oeil* (with a wink), *ouvrez la tête* (open your head), *avec étonnement* (with surprise)—and carries over into his literary work.

Satie and Debussy maintained a mercurial friendship for about thirty years. Though Satie's *Sarabandes*, written in 1887, contain harmonies typical of future Debussy works, his influence on his more famous contemporary is often exaggerated, and by Satie himself.

INTELLIGENCE AND MUSICALITY AMONG THE ANIMALS

From: *Mémoires d'un amnésique*, 1914

The intelligence of animals cannot be questioned. But what does man do to improve the mental level of these long-suffering co-citizens? He offers them a mediocre education, full of holes, incomplete, such as no human child would wish on himself, and he would be right, the little dear. This education aims above all at developing the instincts

357

of cruelty and vice atavistically resident in the individual. In this curriculum questions of art, literature, natural and moral sciences or other matters do not appear. Carrier pigeons are in no way prepared for their mission by the study of geography; fishes are kept innocent of the study of oceanography; cattle, sheep and lambs are kept totally unaware of the scientific arrangements of a modern slaughterhouse, know nothing of the nutritive rôle they play in man-made society.

Few animals benefit from human instruction. The dog, the mule, the horse, the donkey, the parrot and a few others are the only animals to receive a semblance of education. And yet, can you call it education? Compare this instruction if you please, to that given the young human undergraduate by the universities, and you will see it is worthless, it can neither broaden the knowledge nor facilitate the learning which the animal might have acquired through his own labors, by his own devotion. But musically? Horses have learned to dance; spiders have remained under a piano throughout an entire concert—a long concert organized for them by a respected master. So what? So nothing. Now and then we are told about the musicality of the starling, the melodic memory of the crow, the harmonic ingenuity of the owl who accompanies himself by tapping his stomach—a purely artificial contrivance and polyphonically meagre.

As for the perennially cited nightingale, his musical knowledge makes his most ignorant auditors shrug. Not only is his voice not placed, but he has absolutely no knowledge of clefs, tonality, modality or measure. Perhaps he is gifted? Possibly, almost certainly. But it can be stated flatly that his artistic culture does not equal his natural gifts, and that the voice of which he is so inordinately proud, is nothing but an inferior useless instrument.   [1]

THE ORCHESTRA IN OPERA

There is no need for the orchestra to grimace when a character comes onstage. Do the trees in the scenery grimace? What we must do is create a musical scenery, a musical atmosphere, in which the characters move and talk. No "couplets,"—no "leitmotiv," but aim at creating an atmosphere that suggests Puvis de Chavannes.   [2]

YOUTH AND EXPERIENCE [1]

I have always trusted youth. And so far I have not been disappointed. Our epoch is favorable to youth. But let them beware—their youth

[1] Concerning the young musicians in *L'Ecole d'Arceuil*.

will expose them to attack. One need not be very astute to notice that people of a certain age always talk about their "experience". . . . It is very good of them. . . . But one ought, all the same, to be sure that they have really had any worthwhile experience. . . . Human memory is very short—is one not accustomed, whenever the weather behaves erratically, to hear people say: "There's been nothing like this within living memory"? I'm quite ready to believe them. But don't let them talk to me too much about their "experience" . . . I know them only too well. And so these young men will be blamed because they are young. I wrote my *Sarabandes* at the age of twenty-one, in 1887; the *Gymnopédies* when I was twenty-two, in 1888. These are the only works which my detractors—those over the age of fifty, of course—admire. To be logical, they ought to like the works of my maturity. They don't. [3]

JAZZ

What I love about jazz is that it's "blue" and you don't care. [4]

SATIE AND DEBUSSY

From a Lecture on Debussy, no date

When I first met Debussy, he was full of Moussorgsky and was very deliberately seeking a way that wasn't very easy for him to find. In this problem I was well in advance of him. I was not weighed down with the *Prix de Rome*, nor any other prize, for I am a man like Adam (of Paradise) who never won any prizes—a lazy fellow, no doubt.

At that time I was writing *Le Fils des étoiles* to a libretto by Joseph Péladan, and I explained to Debussy that a Frenchman had to free himself from the Wagnerian adventure, which wasn't the answer to our national aspirations. I also pointed out that I was in no way anti-Wagnerian, but that we should have a music of our own—if possible without any *Sauerkraut*.

Why could we not use the means that Claude Monet, Cézanne, Toulouse-Lautrec and others had made known? Why could we not transpose these means into music? Nothing simpler.

That was the origin of a departure which brought results that were safe enough and even fruitful. Who was to show him examples? Reveal new treasures? Suggest the ground to be explored? Give him the benefit of previous considerations? Who? I shan't reply, for I no longer care. [5]

ALBERT ROUSSEL

1869–1937

In his fortieth year, after having won considerable attention as a composer, Erik Satie began taking lessons in counterpoint with Albert Roussel at the Schola Cantorum in Paris. The somewhat younger teacher has noted that Satie was a conscientious student. Roussel himself was for a long time a pupil of D'Indy and came also under the influence of Debussyan Impressionism, yet his personality and original outlook made the later Roussel a highly individual composer. As Norman Demuth says in his book on Roussel: "There is no composer yet to whom one can point and say that he found his roots in Roussel; conversely, there is no composer to whom one can point and say that the mature Roussel had his roots in him."

While still a youngster in the French navy he sailed to India and French Indo-China and was impressed with their ideas and music. The result of these travels was his *Evocations*. A subsequent trip to the Orient was the inspiration for the opera-ballet *Padmâvati* which actually used Hindu scales and is notably free of the quasi-orientalism of most works of this genre. His best known composition, *Le festin d'araignée*, composed as a ballet, is most frequently heard in concert.

The following article is an answer to a questionnaire on the relation of inspiration to musical composition sent to a number of composers by L..Dunton Green of the *Chesterian* after publication of *The Borderland of Music and Psychology* by Frank Howes, in which the question was raised.

INSPIRATION AND COMPOSITION

Answer to a questionnaire, 1928

You ask me what I think about musical inspiration and the manner in which it reveals itself during the composition of a long work. What is by common consent called musical inspiration is, if I am not mistaken, the artist's faculty of conceiving and clearly expressing ideas that should be admirable both for quality and for copiousness. It presupposes the perfect function of a musically organized, sensitive and imaginative brain, and the possession of a technique that enables the composer to solve the problems which will necessarily confront him. That he should be able to keep this faculty intact in the course of a composition on a large scale does not strike me as at all mysterious. It is probable that, once he has written down the last note of his score, he will feel the need of a period of rest before he undertakes a new work; this applies to every profession demanding a high cerebral tension.

You tell me that the author of the book on psychology and music wonders whether, in the process of creation, the composer is influenced more by sentiments of a general nature which he could describe, or by purely musical motives. In my view that depends largely on the character of the work. If it is a question of a symphonic work devoid of a program or commentary, there is no general feeling that could be defined, and the composer is concerned only with the interplay of sound-combinations, the infinite variety of which offers his imagination unlimited scope. It is possible that such music may suggest to certain hearers feelings which the composer himself did not experience in the least, but this is one of the inevitable consequences of the undefined character of the musical language.

In the case of a descriptive or dramatic work, on the other hand, an element foreign to music directs the composer's thought towards some quite definite object, and he is caught up in an atmosphere where musical ideas present themselves in particular forms. Themes, harmony, rhythm and orchestral color are all influenced by it. Although of little account in the case of a symphonic poem without a detailed program, this foreign element may become predominant in program music and in music drama; but whatever the importance, it would be wrong to suppose that the musician remains absorbed in the contemplation of the object of his attention during the whole course of composition of a long work. He will come to a point where his mind will turn in a direction which he will follow almost unconsciously and without effort, and he will then be free to bring his whole intellectual power to bear upon the musical aspect of his work.   [1]

RALPH VAUGHAN WILLIAMS

1872–

When Vaughan Williams first heard the English folk tune "Bushes and Briars," he is said to have remarked that that was the music for him. In his long and active life he has so saturated himself in English national music that his original themes bear the authentic ring of actual folk songs and are at times indistinguishable from them. Direct expression, a vital feature of folk music, is distinctively characteristic of his composition also. Modality, though it exists elsewhere, is a hallmark of old English music, and equally identifies Vaughan Williams' work. He is as English as Morley and Purcell.

Yet he has not been deaf to other influences. An eager student, he has listened to whomever he profitably could, studying as late in his career as 1909 with Ravel, his junior by three years. On his return to England he was even accused of having become an imitator of the French master. He has not avoided the modernistic in music, witness the harsh dissonances in his late works, such as the *F-minor Symphony* (1935) and his stark opera, *Riders to the Sea* (1937). However, his most important works, for example, the *London* and *Pastoral* symphonies and his ballad opera, *Hugh the Drover*, are the apotheosis of Englishness.

When composing *Sir John in Love*, an opera based, as is Verdi's *Falstaff*, on the escapades of the fat toper, he remarked: "I hope it may be possible to consider that even Verdi's masterpiece does not exhaust all the possibilities of Shakespeare's genius." In truth, *Sir John in Love* is no rival of *Falstaff*, for it is almost wholly in the folk song style, redolent of local color and the Shakespeare period.

In the collection of lectures entitled "National Music" and given at Byrn Mawr College in October and November, 1932, Vaughan Williams sketched the history of nationalism in music and its effect on the great composers of the world. He seems to say that if serious composition may not be based on folk material, then much of the greatest music in the world would have to go by the boards.

SHOULD MUSIC BE NATIONAL?

Whistler used to say that it was as ridiculous to talk about national art as national chemistry. In saying this he failed to see the difference between art and science. Science is the pure pursuit of knowledge and thus knows no boundaries. Art, and especially the art of music, uses knowledge as a means to the evocation of personal experience in terms which will be intelligible to and command the sympathy of others. These others must clearly be primarily those who by race, tradition, and cultural experience are the nearest to him; in fact those of his own nation, or other kind of homogeneous community. In the sister arts of painting and poetry this factor of nationality is more obvious, due in poetry to the Tower of Babel and in painting to the fact that the painter naturally tends to build his visual imagination on what he normally sees around him. But unfortunately for the art of music some misguided thinker, probably first cousin to the man who invented the unfortunate phrase, "a good European," has described music as the "universal language." It is not even true that music has a universal vocabulary, but even if it were so, it is the use of the vocabulary that counts and no one supposes that French and English are the same language because they happen to use twenty-five out of twenty-six of the letters of their alphabet in common. In the same way, in spite of the fact that they have a musical alphabet in common, nobody could mistake Wagner for Verdi, or Debussy for Richard Strauss. And, similarly, in spite of wide divergencies of personal style, there is a common factor in the music, say, of Schumann and Weber. And this common factor is nationality.

One of the three great composers of the world (personally I believe the greatest) was Johann Sebastian Bach. Here, you may say, is the universal musician if ever there was one; yet no one could be more local, in his origin, his life work, and his fame for nearly a hundred years after his death, than Bach. He was to outward appearance no more than one of a fraternity of town organists and "town pipers" whose business it was to provide the necessary music for the great occasions in church and city. He never left his native country, seldom even his own city of Leipzig. "World movements" in art were then unheard of; moreover, it was the tradition of his own country which inspired him. True, he studied eagerly all the music of foreign composers that came his way in order to improve his craft. But is not the work of Bach built up on two great foundations, the organ music of his Teutonic predecessors and the popular hymn tunes of his own people?

I am quite prepared for the objection that nationalism limits the scope of art, that what we want is the best, from wherever it comes. My objectors will probably quote Tennyson and tell me that "We must needs love the highest when we see it" and that we should educate the young to appreciate this mysterious "highest" from the beginning. Or perhaps they will tell me with Rossini that they know only two kinds of music, good and bad. So perhaps we had better digress here for a few moments and try to find out what good music is, and whether there is such a thing as absolute good music; or even if there is such an absolute good, whether it must not take different forms for different hearers. Myself, I doubt if there is this absolute standard of goodness. I think it will vary with the occasion on which it is performed, with the period at which it was composed and with the nationality of those that listen to it. Let us take examples of each of these—firstly, with regard to the occasion. The Venusberg music from *Tannhäuser* is good music when it comes at the right dramatic moment in the opera; but it is bad music when it is played on an organ in church. I am sorry to have to tell you that this is not an imaginary experience. A waltz of Johann Strauss is good music in its proper place as an accompaniment to dancing and festivity, but it would be bad music if it were interpolated in the middle of the *St. Matthew Passion*. And may we not even say that Bach's *B minor Mass* would be bad music if it were played in a restaurant as an accompaniment to eating and drinking?

Secondly, does not the standard of goodness vary with time? What was good for the fifteenth century is not necessarily good for the twentieth. Surely each new generation requires something different to satisfy its different ideals. Of course there is some music that seems to defy the ravages of time and to speak a new message to each successive generation. But even the greatest music is not eternal. We can still appreciate Bach and Handel or even Palestrina, but Dufay and Dunstable have little more than an historical interest for us now. But they were great men in their day and perhaps the time will come when Bach, Handel, Beethoven, and Wagner will drop out and have no message left for us. Sometimes, of course, the clock goes round full circle and the twentieth century comprehends what had ceased to have any meaning for the nineteenth. This is the case with the modern revival of Bach after nearly one hundred and fifty years of neglect, or the modern appreciation of Elizabethan madrigals. There may be many composers who have something genuine to say to us for a short time, and for that short time their music may be surely classed as good. We all know that when an idiom is new we cannot detect the difference between the really original mind and the mere imitator. But when the idiom passes into the realm of everyday commonplace, then and then only we can tell the true from the false. For example, any student at a music school can now reproduce the tricks of Debussy's style, and therefore it is now, and only now, that we can discover whether Debussy had something genuine to say or whether, when the secret of his style becomes common property, the message of which that style was the vehicle will disappear.

Then there is the question of place. Is music that is good music for one country or one community necessarily good music for another? It is true that the great monuments of music, the *Missa Papae Marcelli*, or the *St. Matthew Passion*, or the *Ninth Symphony* or *Die Meistersinger*, have a world wide appeal, but first they must appeal to the people, and in the circumstances where they were created. It is because Palestrina and Verdi are essentially Italian and because Bach, Beethoven and Wagner are essentially German that their message transcends their frontiers. And even so, the *St. Matthew Passion*, much as it is loved and admired in other countries, must mean much more to the German, who recognizes in it the consummation of all that he learned from childhood in the great traditional chorales which are his special inheritance. Beethoven has an universal meaning, but to the German, who finds in it that same spirit exemplified in its more homely form in those Volkslieder which he learned in his childhood, he must have a specialized meaning.

I think there is no work of art which represents the spirit of a nation more surely than *Die Meistersinger* of Richard Wagner. Here is no plaything with local color, but the raising to its highest power all that is best in the national consciousness of his own country. This is universal art in truth, universal because it is so intensely national.

[1]

HISTORICAL ASPECTS OF NATIONALISM IN MUSIC

Chopin is generally considered the first of the nationalist composers and he certainly was strongly influenced by the patriotic aspirations of the oppressed country. We must, however, distinguish between the Parisian Chopin of the Waltzes and Nocturnes and the national Chopin of the Mazurkas, Polonaises and Polish songs. But in reality he was no more national than Schumann or Beethoven or Mozart; his inspiration simply came from a new source. His period was the heyday of the romantic movement when everything had to be exotic. One's own time and one's own place were not enough and one sought an escape from reality in the glamor of remote times and remote places, the forests of Poland or the mountains of Scotland. So when Chopin appeared on the scene with his Polish rhythms and cadences, he was hailed as the first nationalist, though he was only building on his own foundations just as Beethoven and Mozart had built on theirs.

The most striking example of a national renaissance comes from Czecho-Slovakia or Bohemia, as it was then called, and it is a clear proof that a self-conscious movement among a few patriots can spread so as to be a living force in the country. The Czech national movement started little more than a hundred years ago with a coterie of Bohemian literateurs; yet now Czech language, Czech culture and Czech music is a natural and spontaneous expression of its people. This would not have been so if the roots had not always been there. The plant had shrivelled under the chill blasts of foreign suppression. Perhaps these March winds were required before the April showers could bring forth the flowers of spring. Those who bring about revivals are often scoffed at by the ignorant as foisting on the people something "unnatural"—if it is "real," we are sure it will come about "naturally."

Smetana, the recognized pioneer of Czech musical nationalism, received his first impulse from 1848, the year of revolutions, when he wrote his choruses for the revolutionary "National Guards." It is curious, however, that Smetana denied that he owed anything to folk song and would indignantly protest that he never committed what he called "forgery." When we think of the polka out of his string quartet, of the dance movement in *Vltava* or the opening chorus of *The Bartered Bride,* this seems difficult to swallow. The truth probably is that Smetana's debt to his own national music was of the best kind, unconscious. He did not indeed "borrow," he carried on an age-long tradition, not of set purpose, but because he could no more avoid speaking his own musical language than he could help breathing his native air.

The national movement in Russia is too well-known for me to have to dwell long on it, but I will call your attention to two points. The Russian movement had small and humble beginnings, as all great artistic movements do, and I believe should do. And the Russian nationalist composers drew frankly and unashamedly on their own folk songs. These are really two aspects of the same factor. The Russian movement started in the late eighteenth century with a revolt against the boredom of the heavy Italian operas which led people to look out for something lighter, some entertainment in which their own popular tunes might have a place.

This led to a series of "people's" operas in which folk tunes were introduced rather after the manner of the *Beggar's Opera*. Then came 1812 and the resultant outburst of Russian patriotism. Thus the way was prepared for Glinka who deliberately, as he said, wanted to write music which would make his own people "feel at home," music which was sneered at by the Frenchified Russian aristocrats as "coachman's music." . . . From Glinka we pass on to the splendors of Moussorgsky, Borodin and Rimski-Korsakov, surpassing their musical ancestor far in power of imagination, but like him, having their roots firmly planted in their native soil. It is a question how far the modern Russian school has not uprooted itself; possibly Stravinsky is too intent on shocking the bourgeois to have time to think about making his own people "feel at home." Cosmopolitanism has to a certain extent ousted nationalism. He seems deliberately to have torn up his roots and sold his birthright, cutting himself off from the refreshing wellspring of tradition. At one time he will toy with jazz, at another time with Bach and Beethoven seen through a distorted mirror. Or he will amuse himself by adding piquant "wrong notes" to the complacent beauty of Pergolesi. This seems to be not the work of a serious composer, but rather that of the too clever craftsman, one might almost say, the feats of the precocious child. But in one branch of our art it is hardly possible for an artist to be untrue to himself, namely, when he writes for the human voice, for then language takes command and the natural rise and fall of the words must suggest the melodic and rhythmic outline. And the human voice is the oldest musical instrument and through the ages it remains what it was, unchanged; the most primitive and at the same time the most modern, because it is the most intimate form of human expression. Instruments are continually being improved and altered, new inventions are continually increasing their capabilities both for good and evil. The pianoforte of today is not the instrument for which Beethoven wrote, the modern chromatic trumpet has nothing to do with the noble tonic and dominant instrument of the classics. Violinists can perform feats on their instruments undreamt of by our forefathers; we can add mutes hard, soft or medium to our brass instruments which change their features so that their own mothers would not know them. But through all this the human voice is connected with our earliest associations and inevitably turns our thoughts back to our real selves, to that sincerity of purpose which it is so difficult to follow and so perilous to leave. And I believe this is especially the case in choral music where the limitations are most severe and the human element is the strongest. When Stravinsky writes for the chorus his mind must surely turn homeward to his native Russia with its choral songs and dances and the great liturgies of its church. And so I believe that it is in *Les Noces* and the *Sinfonie des Psaumes* that we find the real and the great Stravinsky which will remain fresh and alive when all the clevernesses of his instrumental works have become stale from familiarity.   [2]

GENIUS

The great men of music close periods; they do not inaugurate them. The pioneer work, the finding of new paths, is left to smaller men. We can trace the musical genealogy of Beethoven, starting right back from Philipp Emanuel Bach, through Haydn and Mozart, with even such smaller fry as Cimarosa and Cherubini to lay the foundations of the edifice. Is not the mighty river of Wagner but a confluence of the smaller streams of Weber, Marschner and Liszt?

I would define genius as the right man in the right place at the right time. We know, of course, too many instances of the time being ripe and the place being vacant and no man to fill it. But we shall never know of the numbers of "mute and inglorious Miltons" who failed because the place and time were not ready for them. Was not Purcell a genius born before his time? Was not Sullivan a jewel in the wrong setting?   [3]

MAX REGER

1873-1916

Reger, like Brahms whom he so much admired, was a classical romanticist. Like Brahms he wrote only absolute music, avoiding the program music favored by the late nineteenth century followers of the Liszt-Wagner school.

A complete master of technique, he sometimes overloaded and overcomplicated his compositions with free modulations and unconventional progressions.

He was a superb organist and improviser on the organ in the Bach tradition, hence his championship of the classical or what he calls the "German" style of organ composition and his rejection of the English and French schools.

From 1911 to 1914 he was the director of the Meiningen Court orchestra which, under the baton of Hans von Bülow from 1880 to 1885, had become famous for its high level of performance and impeccable style. Reger's most serious orchestral work was composed for the Meiningen orchestra. His letters to George II, Duke of Sachsen-Meiningen, sponsor of the orchestra, frequently discuss style and his efforts to regain the heights reached by the orchestra through Bülow's initiative.

TEMPO, COLOR AND DYNAMICS

Letter to George II of Sachsen-Meiningen,
Meiningen, January 7, 1912

The tempo of a piece is determined not only by the directions of the composer, but also by its harmonic and polyphonic content, by the hall in which it is played and by the principle of utmost clarity. Thus, for example, one can never take an organ fugue as fast in a church as in a concert hall, since the peculiar acoustical conditions in every church might otherwise create noise and chaos. Brahms is so polyphonic that the greatest care must be taken not to drown out important middle voices, thereby suppressing the most beautiful passages.

Besides—now I am committing a sacrilege, but I believe I may receive absolution considering my well-known admiration for Brahms —besides, Brahms too often indicates tempi which are too fast. The inwardly stimulated creator is often misled by his excitement into prescribing overfast tempi. I know from my own experience that I have indicated tempi which I have later taken much more slowly myself! Thus it is impossible to take the first movement of Brahms's *Fourth Symphony* at the tempo he marks it without making a complete hash of it. Particularly Brahms! Only too often did he orchestrate so that the most important passages lie in the "weak" ranges of certain instruments so that it is impossible to bring them out. Naturally such passages do not sound—and Brahms is condemned by detractors as "hard to understand," "confused"! We must make many, many changes, we must make ruthless alterations in some voices in order to fulfill Brahms's true intent. Brahms's treatment of horns is sometimes untenable. He gives passages to bassoons which can only be conceived in the horns. The bassoons blow for dear life and the result is a horrible squeak. Give the identical passages to the horns and they "sound" immediately. Brahms tended to write for horns "conservatively," yet his harmony is sensitive, modern. Hence the dichotomy between "sound" and intent.

An unimaginative interpretation limits itself to forte, piano, crescendo and diminuendo. In my opinion, however, the art of expression begins at the point where one reads "between the lines," where the "unexpressed" is brought to light. I know all too well that my conception will cause considerable opposition among the literal minded. The same thing holds for Bach as for Brahms. Bach can be played in so inhumanly boring a fashion, in such a consciously correct style that it becomes lethal. In my opinion Bach was no cold formalist, but a man of flesh and blood, full of vitality and strength. I resigned publicly from the Bachgesellschaft because I could not sympathize with its prevailing views and because the evangelical religiosity with which it invested him seemed to me too hampering. Bach was certainly a profoundly believing Christian but never the devoted acolyte which the Gesellschaft wants to make of him today. Bach's individuality was too great for that. The Germans have a bad habit of measuring every great creative spirit by their own little yardstick.   [1]

ORGAN MUSIC

From: Letter to Joseph Renner,
Weiden, November 26, 1900

I hail every organ composition which bears the stamp of pure, unadulterated German nationality with particular joy, since unfortunately one too often sees German organ composers aping the French and English styles.

Naturally, what I mean by "German nationality" is not chauvinism and is completely apolitical. We might just as well say "Bach-ish," that is, stemming from the classic spirit. Now one cannot accuse me in the least of reactionary tendencies. On the contrary, I side, if anywhere, with the "left." Only in the case of organ music, I can say on the basis of the most profound study: "Every piece of organ music which is not at bottom related to Bach is impossible." This dictum must naturally not be understood or used pedantically. However, our French and English organ composers are the very antitheses of Bach, and I must therefore reject their music.   [2]

FREE CREATION

From: Letter to Ella Kerndl, Weiden, October 1, 1900

Creation must be completely free. Every fetter one imposes on oneself by taking into account playability or public taste leads to disaster. By this I do not mean that every immature conservatory student should sit down and compose nonsensically. These young gentlemen should first learn something solid.   [3]

BRAHMS

From: Letter to Adalbert Lindner,
Wiesbaden, April 6, 1894

Brahms is the greatest composer since Beethoven, but he also has his mannerisms: Phrygian thirds, Dorian sixths, etc. In the treatment of the piano he stands alone. In his hands, a piano piece takes on a completely orchestral color. To be sure, he makes no use of passages, chromatic scales, etc., but he makes up for it through a pure polyphony and the noblest of melodic lines which is often designated by denigrators as "disregard for sensuous sound." But one must first immerse oneself in the highly expressive power of his melodic line. He is not obvious;

he loves to shroud the beauties of his works with a veil, and one becomes aware of these beauties only after a thorough knowledge of the work. True, his music is somewhat incomprehensible to the average audience; nevertheless, Brahms has carried his art so far that all really discerning musicians must come to consider him as the greatest living composer, if they are not to be considered unknowledgeable. His three symphonies (D major, F major and C minor) place him as a symphonist in a direct line after Beethoven, and he has enriched us considerably with his chamber music and songs.   [4]

SERGEI VASSILIEVITCH RACHMANINOFF

1873–1943

Russian by birth, background and education, Rachmaninoff lived the greater part of his adult life as a cosmopolitan, and died an American citizen. His work is patterned after Tchaikovsky, of whom he was a devoted adherent. Like his model, he made use of his Russian heritage, but his compositions admit no real national feeling. Nor does his music possess the overwhelming Tchaikovskyan emotional drive. That is not to say that his work lacks sentiment or even sentimentality. It has perhaps an overdose of the latter, and suffers from that overabundance of notes resulting from romantic improvisation at the piano.

A member of the Moscow school of composers, which was nearly always at odds with the St. Petersburg school—the "Five" and their disciples—he was, however, a friend and admirer of Rimski-Korsakov and speaks eloquently of him in his reminiscences to Oskar von Riesemann (1934) from which the following quotations are taken.

An atmosphere of gloom and mystery has generally surrounded the man and his work. In these reminiscences, which are clear, forthright and ostensibly happy, this atmosphere is dispelled.

SOUND AND COLOR

From: *Recollections*, 1934

I remember one discussion which took place between Rimski-Korsakov, Scriabin and myself, while we were sitting at one of the little tables in the Café de la Paix. One of Scriabin's new discoveries concerned the relation between musical sound, that is, certain harmonies and keys, and the spectrum of the sun. If I am not mistaken, he was just working out the plan of a great symphonic composition in which he was going to use this relation, and in which, together with the musical incidents, there was to be a play of light and color. He had never reflected upon the practical possibilities of this idea, but that side of the question did not interest him very much. He said

373

he would limit himself to marking his score with a special system of light and color values.[1]

To my astonishment Rimski-Korsakov agreed in principle with Scriabin about this connection between musical keys and color. I, who do not feel the similarity, contradicted them heatedly. The fact that Rimski-Korsakov and Scriabin differed over the points of contact between the sound-and-color scale seemed to prove that I was right. Thus, for instance, Rimski-Korsakov saw E flat major as blue, while to Scriabin it was red-purple. In other keys, it is true, they agreed, as for example, in D major (golden brown).

"Look here!" suddenly exclaimed Rimski-Korsakov, turning to me, "I will prove to you that we are right by quoting your own work. Take, for instance, the passage in *The Miserly Knight* where the old Baron opens his boxes and chests, and gold and jewellery flash and glitter in the light of the torch. Well?"

I had to admit that the passage was written in D major. "You see," said Scriabin, "your intuition has unconsciously followed the laws whose very existence you have tried in vain to deny."

I had a much simpler explanation of this fact. While composing this particular passage I must unconsciously have borne in mind the scene in Rimski-Korsakov's opera *Sadko*, where the people, at Sadko's command, draw the great catch of goldfish out of Lake Ilmen and break into the jubilant shout, "Gold! Gold!" This shout is written in D major. But I could not prevent my two colleagues from leaving the café with the air of conquerors who were convinced that they had thoroughly refuted my opinion.   [1]

THE "SPRING" CANTATA

I shall never forget Rimski-Korsakov's criticism of my work. When the performance was over, he came into the artists' room:

"The music is good, but what a pity! There is no sign of 'Spring' in the orchestra."

I felt at once that his remark hit the nail on the head. How I would like to touch up the orchestration of my *Cantata* today. . . . No, I would alter the whole instrumentation! When I wrote I lacked all understanding of the connections between . . . how shall I put it? . . . orchestral sound and—meteorology, which Rimski-Korsakov handled in such a masterly manner. In Rimski-Korsakov's scores there is never the slightest doubt about the "meteorological" picture the

[1] The Clavier à lumière, in the score of the symphonic poem *Prometheus* for orchestra and pianoforte.—Oskar von Riesemann. [See also p. 53f.]

music is meant to convey. When there is a snowstorm, the flakes seem to dance and drift from the wood instruments and the soundholes of the violins; when the sun is high, all instruments shine with an almost fiery glare; when there is water, the waves ripple and splash audibly through the orchestra, and this effect is not achieved by the comparatively cheap means of a harp glissando; the sound is cool and glassy when he describes a calm winter night with a glittering starlit sky. He was a great master of orchestral sound-painting, and one can still learn from him. It seems strange that a man who handled the secrets of the orchestra in so masterful a fashion, down to the smallest detail, should be so helpless as a conductor. "Conducting is a black art," he says in his book *Chronicles of My Musical Life*. Unfortunately, this thought was not exclusively his own, but presented itself to the audience as he stood at the conductor's desk.   [2]

VALUE OF THE COMPOSER, DEAD AND ALIVE

It is strange how the death of a composer affects the significance of his works. I remember the following incident, which I would like to quote here; it is very instructive. When the talented Russian composer, Vassili Kalinnikov, a slightly older contemporary of mine, died at the early age of thirty-four, he left no money whatever, as he had always been badly paid. His widow, who found herself in very straitened circumstances, asked me for a small loan so that she could erect a tombstone for him. She also brought with her some of Kalinnikov's musical remains, saying:

"It is useless to take them to a publisher. I know his prices."

I took the compositions to the publisher Jurgenson, hoping he might buy one or the other of the pieces.

Without a word Jurgenson added up the prices I had quoted. They made a considerable sum, which was ten times larger than the loan for which I had been asked.

As he went to his safe and opened it, he remarked:

"Don't imagine that I pay this tremendous sum without a definite reason; I pay it because the death of the composer has multiplied the value of his works by ten."   [3]

THE KEEN EAR

My association with Rimski-Korsakov taught me a great deal. I was given more than one opportunity to verify his incredibly fine ear for orchestral detail. One evening after a rehearsal we went to the

Solodovnikov Theatre to hear his opera *A May Night*. The performance had not yet begun. We took seats in the middle row of the stalls.
The conductor and the orchestra, who must have got wind of the
composer's presence, took the greatest pains and fiddled and trumpeted
for all they were worth. Suddenly—Levko was just starting his aria—
I saw Rimski-Korsakov frown, as if he were in great pain: "They are
using B flat clarinets!" he groaned and gripped my knee. Later I
verified from the score that A clarinets are indicated. A similar episode
took place after the last rehearsal of *Pan Voyevoda*. I had asked Rimski-
Korsakov not to attend any previous rehearsals. In the fortune-telling
scene this opera has a fortissimo beat in the dominant chord played
by the whole orchestra. I wondered why the tuba remained silent.
When I mentioned this to Rimski-Korsakov, he answered:

"One would not hear it anyway, and I hate writing down superfluous
notes."

When the rehearsal was over, he expressed his entire satisfaction,
which made me very happy, merely adding:

"Who joins in this fortissimo beat?"

I counted all the players, one after another.

"And why is the tom-tom playing?"

"Probably because the directions say so."

"No, they give only the triangle."

I sent for the musician in question. He produced his part, and there
the tom-tom was marked down.

Rimski-Korsakov asked for the score. It turned out that the tom-tom
was not included in the beat, but had been marked down by mistake,
and that the triangle alone had to play. This striking proof of his sensitive ear convinced me that the tuba would have been inaudible in this
passage.   [4]

ARNOLD SCHOENBERG

1874–1951

Vienna, cradle of some of the most eventful movements in music history, witnessed the inception of Schoenberg's twelve tone technique. The father of this theory and practice began his career as a romantic at the tail end of the Wagnerian hegemony. His most frequently played piece, *Verklärte Nacht* (1899), carries *Tristan* to its ultimate conclusions. It is interesting, in view of Schoenberg's lifelong artistic battles, that one of the Vienna Tonkünstlerverein jury which refused performance to the work remarked of it: "Das klingt ja, als ob man über die noch nasse *Tristan* Partitur darüber gewischt hätte" (It sounds as if one had smeared over the still moist *Tristan* score).

After passing through Atonalism, Impressionism and Expressionism (*Pierrot lunaire* [1912] is the high point of the last), Schoenberg evolved his twelve tone technique. Uncompromising, in spite of the perpetual critical opprobrium heaped upon him, he carried it to its highest development. In his last works, however, he included some tonal writing.

Practically an autodidact except for some formal lessons in counterpoint with Alexander von Zemlinsky, Schoenberg was a great teacher; consequently his enlightening exposition of twelve tone technique is of paramount importance. His essays on Brahms and Mahler, whom he greatly admired, are novel and penetrating, and his *Harmonielehre* (1911) is one of the definitive textbooks on modern music theory.

A group worthy of emulation was the Society for Private Musical Performances which Schoenberg founded and directed, in which modern works of all trends were played before chosen audiences after painstakingly careful preparation. Only so might new works receive considered and just criticism.

THE COMPOSITION WITH TWELVE TONES

From: Essay of same title, 1950

Form in the arts, and especially in music, aims primarily at comprehensibility. The relaxation which a satisfied listener experiences when he can follow an idea, its development, and the reasons for such development is closely related, psychologically speaking, to a feeling of beauty. Thus, artistic value demands comprehensibility, not only for intellectual but also for emotional satisfaction. However, the creator's *idea* has to be presented, whatever the *mood* he is impelled to evoke.

Composition with twelve tones has no other aim than comprehensibility. In view of certain events in recent musical history, this might seem astonishing, for works written in this style have failed to gain understanding in spite of the new medium of organization. Thus, should one forget that contemporaries are not final judges, but are generally overruled by history, one might consider this method doomed. But, though it seems to increase the listener's difficulties, it compensates for this deficiency by penalizing the composer. For composing thus does not become easier, but rather ten times more difficult. Only the better-prepared composer can compose for the better-prepared music lover.

The method of composing with twelve tones grew out of necessity.

In the last hundred years the concept of harmony has changed tremendously through the development of chromaticism. The idea that one basic tone, the root, dominated the construction of chords and regulated their succession—the concept of *tonality*—had to develop first into the concept of *extended tonality*. Very soon it became doubtful whether such a root still remained the center to which every harmony and harmonic succession must be referred. Furthermore, it became doubtful whether a tonic appearing at the beginning, at the end, or at any other point really had a constructive meaning. Richard Wagner's harmony had promoted a change in the logic and constructive power of harmony. One of its consequences was the so-called impressionistic use of harmonies, especially practiced by Debussy. His harmonies, without constructive meaning, often served the coloristic purpose of expressing moods and pictures. Moods and pictures, though extra-musical, thus became constructive elements, incorporated in the musical functions; they produced a sort of emotional comprehensibility. In this way, tonality was already dethroned in practice, if not in theory. This alone would perhaps not have caused a radical change in compositional technique. However, such a change became necessary when there occurred simultaneously a development which ended in what I call the *emancipation of the dissonance*.

The ear had gradually become acquainted with a great number of dissonances, and so had lost the fear of their "sense-interrupting" effect. One no longer expected preparations of Wagner's dissonances or resolutions of Strauss's discords; one was not disturbed by Debussy's non-functional harmonies, or by the harsh counterpoint of later composers. This state of affairs led to a freer use of dissonances comparable to classic composers' treatment of diminished seventh chords, which could precede and follow any other harmony, consonant or dissonant, as if there were no dissonance at all.

What distinguishes dissonances from consonances is not a greater or lesser degree of beauty, but a greater or lesser degree of *comprehensibility*. In my *Harmonielehre* I presented the theory that dissonant tones appear later among the overtones, for which reason the ear is less intimately acquainted with them. This phenomenon does not justify such sharply contradictory terms as concord and discord. Closer acquaintance with the more remote consonances—the dissonances, that is—gradually eliminated the difficulty of comprehension and finally admitted not only the emancipation of dominant and other seventh chords, diminished sevenths and augmented triads, but also the emancipation of Wagner's, Strauss's, Moussorgsky's, Debussy's, Mahler's, Puccini's and Reger's more remote dissonances.

The term *emancipation of the dissonance* refers to its comprehensibility, which is considered equivalent to the consonance's comprehensibility. A style based on this premise treats dissonances like consonances and renounces a tonal center. By avoiding the establishment of a key, modulation is excluded, since modulation means leaving an established tonality and establishing *another* tonality.

The first compositions in this new style were written by me around 1908 and, soon afterwards, by my pupils, Anton von Webern and Alban Berg. From the very beginning such compositions differed from all preceding music, not only harmonically but also melodically, thematically and motivally. But the foremost characteristics of these *in statu nascendi* were their extreme expressiveness and their extraordinary brevity. At that time, neither I nor my pupils were conscious of the reasons for these features. Later I discovered that our sense of form was right when it forced us to counterbalance extreme emotionality with extraordinary shortness. Thus, subconsciously, consequences were drawn from an innovation which, like every innovation, destroys while it produces. New colorful harmony was offered; but much was lost.

Formerly the harmony had served not only as a source of beauty, but, more important, as a means of distinguishing the features of the form. For instance, only a consonance was considered suitable for an ending. Establishing functions demanded different successions of harmonies than roving functions; a bridge, a transition, demanded other successions than a codetta; harmonic variation could be executed intelligently and logically only with due consideration of the fundamental meaning of the harmonies. Fulfillment of all these functions—comparable to the effect of punctuation in the construction of sentences, of subdivision into paragraphs, and of fusion into chapters—could scarcely be assured with chords whose constructive values had not as yet been explored. Hence, it seemed at first impossible to compose pieces of complicated organization or of great length.

A little later I discovered how to construct larger forms by following a text or a poem. The difference in size and shape of its parts and the change in character and mood were mirrored in the shape and size of the composition, in its dynamics and tempo, figuration and accentuation, instrumentation and orchestration. Thus the parts were differentiated as clearly as they had formerly been by the tonal and structural functions of harmony.

Formerly the use of the fundamental harmony had been theoretically regulated through recognition of the effects of root progressions. This practice had grown into a subconsciously functioning *sense of form* which gave a real composer an almost somnambulistic sense of security in creating, with utmost precision, the most delicate distinctions of formal elements.

Whether one calls oneself conservative or revolutionary, whether one composes in a conventional or progressive manner, whether one tries to imitate old styles or is destined to express new ideas—whether one is a good composer or not—one must be convinced of the infallibility of one's own fantasy and one must believe in one's own inspiration. Nevertheless, the desire for a conscious control of the new means and forms will arise in every artist's mind; and he will wish to know *consciously* the laws and rules which govern the forms which he has conceived "as in a dream." Strongly convincing as this dream may have been, the conviction that these new sounds obey the laws of nature and of our manner of thinking, the conviction that order, logic, comprehensibility and form cannot be present without obedience to such laws, forces the composer along the road to exploration. He must find, if not laws or rules, at least ways to justify the dissonant character of these harmonies and their successions.

After many unsuccessful attempts during a period of approximately twelve years, I laid the foundations for a new procedure in musical construction which seemed fitted to replace those structural differentiations provided formerly by tonal harmonies.

I called this procedure *Method of Composing with Twelve Tones Which Are Related Only with One Another.*

This method consists primarily of the constant and exclusive use of a set of twelve different tones. This means, of course, that no tone is repeated within the series and that it uses all twelve tones in the chromatic scale, though in a different order. It is in no way identical with the chromatic scale.[1]

The above example shows that such a basic set consists of various intervals. It should never be called a scale, although it is invented to substitute for some of the unifying and formative advantages of scale and tonality. The scale is the source of many figurations, parts of melodies and melodies themselves, ascending and descending passages, and even broken chords. In approximately the same manner the tones of the basic set produce similar elements. Of course, cadences produced by the distinction between principal and subsidiary harmonies will scarcely be derived from the basic set. But something different and more important is derived from it with a regularity comparable to the regularity and logic of the earlier harmony; the association of tones into harmonies and their successions is regulated by the order of these tones. The basic set functions in the manner of a motive. This explains why such a basic set has to be invented anew for every piece. It has to be the first creative thought. It does not make much difference whether or not the set appears in the composition at once like a theme or a melody, whether or not it is characterized as such by features of rhythm, phrasing, construction, character, etc.

Why such a set should consist of twelve different tones, why none of these tones should be repeated too soon, why, accordingly, only one set should be used in one composition—the answers to all these questions came to me gradually.

---

[1] Curiously and wrongly, most people speak of the "system" of the chromatic scale. Mine is no system but only a method, which means a *modus* of applying regularly a preconceived formula. *A method can, but need not,* be one of the consequences of a system. I am also not the inventor of the chromatic scale; somebody else must have occupied himself with this task long ago. [Author's note.]

Discussing such problems in my *Harmonielehre*, I recommended the avoidance of octave doublings. To double is to emphasize, and an emphasized tone could be interpreted as a root, or even as a tonic; the consequences of such an interpretation must be avoided. Even a slight reminiscence of the former tonal harmony would be disturbing, because it would create false expectations of consequences and continuations. The use of a tonic is deceiving if it is not based on *all* the relationship of tonality.

The use of more than one set was excluded because in every following set one or more tones would have been repeated too soon. Again there would arise the danger of interpreting the repeated tone as a tonic. Besides, the effect of unity would be lessened.

Justified already by historical development, the method of composing with twelve tones is also not without esthetic and theoretical support. On the contrary, it is just this support which advances it from a mere technical device to the rank and importance of a scientific theory.

Music is not merely another kind of amusement, but a musical poet's, a musical thinker's representation of musical ideas; these musical ideas must correspond to the laws of human logic; they are a part of what man can apperceive, reason and express. Proceeding from these assumptions, I arrived at the following conclusions:

The two-or-more-dimensional space in which musical ideas are presented is a unit. Though the elements of these ideas appear separate and independent to the eye and the ear, they reveal their true meaning only through their coöperation, even as no single word alone can express a thought without relation to other words. All that happens at any point of this musical space has more than a local effect. It functions not only in its own place, but also in all other directions and planes, and is not without influence even at remote points. For instance, the effect of progressive rhythmical subdivision, through what I call "the tendency of the shortest notes" to multiply themselves, can be observed in every classic composition.

A musical idea, accordingly, though consisting of melody, rhythm and harmony, is neither the one nor the other alone, but all three together. The elements of a musical idea are partly incorporated in the horizontal plane as successive sounds, and partly in the vertical plane as simultaneous sounds. The mutual relation of tones regulates the succession of intervals as well as their association into harmonies; the rhythm regulates the succession of tones as well as the succession of harmonies and organizes phrasing. And this explains why a basic set of twelve tones can be used in either dimension, as a whole or in parts.

The basic set is used in diverse mirror forms. The composers of the

last century had not employed such mirror forms as much as the masters
of contrapuntal times, at least they seldom did so consciously.

The last century considered such a procedure cerebral and thus incon-
sistent with the dignity of genius. The very fact that there exist classical
examples proves the foolishness of such an opinion. But the validity of
this form of thinking is also demonstrated by the previously stated law
of the unity of musical space, best formulated as follows: *the unity of
musical space demands an absolute and unitary perception.* In this space,
as in Swedenborg's heaven (described in Balzac's *Seraphita*) there is no
absolute down, no right or left, forward or backward. Every musical
configuration, every movement of tones has to be comprehended primarily as a mutual relation of sounds, of oscillatory vibrations, appearing
at different places and times. To the imaginative and creative faculty, relations in the material sphere are as independent from directions or
planes as material objects are, in their sphere, to our perceptive faculties.
Just as our mind always recognizes, for instance a knife, a bottle or a
watch, regardless of its position, and can reproduce it in the imagination
in every possible position, even so a musical creator's mind can operate
subconsciously with a row of tones regardless of their direction, regardless of the way in which a mirror might show the mutual relations,
which remain a given quantity.

The introduction of my method of composing with twelve tones does
not facilitate composing; on the contrary, it makes it more difficult.
Modernistically-minded beginners often think they should try it before
having acquired the necessary technical equipment. This is a great mistake. The restrictions imposed on a composer by the obligation to use
only one set in a composition are so severe that they can only be overcome by an imagination which has survived a tremendous number of
adventures. Nothing is given by this method; but much is taken away.

It has been mentioned that for every new composition a special set
of twelve tones has to be invented. Sometimes a set will not fit every
condition an experienced composer can foresee, especially in those ideal
cases where the set appears at once in the form, character, and phrasing
of a theme. Rectification in the order of tones may then become necessary.

In the first works in which I employed this method, I was not yet
convinced that the exclusive use of one set would not result in monotony.
Would it allow the creation of a sufficient number of characteristically
differentiated themes, phrases, motives, sentences, and other forms? At
this time I used complicated devices to assure variety. But soon I dis-

covered that my fear was unfounded; I could even base a whole opera, *Moses and Aaron*, solely on one set; and I found that, on the contrary, the more familiar I became with this set the more easily I could draw themes from it. Thus, the truth of my first predictions had received splendid proof. One has to follow the basic set; but nevertheless, one composes as freely as before.

In every composition preceding the method of composing with twelve tones, all the thematic and harmonic material is primarily derived from three sources: the tonality, the *basic motive* which in turn is a derivative of the tonality, and the *rhythm*, which is included in the basic motive. A composer's whole thinking was bound to remain in an intelligible manner around the central root. A composition which failed to obey these demands was considered "amateurish"; but a composition which adhered to it rigorously was never called "cerebral." On the contrary, the capacity to obey the principle instinctively was considered a natural condition of a talent.

The time will come when the ability to draw thematic material from a basic set of twelve tones will be an unconditional prerequisite for obtaining admission into the composition class of a conservatory.

The possibility of . . . canons and imitations, and even fugues and fugatos, has been overestimated by analysts of this style. Of course, for a beginner it might be as difficult to avoid octave doubling here as it is difficult for poor composers to avoid parallel octaves in the "tonal" style. But while a "tonal" composer still has to lead his parts into consonances or catalogued dissonances, a composer with twelve independent tones apparently possesses the kind of freedom which many would characterize by saying, "everything is allowed." "Everything" has always been allowed to two kinds of artists: to masters on the one hand, and to ignoramuses on the other. However, the meaning of composing in imitative style here is not the same as it is in counterpoint. It is only one of the ways of adding a coherent accompaniment, or subordinate voices, to the main theme, whose character it thus helps to express more intensively. [1]

GERSHWIN

From: Merle Armitage, *George Gershwin*, 1938

Many musicians do not consider George Gershwin a serious composer. But they should understand that, serious or not, he is a composer, that is, a man who lives in music and expresses everything, serious or not, sound or superficial, by means of music, because it is his native language. There are a number of composers, serious (as they believe) or not (as I know), who learned to add notes together. But they are only serious on account of a perfect lack of humor and soul.

It seems to me that this difference alone is sufficient to justify calling the one a composer, but the other none. An artist is to me like an apple tree. When the time comes, whether it wants to or not, it bursts into bloom and starts to produce apples. And as an apple tree neither knows nor asks about the value experts of the market will attribute to its product, so a real composer does not ask whether his products will please the experts of serious arts. He only feels he has to say something and says it.

It seems to me beyond doubt that Gershwin was an innovator. What he has done with rhythm, harmony and melody is not merely style. It is fundamentally different from the mannerism of many a serious composer. Such mannerism is based on artificial presumptions, which are gained by speculation and are conclusions drawn from the fashions and aims current among contemporary composers at certain times. Such a style is a superficial union of devices applied to a minimum of ideas, without any inner reason or cause. Such music could be taken to pieces and put together in a different way, and the result would be the same nothingness expressed by another mannerism. One could not do this with Gershwin's music. His melodies are not products of a combination, nor of a mechanical union, but they are units and could therefore not be taken to pieces. Melody, harmony and rhythm are not welded together, but cast. I do not know, but I imagine he improvised them on the piano. Perhaps he gave them later the finishing touch; perhaps he spent much time going over them again and again— I do not know. But the impression is that of an improvisation with all the merits and shortcomings appertaining to this kind of production. Their effect in this regard might be compared to that of an oration which might disappoint you when you read and examine it as with a magnifying glass; you miss what touched you so much, when you were overwhelmed by the charm of the orator's personality. One has probably to add something of one's own to re-establish the first effect. But it is always that way with art: you get from a work about as much as you are able to give to it yourself.

I do not speak here as a musical theorist, nor am I a critic, and hence I am not forced to say whether history will consider Gershwin a kind of Johann Strauss or Debussy, Offenbach or Brahms, Lehar or Puccini.

But I know he is an artist and a composer, he expressed musical ideas, and they were new, as is the way in which he expressed them. [2]

CHARLES IVES

A jotting, ca. 1945

There is a great Man living in this Country—a composer.
He has solved the problem how to preserve one's self and to learn.
He responds to negligence by contempt.
He is not forced to accept praise or blame.
His name is Ives. [3]

GUSTAV HOLST

1874–1934

An accident prevented Holst from pursuing a piano virtuoso career, and he took up the trombone. As trombonist in the Carl Rosa Opera Company orchestra, he gained the thorough knowledge of instrumentation so manifest in his best known work *The Planets* (1914–16), a symphonic poem in seven parts depicting the attributes of the great planets.

His early works were chromatic and complex—what he termed "good old Wagnerian bawlings"—but as he developed, he became sparser and more clear. A study of Sanskrit resulted in a one act opera, *Savitri* (1908), and the *Nine Hymns* (1907–08) and *Choral Hymns* (1908–12) from the *Rig Veda*.

As a teacher at Saint Pauls's School and Morley College, he taught and performed sixteenth and twentieth century English choral music (Byrd, Weelkes and Vaughan Williams). His own choral settings are among the best of his compositions.

In his *Four Medieval Lyrics* (1917) for voice and violin, Holst displays his uncanny understanding of English prosody and modality, adding to the latter his own personal twist. His interest in folk song centered on the relation between English music and the English language. Hence his admiration for Purcell, whose mastery of the word and tone was so unerring.

HENRY PURCELL

From: *The Heritage of Music*, 1928

It is generally accepted today, thanks to Barclay Squire's researches, that Purcell's most famous opera *Dido and Aeneas* was written about the year 1689, and not nine years before, as was previously thought. Even so, it is one of the most original expressions of genius in all opera. Mozart remains the greatest prodigy in musical history, but he was brought up in a fine tradition—in opera, as well as in other music. In England there was not then, nor has there ever been, any tradition of opera. Purcell was first a choirboy at the Chapel Royal: then he was organist of Westminster Abbey. Yet at the age of about thirty-one, he wrote the only perfect English opera ever written, and the only opera of the seventeenth century, as far as I know, that is performed as a whole nowadays, for the sheer pleasure it gives as opera. Throughout the whole work not a word is spoken. Between the lovely airs and choruses there are dialogues, set to easy, free and melodious music. Probably the English language has never been set so perfectly, either before or since. Playford said of Purcell: "He had a peculiar genius to express the energy of English words." There is no chance for vocal display in the ordinary sense of the term, but there is every chance to display powers of expression simply and beautifully.

The opera is accompanied either by strings or by a bass to be filled in on the harpsichord. There is beautiful dramatic and lyrical music, and a perfect sense of rhythm in setting the English language, but it is in the final test of all works of art that the *Dido* stands supreme—the test of unity. Many beautiful works fail in this test—Bach's *Christmas Oratorio*, for instance. But if you know *Dido* well, you can feel it as a complete whole. We all know about Dido's "Lament"; it is often sung by itself at concerts, but few listeners realize how much they lose by not hearing all that has gone before. It is impossible to appreciate its full beauty without listening to the whole opera and perceiving Purcell's power to make one beauty a steppingstone to another. Even the "Lament" is not more moving than the preceding recitative, "Thy hand, Belinda, darkness shades me," and it is so perfect that only a real master could have added anything after it. Yet how incomplete it would be without the final chorus, "With drooping wings"!

The libretto by Nahum Tate has been ridiculed for lines such as

> Thus, on the banks of fatal Nile,
> Weeps the deceitful crocodile.

But little or nothing has been said in praise of Tate and Purcell for their power to work up inevitably to the final climax. Then, having achieved, they stopped. What a lesson for the authors of *Orfeo, Don Giovanni* and *Fidelio!*

Dido was written for a girls' school in Chelsea. In any good girls' school in any century, one would expect to find a certain standard of taste and a cultivated language. At the same time, as far as dramatic performances are concerned, all stage effects and all vocal effects must be severely limited. The singers would be expected to pronounce and to phrase their own language well, but sustained dramatic efforts and any sort of vocal display would be out of the question. *Dido* meets these conditions to perfection.

On turning to Purcell's other dramatic works, one realizes how little the London theater has altered since his day. The advertisements of Purcell's later so-called operas read like those of a modern revue—advertisements of enormous expenditure on "stars," scenery, on dresses, on lighting, machinery, and other unessential matters. The one great essential of art is lacking equally in Purcell's later dramatic works, and in all ballad operas, pantomimes and musical comedies. It is never lacking in any real opera. This great essential is unity of style. One could take the "Masque of the Seasons" from Purcell's *Fairy Queen* and put it into his *King Arthur*, just as people have always taken songs from one ballad opera or musical comedy and put them into another. It is impossible to treat real opera in this fashion. Imagine the "Chorus of Peers" from *Iolanthe* transplanted into *The Mikado* or the "Walkürenritt" breaking into the second act of *Tristan!*

It is surely unnecessary nowadays to dwell on Purcell's gift of melody. According to some it is excelled only by Mozart's. Others hold that Purcell's best melodies—and how numerous they are!—are inferior to none. In addition to his gift of melody there are his sense of harmony, his feeling for orchestral color, his humor, his intensity, his lyrical power. We can witness their steady growth to perfection as we compare Purcell's earlier with his later works. Yet all these details of composition were subordinate to his amazing power of dramatic characterization.

This power has been possessed by very few opera composers. Indeed, many do not seem to have been aware of the necessity of cultivating it. They have thought it more important to study the idiosyncrasies of the particular opera singers engaged for a production than to consider the dramatic foundation on which to build the music. Musical characterization is usually looked upon as a modern factor in opera. One instinctively thinks of Wagner. Both Purcell and Wagner used all their gifts of melody and harmony, all their mastery of orchestral color, to give life to their characters and situations. But while Wagner painted huge scenes, each consistent in itself and at the same time part of a vaster whole, Purcell was content to paint little cabinet pictures.

But in one way Purcell is a finer stage composer than Wagner: his music is full of movement, of dance. His is the easiest music in all the world to act. Only those can realize fully the truth of this who have experienced the joy of moving to Purcell's music, whether in the ballroom or on the stage or in the garden, but especially in the garden.

CHARLES EDWARD IVES

1874–1954

For a long time Ives was looked upon as a kind of primitive; today he is regarded rather as a prophet. Before Schoenberg and Stravinsky, he anticipated the means and methods of the most advanced composers, venturing into dissonance, atonality, polyrhythms, polyharmonies, tone clusters, rapid metric changes and jazz or ragtime. Yet his experimentation in novel forms and content was not carried on without a thorough knowledge of established rules. He had a solid musical background. As a youngster he studied with Dudley Buck and Harry Rowe Shelley and finished his training at Yale with Horatio Parker. His father was a music teacher and bandmaster and also an experimenter, so that Ives came by his experimentation legitimately. Wanting to write as he pleased without worrying whether his music sold or not, Ives chose business as a profession. He chose wisely; considering the type of music he wrote and the time when it was written, it would scarcely have sold.

The main source of inspiration for his large output of songs, instrumental solos, chamber and orchestral works is his native New England, its hymn tunes, wheezy church organs, village bands, its outstanding personalities and its history. In the *Concord Sonata*, his best known piano work, each movement centers around New England nineteenth century authors, Emerson, Hawthorne, the Alcotts and Thoreau. His *Essays Before a Sonata* (1920), written as a literary guide or companion piece to the musical work, consists of a prologue, epilogue and four chapters devoted to the characters described in the sonata. The quotations below are taken from the *Essays*.

SUBSTANCE AND MANNER

From: *Essays Before a Sonata*, 1920

In such an abstruse art as music, it is easy for one to point to this as substance and to that as manner. Some will hold, and it is undeniable —in fact quite obvious—that manner has a great deal to do with the beauty of substance, and that to make a too arbitrary division or distinction between them, is to interfere, to some extent, with an art's beauty and unity. There is a great deal of truth in this too. But on the other hand, beauty in music is too often confused with something that lets the ears lie back in an easy chair. Many sounds that we are used to do not bother us, and for that reason, we are inclined to call them beautiful. Frequently—possibly almost invariably—analytical and impersonal tests will show, we believe, that when a new or unfamiliar work is accepted as beautiful on its first hearing, its fundamental quality is one that tends to put the mind to sleep. A narcotic is not always unnecessary, but it is seldom a basis of progress, that is, wholesome evolution in any creative experience. This kind of progress has a great deal to do with beauty, at least in its deeper emotional interests, if not in its moral values. . . . Possibly the fondness for individual utterance may throw out a skin-deep arrangement, which is readily accepted as beautiful—formulae that weaken rather than toughen up the musical muscles. If the composer's sincere conception of his art and of its function and ideals coincide to such an extent with these groove-colored permutations of tried out progressions in expediency that he can arrange them over and over again to his transcendent delight— has he or has he not been drugged with an overdose of habit-forming sounds? And as a result, do not the muscles of his clientele become flabbier and flabbier, until they give way altogether and find refuge only in a seasoned opera box where they can *see* without thinking? [1]

SONATA FORM

The unity of a sonata movement has long been associated with its form, and to a greater extent than is necessary. A first theme, a development, a second in a related key and its development, the free fantasia, the recapitulation, and so on, and over again. Mr. Richter or Mr. Parker [1] may tell us that all this is natural, for it is based on the classic song form, but in spite of your teachers, a vague feeling sometimes creeps over you that the form-nature of the song has been stretched out into deformity. Some claim for Tchaikovsky that his clarity and coherence of design is unparalleled (or some such word) in works for the orchestra. That depends, it seems to us, on how far repetition is an essential part of clarity and coherence. We know that butter comes from cream—but how long must we watch the "churning arm!" If nature is not enthusiastic about explanation, why should

---

[1] Ernst Friedrich Richter (1808–79), author of *Manual of Harmony;* Horatio William Parker (1863–1919), composer, teacher and theorist.

Tchaikovsky be? Beethoven had to churn, to some extent, to make his message carry. He had to pull the ear, hard, and in the same place and several times, for the 1790 ear was tougher than the 1890 one. But the "great Russian weeper" might have spared us.   [2]

MUSICAL TRUTH

The man "born down to Babbitt's Corners" may find a deep appeal in the simple but acute "Gospel Hymns of the New England camp meetin' " of a generation or so ago. He finds in them—some of them—a vigor, a depth of feeling, a natural-soil rhythm, a sincerity, emphatic but inartistic, which, in spite of a vociferous sentimentality, carries him nearer the "Christ of the people" than does the Te Deum of the greatest cathedral. These tunes have, for him, a truer ring than many of those groove-made, even-measured, monotonous, non-rhythmed, indoor-smelling, priest-taught, academic, English or neo-English hymns (and anthems), well-written, well-harmonized things, well-voice-led, well-counterpointed, well-corrected, and well-O.K.'d by well-corrected Mus. Bac. R.F.O.G.'s—personified sounds, correct and inevitable to sight and hearing—in a word, those proper forms of stained-glass beauty, which our over-drilled mechanisms, boy choirs, are limited to. But if the Yankee can reflect the fervency with which "his gospels" were sung—the fervency of "Aunt Sarah" who scrubbed her life away for her brother's ten orphans, the fervency with which this woman, after a fourteen-hour workday on the farm, would hitch up and drive five miles, through the mud and rain to "prayer meetin'," her one articulate outlet for the fullness of her unselfish soul—if he can reflect the fervency of such a spirit, he may find there a local color that will do all the world good. If his music can but catch that "spirit" by being a part with itself, it will come somewhere near his ideal—and it will be American, too, perhaps nearer so than that of the devotee of Indian or Negro melody. In other words, if local color, national color, any color, is a true pigment of the universal color, it is a divine quality; it is a part of substance in art, not of manner.   [3]

RAGTIME

Someone is quoted as saying that "ragtime is the true American music." Anyone will admit that it is one of the many true, natural, and, nowadays, conventional means of expression. It is an idiom, perhaps a "set or series of colloquialisms" similar to those that have added through centuries and through natural means, some beauty to all languages. Every language is but the evolution of slang, and possibly the broad "a" in Harvard may have come down from the "butcher of Southwark." To examine ragtime rhythms and the syncopations of Schumann or of Brahms seems to the writer to show how much alike they are not. Ragtime, as we hear it, is, of course, more (but not much more) than a natural dogma of shifted accents, or a mixture of shifted and minus accents. It is something like wearing a derby hat on the back of the head, a shuffling lilt of a happy soul just out of a Baptist Church in old Alabama. Ragtime has its possibilities. But it does not "represent the American nation" any more than some fine old senators represent it. Perhaps we know it now as an ore before it has been refined into a product. It may be one of nature's ways of giving art raw material. Time will throw its vices away and weld its virtues into the fabric of our music. It·has its uses as the cruet on the boardinghouse table has, but to make a meal of tomato ketchup and horse-radish, to plant a whole farm with sunflowers, even to put a sunflower into every bouquet, would be calling nature something worse than a politician. Mr. Daniel Gregory Mason, whose wholesome influence, by the way, is doing as much perhaps for music in America as American music is, amusingly says: "If indeed the land of Lincoln and Emerson has degenerated until nothing remains of it but a 'jerk and rattle,' then we, at least, are free to repudiate this false patriotism of 'my country right or wrong,' to insist that better than bad music is no music, and to let our beloved art subside finally under the clangor of the subway gongs and automobile horns, dead, but not dishonored."

[4]

DEFINITE MEANING IN MUSIC

A child knows a "strain of joy" from one of sorrow. Those a little older know the dignified from the frivolous—the Spring Song from the season in which the "melancholy days have come" (though is there not a glorious hope in autumn!). But where is the definite expression of late-spring against early-summer, of happiness against optimism? A painter paints a sunset—can he paint the setting sun?

In some century to come, when the school children will whistle popular tunes in quarter-tones, when the diatonic scale will be as obsolete as the pentatonic is now, perhaps then these borderland experiences may be both easily expressed and readily recognized. But maybe music was not intended to satisfy the curious definiteness of man. Maybe it is better to hope that music may always be a transcendental language in the most extravagant sense. Possibly the power

of literally distinguishing these "shades of abstraction"—these attributes
paralleled by "artistic intuition" (call them what you will)—is ever
to be denied man for the same reason that the beginning and end of a
circle are to be denied.   [5]

BEETHOVEN AND STRAUSS

Strauss remembers, Beethoven dreams.

A man may aim as high as Beethoven, or as high as Richard Strauss.
In the former case the shot may go far below the mark; in truth, it
has not been reached since that "thunderstorm in 1827," and there
is little chance that it will bè reached by anyone living today, but that
matters not; the shot will never rebound and destroy the marksman.
But, in the latter case, the shot may often hit the mark, but as often
rebound and harden, if not destroy the shooter's heart—even his soul.
What matters it, men say, he will then find rest, commodity and reputation; what matters it, if he find there but few perfect truths; what
matters (men say), he will find there perfect media, those perfect
instruments of getting in the way of perfect truths.
    This choice tells why Beethoven is always modern and Strauss al-
ways medieval—try as he may to cover it up in new bottles. He has
chosen to capitalize a "talent"—he has chosen the complexity of media,
the shining hardness of externals, repose, against the inner, invisible
activity of truth.   [6]

BRAHMS'S ORCHESTRATION

To think hard and deeply and to say what is thought, regardless of
consequences, may produce a first impression either of great translu-
cence or of great muddiness, but in the latter there may be hidden
possibilities. Some accuse Brahms's orchestration of being muddy. This
may be a good name for a first impression of it. But if it should seem
less so, he might not be saying what he thought. The mud may be a
form of sincerity which demands that the heart be translated, rather
than handed around through the pit. A clearer scoring might have
lowered the thought.   [7]

MAURICE RAVEL

1875–1937

The irony we detect in *La Valse* and the dry humor of his songs, *Histoires Naturelles*, are reflected in Ravel's critical writings. He was a modest person who nonetheless stood firm in his artistic convictions and standards. A keen experimenter, he was a deep-rooted classicist as well, his reasonableness stemming from his eighteenth century models. Like his colleague Debussy, he turned his back on Wagner and the Romanticists to embrace Impressionism. A more complex harmonist than Debussy, whom he has been wrongly accused of imitating, he was also a more confirmed neoclassicist, for his music never exceeded the limits of the tonal.

One of the most brilliant orchestral colorists of our time, Ravel never orchestrated merely for effect, but made his orchestration an integral part of his music. So keen was his feeling for instrumental texture that when he orchestrated his piano pieces, "Alborado del Gracioso," "Pavane pour une Infante défunte" and the "Tombeau de Couperin," they became essentially new works, composed for orchestra.

Half-French, half-Basque, he interested himself in Spanish music, composing his "Habanera," later incorporated into the *Rapsodie Espagnole*, the *Bolero*, a tour de force of orchestration, and his opera, *L'Heure Espagnole*, in the Spanish idiom.

CHOPIN

From an Essay, 1910

> *Rien de plus haïssable qu'une musique sans arrière-pensée.*[1]
> —Frédéric Chopin

Profound statement, this, and too little understood. It is true that Chopin proclaimed it constantly in his work. But did anyone understand? Yes, in retrospect; myriads of underlying meanings were unveiled later! Up to that time music addressed itself to the emotions.

[1] Nothing is more odious than music without hidden meaning.

395

It was then shifted to the understanding, but understanding did not know what to do with it.

Music for musicians, that is the true interpretation of Chopin's idea. Not for the professionals, by God, but for the musician, the creator, the dilettante. You must be sensitive to rhythm, melody, harmony, to the atmosphere which sounds create, to be thrilled with the linking together of two chords, as with the harmony of two colors. The most important element in all the arts is content. The rest flows from it.

Architecture! What a futile comparison! There are rules for making a building "stand up." There is none for constructing modulations. Yes; only one: Inspiration!

The architects trace vast lines. They establish all the modulations in advance . . . Inverted themes . . . Retrograde canons . . . Light and dark modulations. That means nothing to you? Nor to me, for that matter. It doesn't always seem coherent to you, despite all the effort? Then you are really not in the business.

Having something to say, that is what is missing in all this: the hidden meaning of Chopin.

His contribution is striking in the *Polonaises;* before him the polonaise was a festival march, solemn, brilliant, completely exterior. Look at Weber, Moniuszko, etc. Of Chopin's, only one (A major, Opus 40) is in the traditional style. But how superior in inspiration, in harmonic richness, to all those of his contemporaries. The "Grande Polonaise" in E flat with its heroic vehemence, its splendid driving middle section, is already of another calibre. Often he introduces into these dances a dolorous, poignant element, until then unknown (C minor, Opus 26).

At times this tragic sentiment reaches the sublime ("Polonaise-Fantasie in A flat," Opus 61), to such a degree that one may discover in it a complete epic. The sincerity of the expression, grief or heroism, saves it from the bombastic.

The sagacity of the critics has busied itself even with the *Nocturnes* and the *Impromptus.* It is a property of all true music to evoke, incidentally, feelings, landscapes, characters.

Chopin was not content merely to revolutionize piano technique. His figures are inspired. Through his brilliant passages one perceives profound, enchanting harmonies. Always there is the hidden meaning which is translated into poetry of intense despair.

Hints to the artist of genius: Write pieces after the manner of Chopin. To the frequent reproach that Chopin never developed, I answer, so be it. If there is no development, there is certainly a splendid glow: "Polonaise-Fantasie," "Posthumous Prelude" (Opus 46) and the "Barcarolle" (Opus 60).

The "Barcarolle" is the synthesis of the expressive and sumptuous art of this great Slav, Italian by training. This charming Latin school, joyously alive, just a little melancholy, sensual, but of a regrettable facility, abandons voluntarily, in its worst spots, if not soul, at least inspiration, in order to rejoin divinity the more quickly. Chopin achieved all that his teachers, through negligence, expressed but imperfectly.   [1]

NATIONALISM

Letter to the Committee of the National League for the Defense of French Music,[1] Paris, June 7, 1916

Gentlemen: An enforced rest finally allows me to acknowledge receipt of the announcement and statutes of the National League for the Defense of French Music, which reached me quite late. I hope you will excuse my having been unable to write you sooner; my various transfers and my adventurous service have left me scarcely any leisure. Excuse me also for being unable to subscribe to your statutes; a careful reading of them and of your announcement prevents my doing so.

Naturally, I can only laud your "fixed idea of the triumph of the Fatherland," which has also pursued me ever since the opening of hostilities. Consequently I fully approve the "need for action" out of which the National League was born. This need for action has been so strong in me that it forced me to quit civilian life when I was not obliged to.

Where I cannot follow you is where you state the principle that "the role of musical art is economic and social." I have never considered either music or the other arts in that light.

I gladly concede you the "moving pictures," the "gramophone records," the "popular song writers." All these have only a distant relation to musical art. I even grant you the "Viennese operettas," which are, however, more musical and of more careful workmanship than similar products of our own. This material does come under the domain of the "economic."

But I do not believe that "for the safeguarding of our artistic national patrimony" it is necessary to "prohibit the public performance

---

[1] During World War I, the Committee advocated discontinuing the performance of all modern German and Austrian music.

in France of those contemporary German and Austrian works which do not lie within the public domain." If it "cannot be a question of repudiating, for us and for future generations, the classics which constitute one of the immortal monuments of humanity," it should be even less a question of "removing from us, for a long time" interesting works, destined, perhaps, in their turn, to constitute monuments, and from the performing of which we might draw useful lessons.

It might even prove dangerous for French composers systematically to ignore the output of their foreign colleagues, and thus to form a sort of nationalistic group. Our musical art, so rich at the present time, would not be long in degenerating, and immuring itself in commonplace formulas.

It matters little to me that Mr. Schoenberg, for example, is an Austrian. He is nonetheless a musician of great worth, whose very interesting experiments have had a happy influence on certain Allied composers, including our own. Moreover, I am delighted that Messieurs Bartók, Kodály and their disciples are Hungarian, and manifest it in their works with so much relish.

In Germany, aside from Richard Strauss, we hardly see other than second-rate composers, whose equivalents it would be easy to find without crossing our frontiers. But it is possible that shortly some young artists will appear there whom it would be interesting to know here.

On the other hand, I do not think it necessary that all French music be made to predominate in France, or be spread abroad, no matter what its worth.

So you see, gentlemen, that my opinion differs from yours on so many levels that I cannot permit myself the honor of being considered one of you.

I hope, nevertheless, to continue to "act as a Frenchman," and to "count myself among those who mean never to forget that they are Frenchmen." [2]

SELF-CRITICISM

From a Concert Review, 1912

By the irony of chance, the first work which I must review happens to be my "Pavane pour une infante défunte." I feel no embarrassment in discussing it; it is old enough for time to allow the composer to relinquish it to the critic. From such a distance I no longer see its good qualities. But alas! I see all too clearly its faults: the too flagrant influence of Chabrier, and the rather poor form. The remarkable interpre-

tation of this incomplete and unventuresome work contributed much,
I think, to its success. [3]

LISZT

From a Concert Review, 1912

A large part of the public which applauded my *Pavane* did not fail
to show its animosity toward the splendid symphonic poem of Liszt,
Les Idéals. Doubtless these inspired pages must seem a little long on first
hearing, but is the work really any longer than the final scene from the
Twilight of the Gods, which won unanimous success at the same concert?

Of Liszt's entire output, what faults in this work matter to us?
Aren't there virtues enough in this tumultuous, seething, vast and
magnificent chaos of musical matter from which several generations
of illustrious composers drew?

To be truthful: it is in a great measure to these faults that Wagner
owes his declamatory vehemence; Strauss, his over-enthusiasm; Franck,
his tedious loftiness; the Russian school, its sometimes gaudy pic-
turesqueness; the contemporary French school, the excessive coquetry
of its harmonic grace. But do not these so dissimilar authors owe the
best of their qualities to the truly prodigious musical generosity of
their grand precursor? Can one not recognize in this frequently awkward, ever abundant form the embryo of the ingenious, limpid and
easy development of Saint-Saëns? And his dazzling orchestra, of a
sonority at once powerful and light—what a considerable influence it
exercised on the most openly avowed of Liszt's adversaries!

One can't resist a bit of irony when one considers that the majority
of the latter are pupils of Franck, who, of all contemporaries, owes
most to Liszt. These disciples have not guarded against following
the example of their master, whose colorless, heavy orchestra often
spoils the beauty of his idea. [4]

THE CRITICS OF DEBUSSY

From a Concert Review, 1913

Lately, notable "improvements" have been effected in the methods of
music criticism. We are aware that the aim of its official representatives
has always been to weaken the new generation whose tendencies
seem to them dangerous. The rapidity with which these new schools

have succeeded each other in the last half century has necessitated more expeditious means. It is no longer enough to lament the aesthetic of the old master, to feign incomprehension, fury, or hilarity at the discoveries of the new; old and new are contemporary. It's a question of acting as if the old were healthy, the power of the new on the decline.

Actually two schools confront each other: the old comprises the disciples of César Franck, and Claude Debussy may justly be considered the principal initiator of the new.

Composers, generally, are inclined to be tolerant. Thus, Mr. Vincent d'Indy, head of the Franckist group, recognizes the validity of some of his young colleagues, fearing only that future generations will carry on from where these youngsters left off, rather than retrogress. The real dirty work is left to a small army of music scribblers.

On the appearance of *Pelléas and Mélisande*, they ranged themselves in the forefront of Debussy's partisans. At the same time they were planning his downfall. The work is disquieting; they declared it sublime, but erratic. Here was an impasse; they decided to wait.

Whereupon a great number of young people set about investigating the statements of the critics and discovered, behind the "impasse," a wide-open door leading toward a splendid, completely new landscape.   [5]

WEBER

From a Statement to Hélène Jourdan-Morhange, no date

No more fertile spring ever fed German Romanticism! At a time when Italianism invaded music, Weber dammed that fashionable wave with experiments which one might compare to Goethe's, and drew from the folk essence the freshness which was to give his *lieder* a new form. Sensibility and drama were to become the warp and woof of music, if one might so express it.   [6]

THE *BOLERO*

Information given by Ravel to M. D. Calvocoressi and published in the London *Daily Telegraph*, July 16, 1931

I am particularly desirous that there should be no misunderstanding as to my *Bolero*. It is an experiment in a very special and limited direction, and should not be suspected of aiming at achieving anything different from, or anything more than, it actually does achieve. Before the first performance, I issued a warning to the effect that what I had written was a piece lasting seventeen minutes and consisting wholly of orchestral tissue without music—of one long, very gradual *crescendo*. There are no contrasts, and there is practically no invention except in the plan and manner of the execution. The themes are impersonal folk tunes of the usual Spanish-Arabian kind. Whatever may have been said to the contrary, the orchestral treatment is simple and straightforward throughout, without the slightest attempt at virtuosity. In this respect, no greater contrast could be imagined than that between the *Bolero* and *L'Enfant et les Sortilèges*, in which I freely resort to all manners of orchestral virtuosity.

It is perhaps because of these peculiarities that composers do not like the *Bolero*. From their point of view they are quite right. I have done exactly what I set out to do, and it is for the listeners to take it or leave it.   [7]

MANUEL DE FALLA

1876-1946

In 1922, while resident in Granada, Falla organized a festival of *cante jondo* under the auspices of the Centro Artistico de Granada. For its audiences he prepared an essay on the history and characteristics of *cante jondo*, from which several excerpts are quoted below.

Falla had been a student of Felipe Pedrell who, in both his writings and his musical compositions—he also compiled several volumes of folk songs and old Spanish music, secular and religious—tried to reanimate the national musical culture of Spain after two centuries of stagnation. Following his master's road, Falla became the symbol of the regeneration of Spanish music. Pedrell had maintained that each nation should base its art music on its native folk material. For Falla this did not mean the actual borrowing of popular themes; he assimilated Spanish folk music until his own work mirrored it without quoting it. He used actual folk tunes only in his arrangements of the *Seven Spanish Popular Songs*, while fragments of native song appear in several of his more extended pieces, such as the puppet opera, *El Retablo de Maese Pedro*. His works reflect not only Andalusian music with its Moorish, Oriental color, but also the less well known yet thoroughly Spanish, austere Castilian music.

He began his composing career by writing zarzuelas, comic operas of local Spanish color, in the hopes of earning enough money from this popular form to study in Paris. Though these were not successful, he eventually reached Paris where, befriended by Debussy, Dukas and Ravel, his career flowered. He remained in Paris for seven years, returning to Spain as its most celebrated composer. His last years were spent in Argentina where he finished an extensive cantata for soli, chorus and orchestra, *Atlantide*, after an epic by the Catalan poet Jacinto Verdaguer. Never published or performed, it is reputed to mark the apogee of his creative powers.

CANTE JONDO

I. ANALYSIS OF THE MUSICAL ELEMENTS OF "CANTE JONDO"

The name *cante jondo* is applied to a group of Andalusian songs, of which we believe the genuine prototype to be the so-called *siguiriya gitana*, from which proceed others, still preserved by the people, like the *polos*, *martinetes* and *soleares*, which retain marked qualities distinguishing them within the large group formed by the songs commonly called *flamenco*.

This last term should only be strictly applied to the modern group which includes the songs called *malagueñas*, *granadinas*, *rondeñas* (this last an offshoot of the previous two), *sevillanas*, *peteneras*, etc., which can not be considered other than an outgrowth of the ones cited in the preceding paragraph.

Once we admit that the *siguiriya* is the typical song of the *cante jondo* group, and before we emphasize its value from the purely musical point of view, we must state that this Andalusian song is perhaps the only European song which preserves in all its purity—both in structure and style—the highest qualities inherent in the primitive songs of the Orient.

The essential elements of *cante jondo* present the following analogies with some of the songs of India and other Oriental countries:

First: Enharmony as a modulating means. The word *modulating* does not have its modern significance in this case. We designate as modulation the simple passing from one tonality to another like it, but pitched on a different level, the only exception being the change in mode (major to minor), the only distinction established by European music between the seventeenth century and the last third of the nineteenth. These modes or melodic series are made up of whole steps and half steps whose order is unchanging. But the primitive Indian systems and their derivatives do not consider invariable the places in which the smaller intervals (in our tempered scale, semi-tones) occur in the melodic series (the scales), believing rather that the occurrence of these smaller intervals, destructive of similarity of scale movement, must obey the rising and falling of the voice demanded by the expression of the word sung. This explains why the primitive Indian modes were so numerous, as each one of the theoretically determined scales engendered new melodic series through the free alteration of four of its seven tones. In other words, only three of the tones which formed the scale were invariable; moreover, each of the tones susceptible to alteration was divided and subdivided, the results in certain cases being that notes of attack and resolution of some fragments of a phrase were altered, which is exactly what we encounter in *cante jondo*.

Let us add to this the frequent practice, both in Indian songs and in ours, of vocal *portamento*, or the way of handling the voice so as to produce the infinite gradations of pitch lying between two conjunct or disjunct tones.

So then, the real application made of the term *to modulate*, to express the manner in which a singer uses his voice as a means of expression, is much more precise in the case we are studying than that other made by academic treatises on European musical technique.

To sum up, we can state, first, that in *cante jondo*, as in the primitive songs of the Orient, the musical scale is a direct consequence of what we might call the oral scale. Some people have come to believe that speech and song were originally the same thing; Louis Lucas, in his *Acoustique Nouvelle*, in treating of the excellencies of the enharmonic genus says "that it is the first which appears in the natural order of things through imitation of bird songs, animal cries, and the infinite noises of matter."

What we now term enharmonic modulation may be thought of in a certain way as a consequence of the primitive enharmonic genus. This consequence is, nevertheless, more apparent than real, since our tempered scale only allows us to change the tonal functions of a sound, while in enharmony proper this sound is modified according to the natural pull of its attracting functions.

Second: We recognize as a characteristic of *cante jondo* the use of a melodic compass rarely exceeding the limits of a sixth. It is clear that this sixth is not made up merely of nine semi-tones, as in our tempered scale, but that through the use of enharmony, the number of sounds which the singer emits is augmented considerably.

Third: The reiterated and almost obsessive use of the same note, often accompanied by its higher or lower appoggiature. This procedure is characteristic of certain forms of incantation and even of those mumbo-jumbos which we might call prehistoric, and which give rise to the belief, as we have indicated, that song is anterior to the other forms of language. For this reason it has been possible in certain songs of the group which we are studying, especially the *siguiriya*, to destroy all sensation of metrical rhythm, producing the impression of sung prose, when in reality the literary text is verse.

Fourth: Though gypsy melody is rich in ornamental passages, these, just as in primitive Oriental songs, are employed at certain times as elaborations or outbursts suggested by the emotional power of the text. They are to be considered, for the most part, more as extended vocal inflections than as ornamental passages, even though they take on the appearance of ornaments when they are translated into the geometrical intervals of the tempered scale.

Fifth: The sounds and cries with which our people inspire and excite their singers and players also have their origin in the custom which is still observed in analogous cases in races of Oriental origin.

Let no one think, however, that the *siguiriya* and its derivatives are simply songs transplanted from the Orient to the Occident. Here we have, on the contrary, a grafting, or better, a sharing of origins which was certainly not revealed at a single given moment, but which follows, as we said before, the accumulation of folk history evolved in our peninsula. And that is the reason why the song peculiar to Andalusia, though it coincided in its essential elements with that of peoples geographically remote from ours, maintains an intimate character, so peculiar to itself, so national that it can not be confused with any other.[1]

II. THE INFLUENCE OF THESE SONGS ON MODERN EUROPEAN MUSIC

The excellence of natural Andalusian music is revealed by the fact that it is the only music continuously and abundantly used by foreign composers, and though the songs and dances of other nations have been equally utilized in universal music, this use is almost always reduced to the simple application of their characteristic rhythms.

Certainly many of these rhythmic forms have given rise to works of the highest artistic quality, as have some old European dances (gigues, sarabandes, gavottes, minuets), but in addition to the fact that these are few in number, each separate nation is represented by, at most, a

[1] This treasure of beauty—pure Andalusian song—is not only threatened with ruin, but is on the point of disappearing forever.

What is even worse is that, with the exception of some rare singer practicing it, and a few ex-singers already lacking means of expression, what remains of Andalusian singing is no more than a sad and lamentable shadow of what it was and what it should be. The grave, hieratical song of yesterday has degenerated into the ridiculous flamencoism of today. In it the essential elements which constituted its glory, its ancient titles of nobility, are being adulterated and (horrors!) modernized. The sober vocal modulation—the natural inflections of song which give rise to the division and subdivision of the tones of the scale—have been converted into artificial ornamental scrollwork befitting the decadence of the bad Italian epoch more than the primitive songs of the Orient, with which ours can be compared only when they are pure. The limits of the reduced melodic compass in which the songs emerge have been stupidly extended; for the modal wealth of its antique scales they have substituted the tonal poverty caused by the preponderant use of the only two modern modes which have monopolized European music for more than two centuries; finally, the phrase, grossly rhythmized, is losing day by day that rhythmical flexibility which constituted one of its greatest beauties. [Falla's note.]

couple of examples of these purely rhythmic forms, to the exclusion, in the majority of cases, of the rest of their constituent elements.

Our natural music, on the contrary, has not only been the source of inspiration for many of the most illustrious modern foreign composers, but has served to enrich their means of musical expression, revealing to them certain great musical values systematically disregarded by the composers of the so-called classic period. And that is the reason that the moderns (we call those authors modern who date from after the middle of last century) did not limit themselves to taking one element only from our music, but all, absolutely all elements which go to form it, always provided they lent themselves to the tempered scale and the usual notation.

This influence to which we refer is the one directly exercised by popular Andalusian song, the backbone of which is represented by *cante jondo*. Here are some facts which confirm our thesis.

In the *Cancionero musical español*, its eminent author, Felipe Pedrell says, referring to Michael Ivanovitch Glinka and his long sojourn in Spain:

"Later he spent two years in Madrid, Granada, and Seville. What was he looking for there, wandering alone through the Barrio del Avapiés or along the Calle de las Sierpes? The same thing that he was searching for in the Albaicín of Granada when ecstatically following the twangings which Francisco Rodríguez Murciano, the famous guitarist, the popular self-taught artist, with a musical imagination as full of fire as of inexhaustible inspiration, ever alive and fresh, drew from his guitar. Glinka besieged him and they became friends quickly. One of the delights of the great Russian composer was to listen for hours on end while Rodríguez Murciano improvised variations to the accompaniments of *rondeñas, fandangos, jotas aragonesas,* etc., which he noted down with careful persistence, struggling to transcribe them for piano or orchestra.

Glinka's struggles were fruitless; defeated, but hypnotized, he turned back to his companion, listening to him draw from his strings a shower of rhythms, modalities, flourishes, rebellious and refractory to all notation. . . ."

These notations and studies led to the creation of certain orchestral procedures which enrich his *Summer Night in Madrid* and the *Jota Aragonesa,* works written by Glinka during his residence in Spain.

But this, though a great deal, does not suffice to demonstrate the entire importance of the influence on most of the Russian composers who formed the group known as the "Five," direct heirs of the author of *A Life for the Czar*. Other aspects of our music, especially of the old Andalusian music, must have awakened the interest of Glinka during the two years he spent in Spain.

As admirable as was the art with which Rodríguez Murciano translated the songs and dances of Spain on his guitar, this signified no more than an instrumental interpretation. It is obvious that Glinka would not have lost opportunities to enrich his notebooks with an approximation (in the majority of cases it could not have been more) not only of dances and songs gathered directly from the people, but also of its guitar, drumstick, drum and handclapping accompaniments, so much the more since all this vibrated very intensely in the milieu in which he lived and from which he did not separate himself during his long stay in Spain. Since the *cante jondo* songs were those most cultivated in that epoch (1849), they were the ones which exercised the greatest influence on the Russian composers whom we mentioned before. Given the affinity existing between the group of our songs referred to above and the other no less important group of the Russians, the comprehension and assimilation of our songs by those composers must have been effected in the most natural and spontaneous way. A lively interest was awakened in them through their charm and rhythms so closely related to ours, and to this interest was united the idea of incorporating them into art music, mingling the characteristic elements of both types of songs and rhythms, and forming that unmistakable style which represents one of the highest qualities of Russian music of the end of the past century.

Not only Russia was influenced by the music of our country; another great musical nation later followed its example, and that nation was France, in the person of Claude Debussy. Though not a few French composers preceded him along this road, their intentions reduced themselves to making music *a la española*, (in the Spanish manner), and even Bizet in his admirable *Carmen* seems not to have aimed at anything more.

These musicians, from the most middling to the most eminent, contented themselves with the material—in how many cases how unauthentic!—furnished them by this or that collection of songs and dances which offered no guarantee of its national authenticity other than that of listing authors with Spanish names. And since these names unfortunately did not always coincide with that of the artists meriting such a title, the document often lacked any validity.

It is clear that such a procedure could not satisfy a man like Debussy. His music is not written *a la española* but *en español* [in Spanish], or rather *en andaluz*, since it is our *cante jondo*, in its most authentic form, which gave origin not only to his consciously Spanish works, but also to certain musical values in other of his works not intended to be Spanish. We are referring to the frequent use of certain modes, cadences, chord connection, rhythms and even melodic turns which reveal an obvious relation to our natural music.

And yet the great French composer was never in Spain, except for a few hours spent in San Sebastian to see a bull fight. . . .

The knowledge which he acquired of Andalusian music was due to the frequency with which he attended the performances of *cante* and *baile jondo* given in Paris by singers, players and dancers from Seville and Granada at the last two universal expositions held there.

With what better arguments could we demonstrate the enormous importance of our *cante jondo* as an aesthetic force! For we must not forget that the work of that prodigious magician named Claude Debussy represents the point of departure for the most profound revolution recorded in the history of musical art.

But what is more, the case of Debussy in relation to our music does not represent an isolated fact in modern French production; other composers, and Maurice Ravel especially, have made use of not a few essential elements of popular Andalusian lyric.

Ravel is also one of those who have not been content to write music *a la española.* . . . The part of his work in which is revealed, now expressly, now unconsciously, the Andalusian musical idiom, proves in an unequivocal manner to what point Ravel assimilated the purest essence of this idiom. Obviously, in this case as well as in those previously enumerated, it has been translated into the style peculiar to each author.

III. THE GUITAR

We cannot conclude these notes without specifying, be it ever so briefly, the extremely important part which the guitar plays in the influences and ideas to which we have just referred. The popular use of the guitar represents two very definite musical values: external or immediately perceptible rhythm, and purely tonal harmonic value.

The first, combined with some cadential turns easily assimilable, was the only one utilized for a long time by more or less artistic music, while the importance of the second—the purely tonal harmonic value—was hardly recognized by composers, with the exception of Domenico Scarlatti, up to a relatively recent epoch.

The Russian composers to whom we referred before, were, after the old and admirable Neapolitan musician, the first to perceive it; yet

since, with the exception of Glinka, not one of them knew the peculiar
strumming of the Andalusian people except by report, the artistic appreciation of it was necessarily small. Even Glinka paid more attention
to the ornamental forms and to some cadential turns than to the internal
harmonic phenomena produced in what we might call *toque jondo*
(jondo playing).

Claude Debussy was the composer to whom, in a certain way, we owe
the incorporation of these values in art music; his harmonic writing,
his sound texture attest to it in not a few cases.

The example given by Debussy had immediate and brilliant consequences; the admirable *Iberia* of our Isaac Albéniz may be counted
among the most illustrious of them.

And *toque jondo* has no rival in Europe. The harmonic effects which
our guitarists produce unconsciously represent one of the marvels of
natural art. More: we believe that our fifteenth century instrumentalists
were probably the first to accompany vocal or instrumental melody
harmonically (with chords). And it is clear that I am not referring to
Moorish-Andalusian music but to Castilian, since one must not confuse
the Moorish guitar with the Latin guitar. Our fifteenth and sixteenth
century authors refer to both, and what they say proves the distinct
musical use of each instrument.   [1]

ERNEST BLOCH

1880–

Ernest Bloch is best known for his works inspired by Hebrew lore; yet he has composed music in all genres. Early in his career, when his *Macbeth* was produced at the Opéra-Comique in Paris, he was acclaimed by such critics as Romain Rolland, but eighteen years passed before *Macbeth* was again staged. He has had difficulty in finding his rightful place because he does not fit into any of the recognized European schools. He belongs to no school; he is an individualist.

Swiss by birth, he has wandered over Germany and France, finally coming to the United States where he has made his home. He has exerted a strong influence as a teacher—he has taught at the Mannes School in New York, the Cleveland Institute of Music, and the San Francisco Conservatory of Music—numbering among his students one of America's most distinguished composers and teachers, Roger Sessions.

In his Hebrew-inspired compositions—*Schelomo*, the *Israel* Symphony, the *Avodath Hakodesh* (a sacred service for the synagogue) and the *Trois Poèmes Juifs*—he has not used authentic melodies, but has attempted to translate into music the flavor of the Old Testament. Perhaps his most frequently played piece is the first *Concerto Grosso*, a chamber work in neo-classic style, marked by his own impassioned, personal idiom.

THE STATE OF MODERN MUSIC

From an article "Man and Music," March 1917

Only that art can live which is an active manifestation of the life of the people. It must be a necessary, and essential portion of that life, and not a luxury. It must have its roots deep within the soil that brings it forth. Needless to say, it cannot be the direct output of crowds; but, however indirectly, they must have contributed to its substance. A work of art is the soul of a race speaking through the voice of the prophet in whom it has become incarnate. Art is the outlet of the mystical, emotional needs of the human spirit; it is created rather by instinct than by intelligence; rather by intuition than by will. Primitive and elemental races have had marvellous arts; and there have been periods of superior civilization, sterile in this form of expression; particularly those in which the practical and intellectual elements have been dominant. Indeed, it would seem as if certain social states like certain individual conditions give forth an atmosphere that is hostile to art and exclude it. And it is a proper question whether a society, primarily utilitarian like our own, is of a sort to foster art. For art is a completely disinterested function; it is free of all practical compromise and deaf to the law of supply and demand.

In certain epochs of history broad truths, social, political or religious, have set up wide currents of thought and feeling that have swept man along in a unity of action and of faith. In such times, art has been one with life and its expression has stood for humanity. Egypt, Greece, the Middle Ages, the Renaissance knew such an art. It seems to me that the latest example of one of these collective states of soul in music was Richard Wagner: for in him we find incarnate the future dream and development of his race. But since Wagner's time no great conception, no great conviction has fertilized mankind. On the other hand, the critical instinct has developed, the positive sciences have reigned; industrialism and the vulgarization of art, heightened communication and interchange of ideas have foisted on our consciousness a febrile mixture of thought and feeling. We find the most hostile theories living side by side. The old convictions are shattered, and new ideas are not strong enough to become convictions. Everywhere there is chaos. And art indeed has been the mirror of our uncertainties. It is significant to find, in a single epoch, the flourishing of works and styles so varied and so opposed: Reger to Strauss; Mahler to Schoenberg; Saint-Saëns to D'Indy or Debussy; Puccini to Dukas. Our arts tend more and more toward an individualistic, non-representative and non-racial expression. Nor is the factitious renaissance of national arts which manifested itself before the war to be taken seriously. The ardor of these prophets was an affair of the will, of the intellect. Their influence on the real domain of art is negligible.

There can be no doubt, for instance, that a great artist like Claude Debussy stands for the best and purest traditions of the French. But chiefly he is representative aesthetically and in form. The essence of his inspiration has little in common with the present state of France. He stands far less for France than a Rabelais, a Montaigne, a Voltaire, a

Balzac, a Flaubert. He represents in reality only a small part of his country.[1]

Debussy represents the goal of the preraphaelite doctrines propounded by the symbolist poets and painters of France. Above all, he represents Claude Debussy. And it is precisely in this fact that his immense value lies: his personality, his special individuality.

Unfortunately, this is not what musicians have sought in him. Quite the contrary, they appreciate and emulate the exterior part of his work which is of importance only because of what it expresses; so that the fate of Debussy has been the usual one. First, he was ignored. Now, he is understood and admired only through his superficial and trivial qualities. An army of imitators, of second-hand manufacturers, pounced on the technique of Claude Debussy. And through their ironical activities that which was the peculiar asset of a peculiar personality becomes a debased tongue; musicians who have nothing in common with Debussy now think that they must use his words. And criticism which seems perennially unable to distinguish the true work from the pastiche exalts with the same adjectives the authentic expression and the sickening imitation.

Of course, the language of Debussy has become vulgarized and denatured; false usage has emptied it of its native color. It has become a mechanical procedure, without power and without soul. And the consequence, as with Wagner, has been a constant musical depreciation. For the ears of these moderns Debussy is already "vieux jeu." Debussy has had to be outbidden. From one tonal exaggeration to another, we have been hurried along until our ears have become actually perverse and incapable of savoring the clean and fresh beauty of old masterpieces. Our appetite increases for still hotter spices, for still wilder complexities.

First, the Wagnerians created "Wagnerism," a narrow doctrine that declared itself the absolute truth; then the admirers of Debussy forged their "debussysme," a doctrine equally narrow and equally intolerant of the past. And now comes a new aesthetic—that of the *bored ones!* It is based exclusively upon technical considerations. With the charge of rhetoric it denies most of the superb eras of musical history, as if its own rhetoric were better; and it succeeds utterly in confounding the means of art with its end. Its cry is for novelty, and still more novelty. This frenzied search for originality has led to cubism, futurism, all

---

[1] Perhaps it is unjust to seek this manifestation of France in her music. Here poets and novelists, painters and sculptors are certainly more typical. Each race has its arts of predilection. [Author's note.]

those tendencies which above everything are creations of reason and not of feeling.

Here is a new criterion; and all our musicians, artists, critics, are touched by it in some degree. When I say that they are not free, I mean that an intellectual barrier exists between their emotion and their work —a sort of sensory perversion that twists their thoughts, inhibits their inspiration, and warps their taste. They are forever thinking of the development of their art, not as the corollary of a logical growth of thought, not as a spontaneous expression of life, but as a thing-in-itself, apart from life. And the truth is that they neither understand nor are they interested in anything so much as the elaboration of their technique.

[1]

From: Program notes, 1933

ON HIS HEBREW MUSIC

I do not propose nor do I want to attempt the reconstruction of Hebrew music, nor do I base my work on more or less authentic melodies. I am not an archeologist; I believe that the most important thing is to write good and sincere music. It is rather the Hebrew spirit which interests me, the complex, ardent, restless spirit which I feel pulsating throughout the Bible, the freshness and ingenuousness of the Patriarchs, the violence of the books of the Prophets, the fierce love of the Hebrews for justice, the despair in the book of Ecclesiastes, the sorrow and grandeur of the book of Job, the sensuality of the Song of Songs. All this resides in us, all this resides in me, is the best part of me. And this is what I try to feel within me and to translate into my music: the holy fervor of the race which is latent in our soul.   [2]

THE STORY OF SCHELOMO

Here is the story of *Schelomo*. Toward the end of 1915 I was living in Geneva. For years I had had a number of sketches for the book of Ecclesiastes which I wanted to set to music, but the French language was not adaptable to my rhythmic patterns. Nor was German or English, and I hadn't a good enough command of Hebrew. Thus the sketches accumulated and . . . lay dormant.

One day I met the cellist Alexander Barjansky and his wife. I heard Barjansky play and we became friends at once. I played my manuscript scores for them, *Hebrew Poems, Israel* and *Psalms*, all of them unpublished and about which nobody cared. The Barjanskys were profoundly moved. While I played, Mrs. Barjansky, who had asked for a sheet of paper and a piece of chalk, sketched a small statue. "Gratefulness in Sculpture," she called it. Finally, in my terrible loneliness, I had found true and warm friends. My hopes were reborn, and also the desire to write a work for this marvellous cellist. Why shouldn't I use for my Ecclesiastes—instead of a singer limited in range, a voice vaster and deeper than any spoken language—his cello? Thus I took my sketches and, without a plan, without a program, almost without knowing where I was headed, worked day after day on my *Rhapsody*. As I composed, I copied the cello part which Barjansky studied. At the same time Mrs. Barjansky worked at the statue intended for me. At first she had had the idea for a Christ, but later decided on a King Solomon. We finished our works at about the same time. The Ecclesiastes was completed in a few weeks, and since legend attributes this book to King Solomon, I named it *Schelomo*.

As can be seen, I had no descriptive intention. I was saturated with the Biblical text, and above all with the misery of the world for which I have always felt a great compassion. [3]

MACBETH

I composed *Macbeth* in the woods and mountains of Switzerland. I was then twenty-five years old. For a year I immersed myself in the poem, living and dreaming it. Then came the musical work which I completed rather quickly. Much of it was created at fever heat; other sections more slowly with corrections and eliminations. Some scenes gave me an intense joy, but I was frequently discouraged. Sometimes I felt that I had achieved a perfect union between poetry and music; at other times I was overcome with despair. My task was to mirror Shakespeare and at the same time remain true to myself. I could not be Debussy here, Wagner there and elsewhere Franck. I had always and entirely to be myself. In this respect I am a profound egoist. I have no prejudices but I cannot adopt the expressions of others. I can admire, but I cannot imitate. The evolution of an artist is comparable to the development of a baby. As long as it has not reached maturity, come of age, it must imitate. Then comes the time when it must "sing on its own." This is emancipation. Now comes liberation from predilection and prejudice, and one can speak with sincerity and sureness. Until this happens the artist has not expressed his real self; he has only labored to attain experience in the technique of expression. [4]

IX

BARTÓK
MALIPIERO
KODÁLY
STRAVINSKY
WEBERN
BERG
PROKOFIEV
HONEGGER
MILHAUD
HINDEMITH

BÉLA BARTÓK

1881–1945

In 1905, in company with his friend and colleague Kodály, Bartók began intensive research in Hungarian folksong. The two men went out into the field, collecting and recording folk music from the mouths of Hungarian peasants, and returned with thousands of examples of Magyar, Slovak, Transylvanian, Rumanian and other folk themes. In 1924, Bartók published *Hungarian Folk Music*, which discusses the derivation and structure of Hungarian folk song. This preoccupation was in the nature of a revolt against the distortions of gypsy music and the compositions of popular composers which Liszt had utilized in his Rhapsodies, and which, during the nineteenth century and well into the twentieth, represented Hungarian folk music to the general public.

Bartók recognized the spurious in Liszt's Rhapsodies, a fault attributable, as he points out, to the scant knowledge of genuine folk music in Liszt's time; he also understood Liszt's significance for the development of modern music which he considered far greater than the impact of Wagner or Strauss.

Further research led Bartók to North Africa and the Near East where he studied Arab music which he was then able to contrast with his native folk material. His essays and lectures reflect this consummate knowledge, enhanced by an extensive general culture.

His musical works, at first academic, gradually became permeated with the folk spirit of Hungary. He got away from major and minor scales, substituting for them the old scales on which peasant music is based. At the same time, he developed a highly personal idiom, the abstract style of his string quartets, which unfortunately remained almost unaccepted until after his death.

LISZT AS COMPOSER [1]

From an Address, 1934 [2]

If we compare Liszt as a composer with his predecessors and contemporaries, we find characteristics in his works that we seek in vain elsewhere. We see that among all the greater composers of his time and before him, there was not one who was subject to so many different influences as he. Every composer, even the greatest, must start from something that already exists, perhaps one kind of thing, perhaps several related ones. From this, one composer—the innovator—gradually reaches new points, from which it is hardly possible to remember the starting point; another composer—the great traditionalist—develops what already exists to a stage never foreseen, and into a unity never imagined. Liszt, however, did not start from any one point, nor fuse together in his own works several related things; he submitted himself to the influence of the most diverse, contradictory and almost irreconcilable elements.

Let us look at these influences one by one. Of his contemporaries, we feel the influence of Chopin to a very great degree, chiefly in certain kinds of piano works. The imprint of the bel canto style of the Italians of the previous century is plainly to be seen in every work, and it is hardly necessary to mention that he was subject to the influence of the Hungarian so-called gypsy music. He also allowed himself to be influenced by the utterly different, popular, half-folk music of Italy, as his works connected with Italy clearly show. Nor was he untouched by the equivalent Spanish popular music, witness the "Spanish Rhapsody." There is also in manuscript a very little known "Wallachian Rhapsody." Later, chiefly in his religious music, Gregorian influences become apparent. His relationship to Wagner is not easy to make out. A separate study, based on chronological data would be necessary to show which of the elements in Liszt that might be called "Wagnerian" owed their origin to Liszt, and which to Wagner. Probably Wagner had much to thank Liszt for, but on the other hand, in Liszt's later works, such as the last symphonic poem, we may expect to find a certain amount of Wagner's influence. It is, however, quite apparent, and significant, that apart from Wagner's we can hardly find another trace of German influence, whether of folk music or art music, in Liszt's work.

[1] From address "Liszt Problems," delivered on his being elected a member of the Hungarian Academy of Science in 1934.
[2] This is the date given by Bartók; other sources give 1935 and 1936 (see: Halsey Stevens, *The Life and Music of Béla Bartók*, New York 1953, p. 313, note 41).

How did Liszt fit these contradictory elements into a unified structure? First of all, it must be said that whatever Liszt touched, whether it was Hungarian art song, folk song, Italian aria or anything else, he so transformed and so stamped it with his own individuality that it became like something of his own. What he created from these foreign elements became unmistakably Liszt's music. Still more important, however, is the fact that he mixed with these foreign elements so many more that were genuinely drawn from himself that there is no work in which we can doubt the greatness of his creative power. We can say that he was eclectic in the best sense of the word; one who took from all foreign sources, but gave still more himself.

However, there are certain elements that go together ill; for instance, Gregorian music and Italian aria. Such things could not be fused into unity even with all Liszt's art. To quote only one example, there is the *Totentanz* for piano and orchestra. This composition, which is simply a set of variations on the Gregorian melody "Dies Irae," is startlingly harsh from beginning to end. But what do we find in the middle section? A variation hardly eight bars long, of almost Italianate emotionalism. Here Liszt obviously intended to relieve the overwhelming austerity and darkness with a ray of hope. The work as a whole always has a profound effect upon me, but this short section sticks out so from the unified style of the rest that I have never been able to feel that it is appropriate. In many of Liszt's works we find similar little outbursts breaking up the unity of style.

In the end, however, this is not so important; this fleeting disturbance of the unity is merely external, and is dwarfed into insignificance beside the wealth of power and beauty that form the essence of the work. But the general public obviously finds it an insurmountable obstacle; they do not perceive nor understand the beauty, and they miss the compensation of dazzling brilliance, which hardly exists in such works as the *Totentanz*, so they drop the whole work. Another cause, or at least I imagine so, is that tendency to prolixity in Liszt's greater works. This is not the Schubertian "heavenly length" which we forgive without hesitation for the sake of the youthfully exhuberant and astonishingly beautiful ideas. In Liszt's greater works there are certain sequential repetitions of long sections, in the relative major or minor key, for instance, which we today, perhaps because we are used to the faster tempo of life in general, do not always feel to be necessary. But this again is not an essential point. The essence of these works we must find in the new ideas, to which Liszt was the first to give expression, and in the bold pointing towards the future. These things raise Liszt as a composer to the ranks of the great, and for their sake we love his works as they are, weaknesses and all. I say weaknesses and all because there is perhaps not one of the greater works which sustains from beginning to end that perfection that we so much admire in the works we call the great classics.

To explain in detail what it was that was so new and significant that Liszt gave to the world in his works, would lead us too far. One could draw attention to the bold harmonic turns, the innumerable modulatory digressions, such as the juxtaposition, without any transition at all, of the two keys most distant from each other, and to many other points that would require the use of too many technical terms. But all these are mere details. What is more important is the absolutely new imaginative conception that manifests itself in the chief works (the "Piano Sonata," and the two outer movements of the *Faust Symphony*, for instance) by reason of which these works rank among the outstanding musical creations of the nineteenth century. Formally, too, though he did not break with tradition completely, Liszt created much that was new. Thus one finds in him, in the *E-flat major Piano Concerto* for instance, the first perfect realization of cyclic sonata form, with common themes treated on variation principles. After Liszt's time this solution of formal problems came to acquire more and more importance. It was Liszt who, after Berlioz, developed the symphonic poem further, and we may say that the musical form that arose from the juxtaposition of the *lassú* (slow) and the *friss* (fast) was Liszt's innovation, though he was in fact led to it by the usual order of Hungarian folk and semi-folk dances.

His piano technique was at first derived from Chopin's and from that of various less significant composers, but in his maturity it was transformed into something new and individual. He brought his own artistic and expressive medium to such a pitch of perfection that he covered every possible development, in consequence of which his successors in this field could hardly do anything, and were forced to turn in other directions. As an innovator in instrumentation, with his absolutely individual orchestral technique, he stands beside the other two great orchestrators of the nineteenth century, Berlioz and Wagner.

In Liszt's works we find the most exact reflection of his whole mind and outlook. His optimism he expresses best in those magnificent *Verklärung*-like codas that one finds in so many of his greater works. It is humanly very understandable that he did not reject his romantic century, with all its exaggerations. From this comes his own exaggeratedly rhetorical pathos, and no doubt it also explains the concessions he makes to the public, even in his finest works. But whoever picks out only these weaknesses—and there are still some music lovers who do—

does not see the essence behind them. And an unbiased judgment, without the recognition of the essence, is impossible.

From one part of his piano music it seems as if he were intentionally seeking to satisfy public taste. Of course even in these, down to the tiniest details, his great creative artistry is apparent. But from the point of view of content, these brilliant pieces have not half so much to offer us as the other piano works, particularly those from his maturity, which are absolutely free from bombast and frills. Even so, these trivial pieces are formally and technically perfect, often superior in this respect to some of the greater and more significant works. Naturally, in his arrangements and similar works, such as the rhapsodies, he had little opportunity to give expression to his own innermost individuality, and at first only these works were in favor with the public. It is not surprising that his more discerning listeners could not stress enough, sometimes even with exaggeration, what infinitely more valuable things were hidden in his original works. But for the sake of truth, I must stress that the rhapsodies, particularly the Hungarian ones, are perfect creations of their own kind. The material that Liszt uses in them could not be treated with greater artistry and beauty. The value of the material itself is quite another question, and this is obviously one reason why the general value of the works is slight, and their popularity great.

[1]

RACE PURITY IN MUSIC

From an Essay, 1942

There is much talk these days, mostly for political reasons, about the purity and impurity of the human race, the usual implication being that purity of race should be preserved, even by means of prohibitive laws. Those who champion this or that issue of the question have probably studied the subject thoroughly (at least, they should have done so), spending many years examining the available published material or gathering data by personal investigation. Not having done that, perhaps I cannot support either side, may even lack the right to do so. But I have spent many years studying a phenomenon of human life considered more or less important by some dreamers commonly called students of folk music. This manifestation is the spontaneous music of the lower classes, peasants especially. In the present period of controversy over racial problems, it may be timely to examine the question: Is racial impurity favorable to folk (i.e., peasant) music or not? (I apply the word racial here to the music itself, and not to the individuals creating, preserving or performing the music.)

The principal scene of my research has been Eastern Europe. As a Hungarian I naturally began my work with Hungarian folk music, but soon extended it to neighboring territories—Slovakian, Ukrainian, Rumanian. Occasionally I have even made jumps into more remote countries (in North Africa, Asia Minor) to gain a broader outlook. Besides this "active" research work dealing with problems on the spot, I have also made "passive" investigations, studying material collected and published by others.

From the beginning I have been amazed by the extraordinary wealth of melody types existing in the territory under investigation in Eastern Europe. As I pursued my research, my amazement increased. In view of the comparatively small size of the countries—numbering forty to fifty million people—the variety in folk music is really marvellous! It is still more remarkable when compared with the peasant music of other more or less remote regions, for instance North Africa, where the Arab peasant music presents so much less variety.

What can be the reason for this wealth? How has it come to pass? The answer to this question appeared only later, when sufficient material from the various Eastern European peoples was available to permit of scientific analyses. Comparison of the folk music of these peoples made it clear that there was a continuous give-and-take of melodies, a constant crossing and recrossing which had persisted through centuries.

I must now stress a very important fact. This give-and-take is not so simple as many of us might believe. When a folk melody passes the language frontier of a people, sooner or later it will be subjected to certain changes determined by environment, and especially by difference of language. The greater dissimilarity between the accents, inflections, metrical conditions, syllabic structure and so on of two languages, the greater the changes that fortunately may occur in the "emigrated" melody. I say "fortunately" because this phenomenon itself engenders a further increase in the number of types and sub-types.

I have used the term "crossing and recrossing." Now, the "recrossing" generally takes place this way. A Hungarian melody is taken over, let us say, by the Slovakians and "Slovakized"; this Slovakized form may then be retaken by the Hungarians and so "re-Magyarized." But—and again I say, fortunately,—this re-Magyarized form will be different from the original Hungarian.

Scholars doing research in linguistics find many similar phenomena connected with the migration of words. Indeed, the life of folk music and the life of languages have many traits in common.

Numerous factors explain the almost uninterrupted exchange of melodies: social conditions, deliberate or forced migrations and colonizations of individuals and peoples. As everybody knows, Eastern Europe (except for the Russians, Ukrainians and Poles) is inhabited chiefly by small peoples, each numbering about ten million or even less and there are no insurmountable geographical obstacles at the frontiers. Some districts have a completely mixed population, the result of war devastation which has been followed by colonization to fill the gaps. Continued contact between these peoples has been quite easy. And there have been conquests (for instance, of the Balkans by the Turks). Conquerors and conquered have mixed and reciprocally influenced their respective languages and folk music.

Contact with foreign material not only results in an exchange of melodies, but—and this is still more important—it gives an impulse to the development of new styles. At the same time, the more or less ancient styles are generally well preserved, too, which still further enhances the richness of the music.

The trend toward transformation of foreign melodies prevents the internationalization of the music of these peoples. The material of each, however heterogeneous in origin, receives its marked individuality.

The situation of folk music in Eastern Europe may be summed up thus: as a result of uninterrupted reciprocal influence upon the folk music of these peoples, there are an immense variety and a wealth of melodies and melodic types. The "racial impurity" finally attained is definitely beneficial.

And now let us look at the opposite picture. If you visit an oasis in North Africa, for instance Biskra, or one of its surrounding villages, you will hear folk music of a rather unified and simple structure, which is, nevertheless, highly interesting. Then if you go, let us say, as far as fifteen hundred miles to the East and listen to the folk music of Cairo and its surroundings, you will hear exactly the same type of music. I don't know very much about the migrations and history of the Arabic speaking inhabitants of North Africa, but I should say that such uniformity in so huge a territory indicates that there have been comparatively few migrations and changes of population. Also there is another factor. The Arabic people in North Africa many times outnumber those small peoples of Eastern Europe, they live in a far larger territory and, except for the few dispersed islands of Hamitic peoples (Kabyles, Cha-u-yas, Tauregs), are not intermingled with peoples of different race and language.

It is obvious that if there remains any hope for the survival of folk music in the near or distant future (a rather doubtful outcome considering the rapid intrusion of higher civilization into the more remote parts of the world), an artificial erection of Chinese walls to separate peoples from each other bodes no good for its development. A complete separation from foreign influence means stagnation; well-assimilated foreign impulses offer possibilities of enrichment.

There are significant parallels in the life of languages and the development of the higher arts. English is impure in comparison with other Teutonic languages; about forty percent of its vocabulary is of non-Anglo-Saxon origin, nevertheless it has developed incomparable strength of expression and individuality of spirit. As for the development of Europe's higher art music, every musician knows what far-reaching and fortunate consequences have resulted from the transplantation of the fifteenth century musical style of the Netherlands to Italy, and, later, from the spread of various influences from Italy to the Northern countries.   [2]

THE INFLUENCE OF PEASANT MUSIC ON MODERN MUSIC

From an Essay in *Melos*, 1920

At the beginning of the twentieth century there was a turning point in the history of modern music.

The excesses of the romanticists began to be unbearable for many. There were composers who felt: "This road does not lead us anywhere; there is no other solution but a complete break with the nineteenth century."

Invaluable help was given this change (or let us rather call it rejuvenation) by a kind of peasant music unknown up till then.

The right type of peasant music is most varied and perfect in its forms. Its expressive power is amazing, and at the same time it is void of all sentimentality and superfluous ornaments. It is simple, sometimes primitive, but never silly. It is the ideal starting point for a musical renaissance, and a composer in search of new ways cannot be led by a better master. What is the best way for a composer to reap the full benefits of his studies in peasant music? It is to assimilate the idiom of peasant music so completely that he is able to forget all about it and use it as his musical mother tongue.

In order to achieve this, Hungarian composers went into the country and made their collections there. It may be that the Russian Stravinsky and the Spaniard Falla did not go on journeys of collection, and mainly drew their material from the collections of others, but they, too, I feel sure, must not only have availed themselves of books and museums but have studied the living music of their countries.

In my opinion, the effects of peasant music cannot be deep and permanent unless this music is studied in the country as part of a life shared with the peasants. It is not enough to study it as it is stored up in museums. It is the character of peasant music, indescribable in words, that must find its way into our music. It must be pervaded by the very atmosphere of peasant culture. Peasant motifs (or imitations of such motifs) will only lend our music some new ornaments: nothing more.

Some twenty to twenty-five years ago well disposed people often marvelled at our enthusiasm. How was it possible, they asked, that trained musicians, fit to give concerts, took upon themselves the "subaltern" task of going into the country and studying the music of the people on the spot. What a pity, they said, that this task was not carried out by people less qualified for a higher type of musical work. Many thought our perseverance in our work was due to some crazy idea that had got hold of us.

Little did they know how much this work meant to us. We went into the country and obtained first-hand knowledge of a music that opened up new ways to us.

The question is, what are the ways in which peasant music is taken over and becomes transmuted into modern music?

We may, for instance, take over a peasant melody unchanged or only slightly varied, write an accompaniment to it and possibly some opening and concluding phrases. This kind of work would show a certain analogy with Bach's treatment of chorales.

Two main types can be distinguished among works of this character.

In the one case, accompaniment, introductory and concluding phrases, are of secondary importance, they only serve as an ornamental setting for the precious stone: the peasant melody.

It is the other way round in the second case: the melody only serves as a "motto" while that which is built round it is of real importance.

All shades of transition are possible between these two extremes, and sometimes it is not even possible to decide which of the elements is predominant in any given case. But in every case it is of the greatest importance that the musical qualities of the setting should be derived from the musical qualities of the melody, from such characteristics as are contained in it openly or covertly, so that melody and all additions create the impression of complete unity.

At this point I have to mention a strange notion that was wide-spread some thirty or forty years ago. Most trained and good musicians then believed that only simple harmonizations were well suited to folk tunes. And even worse, by simple harmonies they meant a succession of triads of the tonic, dominant, and possibly the subdominant.

How can we account for this strange belief? What kind of folk songs did these musicians know? Mostly new German and Western songs and so-called folk songs made up by popular composers. The melody of such songs usually moves along the triads of tonic and dominant; the main melody consists of a breaking up of these chords into single notes ("Ach, du lieber Augustin"). It is obvious that melodies of this description do not go well with a more complex harmonization.

But our musicians wanted to apply the theory derived from this type of song to an entirely different type of Hungarian song built up on "pentatonic" scales.

It may sound odd, but I do not hesitate to say that the simpler the melody the more complex and strange may be the harmonization and accompaniment that go well with it. Let us, for instance, take a melody that moves on two successive notes only (there are many such melodies in Arab peasant music). It is obvious that we are much freer in the invention of an accompaniment than in the case of a melody of a more complex character. These primitive melodies, moreover, show no trace of the stereotyped joining of triads. That again means greater freedom for us in the treatment of the melody. It allows us to bring out the melody most clearly by building round it harmonies of the widest range varying along different keynotes. I might almost say that the traces of polytonality in modern Hungarian music and in Stravinsky's music are to be explained by this possibility.

Similarly, the strange turnings of melodies in our Eastern European peasant music showed us new ways of harmonization. For instance, the new chord of the seventh which we use as a concord may be traced back to the fact that in our folk melodies of a pentatonic character the seventh appears as an interval of equal importance with the third and the fifth. We so often heard these intervals treated equally in the succession, that it was only natural to give them equal importance when used simultaneously. We sounded the four notes together in a setting which made us feel it was not necessary to break them up. In other words: the four notes were made to form a concord.

The frequent use of the intervals of the fourth in our old melodies suggested to us the use of chords built of fourths. Here again what we heard in succession we tried to build up in a simultaneous chord.

Another method by which peasant music becomes transmuted into modern music is the following: The composer does not make use of a real peasant melody but invents his own imitation of such melodies. There is no true difference between this method and the one described above.

Stravinsky never mentions the sources of his themes. Neither in his titles nor in footnotes does he ever indicate whether a theme of his is his own invention or whether it is taken over from folk music. In the same way the old composers never gave any data: let me simply mention the beginning of the *Pastoral Symphony*. Stravinsky apparently takes this course deliberately. He wants to demonstrate that it does not matter at all whether a composer invents his own themes or uses themes from elsewhere. He has a right to use musical material taken from all sources. What he has judged suitable for his purpose has become through this very use his intellectual property. In the same manner Molière is reported to have replied to a charge of plagiarism: "Je prends mon bien où je le trouve." In maintaining that the question of the origin of a theme is completely unimportant from the artist's point of view, Stravinsky is right. The question of origins can only be interesting from the point of view of musical documentation.

Lacking any data, I am unable to tell which themes of Stravinsky's from his so-called "Russian period" are his own inventions and which are borrowed from folk music. This much is certain, that if among the thematic material of Stravinsky's there are some of his own invention (and who can doubt that there are), these are the most faithful and clever imitations of folk songs. It is also notable that during his Russian period, from *Le Sacre du Printemps* onward, he seldom uses melodies of a closed form consisting of three or four lines, but short motives of two or three bars and repeats them "à la ostinato." These recurring primitive motifs are very characteristic of Russian music of a certain category. This type of construction occurs in some of our old music for wind instruments and also in Arab peasant dances.

This primitive construction of the thematic material may partly account for the strange mosaic-like character of Stravinsky's work during his early period.

The steady repetition of primitive motifs creates an air of strange feverish excitement even in folk music where it occurs. The effect is increased a hundredfold if a master of Stravinsky's supreme skill and his precise knowledge of dynamic effects employs these rapidly chasing sets of motifs.

There is yet a third way in which the influence of peasant music can be traced in a composer's work. Neither peasant melodies nor imitations of peasant melodies can be found in his music, but it is pervaded by the atmosphere of peasant music. In this case we may say, he has completely absorbed the idiom of peasant music which has become his musical mother tongue. He masters it as completely as a poet masters his mother tongue.

In Hungarian music the best example of this kind can be found in

Kodály's work. It is enough to mention the *Psalmus Hungaricus*, which would not have been written without Hungarian peasant music. (Neither, of course, would it have been written without Kodály.)

[3]

THE SIGNIFICANCE OF FOLK MUSIC

From an Essay, Budapest, 1931

Many people think it a comparatively easy task to write a composition round folk tunes. A lesser achievement, at least, than a composition on "original" themes. Because, they think, the composer is freed of part of the work: the invention of themes.

This way of thinking is completely erroneous. To handle folk tunes is one of the most difficult tasks; equally difficult, if not more so, than to write a major original composition. If we keep in mind that borrowing a tune means being bound by its individual peculiarity, we shall understand one part of the difficulty. Another is created by the special character of folk tune. We must penetrate into it, feel it, and bring out its sharp contours by the appropriate setting. The composition round a folk tune must be done in a "propitious hour" or, as is generally said, it must be a work of inspiration just as much as any other composition.

There are many who think the basing of modern music on folk music harmful and not suited to our time.

Before arguing with that school of thought, let us consider how it is possible to reconcile music based on folk music with the modern movement of atonality, or music on twelve tones.

Let us say frankly that this is not possible. Why not? Because folk tunes are always tonal. Atonal folk music is completely inconceivable. Consequently, music on twelve tones cannot be based on folk music.

The fact that some twentieth century composers went back to old folk music for inspiration acted as an impediment to the development of twelve tone music.

Far be it from me to maintain that the only way to salvation for a composer in our day is for him to base his music on folk music. But I wish that our opponents had an equally liberal opinion of the significance of folk music.

It was only recently that one of our reputable musicians held forth like this: "The ulterior motive behind the movement of collecting folk songs, that has spread all over the world, is love of comfort. There is a desire to become rejuvenated in this spring of freshness, a wish to revitalize the barren brain. This desire tries to hide an inner incompetence and to evade the struggle by comfortable and soul-killing devices."

This regrettable opinion is based on erroneous assumptions. These people must have a strange idea of the practice of composing. They seem to think the composer addicted to collecting folk songs will sit down at his writing desk with the intention of composing a symphony. He racks and racks his brain but cannot think of a suitable melody. He takes up his collection of folk songs, picks out one or two melodies and the composition of his symphony is done without further labor.

Well, it is not so simple as all that. It is a fatal error to attribute so much importance to the subject, the theme of a composition. We know that Shakespeare borrowed the plots of his plays from many sources. Does that prove that his brain was barren and that he had to go to his neighbors, begging for themes? Did he hide his incompetence? Molière's case is even worse. He not only borrowed the themes for his plays, but also part of the construction, and sometimes took over from his source expressions and whole lines unchanged.

We know that Handel adapted a work by Stradella in one of his oratorios. His adaptation is so masterly, so far surpassing the original in beauty, that we forget all about Stradella. Is there any sense in talking of plagiarism, of barrenness of brain, of incompetence in these cases?

In music it is the thematic material that corresponds to the story of a drama. And in music, too, as in poetry and in painting, it does not signify what themes we use. It is the form into which we mould them that makes the essence of our work. This form reveals the knowledge, the creative power, the individuality of the artist.

The work of Bach is a summing up of the music of some hundred-odd years before him. His musical material consists of themes and motives used by his predecessors. We can trace in Bach's music motifs and phrases which were also used by Frescobaldi and many others among Bach's predecessors. Is this plagiarism? By no means. For an artist it is not only right to have his roots in the art of some former time, it is a necessity.

Well, in our case it is peasant music which contains our roots.

The conception that attributes so much importance to the invention of a theme originated in the nineteenth century. It is a romantic conception which values originality above all.

From what has been said above, it must have become clear that it is no sign of "barrenness" or "incompetence," if a composer bases his music on folk music instead of taking Brahms and Schumann as his models.

There exists another conception of modern music which seems exactly the opposite of the former.

There are people who believe that nothing more is needed to bring about the full bloom in a nation's music than to steep oneself in folk music and to transplant its motives into established musical forms.

This opinion is founded on the same mistaken conception as the one discussed above. It stresses the all-importance of themes and forgets about the art of formation that alone can make something out of these themes. This process of moulding is part of the composer's work which proves his creative talent.

And thus we may say: folk music will become a source of inspiration for a country's music only if the transplantation of its motifs is the work of a great creative talent. In the hands of incompetent composers neither folk music nor any other musical material will ever attain significance. If a composer has no talent, it will be of no use to him to base his music on folk music or any other music. The result will in every case be nothing.

Folk music will have an immense, transforming influence on music in countries with little or no musical tradition. Most countries of southern and eastern Europe, Hungary, too, are in this position.

May I, to conclude my thoughts, finish by quoting what Kodály once said in this context about the importance of folk music.

"So little of old written Hungarian music has survived, that the history of Hungarian music cannot be built up without a thorough knowledge of folk music. It is known that folk language has many similarities with the ancient language of a people. In the same way folk music must for us replace the remains of our old music. Thus, from a musical point of view, it means more to us than to those peoples that developed their own musical style centuries ago. Folk music for these peoples became assimilated into their music, and a German musician will be able to find in Bach and Beethoven what we had to search for in our villages: the continuity of a national musical tradition." [4]

GIAN FRANCESCO MALIPIERO

1882–

In the world of music Malipiero is as well known for his scholarship and skill as an author as for his compositions. Commanding an encyclopedic knowledge of music, he has published essays, reviews and articles in numerous international magazines. He has written his own libretti for his operas.

Besides editing the works of Marcello, Galuppi, Tartini, Corelli and other Italian masters, he has published the definitive edition of Monteverdi. Through his profound study of these composers, particularly Monteverdi, he has developed a mastery of vocal writing which reflects itself in his own musical works.

Malipiero belongs to that group of modern Italian composers—Casella, Pizzetti, Respighi—who, though they have followed the Italian tradition of opera composition, have written music in every genre. All his works, uncompromisingly modern in idiom, are infused with that chief characteristic of Italian music—melody.

From: *L'orchestra*, 1920

THE ORCHESTRA

The rudimentary instruments from which descended the heads of the various families that have helped constitute an orchestra may be considered to have undergone a national evolution, almost like the voice. The orchestra has always existed; it merely had to be discovered. It represents, therefore, not so much an invention as a human conquest, made under the impulse of musical intuition and overcoming all the purely material obstacles. In the same measure as the construction of the instruments perfected itself, the ability of the players progressed.

[1]

In order to demonstrate that the primitive orchestra stood in no just proportion to the musical substance of the works of which it formed the expressive medium—although many learned people would have us

431

believe the contrary, and although there is no doubt that a certain
sensibility characteristic of the taste of the period must have produced
a sonority which we, lacking reliable evidence, cannot imagine or re-
construct—it has remained necessary, in the absence of full scores, to
rely solely on whatever information has been left to us by the early
composers who first introduced the musical instruments. It is likely that
at a time when it was the custom to complete the composer's idea by
improvisation, there may have occurred, simultaneously with the development of music, some changes in the art of accompanying from
the figured bass. These changes constitute the progressive phase between the primitive indefinite orchestra, and the period which we
know through the first complete scores.   [2]

It would be absurd to imagine that any rules could be established for
the blending of orchestral instruments. The theories of combination
cannot be set up according to empiric criterions; they represent the
individual and inimitable expressions of the composers by whom they
have been invented. The possibilities of instrumental combination are
infinite, both as regards difference of register and variety of harmony
and rhythm. Each musical thought, symphonically expressed, is remarkable for the manifold properties that constitute its essence. Even
though the classical orchestra is not surpassingly rich in color, it has
nevertheless almost greater instrumental than rhythmic and harmonic
variety.   [3]

SONORITY

The sonority of an orchestral work infallibly reveals as much of its
composer's individuality as the harmonic and thematic context. It is
sufficient to compare a few symphonic fragments of different composers who have a certain affinity of intention, to demonstrate their
orchestral characteristics which are immediately perceptible to a refined ear. Beethoven, for instance, without the continuous doubling
indispensable to Anton Bruckner and without the harmonic support
favored by Wagner, attains to an orchestral intensity equal to that
of these two composers. Nothing could be added to the orchestra of
Beethoven and nothing subtracted from that of Bruckner or Wagner
without causing, respectively, heaviness or emptiness.

A curious change, which possibly might make his own work unrecognizable to the composer, has come about in the Beethoven orchestra: it is no longer possible to tolerate a performance of one of his
symphonies with the small number of strings originally intended.

Today the body of violins, violas, violoncellos and double basses is more than twice as numerous in relation to the proportion desired by the composer. And yet (with the exception of those cases where it has been found necessary to double the wind also, when in a *forte* a theme or fragment of theme is assigned to them) no unbalanced combination ever occurs.   [4]

RICHARD STRAUSS

The personality of this Meyerbeer of the twentieth century is of undeniable importance because he occupies the foremost position among the post-Wagnerians. Musically speaking, Strauss has an abundant selection of uniforms, liveries and costumes which he dons according to the occasion. In his *Lieder*, small music for the general public, he dresses negligently and seems to be masquerading perfunctorily as Tosti, Schumann, Verdi or Hugo Wolf rather than looking like himself. In the symphonic poem and in the music drama, on the other hand, he appears clad in his most dazzling uniforms in order to conceal the poverty of his Wagnerian lyricism, or poses as humorist worthy of his namesake Johann, the pirouetting Viennese. The operas of Richard Strauss are full of old, stale tricks propped up by clever orchestral devices in order to distract the hearer's attention from all these commonplaces. He prefers the crude colors of the extreme registers to which he assigns strongly reinforced thematic material, while gliding arpeggios, scales and other superficialities (varnish and polish) are lavished with great profusion to mitigate the roughness of certain combinations which he uses with undue frequency, or to infuse life in the symphonic line, which too often languishes in a vulgar welter devoid of ideas. Although the music drama of Richard Strauss fails to make any deep impression and its orchestral orgies leave an almost disgusting aftertaste, the significance of this baroque symphonist is none the less remarkable because, in the Wagnerian parabola, he marks the extreme limit of this precipitate decadence.   [5]

A PLEA FOR TRUE COMEDY

From an article in *Modern Music*, 1929

One of the greatest obsessions of contemporary criticism is trying to figure out whether the works that are liked—and those that are not—are going to survive; or whether, in centuries to come, they will fall into complete oblivion. This is illogical not only in regard to music but all the other arts. Paint and paper made today are destined to a chemical disintegration, and thousands of volumes accumulating on library shelves will fall in shreds before the century is over, as bodies preserved in hermetically sealed tombs crumble to dust on contact with the air. The sciences of chemistry and physics represent the great triumphs of our age, but chemistry is the science which has destroyed the durability of modern art. Thanks to the chemist, our civilization will disappear and all the critical essays, intended to survive the arts, will themselves vanish, the victims of chemistry.

In opposition to this critical concern with the future, we see a fervent desire to return to the sources of music, every effort to find a new road having been exhausted. The wisest hope to create a new language by drawing on the beautiful period of the Renaissance, which, in music, ended with the seventeenth century. Others are returning to the works of the end of the eighteenth or the beginning of the nineteenth century.

Some time ago, one of my friends asked me: "What are the possibilities of the *opera buffa* and of the *cantata buffa*, like the *Amfiparnasso* of Orazio Vecchi? Can we find its traces in certain modern works and is the resurrection of that form possible?

The *opera buffa* represents the spirit of an era which did not support intense drama and which liked good cheer without vulgar degeneration. It was formed in a musical language harmonious with the spirit of its age and consequently with the comedy on whose words it was constructed. Is it possible that the musical material of the time of the *opera buffa* can belong to today? Can the spirit of the eighteenth be revived in the twentieth century? Musical development must be the spontaneous expression of its age. The most powerful artists have been unable to avoid the influences of their time. Despite his conquering personality, Johann Sebastian Bach remains a man of the eighteenth century. Richard Wagner is the heir of Beethoven; he is a romanticist who gained recognition through his personality, but he is fundamentally the contemporary of Johannes Brahms and Schumann.

Wagner is the most important figure in the present and future development of music because he took such vigorous possession of the current language that he squeezed it out like a lemon and left nothing for his successors. Debussy represents a digression; this exquisite musician, this super-aristocrat could not be the starting point for a school. We may consider Monteverdi the father of the whole Italian melodramatic school, even of those who have no spiritual link with him, because everything he invented could be assimilated and exploited by his heirs. But the Italian melodrama, as it has endured until our day, can no longer be considered a fruitful musical form because of its subordination to the singers.

The *opera buffa*'s development in France and Italy owed its impetus to those writers who created the gay comedies of the eighteenth century. The best Italian *opera buffa* librettos are quite good comedies which might amuse us even today if the music did not drag them out so, and if the faults of a precocious improvisation, masquerading as genius, were not so obvious. But this, fundamentally, is the shortcoming of all music dramas from about 1750 to 1850. Giambattista Lorenzi's *Socrate immaginario* is one of the best Italian comedies. But Paisiello's music is the feeblest he has ever written. Girolamo Gigli, Carlo Goldoni, Casti, Ranieri Calzabigi wrote librettos for *opera buffa* which no musician immortalized. On the other hand, the *opera buffa* which has survived is based on libretti of slight literary value, for example, Pergolesi's *Serva padrona*, Cimarosa's *Matrimonio segreto*, even Rossini's *Barbiere di Siviglia*, which represents an eighteenth century that already had the Napoleonic era behind it.

Today the great foe of *opera buffa* is the musical pastiche called operetta. To study the modernization of the *opera buffa* is to study the modern spirit. When Carlo Goldoni and Carlo Gozzi enthused Venice, there were no "pochades." They had the refinement and depth of spirit of Molière, Marivaux, Regnard, Beaumarchais and others in France. The banal platitudes of the "pochades" would not have amused the audiences which laughed at the masterpieces of these authors. Consequently *opera buffa* maintained a level with comedy.

Up to the first half of the nineteenth century, musical art appeared only in the form of chamber music, symphonies, oratorios, and comic and serious melodramas. Popular music was a thing apart, distinct from authentic art. The songs and dances of village fêtes were fine in character and relied on folklore; from the dances of the aristocracy all vulgarity was banished. It is the second half of the nineteenth century which caused the mischief in music. The banal novelties of music and concert halls have spread like wildfire over the world. The most worthless cabaret song, if it is a hit, is distributed even by airplane. The composer is often a man who knows nothing about music and will never be able to learn anything about the art. It is strange to see how these slight, feeble works, whose words moved the whole world to tears a few years ago, now seem silly and antiquated, a ridiculous and grotesque effusion. Stravinsky has, it is true, invented a musical grotesque (see *Petrouchka*) which bases itself properly on a conflict of words (or the dramatic situations which take their place) and music, but cases like this are rare. Stravinsky, though always attempting something new, was unable to ignore the *Amfiparnasso*. The book of that madrigal drama is constructed in a synthetic and purely musical fashion which enables the author to create a symphonic atmosphere with the voices while the mimed comedy is developed separately on the stage. *Renard, Les Noces,* and *L'Histoire du soldat* are thus fundamentally related to the *Amfiparnasso*.

Before the resurrection of the *opera buffa* can take place, the grossness of the operetta and of the pochade will have to be renounced. Music is a delicate art; demoralized by vulgarity it falls into the deepest pit of degradation. It is really time to end this confusion; let us stop calling certain productions of sound by the name of music.

Vecchi's *Amfiparnasso* is a perfect masterpiece because its beauty is not limited to the historical presentation of a period but has the qualities of immortal art which enable it to survive its era. *Opera buffa* has been completely abandoned in Italy. Even Donizetti's *Don Pasquale* and Verdi's *Falstaff* have not achieved the popularity of the musical melodramas that are full of preposterous episodes. The possibilities of the *opera buffa* depend on a revival of the spirit. If the spirit merely sleeps, a revival will be possible but if it is dead, the *opera buffa* is dead too.   [6]

ZOLTÁN KODÁLY

1882–

Perhaps Kodály's scientific study of Hungarian folk song was helped, as to method, by the fact that he had originally planned on a scientific career, and indeed attended the University of Budapest while studying at the Conservatory.

Feeling that what generally passed for Hungarian folk music was a corruption of the authentic material by gypsy and foreign adaptations, he betook himself to its source, travelling through the countryside, collecting songs and dances, writing down some and recording others. Partly, in collaboration with his friend Bartók, he published his findings.

His original musical compositions reflect the Hungarian folk idiom. *Háry János*, his humorous opera based on the experiences of a kind of Hungarian Tyl Eulenspiegel, and *The Spinning Room* are both national in character, as are the orchestral works, *Dances of Marosszék* and the *Dances of Galánta*.

Especially prolific in choral writing, his children's choruses, the *Pictures of the Matra Region*, the *Te Deum* and the *Psalmus Hungaricus*—he was commissioned to compose the last in 1923 to celebrate the fiftieth anniversary of the union of Buda and Pest—have been performed with success all over the Western world.

To the Hungarian background of his music he has added his own extraordinary melodic gift, and a feeling for the picturesque and for modern harmony. Together with Bartók, he is Hungary's great gift to contemporary music.

NEW MUSIC FOR OLD

From an Article in *Modern Music*, 1925

There are many who dispute the importance of the folk song to the higher forms of music. These are usually people of a special intellectual type whose approach is purely rationalistic. To maintain that the average European folk song is too primitive to have a relation to

437

higher art, or to serve as the expression of a differentiated and complex spiritual life, is doubtless correct. Most of the German, French or Slavic folk songs are not above the level of pleasantness and grace. They are pretty and without depth.

There are Hungarian melodies, however, which have given me and many others the same profound aesthetic experience as a motif of Beethoven.

To the Hungarian composer, a knowledge of his native music offers greater inspiration than do the German, French or Italian songs to composers of these nationalities. In all countries of an older cultural tradition, the substance of folk music has long since been absorbed into the masterpieces. Great artists have always been huge reservoirs of racial power. Bach is a condensation of German music such as no other nation has. The German student who knows his Bach need not concern himself long with folk songs.

This is not our situation. Our only tradition is folk music. And though it cannot replace Bach, it may yet produce a great interpreter. Our folk music is not that of a crude unlettered class. It is, or has been until very recently, the music of the whole nation. Elsewhere in Europe, great music flourished at the courts, or under the protection of rich communities. In Hungary no foreign dynasty ever encouraged the idea of a national culture. The aristocracy cherished only foreign art. During the centuries of continuous fighting, the middle classes and the peasantry, left entirely to their own resources, had no opportunity to create a great art themselves. This was a period of flowering of folk art. Later, when the middle classes "elevated" themselves sufficiently to do homage to foreign ideas, when they were denationalized and mixed with foreign immigrants, the old music became the exclusive treasure of the peasantry.

Certain modern Hungarian works apparently have created the impression abroad of a musical revolution. They are more accurately to be described as conservative. Our intention has been not to break with the past, but to renew and strengthen the links by recreating the atmosphere of the ancient, forgotten melodies, by erecting new structures from their scattered stones. These old songs are our heirlooms; their creators, long since silent, are our true ancestors.

It is but natural that our new works should be markedly different from any other music. Those who find in the German classical style the single mold of real music—and there are many such—unconsciously accept the mother tongue of Germanic-Italian folk music, on which it is based, as the only orthodox foundation for music. It is necessary to decide at the outset for or against the right to existence of other musical idioms, before further considering modern Hungarian music. Much that is strange in it can be traced back to the peculiarities of the old songs.

I have often had occasion to observe that these strange sounds and inflections are, at first hearing, repellent to ears attuned only to Italian-German melodies. Repeated hearings render them natural. A foreign language must be studied. It is necessary to learn even a slight variant of one's own language. Ady, a modern Hungarian poet, reconstructed a remarkable speech of his own out of the old racial tongue. At first criticized as absurd, unclear, incomprehensible, even un-Hungarian, it later converted the sceptics into enthusiasts. From the foreigner our music exacts an effort both in interest and understanding. It is only after mastering its idiom that he can discover therein the portrait of the nation, and can respond to its expressive power and heroic emotional force.   [1]

BARTÓK THE FOLKLORIST

From an article in *La Revue Musicale*, 1952

> I want to devote my life at all times, at all costs and in every sphere to but one cause: the welfare of the Hungarian nation, the welfare of my Hungarian fatherland.
>
> —Bartók, 1903

Three periods may be distinguished in the evolution of Bartók's collections of folk songs. In the first his transcriptions are sketchy; even the transcription of those sections recorded on the phonograph is defective (*Ethnograpia*, 1908). Later, in revising them, he included details down to the slightest ornaments. He made a new revision of his entire collection from 1934 to 1940, while working three times a week on the preparation of the Academy's large collection of folk songs. On the one hand, his knowledge of Arab, Rumanian and other songs, and on the other, the use of earphones, revealed to him details heretofore undiscovered. His transcriptions represent the ultimate limits to be attained by the human ear without the aid of instruments. Beyond that, there is only sound photography.

He did not bother with measuring sound down to its infinitesimal degrees. The task of the future will be the re-examination of the results obtained through the ear alone. The question will have to be answered as to whether or not elements exist in live music which escape our perceptions in passing from the sounding body to our ears, and if they do, whether or not they remain in the subconscious. There is no doubt that the apparatus of the phonetic microscope will cast a new light on many unresolved problems. However, there is little likelihood that these researches will change the fundamental character of our auditory impressions.

The largest part of Bartók's work will endure. Every period in the history of science is generally characterized by the fact that it brings new inventions, modifications in relation to the results achieved by preceding periods. Thanks to his good sense Bartók succeeded in steering clear of all romantic theories. His principal aim was the most exact reproduction and interpretation of his material. Here, then, is no theory, but life, and a guarantee of permanence even if the theories based on this work collapse with time like a house of cards.

He also had ideas about certain relationships among the folk songs of diverse nations, but he developed them with many reservations, mindful that truth can be attained only from clear evidence. Whoever swerves from the path of reality is irrevocably lost in the emptiness of illusions.

The complete value of his folkloristic activity can not yet be appreciated. His single important book, which appeared under the title *A magyar népdal* [*Hungarian Folk Music*], was published in German and English. The notes gathered in Rumania, Slovakia and Yugoslavia are still unpublished. He took the notes which he collected in Rumania and Slovakia to America, because he could not find a publisher in chauvinistic Europe. Though he worked for years on his Yugoslav material for Columbia University, and though it was ready for publication in 1944, and, as he wrote in one of his letters, the employees at Columbia University Press had taken great pains in editing his manuscripts, it still remains unpublished today.[1]

When in the future we are acquainted with all of his work, we will know better how to appreciate the universal importance of him who, from his youth, believed only in serving his own country.   [2]

[1] This article was written in 1950. Bartók's book was published in 1951 (Bartók, Béla, and Lord, Albert B., *Serbo-Croatian Folk Songs;* with a foreword by George Herzog, New York, Columbia University Press, 1951).

IGOR STRAVINSKY

1882–

Twice atonality has occasioned audience riots: in Vienna, in 1913, when Schoenberg's atonal orchestral works received their initial performance, and again in Paris, in 1913, when the *Sacre du printemps*, probably Stravinsky's nearest approach to atonality, had its première. However, atonality has been only a way-station in Stravinsky's stylistically varied career. Beginning with a symphony of a marked Brahmsian flavor, he has passed through the Russian National School with its folkloristic manner to polytonality, jazz, liturgical music and neoclassicism.

Křenek, in *Music Here and Now*, maintains that Stravinsky never explains how he "journeyed from the *Sacre du Printemps* to the *Jeu de Cartes*." Stravinsky's urbane autobiography, *Chroniques de ma vie*, states very simply that he did not feel bound to remain in one groove all the time, that each change in style meant an advancement in his musical thinking. In this same volume Stravinsky made the fiercely attacked observation that music is incapable of expressing anything at all.

The *Poetics of Music*, selections from which are quoted here, consists of a series of six lectures delivered at Harvard University in 1939, in which the composer discusses the aesthetics and philosophy of music, and stylistic trends from early music through the miasma of Wagnerism to the clearing of the air in the twentieth century.

From: *Chroniques de ma vie*, 1935

COMPOSING AT THE PIANO

I should like to quote a remark of Rimski-Korsakov's that he made when I became his pupil. I asked him whether I was right in always composing at the piano. "Some compose at the piano," he replied, "and some without a piano. As for you, you will compose at the piano." As a matter of fact, I do compose at the piano and I do not regret it. I go further; I think it is a thousand times better to compose in direct

contact with the physical medium of sound than to work in the abstract
medium provided by one's imagination.   [1]

MUSIC AND EXPRESSION

I consider that music, by its very nature, is essentially powerless to
express anything at all, whether a feeling, an attitude of mind, a psychological mood, a phenomenon of nature, etc. . . . *Expression* has
never been an inherent property of music. That is by no means the
purpose of its existence. If, as is nearly always the case, music appears
to express something, this is only an illusion and not a reality. It is
simply an additional attribute which, by tacit and inveterate agreement,
we have lent it, thrust upon it, as a label, a convention—in short, an
aspect which, unconsciously or by force of habit, we have often come
to confuse with its essential being.

Music is the sole domain in which man realizes the present. By the
imperfection of his nature, man is doomed to submit to the passage
of time—to its categories of past and future—without ever being able
to give substance and, therefore, stability, to the category of the
present.

The phenomenon of music is given to us with the sole purpose
of establishing an order in things, including particularly the coördination between *man* and *time*. To be put into practice, its indispensable
and single requirement is construction. Construction once completed,
this order has been attained, and there is nothing more to be said. It
would be futile to look for, or expect anything else from it. It is precisely this construction, this achieved order, which produces in us a
unique emotion having nothing in common with our ordinary sensations and our responses to the impressions of daily life. One could not
better define the sensation produced by music than by saying that it is
identical with that evoked by contemplation of the interplay of architectural forms. Goethe thoroughly understood that when he called
architecture frozen music.   [2]

LISTENING AND LOOKING AT MUSIC

I have always had a horror of listening to music with my eyes shut,
with nothing for them to do. The sight of the gestures and movements
of the various parts of the body producing the music is fundamentally
necessary if it is to be grasped in all its fullness. All music created or
composed demands some exteriorization for the perception of the listener. In other words, it must have an intermediary, an executant. That

being an essential condition, without which music cannot wholly reach us, why wish to ignore it, or try to do so—why shut the eyes to this fact which is inherent in the very nature of musical art? Obviously one frequently prefers to turn away one's eyes, or even close them, when the superfluity of the player's gesticulations prevents the concentration of one's faculties of hearing. But if the player's movements are evoked solely by the exigencies of the music, and do not tend to make an impression on the listener by extramural devices, why not follow with the eye such movements as those of the drummer, the violinist or the trombonist, which facilitate one's auditory perceptions? As a matter of fact, those who maintain that they only enjoy music to the full with their eyes shut do not hear better than when they have them open, but the absence of visual distractions enables them to abandon themselves to the reveries induced by the lullaby of its sounds, and that is really what they prefer to the music itself.   [3]

MECHANICAL MUSIC

In the domain of music the importance and influence of its dissemination by mechanical means, such as the record and the radio—those redoubtable triumphs of modern science which will probably undergo still further development—make them worthy of the closest investigation. The facilities they offer to composers and executants alike for reaching great numbers of listeners, and the opportunities they give those listeners to acquaint themselves with works they have not heard, are obviously indisputable advantages. But one must not overlook the fact that such advantages are attended by serious danger. In Johann Sebastian Bach's day, he had to walk ten miles to a neighboring town to hear Buxtehude play his works. Today anyone, living no matter where, has only to turn a knob or put on a record to hear what he likes. Indeed, it is in just this incredible facility, this lack of necessity for any effort, that the evil of this so-called progress lies. For in music, more than in any other branch of art, understanding is given only to those who make an active effort. Passive receptivity is not enough. To listen to certain combinations of sound and automatically become accustomed to them, does not necessarily imply that they have been heard and understood. For one can listen without hearing, just as one can look without seeing. The absence of active effort and the liking acquired for this facility make for laziness. The radio has got rid of the necessity which existed in Bach's day for getting out of one's armchair. Nor are listeners any longer impelled to play themselves, or to spend time on learning an instrument in order to acquire a knowledge of musical literature. The wireless and the gramophone do all that. And thus the active faculties of listeners, without which one cannot assimilate music, gradually become atrophied from lack of use. This creeping paralysis entails very serious consequences. Oversaturated with sounds, *blasé* even before combinations of the utmost variety, listeners fall into a kind of torpor which deprives them of all power of discrimination and makes them indifferent to the quality of the pieces presented. It is more than likely that such irrational overfeeding will make them lose all appetite and relish for music. There will, of course, always be exceptions, individuals who will know how to select from the mass those things that appeal to them. But for the majority of listeners there is every reason to fear that, far from developing a love and understanding of music, the modern methods of dissemination will have a diametrically opposite effect—that is to say, the production of indifference, inability to understand, to appreciate, or to experience any worth-while reaction.

In addition, there is the musical deception that arises when a reproduction, whether on record or film or by wireless transmission from a distance, is substituted for actual playing. It is the same difference as between the *ersatz* and the authentic. The danger lies in the very fact that there is always a far greater consumption of the *ersatz*, which, it must be remembered, is far from being identical with its model. The continuous habit of listening to changed and sometimes distorted timbres spoils the ear, so that it gradually loses all capacity for enjoying natural musical sounds.

All these considerations may seem unexpected from one who has worked so much, and is still working, in this field. I think that I have sufficiently stressed the instructional value I unreservedly ascribe to this means of musical reproduction; but that does not prevent me from seeing its negative sides, and I anxiously ask myself whether they are sufficiently outweighed by the positive advantages to enable one to face them with impunity.   [4]

BEETHOVEN

In our early youth we were surfeited by his works, his famous *Weltschmerz* being forced upon us at the same time, together with the "tragedy" and all the commonplaces voiced for more than a century about this composer who must be recognized as one of the world's greatest musical geniuses.

Like many other musicians, I was disgusted by this intellectual and sentimental attitude, which has little to do with serious musical appreciation. This deplorable pedagogy did not fail in its result. It alienated me from Beethoven for many years.

Cured and matured by age, I could now approach him objectively so that he wore a different aspect for me. Above all I recognized in him the indisputable monarch of the instrument. It is the instrument that inspires his thought and determines its substance. The relations of a composer to his sound medium may be of two kinds. Some, for example, compose music *for* the piano; others compose *piano music*. Beethoven is clearly in the second category. In all his immense pianistic work, it is the "instrumental" side which is characteristic of him and makes him infinitely precious to me. It is the giant instrumentalist that predominates in him, and it is thanks to that quality that he cannot fail to reach any ear that is open to music.

But is it in truth Beethoven's music which has inspired the innumerable works devoted to this prodigious musician by thinkers, moralists, and even sociologists who have suddenly become musicographers? In this connection, I should like to quote the following passage taken from an article in the great Soviet daily, *Izvestia:*

"Beethoven is the friend and contemporary of the French Revolution, and he remained faithful to it even when, during the Jacobin dictatorship, humanitarians with weak nerves of the Schiller type turned from it, preferring to destroy tyrants on the theatrical stage with the help of cardboard swords. Beethoven, that plebeian genius, who proudly turned his back on emperors, princes and magnates—that is the Beethoven we love for his unassailable optimism, his virile sadness, for the inspired pathos of his struggle, and for his iron will which enabled him to seize destiny by the throat."

This chef-d'oeuvre of penetration comes from the pen of one of the most famous music critics in the U.S.S.R. I should like to know in what this mentality differs from the platitudes and commonplaces uttered by the publicity-mongers of liberalism in all the bourgeois democracies long before the social revolution in Russia.

I do not mean to say that everything that has been written on Beethoven in this sense is of the same quality. But, in the majority of these works, do the panegyrists not base their adulation far more on the sources of his inspiration than on the music itself? Could they have filled their fat volumes, if they had not been able to embroider to their hearts' content all the extra-musical elements available in the Beethoven life and legend, drawing their conclusions and judgments on the artist from them?

What does it matter whether the *Third Symphony* was inspired by the figure of Bonaparte the Republican or Napoleon the Emperor?

It is only the music that matters. But to talk music is risky, and entails responsibility. Therefore some find it preferable to seize on side issues. It is easy, and enables you to pass as a deep thinker. . . .

It is in the quality of his musical method and not in the nature of his ideas that his true greatness lies.

It is time that this was recognized, and Beethoven was rescued from the unjustifiable monopoly of the "intellectuals" and left to those who seek nothing in music but music. It is, however, also time—and this is perhaps even more urgent—to protect him from the stupid drivel of fools who think it up-to-date to giggle as they amuse themselves by running him down. Let them beware; dates pass quickly.

Just as in his pianistic work Beethoven lives on the piano, so in his symphonies, overtures and chamber music, he draws his sustenance from his instrumental ensemble. With him the instrumentation is never apparel, and that is why it never strikes one. The profound wisdom with which he distributes parts to separate instruments or to whole groups, the carefulness of his instrumental writing, and the precision with which he indicates his wishes—all these testify to the fact that we are in the presence of a tremendous constructive force.

I do not think I am mistaken in asserting that it was precisely his manner of moulding his musical material that led logically to the erection of those monumental structures which are his supreme glory.

There are those who contend that Beethoven's instrumentation was bad and his tone color poor. Others altogether ignore that side of his art, holding that instrumentation is a secondary matter and that only "ideas" are worthy of consideration.

The former demonstrate their lack of taste, their complete incompetence in this respect, and their narrow and mischievous mentality. In contrast with the florid orchestration of a Wagner, with its lavish coloring, Beethoven's instrumentation will appear to lack luster. It might produce a similar impression if compared with the vivacious radiance of Mozart. But Beethoven's music is intimately linked with his instrumental language, and finds its most exact and perfect expression in the sobriety of that language. To regard it as poverty-stricken would merely show lack of perception. True sobriety is a great rarity, and most difficult of attainment.

As for those who attach no importance to Beethoven's instrumentation, but ascribe the whole of his greatness to his "ideas"—they obviously regard all instrumentation as a mere matter of apparel, coloring, flavoring, and so fall, though following a different path, into the same heresy as the others.

Both make the same fundamental error of regarding instrumentation as something extrinsic from the music for which it exists.

This dangerous point of view concerning instrumentation, coupled with today's unhealthy greed for orchestral opulence, has corrupted the judgment of the public, and, being impressed by the immediate effect of tone color, people can no longer solve the problem of whether it is intrinsic in the music or simply "padding." Orchestration has become a source of enjoyment independent of the music, and the time has surely come to set things to rights. We have had enough of this orchestral dappling and these thick sonorities; we are tired of being saturated with timbres, and want no more of all this overfeeding, which deforms the entity of the instrumental element by swelling it out of all proportion and giving it an existence of its own. There is a great deal of re-education to be accomplished in this field.   [5]

From: *Poétique musicale*, 1939

DISSONANCE AND ATONALITY

Consonance, says the dictionary, is the combination of several tones into an harmonic unit. Dissonance results from the deranging of this harmony by the addition of tones foreign to it. One must admit that all this is not clear. Ever since it appeared in our vocabulary, the word dissonance has carried with it a certain odor of sinfulness.

Let us light our lantern: in textbook language, dissonance is an element of transition, a complex or interval of tones which is not complete in itself and which must be resolved to the ear's satisfaction into a perfect consonance.

But just as the eye completes the lines of a drawing which the painter has knowingly left incomplete, just so the ear may be called upon to complete a chord and coöperate in its resolution, which has not actually been realized in the work. Dissonance, in this instance, plays the part of an allusion.

Either case applies to a style where the use of dissonance demands a resolution. But nothing forces us to be looking constantly for satisfaction that resides only in repose. For more than a century, music has provided repeated examples of a style in which dissonance has emancipated itself. It is no longer tied down to its former function. Having become an entity in itself, dissonance often neither prepares nor anticipates anything. Dissonance is thus no more an agent of disorder than consonance is a guarantee of stability. The music of yesterday and of today unhesitatingly unites parallel dissonant chords that thereby lose their functional value, and our ear quite naturally accepts their juxtaposition.

Of course, the instruction and education of the public have not kept pace with the evolution of technique. The use of dissonance, for ears ill-prepared to accept it, has not failed to confuse and enfeeble the listener's response until the dissonant is no longer distinguished from the consonant.

We thus no longer find ourselves in the framework of classic tonality, in the scholastic sense of the word. It is not we who have created this state of affairs, and it is not our fault, if we find ourselves confronted with a new logic of music that would have appeared unthinkable to the masters of the past. And this new logic has opened our eyes to riches whose existence we never suspected.

Having reached this point, we must obey, not new idols, but the external necessity of affirming the axis of our music, and we must recognize the existence of certain poles of attraction. Diatonic tonality is only one means of orienting music towards these poles. The function of tonality is completely subordinated to the force of attraction of the pole of sonority. All music is nothing more than a succession of impulses that converge towards a definite point or repose. That is as true of Gregorian chant as it is of a Bach fugue, as true of Brahms's music as it is of Debussy's.

This general law of attraction is satisfied in only a limited way by the traditional diatonic system, for that system possesses no absolute value.

There are few present-day musicians who are not aware of this state of affairs. But the fact remains that it is still impossible to lay down the rules that govern this new technique. Nor is this at all surprising. Harmony, as it is taught today in the schools, dictates rules that were not fixed until long after the publication of the works upon which they were based, rules which were unknown to the composers of these works. So it is that our harmonic treatises take as their point of departure Mozart and Haydn, neither of whom ever heard of harmonic treatises.

Our chief concern is not so much what is known as tonality, as what one might term the polar attraction of sound, of an interval, or even of a complex of tones. The sounding tone constitutes, in a way, the essential axis of music. Musical form would be unimaginable without elements of attraction which make up every musical organism and which are bound up with its psychology. The articulations of musical discourse betray a hidden correlation between the tempo and the interplay of tones. All music being nothing but a succession of impulses and repose, it is easy to see that the drawing together and separation of poles of attraction in a way determine the respiration of music.

In view of the fact that our poles of attraction are no longer within the closed system which was the diatonic system, we can bring the poles together without being compelled to conform to the exigencies of tonality. For we no longer believe in the absolute value of the major-minor system, based on the entity which musicologists call the c-scale.

The tuning of an instrument, of a piano, for example, requires that the entire musical range available to the instrument should be ordered according to chromatic steps. Such tuning prompts us to observe that all these sounds converge towards a center which is the *a* above middle *c*. Composing, for me, is putting into an order a certain number of these sounds according to certain interval relationships. This activity leads to a search for the center upon which the series of sounds involved in my undertaking should converge. Thus, if a center is given, I shall have to find a combination that converges upon it. If, on the other hand, an as yet unoriented combination has been found, I shall have to determine the center towards which it should lead. The discovery of this center suggests to me the solution of my problem. It is thus that I satisfy my very marked taste for such a kind of musical topography.

The superannuated system of classic tonality, which has served as the basis for musical constructions of compelling interest, has had the authority of law among musicians for only a short period of time—a period much shorter than is usually imagined, extending only from the middle of the seventeenth century to the middle of the nineteenth. From the moment when chords no longer serve to fulfill merely the functions assigned to them by the interplay of tones but, instead, throw off all constraint to become new entities free of all ties—from that moment, one may say that the process is completed: the diatonic system has lived out its life cycle. The work of the Renaissance polyphonists had not yet entered into this system, and we have seen that the music of our times abides by it no longer. A parallel progression of ninth-chords would suffice as proof. It was here that the gates opened upon what has been labelled with the abusive term: *atonality*.

The expression is fashionable. But that doesn't mean that it is very clear. And I should like to know just what those persons who use the term mean by it. The negating prefix *a* indicates a state of indifference in regard to the term, negating without entirely renouncing it. Understood in this way, the word *atonality* hardly corresponds to what those who use it have in mind. If it were said that my music is atonal, that would be tantamount to saying that I had become deaf to tonality. Now it well may be that I remain for a considerable time within the bounds of the strict order of tonality, even though I may quite consciously break up this order for the purposes of establishing a new one. In that case I am not *a*-tonal, but *anti*-tonal. I am not trying to argue pointlessly over words but essentially to discover what we deny and what we affirm. [6]

CACOPHONY

Our vanguard elite, sworn perpetually to outdo itself, expects and requires that music should satisfy the taste for absurd cacophony.

I say *cacophony* without fear of being classed with the conventional *pompiers*, the *laudatores temporis acti*. And in using the word, I am certain I am not in the least reversing myself. My position in this regard is exactly the same as it was at the time when I composed the *Rite*, and when people saw fit to call me a revolutionary. Today, just as in the past, I am on my guard against counterfeit money and take care not to accept it for the true coin of the realm. Cacophony means bad sound, counterfeit merchandise, uncoördinated music that will not stand up under serious criticism. Whatever opinion one may hold about the music of Arnold Schoenberg (to take as example a composer evolving along lines essentially different from mine, both aesthetically and technically), whose works have frequently given rise to violent reactions or ironic smiles—it is impossible for a self-respecting mind equipped with genuine musical culture not to feel that the composer of *Pierrot Lunaire* is fully aware of what he is doing and that he is not trying to deceive anyone. He adopted the musical system that suited his needs and, within this system, he is perfectly consistent with himself, perfectly coherent. One cannot dismiss music that one dislikes by labelling it cacophony.

Equally degrading is the vanity of snobs who boast of an embarrassing familiarity with the world of the incomprehensible, and who delightedly confess that they find themselves in good company. It is not music they seek, but rather the effect of shock, the sensation that befuddles understanding.

So I confess that I am completely insensitive to the prestige of revolution. All the noise it may make will not call forth the slightest echo in me. For revolution is one thing, innovation another. And even innovation, when not presented in an excessive form, is not always recognized by its contemporaries. [7]

STYLE

Style is the particular way a composer organizes his conceptions and speaks the language of his craft. This musical language is the element common to the composers of a particular school or epoch. Certainly the musical physiognomies of Mozart and Haydn are well known to you, and certainly you have not failed to notice that these composers are obviously related to each other, although it is easy for those familiar with the language of the period to distinguish them.

The attire that fashion prescribes for men of the same generation imposes upon its wearers a particular kind of gesture, a common carriage and bearing, that are conditioned by the cut of the clothes. In a like manner, the musical apparel worn by an epoch leaves its stamp upon the language, and, so to speak, upon the gestures of its music, as well as upon the composer's attitude towards tonal materials. These elements are the immediate factors of the mass of particulars that help us to determine how musical language and style are formed.

There is no need to tell you that what is called the style of an epoch results from a combination of individual styles, a combination which is dominated by the methods of the composers who have exerted a preponderant influence on their time.

We can notice, going back to the examples of Mozart and Haydn, that they benefited from the same culture, drew on the same sources, and borrowed each other's discoveries. Each of them, however, works a miracle all his own.

One may say that the masters, who in all their greatness surpass the generality of their contemporaries, send out the rays of their genius well beyond their own day. In this way they appear as powerful signal fires—as beacons, to use Baudelaire's expression—by whose light and warmth is developed a sum of tendencies that will be shared by most of their successors and that contributes to form the parcel of traditions which make up a culture.   [8]

TRADITION

It is culture that brings out the full value of taste and gives it a chance to prove its worth simply by its application. The artist imposes a culture upon himself and ends by imposing it upon others. That is how tradition becomes established.

Tradition is entirely different from habit, even from an excellent habit, since habit is by definition an unconscious acquisition and tends to become mechanical, whereas tradition results from a conscious and deliberate acceptance. A real tradition is not the relic of a past that is irretrievably gone; it is a living force that animates and informs the present. In this sense the paradox which banteringly maintains that everything which is not tradition is plagiarism, is true. . . .

Far from implying the repetition of what has been, tradition presupposes the reality of what endures. It appears as an heirloom, a heritage that one receives on condition of making it bear fruit before passing it on to one's descendants.

Brahms was born sixty years after Beethoven. From the one to the other, and from every aspect, the distance between them is great; they do not dress the same way, but Brahms follows the tradition of Beethoven without borrowing one of his habiliments. For the borrowing of a method has nothing to do with observing a tradition. "A method is replaced; a tradition is carried forward in order to produce something new." Tradition thus assures the continuity of creation. The example that I have just cited does not constitute an exception but is one proof out of a hundred of a constant law. This sense of tradition which is a natural need must not be confused with the desire which the composer feels to affirm the kinship he finds across the centuries with some master of the past.

My opera *Mavra* was born of a natural sympathy for the body of melodic tendencies, for the vocal style and conventional language which I came to admire more and more in the old Russo-Italian opera. This sympathy guided me quite naturally along the path of a tradition that seemed to be lost at the moment when the attention of musical circles was turned entirely towards the music drama, which represented no tradition at all from the historical point of view and which fulfilled no necessity at all from the musical point of view. The vogue of the music drama had a pathological origin. Alas, even the admirable music of *Pelléas et Mélisande*, so fresh in its modesty, was unable to get us into the open, in spite of so many characteristics thanks to which it shook off the tyranny of the Wagnerian system.

The music of *Mavra* stays within the tradition of Glinka and Dargomijsky. I had not the slightest intention of reëstablishing this tradition. I simply wanted in my turn to try my hand at the living form of the *opéra bouffe* which was so well suited to the Pushkin tale which gave me my subject. *Mavra* is dedicated to the memory of composers, not one of whom, I am sure, would have recognized as valid such a manifestation of the tradition they created, because of the novelty of the language my music speaks a hundred years after its models flourished. But I wanted to renew the style of these dialogues-in-music whose voices had been reviled and drowned out by the clang and clatter of the music drama. So a hundred years had to pass before the freshness of the Russo-Italian tradition could again be appreciated, a tradition that continued to live apart from the main stream of the present, and in which circulated a salubrious air, well adapted to delivering us from the miasmic vapors of the music drama, the inflated arrogance of which could not conceal its vacuity. [9]

MODERNISM AND ACADEMICISM

What is modern is what is representative of its own time and what must be in keeping with and within the grasp of its own time. Sometimes artists are reproached for being too modern or not modern enough. One might just as well reproach the times with not being sufficiently modern or with being too modern. A recent popular poll showed that, to all appearances, Beethoven is the composer most in demand in the United States. On that basis one can say that Beethoven is very modern and that a composer of such manifest importance as Paul Hindemith is not modern at all, since the list of winners does not even mention his name.

In itself, the term modernism implies neither praise nor blame and involves no obligation whatsoever. This is precisely its weakness. The word eludes us, hiding under any application of it one wishes to make. True, it is said that one must live in one's own time. The advice is superfluous; how could one do otherwise? Even if I wanted to relive the past, the most energetic strivings of my misguided will would be futile.

It follows that everyone has taken advantage of the pliability of this vacuous term by trying to give it form and color. But, again, what do we understand by the term modernism? In the past the term was never used, was even unknown. Yet our predecessors were no more stupid than we are. Was the term a real discovery? We have shown that it was nothing of the sort. Might it not rather be a sign of a decadence in morality and taste? Here I strongly believe we must answer in the affirmative.

My fondest hope, to conclude, is that you may be as embarrassed by the expression as I myself am. It would be so much simpler to give up lying and admit once and for all that we call anything modern that caters to our snobbishness, in the true sense of the word. But is catering to snobbishness really worth the trouble?

The term modernism is all the more offensive in that it is usually coupled with another whose meaning is perfectly clear: I speak of academicism.

A work is called academic when it is composed strictly according to the precepts of the conservatory. It follows that academicism considered as a scholastic exercise based on imitation is in itself something very useful and even indispensable to beginners who train themselves by studying models. It likewise follows that academicism should find no place outside of the conservatory, and that those who make an ideal of academicism when they have already completed their studies, produce stiffly correct works that are bloodless and dry.

Contemporary writers on music have acquired the habit of measuring everything in terms of modernism, that is to say in terms of a nonexistent scale, and promptly consign to the category of "academic" —which they regard as the opposite of modern—all that is not in keeping with the extravagances which in their eyes constitute the thrice-distilled quintessence of modernism. To these critics, whatever appears discordant and confused is automatically relegated to the pigeonhole of modernism. Whatever they cannot help finding clear and well-ordered, and devoid of ambiguity which might give them an opening, is promptly relegated in its turn to the pigeonhole of academicism. Now we can make use of academic forms without running the risk of becoming academic ourselves. The person who is loath to borrow these forms when he has need of them clearly betrays his weakness. How many times have I noticed this strange incomprehension on the part of those who believe themselves good judges of music and its future! What makes this all the more difficult to understand is the fact that these same critics admit as natural and legitimate the borrowing of old popular or religious melodies harmonized in ways incompatible with their essence. They are not at all shocked by the ridiculous device of the leitmotiv and let themselves be inveigled into musical tours conducted by the Cook Agency of Bayreuth. They believe themselves up to the minute when they applaud the very introductory measures of a symphony employing exotic scales, obsolete instruments, and methods which were created for entirely different purposes. Terrified at the thought of showing themselves for what they are, they go after poor academicism tooth and nail, for they feel the same horror of forms consecrated by long use that their favorite composers feel, who are afraid to touch them.   [10]

ANTON VON WEBERN

1883–1945

As Schoenberg explains in his discussion of twelve tone technique, the initial efforts in this medium were perforce short. Schoenberg, Berg and Krenek subsequently developed the technique to the point where it could carry long works. The compositions of Webern, who, with Berg, was one of the best known of Schoenberg's students and disciples, are practically all brief, some of them not exceeding a scant few measures.

According to Humphrey Searle, who studied with him in Vienna during the season 1937–38, he invariably used the piano when composing, and his sketch books are full of variants which would all be equally possible according to twelve tone technique. Webern was a profound theorist, yet his works are more than the solutions of mathematical problems.

Webern was for a time conductor of the Vienna Workers' Symphony Orchestra; after 1918 he lived in the country devoting his time to composition and teaching.

SCHOENBERG AS TEACHER

From the Symposium *Arnold Schönberg*, 1912

> The belief in technique as the only means of salvation must be suppressed, the striving toward truth furthered.
> —Arnold Schoenberg, in "Problems of Art Instruction"

In his essay, "Problems of Art Instruction," Arnold Schoenberg himself has presented the most brilliant refutation of all the malicious, envious persecution and slander which backward minds have contrived against him as a teacher.

Never were more penetrating, truer words spoken on the subject. And what Schoenberg expresses therein, every one of his students could and can experience for himself. It is believed that Schoenberg teaches his style and forces his students to adapt themselves to it. This is absolutely untrue.

Schoenberg teaches no style whatsoever; he preaches neither the use of old nor new artistic means. In the same essay, he says: "What sense is there in teaching the mastery of the commonplace? The student learns to use something he may not employ if he wishes to be an artist. But the most important thing one cannot give him: the courage and the strength to put himself in a position, from which everything he views becomes, through the manner in which he views it, unique."

However, this "most important thing" is what the Schoenberg student learns. Schoenberg demands above all that, in his exercises, the student write not merely any notes whatsoever in order to fill an academic form, but that he complete these exercises out of the necessity for expression.

Hence, he must actually create, even in the most primitive beginnings of musical movement construction. What Schoenberg explains to the student is altogether bound up, then, with the work in hand; he brings in no external dogmas.

Thus Schoenberg educates actually through creating.

He follows the traces of the student's personality with the utmost energy, tries to deepen them, to help them break through, in short, to give the student "the courage and the strength to put himself in a position, from which everything he views becomes, through the manner in which he views it, unique."

This is a training toward the most complete honesty with oneself. It affects not only the purely musical aspect, but every other realm of human life as well.

Yes, with Schoenberg one truly learns more than art rules. Whosoever's heart is open is here shown the road to the Good.

However, how can one explain that every one of his students who works independently today composes in a manner which brings the style of his compositions into immediate proximity with the work of Schoenberg? This is the chief reason for the misunderstanding of Schoenberg's teaching mentioned at the start. One cannot explain this. The secret of artistic creation is especially involved in this question.

Who can explain it?

It cannot at all be a question of a mere external appropriation of these artistic means.

What then is it?

Here reigns a necessity, the reasons for which we do not know, but in which we must believe.   [1]

KNOWLEDGE

Remark to Humphrey Searle, 1939

Don't write music entirely by ear. Your ears will always guide you aright, of course, but you must *know* why one progression is good and another bad. [2]

VARIATIONS FOR ORCHESTRA, OP. 30

From: Letter to Willi Reich, May 3, 1941

The first reaction to this score may well be: "There is nothing in it." One looks in vain for the many, many notes one is used to. But this touches upon the most essential point: the basic thing is that here (in my score) a different style is employed. . . . And I believe it is a new style. Its material is ruled by physical laws exactly as were the earlier forms of tonality. It too forms a tonality, but this tonality uses the possibilities offered by the nature of tone in a different manner: it is based on a system in which the twelve separate tones as we know them from Western music are "related to each other," as Schoenberg expressed it. Nevertheless, this new system does not overlook the laws that are inherent in the nature of tone. This would indeed be impossible if what is expressed in tones is still to make sense. And no one will seriously maintain that we would not want to make sense. [3]

ALBAN BERG

1885–1935

Though Berg forged new paths in his own music, he always felt indebted to his master, Schoenberg, and so expressed himself in his writings. Schoenberg, in turn, wrote in high praise of his most famous pupil. The eulogy quoted here is Berg's summation of Schoenberg's attributes and is found in an essay minutely analyzing the first ten measures of his master's *D minor String Quartet*.

The first performance of Berg's complex opera *Wozzeck* gave rise to a tide of literature analyzing, condemning and praising it. He at once became one of the most discussed of contemporary composers. Universal Edition, which published the score, has collected a number of these polemics in a brochure entitled *Alban Berg's Wozzeck und die Musikkritik*. His techniques, twelve tone and otherwise, his musical forms and dramatic procedures were microscopically dissected. As is usual in such cases, the critics read into the work much of which Berg never dreamed. One of his own comments on the opera, quoted below, is helpfully direct and simple.

WHY IS SCHOENBERG'S MUSIC SO HARD TO UNDERSTAND?

From: Essay of the same title, 1924

It is not so much so-called, "atonality," which has by now become the mode of expression of so many contemporaries, that makes Schoenberg's music so difficult to understand; it is rather Schoenberg's musical structure, the abundance of the artistic means everywhere employed in this harmonic style, the application of all compositional possibilities presented by music throughout the centuries—in a word: its immeasurable richness.

Here, too, we find the same diversity in harmony, the same variety of chord progression characterizing the cadence;

here again the melodic line suitable to such harmony, melody which makes the most daring use of the potentialities of the twelve tones;

here, too, the asymmetrical and quite free construction of themes with their never flagging development of the motive;

here again the art of variation, which in this music is developed
thematically as well as harmonically, contrapuntally as well as rhythmically;

here again polyphony permeating the entire work, and unequalled
contrapuntal part writing;

finally, here again the diversity of form and differentiation of
rhythms of which one can only say that, besides being subject to
their own laws, they are also subject to the rules of variation, thematic
development, counterpoint and polyphony. Thereby an art of construction is attained in this field also, which shows how erroneous
it is to speak of an "undefined rhythm," especially in Schoenberg's
work.

How fundamentally different—viewed from a universal standpoint—
the picture of other contemporary composers appears, even when
they have broken with the sovereignty of the triad in their harmonic
speech. Naturally, the musical means just enumerated are demonstrable
in their music also. Never, however, do we find them united in the
works of a single personality, as in Schoenberg, but always divided
among various groups, schools, movements, nations and their representatives of a given moment.

One favors the polyphonic method of writing, while reducing
thematic development and the art of variation to a minimum; another
prefers daring harmony which shrinks from no clash, but in which
only a melody line going scarcely beyond homophony has a place—
a melody line which is also characterized for the most part by the
use of merely two- and four-measure phrases. The "atonality" of one
consists in his setting wrong basses to primitively harmonized periods;
still others employ two or more (major or minor) keys simultaneously,
though the musical procedure within each key often shows a frightening poverty of invention. Some music distinguished by a more richly
moving melodic line and unconfined thematic construction suffers
from harmonic inertia which manifests itself in a dearth of harmonic
variety, endlessly held chords, endless organ points and ever recurring
harmonic patterns. I am inclined to say that music so built cannot do
without more or less mechanical repetitions, often even primitive se-
quences. This stands out in rhythmical aspects particularly. Here we
find a rhythm, sometimes rigid, sometimes hammered, sometimes dance-
like or otherwise lilting, which continues almost to the point of
monotony, and, among the otherwise reigning poverty, creates an
illusion of richness mainly through plentiful changes and dislocations
of meter. Such a rhythm, more often than one might believe, furnishes
the only element of cohesion in an otherwise inconsequential music.

The representatives of this technique of composition are preferably known as "stark rhythmists."

This adherence to such more or less firmly laid down principles, this one-sidedness which frequently degenerates into mannerism, this complacency, this being modern, but not too "ultra" (as it is so neatly termed), helps even "atonal" as well as otherwise "progressively oriented" music toward being accepted and relatively liked. For the most part, even when in one or more respects it poses some difficult problems for the listener, it deviates so little from tradition in every other regard, it often is so consciously "primitive" that, thanks precisely to those negative characteristics it can also speak to the ears of the musically uninitiated: in short, it pleases. This, all the more, since the authors of such music, in order to be stylistically pure, must keep in mind only the consequences of their special type of modernity, and therefore are not forced to come to terms with all these possibilities combined.

When I say that such an inescapable necessity, which, I repeat, consists in drawing the ultimate consequences from a self-imposed universality is to be found but once, and that in the compositions of Schoenberg, I believe that this conveys the final and most potent reason for the difficulty of their comprehension. The fact that this lofty necessity is combined with a mastery granted, I might say, to genius alone, also gives one the right, as does everything else I have said about Schoenberg's unequalled knowledge, to assume, nay, to be certain, that here we have the work of a master who—once the "classicists" of our era belong to history—will be one of the very few who will be termed classicists for all time. For he has not only, as Adolf Weissmann in his book *Die Musik in der Weltkrise* (Music in the World Crisis) so aptly says, "drawn from German musical culture the final, most daring conclusions"; he has also advanced further than those who, without foundation, searched for new ways and, consciously or unconsciously, more or less denied the art of this musical culture. So that today, on Schoenberg's fiftieth birthday, one can say, without being a prophet, that through the work he has brought to the world up to now, not only the predominance of his own personal art seems assured, but what is more, that of German art for the next fifty years. [1]

A WORD ABOUT *WOZZECK*

From: "Das Opernproblem," 1928

I never entertained the idea of reforming the artistic structure of the opera with *Wozzeck*. Neither when I started nor when I completed this work did I consider it a model for further operatic efforts, whoever the composer might be. I never assumed or expected that *Wozzeck* should in this sense become the basis of a school.

I wanted to compose good music, to develop musically the contents of Büchner's immortal drama, to translate his poetic language into music; but other than that, when I decided to write an opera, my only intentions, including the technique of composition, were to give the theater what belongs to the theater. In other words, the music was to be so formed as consciously to fulfill its duty of serving the action at every moment. Even more, the music should be prepared to furnish whatever the action needed to be transformed into reality on the stage. It was the function of the composer to solve the problems of an ideal stage director. And at the same time, this aim must not prejudice the development of the music as an absolute, purely musical entity. There was to be no interference by externals with its individual existence.

That these purposes should be accomplished by use of musical forms more or less ancient (considered by critics as one of the most important of my ostensible reforms of the opera) was a natural consequence. For the libretto it was necessary to make a selection from twenty-six loosely constructed, sometimes fragmentary scenes by Büchner. Repetitions that did not lend themselves to musical variations had to be avoided. Finally, the scenes had to be brought together, arranged and grouped in acts. The problem therefore became, utterly apart from my will, more musical than literary, one to be solved by the laws of musical structure rather than by the rules of dramaturgy.

It was impossible to take the fifteen scenes I selected and shape them in different manners so that each would retain its musical coherence and individuality, and at the same time follow the customary method of developing the music along the lines of their literary content. An absolute music, no matter how rich structurally, no matter how aptly it might fit the dramatic events, would, after a number of scenes so composed, inevitably create musical monotony. The effect would become positively boring with a series of a dozen or so formally composed entr'actes, which offered nothing but this type of illustrative music. Boredom, of course, is the last thing one should experience in the theater.

I obeyed the necessity of giving each scene and each accompanying piece of entr'acte music, whether prelude, postlude, connecting link or interlude, an unmistakable aspect, a rounded and finished character. It was therefore imperative to use every warranted means to create individualizing characteristics on the one hand, and coherence on the other; thus the much discussed utilization of old and new musical forms, including those used only in absolute music.

In one sense, the use of these forms in opera, especially to such an extent, was unusual, even new. But certainly, as conscious intention, it is not at all to my credit, as I have already demonstrated, and consequently I can and must reject the claim that I am a reformer of the opera through such innovation. However, I do not wish to depreciate my work through these explanations. Others who do not know it so well can do it much better. I therefore would like to suggest something which I consider my particular accomplishment.

No matter how cognizant any particular individual may be of the musical forms contained in the framework of this opera, of the precision and logic with which everything is worked out and the skill manifested in every detail, from the moment the curtain parts until it closes for the last time, there must be no one in the audience who pays any attention to the various fugues, inventions, suites, sonata movements, variations and passacaglias—no one who heeds anything but the idea of this opera which by far transcends the personal destiny of Wozzeck. This I believe to be my achievement.   [2]

HANDEL AND BACH

From: *Eine Wiener Musikzeitschrift*, March, 1935

It is lucky that Handel and Bach were born in 1685 and not two hundred years later. Else the citizenship of the one might have been questioned, just as the music of the other might have been found "bolshevistic." Prepared to prove which is the undersigned,

Alban Berg   [3]

SERGEI PROKOFIEV

1891–1953

Prokofiev's musical career not only spanned pre- and post-revolutionary Russia, but was influenced by years of living and extensive travel in Western Europe and the United States. He was one of the most sophisticated of Russian composers, what with his variety of styles, his humor, and his keen sense of the grotesque or "scherzoness" as he calls it in his autobiography. This capacity for laughter and mockery extends itself through some of his best known works, such as *The Love for Three Oranges*, the first of his operas to be staged, the première of which he conducted in Chicago in 1921.

Though the dissonant predominates in his early *Scythian Suite* and the ballets, *Chout* and *Le Pas d'acier*, written for Diaghilev, he approached the atonal and polytonal only in his cantata, *Seven, They Are Seven*.

In contrast to the brash harmonies and aggressive rhythms of the above pieces stands the lyricism of his violin concertos and the *Classical Symphony*, composed in Haydnesque-Mozartean style. Yet even here the hallmark of his overall manner, i.e., the abrupt, unexpected modulation, emerges slyly.

In 1934 Prokofiev settled in Moscow, but still continued his tours in Western Europe and the United States as pianist and conductor. With a number of his contemporaries he was criticized sharply in 1948 by the Soviet press for his "formalism," a fault not too clear to Western musicians. His opera, *A Tale of a Real Man* (1948), was considered by his critics as unmelodic, thematically deficient. What he wrote thereafter we scarcely know, but he has left enough important works to place him as one of the most gifted composers of the twentieth century.

From: *Autobiography*, 1948

ENCOUNTERS WITH RACHMANINOFF AND MEDTNER

In 1915 I met Rachmaninoff. He was very pleasant, took my hand in his huge paw, and talked to me in a most friendly fashion. In the autumn he gave a concert dedicated to the memory of Scriabin, in which, among other pieces, he played the "Fifth Sonata." When Scriabin played this sonata his music soared into ethereal realms, but with Rachmaninoff every tone, precise and solid, remained entirely earthbound. Great excitement among Scriabin's friends in the audience! The tenor Altschevski, whom we had to hold back by his coattails, cried: "Just wait, I must have this out with him!" I felt that I had to remain objective, and replied that though we were accustomed to the composer's interpretation of the sonata, it was obvious that another presentation was also permissible.

When I entered the green room, I remarked quite ingenuously to Rachmaninoff: "And nevertheless, Sergei Vassilievitsch, you played very well." Rachmaninoff answered with a forced smile: "And did you think that I would play badly?" immediately turning his back on me to greet somebody else. And with that our good relations ceased. In addition, there was the fact that he did not like my music; in some curious way it irritated him.

Somewhat later an unfortunate episode occurred with Medtner. I had hoped that at his concert he would play his great "C-major Sonata" in which I was interested. Instead, he chose one of his simpler sonatas for which the composer's interpretation was hardly necessary. I told him that I was disappointed in his choice.

"And the sonata which I played?"

"Well, that one is more suitable for home use."

On the basis of this incident as related by Medtner, Rachmaninoff later indignantly broadcast the story that Prokofiev divided sonatas into real sonatas and sonatas for home consumption. [1]

SCYTHIAN SUITE PERFORMANCE

During the autumn of 1915 I directed my *Sinfonietta* in its revised version and on January 29, 1916, my *Scythian Suite* at the Siloti Concerts [in Petrograd]. After the *Suite* there was an uproar similar to the one following my first appearance in the second concert at Pavlovsk, except that this time the whole of musical Petrograd was assembled. Glazounov, whom I had looked up for the express purpose of inviting him to the concert, flew into a rage, and left the hall eight measures before the end because he could no longer listen to the "Dawn" section. . . . The tympanist tore the kettle drum head with his heavy blows, and Siloti promised me that he would send me the mangled piece of leather as a keepsake. In the orchestra itself there were noticeable signs of antagonism. "Just because I have a sick wife and three children, must I be forced to suffer this hell?" grumbled the cellist, while behind him the trombonists blew fearful chords right into his ears. Siloti, in fine fettle, walked up and down the hall, repeating, "Right on the nose, right on the nose!" which was as much as to say that he and Prokofiev had given the public a slap in the face. "A scandal in high society," remarked the critic in the magazine *Music,* not without a certain malicious pleasure. [2]

ORCHESTRATING *THE GAMBLERS*

I spent the entire summer of 1916 orchestrating, scoring about ten pages a day; in the uncomplicated sections I even did as many as eighteen. My mother chanced to ask Tcherepnin how many pages a day he could orchestrate. "Sometimes only one chord," he answered, seeking to impress her with his careful workmanship. "My son does eighteen pages a day," declared my mother, quite proudly. [3]

COMPOSING AWAY FROM THE PIANO

I spent the summer of 1917 in complete solitude in the environs of Petrograd; I read Kant and worked hard. I had purposely not had my piano moved to the country because I wanted to try composing without it. Up to now I had generally written at the piano, but I wanted to establish the fact that thematic material worked out without a piano is better. When transferred to the piano it seems at first glance rather strange, but after several tryouts it becomes clear that only in this way and in no other must it be done.

The idea occurred to me to compose an entire symphonic work without the piano. Composed in this fashion, the orchestral colors would of necessity be clearer and cleaner. Thus the plan of a symphony in Haydnesque style originated, since as a result of my studies in Tcherepnin's classes, Haydn's technique had somehow become especially clear to me, and with such intimate understanding it was much easier to plunge into the dangerous flood without a piano. It seemed to me that were he alive today, Haydn, while retaining his own style of composition, would have appropriated something from the modern. Such a symphony I now wanted to compose: a symphony in the classic manner. As it began to take on actual form I named it *Classical Symphony;* first, because it was the simplest thing to call it; second, out of bravado, to stir up a hornet's nest, and finally, in the hope that should the symphony prove itself in time to be truly "classic," it would benefit me considerably. [4]

ARTHUR HONEGGER

1892–1955

Of Swiss extraction, Honegger was born in France where he lived most of his life. Serious, austere, unlike most of his colleagues of "Les Six" [1] whose compositions are redolent of music hall and street song, he tended toward chamber and symphonic music. A profound study of Bach made his writing firm, concise and contrapuntally well-knit. From Wagner, Strauss and the German Romanticists he acquired a brilliant orchestral technique and largeness of scope. His intense dramatic talent created such masterworks as *Le Roi David*, *Judith* and *Jeanne d'Arc au bûcher*. His sense of realism manifested itself in *Rugby* (he was very interested in sports) and *Pacific 231*. Yet he cannot be called a descriptive composer for he was interested in music *per se*.

In the source of the following quotations, *Je suis compositeur* (1951) —a volume in which he answers questions on music put to him by Bernard Gavoty—his native gravity deepens almost to pessimism. His outlook on present-day life and the future for the professional musician, particularly the composer, was gloomy, if not negative.

From: *Je suis compositeur,* 1951

ORIGINALITY

Absolute originality does not exist. Despite the prodigious novelty of his contributions, Debussy had his precursors. Certain of the last piano pieces of Liszt are not so distant from Debussy's *Préludes*. Before our Claude Achille, the great Richard had carried harmonic invention quite far; contemporary with Debussy, another Richard, author of *Elektra*, discovered treasures in the realm of harmony; with the instinct of genius, Moussorgsky had prospected in the domain from which Debussy borrowed. Thus, Debussy did not suddenly emerge from the void. But his works have such personality that they undeniably reflect a powerful genius and have revolutionized the musical world.   [1]

[1] See p. 475.

HIT OR MISS

Surprise is, on the whole, proof of insecurity, of the fact that the musician does not know his business. A composer worthy of the name must foresee everything. Once he does, it is enough for him to verify with his ear what his brain has conceived. Were I to benefit by the privileges accorded to painters, I would have an orchestra at my disposal, to play my rough sketches one after the other. That would be like taking a perspective at my leisure. Unfortunately, it is impossible. I must wait for the dress rehearsal. By that time the orchestral material is set, the parts are copied, and any serious corrections entail considerable work. True, there are some publishers willing to re-engrave entire pages after a first edition. But they are few and far between, you may be sure! For the rest, one must know how to accept risks.

The most appropriate comparison seems to me to be with the builder of boats who, at the moment of launching, risks seeing the boat turn over. Luckily, in music the same accident doesn't offer the same kind of evidence. Many modern scores float upside down. Very few people are aware of it.   [2]

MIND AND MATTER

The fact is that, to the lay mind, the act of composing music remains an incomprehensible thing. "When you are composing, do you figure out on the piano what will make a piece? But if it is a piece for orchestra, how can you play all the instrumental parts at the same time?"

I try to explain that musical construction must first be done in the mind, then be noted on paper in its large lines.

"But without hearing the notes played?"

"Naturally, since I don't, so to speak, play the piano."

"Then you are obliged to have it played by someone else?"

"No, because composing is a mental operation which takes place in the brain of the composer. However, I don't claim that to check certain passages at the piano is not useful, if only as an aid or guide in the linking of certain elements."

When you read a book, you do not have to pronounce the words aloud; they sound in your mind. It is the mind, the thought, which must create the music, and not the fingers wandering at random on the keys. Nevertheless, searching at the piano can be fruitful, especially when the composer is a skillful instrumentalist who gives himself over to improvisation. Schumann condemned this technique, but it is probable that a Chopin or a Liszt practiced it. It can produce excellent results. Thus, chance becomes inspiration, since the first spurt is caught, worked over, improved, made precise by the musical knowledge of the author. I can very well envisage the following case: The composer is seated at the piano experimenting with chords. He may suddenly become fascinated by a chain of two or more of these chords. They serve him as a basis for the entire harmonic character of a piece. Berlioz conceived a melodic line and searched for its harmonization on his guitar. That explains the tendency toward homophony which is peculiar to him. Bach and the polyphonists must have rarely used this method.

The reading of a musical text without an instrument seems a feat to the uninitiate. A friend told me in a tone of wonder how, in the train, he had seen a singer learning her rôle despite the absence of a piano! We must realize, moreover, that the reading of an orchestral score is infinitely harder than the reading of a literary text, and that it takes long training to succeed in doing it. Simply to watch the manner in which certain orchestral conductors read these scores is to marvel. The notes are numberless, and the eye must cover a very large area, since one must read simultaneously the top and the bottom of a page which comprises about thirty staves. In the main, it is normal enough that the layman should be surprised at what constitutes precisely the peculiarity of our profession, and that we should be asked: "You look at the notes and you really hear what is there?"

All this need not necessarily appertain to light music. There we very often find composers who have no technical knowledge at all. They play "tunes" which they have made up at the piano, and which may soon after be "on everybody's lips." They are generally fairly short pieces, nearly always in the same form: couplet-refrain. These authors depend on collaborators who edit their improvisations, harmonize them, orchestrate them. There is, on the one hand, the inventor of ideas; on the other, the technician who builds the piece with these ideas.

In American film music all this has become tradition. It is perfectly legitimate, for men who have the gift of melodic invention are not necessarily the most expert of practitioners. When music becomes a branch of industry, all values change. We have never demanded of Messrs. Ford and Citroën that they mount bodies on chassis themselves, simply because they personally conceived and perfected the motor. Nevertheless, the cars bear their names.

Let us get back to symphonic music. What has always astounded people is the existence of the deaf composer. It is not improbable that a great part of the admiration bestowed on Beethoven stems from his infirmity. Actually, apart from the tragic aspect of this situation, the fact that a creator can never hear the *execution* of his work should remove great technical restrictions for him. Beethoven had gradually forgotten the purely aural qualities of certain combinations of tones. We discover this in the vocal writing of the *Missa Solemnis* and the *Ninth Symphony*. We also observe it in the great interval between the right hand and the left in his piano writing and especially in the paradoxical harmonization of up-beats.

However, this had no influence whatsoever on the essence of his thought. I should be tempted to say that his deafness, which immured him in himself, helped him in the concentration of his genius and detached him from the tastelessness and banalities of his time.

I found, by chance, in an old number of the magazine *Die Musik*, devoted to Beethoven, an article by Dr. J. Niemack on the master's deafness. He takes one particular example—the middle passage of the Cavatina from the *Opus 130 Quartet* where the first violin declaims, over a strangely broken rhythm, a melodic line which Beethoven marked *Beklemmt* (anguished). "Let a cardiologist hear this passage," says Dr. Niemack, "and ask him if he knows the rhythm."

"Naturally," he will answer, "it is the heartbeat of an arteriosclerotic whose organ is affected by compensatory insufficiency." Beethoven's deafness rendered him more sensitive to the sound of his heartbeats. In consequence, Dr. Niemack asks whether the aesthetician might not take into consideration reflections of the phenomena of illness. [3]

OUR MUSICAL AGE (TWELVE-TONE MUSIC)

What strikes me about it [our age] is the haste of reactions, the premature discarding of methods. It took centuries, from Monteverdi to Schoenberg, to arrive at the free use of twelve tones. After this discovery, evolution suddenly became very rapid. We all face a wall; this wall, consisting of all the materials piled up little by little, stands before us today, and everybody is trying to find an opening in it; each one searches for it according to his own intuition.

There are, on the one hand, the champions of Satie's method: they extol the return to simplicity—*sancta simplicitas!*—on the other hand, those who, returning to Schoenberg's researches forty years later, look for an exit by way of atonality, setting up, more arbitrarily still, the twelve tone system. This system boasts a very narrow codification; the dodecaphonists remind me of convicts who, having broken their chains, voluntarily attach two-hundred-pound balls to their feet in order to run faster. Their dogma is entirely comparable to that of classroom counterpoint, with this difference, that while the aim of counterpoint is merely to facilitate the pen and stimulate invention through its exercise, the serial principles are presented, not as a means, but as an end!

I believe that there is here no possibility of expression for a composer, because his melodic invention is subject to intransigent laws which hinder the free expression of his thought. I am not at all opposed to discipline freely accepted, or even sought out, for artistic ends. But such discipline must have direction and not be arbitrary and despotic.

On the other hand, anarchic freedom, from the point of view of the harmonies resulting from superimposed lines, opens the road to the most dangerous fantasies. Here is what René Leibowitz, the eminent theoretician of the twelve tone system says: "It follows that the composer's thinking can finally function in an entirely linear (horizontal) manner, *since no vertical restriction can have any hold on him.* No forbidden dissonances, no fixed harmonic formulae (such as the cadences of model counterpoint, or the harmonic steps in tonal counterpoint); in other words, the composer can give free rein to the invention of his voices, which thus acquire at the same time a total individual freedom and the faculty of superimposing themselves one above the other." And further: "The imminent possibility [exists] for the composer to write in a purely horizontal manner, without any a priori vertical concern."

Evidently the restrictions imposed by the formation of an orthodox "set" are largely compensated for by this freedom. That explains why young people not too well-endowed with musical invention have thrown themselves enthusiastically into this technique. However, it must not be forgotten that the listener hears music vertically, and that the most complex contrapuntal combinations lose all interest and acquire an elementary facility when they dispense with all discipline.

Another inconvenience of the twelve tone system is the suppression of modulation, which offers so many, endlessly renewed, possibilities. "Passing from one region to another," maintains Leibowitz, "is vaguely equivalent to what modulation signifies in the realm of tonal architecture."

Finally, I fear the poverty of form . . . "since one might say that every twelve tone piece is only a suite of variations on the initial 'set.' "

The aim of conquest is to widen horizons, to abolish frontiers, not to narrow them. The efforts of creators have always been in the direction of liberation from formulae and conventions. But what examples of the reverse all around us! The demagogies have evolved toward an imperialism more autocratic than the one they have destroyed, while the dictators return to demagogy. I am very much afraid that the forced growth of the twelve tone system—incidentally we see it on the decline—is producing a reaction toward a too simplified, too rudimentary music. The cure for having swallowed sulphuric acid will be to drink syrup. The ear, fatigued by intervals of the ninth and the seventh, will welcome with delight accordion music and sentimental songs! [4]

THE FUTURE OF MUSIC

I have a strong feeling that we are at the end of a civilization. Decadence lies in wait for us, it already has a hold on us. Our arts are on the decline; they are disappearing. . . . I fear that music will be the first to depart. The more I look about me, the more I see it deviating from its calling—from that magic, that incantation, that solemnity which should surround artistic expression. It is not the fault of musicians, but of our musical life, which has changed. Formerly, a concert was a kind of celebration, a reunion where this magic came alive before people assembled as for a religious ceremony.

———————————

In 1919, Satie advocated *musique d'ameublement*—music to be played without being listened to, like looking at wallpaper without seeing it. Today we have lowered the *B minor Mass* or the *Opus 132 Quartet* to this level. Concerts are more numerous than ever. But they have become performances for piano or baton champions. The impresario demands orthodox programs—Beethoven festivals for orchestra conductors and Chopin recitals for the pianist. The public rushes to the box office without even knowing the programs. Here again, it is not the music that counts; it is the virtuosity of its execution. We are in an age where one sets a six-year-old girl in front of an orchestra in order to be staggered by her extravagant gesticulations.

One wonders why so many great masters of the past should have written so many works, since they never provoke the curiosity of performers. Even more, why should young unknowns wish to enter such an overcrowded field?

Here we have the curse—the word is not too strong—of our profession. Music is not dying of anemia, but of plethora. There is too much production, too much supply and too little demand. In addition to French composers who live in Paris there are, in other countries, men of great talent (genius is reserved for the dead) like Hindemith, Prokofiev, Malipiero, Dallapiccola, Hartmann, Toch, Egk, Orff, Britten,

Walton, Absil, Frank Martin, Beck, Nabokov, Barber, Copland, Shostakovitch . . . many more still, scorned by the orchestras. Let us surrender to the evidence of a manifestly comatose state of affairs.

I want to be clearly understood; it is not for myself that I am frightened. It is for those who are entering on a career that grows more inaccessible every day and is dominated by routine. Just as one faces death, so must one have the courage consciously to face the end of our musical civilization, which is only a step behind the end of civilization as a whole.

To deny it would be nothing less than lack of foresight. There is no use fighting against it. It must be accepted coldly. Thereafter one may console oneself with the thought that out of the ruins of this civilization another will be born.

Young composers, don't think of me as an old fossil who is content to leave you behind on earth, so long as I can poison your sojourn in advance. Just be aware that the "business of composing" can give you but little material reward. If your works are savored by a few friends and contemporaries, that in itself should be enough recompense and inner joy to you. This is the one privilege which cannot be taken from the creator.   [5]

DARIUS MILHAUD

1892–

An enthusiastic traveller, Milhaud has been influenced by the music of practically every country he has visited; an avid experimenter, he has tried his hand at almost every musical style and medium. As a consequence of this sensitivity to ever-varying stimuli, his tremendous output includes Jewish music, Brazilian music, jazz, atonality, polytonality and even *musique d'ameublement*, music as a background to be heard but not listened to as thought up by Satie. Symphonies, chamber music for odd as well as conventional combinations of instruments, ballets, full-length and minute operas, songs and instrumental solos, have flowed from his pen in profusion. His subject matter has ranged from Greek drama to a florist's catalogue.

Following the Nazi conquest of France, he emigrated to the United States, where he has exerted a beneficent influence on young American composers.

In his autobiography, *Notes sans musique* (1949), Milhaud gives a vivid and complete picture of French music from the First World War to the present.

From: *Notes sans musique,* 1949

POLYTONALITY

I had undertaken a thoroughgoing study of the problems of polytonality. I had noted—and interpreted for myself—that a little duet by Bach written in canon at the fifth really gave one the impression of two separate keys succeeding one another, and then becoming superimposed and contrasted, though of course the harmonic texture remained tonal. The contemporary composers, Stravinsky or Koechlin, made use of chords containing several tonalities, often handled contrapuntally or used as a pedal. I set to work to examine every possible combination of two keys superimposed and to study the chords thus produced. I also studied the effect of inverting them. I tried every imaginable permutation by varying the mode of the tonalities making up these chords. Then I did the same thing in three keys. What I could not understand was why, though the harmony books dealt with chords and their inversions and the laws governing their sequence, the same thing could not be done for polytonality. I grew familiar with some of these chords. They satisfied my ear more than the normal ones, for a polytonal chord is more subtly sweet and more violently potent.

[1]

BRAZILIAN FOLKLORE

My first contact with Brazilian folklore was very sudden. I arrived in Rio in the middle of the Carnival [of 1917] and immediately sensed the mood of crazy gaiety that possessed the whole town. . . . Six weeks before the Carnival is due to begin, the *cordoes* perambulate the streets on Saturday and Sunday evenings, select a little square and dance to the music of the *violaõ* (a kind of guitar) and a few percussion instruments like the *choucalha* (a kind of round, copper container filled with iron filings and terminating in a rod which is rotated, thus producing a continuous rhythmical sound). One of the dancers' favorite amusements is to improvise words to a tune repeated over and over again. The singer must keep on finding new words, and as soon as his imagination begins to flag, someone else takes his place. The monotony of this never ending chorus and its insistent rhythm end by producing a sort of hypnosis to which the dancers fall victim. . . .

For six weeks the whole populace is passionately given over to singing and dancing; there is always one song which wins more favor than the others, and thereby becomes the "Carnival Song." Thus *"Pelo Telefono,"* the Carnival song for 1917, was to be heard wherever one went, ground out by little orchestras, churned out by pianolas and gramophones, whistled and sung after a fashion in every house—and it haunted us all winter.

I was fascinated by the rhythms of this popular music. There was an imperceptible pause in the syncopation, a careless catch in the breath, a slight hiatus that I found very difficult to grasp. So I bought a lot of maxixes and tangos, and tried to play them with their syncopated rhythms that run from one hand to the other. At last my efforts were rewarded, and I could both play and analyze this typically Brazilian subtlety. One of the best composers of this kind of music, Ernesto Nazareth, used to play the piano at the door of a cinema in the Avenida Rio Branco. His elusive, mournful, liquid way of playing also gave me deeper insight into the Brazilian soul. [2]

THE "SIX"

After a concert at the Salle Huyghens [in 1919], at which Bertin sang Louis Durey's *Images à Crusoë* on words by Saint-Léger Léger and the Capelle Quartet played my *Fourth Quartet,* the critic Henri Collet published in *Comœdia* a chronicle entitled "Five Russians and Six Frenchmen." Quite arbitrarily he had chosen six names: Auric, Durey, Honegger, Poulenc, Taillefaire and my own, merely because we knew each other, were good friends, and had figured on the same programs; quite irrespective of our different temperaments and wholly dissimilar characters. Auric and Poulenc were partisans of Cocteau's ideas, Honegger derived from the German Romantics, and I from Mediterranean lyricism. I fundamentally disapproved of joint declarations of aesthetic doctrines and felt them to be a drag, an unreasonable limitation on the imagination of the artists who must for each new work find different, often contradictory means of expression. But it was useless to protest. Collet's article excited such worldwide interest that the "Group of Six" was launched, and willy-nilly I formed part of it.

This being so, we decided to give some *Concerts des Six.* The first was devoted to my works; the second to foreign music. The latter program consisted of works by Lord Berners, Casella, Lourié, who was then People's Comissar for the Fine Arts in Soviet Russia, and Schoenberg and Bartók, whose latest works we had been unable to hear owing to the war. Satie was our mascot. He was very popular among us. He was so fond of young people that he said to me one day: "I wish I knew what sort of music will be written by the children who are four years old now." The purity of his art, his horror of all concessions, his contempt for money, and his ruthless attitude toward the critics were a marvellous example for us all.

The formation of the Group of Six helped to draw the bonds of friendship closer among us. For two years we met regularly at my place every Saturday evening. . . . We were not all composers, for our number also included performers . . . painters . . . and writers. . . . The poets would read their poems, and we would play our latest compositions. Some of them, such as Auric's *Adieu New York,* Poulenc's *Cocardes* and my *Bœuf sur le toit* were continually being played. We even used to insist on Poulenc's playing *Cocardes* every Saturday evening; he did so most readily. Out of these meetings, in which a spirit of carefree gaiety reigned, many a fruitful collaboration was to be born; they also determined the character of several works strongly marked by the influence of the music hall.   [3]

MUSIQUE D'AMEUBLEMENT

Just as one's field of vision embraces objects and forms, such as the pattern on the wallpaper, the cornice of the ceiling, or the frame of the looking glass, which the eye sees but to which it pays no attention, though they are undoubtedly there, Satie thought that it would be amusing to have music that would not be listened to, *musique d'ameublement* or background music, that would vary like the furniture of the rooms in which it was played. Auric and Poulenc disapproved of this suggestion, but it tickled my fancy so much that I experimented with it, in cooperation with Satie, at a concert given in the Galerie Barbazange [in 1921]. During the program, Marcelle Meyer played music by *Les Six*, and Bertin presented a play by Max Jacob called *Un Figurant au théâtre de Nantes*, which required the services of a trombone. He also sang Stravinsky's *Berceuse du chat* to the accompaniment of three clarinets, so Satie and I scored out music for the instruments used in the course of these various items on the program. In order that the music might seem to come from all sides at once, we posted the clarinets in three different corners of the theater, the pianist in the fourth, and the trombone in a box on the first floor. A program note warned the audience that it was not to pay any more attention to the ritornelles that would be played during the intervals than to the candelabra, the seats, or the balcony. Contrary to our expectations, however, as soon as the music started up, the audience began to stream back to their seats. It was no use for Satie to shout: "Go on talking! Walk about! Don't listen!" They listened without speaking. The whole effect was spoiled—Satie had not bargained on the charm of his own music. Nevertheless, Satie wrote another *ritournelle d'ameublement* for Mrs. Eugene Meyer of Washington, when she asked him, through me, to give her an autograph. But for this *Musique pour un cabinet préfectoral* to have its full meaning, she should have had it recorded and played over and over again, thus forming part of the furniture of her beautiful library, adorning it for the ear in the same way as the still life by Manet adorned it for the eye. In any case, the future was to prove Satie right; nowadays, children and housewives fill their homes with unheeded music, reading and working to the sound of the radio. And in all public places, large stores and restaurants, the customers are drenched in an unending flood of music. In America, every cafeteria is equipped with a sufficient number of machines for each client to be able, for the modest sum of five cents, to furnish his own solitude with music or supply a background for his conversation with his guest. Is this not *musique d'ameublement*—heard, but not listened to?   [4]

JAZZ

It was during this visit to London [in 1920] that I first began to take an interest in jazz. Billy Arnold and his band, straight from New York, were playing in a Hammersmith dance hall.

In his *Coq et l'Arlequin*, Cocteau described the jazz accompaniment to the number by Gaby Deslys at the Casino de Paris in 1918 as a "cataclysm in sound." In the course of frequent visits to Hammersmith, where I sat close to the musicians, I tried to analyze and assimilate what I heard. What a long way we had travelled from the gypsies who, before the war, used to pour their insipid, treacly strains intimately into our ears, or the singers whose questionably tasteful glides were borne up by the wobbly notes of the cimbalom, or the crudity of our bals-musettes with the unsubtle forthrightness of cornet, accordion and clarinet! The new music was extremely subtle in its use of timbre: the saxophone breaking in, squeezing out the juice of dreams, the trumpet, dramatic or languorous by turns, the clarinet, frequently played in its upper register, the lyrical use of the trombone, glancing slidingly over quarter-tones in crescendos of volume and pitch, thus intensifying the feeling. The whole, various yet not disparate, was held together by the piano, subtly punctuated by the complex rhythm of the percussion, a kind of inner beat, the vital pulse of the rhythmic life of the music. The constant use of syncopation in the melody was of such contrapuntal freedom that it gave the impression of unregulated improvisation, whereas, in actual fact, it was elaborately rehearsed daily, down to the last detail. I had the idea of using these timbres and rhythms in a work of chamber music, but first I had to penetrate more deeply into the arcana of this new musical form, whose technique still baffled me. The musicians who had already made use of jazz had confined themselves to what were more or less interpretations of dance music. Satie, in the "Rag-Time du Paquebot" of *Parade*, and Auric in the fox-trot *Adieu New York* had made use of an ordinary symphony orchestra, and Stravinsky had written his *Rag-Time* for eleven solo instruments, including a cimbalom. [5]

DECADENCE OF JAZZ

I disappointed the American reporters by telling them that I was no longer interested in jazz. It had now [by 1926] become official, and won universal recognition. The Winn School of Popular Music had even published three methods: *How to play Jazz and the Blues*, in which syncopation was analyzed—I might even say dissected. The various ways of assimilating jazz were taught, as well as jazz style for the piano, and improvisation; its freedom within a rigid rhythmic framework, all the breaks and passing discords, the broken harmonies, arpeggios, trills and ornaments, the variations and cadences that can return ad lib in a sort of highly fantastic counterpoint. You could also find instructions on playing the trombone, including the principal types of glissando and the way to make the sound quiver by a rapid little to-and-fro movement of the slide, and there were clarinet manuals exploiting all the new technical possibilities opened up by jazz. Even in Harlem, the charm had been broken for me. White men, snobs in search of exotic color, sightseers curious to hear Negro music, had penetrated to even the most secluded corners. That is why I gave up going.

[6]

PAUL HINDEMITH

1895-

One of the most versatile and practical of contemporary musicians, Hindemith excels as composer, performer, conductor, and teacher. Skilled on a variety of musical instruments, he has written sonatas for all manner of them, with and without piano. His main instrument is the viola, for which he has composed prolifically.

Hindemith's knowledge of music past and present is encyclopedic. He has made researches into a vast amount of old music, both instrumental and vocal, which his Collegium Musicum at Yale University has performed both in New Haven and New York. His erudition is enlivened by a keen sense of humor, which he exhibits both in his compositions and in his writings. A lively example is his *Kleine Kammermusik*, Op. 24, No. 2, for winds; in criticism his humor becomes particularly biting when he discusses twelve tone technique. He has written a number of books on musical theory, the best known of which is his *Unterweisung im Tonsatz* (Instruction in Composition).

Having played in opera house, movie house and theater orchestras, Hindemith is averse to art for art's sake. He feels that the composer should write with a purpose; his own *Gebrauchsmusik* or "workaday music," as Eric Blom calls it, was composed to give reality to this thesis.

From: *A Composer's World,* 1952

THE LIMITS OF NOVELTY

A musical structure which due to its extreme novelty does not in the listener's mind summon up any recollections of former experiences . . . will prevent his creative coöperation. He cannot adjust his sense of proportion to the unfolding structure, he loses the feeling for his position in the sounding terrain, he does not recognize the significance of the single structural members in reference to the entity, he even loses the feeling for the coherence of these members. For him, music goes astray, disappears in chaos; it deteriorates into the mere amorphous assembly of sound it was before it entered the zone of active coöperation in the listener's mind.

In view of all this, we may conclude that there is—strange as it may sound in the face of countless attempts at modernization of the musical means of expression—in principle never anything new in the general order, shape, and mutual relationship of musical successions. We may even go so far as to say that, basically, nothing new can ever be introduced into such successions—if we do not want to see the participant in music degraded to a dull, apathetic receptacle, an absorbent sponge reaching the point of saturation without showing any sign of reaction.

Once we agree to this statement, our opinion in respect to musical facts will undergo significant changes. What, then, remains of the importance which we customarily ascribe to all questions of a composer's style? We prefer to think of his tone-combining craft as possessing an infinite variability, even power of eternal regeneration; but it merely permits a limited number of variations within the given limitations of its sounding ingredients. The building material cannot be removed very far away from certain structural, harmonic-tonal, and melodic prototypes, so that the listener can assume an active part in the process of musical realization.

Furthermore, the continual accumulation of experience in a listener's mind should not be overrated. Once he reaches a certain point of versatility in his power of musical co-construction, no further progress seems to be possible. . . . All musical structures that stand entirely without his previous experience will have to exert their impact many times on his physical and mental receptivity if they are to be added to his stock of accumulated knowledge. We know how the more performances a listener needs for the comprehension of music complex in texture, the less chance he seems to be given of a sufficient number of hearings. Even if he were to have such hearings, the final effect would not be a sensation of constantly accumulating novel experiences. Rather, the more familiar he became with the piece, the more he might continue to discover in it similarities to compositions already heard.

However, we must admit that the amassment of many listeners' experiences in the course of decades and centuries causes some kind of so-called progress which expresses itself in the acknowledgment of hitherto unknown stylistic patterns or technical novelties. This progress does not greatly exceed the very banal but ever newly experienced and always overrated fact that Ockeghem's style is different from Schoenberg's . . . Beyond the ever-changing aspects of stylistic and technical evaluation, this "progress" does not affect the essential qualities of music, its meaning and its emotional effects on the recipient, or its everlasting values. Although the recipient may derive certain advantages from the accumulated experiences of generations, just as in turn these generations profit from individual contributions, the music of our day cannot touch regions of our intellectual and emotional life other than those touched in participants of the past by their own contemporary music. In this respect a modern symphony concert is neither more advanced nor better than the simple tune a stone-age man created musingly on the bone flute. [1]

EMOTION IN MUSIC

There is no doubt that listeners, performers and composers alike can be profoundly moved by perceiving, performing or imagining music, and that, consequently, music must touch on something in their emotional life that brings them to this state of excitation. But if these mental reactions were feelings, they could not change as rapidly as they do; they would not begin and end precisely with the musical stimulus that aroused them. If we experience a real feeling of grief—that is, grief not caused or released by music—it is not possible to replace it, at a moment's notice and without plausible cause, with a feeling of wild gaiety; gaiety, in turn, cannot be replaced by complacency after a fraction of a second. Real feelings need a certain interval of time to develop, reach their climax, and fade again; reactions to music, however, may change as fast as musical phrases do; they may spring up in full intensity at any given moment and disappear entirely when the musical pattern that provoked them ends or changes. Thus these reactions may, within a few instants, skip from the most profound grief to utter hilarity and on to complacency, without causing any discomfort to the mind experiencing them, as would be the case with a rapid succession of real feelings. In fact, if it happened with real feelings, we could be sure that it could be only in the event of slight insanity. The reactions music evokes are not feelings; they are the images, the memories of feelings. We can compare these memories of feelings to the memories we have of a country in which we have travelled. The original journey may have taken several weeks or months, but in conjuring up in our memory the events of it, we may go through the entire adventure in a few seconds and still have the sensation of a very complete mental reconstruction of its course. It is the same trick dreams play on us. They, too, compress the reproductions of events that in reality would need long intervals of time for their development into fractions of a second, and yet they seem to the dreamer as real as adventures he has when he is wide awake. In some cases, these dream-events may even be the "real" life of the individual, while the facts they reflect, distort, or rearrange are nothing but inconsequential and sober successions of trifles.

Dreams, memories, musical reactions—all three are made of the same stuff. We cannot have musical reactions of any considerable intensity if we do not have dreams of some intensity, for musical reactions build up, like dreams, a phantasmagoric structure of feelings that hits us with the full impact of real feeling. Furthermore, we cannot have any musical reactions of emotional significance, unless we have once had real feelings, the memory of which is revived by the musical impression. . . .

If music did not instigate us to supply memories out of our mental storage rooms, it would remain meaningless; it would merely have a certain tickling effect on our ears. We cannot keep music from uncovering the memory of former feelings, and it is not in our power to avoid them, because the only way to "have"—to *possess*—music, is to connect it with those images, shadows, dreamy reproductions of actual feelings, no matter how realistic and crude or, on the contrary, how denatured, stylized, and sublimated they may be. If music we hear is of a kind that does not easily lend itself or does not lend itself at all to this connection, we still do our best to find in our memory some feeling that would correspond with the audible impression we have.

[2]

"GOOD" AND "BAD" MUSIC

If all music ever written could only be classified as "good" or "bad," with some pieces perhaps occasionally falling short of either extreme, what would a singer or player do with a composition of the highest quality, viewed objectively, but not serving his personal purposes? Take one of the .more florid Gregorian melodies, such as those sung at Easter or Whitsunday, which will doubtless be considered by every musician of some taste the most perfect, convincing one-line compositions ever conceived. Of course, fully to understand their overwhelming linear power, you cannot restrict yourself to just reading or hearing them. You must participate in singing these melodic miracles, if you want to feel how they weld the singing group into a spiritual unit, independent of the individualistic prompting of a conductor, and guided only by the lofty spirit and technical excellence of the structure. Now, imagine that you are forced to sing them by yourself—

solo, that is—transplanting those immaculate creations into another environment. Don't you feel as if you were expelled from a community of worthy friends? Has the music not lost its savor and assumed a taste of bitterness instead? And then play these same melodies, which were the precious vessels of highest linear revelations, on a wind instrument, then on a fiddle, and finally on the piano. The quality of the melodic line seems gradually to disappear, greatness turns into inexpressive melismatism, then becomes insipid passage work, and finally ends in ridicule. If . . . perfection remained perfection under all circumstances, how could such a disintegration of values take place merely by altering the means of performance?

Let us once more illustrate our point, this time with an example in which the change of the means of expression is not quite as drastic as in the gradual metamorphosis of a chorus into a piano [piece], but which, due to its closeness to our everyday musical experience, is perhaps even more convincing. We all agree that, in a fugue, the linear arrangement of the musical material must be strongly emphasized, and this is often carried to the highest degree of contrapuntal rigidity. Consequently, any group of instruments that allows this contrapuntal fabric to appear in transparent lucidity should in principle be preferable to all others. Since linear writing for pianos or other keyboard instruments can only be an artificial projection of several independent melodic planes into one single plane, a keyboard fugue played on non-keyed melodic instruments should reveal its linear spirit in a more appropriate and therefore more convincing manner than the original form could ever do. Now play some of the undisputed masterpieces of this species, namely, fugues from Bach's *Wohltemperiertes Klavier*, as string trio or string quartet pieces. You will have a queer and rather disagreeable sensation: compositions which you knew as being great, heavy, and as emanating an impressive spiritual strength, have turned into pleasant miniatures. With the increase in contrapuntal clarity, we have had to accept a deplorable loss of majesty and gravity. Although the supremacy of the piece has remained the same, the pieces have shrunk, despite the improved reproduction, and their structural and spiritual relation to the original keyboard form has become that of a miniature mummified Incan head to its previous animate form. In our fugues we have reduced to almost nothing the heavy technical resistance that a player of polyphonic keyboard music has to overcome, since the string players have produced their isolated lines without noticeable effort.

This example shows clearly that, with the artless classification of good and bad, nothing is said about the real technical quality of a composition so long as no further criteria are introduced. One of these criteria is, as our experiments in the transformation of Gregorian and Bach pieces have demonstrated, the degree of resistance that the particular technical form of a composition offers to the players' or singers' technique of performance, a factor which the performer has to cope with before either the listener or the producer need be aware of it.   [3]

MODERN MUSIC: TWELVE-TONE TECHNIQUE

Let us investigate briefly some of those allegedly "modern" achievements. The best known and most frequently mentioned is the so-called twelve-tone technique, or composition in pre-established tone series. The idea is to take the twelve tones of our chromatic scale, select one of its some four hundred million permutations, and use it as the basis for the harmonic (and possibly melodic) structure of a piece. This rule of construction is established arbitrarily and without any reference to basic musical facts. It ignores the validity of harmonic and melodic values derived from mathematical, physical, or psychological experience; it does not take into account the differences in intervallic tensions, the physical relationship of tones, the degree of ease in vocal production, and many other facts of either natural permanence or proven usefulness. Its main "law" is supplemented by other rules of equal arbitrariness, such as: tones must not be repeated; your selected tone series may skip from one stratum of the texture to any other one; you have to use the inversion and other distortions of this series; and so on—all of which can be reduced to the general advice: avoid so far as possible anything that has been written before.

The only segment of our conventional body of theoretical musical knowledge which the dodecaphonists have deigned to admit and which, in fact, alone makes their speculations possible, is the twelve-tone tempered scale. We have already been told of this scale's weakness: because of its basic impurity it can be used only as a supplementary regulative to a tone system containing natural intervals—at least, so long as we want to save our music from total instrumental mechanization and have human voices participate in its execution. True, some kind of a restricted technique of composition can be developed on a foundation of compromise scales and arbitrary working rules, but doubtless the general result will always be one similar to the kind of poetry that is created by pouring written words out of a tumbler without calling in grammar and syntax. A higher tonal organization is not attempted and cannot be achieved, especially if one permits the technical working rules to slip off into the aforementioned set of supplementary statutes which are nothing but stylistic whims, and as such, not subject to any controlling power of general validity.

[4]

PIANO TONE

The worst blow the admirers of the hammer keyboard ever received was the discovery by physicists that in the sound tracks of an oscillator no difference can be detected between tones produced by the adept touch of a great artist's hand and those stemming from manipulation with an umbrella. Piano antagonists liked to gloat over this humiliating experiment which, by the mere fact that it could be performed, seemed to prove the uncouthness of the mechanism in question.

The scientifically proven fact cannot be doubted, in spite of all disavowals by the pianists. There is no mysterious power acting in a key and no reason can be found why an arrangement of several levers should be more than a device for the transmission of physical energy. In my opinion, both the clavier addicts and the umbrella conspirators are arguing facts that have no bearing on music and musical effects. It is of no importance whether a single tone is produced by Franz Liszt or by Mr. Smith's umbrella. A single tone, as we have stated repeatedly, has no musical significance, and the keyboard does not provide any exception to this rule. The tones released by the keyboard receive musical value only if brought into temporal and spatial relations with each other. Then the infinitely subtle gradation in the application of pressure, the never-ceasing interplay of minutest dynamic hues and temporal length proportions, all the bewitching attractions of good piano playing—only the artist can produce them convincingly; and it certainly is not his hand that reigns within the microcosm of musical diversity but his musical intellect as the master of his playing hand. Even the application of the world's most perfect umbrellas could never cope with this diversity, gradation and interplay.   [5]

X

THOMSON
SESSIONS
GERSHWIN
POULENC
AURIC
CHAVEZ
ANTHEIL
KRENEK
COPLAND

VIRGIL THOMSON

1896–

"He was terrifyingly articulate both as a composer and as a critic." In this sentence from his essay, "The Berlioz Case," Thomson has summed up himself as well as Berlioz. As composer, conductor, critic and organist he has left hardly a facet of music untouched. His musical works range through opera, ballet, film, chamber music, choruses, solo songs and all manner of instrumental solos with and without orchestra. His opera, *Four Saints in Three Acts* launched a new departure in that field, and his film scores, *The Plough That Broke the Plains, The River* and *Louisiana Story* not only supplied a meaningful background for the pictures they accompanied, but turned out to be successful orchestral suites in their own right.

Years of study and living in France and the influence of Satie and "the Six" gave him a predilection for French music, its reasonableness, its clarity, and its daring. His music also reflects the American scene, with its simple hymn and folk tunes.

In over a decade of reviewing for the New York *Herald Tribune* and in contributions to magazines such as *Modern Music,* he has covered practically every phase of music in America both in and outside New York, as well as an appreciable portion of concerts in Europe. His opinions, not always orthodox, are decided, the result of years of music making and listening.

The State of Music (1939), his first book, is a series of discussions of music in general and the modern American composer in particular. Three other volumes, *The Musical Scene* (1945), *The Art of Judging Music* (1948), and *Music Right and Left* (1951), consist of pieces chosen from his daily reviews and Sunday articles in the *Herald Tribune*, the accent of the last book being on contemporary music of which he is a staunch champion.

BACH

December 31, 1940

The closer the performing conditions for Sebastian Bach's concerted music are approximated to those of early eighteenth-century provincial Germany, the more that music sounds like twentieth-century American swing. The exactitude with which a minimum time unit is kept unaltered at all times, the persistence of this unit as one of exactly measured length rather than of pulsation, the omnipresence of the harpsichord's ping, like a brush on a cymbal, the constant employment of wiggly counterpoint and staccato bass, all make it a matter of preference between anachronisms whether one puts it that Bach has gone to town or that some of the more scholarly jitterbugs of the town have wandered into a church.   [1]

CHOPIN AND RUBATO

October 26, 1940

Chopin's prescription for rubato playing, which is almost word for word Mozart's prescription for playing an accompanied melody, is that the right hand should take liberties with the time values, while the left hand remains rhythmically unaltered.[1] This is exactly the effect you get when a good blues singer is accompanied by a good swing band. It is known to the modern world as *le style hot*. The Paderewski tradition of Chopin-playing is more like the Viennese waltz style, in which the liberties in the melody are followed exactly in the accompaniment, the two elements keeping always together and performing at the same time a flexible distortion of strict rhythm that manages by its very flexibility to keep the procedure from seeming arbitrary or the continuity from collapsing. Mr. Rubinstein is skillful with this kind of rubato. He keeps the music surging. But I don't believe for a moment it resembles anything Frédéric Chopin ever did or had in mind.   [2]

INTERPRETING BRAHMS

November 12, 1944

It is a strange anomaly that although Brahms's symphonic music is extremely popular (in some years it tops even that of Beethoven for frequency of performance), almost nobody's rendition of it is thoroughly satisfactory. How to discern the rhythm that underlies its slow and its energetic passages, to make these sound in any given piece as if they are all parts of the same piece, is one of the unsolved problems in music. Certainly the meditative ones require to be read as inward rather than as extrovert sentiment. And certainly the animated ones

[1] See p. 78.

and the passages of broad eloquence, such as the codas and finales, tempt any conductor to make oratory out of them. But alternations of introversion and extraversion do not make a unity in the reading of anything, and there is no reason to suppose that so experienced and so consecrated a musician as Brahms was basically incoherent in thought. It is far more likely that his exact poetic temper, being profoundly personal, escapes us.   [3]

MAHLER AND STRAUSS

March 14, 1941

Gustav Mahler is to Richard Strauss as Bach to Handel, or Debussy to Ravel. All such pairs of contemporaries have a common background of style and material that gives to their contrasted temperaments the ability to define and enclose an epoch, as the heads and the tails of a coin define and enclose between them its content.

Mahler's music is the more introspective. It is meditative, visceroemotional, all about himself. Strauss's is declamatory, objective, descriptive of everything in the world but himself. Mahler's has the power of attracting fanatical devotion to itself and to the personality of its author. Strauss's gives a ripsnorting good time to all without provoking the slightest curiosity anywhere about its author's private life. Mahler wrote as if the material of Viennese music itself were so bound up with his own soul that only by integrating the two in a practically marital union could a work be created that would be a valid expression of either. Strauss wrote his pieces very much as a theatrical producer cooks up a show.

And yet the musical material and technique of the two are almost identical. Their themes might have been written by either, so characteristically do they consist of descending appoggiaturas and upward skips of the sixth. The two have an equal freedom of modulation and the same habit of playing their chromatics wild, not limiting the use of these to modulatory or to melodic purposes, but throwing them in anywhere they feel like it or for any reason whatsoever.

Both orchestrate, of course, with a sure hand and with wide resources of imagination and fancy. Mahler's orchestra, however, is the more elegant of the two by far, as is likewise his harmonic and contrapuntal fabric. His concentration on personal sincerity gave him an integrated manner of expressing himself, at his best, that is stylistically more noble than anything Strauss, with all his barnstorming brilliance, ever achieved. The Strauss heavy doublings and unashamed use of

mere orchestral hubbub belong to a less refined and a less responsible
order of musical expression. Mahler keeps his colors clean, and he
never writes a middle part that hasn't in itself some intensity of expression or some grace.

The *Ninth Symphony* (considered by most Mahler devotees to be
the finest of his works, though *Das Lied von der Erde* has its wor-
shippers and so have the *Kindertotenlieder*) is beautifully made and
beautifully thought. It is utterly German and Viennese and strangely
not so at the same time. In reviewing *Das Lied von der Erde* some time
back, I opined that there were some French influences in the particular contrapuntal approach Mahler employed. Naturally, I pulled down
on my head a flood of abusive correspondence from the Mahlerites,
who will have no analyzing of their idol and certainly no aspersions
cast upon his hundred-per-cent Germanism. I suppose they don't count
his Israelite birth or his professional travels (he conducted here at the
Metropolitan Opera House and at the Philharmonic for something like
three years) as factual evidence of a certain internationalism in his
culture. Nevertheless, as I listened to the *Ninth Symphony* last night,
I was still aware of French influences. Certain of these are technical,
like the no-doubling orchestration. Others are aesthetic. I know the
protest mail I shall get for saying this, but I must say it. Mahler has
a great deal in common with the French Impressionists. As an Italian
musician to whom I mentioned the matter put it: "He comes as near
being an Impressionist as a German could."   [4]

MACDOWELL'S MUSIC

November 5, 1944

Revisiting the music of Edward MacDowell, through copies found
in a borrowed house, was one of the pleasures of your reviewer's late
summer vacation. What the larger works would sound like nowadays
—the two suites for orchestra, the two piano concertos, and the four
piano sonatas—he does not know, because he has not for many years
handled their scores; and they have almost disappeared from our metropolitan programs. But the shorter piano works—the *Woodland
Sketches*, the *New England Sketches*, and the *Sea Pieces*—have kept
an extraordinary freshness through the years. Rereading them brought
the reflection that although no living American would have written
them in just that way (the Wagnerian harmonic texture having passed
out of vogue), no living American quite *could* have written them,
either.

Let us take them for what they are, not for what they are not. They are landscapes mostly, landscapes with and without figures, literary or historical evocations, *morceaux de genre*. The test of such pieces is their power of evocation. Couperin, Mendelssohn, Schumann, and Debussy are the great masters of genre painting in music; Grieg, Smetana, and possibly Albeniz or Villa-Lobos its lesser luminaries. MacDowell might well rank with these last if he had had access to a body of folklore comparable in extent to theirs, an access that Americans do have, in fact, now. He divined the problems of style that face American composers, but he was not able to solve them single-handed. So he borrowed more from German sources than he would have liked, I think, and more than anybody has to do today.

Nevertheless, the scenes he describes are vivid. His rhythmic contours evoke the stated subject quickly, accurately. No other American composer has painted a wild rose, or an iceberg, a water lily or a deserted farmhouse so neatly. The rendering is concise, the outline definite. No piece is a rewriting of any other. Each is itself, economical, elegant, clearly projected. The impersonality of the procedure is proof of the author's sincerity; its evocative power is proof of his high skill as a craftsman. MacDowell did not leave his mark on music as a stylist; he left us merely a repertory of unforgettable pieces, all different from one another and all charming. And he left to American composers an example of clear thought and objective workmanship that has been an inspiration to us all.

There is a movement on foot toward influencing the American Academy of Arts and Sciences to place his bust in the Hall of Fame at New York University. Stephen Foster is the only writer of music there honored at present. MacDowell could not be in better company, because his music, like that of Foster, is part of every American's culture who has any musical culture. Everybody has played it, loved it, remembered it. Just as no student who ever attended MacDowell's classes at Columbia University ever forgot the master's penetrating observations about music, no musician or no music lover has ever forgotten the delicate firmness of MacDowell's melody, the exactitude with which his rhythm (and his piano figuration, too) depicts the picturesque. To have become, whether by sheer genius for music making, as in Foster's case, or, as in MacDowell's, by the professional exercise of a fully trained gift and by an integrity of attitude unequalled in our musical history, part and parcel of every musical American's musical thought is, in any meaning of the term, it seems to me, immortality.

[5]

TEMPO

June 11, 1944

No element of musical execution is more variable from one interpreter to another than tempo. No problem, indeed, is more bothering to any musician, even to the composer, than that of determining the exact metronomic speed at which he wishes or advises that a piece be made to proceed in performance, unless it is that of sticking to his tempo once he has decided on it. Many musical authors, beginning with Beethoven, have indicated in time units per minute their desires in this matter. And yet interpreters do not hesitate to alter these indications when conviction, based on reasoning or on feeling or on executional circumstances, impels them to do so.

The truth of the matter is that very few pieces require to be played at a given speed in order to make sense. Serge Koussevitzky gave an excellent performance of the Berlioz *Symphonie Fantastique* that took a good ten minutes more of actual playing time than Monteux or Beecham or Toscanini ever needs for this piece. Toscanini himself once angered Ravel considerably by sweeping brilliantly through his *Bolero*, which is not a long piece, in four minutes less time than the composer considered legitimate. I have heard the fugues and toccatas of Sebastian Bach played by organists at the Cathedral of Notre Dame in Paris, which has some of the most complex echoes and reverberations of any building in the world, at tempos twice, thrice, and even four times as slow as those the same organists employ in churches of drier acoustic properties. They sounded perfectly well, too.

The reason why such variations shock us as little as they do is that speed itself is not nearly so expressive an element in musical communication as clear phraseology and exact rhythmic articulation are. These matters require, in the course of studying a work and preparing its execution, a great deal of thought on the interpreter's part and no small amount of adjustment to instrumental limitations—to practicability, in short. But once set in the artist's understanding, they are not likely to change for many years. They constitute the whole shape and substance of what is correctly called his "interpretation" of any score.   [6]

MASTERPIECES

June 25, 1944

The enjoyment and understanding of music are dominated in a most curious way by the prestige of the masterpiece. Neither the

theater nor the cinema nor poetry nor narrative fiction pays allegiance
to its ideal of excellence in the tyrannical way that music does. They
recognize no unbridgeable chasm between "great work" and the rest
of production. Even the world of art painting, though it is no less
a victim than that of music to Appreciation rackets based on the
concept of gilt-edged quality, is more penetrable to reason in this regard, since such values, or the pretenses about them advanced by investing collectors and museums, are more easily unmasked as efforts
to influence market prices. But music in our time (and in our country)
seems to be committed to the idea that first-class work in composition
is separable from the rest of music writing by a distinction as radical
as that recognized in theology between the elect and the damned. Or
at the very least by as rigorous an exclusion from glory as that which
formerly marked the difference between Mrs. Astor's Four Hundred
and the rest of the human race.

This snobbish definition of excellence is opposed to the classical
concept of a Republic of Letters. It reposes, rather, on the theocratic
idea that inspiration is less a privilege of the private citizen than of
the ordained prophet. Its weakness lies in the fact that music, though
it serves most becomingly as religion's handmaiden, is not a religion.
Music does not deal in general ideas of morality or salvation. It is an
art. It expresses private sentiments through skill and sincerity, both
of which last are a privilege, a duty, indeed, of the private citizen, and
no monopoly of the prophetically inclined.

In the centuries when artistic skills were watched over by guilds of
workmen, a masterpiece was nothing more than a graduation piece, a
work that marked the student's advance from apprenticeship to master
status. Later the word was used to mean any artist's most accomplished work, the high point of his production. It came thus to represent no corporate judgment, but any consumer's private one. Nowadays most people understand by it a piece differing from the run of
repertory by a degree of concentration in its expressivity that estab-
lishes a difference of kind. And certain composers (Beethoven was the
first of them) are considered to have worked consciously in that
vein. The idea that any composer, however gifted and skillful, is
merely a masterpiece factory would have been repellent to Bach or
Haydn or Handel or Mozart, though Gluck was prone to advertise
himself as just that. But all the successors of Beethoven who aspired
to his position of authority—Brahms and Bruckner and Wagner and
Mahler and Tchaikovsky—quite consciously imbued their music with
the "masterpiece" tone.

This tone is lugubrious, portentous, world-shaking; and length, as

well as heavy instrumentation, is essential to it. Its reduction to ab-
surdity is manifest today through the later symphonies of Shostakovitch. Advertised frankly and cynically as owing their particular
character to a political directive imposed on their author by state disci-
plinary action, they have been broadcast throughout the United Nations as models of patriotic expression. And yet rarely in the history
of music has any composer ever spread his substance so thin. Attention
is not even required for their absorption. Only Anton Rubinstein's
once popular symphony, *The Ocean*, ever went in for so much water.
They may have some value as national advertising, though I am not
convinced they do; but their passive acceptance by musicians and
music lovers can certainly not be due to their melodic content (in-
offensive as this is) or to their workmanship (roughly competent as
this is, too.)

What imposes about them is their obvious masterpiece-style one-
trackness, their implacable concentration on what they are doing.
. . . But that what these pieces are up to in any musical sense, chiefly
rehashing bits of Borodin and Mahler, is of much intrinsic musical
interest I have yet to hear averred by a musician. And that is the whole
trouble with the masterpiece cult. It tends to substitute an impressive
manner for specific expression, just as oratory does.   [7]

AMERICANISMS

January 27, 1946

For all the vaunted virtuosity of the American symphony orchestras, your correspondent has long wondered what, if any, has been,
or is likely to be, their contribution to art. American ensemble playing
on the popular level has given to the world two, perhaps three, expressive devices of absolute originality. One is a new form of tempo
rubato, a way of articulating a melody so loosely that its metrical
scansion concords at almost no point with that of its accompaniment,
the former enjoying the greatest rhythmic freedom while the latter
continues in strictly measured time. Another characteristically American device is playing "blue," using for melodic expression constant
departures from conventionally correct pitch in such a way that these
do not obscure or contradict the basic harmony, which keeps to
normal tuning. Simultaneous observance of these two dichotomies,
one metrical and one tonal, constitute a style of playing known as
"hot." And although precedents for this are not unknown in folklore

and even in European art custom, our systematization of it is a gift to music.

Another device by which our popular ensembles depart from European habits is the execution of a volume crescendo without any acceleration of tempo. It is possible that Sebastian Bach may have played the organ without speeding up the louder passages, but Bach did not know the volume crescendo as we conceive it. He only knew platforms of loudness. The smooth and rapid increase of sound from very soft to very loud and back again is a Romantic invention. It is possible, even today, only with a fairly numerous orchestra or chorus, on a pianoforte or on the accordion. It is the basic novelty of musical Romanticism; and the nineteenth century invented a fluid rhythmic style, in which pulsations were substituted for strict metrics, to give to the planned crescendo a semblance of spontaneity.

It was the conductor Maurice Abravanel who first called my attention to the rarity of the non-accelerating crescendo in European musical execution. It has long been used to suggest armies approaching and then going off into the distance, its rhythmic regularity being easily evocative of marching. But aside from this special employment, it is foreign to Romantic thought. If you want to get a laugh out of yourself, just try applying it to Wagner or Chopin or Liszt or Brahms or Beethoven or even Debussy. These authors require a fluid rhythmic articulation. And though one may, for rhetorical purposes, as when approaching a peroration, get slower instead of faster as the volume mounts, it is obviously inappropriate in Romantic music to execute a subjectively expressive crescendo or decrescendo without speeding up or slowing down.

The modern world, even in Europe, has long recognized the rhythmically steady crescendo as, in theory, a possible addition to the terraced dynamics of the eighteenth century symphony. In fact, however, European composers have never, to my knowledge, used it without a specifically evocative purpose. Of the three most famous crescendos in modern music not one is both tonally continuous and rhythmically steady. Strauss's *Elektra* is tonally continuous, rising in waves from beginning to end; but it presupposes no exact metrics. Stravinsky's "Dance of the Adolescents" (from *The Rite of Spring*) and Ravel's *Bolero* do presuppose a metrically strict rendering, but they are not tonally steady crescendos. They are as neatly terraced as any Bach organ fugue.

The completely steady crescendo is natural to American musical thought. Our theater orchestras execute it without hesitation or embarrassment. Our popular orchestrators call for it constantly and get it. Our symphonic composers call for it constantly and rarely get it. The conductors of European formation, who lead most of our symphonic ensembles, simply do not understand it. Very few of them understand metrical exactitude in any form. American music, nevertheless, requires a high degree of metrical exactitude, emphasized by merely momentary metrical liberties. Also lots of crescendo, which is our passion. The music of Barber and Schuman and Piston and Hanson and Copland and Harris and Bernstein and Gershwin and Cowell and Sowerby and Randall Thompson and William Grant Still is full of crescendos. It is also full of rhythmic and metrical irregularities. But none of it is romantic music in the European sense, because the crescendos and the rhythmic irregularities are not two aspects of the same device. The separation of these devices is as characteristic of American musical thought as is our simultaneous use of free meter with strict meter and free with strict pitch. These three dichotomies are basic to our musical speech.

Hearing Howard Hanson or Leonard Bernstein conduct American music is a pleasure comparable to hearing Pierre Monteux conduct French music or Bruno Walter interpret Mahler and Bruckner. The reading is at one with the writing. Our foreign-born conductors have given the American composer a chance to hear his own work. Also, they have built up among the public a certain toleration of American music, or encouraged, rather, a toleration that has always existed. But they have built up also a certain resistance to it which did not exist here previous to the post-Civil War German musical invasion. That resistance comes from a complete lack of adaptation on the part of the European-trained to American musical speech. They understand its international grammar, but they have not acquired its idiom and accent.

In so far as they are aware that there are an idiom and an accent (as several of them are), they are likely to mistake these for localisms of some kind. They are nothing of the sort, they are a contribution to the world's musical language, as many postwar Europeans are beginning to suspect. American popular music has long been admired abroad, but American art music is just beginning to be discovered. It would probably be a good idea for us here to keep one step ahead of the foreign market by building up a record library of American works in authoritative renderings by American-trained artists. Also to accustom our own public to this kind of authoritative collaboration. We shall need both a professional tradition and broad public support for it if we are to accept with any confidence the world-wide distribution of

American music that seems to be imminent, in view of the world-wide demand.

Actually we are producing very nearly the best music in the world. Only France, of all the other music-exporting countries, operates by stricter standards both of workmanship and of originality. Not Germany nor Italy nor Russia nor England nor Mexico nor Brazil is producing music in steady quantity that is comparable in quality to that of the American school. And we are a school. Not because I say so, but because we have a vocabulary that anybody can recognize, I think, once it is pointed out, as particular to us. [8]

ROGER SESSIONS
1896–

Not a prolific composer, Sessions polishes all his works to a high degree. Frequently their complexity makes them hard to understand on first hearing, but as he says in *The Musical Experience* (1950): "The key to the understanding of contemporary music lies in repeated hearing; one must hear it till it sounds familiar."

Logic and clarity are the outstanding characteristics of his music and writing. Consequently, he is an extraordinary pedagogue, and has spent many years teaching theory and composition at Smith College, the Cleveland Institute—here he was assistant to his own teacher, Ernest Bloch—Princeton University and the University of California. His textbook, *Harmonic Practice* (1951), written as a result of his wide teaching experience, is one of the most excellent of contemporary works on musical theory. His point of view is always fresh and original, as the following excerpts effectively suggest.

A champion of modern music, he collaborated with Aaron Copland in the Copland-Sessions Musicals, in 1928. He has served on the jury of the International Society for Contemporary Music, on the executive board of the League of Composers, and is also a member of the executive committee of the American Composers' Alliance.

THE AMERICAN FUTURE

From: A Letter to *Modern Music*, 1940

A certain number of our musicians, together with a not negligible part of our musical press, is demanding with a voice quite reminiscent of various totalitarian phrases which we have heard, that music which shall "express the national feeling," "reflect the American scene," "establish an American Style"—as if these were in any sense measurable or specific quantities, or as if they were in any sense criteria or even basic ingredients of musical quality. We hear frequent statements to the effect that "European music is played out," that "American composers are doing in every way better work than their European contemporaries."

The demand for "national" art is fundamentally a defensive attitude, the reflex action of a pervasive inferiority complex. If American composers tend to think of musical life in terms of competition, it is not merely a quite false analogy taken over from the business world, but a sign of their own self-consciousness which may make them think of musical development in egocentric terms rather than in terms of music itself. If they are self-conscious and hypersensitive with respect to "European" music, it is only to a very small extent because of real or fancied slights which have been dealt them in the name of European tradition; for these would prove largely quite illusory and in any case quite negligible if they had really found themselves and were primarily absorbed in their own creative impulses. But just as the valetudinarian frequently becomes, through excessive preoccupation with his health, the victim of his own hypochondria, the artist who is excessively afraid of "influences" or insistent on the purity of his origins tends to wither from lack of nourishment. A consciously "national" style, in any field, inevitably becomes a picturesque mannerism, a kind of trade-mark, devoid of significant human content, irremediably outmoded the moment its novelty has gone. Of the Russian "Five," how much music remains in the vital repertory? And in the music of Moussorgsky himself, is it not precisely what is most specifically "Russian" which has aged most quickly? How much remains of the French "School" which throve with such apparent luxuriance as a spiritual result of the disaster of 1870, in seeming unawareness that Chopin and Berlioz and Bizet were also Frenchmen, though quite unpreoccupied with the idea of a "national" style?

For vital music is characterized far less by somewhat academic purity than by the range and depth of its expression; great composers have been so by virtue of influences absorbed and transcended, not through scrupulous avoidance of contagion or through self-conscious direction of their impulses into channels "national" or otherwise. They have expressed themselves, in other words, as men, and have not scrupled to draw their nourishment from all promising sources, since it would never have occurred to them to question their own digestive capacities.

My second cause for concern is that the nationalistic attitude tends to remove composers, through the artificial isolation which they thereby assume, from the realities of their art, since it is indeed to a considerable extent a pretext for escape from those realities. Especially in a country like ours, in which development has been inevitably so rapid, there is always the danger of superficiality; and the establishment of specialized criteria leads all too easily to a neglect of the fundamental requirements of the art. Hence in asking that music be American we almost inevitably neglect to demand that it be music—that it spring from a genuine and mature impulse on the part of the composer and be more than simply a more or less promising attempt. I am not speaking here of technical inadequacy but of the half-baked quality, the undefiniteness, which we so often tend to mistake for vitality. No amount of "technical" proficiency can compensate for a lack of the basic spiritual discipline which alone can produce a mature artist. Composers, to be sure, are born, not made. But once born, they must grow; and far more composers are born than ever come to real fruition. "Talent" and "promise" are exceedingly common, and one need not be unduly impressed by them when they so often remain at that primitive stage. They can never get past that stage unless artists demand of themselves something more than provincialism.

For nationalistic criteria are, in the last analysis, quite unreal. I do not really believe that our advocates of "American" music would be seriously content with a picturesque folklore or with the musical reproduction, either specific or general, of American scenes or landscapes —we are quite adequately supplied with these in our popular music and various other manifestations. A nation is something far greater than that: it is, rather, the sum of a great many efforts towards goals which are essentially human and not parochial. It gains much of its character, no doubt, from the conditions of time and space under which those efforts are made. But it is the efforts and the goals which are really essential. So how on earth can we demand in advance, qualities which can reveal themselves only gradually, in works, the products of clear artistic vision? It is such works which, if and when they come into existence, will reveal America to us, not as the mirror of things already discovered, but as a constantly renewed and fresh experience of the realities which music alone can reveal. It seems to me so clear that this was the real achievement of the great music of the past. Bach and Mozart and Beethoven did not *reflect* Germany, they helped to create it; they brought in each instance new and unexpected, but essential materials to its construction. And only after the picture had really begun to take clear shape, through the influence of their finished work, was it possible to point with some certainty to specifically German characteristics in their art. It is not, moreover, as "German" composers that we value them, but rather we value Germany because of them, as creators of immortal music. What is "German" in their works and that of their lesser colleagues is purely incidental, an inevitable but unimportant by-product of music that is real and complete. So what we most ask of our composers is not "American" music, but something much more exacting and at the same time essentially simpler—*music* in the only real sense of the word—music, that is, which is deeply and completely conceived, the product of a mature vision of life.   [1]

From: Lectures held in the summer of 1949

LISTENING TO MUSIC

We find that listening to music, as we understand it, is a relatively late, a relatively sophisticated, and even a rather artificial means of access to it, and that even until fairly recent times composers presumably did not think of their music primarily as being listened to, but rather as being played and sung, or at most as being heard incidentally as a part of an occasion, of which the center of attention for those who heard it lay elsewhere than in the qualities of the music as such.

In fact, composer, performer and listener can, without undue exaggeration, be regarded not only as three types or degrees of relationship to music, but also as three successive stages of specialization. In the beginning, no doubt, the three were one. Music was vocal or instrumental improvisation; and while there were those who did not perform, and who therefore heard music, they were not listeners in our modern sense of the word. They heard the sounds as part of a ritual, a drama, or an epic narrative, and accepted it in its purely incidental or symbolic function, subordinate to the occasion of which it was a part. Music, in and for itself can hardly be said to have existed, and whatever individual character it may have had was essentially irrelevant.

Later, however, as certain patterns became fixed or traditional, the functions of composer and performer began to be differentiated. The composer existed precisely because he had introduced into the raw material of sound and rhythm patterns that became recognizable and therefore capable of repetition—which is only another way of saying that composers began to exist when music began to take shape. The composer began to emerge as a differentiated type exactly at the moment that a bit of musical material took on a form that its producer felt impelled to repeat.

The same event produced the performer in his separate function; the first performer was, in the strictest sense, the first musician who played or sang something that had been played or sung before. His type became more pronounced in the individual who first played or sang music composed by someone other than himself. At both of these points the performer's problems began to emerge, and whether or not he was aware of the fact, his problems and his characteristic solutions and points of view began to appear at the same time.

It hardly need be pointed out that the relation to music of the listener is even more complex than that of the performer. As I have pointed out, the listener, as we think of him today, came fairly recently on the musical scene. Listening to music, as distinct from reproducing it, is the product of a very late stage in musical sophistication, and it might with reason be maintained that the listener has existed as such only for about three hundred and fifty years. The composers of the Middle Ages and the Renaissance composed their music for church services and for secular occasions, where it was accepted as part of the general background, in much the same manner as were the frescoes decorating the church walls or the sculptures adorning the public buildings. Or else they composed it for amateurs, who had received musical training as a part of general education, and whose relationship with it was that of the performer responding to it through active participation in its production. Even well into the nineteenth century the musical public consisted largely of people whose primary contact with music was through playing or singing in the privacy of their own homes. For them concerts were in a certain sense occasional rituals which they attended as adepts, and they were the better equipped as listeners because of their experience in participating, however humbly and however inadequately, in the actual process of musical production. By the "listener," I do not mean the person who simply hears music, who is present when it is performed and who, in a general way, may either enjoy or dislike it, but who is in no sense a real participant in it. To listen implies rather a real participation, a response, a real sharing in the work of the composer and of the performer, and a greater or less degree of awareness of the individual and specific sense of the music performed. For the listener, in this sense, music is no longer an incident or an adjunct but an independent and self-sufficient medium of expression. His ideal aim is to apprehend to the fullest and most complete possible extent the musical utterance of the composer as the performer delivers it to him.   [2]

THE COMPOSER'S INDICATIONS

Composers have always, I believe, set down in scores everything they considered necessary for the performer's guidance; and the evolution of musical notation, the development of increasing subtlety, has been the result not of an independent effort but of the development of music itself. Certainly this has been true in recent history. If Bach, for instance, was sparing in dynamic indications, this was only partly owing to the fact that he himself was able to supervise the performance of his works and therefore could afford to neglect such matters. Still less, certainly, is it the result, as has sometimes been assumed, of any taboo against so-called expressive performance. One must assume that musicians of Bach's generation and before were as sensitive to the expressive modelling of phrases, to clear and discriminating stressing of accents, to the throwing of contrasts into relief, even to subtle inflections in tempo, as musicians have always been. In a similar sense it is impossible to conceive of composers like Josquin des Près, Orlando di Lasso, even Palestrina, urging their singers to suppress the natural eloquence of vocal inflection in order to achieve the complete neutrality of effect which is sometimes even today demanded as requisite for the performance of this music, and for which the composers of the Renaissance are sometimes held up as models.

Yet why did they not indicate minute dynamic changes and inflections of movement in their texts, as later composers learned to do? Was it, perhaps, because they simply had not thought of doing so, either because, as I have pointed out in connection with Bach, they were so frequently involved in the performance of their works and therefore inclined to rely on something like a so-called "oral tradition" passed from one musician to another? Or was it because the musical sense was at that time so fresh, so sure of its roots, and so uncontaminated by various influences that have in later ages tended to corrupt it, that it never occurred to these early composers that their interpreters could go astray?

I am not a music historian, and though I am not unacquainted with various phases of music history, I shall not attempt to answer these questions from an historical point of view. Furthermore, I feel that the historical approach to all such matters is not likely to give us the real answer. We would do better to start with the fairly plausible premise that the best composers were serious and mature musicians who brought to their work the whole, and not merely a part of their powers, and on that basis to try to see the situation as it appeared to them.

By this approach to the question we come, I think, to the following conclusions: First of all, composers of all times have demanded of performers whatever liveliness and eloquence the latter could give. They have not, however, attempted to indicate the intangible factors in performance, and being men of experience as well as common sense, they have known full well that these factors, which make all the difference, indeed, between a good performance and a bad one, cannot conceivably be indicated in any score.

What composers have always tried to indicate in the clearest possible manner are the essential contours of the music, and the means required of the performer in order to make these clear. Whatever tempo and dynamic indications the composer gives are those he considers quite necessary for this purpose. They are functional in intent and are included because the composer feels they are needed in order to lay bare the proportions, to underline the contrasts, and to clarify, through articulation and through various types and gradations of accent, the rhythmic outlines of his score. Their function is to illuminate the form of the work by throwing its outlines into sharper relief.

Bach frequently, though by no means always, set off his contrasts by dynamic indications of the very simplest type: piano and forte, which always indicate generalized and large scale contrasts. In the music of later composers, the sharper the essential contrasts on which the music is built, the more carefully the composer indicates and emphasizes these contrasts by nuances of all kinds. The tendency to minute indications runs in the most striking parallel to the development of minute elaboration and sharp contrast in musical detail, and the nuances are in the score, as always, for the purpose of throwing the detail into more drastic relief.

Any composer of the first magnitude may be cited in illustration of this fact. Possibly Beethoven's scores offer as good an illustration as any, since Beethoven stands, as it were, on the peak dividing the eighteenth and the nineteenth centuries and certainly partakes of both. His vast musical designs are not only completely integrated but, far more than those of any composer before him, they are extraordinarily rich in contrast and detail. It is for this reason that he carried the use of so-called expressive nuance so far, and what is amazing, and in itself worth years of study, is the absolute mastery—of one piece with his mastery of the design as a whole, and in fact one aspect of it—with which, by means of the nuances, he illuminates every essential detail of the whole and always in relation to this whole, that is, to the largest line.

To speak of dynamic and rhythmic nuances in this connection as "functional" is not to deny that they are essentially expressive. My intention is rather to demonstrate what is certainly obvious to all mature musicians: the expression, or espressivo, or expressivity, is in the music itself from the beginning and is not imposed from without. To perform a piece of music correctly, one plays not only the notes; one plays, in the first place, not so much notes as motifs, phrases, periods, sections, the rhythmic groups or the impulses of which the music is composed. One sets them in the relationship to each other which the composer has indicated. And I firmly believe that a certain type of instrumental instruction which teaches students first to learn notes and then, as it is quaintly put, to "put in the expression," is not only musically but instrumentally false. But what is 'espressivo,' if not the accentuating of contrasts, the throwing of contours into relief? In the music of Beethoven and those who came after him—in fact one may eventually say all the music of the tonal and the post-tonal period—the espressivo is in the music itself and nowhere else. It is in the structure of the music and, in the last analysis, is identical with this structure.   [3]

THE PERFORMER'S FUNCTION

What, then, is the task of the performer? Is it simply fidelity to the composer's text, or is the performer himself a creative artist for whom the music performed is simply a vehicle for the expression of his personality?

Stated thus, the most obvious comment is that it is not 'simply' either one of these things, or, in fact, simply anything at all. In what consists 'fidelity' to the text? What constitutes 'personality'? Let us acknowledge at the outset that fidelity is fidelity, or truth; infidelity is falsehood. Are we to be understood, then, as asking whether or not the performer shall give a true or a false performance of the music? For after all, if the performer plays, let us say, a crescendo where a diminuendo is indicated, he is playing as surely falsely as he would should he sound F sharp where the composer has asked for G.

What makes both of the above questions absurd is the word 'simply.' For in the first place, fidelity to the composer's text is anything but simple, since the text itself is already very complex. It is complex because the composer has attempted to indicate (I can find no better word) by means of a vastly complex system of symbols the essentials of what I have called a musical gesture. And yet, as I have also tried to imply, a gesture, if it is to be living and genuinely expressive, must be unique; it must go beyond mere mechanical repetition and be invested with fresh energy if it is to live in time. Paradoxically enough, it cannot be really perpetuated in any other way; this is the very condition of its existence and, above all, of its endurance. For the listener—the person who responds to the music, who re-creates it, either internally or externally—will respond to the musical gesture only as long as it strikes him freshly, or as long as he is capable of apprehending it as created anew and not as something mechanically repeated.

The agent of this re-creation is the imagination of the performer, or, if you will, his "personality." It is his task, and I believe his whole task, to apply his imagination to discovering the musical gestures inherent in the composer's text, and then to reproducing them according to his own lights; that is, with fullest participation on his own part. This is only another way of saying that, having discovered as well as he can the composer's intentions, he must then apply himself to the task of reproducing them with the utmost conviction. It seems to me clear and beyond all doubt that both elements—fidelity, not so much to the text as to the music as expressed in the text, and conviction as animated by the musical nature of the performer—are essential. Without fidelity, a performance is false; without conviction, it is lifeless; in other words, it is hardly music.   [4]

MECHANICAL REPRODUCTION

The point which cannot be made too clear or understood too thoroughly is that music, just because it is an art in which time and movement are the basic elements, needs constant renewal. This principle is extremely difficult to formularize and is full of pitfalls; but it is none the less real for that reason. Perhaps we can understand it most clearly if we consider a certain inherent limitation of that most useful instrument, the gramophone. I need not dwell on the fact of its usefulness, nor expatiate on the incredible advantages won through its invention and development. Any musician could add to the list of those advantages; and we of the mid-twentieth century are acquainted enough with the ordinary facts of technology to take it for granted that purely technical limitations can either be ignored or overcome. We may be sure that machines will be constantly improved and that reproductions will be constantly perfected. But what will never be overcome are the diminishing returns inherent in mechanical reproduction as such. We can listen to a recording and derive a maximum of pleasure from it just as long as it remains to a degree unfamiliar. It ceases to have interest for us, however, the instant we become aware of that fact of literal repetition, of mechanical reproduction, when we know and can anticipate exactly how a given phrase is going to be modelled, exactly how long a given fermata is to be held, exactly what quality of accent or articulation, of acceleration or retard, will occur at a given moment. When the music ceases to be fresh for us in this sense, it ceases to be alive, and we can say in the most real sense that it ceases to be music. [5]

CONTINUITY IN MUSICAL THOUGHT AND FORM

The past is never, as our jargon implies, a fixed quantity; it is in movement. If we regard it clearly, we see it moving toward us, and if we set out to meet it, we find that it sees itself quite differently from the way we see it. Mozart, for his contemporaries, was not the serene classic, the apostle of measure and perfection, that so many of his admirers of the nineteenth century, and even some of those of today, have liked to conjure up. On the contrary, he was for them a painter of intense and even sombre canvases, of large scope and vast design, whom Lorenzo da Ponte is said on one occasion to have coupled in comparison with Dante of the *Inferno*. [6]

UNDERSTANDING CONTEMPORARY MUSIC

The key to the understanding of contemporary music lies in repeated hearing; one must hear it till it sounds familiar, until one begins to notice false notes if they are played. One must make the effort to retain it in one's ear, and one will always find that the accurate memory of sounds heard coincides with the understanding of them. In fact, the power to retain sounds by memory implies that they have been mastered. For the ear by its nature seeks out patterns and relationships, and it is only these patterns that we can remember and that make music significant for us. [7]

GEORGE GERSHWIN

1898–1937

On the evening of February 12, 1924, a musical event at Aeolian Hall in New York caused a greater stir in the United States than almost any American concert before or since. It was the première of George Gershwin's *Rhapsody in Blue*, one of the first efforts to pour jazz music into a symphonic mold. The form of the *Rhapsody in Blue* was practically that of Liszt's *Hungarian Rhapsody*, for piano and orchestra. Its racy, jazzy first theme, its very opening clarinet glissando upswing (not actually Gershwin's, but the discovery of a clever jazz clarinet player), its nostalgia, and its raucousness instantly captured the imagination of its hearers.

Gershwin had begun as a "song plugger" for Jerome H. Remick and Co., and had written a number of successful popular tunes, followed by equally successful show tunes in musical comedies. The reception of the *Rhapsody in Blue*, commissioned by Paul Whiteman who wanted a "classical" piece for his Aeolian Hall concert, gave Gershwin serious ambitions. He began the study of orchestration (Ferde Grofé had scored the *Rhapsody*) and followed his first triumph with the *Concerto in F*, commissioned and first conducted by Walter Damrosch, with Gershwin at the piano. A trip to France resulted in *An American in Paris*. His opera, *Porgy and Bess*, to DuBose Heyward's libretto, has had as great applause in Europe as in the United States.

Whether, as his staunch admirers believe or his critics deny, Gershwin was or would have become one of America's very great composers is of less concern than the fact that his music does express, as Merle Armitage says in his memorial volume to Gershwin, "the excitement, the nervousness and the movement of America."

From an Article written in 1933
AMERICAN AND EUROPEAN RECIPROCAL INFLUENCES

Unquestionably modern musical America has been influenced by modern musical Europe. But it seems to me that modern European composers, in turn, have very largely received their stimulus, their rhythms and impulses from Machine Age America. They have a much older tradition of musical technique which has helped them put into musical terms a little more clearly the thoughts that originated here. They can express themselves more glibly.

The Machine Age has influenced practically everything. I do not mean only music, but everything from the arts to finance. The machine has not affected our age in form as much as in tempo, speed and sound. It has affected us in sound whenever composers utilize new instruments to imitate its aspects. In my *American in Paris* I used four taxi horns for musical effect. George Antheil has used everything, including aeroplane propellers, door bells, typewriter keys, and so forth. By the use of the old instruments, too, we are able to obtain modern effects. Take a composition like Honegger's *Pacific 231*, written and dedicated to a steam engine. It reproduces the whole effect of a train stopping and starting, and it is all done with familiar instruments.

IDEAS AND FEELING

There is only one important thing in music and that is ideas plus feeling. The various tonalities and sound mean nothing unless they grow out of ideas. Not many composers have ideas. Far more of them know how to use strange instruments which do not require ideas. Whoever has inspired ideas will write the great music of our period. We are plowing the ground for that genius who may be alive or may be born today or tomorrow. If he is alive, he is recognized to a certain degree, although it is impossible for the public at large to assimilate real greatness quickly. Take a composer like Bach. In his lifetime, he was recognized as one of the greatest organists in the world, but he was not acclaimed as one of the greatest composers of his time or of all time until generations after his death.

JAZZ

It is difficult to determine what enduring values, aesthetically, jazz has contributed, because jazz is a word which has been used for at least five or six different types of music. It is really a conglomeration of many things. It has a little bit of ragtime, the blues, classicism and spirituals. Basically, it is a matter of rhythm. Intervals come after rhythm in importance, music intervals which are peculiar to the rhythm. After all, there is nothing new in music. I maintained years ago that there is very little difference in the music of different nations. There is just that little individual touch. One country may prefer a peculiar rhythm or a note like the seventh. This it stresses, and it becomes identified with that nation. In America this preferred rhythm is called jazz. Jazz is music, it uses the same notes that Bach used. When jazz is played in another nation, it is called American. When it is played in another country it sounds false. Jazz is the result of the energy stored up in America. It is a very energetic kind of music, noisy, boisterous and even vulgar. One thing is certain. Jazz has contributed an enduring value to America in the sense that it has expressed ourselves. It is an original American achievement which will endure, not as jazz perhaps, but which will leave its mark on future music in one form or another. The only kinds of music which endure are those which possess form in the universal sense of folk music. All else dies. But unquestionably folk songs are being written and have been written which contain enduring elements of jazz. To be sure, that is only an element, it is not the whole. An entire composition written in jazz could not live.

EMOTION

Music is a phenomenon that to me has a very marked effect on the emotions. It can have various effects. It has the power of moving people to all of the various moods. Through the emotions, it can have a cleansing effect on the mind, a disturbing effect, a drowsy effect, an exciting effect. I do not know to what extent it can finally become a part of the people. I do not think music as we know it now is indispensable, although we have music all around us in some form or other. There is music in the wind. People can live more or less satisfactorily without orchestral music, for instance. And who can tell that we would not be better off if we weren't as civilized as we are, if we lacked many of our emotions? But we have them, and we are more or less egotistic about them. We think that they are important and that they make us what we are. We think that we are an improvement over people of other ages who didn't have them. Music has become a very important part of civilization, and one of the main reasons is that one does not need a formal education to appreciate it. Music can be appreciated by a person who can neither read nor write, and it can also be appreciated by people who have the highest form of intelligence. For example, Einstein plays the violin and listens to music. People in the underworld, dope fiends and gun men, invariably are music lovers, or at least they are affected by it. Music is entering into medicine. Music sets up a certain vibration which unquestionably results in a physical reaction. Eventually the proper vibration for every person will be found and utilized. I like to think of music as an emotional science.

MECHANICAL MUSIC

The composer, in my estimation, has been helped a great deal by the mechanical reproduction of music. Music is written to be heard, and any instrument that tends to help it to be heard more frequently and by greater numbers is advantageous to the person who writes it. . . .

The radio and the phonograph are harmful to the extent that they bastardize music and give currency to a lot of cheap things. They are not harmful to the composer. The more people listen to music, the more they will be able to criticize it and know when it is good. When we speak of machine-made music, however, we are not speaking of music in the highest sense, because, no matter how much the world becomes a Machine Age, music will have to be created in the same old way. The Machine Age can affect music only in its distribution. Composers must compose in the same way the old composers did. No one has found a new method in which to write music. We still use the old signatures, the old symbols. The composer has to do every bit of his work himself. Handwork can never be replaced in the composition of music. If music ever became machine-made in that sense, it would cease to be an art. [1]

FRANCIS POULENC

1899–

From the outset of his career Poulenc created a stir with his clever, effective compositions. His *Rapsodie nègre*, *Cocardes* and the three *Mouvements perpétuels* for piano, written at the age of 19, attracted universal attention. Spare, using only the most necessary notes, his music contrasted sharply with the Impressionistic music which had preceded it. This youthful prodigy, almost completely self-taught, and strongly influenced by music hall and popular tunes, gave French music a fresh, lively, if superficial turn.

Since the war, however, his music has taken on a more serious character. To the text of Paul Eluard he has written a profound choral work, *Figure humaine* (1943), and his songs, notably *Le Pont de C*, are earnest, moving, and may be ranked with many of the finest German lieder.

In recent years Poulenc twice toured the United States as accompanist for the baritone Pierre Bernac, who interpreted many of the composer's songs. The following notes are culled from interviews with critics and his own American diary.

From: *Feuilles Americaines*, 1950

TRADITION

We come to the problem of tradition and must deplore the fact that tradition is such a precarious thing. It is really astonishing how, only thirty years after Debussy's death, the exact meaning of his message has been lost. How many of his interpreters, themselves lacking in sensuality, betray Debussy! The word 'sensuality' stuns my interviewer. I perceive that this is a term which he is not in the habit of applying to music.

"You undoubtedly mean eroticism?"

"Not necessarily, sensuality sometimes being a more gratuitous form of eroticism."

Then, passing over to a more concrete example, I explain to him that if Toscanini has revealed *La Mer* and Sabata has revealed *Jeux* to the public, it is because, as true Italians not blushing for Puccini (bravo!), they do not understand how we can escape the Massenet aspect of many pages of Debussy. I must add that a conductor, by placing *Jeux* in a refrigerator, and another, placing it in a sterilizer, do more harm to this jewel than silence.   [1]

YOUNG AMERICAN COMPOSERS

Heard this afternoon some works by young American composers. Gifted, certainly, lots of health, some technique, drive; but how dangerous are the lessons taken from the great composer-teachers. In Los Angeles the young musicians write like Schoenberg, in Boston like Hindemith. Milhaud alone, to the gratitude of his students, maintains in San Francisco a climate of eclecticism. I could wish for American youth more masters like Gédalge and Leroux.[1]   [2]

MENOTTI'S *CONSUL*

What a strange success is *The Consul*, a three-act opera by Menotti! What an astounding instinct for the stage! Menotti has served at once as composer, librettist and director. From this ensemble results a prodigious cohesion, but one which is not without injury to the music. In my opinion this is a grave defect. In Verdi or Puccini the music is always sovereign. Here not. But what ingenuity, what strength, what power of persuasion! Seized by the drama, an audience of stylish first-nighters forgot, for once, to look one another over, left the theater with eyes red and beating hearts.   [3]

THE CHARACTER OF FRENCH MUSIC

Statement to Roland Gelatt, 1950

You will find sobriety and dolor in French music just as in German or Russian. But the French have a keener sense of proportion. We realize that sombreness and good humor are not mutually exclusive. Our composers, too, write profound music, but when they do, it is leavened with that lightness of spirit without which life would be unendurable.   [4]

[1] André Gédalge (1856–1926), professor at the Paris Conservatoire, where Honegger, Milhaud, Ravel, and Poulenc's teacher Koechlin were among his pupils; Xavier Leroux (1863–1919), also professor at the Conservatoire, teacher of Milhaud.

GEORGES AURIC

1899–

Among the most arresting film scores to come out of France of late years are those of Auric, the youngest member of "Les Six." *Moulin Rouge*, the American film depicting the life of Toulouse-Lautrec, is also accompanied by an Auric score.

One of Auric's first claims to public notice was *Les Fâcheux* (1923), incidental music to the Molière play, later transformed into a ballet for Diaghilev's Ballets Russes. *Les Matelots* (1925) is another of his best-known works.

A pupil of D'Indy, as a young lad Auric came under the influence of Satie. He idolized Satie and wrote a laudatory preface to the older man's ballet *Parade*, but theirs was a mercurial friendship. A quarrel between them led to a break which Auric tried to mend, but which Satie quietly allowed to remain.

The warm essay, "Découverte de Satie," which appeared in the issue of the *Revue Musicale* entirely devoted to Satie, is a tribute to the wit, integrity and musical gifts of Auric's "bon maître."

DISCOVERY OF SATIE

From: *Revue Musicale*, Paris, June 1952.

"Will I be a 'great pianist' some day?"—The serious, eager boy I was at twelve asked himself this question while spinning out scale after scale, indefatigably repeating the same measures of a Bach partita, a Beethoven sonata or a Mendelssohn concerto.

I was living at Montpellier, where the masterpieces of Lassus, Jannequin and Costeley had been revealed to me at an excellent provincial schola . . . Mlle Blanche Selva, definitely an extraordinary artist, too soon forgotten, had kindly given me some lessons. Yes, to become a "great pianist" later would certainly be grand! But, after all, why not become—perhaps—a composer?

I was not long in discovering Debussy and Ravel, whose most daring works (these were still far from winning the audience and enthusiastic approval they now enjoy) I tried to read off at sight quickly. Playing truant from my harmony class, I rushed to a music shop whose owner, as soon as he saw me, handed me, with a conspiratorial smile, the first volume of Debussy *Préludes*. Alfred Cortot, I believe, had just introduced them to the Parisian public. And I was amazed at the *Valses nobles et sentimentales* which this same public had received with chaste reserve inexplicable to me.

A little later I happened on an issue of the magazine *Musica*. How could I immediately have foreseen the importance this author was to have for me? Although later I was to have the chance to read and re-read his *Sarabandes*, they made an immediate impression on me. I had already learned to admire another "Sarabande" in the lovely suite *Pour le piano* by Claude Debussy. How could I have explained to myself (and who could have explained to me) the strange relation in their harmonies, their character and their development?

Erik Satie: this obscure and bizarre name puzzled me, intrigued me . . . I had to wait several months before rediscovering it, but now I was faced with some disconcerting little problems. The few pieces I had managed to collect had been composed at widely separated dates. The same imagination governed the choice of their titles. "Airs à faire fuir" and "Danses de travers" (1897); "Morceaux en forme de poire" (1903); "Déscriptions automatiques" or "Embryons dessechés" (1913) . . . All this obviously went beyond the "Sites auriculaires" or the "Pavane pour une Infante défunte" of Ravel (this last a "classic" today, but a work one hardly dared place on a program at first) . . . And then, wasn't there also *Pas sur la neige* which Debussy had disconcertingly marked, "this rhythm must have the sonorous value of a mournful and icy landscape?"

I soon learned that the great Ricardo Viñes, for whom the entire younger school professed an admiration and gratitude easy to understand today, had just introduced the latest pages of Satie in Paris. The few squibs I read were rather guarded. This bizarre M. Satie seemed to be received without great enthusiasm. How could "these gentlemen," as he so politely referred to them, have consented to speak even a little seriously about a composer who did not hesitate to compromise his chances by writing in this way? The legend of a musical comedian and jokester quickly took hold and grew. Now, perhaps one should be able to pardon and somewhat understand the confusion engendered by titles which so readily suggested provocation, irony, or, dare I say, serious intent.

However, was it really out of line to recognize what gave these pages an accent, a color, a style until then unique? I have always believed—and I still believe—that very little art pleads for spontaneous acceptance more than does that of Satie. I hardly think his work requires any "initiation" and I can't imagine how one can *teach* a love for such an author or such an art. The two-part writing in the "Préludes flasques," their light counterpoint kept to its bare essentials, contrasted radically with the exquisite subtleties, the learned tricks which were enchanting the best ears of the day. One must not be hypocritically surprised at their astonishment, their reticence, their rejection of an author who dared present himself so modestly. His technique doubtless baffled his epoch by offering a lesson in simplification and renunciation which could not yet be appreciated at its full worth or in all its aspects.

In 1913 the "Satie case" was quickly judged, and back in my province, I followed the judgment of the capital with interest. Here, I learned, was an amateur, certainly "talented" but of a disturbing, lightweight turn of mind, and quite lazy—despite his strange idea of starting school again at forty, and attending classes at D'Indy's Schola Cantorum. His last works were of no value whatsoever, but a point was made of citing a few prophetic "finds" (his first efforts) which he had jotted down around his twentieth year. Concerning this, a letter to his brother in 1910 brings us—with a surface irony that need not fool us—the most moving testimony . . . "I was tired of being reproached for an ignorance of which I believed myself guilty, since competent people pointed it out in my works. After three years of unremitting labor I obtained a diploma in counterpoint at the Schola Cantorum. Proud of my knowledge, I began composing . . . I have been tongue-lashed in my poor life, but never was I so scorned. What right had I to have anything to do with D'Indy? I had written things of such profound charm before . . . Whereupon the "young bloods" organized an anti-D'Indy movement and played the "Sarabandes," the "Fils des étoiles," etc., works formerly and wrongly, according to the youngsters, considered the fruit of great ignorance. That's life, old man. Who can make head or tail of it?"

Yes, who could really make "head or tail of it"—and they didn't fail to let him feel it. Here was a man past forty who, wishing to revitalize himself, found the most unlikely way to offend "modern" ideas of beauty: a few short sketches, a transparent, quizzical art, a calm assurance in its presentation, and despite his obvious humility, that disconcertingly little, bantering touch which left no room for any aestheticism . . . At whom were they poking fun here?

As for me, I was immediately won over and held, not only because I was made aware of an art so remote from what I had admired until then, but also because of the new vistas it promised.

On my arrival in Paris in October, 1913, I wrote to Satie, sent him an article which Léon Vallas had just published in his *Revue Française de Musique*, and tried to express as best I could my juvenile admiration.

Unfortunately, I have lost his reply, the first letter from him whom I, with Roland-Manuel, was soon calling my "bon maître." It had a tone which I have never forgotten. "Your article, which is a study, is much too beautiful for me . . . I am not accustomed to such eulogies." He promised me a visit shortly which I awaited with easily imagined impatience. The day having come, I listened impatiently for the sound of the bell and rushed to open the door for him. "M. Auric?" my visitor inquired politely, surprised by this unexpected big boy who received him and who, he was pleased to discover, was the author of that famous "study."

Satie already had that beautiful passion for youth which he miraculously preserved until his death, and which made him generously greet every newcomer. I was soon proud of the friendship and the confidence which he showed me, and which I cannot separate, in my memory, from the long trousers I had been wearing but a few months.

So began the long visits which my "bon maître" got in the habit of making me, and which taught me, without doubt, much more than the majority of lessons and discussions of all the styles and genres in which I have taken part since. How describe a lunch with Satie? They lasted for hours, mingling funny recollections, reflections, sketches, the most unexpected bon mots which, despite apparent drollery, were intended to awaken curiosity and a passion for his field in an adolescent as unsettled as I still was. All this finished with long walks across Paris to the Place Denfert-Rochereau where I left him after a few stops in those saloons where Satie bravely mixed beer and calvados! Whereupon he would take off, always on foot, to reach his poor little room in Arceuil where he had lived since 1898.

Wearing the same bowler hat from one year's end to the next, his monacle set in his lively and amused eye, his beard carefully trimmed, his umbrella in his hand, so I still see that familiar, irresistible Socrates to whom I could have listened indefinitely. The "great" days were those on which he brought me one of the small notebooks in which he had copied, with extraordinary care, his latest compositions. Modest but sure of himself, knowing quite the true value of his work, and much more sensitive than one might have imagined to its reception, he was not too surprised at the reserve of his closest companions, and I am sure he was happy to feel the lively confidence of my friends and myself.

However, everything began to change for Satie during the war of 1914. Through Valentine Gross he had met Jean Cocteau, and the latter had immediately spoken about him to Serge Diaghilev. A ballet project quickly developed for which Picasso was asked to do the sets and costumes. For our "bon maître" a great day was dawning, a day which was in fact to prove quite sensational. What would this mysterious "great public" in Paris which combined balletomanes, dilettantes, and just simple souls who cannot resist the appeal of a poster and an attractive program, think of him?

Satie, without hurrying, worked at his score [*Parade*], bringing me each of his "numbers" as soon as it was completed, and playing and re-playing it with me I don't dare think how many times. I was astonished how much freshness this music brought me, opening wide the windows of the studios where the best of us were threatened with sterility. Leonide Massine, so Cocteau told us, was rehearsing the dancers chosen by Diaghilev with exemplary zeal, and Picasso, for his part, was preparing himself for his discovery by the theater world (the success which this truly magical début meant for him is now history).

The great day having arrived (May 18, 1917), with the auditorium of the Châtelet filled to the last aisle seat, the scandal broke, surpassing our worst conjectures. "To Berlin!" shouted respectable people, a prey to a kind of hysteria which, with the passing years, I can scarcely understand. No music, it seemed to me—it still seems to me—could have been clearer, and it certainly took M. Pierre Lalo to discover "insolence" in it. "Had I known it was so silly, I would have taken along the children!" This anonymous remark, overheard by Jean Cocteau, sums up rather benevolently the surprise and stupefaction of many simple souls . . . On top of which, as can be imagined, the press was judge and executioner, blasting the "three Boches": Satie, Picasso and Cocteau.

Our "bon maître," for once taking certain criticisms badly, replied with some incautious postcards (never write!), and had to suffer the thunderbolts of the courts as well as those of the newspapers. A shameful lawsuit led him to the dock and saw him condemned to a week in jail. "Public injury and defamation of character." For once the "Boche" paid. True, it concerned only a great French artist.

When all this had been forgotten and Diaghilev remounted *Parade*—finally received by a friendly public—Igor Stravinsky confided to me, on leaving the theater: "There are Bizet, Chabrier and Satie . . ."

This must have surprised some of the admirers of the *Sacre* when I repeated it to them. But, as for me, I thought of 1917, of the "boos" at the Châtelet, of the articles by "these gentlemen." I also thought of the "bon maître."

Could he have wished for more?   [1]

CARLOS CHAVEZ
1899–

In the March–April, 1936, issue of *Modern Music*, Chavez published an article, "Revolt in Mexico," in which he discussed his reorganization of Mexican musical education, the substitution for the traditional classical European courses of an intensive study of native Mexican Indian music and instruments. This change, he felt, would develop truly Mexican composers. The intervening years have substantiated his theories. A new group of young Mexican composers has arisen, which has enriched and vitalized Mexican music enormously. Chavez' own compositions, notably the ballet *HP* (1927), and the *Sinfonía India* (1936), have caught the spirit of ancient Mexico and created a new dynamic Mexican idiom.

While invigorating Mexican composition, Chavez proceeded to facilitate its performance by establishing the Orquesta Sinfónica de México which played not only the best of Mexican music but the classical and modern repertoire of other nations. As Director General of Fine Arts, he also sponsored exhibitions of the works of modern Mexican painters; like Mexican music, this art strikingly portrays the Mexico of yesterday, today and tomorrow.

The same forward-looking attitude pervades his book, *Toward a New Music* (1937), which is a study of the effects of electricity on music. He discusses in detail the new instruments of sound production and reproduction which have changed and continue to change the art of music. Separate chapters are devoted to a study of radio, phonograph recording and sound film, and their far-reaching artistic, social and economic effects on contemporary life. An interesting token of the speed of present-day invention is the fact that the book devotes only one footnote to wire and tape recording which in less than two decades have become altogether commonplace.

From: *Toward a New Music*, New York, 1937

MUSIC AND ELECTRICITY

There have always been difficult periods of transition, both for the public and for the artist, when the current forms of expression begin to crumble, and the new forms have not yet been consolidated. The present epoch is a typical case of this painful frustration; the opera and operetta have not finished dying, and the sound film has not finished being born.

It is not easy for the general public to comprehend that an era of electricity and great mechanical inventions may inspire profound works of art, works worthy of being classed with the symphonies of Beethoven and the cantatas of Bach. It is difficult to realize that the great contemporary advance of science will result in a marvellous artistic flowering.

However, a moment's consideration will reveal that any given epoch seemed at the time more prosaic than its predecessor exactly because of its greater material and scientific development. The Periclean age, the Renaissance, and the eighteenth and nineteenth centuries—glorious periods in art—seemed thus prosaic when they were the present. The general notion has always been that the present is commonplace. We must purify this concept, search out a more useful perspective. The present age, with its fertile agitation, its portentous scientific development, is perfecting, in electricity, its own organ of expression, its own voice. This, clarified and matured, will become the legitimate art of our era, the art of today.

I have always thought that an analysis of our present artistic situation and its expressive potentialities must begin with the study of its determining causes, a retrospective study of the development of art in relation to man's dominion of physical means. It seems to me, in short, that history and physics will well explain the artistic phenomena of today. Only by their study may we obtain a much-needed perspective on the present, just as a mariner, to confirm his route, must first ascertain his position on the vastness of the ocean.

Sound, by the very nature of its production, acquires from the human touch a living quality no machine has yet equalled. Human touch is a decisive factor in sound production on all existing instruments. On wind instruments it is the pressure of the lips on the mouthpiece, the special consistency of the tongue, the inflections of breath, the hands' support of the instrument in adjusting it against the lips. Each of these factors is a particular quality in each individual, and determines the beauty of sound according to the ability, experience, and musical feeling of each instrumentalist. On stringed instruments, as on the piano, it is the weight of the hand and arm, the elasticity of the muscles, the shape of the fingers, and many other individual attributes of each performer which determine the special color and quality of the sounds he produces. Up to the present day this has been man's privilege as against the machine in direct performance.

However, nothing indicates that electric mechanical instruments cannot eventually render the high qualities of touch which have heretofore been man's privilege . . . The precision obtainable by electromechanical means is incomparably greater than that achieved by men.

Musical instruments have not changed substantially in seven thousand years. In the course of this long period of time there has been great improvement in the construction and playing of the instruments, so that now we have far better control of them than was possible in remote antiquity. But during seventy centuries there did not appear a single musical instrument containing a new sound agent, or showing a new procedure of vibrating its agent. We received our present sound material complete from pre-history. Electric instruments of sound production offer the first case in history of a new musical instrument. They contain (a) a new sound agent, (b) a new manner of vibrating that agent, and (c) a new means of controlling that vibration—in frequency (pitch), amplitude (intensity), and form (timbre).

This electromechanical way of playing instruments not only makes it possible to obtain from each a rendition now unthinkable, but also makes possible the most perfect coördination of any number of them. It is easy to imagine the prodigies of polyphony and polyrhythm, of contrasts and amalgamations of sounds, which can be obtained by a large automatic electric symphony orchestra playing a music which only a roll, and no man or group of men, could possibly play. A composer taking advantage of all these resources to give form to his conceptions will be creating a new art, one still unforecast.   [1]

THE TRAINING OF THE NEW COMPOSER

We are used to thinking that the places in which composers start and are educated are conservatories and music schools. Speaking in general terms, the conservatory has been good for developing performing musicians, but has not been exactly the place in which the great composers, the masters of music, have been formed. They have never, in reality, needed a school, properly speaking, with its conventional organization, plan of studies divided into years of grades at the close of which there are examinations, etc., etc. The great masters of music have developed their natural faculties in the practice of music itself. Handel was not only a composer writing his works down on paper; he lived the life of the theater. He himself was an impresario. He wrote his operas for immediate performance. He lived in the orchestra, in the theater, in the whole organization of the musical life of his time. Bach was a religious composer because he lived in the church. He wrote chorales, oratorios, motets, masses and cantatas, which were needed for the Church's services. He wrote for the organ because it was the Church instrument and because it was the instrument at hand, the one he had to play. Nor need it be said that the composers of the Roman Catholic Church were always formed in the atmosphere and constant practice of religious music.

The conservatories and schools of music, even though they may give their students of composition a theoretical instruction (necessarily static) of more or less breadth, do not provide the composer with the real stage for his work. They do not provide practical resources for his work, for the simple reason that their function is not to practice music, but to teach the theoretical part of it. It is in this sense that the schools for composers foment the sterile, ivory tower attitude which creates musicians on a theoretical level. History shows that all the great masters of music constantly perfected their art through practice, that they always wrote for public performance; their music, however revolutionary it was considered in its day, responded to a demand and had commercial value to publishers and managers.

The esteem in which great artists are held grows constantly after their death, yet we do not know of a single Bach unknown in his lifetime, but discovered and glorified after his death. Great composers never learned their art in an ivory tower, but in its constant practice. At the present time the conservatories and schools of music cannot provide the proper surroundings for the development of the great composers of today. On the other hand, the policy of the great radio organizations consists of only the means of musical performance. This will one day inevitably lead to a shortage of adequate repertoire which will be a serious problem.

The radio, as the social institution of our day controlling the whole musical movement, should see that one of the important departments of its organization include the means needed for the production of new musical creations. The whole structure of musical activity will undergo a gigantic transformation because of the radio. We must reach a point from which we can get the whole perspective. This is exactly what interests me more and more in an attempt at a general interpretation of the effects which the great achievements of electro-mechanics will have on the music of the present.   [2]

FILMS AND MUSIC

After having glanced at the new instruments which today are within our reach, we might have some doubt that an artist, in order to produce his new creations, could dominate such complicated apparatus as the sound film, for example, in all its details. But let us note that the composer has always been capable of managing his mechanical instruments. If Chopin had not managed the piano as perfectly as he did, he would not have produced the marvellous piano music we all know and admire. In the same way, the composers who will make a true musical drama of the cinema will be those who know how to manage its various instrumentalities as perfectly as Chopin dominated the piano. . . .

If we look at the problem implied for the composer in conceiving a complex filmed music drama, we find that it is, in different manner and degree, the same problem presented in the case of an opera or a symphony: that of familiarizing himself with the instrumental means. In a classical symphony, each musical part is decided in relation to the instrumental possibility. The part played by the violin fits that instrument, and is inappropriate for the tuba. This propriety of music in relation to the instrument which produces it is what a musician means when he talks about a violinistic, unviolinistic, pianistic, or unpianistic passage.

A composer who knew only the mechanism of the violin would be unable to write for orchestra or opera. It may seem too difficult, this achieving of an understanding of very varied and complex mechanisms, but intellect and practice make it possible. In the particular case of the cinema, the new "apprenticeship" will not begin while musicians continue making only adaptations. The musical adaptations for cinematographic films are not more or less satisfactory than any other adaptations. Every adaptation implies the use of a thing originally conceived for another purpose. The music of *Tristan* fits the opera better than any other.

The dreadful salads of sections of classic works, sentimental melodies, and popular songs which are generally confected to accompany films prove nothing but the inability of producers to conceive original cinematographic works with their own music. The same thing happened in the seventeenth and eighteenth centuries, when the famous pasticcio music for operas was made, pasting the "favorite" airs of the period together without rhyme or reason.

The apprenticeship is slow. New art forms are not made in a day. The function of the true composer for the cinema is not that of superimposing music on the scenes to the order of the director of the production. He should have a conception of the cinematographic work as a whole, and of music's fulfilling an integral function within it. So that the artist may be capable of such conceptions, he must have a profound understanding of the potentialities of all the cinematographic instruments. [3]

THE FUNCTION OF THE COMPOSER

The composer should be integrated into the musical life of the present, and should have in himself a full sense of reality about his work and about the meaning it will have for the public at whom it is directed. I might say, in default of a better expression, that music ought always to be playable and audible. The composer will understand this only when he lives constantly in the actual presence of music. On this point the case of Bach is profoundly illustrative. [4]

GEORGE ANTHEIL

1900–

Antheil's career as a musician and writer has been colorful and varied. His compositions include symphonic, chamber, choral and film music as well as operas. In his writings he has delved not only into musical topics, but astronomy, the functioning of glands, advice to the lovelorn, and much more.

Beginning his career as a concert pianist, Antheil toured Central Europe, England and France. During several years' stay abroad, he acted as assistant conductor at the Berlin Stadttheater where he became thoroughly familiar with German opera and where, in 1929, he composed *Transatlantic*, one of the first American operas to be mounted in Germany (in Frankfurt a/M) with success. His *Ballet mécanique*, a score introducing several mechanical pianos and electrical appliances, created a furore at its première and earned him the reputation of *enfant terrible* of the twenties, a reputation hardly lived down to this day. His next full length opera, *Helen Retires* (1932), composed to a libretto by John Erskine, was written for the most part in Europe, but was produced in New York at the Juilliard School of Music.

The article on American opera quoted below, which appeared in *Modern Music* in 1930, is as pertinent today as it was then. Though he uses Kurt Weill's *Dreigroschenoper* (1928)—today a classic—and Krenek's *Jonny spielt auf* (1927)—now practically forgotten—as examples of the new and progressive in theater music, the situation both here and abroad is nearly the same as it was at that time. Then, as now, the many German opera houses were experimenting with new and daring works, while indigenous American opera flourishes only a little more today than it did then.

Antheil's autobiography, *Bad Boy of Music*, the source of the other quotations, is a racy survey of music and musicians in the second quarter of this century.

WANTED—OPERA BY AND FOR AMERICANS

From: *Modern Music*, 1930

The national school of Russia was given its chief impetus by the operas of Moussorgsky, Borodin, Rimski-Korsakoff and Glinka. The new French school of "Les Six" devoted itself mostly to ballets for Diaghilev, Rolf de Mare and Ida Rubinstein; and the latest German school gives by far the largest share of its attention to modern opera. Each of these three important groups has been nourished mainly in the atmosphere of the theater.

The reason is obvious. The "modern music" of every epoch is more easily assimilated by the general public in theatrical garb wherein the eye may help the ear over the difficult places until every part of a new score has become part of the common popular musical language of all time, no matter how modern it may have seemed in the beginning.

In the development of modern music one thing must by now be obvious to all: its newest and strongest tendency is to educate rather than flout the public. That composer whose scores cannot be abstract, reserved or cacophonous enough finds himself more and more limited to his special followers and his solitary conductor. Even these tightly enclosed little groups are beginning to break up, as their futility becomes apparent. Modern music faces a new boundary and a new epoch. All former groups are taking part in the vast revolution and all far-flung dialects are gradually combining into a common language. This evolving of music today towards an inner norm is merely a preparation to speak the international tongue that it once commanded, to a large public.

Several practical steps have been taken in this direction by the young German school. One example is Kurt Weill's *Beggar's Opera* which was a sensational success throughout Germany and is now being played everywhere in Europe, even in reactionary centers like Rome. The music of this work is, without question, extremely modern. Nevertheless all over the Continent one can hear almost every shop-girl singing its melodies. *Jonny spielt auf*, in spite of obvious limitations, was the first move in this direction, and a bold and daring move it was, to be applauded as such. It made a bad impression in America, because our critics failed to realize that it was not intended to represent American jazz but was a European burlesque of our atmosphere. With his new opera, *Leben des Orest*, Křenek has proved to be one of the most talented of all the young European operatic school.

A renaissance of opera is at hand. A few years ago the opera houses of Europe were dying in their own dust, maintaining, towards no end, huge and costly personnels. Today, in spite of recent theater crises, nearly every one of them is a live and going institution with box office receipts, a direction, and a soul. Brilliant young directors scarcely thirty years of age, and often in their twenties, are in charge of their destinies, and brilliant destinies they are. Musical Europe, stunned after the war, is awakening; and how! There are eighty-two intensely active opera houses in Germany alone. If America wishes to remain within the circle of foremost musical nations, it will have to do some quick thinking.

For "modern" music must continue to belong to the people, as it has in the great operatic periods of the past. A public of music lovers should come to the music theater from all walks of life in America. From this vast group, trained through the theater to understand the essence and reason of modern music, a new symphonic public will gradually be formed, a public that is able to project itself completely into the abstraction of symphonic music. But to put the cart utterly before the horse means the complete suppression of the organic growth of an individual American school of music. In painting, as in all art, abstraction is impossible before the literal has been achieved.

American music to date has had a curious, quixotic development. There is a tremendous musicality here such as very few nations possess, yet its cultivation has been haphazard and we find ourselves today making excuses that we are still a young nation musically, which is obviously hokum. Music in America has been going on a long time, and there is no doubt whatsoever in my mind that a large share of the dissipation of our energies is due to the rafts of ultra-conservative European musicians who have flooded to our shores in past decades, ensconced themselves in positions of power and trust, and betrayed a good deal of the musical future of America. In this they have been aided by the American musical critic. As a boy of sixteen, I was so embittered by this situation that I swore never to write anything but the most revolutionary music possible—'revolution' being somewhat confused in my youthful mind with cacophony. In my late twenties, I see the error of these earlier ways, but I am convinced that there still are other musicians in America who feel as I once did, who are still going to an unnecessary extreme, often within the scope of an iconoclastic theory of an aesthetic that long since has either been exploded or accepted. There is something depressing about this fine futility, this clashing of swords upon one's own armor, this shouting of battle cries alone, when the battle has already been won and the armies have already gone home. Such self-delusion would be impossible in Europe.

Opera we must have, but I am not so fantastic as to suppose that we will *soon* have a music springing from the people and patronized by them, nor that state legislatures will immediately establish state operas everywhere. My suggestions are entirely practical. I know that all the musical schools in America are turning out really splendid operatic material . . . I am sure that a dozen personnels could instantly be found in America for a dozen new opera houses. But—where do all these gifted young graduates go, year after year? Do they, these fine talents, merely become teachers who teach other young people, who also in turn become teachers?

Short operas of one act, interesting as plays or as "talkies," with no heavy "literary merit," stripped of the false operatic poetry of a decade past, with no long philosophical speeches and no slowly moving psychological drama devoid of action, and without tedious and impossible arias, should be given on Broadway and in the legitimate theaters. There is a sufficient dearth of stage material or novelty to assure a welcome to such experiments. But remember! The present-day public, spoiled or educated, as you please, by the rapidity of the movie screen and the real excellence of the contemporary legitimate theater, will put up with no démodé, "artistic," operatic monkey-business. The composers will have to get to work without too much accessory baggage. In this way only, I am convinced, can we soon have a real American school of opera.

For the seemingly unattainable Elysia can be captured by American composers alone; it is with them exclusively that the hope of an American musical future rests. They should no longer entrench themselves behind some tightly encircled group to devote themselves solely to the production of one more or less short orchestral composition a year. Let them remember that the elderly "promising young composer" is a purely American phenomenon. Some day he wakes up definitely past the middle-age mark, scarcely further than his starting point, just one more of those innumerable, finicky, dry, cautious, and fairly unimportant men with whose names our music lexicons and *Who's Who* are filled.

I suggest that we incorporate the daring and the friendly spirit of the Russian Five in our striving towards a national goal. Though living in Europe, I feel myself as American as anyone who has never left its shores and that I am needed as each one of us should feel he is needed. It is towards a national goal and competition with Europe that all of us should bend our thoughts. The new public will listen to something new. Living constantly in the movie theaters, it is astonished at nothing in the way of dramas. It will listen to anything that seems to be going somewhere and has a head and a tail. A score can be amazingly modern and yet will be swallowed without question by the public when the action explains the music. Serious opera, written in excellent scenario, with rapid cinema technique or at least a new stage technique, with a good story, dramatically heightened by music, should be comprehended by everybody. I can readily understand that the usual business man is not interested in the usual wooden opera story in a foreign language about people and an epoch he cares little about. Why not an opera about this business man himself, his surroundings, New York, factories, the romance of the West, whatever is of absorbing interest in America? Or if one must write about ancient Greece, why not write as though one were born on the same soil that produced Hollywood or Ernest Hemingway?

But if the new operatic movement is to get off only to a halfhearted start, it is better not to begin. For American critics in general are only too glad to knife any dangerous idea right off the bat when it is still weak and in its infancy, thus saving themselves any future trouble with a possibly irritating and new aesthetic. The experiment, if undertaken, deserves a fair chance.

One thing is certain; the newly developing relation of modern music toward the public requires the breaking up of all narrowly enclosed musical circles and aesthetics. America, just beginning to accept and understand modern music, has a difficult but unavoidable problem to solve. Nevertheless we should be completely optimistic.   [1]

From: *Bad Boy of Music*, 1945

CLASSICISM, ROMANTICISM AND NEO-CLASSICISM

Throughout the history of art there have been but two basic phenomena, an *inhalation* and an *exhalation*. The first produces one series of art movements, among which we can include the so-called "classic." It inhales, pulls in, restricts. The second produces an equally different general kind of art, into which we may place the "romantics."

It might not be too dangerous, now, to liken all art of all ages to a "classic" inhalation after which comes a romantic exhalation, then again the classic inhalation, ad infinitum.

Art remains healthy and alive only so long as its normal in-and-out breathing is not too long restricted, inhalation or exhalation not too long held up at any one point of breathing.

Art cannot hold its breath too long without dying.

The "classic" period of Haydn, Mozart and early Beethoven commenced circa 1725 with the words of Johann Josef Fux, who, in his foreword to his *Gradus ad Parnussum*, wrote: "Composers most unfortunately no longer permit themselves to be bound by the laws and rules, but avoid the names of School and Law as they would Death itself. . . ."

A few years later, in 1732, Josef Haydn was born, and with him the final, most classic, *limiting* version of the superb sonata-allegro form, that great nucleus of all classic symphonic music of the Haydn-Mozart-Beethoven period. Note, here, Fux's A.D. 1725 irritation with those romantic lawbreakers who then everywhere thumbed their noses at musical law, rhetoric, grammar, basic principle. His textbook was to become the basis for whole generations of future music scholars, among whom were to be the greatest "classic" names in music: Haydn, Mozart, Beethoven, Brahms.

Until Schumann, Chopin, and Wagner came along to break it up, basic fun in music (from 1730 to well past 1840) consisted mostly in making new restrictions and keeping them. Indeed Beethoven alone added volumes to the rules of symphonic form, although he did so in the spirit of liberating symphonic music from the purely abstractionist to the human, the feeling, the dramatic, the spiritual.

It would not be too farfetched to compare this particular classic period to a man balancing first a single walking stick, then adding a plate, then a vase of flowers, and then a whole table. *The interest of classic design usually increases as its hurdles increase;* Mozart, Beethoven, and even Brahms added rather than subtracted to their hurdles.

The "fun" in a Mozart symphony is not entirely unlike that of a baseball game. In baseball all plays are severely within the rules; what would you think of a baseball team that had twenty-seven players instead of nine? Baseball operates strictly within the rules, and to make certain that the rules are kept, umpires stand right on the field.

The composers of the hundred or more years preceding the overlap of the Chopin-Schumann-Wagner romantic period derived their main excitement, their top spiritual exaltation, from the masterly way in which they could knock out home runs or move and skip about inside of these binding, limiting classic rules.

Mozart's mastery was so superb, so utterly top-notch, that Mozart fans experienced exactly the same sensation which a modern baseball audience might feel today should its home-town team be blindfolded and still win hands down against a superexcellent non-blindfolded visiting team!

So much for what classicism is, now for what "neo-classicism" is.

The idea of a truly *new* classicism is certainly all right, for a "new" classicism will forever follow an old romanticism, and if Debussy, Ravel, and early Stravinsky were not romantics, I'd like to know what is romantic. But here, within Stravinsky's new "Pulcinella," there was no new operating within severely prescribed limits (as, for instance, there was in the contemporary Schoenberg school's atonalism). The entire process was, with Stravinsky, purely arbitrary, "anti-classic" even; it only employed classic *sounds,* musical stuff which we have long associated with the classic periods. It was classic only in the sense that Dali's surrealist paintings are often *like* Vermeer without at all *striking* at Vermeer's objectives.

"Pulcinella" reminded me of perfume distilled in Bulgaria: two hundred pounds of the petals of Bulgarian roses to make an ounce of quintessence; a lifetime of Pergolesi is boiled down into one single Stravinsky "Pulcinella." (Later, it was to be worse; seven thousand pages of Bach and Handel to make a single Stravinsky piano concerto, a serenade, or a piano sonata!) The boiling-down process was contractionist, therefore *superficially* similar to the classic principle, *but* here its similarity to true classicism stopped; it was as like a true Mozartian baseball game as is one of those ultra-synthesized table baseball games which one buys nowadays.

To cut to the chase: Stravinsky's "neoclassicism" was no new classicism at all, but a primitivism-romanticism, if for no other reason than that Stravinsky so violently opposed all limiting rules except those which he made and destroyed daily for himself. . . .

I watched Stravinsky romp merrily through the classic masters, Bach, Mozart, Weber, and any number of others, each one in turn to become his "prince of music," his star, his basis for his synthesizing operations, so to speak; each star in turn to be succeeded by a new favorite as the old one fell exhausted, drained of essence. The *Psalms Symphony,* the *Capriccio,* lately even the *Symphony in C,* and, in the last analysis, that is all that is important. Beyond question he is a genius, especially when it comes down to composing directly into the orchestra.

But he is no classicist, no classicist at all. [2]

THE FATHER OF IMPRESSIONISM

My old teacher in Philadelphia, Constantine von Sternberg, had not liked the Debussy-Ravel school and had once attempted to discredit them with me by claiming that they, including Satie, had stolen their entire impressionistic technique from an Italian, Ernest Fanelli.[1] Fanelli was an older composer living in Paris during the 1880's.

I wondered now whether it was true because, if it were, it might mean that a young foreign-born composer like myself, inventing a whole new music such as I now intended to invent, might easily find his work voraciously pre-devoured, then reassimilated, finally to be given out to the Parisian public under other names than his own.

I decided to investigate the Fanelli case. To see if any traces of him still remained in Paris. Among the biographers of the French musical Impressionists, I found little or nothing. But in an old musical dictionary I found his former address.

The address at least supplied me with a trail which led me to his widow—for he was dead. His son (my age) and the younger daughter also lived in the same apartment.

I explained to Mme Fanelli that I was an American music critic (a lie), anxious to write an article on the true worth of Ernest Fanelli. Whereupon they innocently took me into their household, where I was permitted to peruse Fanelli's manuscripts at leisure.

I soon discovered that Constantine von Sternberg had been right, at least in one regard: the works of Fanelli *were* pure *Afternoon of a Faun* or *Daphnis and Chloë, at least in technique,* and they predated the Debussy-Ravel-Satie works by many years.

But, as I also soon discovered, they were not as talented as the works of the two slightly younger men, although they had had the advantage of being "firsts." In my recent investigations I had somewhere read that young Debussy, Satie and Ravel had known old Fanelli well, had visited him and even borrowed his scores. I asked Mme Fanelli if this were so.

"Oh yes," she said, "it was so; nice young Claude Debussy was very enthusiastic about my poor husband's work!"

I left the Fanellis in quite a quandary. To write an article about Fanelli now would be to unbury a possibly unpleasant body—who in Paris wanted to hear such a thing! Besides, frankly, the worth of Fanelli—his intrinsic musical worth—hardly merited the sacrifice this would quickly prove to be. Debussy was the genius who had distilled Fanelli into immortality!

As I wandered home, I recollected bits of Mme Fanelli's answers. For instance, I had asked her when his *Tableaux Symphoniques* was written; I saw that the date of publication was 1884.

[1] Ernest Fanelli (1860–1917), actually a born Frenchman, studied with Alkan and Delibes, and made his living as a percussion player; in his twenties he composed a quintet and several orchestral pieces, but ceased composing in 1893.

"He wrote it around 1880," she said.

"And when was it first performed?"

"In 1912."

Thirty-two years, during which time Debussy, Ravel, and Satie had visited him, borrowed his scores!

Finally, out of bad conscience, I did write an article on Fanelli . . . but it was a wishy-washy article, said nothing about the score borrowing; if it had, it would have instantly made me the most disliked fellow in Paris. . . .

I did not feel like being hung for a principle I had never believed in—the eternal question of who invented what first.

Art is not a question of precedence, but of excellence.   [3]

NATIONALISM

In the light of mature consideration and twenty-three years' thought devoted to the subject, I have at last come to the conclusion that the biggest musical criminal the world has ever seen was Balakirev, inventor and protector of "The Russian Five," the Russian nationalist school. For, aside from the fact that its one indisputable genius, Moussorgsky, hardly needed a Balakirev or a "school" in order to create what he did create, the intriguing old rascal, Balakirev, and his doting satellites very nearly wrecked the career of one of the greatest of all musical geniuses, Tchaikovsky.

The thing becomes very plain in the Rimski-Korsakov autobiography. Rimski, an excellent technician and painter of Russian fairy tales in musical color, was one of the group and, as all of his life and works prove, fairly well sold on its central idea, which was that if one's music wasn't one hundred per cent Russian, it wasn't anything, and that was that. Rimski didn't want the composers of other countries to be Russian; he wanted them to be as national as their own soil and folk song; and here we encounter again one of those odious strait-jackets which, from the very beginning of musical composition in the larger forms, have destroyed the soul of music, killed its initiative in all pathways except the pathway fortunate enough to obtain the widest publicity—which is where the critics who exalt such "schools" come in.

For, indeed, how can one in one's musical composition be *intentionally* nationalistic? Or, for that matter, an *intentional* Cubist painter: Or an *intentional* Surrealist, or what have you? To superimpose a "school" upon one's personal method of artistic creation is, surely, the greatest of nonsense, the most flagrant of artistic forgeries! When a painter, for instance, as great and gifted as Picasso, turned to Cubism during the frightened, angular days of 1914–18, it is at least possible (indeed highly probable) that he *could* have done so because of a most insistent and sincere artistic pressure from within. But when, in 1920, one hundred or more other Cubist painters also emerged, is it not too unreasonable to suppose that a goodly portion were fakers, frauds, or simply imitators? That, for instance, most of them were very conscious indeed that Picasso's cube paintings were selling on the Rue de la Boétie for more than several thousand dollars apiece?

Many critics seem readily to fall for this "school" situation, particularly when the school is a chauvinistic one. What is more glorious on the surface than nationalism? History tells us that at first they resist, then gradually become convinced of the righteousness of the new "school" and particularly if it is nationalist, eventually its most fatuous publicists.

And may God help any new painters, composers or authors who from now on fail to identify their work with this accepted "movement!" This is as true today as it was in Balakirev's day.

In my humble opinion, therefore, the "school" proposition is—in art—the most unadulterated, vicious nonsense. And yet, today, in modern 1945–50, America still wants and assiduously seeks after an "American school" in music; may God forgive its sophomoric naïveté, its infantile anxiety to appear as advanced and sophisticated as decaying Europe!

An "American school" of music will come about only when, finally we stop planning methodically to catch ourselves one. And, in the meantime, perhaps many a budding American Tchaikovsky may be utterly discouraged, or at least greatly restrained, by that method of critical analysis which rejects a lamp because you cannot sit on it.   [4]

ERNST KRENEK

1900–

Nearly as prolific a writer as he is composer, Krenek has produced many books and monographs on music and musicians, as well as the librettos for his own operas.

Musik im goldenen Westen, published in Vienna in 1949, is a record of his more than ten years' residence in America, where he has taught, lectured, written and composed. This volume discusses American composers, orchestras, radio, films, publishers, recordings, music education, emigré composers and their influence on American composition, and jazz. His interest in this last antedates his emigration to the United States, his once popular and most controversial opera, *Jonny spielt auf* (1927), having been composed in the jazz idiom. In his sketches of American composers since the First World War, he presents the view that they stem primarily from what he considers the two most important European schools, the Schoenberg or central European, and the French, neoclassic school of Stravinsky. A twelve tone composer himself for many years, he favors the Schoenberg influence.

Music Here and Now is a comprehensive structural history of music, from church modes through tonal and atonal harmony to the twelve tone technique, and in it Krenek develops the thesis that the only true musical innovation in the past three centuries has been atonal or, more strictly, twelve tone music.

From: *Music Here and Now*, 1949

STRAVINSKY AND SURREALISM

Stravinsky appeared with dramatic suddenness, a crudely prominent personality, sharply and vigorously outlined, vibrant with barbaric force.

Two qualities gave this newcomer a revolutionary and progressive aspect. When Stravinsky used the musical language of atonality in his middle period, particularly in his *Sacre du printemps*, he seemed

537

to take his place alongside Schoenberg as a pioneer of a new type of music. On the other hand, his relation to the sophisticated Jean Cocteau helped to give his utterances an exciting spiritual background. Probably Cocteau knows more about the real situation in music than many of the French musicians, who mostly are content to play around outside the walls of his thought structure, which frequently look mysterious and hard to penetrate.

From this point of departure sprang many efforts proposing to transmit surrealism into the field of music. Stravinsky's *Histoire du soldat* may be the first and most important of these, apart from the curiosity cabinet of Eric Satie, that extravagant but limited musician. Here the clinging to traditional means is just as systematic as in the case of neoclassicism, although the share of progressiveness is larger here than in the latter, since destruction, not restoration, is the object. The old material is not treated as if it were still intact and as useful as before, but is regarded as a conglomeration of wreckage, to be built up into a system contradicting the original arrangement. Surrealism causes a shock very similar to that produced by the introduction of really new features. But while the latter is legitimated by the direct impact of something truly novel, the shock felt in Surrealism is obtained indirectly by the distortion of old material into a newfangled structure.

Musical Surrealism has not found many adherents. Except for what has been produced by a few young French composers, such as Henri Sauguet, by far the most original work of this kind is *Mahagonny* by Kurt Weill. Generally speaking, it is the text accompanying the music which plays an important and even decisive part in giving Surrealism its peculiar stamp. The musical substance, viewed as such, only too soon turns out to be simply reactionary; of attack and shock nothing much remains . . . The movement has deteriorated until it has become a craft, and by this deterioration has surrendered the essential individuality required for a really new style in art.

Stravinsky shakes hands with neoclassicism by way of Jean Cocteau and Surrealism. And here is the start of that comedy masquerade in which he hides behind Pergolesi, Bach, Weber, and Tchaikovsky for so long that when he finally emerges again as Stravinsky, one does not recognize him for himself. His individuality can always be identified in the unmistakable gestures with which his genius animates his figures, but no one knows what has become of his real personality—perhaps he does not know himself, possibly he does not want to know. In his autobiography, written so coolly and with such conscious detachment, Stravinsky speaks of many people and things but is silent about

the only cardinal fact of his mysterious career: namely, how he journeyed from the *Sacre du printemps* to the *Jeu de cartes*.   [1]

SCHOENBERG AND ATONALITY

Reservations must be made in awarding the title "new" to contemporary composers mentioned thus far [Stravinsky, Hindemith, Bartók,
the Russians, etc.]. The one quality common to them all is their more
or less strict adherence to the traditional material of tonality—in other
words, to the sound language based on the system of major and minor
keys and formulated by the device of the tonal cadence which has had
undisputed reign since 1600. It follows that the outstanding characteristic of the type of music we shall designate as "new" will probably
be its failure to adhere to this principle of tonality.

Such music does exist, being, in fact, none other than the so-called
atonal music . . . Although atonal music has been in existence for
about thirty years and has caused a great deal of commotion for at
least a considerable part of this period, it has not deteriorated into a
craft. It does not fit in with the character of merchandise demanded
by our present economic conditions, because it is not popular and
therefore is difficult to sell.

As we know, this type of music was originated by Arnold Schoenberg in a city which was, until recently, considered the capital of the
musical world and which at that time [thirty years ago] certainly had
the right to that proud title. We refer to Vienna. Neither the accident
that one of the most radical revolutions in many centuries took place
in that city, nor the concrete changes carried on by that revolution
mitigate the fact that Vienna was the focal point of the holiest musical
traditions and for a long time had been averse to any innovation in the
field. The Austrian character is not accurately pictured along the lines
so incessantly followed in the Viennese operetta "zoo"—from *The
Bat* to *The White Horse Inn*. Involved for decades in a discouraging
struggle for life, the average Austrian was imbued with a deep skepti-
cism, an epicurean pessimism, a complete lack of nationalistic feeling,
and a rather primitive sense of reality, balanced by a licentious pro-
pensity for unrestrained speculation. This unique combination of conservative and radical constituents, whose origin can be explained in
detail by the peculiar history of the country, can naturally be preserved only in certain individuals under the present circumstances, for
in reality it represents an extremely humane pattern of life; as a
type, it has been long since condemned to an accepted oblivion. The

"new" music is practically the last thing which Austria contributed to the world's cultural development before her destruction; and the impending catastrophe was clearly presaged in this music. If the prophecy is correctly interpreted, then the destruction may have at least some justification. If thinkers can learn from this phenomenon the direction of the road leading to a world music, then the world will perhaps have derived from its catastrophe the only tangible advantage accessible to it today.

The step from the later tonality to atonality proper was at once recognized as an undefinable radical measure. That was seen in the turbulent reactions which followed the initial performance of atonal music. Even today—and in spite of all the other and (from a material standpoint) incomparably greater distress they have known—witnesses speak with shudders of that formidable concert in Vienna in 1911, when atonal orchestral works were heard for the first time, causing such a riot that the police were called in to separate the fighting factions, and ambulances were summoned that victims with bloody heads could be cared for. Certainly people were justified in their horror as well as in their fury. The handwriting on the wall may be more horrible in its appearance than what it forebodes; and the prophet announcing the disaster is invariably stoned. Small wonder that this radical step was taken in the very place where the pressure of tradition was the strongest; small wonder, also, that the reaction here should be most violent. In fact, the appearance of Schoenberg had a decisive influence on the musical fate of Vienna, even though the ubiquitous "conquerors" there refused to recognize it. Those who did not want to take part in Schoenberg's innovations—and they, under the pressure of public condemnation, were just about everybody—experienced something like a pathological repression which permanently inhibited the normal use of their musical powers. There is no doubt that the ornate, fat, jellylike, bloated character of the newer Viennese style is a kind of sickly degeneration resulting from repressed atonality.   [2]

From: *Musik im goldenen Westen*, 1949

SOME OUTSTANDING AMERICAN COMPOSERS

AARON COPLAND

If among the various known styles in Europe, we consider those of Stravinsky and Schoenberg as distinct opposites, and can view them as the extreme limits of a continuous gamut of writing methods, we can say that Aaron Copland stands nearest to Stravinsky and Roger Sessions nearest to Schoenberg. This should serve the European reader as a general orientation rather than imply that these composers actually imitate those European models.

Aaron Copland, an extremely facile, skillful and sophisticated musician, created perhaps his most important work in his *Variations* for piano (1930). Stravinsky's influence is obvious enough in the harsh, consistently percussive handling of the piano and in the rhythmic groupings, in which a relatively short motive with but few variants is incessantly repeated, and driven through a succession of irregular meters by means of changing, delayed, syncopated accents. At the same time, however, the theme of the *Variations* which, through being limited to a few tones, reminds one of some of Schoenberg's "basic forms," is inflected with an austerity and a logic which makes us think of middle-European models rather than of the discursive manner of Stravinsky. In other works of this period Copland also favored an aggressive handling of dissonance which is closely related to the early attempts of the atonal school, although they derive presumably consciously from the Stravinsky of the *Sacre*. At that time Copland was known as a battling modernist, and when his music occasionally appeared in traditional concerts, it was often received with rebuffs. . . .

Copland followed the "folk" trend when, in his *El Salón México*, he produced an effective, if at the same time considerably superficial potpourri of Mexican dance rhythms. He has since written several similar works. While these pieces belong to a kind of elevated entertainment music, his piano *Sonata* may be viewed as an attempt to employ this style to higher ends. Without criticizing this style as such, since it is undoubtedly possible to create something significant in any style, one must admit that this manner makes it gratuitously difficult for the composer to produce something truly valid since it imposes great limitations upon him. While the earnest aim and the urge towards true greatness should not go unrecognized, one cannot overlook the fact that the use of the piano as a percussion instrument is too one-sided to lend a piece of considerable length the variety necessary to a truly expressive composition.   [3]

ROGER SESSIONS

Roger Sessions is one of the few American composers of his generation who did not spend his European stay in Paris as a pupil of Nadia Boulanger. He stopped frequently in Italy and travelled in central Europe. A relatively slow and conscientious worker, Sessions has, as we shall see, unquestionably developed into the most important composer in contemporary America. Among the works of his first period we might mention his first piano *Sonata*, a one movement piece of considerable pianistic difficulty, not altogether uniform stylistically, since it shows the influence of both the opposing European schools. Nevertheless, his wealth of ideas and the compactness of his structure make one recognize the originality and the profound seriousness of this composer. . . .

No one among American composers more clearly perceived the dangers inherent in nationalistic tendencies. With noteworthy courage and unmistakable integrity he has pointed out both in word and in composition that musical isolationism and the crabbed search for independent expression might lead not so much to a significant national style as to provincialism and the dictatorship of mediocrity. Consequently Roger Sessions is rejected by some nationalistic critics as an "un-American" type of composer dependent upon European models, and treated by concert organizations almost like a European, that is, quite seldom performed. When his critics speak of a European influence, they naturally refer to a more specific, quite definitely central-European influence. Certainly his style is nearer to the Schoenberg school than that of most other American composers, since Sessions strives for a more dynamic intensity, and also practices a much more compact and ingenious contrapuntal manner of writing than they do. Apart from these characteristics, his music has much less to do with Schoenberg or anybody else than that of his more successful neoclassic and "folk-like" colleagues does with Stravinsky and his imitators, although the latter believe themselves completely emancipated from all European models. In his string quartet and his duo for violin and piano Sessions has contributed distinguished additions to modern chamber music. Here and there in his music one may miss a certain amount of penetrating vitality, but this is always more than compensated for by a wealth of ideas, a fullness of expression, an original tonal speech and a deep earnestness. His three symphonies and the violin concerto deserve far greater attention than they have hitherto received. An opera project of monumental dimensions on which Sessions has been working for years with the Italian emigré author, Borgese, will be of quite special interest. It deals with the conquest of Mexico by Cortes and the tragic end of Montezuma. Together with Darius Milhaud's *Christophe Colomb* and my *Karl V*, this work would comprise a trilogy which, as few other operas of our time, would offer a monumental picture of modern music drama in the grand

style. Unfortunately the outlook for modern opera production of this
type in America is at the moment quite dim. [4]

GEORGE ANTHEIL

George Antheil has spent more time than most of his colleagues in
Paris, and his work clearly reflects the atmosphere of the French capital of the period—the dominating influence of Stravinsky and the
rapidly changing artistic styles. Probably it was not of particular advantage to the development of this composer that he excited a premature stir with a work entitled *Ballet mécanique*, and owed his initial
notoriety primarily to the fact that vacuum cleaners and typewriters
were used in the orchestra. Doubtless it would have been better for
the composer (and he himself was the first very quickly to recognize
this), if not much attention had been paid to these childish tricks,
and the emphasis had been laid on the musical worth of his opus. As
usual, critics fixed on externals, and while some saw in the introduction of those noise instruments the beginning of a new era, others
were inclined to view it as the impending end of the world. It took
Antheil many years to overcome this distortion of his perspectives,
and his earnest efforts to achieve a clear and meaningful style were
repeatedly confounded by that youthful prank. [5]

VIRGIL THOMSON

The Paris adventure left its lasting effects on Virgil Thomson also.
He shows himself influenced less by Stravinsky than by Erik Satie,
that precursor of French modernism who possessed the remarkable
gift of lending completely empty and worn-out material an exaggerated
profundity. In Satie's work music comes closest perhaps to the ideas
of Dadaism and Surrealism. In Thomson as well, it is at times hard
to decide whether one is dealing with ironically masked significance
or with kindergarten stuff. Virgil Thomson's most interesting work,
Four Saints in Three Acts, is a product of that Paris period. It is
written to a text of that American poet so closely related in spirit to
him, Gertrude Stein, who remained in France through the Second
World War. The contents of this opera defies rational description.
The text consists for the most part of conversations reminiscent of
childish chatter by characters who are introduced into the dramatis
personae as saints. Thomson's music, which leans essentially on the
most elementary triad combinations, lends this improbable theater
piece an undeniable if not easily explainable charm. A lot of it sounds

like primitive church music, other parts are like a parody on hackneyed Italian opera. In its conscious unoriginality the piece gives the effect of decided originality, without its ever being quite clear what its meaning is or if it has one. [6]

CHARLES IVES

Charles Ives, a contemporary of Arnold Schoenberg, is one of the most original and important phenomena in new American music. One would hardly guess by looking over his compositions that Ives enjoyed a solid training in the tradition of the nineteenth century. Much of his work resembles the attempts of an amateur of genius who, unconcerned with convention and practical usability, simply writes what comes into his head. The amateurish character of Charles Ives's creation may perhaps be explained in part by the fact that this composer actually need not concern himself very much about the practical aspects of his works, since he derives his considerable income from a directorial position in the insurance business. The material independence which he thus enjoys likewise permits him a degree of intellectual independence for which only a few other American composers have found courage.

Ives has produced by fits and starts and in completely unpredictable curves. Throughout his work inspirations of genius and dilettantish stuff are indifferently juxtaposed. In this respect, his more than one hundred and fifty songs are richly revealing. The choice of text alone shows an unusual and almost unselective breadth of literary interest. One finds English, American, German, Italian poems of all epochs and styles, quotations from philosophic prose texts, and some curious literary attempts from the pen of the composer himself. His lively literary interest is documented in numerous explanatory marginal notes and footnotes. The musical style of the songs ranges from childish imitations of Schumann to improbable anticipations of the later Schoenberg. There is a satirical song from 1907 bearing the subtitle *Studies in Sevenths, etc.* which uncannily forecasts the musical language of Schoenberg's *Erwartung*. But Surrealistic fare and the chaotic experiments of Stravinsky are demonstrated in Ives years before these fashions became "official."

The orchestral scores of Charles Ives frequently present quite a frightening spectacle. Without the slightest consideration for practical feasibility, he writes two or three different tempi and meters for various groups of instruments at the same time. Ives also anticipated musical Americanism, so that he is often cited by nationalistic critics as the archetype of the so passionately wished-for American genius. Nevertheless, his music is seldom played and is all but inaccessible.

One of his main works is the *Concord Sonata* for piano, so named because its four movements are dedicated to several of the most important personages of that literary group which lived in Concord, Massachusetts, in 1830. Their most significant representatives were Emerson, Thoreau and Hawthorne. The *Sonata*, about fifty minutes in length, follows no recognizable pattern rooted in tradition, but consists of an imaginative, unpredetermined succession of ideas which are alternately profound and banal. Nevertheless, the work, from its first to its last measure, is arresting—no small achievement when one considers that for almost a full hour one is listening to pretty much planless piano playing. As regards the gift of invention and vitality, Ives probably stands at the head of American composers. [7]

AARON COPLAND

1900–

Perhaps no one American musician has played so influential and important a rôle in the contemporary American musical scene as Aaron Copland. As composer, teacher, lecturer and writer, he has struggled unceasingly for the recognition and performance of modern music, and there is scarcely an American composer of any worth who has not been helped directly or indirectly by Copland's indefatigable sponsorship.

Before the First World War, the American musician who went abroad to study went inevitably to Germany and returned to continue the German tradition at home, adding little to American music itself. Copland was one of the first to study in Paris. However, as he says in his latest book, *Music and Imagination* (1952), he came back not a francophile, but filled with the idea of expressing his native country, which he has done.

His youthful works, *Music for the Theatre* and the *Piano Concerto*, employ jazz and sharp dissonance, and are rhythmically and harmonically complex. In late years his music, much of it based on American folk tunes, has become clearer, simpler and more consonant. The ballets, *Billy the Kid*, *Rodeo*, *Appalachian Spring*, and the film scores for *The City*, *Of Mice and Men* and *Our Town* have a spare, almost stark quality. He has dipped into Latin American popular music with his *El Salón México*.

His literary work has the clarity, conciseness and cogency characteristic of his music. In newspaper and magazine articles, in his books, *What to Listen for in Music* (1938), *Our New Music* (1941), as well as in the latest volume mentioned above, he has allotted illuminating sections to the American composer and his environment.

A MODERNIST DEFENDS MODERN MUSIC

Article in the New York *Times*, December 25, 1949

There seems to be no doubt about it—after almost fifty years of so-called modern music, there are still thousands of well-intentioned music lovers who think it sounds peculiar. The only way I can get the full impact of what modern music must sound like to such people is to stand in front of Picasso's more controversial paintings—the two-headed women, for example. I suppose that the more radical new music hits the ear with something like the violence that hits the eye in modern painting. Keeping these paintings in mind, I can sympathize with the musical layman who fails to comprehend contemporary music, although, as a composer myself, most recent music sounds quite natural and normal to me.

It occurred to me to wonder whether it wasn't possible to help the listener of good will to hear it my way. Perhaps I should start by clearing up one possible source of confusion as to terminology. There really isn't any modern music any more because the term "modern music" has been taken over by the bebop boys. When Bop City on Broadway began advertising concerts of "modern music," that just about finished off a name that had outlived its usefulness anyway. Contemporary music, or new music, is what the recent works of living composers are called nowadays. It's not a glamorous cognomen, perhaps, but at least it is exact.

Formerly—up to about 1925—the kind of music I have in mind was called 'ultra-modern.' It was under continuous attack by the more conservative members of the press; more significant, it was heard only by the comparatively small group of people who attended concerts. The rest of the world may have read about it, but rarely had any direct contact with it. Nowadays the situation has radically changed; the press is more open-minded, and anybody casually twisting a radio dial is in danger of getting an earful of it.

However one calls it, almost anyone can identify it as music that falls strangely on the ear; music that is different. To the old-fashioned listener its musical purpose seems different, and its methods are obviously different. Such a listener would probably tell you that, whereas the older music—the classics—seems designed to caress and invite the soul, the newer music is disconcerting in effect, the idea being apparently to upset and disturb one's equanimity of soul. Otherwise, how is one to explain the cacophonous harmonies, the tuneless melodies, the head-splitting sonorities, the confusing rhythms and cerebral forms?

It is natural enough for the uninitiated to imagine that all problematical music may be safely damned under a single heading. But actually, even in the old days of "ultra-modern" music, a great many different kinds of music were grouped indiscriminately together, and especially today the newer music may be said to include an unusually variegated experience. It might be helpful, therefore, to start by trying to bring some order into the apparent chaos of contemporary composition by dividing its leading exponents according to the relative degree of difficulty in the understanding of their respective idioms:

Very easy: Shostakovitch and Khatchaturian, Francis Poulenc, Erik Satie, early Schoenberg and Stravinsky, Vaughan Williams, Virgil Thomson.

Quite approachable: Prokofiev, Roy Harris, Villa-Lobos, Ernest Bloch, William Walton.

Fairly difficult: late Stravinsky, Béla Bartók, Chavez, Milhaud, William Schuman, Honegger, Britten, Hindemith, Walter Piston.

Very tough: middle and late Schoenberg, Alban Berg, Anton Webern, Varèse; Krenek, Charles Ives, Roger Sessions.

It would be miraculous if anyone agreed with the comparative estimates of this list, but that is not its purpose. It demonstrates merely that not all new music ought to be thought of as equally inaccessible; Schoenberg in his latest manner, and the members of his twelve-tone school, are the hardest nut to crack, even for musicians. One needs a contrapuntal ear for Hindemith and Piston, a feeling for the lushly colorful Villa-Lobos, a sharp wit for Poulenc and Thomson. For the later Stravinsky you need a love of style, precision, personality; for Milhaud a love of tartly seasoned sonorities. One of the toughest of all is Varese; and the easiest, certainly Shostakovich.

But whether the style of a contemporary composer is easy or hard to comprehend, it would be wise for the lay listener to keep the composer's objective well in mind. The objective is not necessarily to make beautiful sounds like Chopin or Mozart. Much as one should like to do just that, it isn't possible, because one doesn't write the music of one's choice but of necessity.

If forced to explain the creative musician's basic objective in elementary terms, I would say that a composer writes music to express and communicate and put down in permanent form certain thoughts, emotions and states of being. These thoughts and emotions are gradually formed by the contact of the composer's personality with the world in which he lives. He expresses these thoughts (musical thoughts, which are not to be confused with literary ones) in the musical language of his own time. The resultant work of art should speak to the men and women of the artist's own time with a directness and immediacy of communicative power that no previous art expression can give.

My love of the music of Chopin and Mozart is as strong as that of the next fellow, but it does me little good when I sit down to write my own, because their world is not mine and their language not mine. The underlying principles of their music are just as cogent today as they were in their own period, but the essential point is that with these same principles, one may and one does produce a quite different result.

The uninitiated music lover will continue to find contemporary music peculiar only as long as he persists in trying to hear the same kinds of sounds or derive the same species of musical pleasure that he gets from the great works of the past. When approaching a present day musical work of serious pretensions, one must first realize what the objective of the composer is and then expect to hear a different treatment of the elements of music—harmony, melody, timbre, texture —than was customary in the past.

Perhaps the best way to elucidate some of the peculiarities of new music is to attempt an answer to a few of the most frequently asked questions:

Why must new music be so dissonant?

A satisfactory reply to this troublesome question is exceedingly difficult because of the fact that a dissonance in music is a purely relative thing. What sounds dissonant to you may sound quite mellifluous to me. The whole history of Western music proves that our ear tends to increase its capacity for considering chords pleasurable which in former times were considered painfully discordant. Harmonies thought to be unusual or bizarre in the time of Monteverdi or Wagner are accepted as current usage by later generations of ordinary music lovers. Our period has hastened this historical process, since nowadays any chord, no matter what its degree of dissonance, is considered usable if it sounds "right" to the composer (that is, right for its expressive purpose), and is handled well within its context. If you find yourself rejecting music because it is too dissonant, it probably indicates that your ear is insufficiently accustomed to contemporary musical vocabulary and needs more training—that is, listening. Reading about a dissonant chord doesn't make it sound any sweeter, but repeated hearing certainly does. It is interesting to note in this connection that bebop, the latest jazz manifestation, has been introducing more and more dissonant harmonic textures into popular music, thereby arousing some of the same resistance from the mass public as was encountered by the serious composers in their field.

Is it true that the new composers care little about melody?

No, it definitely is not true. The greater proportion of today's music is melodically conceived, but it must be remembered that conceptions of melodic writing have changed. Here again it is not easy to agree upon a common ground for discussion, since the average person's idea of melody is so limited in scope. A melody is not merely something you can hum. It may be too complex for that, too tortuous or jagged or fragmentary, and in instrumental writing, it may go far beyond the limitations of the human voice. You must broaden your conception of what a melody may be if you want to follow what goes on in the composer's mind.

Part of the difficulty, as it concerns modern melody, may be traced to the harmonic problem. Many listeners become so lost in the web of unfamiliar harmonies that they never manage to hear the tunes that *are* being played. Since most music of serious pretensions deals in simultaneously sounded independent melodies, forming a contrapuntal texture that requires wide-awake listening even if the melodies are conventionally cast, it follows that a similar structure made of more recondite melodic writing will imply even more attentive listening. (Composers—and not only contemporary ones—have sometimes exaggerated in that direction, forgetting that the human ear is limited in absorbent capacity.) In general I would say that the melodies are there, but they may not always be of the immediately recognizable variety.

Is contemporary music supposed to be without sentiment or feeling, cerebral and clever rather than romantic?

A brief paragraph can hardly suffice to deal adequately with so persistent a misconception. If a contemporary composer's work strikes you as cold and intellectual, it may be that you are using standards of comparison that really do not apply. Most music lovers do not appreciate to what an extent they are under the spell of the romantic approach to music. Our audiences have come to identify nineteenth century musical romanticism as analogous to the art itself. Because it was, and still remains, so powerful an expression, they tend to forget that great music was written for hundreds of years before the romantics flourished.

It so happens that a considerable proportion of present day music has closer aesthetic ties with that earlier music than it has with the romantics. The way of the uninhibited and personalized warmth and surge of the best of the romanticists is not our way. That may be regrettable from your angle, but it remains a fact nevertheless—unavoidable fact probably, for the romantic movement had reached its apogee by the end of the last century, in any case, and nothing fresh was to be extracted from it.

Even composers found it difficult to break the spell, so it is hardly to be wondered at that the public should have been slow to grasp the full implication of what was happening. The literary world does not expect Gide or Mann or T. S. Eliot to emote with the accents of Victor Hugo or Walter Scott. Why, then, should Bartók or Milhaud be expected to sing with the voice of Schumann or Tchaikovsky? When a contemporary piece seems dry and cerebral to you, when it seems to be giving off little feeling or sentiment, there is a good chance that you are not willing to live in your own epoch, musically speaking.

Before concluding, I should like to ask a question of my own. Why is it that the musical public is seemingly so reluctant to consider a musical composition as, possibly, a challenging experience? When I hear a new piece of music that I do not understand, I am intrigued— I want to make contact with it again at the first opportunity. It's a challenge—it keeps my interest in the art of music thoroughly alive.

But I've sadly observed that my own reaction is not typical. Most people use music as a couch; they want to be pillowed on it, relaxed and consoled for the stress of daily living. But serious music was never meant to be used as a soporific. Contemporary music, especially, is created to wake you up, not put you to sleep. It is meant to stir and excite you—it may even exhaust you. But isn't that the kind of stimulation you go to theater or read a book for? Why make an exception of music?

It may be that new music sounds peculiar for the sole reason that, in the course of ordinary listening, one hears so little of it by comparison with the amount of conventional music that is performed year in and year out. Radio and concert programs, the advertisements of the record manufacturers, our school curricula—all emphasize the idea, unwittingly perhaps, that "normal" music is music of the past, familiar music that has proved its worth. A generous estimate indicates that only one-eighth of the music we hear can be called contemporary— and that estimate applies mostly to music heard in the larger musical centers. Under such circumstances, contemporary music is likely to remain peculiar, unless audiences demand that the music producers let them hear more of it. From where I sit that sounds like the millennium.

[1]

From: Music and Imagination, 1952

THE GIFTED LISTENER

An important requirement for subtle listening is a mature understanding of the natural differences of musical expression to be anticipated in music of different epochs. An awareness of musical history should prepare the talented listener to distinguish stylistic differences, for example, in the expression of joyousness. Ecstatic joy as you find it in the music of Scriabin ought not to be sought for in the operas of Gluck, or even of Mozart. A sense of being "at home" in the world of the late fifteen hundreds makes one aware of what not to seek in the music of that period; and in like fashion, being "at home" in the musical idioms of the late baroque period will immediately suggest parallelisms with certain aspects of contemporary music. To approach all music in the vain hope that it will soothe one in the lush harmonies of the late nineteenth century is a common error of many present day music lovers. [2]

THE SONOROUS IMAGE

The ability to imagine sounds in advance of their being heard in actuality is one factor that widely separates the professional from the layman. Professionals themselves are unevenly gifted in this respect. More than one celebrated composer has struggled to produce an adequate orchestral scoring of his own music. Certain performers, on the other hand, seem especially gifted in being able to call forth delicious sonorities from their instrument. The layman's capacity for imagining unheard sound images seems, by and large, to be rather poor. This does not apply on the lowest plane of sound apprehension where, of course, there is no difficulty. Laboratory tests have demonstrated that differences in tone color are the first differences apparent to the untrained ear. Any child is capable of distinguishing the sound of a human voice from the sound of a violin. The contrast between a voice and its echo is apparent to everyone. But it bespeaks a fair degree of musical sophistication to be able to distinguish the sound of an oboe from that of an English horn, and a marked degree to imagine a whole group of woodwinds sounding together. If you have ever had occasion, as I have, to perform an orchestral score on the piano to a group of non-professionals, you will have soon realized how little sense they have of how this music might be expected to sound in an orchestra.

It is surprising to note how little investigation has been devoted to this whole sphere of music. There are no textbooks solely designed to examine the sound stuff of music—the history of its past by comparison with its present; or its future; or its potential. Even so-called orchestration texts, written ostensibly to describe the science of combining orchestral instruments, are generally found to steer shy of their subject, concentrating instead on instrumentation, that is, on the examination of the technical and tonal possibilities of the individual instrument. The sonorous image appears to be a kind of aural mirage, not easily immobilized and analyzed. The case of the individual sound is rather different, since it is more comparable to that of the primary colors in painting. It is the full spectrum of the musician's "color" palette that seems to lend itself much less well to discussion and consideration than that of the painter. [3]

ORCHESTRATION

It is axiomatic that no one can satisfactorily orchestrate music which was not conceived in orchestral terms in the first place. The music must, by its nature, belong to the orchestra, so to speak, even before one can tell in exactly what kind of orchestral dress it will appear. Assuming that one does have orchestrable music, what governs the choice of instruments? Nothing but the composer's expressive purpose. And how does one give expressive purpose through orchestral color? Through the choice of those timbres, or combination of timbres, that have closest emotional connotation with one's expressive idea. . . .

But even when the composer's expressive purpose is clearly before him, there appear to be two different approaches to the problem of orchestration: one is to "think in color" at the very moment of composition, the other is to "choose color" after a sketch of the work is at hand. Most composers of my acquaintance make a virtue of the first system; that is, they claim to think coloristically. A feat is, of course, implied. If, at the instant the composer conceives a melody, he at the same instant knows what its orchestral dress will be, he has performed two operations simultaneously. Some few composers have told me that they prepare no sketch; they compose directly into score, thinking the timbre and the notes together. It seems to me, however, that there are definite advantages to be gained from separating these two functions. The method of choosing colors only at the moment when one begins deliberately to orchestrate makes it possible to plan out an entire score in terms of its overall effect. It counteracts the tendency to orchestrate page by page, which is certain to lead to poor results, for the decisions made on any single page are valid only in relation to what has gone before and what is to follow. Since balance and contrast of instrumental effect are prime factors in good orchestration, it follows that any decision as to timbre, too quickly arrived at, is itself a limitation, since it prevents freedom of action on other pages. This greater freedom of choice, it would appear, is possible only if the composer deliberately prevents himself from thinking in color until the moment comes for applying himself solely to that purpose. This isn't always possible, for there are times when a phrase or a section suggests its orchestral form so forcibly as not to be ignored. These moments, when they really impose themselves, act as a catalytic in the general orchestral scheme. But, in general, I belong to the category of instrumentator whose orchestral framework and detail is carefully planned so as to carry out more faithfully the expressive purpose inherent in the entirely completed ground plan of the work. If I stress this unduly it is only to counteract what is generally supposed to be normal procedure in orchestration.   [4]

CONDUCTOR AND COMPOSER

A well-known conductor once confided to me that he invariably learned something from watching a composer conduct his own composition, despite possible technical shortcomings in conducting, for something essential about the nature of the piece was likely to be revealed . . . If my conductor friend was right, the composer ought to bring an awareness and insight to the understanding of music that critics, musicologists, and music historians might put to good use, thereby enriching the whole field of musical investigations.   [5]

IMPROVISATION

If one looks up the word 'improvisation' in the music dictionaries, reference will be made to the ability of composers, at certain periods of musical history, to improvise entire compositions in contrapuntal style. The art of improvising an accompaniment from a figured bass line was an ordinary accomplishment for the well-trained keyboard instrumentalist during the baroque period. But the idea of *group* improvisation was reserved for the jazz age. What gives it more than passing interest is the phonograph, for it is the phonograph that makes it possible to preserve and thereby savor the fine flavor of what is necessarily a lucky chance result. It is especially this phase of our popular music that has caused the French *aficionado* to become lyrical about *le jazz hot*.

When you improvise, it is axiomatic that you take risks and can't foretell results. When five or six musicians improvise simultaneously, the result is even more fortuitous. That is its charm. The improvising performer is the very antithesis of that tendency in contemporary composition that demands absolute exactitude in the execution of the printed page. Perhaps Mr. Stravinsky and those who support his view of rigorous control for the performer have been trying to sit on the lid too hard. Perhaps the performer should be given more elbow room and a greater freedom of improvisatory choice. A young composer recently conceived the novel idea of writing a "composition" on graph paper which indicated where a chord was to be placed in space and when in time, but left to the performer freedom to choose whatever chords happened to strike his fancy at the moment of execution. Most jazz improvisers are not entirely free either, partly because of the conventionality of jazz harmonic formulas, and partly because of overused melodic formulas. Recent examples of group improvisations by Lennie Tristano and some few other jazz men are remarkable precisely because they avoid both these pitfalls. When American musicians improvise thus freely, and we are able to re-hear their work through recordings, the European musician is the first to agree that something has been developed here that has no duplication abroad.   [6]

A NATIONAL MUSIC

Actually, it seems to me that, in order to create an indigenous music of universal significance, three conditions are imperative. First, the composer must be part of a nation that has a profile of its own—that is the most important; second, the composer must have in his background some sense of musical culture and, if possible, a basis in folk or popular art; and third, a superstructure of organized musical activities must exist—to some extent, at least—at the service of the native composer.   [7]

OBSERVATIONS

It is quite evident that there is no further revolution possible in the harmonic sphere, none, at any rate, so long as we confine ourselves to the tempered scale and normal division by half tones. There is no such thing any longer as an inadmissible chord, or melody, or rhythm —given the proper context, of course. Contemporary practice has firmly established that fact.   [8]

Music is in a continual state of becoming.   [9]

LIST OF SOURCES

This list gives full bibliographical details for each source, followed by the number (in square brackets) corresponding to the number of the excerpt in the text, and then by the page number in the original source. For example, under Chapter VI, the selection [10] of Puccini will be found on page 169 of Giuseppe Adami, *Letters of Giacomo Puccini*, etc.

All selections from foreign-language editions here cited have been translated by the editor, and in some cases existing translations were slightly revised on the basis of the original texts or in order to adjust them to current linguistic usage.

Following is the full information for certain recurring sources which are given in abbreviated form in the list:

La Mara, *Briefe hervorragender Zeitgenossen an Franz Liszt*, Leipzig, Breitkopf & Härtel, 1895 (La Mara, *Briefe*).

Jay Leyda and Sergei Bertensson, *The Musorgsky Reader*, New York, W. W. Norton, 1947 (Leyda and Bertensson, *The Musorgsky Reader*).

Ludwig Nohl, *Letters of Distinguished Musicians*, tr. Lady Wallace, London, Longmans, Green, 1867 (Nohl, *Letters*).

Marc Pincherle, *Musiciens peints par eux-mêmes*, Paris, Pierre Cornuau, 1939 (Pincherle, *Musiciens*).

Chapter 1

PALESTRINA
Henry Coates, *Palestrina*, New York, Pellegrini and Cudahy, 1949. [1] 22 – [2] 4 – [3] 18

BYRD
Edmund H. Fellowes, *William Byrd*, 2nd ed., London, Oxford University Press, 1948. [1] 149
————— ed., *The Collected Vocal Works of William Byrd*, Vol. XIV, London, Stainer & Bell, 1949. [2] IX

CACCINI
Francisco Mantica, ed., *Prima Fiorituri del Melodramma Italiano*, Vol. II, Rome, Raccolte Claudio Monteverdi, 1930. [1] 1

MORLEY
Thomas Morley, *A Plaine and Easie Introduction to Practicalle Musicke*,

reprint, London, Oxford University Press, 1937. [1] 180 – [2] 162 –
[3] 1 – [4] 121 – [5] 166 – [6] 177 – [7] 179

MONTEVERDI
G. Francesco Malipiero, ed., *Tutte le Opere di Claudio Monteverdi*, Asola;
[1] Vol. V (1927) Preface – [4] Vol. VIII (1929) Preface
Louis Schneider, *Claudio Monteverdi*, Paris, Perrin & Co., 1921. [2] 138
Henry Prunières, *Monteverdi, His Life and Work*, New York, E. P.
Dutton, 1926. [3] 284

FRESCOBALDI
Claudio Sartori, *Bibliografia della Musica Strumentale Italiana*, Florence,
Leo S. Olschki, 1952. [1] 219, 357 – [2] 344

SCHÜTZ
Erich H. Müller, ed., *Heinrich Schütz: Gesammelte Briefe und Schriften*,
Regensburg, Gustav Bosse, 1931. [1] 64 – [2] 82 – [3] 178 – [4] 192

PURCELL
J. A. Westrup, *Purcell*, New York, Pellegrini & Cudahy, 1949. [1] 47 –
[2] 69
John Playford, *Introduction to the Skill of Music*, London, 1697. [3] 134

COUPERIN
François Couperin, *Oeuvres complètes*, Vol. I, Paris, Editions de l'Oiseau
Lyre, 1933. [1] 25 – [2] 28 – [3] 28 – [4] 41

TELEMANN
Hans Hörner, *Gg. Ph. Telemann's Passionsmusiken*, Borna-Leipzig, Noske,
1933. [1] 66
Willi Kahl, *Selbstbiographien deutscher Musiker des xviii. Jahrhunderts*,
Cologne, Staufen-Verlag, 1948. [2] 205 – [3] 206
Romain Rolland, *Musikalische Reise ins Land der Vergangenheit*, Frank-
furt o/Main, Rütten & Loening, 1922. [4] 124

RAMEAU
Jean Philippe Rameau, *Nouveau système de musique théorique*, Paris,
1726. [1] 106 – [2] 42 – [3] 43 – [4] 105
————, *Observations sur notre instinct pour la musique et son principe*,
Paris, 1734. [5] 3 – [6] 21 – [7] 2 – [8] 61

MARCELLO
Benedetto Marcello, "Il teatro alla moda," tr. Reinhard G. Pauly, *The
Musical Quarterly*, New York, G. Schirmer Inc., XXXIV (July 1948).
[1] 372 – [2] 380 – [3] 382

Chapter 2

ROUSSEAU
Jean Jacques Rousseau, *Ecrits sur la musique*, Paris, 1838. [1] 227 –
[2] 234 – [3] 238

CARL PHILIPP EMANUEL BACH
C. Ph. E. Bach, *Essay on the True Art of Playing Keyboard Instruments*,
tr. & ed. William J. Mitchell, New York, W. W. Norton, 1949.
[1] 79 – [2] (with notes) 147 – [3] 367 (with omissions)
Nohl, *Letters*. [4] 54 – [5] 55
Dragan Plamenac, "New Light on the Last Years of Carl Philipp Emanuel
Bach," *The Musical Quarterly*, XXXV (October 1949). [6] 582

GLUCK
Nohl, *Letters*. [1] 3 – [2] 8 (with omissions) – [3] 13

HAYDN
Willi Reich, *Joseph Haydn: Leben, Briefe, Schaffen*, Lucerne, Stocker,
1946. [1] 85 – [4] 86 – [5] 87 – [7] 160 – [8] 161 – [9] 162
Ludwig Nohl, *The Life of Haydn*, tr. George P. Upton, Chicago, 1883.
[2] 83 – [3] 86
Nohl, *Letters*. [6] 107
Joseph Haydn, *Die Sieben Worte des Erlösers am Kreuze*, Leipzig, Breit-
kopf & Härtel, 1801. [10] III

GRÉTRY
André Grétry, *Mémoires ou Essais sur la musique*, Liége, Vaillant-Car-
manne, 1914. [1] 64 – [2] 354 – [3] 356 – [4] 124 – [5] 368

MOZART
W. A. Mozart, *The Letters of Mozart and his Family*, tr. and ed. Emily
Anderson, London, Macmillan & Co., 1938. [1] I, 478 – [2] II, 497 –
[3] II, 662 – [4] II, 937 – [5] II, 736 – [6] III, 1143 – [7] III, 1150 –
[8] III, 1242 – [9] III, 1267 – [10] III, 1294 – [11] III, 1329

BEETHOVEN
Michael Hamburger, ed. and tr., *Beethoven: Letters, Journals and Conversations*, New York, Pantheon Books, 1952. [1] 35 – [2] 72 –
[5] 198 – [6] 164 – [7] 194 – [9] 212 – [10] 68 – [11] 237 – [12] 46 –
[13] 55 – [14] 34 – [15] 76 – [16] 36 – [17] 153 – [18] 161
Ernst Bücken, ed., *Musikerbriefe*, Wiesbaden, Dieterich, n.d. [3] 84
A. C. Kalischer, ed., *Beethoven's Letters*, London, J. M. Dent, 1909.
[4] 140
Friedrich Kerst, *Beethoven, the Man and the Artist as Revealed in His*

Own Words, tr. Henry E. Krehbiel, New York, B. W. Huebsch, 1905. [8] 26

SPOHR

Louis Spohr, *Autobiography*, tr. anon., London, 1865. [1] I, 45 – [2] I, 186 – [3] II, 81

WEBER

Carl Maria von Weber, *Sämmtliche Schriften*, ed. Georg Kaiser, Berlin, Schuster & Loeffler, 1908. [1] 128 – [2] 252 – [3] 372 – [4] 224 – [6] 397
Nohl, *Letters*. [5] 209
Alfred Kohut, *Weber-Gedenkbuch*, Reudnitz-Leipzig, 1887. [7] 57

ROSSINI

G. Mazzatinti and F. G. Manis, eds., *Lettere di G. Rossini*, Florence, Barbera, 1902. [1] 2 – [2] 190 – [3] 251 – [4] 342
La Mara, *Briefe*. [5] 305

SCHUBERT

O. E. Deutsch, *Franz Schubert's Letters and Other Writings*, tr. Venetia Saville, New York, Alfred A. Knopf, 1928. [1] 28 – [2] 96
O. E. Deutsch, *Franz Schuberts Briefe und Schriften*, Munich, Georg Müller, 1922. [3] 62

DONIZETTI

Guido Zavadini, *Donizetti: vita, musiche, epistolario*, Bergamo, Istituto Italiano d'arti grafici, 1948. [1] 287 – [2] 506 – [3] 718

Chapter 3

BERLIOZ

Hector Berlioz, *Memoirs*, tr. Rachel Holmes and Eleanor Holmes, annot. and rev. Ernest Newman, New York, Alfred A. Knopf, 1932. [1] 13 – [2] 408 – [3] 98 – [4] 154 – [5] 323 – [6] 318 [7] 65 – [8] 59 – [9] 289 – [10] 376 – [11] 487

GLINKA

Octave Fouque, *Glinka d'après ses mémoires et sa correspondance*, Paris, Heugel, 1880. [1] 10 – [4] 83
Oskar von Riesemann, *Monographien zur Russischen Musik*, Munich, Drei-Masken-Verlag, 1923. [2] 79 – [3] 98

MENDELSSOHN

Felix Mendelssohn-Bartholdy, *Letters*, ed. Gisella Selden-Goth, New

York, Pantheon Books, 1945. [1] 27 – [2] 81 – [3] 120 – [4] 313 –
[5] 277 – [6] 260 – [8] 296
Peter Sutermeister, *Felix Mendelssohn-Bartholdy: Lebensbild mit Vorge-schichte*, Zurich, Ex-Libris-Verlag, 1949. [7] 210

CHOPIN
Chopin's Letters, coll. by Henryk Opieński, tr. E. L. Voynich, New
York, Alfred A. Knopf, 1931. [1] 129 – [2] 133 – [3] 154 – [4] 394

SCHUMANN
Robert Schumann, *On Music and Musicians*, ed. Konrad Wolff, tr. Paul
Rosenfeld, New York, Pantheon Books, 1946. [1] 30, 31, 33 – [2] 38, 42,
44 – [3] 59 – [4] 70, 72 – [5] 83 – [6] 92 – [7] 93 – [8] 87 – [9] 102 –
[10] 106 – [11] 114 – [12] 142 – [13] 155 – [14] 157 – [15] 158 –
[16] 172 – [17] 173 – [18] 176 – [19] 177 – [20] 250 – [21] 252

Chapter 4

LISZT
Franz Liszt, *Gesammelte Schriften*, Leipzig, 1880–82. [1] VI, 51 –
[2] VI, 267 – [3] V, 231 – [4] III, 32 – [6] III, 44 – [7] I, 10
Franz Liszt, *Briefe*, Leipzig. 1893. [5] I, 123
Arthur Holde, "Unpublished Letters by Beethoven, Liszt and Brahms,"
The Musical Quarterly, XXXII (1946). [8] 283

DARGOMIJSKY
Oskar von Riesemann, *Monographien zur Russischen Musik*, Munich, Drei
Masken, 1923. [1] 283 – [2] 274 – [3] 256 – [4] 231 – [5] 257

WAGNER
Richard Wagner, *Prose Works*, tr. William Ashton Ellis, London, Kegan
Paul, Trench, Trubner & Co., Ltd., 1895. [1] II, 14 – [2] II, 23 (transla-tions revised)

VERDI
Franz Werfel and Paul Stefan, *Verdi: the Man in His Letters*, New York,
L. B. Fischer, 1942. [1] 124 – [2] 145 – [3] 173 – [4] 175 – [5] 185 –
[6] 251 – [7] 303 – [8] 336 – [9] 343 – [10] 364 – [11] 301 – [12] 299 –
[13] 362 – [14] 402 – [15] 431 – [16] 363 – [17] 365 – [18] 346 –
[19] 372 – [20] 261

Chapter 5

GOUNOD

Charles François Gounod, *Mémoires d'un artiste*, Paris, Calmann-Levy, 1896. [1] 100 – [2] 56 – [3] 333

LALO

Pincherle, *Musiciens*. [1] 179 – [2] 172 – [3] 181

SMETANA

Ernst Rychnowsky, *Smetana*, Stuttgart, Deutsche Verlagsanstalt, 1924. [1] 263 – [2] 171 – [3] 173 – [4] 264
La Mara, *Briefe*. [5] II, 121

BRAHMS

Berthold Litzmann, ed., *Letters of Clara Schumann and Johannes Brahms*, tr. anon., New York, Longmans, Green, 1927. [1] I, 67 – [3] II, 16 – [5] I, 241
Johannes Brahms in Briefwechsel mit Joseph Joachim, Berlin, Deutsche Brahms-Gesellschaft, 1912. [2] I, 150
Max Kalbeck, ed., *Johannes Brahms, the Herzogenberg Correspondence*, tr. Hannah Bryant, New York, E. P. Dutton, 1909. [4] 286
Eduard Hanslick, *Am Ende des Jahrhunderts*, Berlin, Allgemeiner Verein für deutsche Literatur, 1899. [6] 379

BORODIN

V. V. Stassov, *Alexandre Borodine*, tr. A. Habets, Paris, Fischbacher, 1893. [1] II, 118 – [3] II, 121   .
Alfred Habets, *Borodin and Liszt*, tr. Rosa Newmarch, London, Digby, Long & Co., 1896. [4] 30
Leyda and Bertensson, *The Musorgsky Reader.* [2] 173

CUI

César Cui, *La Musique en Russie*, Paris, Fischbacher, 1880. [1] 4 – [2] 73

SAINT-SAËNS

Camille Saint-Saëns, *Musical Memories*, tr. Edwin Gile Rich, Boston, Small, Maynard & Co., 1919. [1] 14 – [4] 61, 67, 74
———, *Au courant de la vie*, Paris, Dorbon-Aîné, 1914. [3] 16; 18
———, *École buissonnière*, Paris, Lafitte, 1913. [2] 189
"Lettres de Saint-Saëns et Camille Bellaigue," Paris, *Revue des deux mondes*, période 8, tome 32, (1936). [5] 539 – [6] 535 – [8] 538
Pincherle, *Musiciens*. [7] 155

BALAKIREV

M. A. Balakirev and P. I. Tchaikovsky, *Correspondence*, St. Petersburg,

J. H. Zimmermann, 1912. [1] 28 (tr. Jean Karsavina) – [2] 48f (tr. Harry Cumpson)

BIZET
Georges Bizet, *Lettres*, ed. Louis Ganderax, Paris, Calmann-Levy, 1908. [1] 118 – [2] 123 – [3] 135 – [4] 144 – [8] 311 – [9] 322
————, *Lettres à un ami, 1865–72*, ed. Edmond Galabert, Paris, Calmann-Levy, 1909. [7] 184
Hugues Imbert, *Portraits et études*, Paris, Fischbacher, 1894. [5] 164 – [6] 180

Chapter 6

MOUSSORGSKY
Leyda and Bertensson, *The Musorgsky Reader*. [1] 111 – [2] 138 – [3] 192 – [4] 199 – [5] 359 – [6] 419

TCHAIKOVSKY
Modeste Tchaikovsky, *Life and Letters of Peter Ilyich Tchaikovsky*, tr. Rosa Newmarch, New York, Dodd, Mead & Co. [1] 250 – [2] 259 – [3] 372 – [4] 382 – [5] 306; 308 – [6] 311 – [7] – 281

DVOŘÁK
Antonin Dvořák, "Music in America," *Harper's Magazine* (1895). [1] 429

GRIEG
Edvard Grieg, "Mozart," *The Century Magazine*, LV (1897). [1] 140, 142
————, "Robert Schumann," *ibidem*, XLVII (1894). [2] 440, 442, 444, 447 – [3] 447

RIMSKI-KORSAKOV
Nicolas Rimsky-Korsakov, *Principles of Orchestration*, tr. Edward Agate, London, Russian Music Agency, 1922. [1] 2
Leyda and Bertensson, *The Musorgsky Reader*. [2] 406

FAURÉ
Gabriel Fauré, *Opinions musicales*, Paris, Rieder, 1930. [1] 50 – [2] 94 – [4] 24 – [6] 101 – [7] 139
————, "Camille Saint-Saëns," *La Revue Musicale*, III (1922). [3] 97
————, "Souvenirs," *La Revue Musicale*, III (1922). [5] 3

D'INDY
Vincent d'Indy, *César Franck*, tr. Rosa Newmarch, London, John Lane (The Bodley Head), 1909. [1] 97 – [3] 182 – [4] 73
————, "Concerts Lamoureux," *La Revue S.I.M.*, X (1914). [2] 52

PUCCINI
Giuseppe Adami, *Letters of Giacomo Puccini*, tr. Ena Makin, Philadelphia, J. B. Lippincott, 1931. [1] 164 – [2] 177 – [3] 243 – [4] 90 – [5] 91 – [6] 130 – [8] 144 – [9] 146 – [10] 169 – [11] 176
Dante del Fiorentino, *Immortal Bohemian*, New York, Prentice-Hall, 1952. [7] 104
Vincent Seligman, *Puccini Among Friends*, London, Macmillan, 1938. [12] 138 – [13] 319

Chapter 7

WOLF
Hugo Wolf, *Musikalische Kritiken*, Leipzig, Breitkopf & Härtel, 1912. [1] 10 – [2] 35 – [3] 96 – [5] 125 – [6] 212
Frank Walker, *Hugo Wolf*, New York, Alfred A. Knopf, 1952. [4] 155 – [7] 159

MAHLER
Alma Maria Mahler, *Gustav Mahler: Briefe*, Vienna, Zsolnay, 1924. [1] 146 – [2] 296 – [3] 187 – [4] 191 – [5] 462 – [10] 228 – [11] 162
————, *Gustav Mahler: Erinnerungen und Briefe*, Vienna, Bermann-Fischer, 1949. [6] 69 – [7] 308 – [8] 367 – [9] 374

MACDOWELL
Edward Alexander MacDowell, *Critical and Historical Essays*, Boston, Arthur P. Schmidt, 1912. [1] 145 – [2] 14 – [3] 146 – [4] 193 – [5] 267

DELIUS
Frederick Delius, "At the Crossroads," *The Sackbut* I (1920). [1] 205
Clare Delius, *Frederick Delius: Memories of my Brother*, London, Nicholson & Watson, 1935. [2] 198

DEBUSSY
Claude Debussy, *Lettres à son éditeur*, Paris, Durand, 1927. [1] 179 – [2] 164 – [4] 150 – [6] 85 – [8] 55 – [9] 65 – [10] 176
————, *Monsieur Croche, the Dilettante Hater*, tr. B. N. Langdon-Davies, New York, Viking Press, 1938. [3] 33 – [5] 130
Edward Lockspeiser, *Debussy*, New York, Pellegrini and Cudahy, 1949. [7] 56

RICHARD STRAUSS
Richard Strauss, *Betrachtungen und Erinnerungen*, Zurich, Atlantis, 1949. [1] 44 – [2] 45 – [3] 47 – [4] 101 – [5] 134 – [6] 91

Richard Strauss und Hugo von Hofmannsthal, *Briefwechsel*, Zurich, Atlantis, 1952. [7] 343 - [8] 348 - [9] 362 - [10] 485 - [11] 499

DUKAS
Paul Dukas, *Les écrits de Paul Dukas sur la musique*, Paris, Société d'éditions françaises et internationales, 1948. [1] 198

BUSONI
Ferruccio Busoni, *Sketch of a New Esthetic of Music*, tr. Dr. Th. Baker, New York, G. Schirmer, 1911 (tr. revised after 2nd German edition). [1] 43 - [4] 25 - [5] 23
Ferruccio Busoni, *Letters to His Wife*, tr. Rosamund Ley, London, Edward Arnold & Co., 1938. [2] 27 - [3] 229 - [6] 188 - [7] 78 - [8] 83 - [9] 287

Chapter 8

SATIE
Erik Satie, "Mémoires d'un amnésique," *La Revue S.I.M.*, X (1914). [1] 69
Rollo H. Myers, *Erik Satie*, London, Dennis Dobson, 1948. [2] 32 - [3] 65 - [5] 32

ROUSSEL
L. Dunton Green, "On Inspiration," *The Chesterian*, IX (1928). [1] 116

VAUGHAN WILLIAMS
Ralph Vaughan Williams, *National Music*, London, Oxford University Press, 1934. [1] 3, 13, 129 - [2] 98 - [3] 92

REGER
Hedwig und E. Müller von Asow, eds., *Max Reger: Briefwechsel mit Herzog Georg II. von Sachsen-Meiningen*, Weimar, Hermann Böhlaus Nachfolger, 1947. [1] 91
Max Reger, *Briefe eines deutschen Meisters*, ed. Else von Hase-Koehler, Leipzig, Koehler und Amelang, 1928. [2] 83 - [3] 77 - [4] 39

RACHMANINOFF
Oskar von Riesemann, *Rachmaninoff's Recollections*, New York, Macmillan, 1934. [1] 146 - [2] 144 - [3] 182 - [4] 127

SCHOENBERG
Arnold Schoenberg, *Style and Idea*, tr. Dika Newlin, New York, Philosophical Library, 1950. [1] 103, 106, 107, 114, 116, 130
Merle Armitage, *George Gershwin*, New York, Longmans, Green & Co., 1938. [2] 97

Henry and Sidney Cowell, *Charles Ives and His Music*, New York, Oxford University Press, 1955. [3] 114n

HOLST

Hubert J. Foss, *The Heritage of Music*, I, New York, Oxford University Press, 1926. [1] 47

IVES

Charles E. Ives, *Essays Before a Sonata*, New York, Knickerbocker Press, 1920. [1] 118 – [2] 120 – [3] 95 – [4] 113 – [5] 81 – [6] 98, 102 – [7] 25

RAVEL

Maurice Ravel, "L'oeuvre de Chopin," *Le Courrier Musical*, XIII (Jan. 1910). [1] 31

————, "Lettre au Comité de la Ligue Nationale pour la défense de la musique française," *La Revue Musicale*, XIX (Dec. 1938). [2] 70

————, "Concerts Lamoureux," *Revue S.I.M.*, VIII (1912). [3] 62 – [4] 63

————, "À propos des *Images* de Claude Debussy," *Cahiers d'aujourd'hui*, (Feb. 1913). [5] 135

Hélène Jourdan-Morhange, *Ravel et nous*, Geneva, Editions du milieu de monde, 1945. [6] 81

M. D. Calvocoressi, "Ravel's Letters to Calvocoressi," *The Musical Quarterly*, XXVII (1941). [7] 17

FALLA

Manuel de Falla, *Escritos*, Madrid, Publicaciones de la Comisaria General de la Música, 1947. [1] 122

BLOCH

Ernest Bloch, "Man and Music," tr. Waldo Frank, *Seven Arts Magazine*, (1917). [1] 495, 498

Mary Tibaldi-Chiesa, *Ernest Bloch*, Turin, Paravia & Co., 1933. [2] 29 – [3] 30 – [4] 47

Chapter 9

BARTÓK

Béla Bartók, "The Liszt Problem," tr. Colin Mason, *Monthly Musical Record*, Vol. 78 (1948). [1] 200, 237

————, "Race Purity in Music," *Modern Music*, XIX (1942). [2] 153

————, "The Influence of Peasant Music on Modern Music," *Tempo*, No. 14 (Winter 1949-50). [3] 19 – [4] 22

MALIPIERO
G. Francesco Malipiero, *The Orchestra*, tr. Eric Blom, London, J. & W. Chester, 1921. [1] 10 – [2] 16 – [3] 17 – [4] 18 – [5] 24
————, "A Plea for True Comedy," tr. anon., *Modern Music*, VI (1929). [6] 10

KODÁLY
Zoltán Kodály, "New Music for Old," *Modern Music*, III (1925). [1] 27
————, "Bartók, le folkloriste," *La Revue Musicale*, No. 212 (Apr. 1925). [2] 37

STRAVINSKY
Igor Stravinsky, *Chronicle of My Life*, London, Victor Gollancz, 1936. [1] 14 – [2] 91 – [3] 122 – [4] 247 – [5] 189
————, *Poetics of Music in the Form of Six Lessons*, tr. Arthur Knodel and Ingolf Dahl, Cambridge, Harvard University Press, 1947. [6] 34 – [7] 12 – [8] 70 – [9] 56 – [10] 81

WEBERN
Arnold Schönberg, Munich, Piper, 1912. [1] 85
Humphrey Searle, "Conversations with Webern," *Musical Times*, (1940). [2] 405
Josef Rufer, ed., *Musiker über Musik*, Darmstadt, Stichnote, 1956. [3] 216

BERG
Willi Reich, *Alban Berg*, Vienna, Reichner, 1937. [1] 152 – [2] 175 – [3] 193

PROKOFIEV
H. H. Stuckenschmidt, *Neue Musik*, Berlin, Suhrkamp, 1951. [1] 338 – [2] 340 – [3] 342 – [4] 347

HONEGGER
Arthur Honegger, *Je suis compositeur*, Paris, Editions du Conquistador, 1951. [1] 96 – [2] 102 – [3] 86 – [4] 164 – [5] 175

MILHAUD
Darius Milhaud, *Notes Without Music*, tr. Donald Evans, New York, Alfred A. Knopf, 1953. [1] 55 – [2] 62 – [3] 82 – [4] 105 – [5] 102 – [6] 164

HINDEMITH
Paul Hindemith, *A Composer's World*, Cambridge, Harvard University Press, 1952. [1] 19 – [2] 38 – [3] 104 – [4] 121 – [5] 164

Chapter 10

THOMSON
Virgil Thomson, *The Art of Judging Music*, New York, Alfred A. Knopf,
1948. [1] 305 – [3] 279 – [7] 17 – [9] 145
————, *The Musical Scene*, New York, Alfred A. Knopf, 1945.
[2] 272 – [4] 277 – [5] 62 – [6] 187 – [8] 249

SESSIONS
Roger Sessions, "On the American Future," *Modern Music*, XVII (1940).
[1] 72
————, *The Musical Experience of Composer, Performer and Listener*,
Princeton, Princeton University Press, 1950. [2] 4 – [3] 72 – [4] 77 –
[5] 70 – [6] 123 – [7] 99

GERSHWIN
Merle Armitage, *George Gershwin*, New York, Longmans, Green & Co.,
1938. [1] 225

POULENC
Francis Poulenc, "Feuilles Americaines," *La Table Ronde*, No. 30 (1950).
[1] 68 – [2] 74 – [3] 75
Roland Gelatt, "A Vote for Francis Poulenc," *The Saturday Review of
Literature*, (1950). [4] 57

AURIC
Georges Auric, "Découverte de Satie," *La Revue Musicale*, No. 214
(1952). [1] 119

CHAVEZ
Carlos Chavez, *Toward a New Music*, tr. Herbert Weinstock, New York,
W. W. Norton, 1937. [1] 113, 15, 61, 139, 49 – [2] 135 – [3] 167 –
[4] 169

ANTHEIL
George Antheil, "Wanted—Opera by and for Americans," *Modern Music*,
VII (1930). [1] 11
————, *Bad Boy of Music*, Garden City, Doubleday Doran, 1945.
[2] 101 – [3] 128 – [4] 61

KRENEK
Ernst Krenek, *Music Here and Now*, New York, W. W. Norton, 1949.
[1] 71 – [2] 80
————, *Musik im goldenen Westen*, Vienna, Hollinek, 1949. [3] 14, 28 –
[4] 15, 26 – [5] 16 – [6] 16 – [7] 18

COPLAND

Aaron Copland, "A Modernist Defends Modern Music," *New York Times Magazine*, December 25, 1949. [1] 11

————, *Music and Imagination*, Cambridge, Harvard University Press, 1952. [2] 14 – [3] 24 – [4] 32 – [5] 3 – [6] 89 – [7] 79 – [8] 62 – [9] 2

ACKNOWLEDGMENTS

Grateful acknowledgment is made to the following for the use of material quoted, and in some cases newly translated, in this book. Detailed bibliographical information will be found in the List of Sources.

Edward Arnold, Ltd., for Ferruccio Busoni, *Letters to His Wife*, tr. Rosamund Ley; Berthold Litzmann, *Letters of Clara Schumann and Johannes Brahms*.

Erich H. Müller von Asow, for *Max Reger: Briefwechsel mit Herzog Georg Il. von Sachsen Meiningen*.

Atlantis Verlag, for Richard Strauss, *Betrachtungen und Erinnerungen;*[1] Richard Strauss and Hugo von Hofmannsthal, *Briefwechsel*.[2]

Ernest Bloch, for "Man and Music," *Seven Arts Magazine*, tr. Waldo Frank.

Victor Bator, trustee of the Béla Bartók estate, for "The Influence of Peasant Music on Modern Music," *Tempo* Magazine.

Braun & Cie, for Maurice Ravel, "A propos des *Images* de Claude Debussy," *Cahiers d'Aujourd'hui*.

J. & W. Chester, Ltd., for G. Francesco Malipiero, *The Orchestra*, tr. Eric Blom; L. Dunton Green, "On Inspiration," *The Chesterian*.

Wm. Collins Sons & Co., Ltd., and trustees of the Strauss-Hofmannsthal estate, for Richard Strauss und Hugo von Hofmannsthal, *Briefwechsel*.

Éditions du Conquistador, for Arthur Honegger, *Je suis compositeur*.

Aaron Copland, for "A Modernist Defends Modern Music," *New York Times Magazine*.

Éditions Cornuau, for Marc Pincherle, *Musiciens peints par eux-mêmes*.

J. Curwen & Sons, Ltd., for Frederick Delius, "At the Crossroads," *The Sackbut*.

Dennis Dobson, Ltd., for Rollo H. Myers, *Erik Satie*.

Dodd, Mead & Co., for *Life and Letters of Peter Ilyich Tchaikovsky*, tr. by Rosa Newmarch.

Dorbon-Aîné, for Camille Saint-Saëns, *Au courant de la vie*.

Doubleday & Co., for George Antheil, *Bad Boy of Music*. Copyright 1945 by George Antheil, reprinted by permission of Doubleday & Co.

Durand & Cie, Paris, copyright owners, and Elkan-Vogel Co., Philadelphia, agents, for Claude Debussy, *Lettres à son éditeur*.

Éditions du milieu de monde, for Hélène Jourdan-Morhange, *Ravel et nous*.

E. P. Dutton & Co., for Max Kalbeck, *Johannes Brahms, the Herzogenberg Correspondence*, tr. Hannah Bryant.

Ex-Libris-Verlag, for Peter Sutermeister, Felix Mendelssohn-Bartholdy, *Lebensbild mit Vorgeschichte*.

Faber & Faber, Ltd., for O. E. Deutsch, *Franz Schubert's Letters and Other Writings*, tr. Venetia Saville.

[1] A complete English version, by L. J. Lawrence, is available through Boosey & Hawkes, London and New York. Copyright 1949 by Atlantis-Verlag, Zurich. English translation by permission of Boosey & Hawkes, Inc.

[2] An English translation of this correspondence is being prepared for publication by Wm. Collins Sons & Co., Ltd., London.

Farrar, Straus & Cudahy, Inc., for Henry Coates, *Palestrina;* Edward Lockspeiser, *Debussy.*

Waldo Frank, for his translation of Ernest Bloch, "Man and Music," *Seven Arts Magazine.*

Harvard University Press, for Aaron Copland, *Music and Imagination,* copyright 1952 by the President and Fellows of Harvard College; Paul Hindemith, *A Composer's World,* copyright 1952 by the President and Fellows of Harvard College; Igor Stravinsky, *Poetics of Music, in the Form of Six Lessons,* tr. Arthur Knodel and Ingolf Dahl, copyright 1947 by the President and Fellows of Harvard College.

Brüder Hollinek, for Ernst Krenek, *Musik im goldenen Westen.*

Mrs. Charles E. Ives, for Charles E. Ives, *Essays Before a Sonata.*

Koehlers Verlagsgesellschaft Biberach/Riss for Max Reger, *Briefe eines deutschen Meisters,* ed. Else von Hase-Koehler.

Alfred A. Knopf, Inc., for Hector Berlioz, *Memoirs,* tr. Rachel Holmes and Eleanor Holmes, annot. and rev. Ernest Newman, copyright 1932 by Alfred A. Knopf, Inc.; Darius Milhaud, *Notes Without Music,* tr. Donald Evans, copyright 1953 by Alfred A. Knopf, Inc.; *Chopin's Letters,* collected by Henryk Opieński, tr. E. L. Voynich, copyright 1931 by Alfred A. Knopf, Inc.; Virgil Thomson, *The Art of Judging Music,* copyright 1948 by Virgil Thomson; Virgil Thomson, *The Musical Scene,* copyright 1945 by Virgil Thomson; Frank Walker, *Hugo Wolf,* copyright 1952 by Frank Walker.

Ernst Křenek, for *Music Here and Now,* published by W. W. Norton Co.

League of Composers, for selections from articles in the magazine *Modern Music:* George Antheil, "Wanted—Opera by and for Americans"; Béla Bartók, "Race Purity in Music"; Zoltán Kodály, "New Music for Old"; G. Francesco Malipiero, "A Plea for True Comedy."

J. B. Lippincott Co., for Giuseppe Adami, *Letters of Giacomo Puccini,* tr. Ena Makin, copyright 1931 by J. B. Lippincott Co.

Longmans, Green & Co., for Merle Armitage, *George Gershwin;* Berthold Litzmann, *Letters of Clara Schumann and Johannes Brahms.*

Macmillan Co., New York, for Oskar von Riesemann, *Rachmaninoff's Recollections.*

Alma Mahler-Werfel, for *Gustav Mahler: Briefe; Gustav Mahler: Erinnerungen und Briefe;* Franz Werfel and Paul Stefan, *Verdi: the Man in His Letters.*

Colin Mason, for his translation of Béla Bartók, "The Liszt Problem," in the *Monthly Musical Record.*

Novello and Co., Ltd., for Humphrey Searle, "Conversations with Webern," in *Musical Times.*

New York Times Magazine, for Aaron Copland, "A Modernist Defends Modern Music."

W. W. Norton & Co., for C. P. E. Bach, *Essay on the True Art of Playing Keyboard Instruments,* tr. and ed. William J. Mitchell, copyright 1949 by W. W. Norton & Co., Inc.; Carlos Chavez, *Toward a New Music,* tr. Herbert Weinstock, copyright 1937 by W. W. Norton & Co., Inc.; Jay Leyda and Sergei Bertensson, *The Musorgsky Reader,* copyright 1947 by W. W. Norton & Co., Inc.

Oxford University Press, for Henry and Sidney Cowell, *Charles Ives and His Music;* Edmund H. Fellowes, *William Byrd* (2nd ed.); Hubert J. Foss, *The Heritage of Music,* Vol. I; Ralph Vaughan Williams, *National Music.*

572   ACKNOWLEDGMENTS

Paravia & Co., for Mary Tibaldi-Chiesa, *Ernest Bloch.*

Philosophical Library, for Arnold Schoenberg, *Style and Idea,* tr. Dika Newlin.

Francis Poulenc, for "Feuilles Américaines," in *La Table Ronde.*

Prentice-Hall, for Dante del Fiorentino, *Immortal Bohemian,* copyright 1952 by Prentice-Hall, Inc.

Presses Universitaires de France, for Gabriel Fauré, *Opinions musicales.*

Princeton University Press, for Roger Sessions, *The Musical Experience of Composer, Performer and Listener.*

Publicaciones de la Comisaria General de la Música, for Manuel de Falla, *Escritos.*

Mrs. Antonio Puccini, for Vincent Seligman, *Puccini Among Friends.*

Herbert Reichner, for Willi Reich, *Alban Berg.*

Revue des Deux Mondes, for "Lettres de Saint-Saëns et Camille Bellaigue."

La Revue Musicale, for Zoltán Kodály, "Bartók, le folkloriste"; Georges Auric, "Découverte de Satie."

G. Schirmer, for Ferruccio Busoni, *Sketch of a New Esthetic of Music,* tr. Dr. Th. Baker, and for the following articles in *The Musical Quarterly:* M. C. Calvocoressi, "Ravel's Letters to Calvocoressi"; Arthur Holde, "Unpublished Letters by Beethoven, Liszt and Brahms"; Benedetto Marcello, "Il teatro alla moda," tr. Reinhard G. Pauly; Dragan Plamenac, "New Light on the Last Years of Carl Philipp Emanuel Bach."

St. Martin's Press, for *Letters of Mozart and His Family,* tr. and ed. Emily Anderson.

Saturday Review, for Roland Gelatt, "A Vote for Francis Poulenc."

Revue S. I. M., for Erik Satie, "Mémoires d'un amnésique"; Maurice Ravel, "Concerts Lamoureux."

Arthur P. Schmidt Co., for Edward MacDowell, *Critical and Historical Essays.*

Small, Maynard & Co., for *The Musical Memories of Camille Saint-Saëns,* tr. Edwin Gile Rich.

Verlag Stichnote, for *Musiker über Musik,* ed. Josef Rufer.

Société d'éditions françaises et internationales, for Paul Dukas, *Les écrits de Paul Dukas sur la musique.*

Igor Stravinsky, for *Chronicle of My Life,* published by Victor Gollancz, London.

Suhrkamp Verlag, for H. H. Stuckenschmidt, *Neue Musik.*

Viking Press, for Claude Debussy, *Monsieur Croche, the Dilettante Hater,* tr. B. N. Langdon-Davies, copyright 1928, 1956 by The Viking Press, Inc.

INDEX

Works mentioned only in the editor's introductions are not indexed, nor are the names of recipients of letters and dedicatees.